Diderot

P. N. Furbank was born in Surrey in 1920 and has worked as an academic, in publishing and as a freelance writer and critic. In 1992 he was appointed Emeritus Professor in Literature at the Open University. His publications include *Samuel Butler (1835–1902)*, *Italo Svevo: The Man and the Writer*, *Reflections on the Word 'Image'*, *E. M. Forster: A Life*, *Unholy Pleasure: The Idea of Social Class* and (with W. R. Owens) *The Canonisation of Daniel Defoe*. He lives in London.

P. N. FURBANK

DIDEROT

A Critical Biography

Minerva

A Minerva Paperback
DIDEROT

First published in Great Britain 1992
by Martin Secker & Warburg Ltd
This Minerva edition published 1993
by Mandarin Paperbacks
an imprint of Reed Consumer Books Ltd
Michelin House, 81 Fulham Road, London SW3 6RB
and Auckland, Melbourne, Singapore and Toronto

Copyright © 1992 by P. N. Furbank

A CIP catalogue record for this title
is available from the British Library
ISBN 0 7493 9887 6

Printed and bound in Great Britain
by Cox & Wyman Ltd, Reading, Berks

For JACK BUDGEN

Contents

Illustrations

Preface

The world has always paid homage to Diderot's *Rameau's Nephew*, as a work, like Dostoevsky's *Letters from Underground* or certain stories of Kafka's, that can never finally be taken possession of and always remains a step, or several steps, ahead of the reader. It has certainly had some distinguished champions. Goethe formed an intense attachment to it, as did Hegel and Marx: and on three separate occasions Freud drew attention to the oddity that this eighteenth-century writer seemed to have forestalled him. "Nor should it be allowed to pass unnoticed", he said in his *Introductory Lectures*, "that the two criminal wishes of the Oedipus complex were recognised as the true representatives of the uninhibited life of the instincts long before the time of psycho-analysis. Among the writings of the Encyclopaedist Diderot you will find a celebrated dialogue, *Le Neveu de Rameau*, which was rendered into German by no less a person than Goethe. There you may read this remarkable sentence: 'If the little brute were left to his own devices, and remained in all his ignorance, combining the undeveloped mind of a child in its cradle with the violent passions of a man of thirty, he would wring his father's throat and go to bed with his mother.' "

Something of the profound strangeness of *Rameau's Nephew* is also to be found in Diderot's two other novels, *The Nun* and *Jacques the Fatalist*, and in his philosophical fantasy *D'Alembert's Dream*. He is a writer whose works speak to us today in a way that Voltaire's, apart from *Candide*, do not. But then . . . Diderot, as everybody knows, was a polymath, fought side by side with Voltaire and D'Alembert against superstition and despotism, and edited the great *Encyclopédie*, siege-engine or bible of "enlightenment". These facts are important but rather hard for the

ordinary reader, especially the English-speaking one, to do much
about, imaginatively or otherwise. He or she is hardly like to go
and read the *Encyclopédie*. It seems like a story that it can safely be
left to the textbooks to take care of.

I have mentioned two different responses to the name
"Diderot", and the list is not yet complete. For it is a commonplace among art historians, but not so much for other readers,
that Diderot was (more or less) the inventor of modern art
criticism; and well-known to French readers, but not so to
English-speaking ones, that he was one of the world's great
letter-writers. Then: it is notorious that some bloodthirsty
Jacobin once spoke with relish of strangling the last king with the
guts of the last priest, but not everyone is aware that it was the
benevolent Diderot who composed the phrase, in a festive New
Year's Eve poem, nearly twenty years before the Revolution.

All in all, there is some disconnection in the received notions
about Diderot, and this is not just a later phenomenon, it was true
of him even in his own time. There are, I think several reasons for
this, but an all-important one is plainly the fact that he simply did
not publish *Rameau's Nephew*, or indeed any of his most truly
original writing. There was thus a side of him that was not known
to his contemporaries and that might have puzzled them
considerably if they had known it. My purpose in the present
book is to see if I can help a little towards connecting up the
different ideas suggested by Diderot's name.

Anyone undertaking a new study of Diderot is bound to be
indebted to, and feel rather overawed by, Arthur Wilson's
magnificent two-volume biography of thirty years or so ago; and I
certainly cannot pretend to know as much about the subject as
Wilson did. However, my book attempts something slightly
different from his. For one thing, it is a "critical biography": that
is to say the narrative chapters are interspersed – and increasingly so as the book goes on – with chapters of literary
criticism. It is an awkward form (and as a matter of fact I have
said some rude things about it in the past), but it seemed
somehow to be called for in the present case. I am not altogether
clear why this is; but the reason is partly, certainly, that the thing
that interests me about Diderot is not so much what he

"represented" as what he achieved. The works he will live by, *has* lived by – even including his art criticism – are really quite few; but to me, at least, they are astounding.

I should like to give my warmest thanks to the following, for their advice and help: Andrew Best, Peter Biller, Piers Brendon, Tony Coulson, the Revd. John Fellows, Tony Lentin, Douglas Matthews, Derwent May, Bob Owens, Ben Spackman. I would, further, like to express particular gratitude to my editor John Blackwell, and to Elisabeth Sifton, for a whole series of constructive suggestions and comments.

Introduction

The star attraction of the Paris *Salon* exhibition[1] of 1765 was Fragonard's canvas "The High Priest Coresus Immolates Himself to Save Callirhoë."[2] The lurid subject of this painting derives originally from Pausanias's *Description of Greece* and concerns the plague of madness brought upon Calydon by the maiden Callirhoë, when she spurns the love of the high priest Coresus, and the sublime gesture of Coresus when, instructed by the god Dionysus to sacrifice Callirhoë, he turns the knife upon himself. Fragonard had probably taken the story from a current opera, and his large and operatic canvas, which was his Académie admission-piece, had already been bought by Louis XV on behalf of the Gobelins tapestry-factory.

A few years earlier, Denis Diderot, the atheist philosopher, dramatist, polymath and co-editor of the great *Encyclopédie*, had embarked on a new career as an art critic. Thus he had been commissioned to review the present exhibition, as he had done the three preceding ones, for a small-circulation subscription-journal, the *Correspondance littéraire*, run by his friend Melchior Grimm. His review took the form of a letter to Grimm. However, so Diderot reports in it, he will not be able to discuss Fragonard's painting, for by the time he arrived at the exhibition it was no longer on show. He will thus have to fill up his article by describing a disturbing dream he has had, as the fruit of a morning at the exhibition and an evening spent reading Plato.

> It seemed that I was enclosed in the place known as Plato's cave.
> It was a long and gloomy cavern. I was sitting in the midst of a
> crowd of men, women and children. We all had our feet and hands
> in chains and our heads so firmly fastened by wooden clamps that

it was impossible to look round. But the thing which surprises me
was that the majority of my fellow-prisoners were drinking,
laughing and singing, not seeming in the least troubled by their
chains, and you would have said, so far as appearances went, that
it was their natural situation in life and they had no desire for
anything different. It even seemed to me that people looked rather
hostile at those who tried to free their feet or hands or head or help
others to do so; that they called them evil names; that they shrank
away from them, as if they had an infectious disease; and that,
when any mishap occurred in the cave, these would be the first to
be blamed. Installed in the way that I have explained to you, we
all had our backs turned to the entrance of this habitation and
were only able to look at its far end, which was hung with an
immense canvas or curtain.

Behind us, there were kings, ministers, priests, doctors, apostles,
prophets, theologians, politicians, rogues, charlatans, makers of
illusions, and the whole troupe of merchants of hopes and fears.
Each had a supply of little coloured and transparent images, of the
kind suitable to their own condition; and these images were so well
constructed, so well painted, so numerous and so varied, that
there was all that was needed to represent every scene of life,
comic, tragic, or burlesque.

These charlatans, I then realised – placed as they were between
us and the entrance to the cave – had hanging behind them a
great lamp, to the light of which they exposed their images; and
the shadows of these latter, passing over our heads and growing in
size as they travelled, were cast upon the great screen at the end of
the cavern, forming whole scenes – scenes so natural, so true to life
that we took them for real. Sometimes they made us laugh, till we
split our sides; sometimes they made us weep salt tears – a fact
which will seem less strange to you when I say that behind the
screen other subordinate rogues, in the pay of the former ones,
supplied these shadows with the voices, the accents, the speech
appropriate to their roles.[3]

This Platonic cinema of Diderot's captures the imagination. But
then, a decade earlier, in his theatrical homily *Conversations on
"The Natural Son"*, he had already put forward the very cinematic
notion of a mobile *mise-en-scène*, as many *mises-en-scène* as there
were moments of dramatic concentration. ("Ah", he had sighed
there, "if only we had theatres where the décor changed
whenever the scene did!") As Roland Barthes rightly points out

in his "Diderot/Brecht/Eisenstein", this, and Diderot's whole conception of a perfect play as "a succession of tableaux, a gallery, an exhibition", is a foreshadowing of Eisenstein.[4] It is an unusual fate, one cannot help thinking, to have invented the cinema twice over, once as an aesthetic innovation, and on another occasion, with hints from Plato, as a symbol of oppression and obscurantism and the self-indulgence and self-stultification that go with them.

I shall come back often to this Platonic allegory of Diderot's, for it impresses me, and one could not ask for a better expression of his purposes as a writer and thinker. His theory of epistemology is related to it, as are his aesthetic theories; and the hero, or anti-hero, of his novel *Rameau's Nephew* is precisely one of those who have a vision of the world as a tyrannical system of illusion and cliché and are called evil names by their fellows for proclaiming it.

But what also tells us something about Diderot is his own attitude towards this *Salon* review of 1765. He wrote it (the whole thing is some eighty thousand words in length) in a fortnight's burst of energy, and he considered it the best work he had done in his twenty years as a man of letters. There were thoughts in it, he told his mistress Sophie Volland (for he believed in self-praise), that could have entered no one else's head. "Sometimes it is genuine conversation, such as one might have at the fireside. At all other times it is all that can be imagined in the way of profundity and eloquence." He felt quite torn about it, he told her, and sometimes he longed to see it published – properly published, and "dropping from the skies, all printed, into the middle of Paris". (To circulate in handwritten copies among some fifteen readers, most of them foreign princes, could hardly be called "publication".) More often, though, he said, he thought of the injury his criticisms might give to struggling artists – poor wretches who did not deserve to be cruelly punished, and have the bread torn from their lips, for failing to please. So he would have to content himself with the thought that he had given a lesson or two (not that they would have any effect) to his masters, to the princes who subscribed to Grimm's journal – had told them that they were "fabricators of unhappiness and illusions, and salesmen of fear and hope".

Thus I condemn to obscurity a work from which it would not be difficult to reap glory and profit . . . All the same, writing this essay has been a real pleasure to me. I have convinced myself that the fire and imagination of my thirties are still there, complete and intact – and with a weight of knowledge and judgement that I did not have then . . . I have learned, too, that my self-love does not insist on public rewards, and it does not even greatly matter to me how much, or how little, I am appreciated by those around me, so long as there is one man in the world whose judgement I respect and who knows what I am worth.[5]

There is some truth and some self-persuasion here, but plainly the drive to fame and publication is not all that strong in him. In an earlier version of his Platonic allegory he imagines a rebel who breaks his fetters and scales the wall of the cave to make his escape; and he says that this man, if he ever returns to the cave, had better keep his mouth shut as to what he has seen. It was perhaps a simile which came naturally to Diderot, who once (and possibly more than once) made his own escape over a real-life prison wall. At all events a mixture of prudence, compunction and a sense of the possible seems to have worked on him strongly as a writer and kept him partly hidden from his contemporaries.

Certainly, Diderot, the most talkative man of his generation, and one of the most committed to the spreading of Enlightenment, had a considerable capacity for silence. So far as is known he did not show his masterpiece *Rameau's Nephew* to a single person, nor was it published till twenty years after his death – and then in a German translation by Goethe![6] Nor is the situation much different with the other works of his that most count for the modern reader. Neither *The Nun*, nor *Jacques the Fatalist*, nor his triptych of stories, nor his philosophical fantasy *D'Alembert's Dream* was written to influence anybody or in the hope of fame.

It is true, as Michael Butor has pointed out,[7] that the issue of censorship looms extraordinarily large with Diderot. In his work on the *Encyclopédie* he not only had to cope with official censors but eventually discovered that his own publisher had been censoring him in secret. D'Alembert demanded that he should destroy *D'Alembert's Dream*; his literary executor Naigeon censored his work; his daughter and son-in-law censored and rewrote his manuscripts; and Goethe bowdlerised *Rameau's Nephew*. Moreover, not only did Diderot become an expert in literary self-censorship, he became absorbedly interested in the general phenomenon of self-censorship and found in it a precious clue to the workings of the mind and the nature of reality.

Diderot's reserve as a writer, one feels, did not spring from secretiveness, for he disapproved on principle of secrecy. No doubt it had to do with a feeling, probably well-founded, that he would not have been understood. But other considerations seem also to have entered in. He was a man enormously in the public eye, and earnestly and vociferously concerned to promote the public good, yet, unlike his friend Rousseau and unlike Voltaire, he did not have the gift for establishing a *rapport* with a "public". His thoughts only ran free when he could feel he was writing for the eye of friends, and even that friendly audience was for him no more than a useful fiction. Essentially, it is one's impression, he designed his best works as messages in a bottle addressed, if with no great urgency, to a future age. If so, they have reached their destination, though only with the aid of various strokes of luck. What a terrible reflection on the judgement of posterity, remark the Goncourts in their *Journal* for April 1858, that Diderot, "the Homer of modern thought", should enjoy a second-order popularity as compared with the commonplace Voltaire!

Let me sketch the rest of Diderot's critique of Fragonard's "Coresus and Callirhoë" without pressing it too hard for its message, but rather to catch the feel of Diderot's mind when in full flight of fantasy. The screen at the end of the cave seems at first filled with mere chaos; human beings weeping, laughing, gambling, drinking, singing, gnawing their knuckles, tearing their hair, caressing and whipping one another. "At the moment one is drowning himself, another is being hanged, and a third is being placed on a pedestal." At last, however, the screen clears and a story begins to unfold before Diderot's hallucinated eyes. A young priest of Bacchus appears, ivy-garlanded and bearing a *thyrsus*. He is serving great beakers-full of wine to a group of dishevelled Maenads, and all grow drunk, the priest included, and rush through the streets with cries of fury and joy, while the citizens cower in their homes. Next the young priest is seen "plunged in intoxication more dangerous than that of wine" and making passionate advances to a young woman, who refuses him with scorn. Meanwhile from the houses loud cries are heard, and the citizens, who by now have caught the infection, fill the streets in a mob – "fathers assaulting their daughters, who are lost to shame, mothers making love to their unrecognised sons, and children of both sexes rolling, a confused mass, upon the ground". ("Ah! if only I were a painter," remarks Diderot in his review. "Every one of those faces is still there, before my very eyes.")

In the midst of the tumult, some old men, untouched by the epidemic, are seen in a temple. They are weeping and beating their heads upon the floor when a loud voice – which is that of the god, "or perhaps of the subordinate rogue behind the screen" – is heard proclaiming: "She must die, or another die in her place!" ("But my friend," the review quotes Grimm as exclaiming, "at the rate you are dreaming, do you not realise that one of your dreams would be enough to fill an entire art gallery?" "Wait," replies Diderot, "you are not at the end yet.")

Before Diderot's anxious eyes the wall of the temple falls away, revealing a tremendous tableau. The temple floor is covered with a rich red gold-fringed carpet, falling over a long step which runs the length of the façade. To the right is a grand sacrificial vessel and on either side stand great towering columns of white marble. There is an urn of black marble, half-draped with bloodstained cloths, a giant candelabrum, an altar and a brazier, the fumes from which partly veil the recesses of the temple. "But tell me, my friend," Grimm is made to comment, "have you not told your dream to anybody?" DIDEROT: "No. Why do you ask?" GRIMM: "Because the temple you describe is in every detail the scene shown in Fragonard's painting." DIDEROT: "It could be so. I had heard so much talk of the painting in the last few days that, having to dream of a temple, I may have dreamed his."

There now enters the high-priest Coresus, with dragging steps, first with his head bent and then raising his eyes to heaven and uttering a cry which draws an answering groan from the dreaming Diderot. Next on the scene is a young woman, and one we have already encountered, now trembling and pale as death, for she is the destined sacrificial victim; meeting the high-priest

Coresus, her lover ("Ah, a thousand times unhappier even than she"), she sinks to the floor. Amidst this scene of "the unhappy face of men and the cruelty of the gods – or of their ministers, for the gods are nothing" – there enter young acolytes, one especially of amazing beauty. "I do not know," says Diderot, "if it was his modesty, his youth, his sweetness or his nobility which so touched me, but he outshone the priest himself."

As the act of sacrifice is prepared, the temple fills up with spectators. The priest raises his knife and . . . turns it upon his own breast. All watch thunderstruck as the chill of death creeps over his noble and tender features; and even the aged priests, "whose cruel regard must often have fed on the vapour of the blood shed at altars", cannot withhold their tears. But of all the sorrowing crowd, a grey-haired old man, his arms spread out tragically above the altar, strikes Diderot with most force: "I see his eyes, I see his mouth, I see him start forwards, I hear his cries, they wake me up, the screen rolls up and the cavern disappears."

All this game or mystification played with Fragonard's painting, we perceive, is a continuation of the allegory of the cave. Human life is being depicted by Diderot as an enthralling but spurious scene of passion, superstition and cruelty, devised by charlatans – a scene which, however, being human, we are incapable of not responding to. "Human beings, being born compassionate," remarks Diderot in his review, "seek in cruel spectacles the exercise of this quality" – a thought which, elsewhere, he uses to justify public executions.

What Diderot has done is to lead us out, in an entirely coherent fashion, from this philosophic allegory into the realm of aesthetics. He has, in fact, attempted a curious feat, no less than to re-invent Fragonard's painting for him, together with all that led up to it. He has tried to retrace Fragonard's whole creative process; and this in turn has broadened into an image of the creative process in general, which begins from formlessness and chaos and prodigally throws off many unfulfilled painterly conceptions *en route* to its goal.

But, we find further that Diderot is re-enacting not just the creative process but the critical one also. Good criticism, it is implied, has to be a two-stage enterprise: first a whole-hearted

find Fragonard's picture

and generous, even credulous, response; and then a re-appraisal in colder blood. Thus Diderot is, at first impact, quite overwhelmed by the beauty of the young acolyte; but in his later critical phase he sees faults, finding the acolytes too androgynous and hermaphroditic. We have in this an example of something which, as we shall see, was fundamental to Diderot: a capacity for combining the advantages of getting "carried away" with those of self-possession and detachment. The whole elaborate game played with Fragonard's painting is revealed as, among other things, a most telling piece of art-criticism. The weakness of this brilliant painting, which was so enormously admired when first put on show, lies, so Diderot conveys, in its contrived, overtheatrical and ephemeral quality. "When one loses sight of his canvas for a moment, one is always afraid that it will roll up like that in the dream, and these engaging and sublime phantoms will dissolve like those of the night." It is the sort of sensation-mongering painting, he implies, that is encouraged by a bad social system.

I can think of no one else who could have written that review; and even in my précis it must surely strike the reader as strangely brilliant and attractive, full of the most liberating cleverness, profundity and gaiety. The Diderot whom it reveals is, however, not the one his contemporaries knew. They were aware of him as the author of one or two early philosophical works and as a not too successful dramatist, and above all as the director of the great multi-volume *Encyclopédie* which, for good or evil, represented the bible of "enlightenment" in France. But as for this other more elusive and more "modern" writer, they were not given the chance to read him, and they might not have relished him if they had done so.

Diderot in Youth

Denis Diderot was born on 5 October 1713 in Langres, a fortified hill town in Champagne of ancient Roman origins, where his father Didier was a master cutler. Denis was the eldest surviving child and was followed by three sisters and a brother. The Diderots had been cutlers in Langres for two centuries, and his father had a high reputation; indeed his surgical lancets enjoyed national fame. Didier had acquired a certain amount of land, and thus the family was in easy circumstances and carried weight in the locality. They were well looked upon by the local clergy, who set the social tone in Langres, and Denis's maternal uncle was a canon of the neighbouring cathedral of Saint-Mammès. It seems moreover, at least at this period, to have been a harmonious family. Denis was greatly attached to his father (as indeed he seems to have been to his mother, but not much is known about her), and later, despite various ferocious quarrels between them, he was inclined to idealise his father as a model of industry and moral probity.

At the age of ten Diderot was sent to the Jesuit college at Langres, where he received an excellent humanist education. It was the practice of Jesuit schools to organise their pupils, for work purposes, into two very large rival camps, the "Romans" and the "Carthaginians"[1]; at Langres this custom spilled over into the boys' leisure time, and they would stage ferocious mock-military battles, sometimes as many as a hundred boys to a side. The young Diderot, who was sturdy and physically reckless, threw himself into these combats with great zest and carried the scars of ten slingshot wounds to his grave. It was been said of Voltaire that he pictured himself and his fellow *philosophes* as a "Macedonian phalanx", a "square, compact and united little battalion"; and one may imagine that both Diderot and Voltaire, in their warfare with the church, were remembering their Jesuit schooling.

At school Diderot was often in trouble for unruliness and carelessness, and he once told his father he wanted to leave. His father asked him if he would like to be a cutler, "Yes, with all my heart," he replied; so he donned an apron and began to work at his father's side. The experiment lasted four or five days, during which he wrecked every blade that he touched, and thereupon he collected his books and returned to school, remarking that he "preferred irritation to boredom".[2]

Back at school he had some quarrel with another boy, violent enough for him to be forbidden the school premises on the annual prize-giving day, when he was due to receive several awards. It was too much for him to stay at home, so he mingled with the crowd at the school entrance and slipped in. The porter spotted him and chased after him with some kind of weapon, giving him a nasty wound in his side, but, bleeding as he was, he took his due place on the platform. He remembered afterwards, as one of the "sweetest moments of his life", his father's joy at seeing him come home from school "with my arms laden with prizes I had won: and around my neck the academic garlands I had received, which, being too wide for my brow, had slipped down onto my shoulders. From the farthest distance he saw me; he left his work, came to the door, and burst into tears."

His uncle the canon, who was getting on in years, planned for Denis to succeed to his lucrative prebend; and with this in view Denis, at the age of thirteen, was inducted into minor orders and given the tonsure, which bestowed on him the right to the title *abbé* and meant dressing in the appropriate ecclesiastical garb. He thus might, in the manner of so many of his fellow-intellectuals, have gone down to history as "the *abbé* Diderot".

It is, though, worth being clear about the ubiquitous term *abbé*. It means, literally, "abbot", but one could earn the title of *abbé* in a variety of ways. One might do so by receiving a commendatory abbacy, for which one did not have to be a priest and might even be a layman. But it was also a courtesy title loosely applied to any non-attached priest or to a member of the cloth in general. The

Jesuit Barruel, writing after the Revolution in his *History of Jacobinism*,[3] complained of "all that class of men who wore the half-livery of the church and styled themselves 'Abbé' " but said that "the people, on the whole, did not confuse them with the clergy."

Diderot's uncle's plan for him went awry. The cathedral chapter greatly disliked the old man, who had a savage tongue, and did everything they could to thwart him in the project. In retaliation he conceived the scheme of remitting the whole question to Rome and despatched a document to the Vatican formally surrendering his prebend into the Pope's hands in favour of the fourteen-year-old "Denis Diderot, tonsured cleric of the diocese of Langres." A few hours, though, before his emissary could have been thought to have reached the Vatican, the canon died. The event raised a problem of conscience for the Diderot household: should they delay reporting the death? The women argued for doing so, but Diderot senior, with great and characteristic firmness, sent instructions for the news to be announced at once by the ringing of the church bells.

Somewhere about the same time – or so in old age he told his daughter – Diderot went through a phase of extreme piety, adopting a hair shirt and sleeping on straw. At this period one of his Jesuit instructors persuaded him that he should abscond from his home and join their order. Diderot revealed his plans to a cousin, who volunteered to come with him, but the cousin then grew scared and betrayed the secret to Diderot's father. Thus, as Diderot crept downstairs on the appointed night, he found his father barring his way and demanding to know where he was going at midnight. "To Paris, to join the Jesuits," said Diderot. "Your wishes shall be granted," replied his father gravely, "but it will not be tonight."

Soon afterwards, in 1728 or early 1729, and perhaps as a result of this incident, Diderot was sent to Paris to complete his education. For some reason, though (the evidence is rather confused), he appears to have gone not to the famous Jesuit college of Louis-le-Grand, but to the strongly Jansenist Collège d'Harcourt.[4] His father came with him upon his journey to Paris, and after their farewells – it was a characteristic gesture – he stayed on in the city for another fortnight, unbeknown to Denis, and suffering agonies of boredom, to make sure that the boy would be happy and that he was making a good impression on his teachers. Father and son were not to see each other again for thirteen years.

The following ten years, crucial in Diderot's development, are the least known part of his life. In 1732 he graduated as master of arts in the University of Paris, and thereupon he embarked on the course of studies leading to a Doctorate in theology. At the age of nineteen or twenty, or so he tells us, he had thoughts of becoming a Carthusian novice. Plainly, therefore, though at some stage he must have abandoned his *abbé*'s costume, and with it all thoughts of a clerical career, this could not have happened at once; and when it did so, it seems to have meant rejecting the whole idea of a career. What he wanted was to go on studying the classics, to master mathematics, and to teach himself English and Italian; and, with a great deal of undisciplined energy, this is what he did.

It was arranged that a Paris solicitor of Langres origins, Clément de Ris, should take him into his household and give him training in the law. After some time, though, M. Clément had to report that Diderot was making no progress at all. At this, Diderot senior instructed M. Clément to ask Denis what profession he *would* prefer; to which his reply was, quite simply, "None. I enjoy study. I am well provided for and extremely content with life. I ask for nothing more." This reply was relayed to his father, who responded with vigour, cutting off all money and ordering him to return home within the week. It did not really enter Diderot's head to obey. However, it made it awkward for him to lodge any longer with the kindly M. Clément; so he moved out and, being now penniless, looked round for some way of supporting himself in Paris.

There are numerous legends as to how he managed this. His greatest standby was teaching mathematics, as a tutor in private households. At first, according to his own account, he did it very inefficiently, rarely being more than one step ahead of his pupils. Certainly he was always capricious. He would not care how many hours he spent with a pupil he found congenial, but he might drop a stupid or unresponsive one after a single lesson. His fee sometimes came in money and sometimes, which suited him just as well, in books or linen.

At some stage he became a tutor in the household of a wealthy financier, who paid him very generously but expected him to spend the whole day with the children. Before long, Diderot had to announce that the post would never do for him. "Monsieur, look at me," he said to his employer. "No lemon could be yellower than my complexion. I am making men out of your children, but it means that every day I must become a child myself. I am a thousand times too well-paid and too comfortable in your home, and I shall have to leave."

Occasionally some hack journalism came his way. He also made a profitable line out of sermon-writing: on one occasion he sold six sermons, at the very handsome price of fifty *écus* apiece, to a missionary just off to the Portuguese colonies. He had a passion for the theatre, attending it whenever he could afford it, and had fantasies of becoming an actor. His friends were as poverty-stricken as himself, and when he happened to have an apartment he would let them doss down on his spare mattresses. At other times they would do the same for him.

His churchy training had its uses, and on more than one occasion he found it convenient to pose as an aspiring seminarist or potential monk. His daughter relates, as a good story, his fleecing of a certain Brother Angel, a Carmelite friar in Paris distantly related to the Diderots. The friar kept a look-out for recruits for his monastery, from among just such young men as Diderot – youths of good education but estranged from their parents – and he would tempt them by discreet offers to settle their debts. It was too much for Diderot to resist, and on a visit to Brother Angel he dropped hints about his yearning for a haven from the hurly-burly of the world: perhaps some monastery in the provinces. At this Brother Angel pressed the claims of his own excellently run establishment. A second visit followed, and at this, under the delicate urging of the friar, Diderot confessed to the one obstacle to his hoped-for change of life: he had led a young woman into sin, and if he were to part from her, he was in duty bound to leave her some provision, for otherwise what was left for her but a life of shame? He mentioned the sum of 1,200 francs,

which would take him some years to earn, but he was young . . .
Upon this, seizing his moment, the friar exclaimed "Why delay?"
and insisted on advancing the 1,200 francs, feeling sure that
Diderot's father would gladly repay it when he heard of its
edifying employment. Further encounters took place, and
Diderot admitted to some debts which were troubling his
conscience; these too the friar paid. Then there arose the question
of his outfit; as the son of a respectable family, Diderot said, he
would hate to enter the order like a beggar. This was too much for
Brother Angel, who testily refused further supplies; and at this, to
the friar's extreme fury, Diderot coolly announced that he had
lost his vocation for the monastic life, advising the friar to recoup
his outlay from Diderot senior.

From time to time Diderot came near to destitution, and on
three occasions his mother, who was less of a stickler for principle
than his father, secretly sent him some money. For this purpose
she despatched her maid, who did the whole journey to Paris and
back, some 250 miles, on foot and, being extremely attached to
Diderot, added some of her own savings to the remittance. On
one Shrove Tuesday Diderot found himself without the price of a
meal. Not wanting to trouble his friends on a public holiday, he
tried to study, but this proved impossible, so he went for a long
walk, returning to his inn-lodgings feeling quite ill and desperate.
His landlady gave him a little toast in wine, and he went
disconsolately to bed. The recollection of this appalling day
caused him to vow that "if ever I possessed anything, never in my
life would I refuse a person in need."

Paris harboured quite a colony of hard-up and unattached
intellectuals, young men like Diderot, unsupported by patrons,
or at all events not "owned" by one, and surviving from day to
day by tutoring, translating, pamphleteering, the writing of
pornographic fiction and the like. Their outlook, in general,
tended to be freethinking and subversive, and the police kept a
close eye on them through their informers. One of Diderot's
friends at this time was his college acquaintance the gentle and
ingenuous François-Vincent Toussaint. Toussaint was the son of
a poor and pious Jansenist family and had once written a Latin
hymn in honour of the miracle-working Jansenist deacon Pâris.

He had, however, become a convert to "enlightened" ideas and was to earn fame as the author of an admired and scandal-making *Treatise on Morals* (1748), a work which argued for a non-religious system of ethics. He was totally incapable of supporting himself, and Diderot would share his purse with him. Another friend was the rancorous Fougeret de Monbron, a one-time royal *valet de chambre*, dismissed for bad character, and now an anti-patriotic satirist and Hobbesian misanthrope. During his court days Monbron had travelled widely, and he claimed that the great fruit of his travels was to "have learned to hate by reason what I already hated by instinct." In 1748 he would be arrested and exiled from Paris for his satirical and pornographic novel *Margot la Ravaudeuse*.

Diderot's own favourite study at this period, and the one to which he always came back, was mathematics. It brought him into contact with Le Guay de Prémontval (1716–64), who in 1738 began a celebrated series of mathematical lectures in Paris. He delivered them free of charge, and, what was rather a novelty, they attracted a number of women. Indeed, Prémontval fell in love with, and eventually married, one of his pupils, a Mademoiselle Pigeon. Diderot would evoke her in *Jacques le Fataliste* (*Jacques the Fatalist*), "going to her lessons every morning with her portfolio under her arm and a box of mathematical instruments in her muff." Franco Venturi, in his *La Jeunesse de Diderot* (*Diderot's Youth*), describes de Prémontval's centre for mathematical studies as "a veritable little pre-*Encyclopédie*."[5] Prémontval was a quarrelsome and spendthrift character, and in the end he was forced to flee France and his creditors. He set off on foot for Geneva with his mistress Mlle Pigeon, and after various vicissitudes he ended up, as did Toussaint (and as did many other French intellectuals on bad terms with the authorities), in the employment of Frederick the Great. He had conceived a violent hatred for Toussaint's *Treatise on Morals*, satirising it wildly in his own *Panagiana*, and he died of fever and obsession when Toussaint was preferred for the chair of French at the Berlin military academy.

With all its problems, Diderot's Bohemian existence suited him very well. He was an ebullient, vociferous and sociable

character, physically sturdy ("built like a porter," his friends
said) and with a handsome, massive-browed, beaky-nosed face,
full of expressiveness and charm. At this time (his mid-twenties)
he wore his own hair and would often dress in a torn old overcoat
and black woollen stockings mended with white thread. He was
attractive to women and years later would write nostalgically of
his golden-haired younger days:

> In the mornings, when the collar of my shirt was open and I took
> off my nightcap, my hair fell in great untidy locks over shapely
> and very white shoulders. My neighbour would leave her
> husband's side, early in the morning, and half-open her window-
> curtains, intoxicating herself with the sight, and I would watch
> her. In this way I seduced her from across the street. When I was
> with her, for in due course we got to know each other, I acted with
> candour and innocence and in a gentle, simple, modest and true
> manner. It has all gone: the golden hair, the candour and the
> innocence.[6]

One or two accounts of him from the end of these "lost" years
paint a cheerful picture. In 1742 the German artist and engraver
Johann Georg Wille took lodgings in a house in the rue de
l'Observance (near the present Ecole de Médecine) and introduced himself to Diderot, who lived on the floor below. He found
Diderot "a very affable young man", who professed the highest
regard for artists and the arts and told Wille that, for himself, "he
wanted to be a good writer, and, if possible, an even better
philosopher." He possessed a "very pretty library" and eagerly
pressed books on Wille, taking it for granted that they would
become close friends.[7]

Another witness is the writer Baculard d'Arnaud, a protégé of
Voltaire, who describes Diderot in a poem published in 1741 as
"philosopher by taste and not by habit, mingling the sweets of
pleasure with virtue, foe to vain study, flitting from desire to
desire, learned critic, equitable judge, master of his own intellect
and even more of his own heart, lover of Iris amidst the pleasures
of the table."[8] Allowing for some cliché or nonsense, one discerns
a figure not too much unlike the Diderot of later years. One
notices especially the kind of easy dominance (as "learned critic"

and "equitable judge") that he established over his friends. Where d'Arnoud may have been wrong is in portraying Diderot as indolent. One senses, on the contrary, that he was always, in his undisciplined way, an enormously hard worker, a passionate rather than a dilettante self-educator.

It was in these circles that Jean-Jacques Rousseau would first encounter Diderot. They met in 1742, when a mutual friend named Samuel Roguin introduced Rousseau, "a young chess-player" as he called him, to Diderot, at the Café de la Régence. Rousseau had only recently arrived in Paris. He had brought with him a new mathematical scheme for musical notation, with which he expected to make his fortune, till the great Rameau pointed out its fatal flaw, its visual inefficacy. Meanwhile he had been scraping a living by teaching music, but about this time he had become a sort of secretary and research assistant to a wealthy dilettante, Mme Dupin, and her stepson Dupin de Francueil. Diderot and he were of much the same age and, according to Rousseau, they first found a bond in music and musical theory. The two quickly developed a warm friendship, one which would be of enormous importance to both of them but which ended, as did most of Rousseau's friendships, in havoc and recrimination. They might have remained friends for ever, would be Rousseau's bitter comment in his *Confessions*, if Diderot had not unwisely encouraged him to become a philosopher, and thus a rival.[9] Diderot, looking back, would make a telling comment too. "Man is keen to achieve superiority, even in the most trifling things. Jean-Jacques Rousseau, who always beat me at chess, refused to grant me a 'handicap' to make the game more equal. 'Does it upset you to lose?' he asked. 'No,' I said, 'but I would be able to give you a better game.' 'That may be,' he replied. 'Still, let us leave things as they are.' "[10]

In 1741 Diderot fell in love. He had encountered a ravishingly beautiful and pious young woman named Anne-Toinette Champion: not so young, indeed, for she was three years older than himself. She lived with her widowed mother in a garret in the nearby parish of Saint-Séverin, and the two supported themselves by a little business in linen and lace. They lived in great seclusion, but once again Diderot's supposed religious vocation came to his aid. He was, he explained to them, shortly to enter a seminary and would need a proper outfit of linen. His mother had recently sent him some shirts, but he would like the Champions to make alterations to them. Meanwhile he sent a message to his mother, via a family friend, that in future it might be better if she did not send him shirts but merely the cloth, so that he could have it made up in Paris.

The linen was an excellent pretext for repeated visits to the Champions. The two women took a warm interest in the pious youth; and before long he was talking not of the seminary, but of marriage, and was accepted as a suitor for Anne-Toinette's hand. Her mother declared that Anne-Toinette would be mad to marry such a wild fellow, a man who did nothing and whose only talent was a "golden tongue". However, she was as much taken with Diderot as her daughter.

If he and Nanette were to marry, his father's consent would be needed, for he was under thirty, and presumably he would also have to find himself a more definite career. The idea of the law had recently come up again, and Diderot gave Nanette a disrespectful description of a letter he had just received from "Papa".

> After a sermon two ells longer than usual, *carte blanche* to do whatever I choose, so long as I do *something*.
>   Am I still considering entering the *procureur*'s office? If so, I am to choose a good one and to pay the first quarter's fee on the nail. – But on perfectly comical conditions. "That I do not fail to invoke the Holy Ghost before proceeding and take the most holy sacrament of the eucharist." Have you ever heard of such a thing . . . invoke the Holy ghost to enter a *lawyer's office*? You have my permission to laugh, Mademoiselle.[11]

Fortunately, not long before this he had received a commission to translate a history of Greece from the English of Temple Stanyan,[12] so he could at least claim not to be unemployed.

It was agreed that he should make a visit to Langres, to break the news of his marriage plans to his parents – something which would need careful handling – and, if possible, to find out more about his financial expectations. He set off early in December 1742, finding a rather depleted household, for his brother had just entered a seminary and the younger of his two sisters, Angélique, had, much against her parents' advice, gone into a nunnery. Fortunately for him, his favourite sister Denise was there. She was now twenty-six, a free-spoken, downright and independent-minded spinster: a sort of "female Diogenes" was Denis's later description. She adored him and took a passionate interest in all his doings. Indeed he believed he was the only man she had ever loved, and certainly she showed no signs of getting married.

His arrival was a great event in the Langres circle, and at first all went very well, as may be seen from a letter to Nanette of 17 December:

> Dear Nanette, set your mind at rest. I have arrived. I had a good journey. I am well, and it would seem that people are very pleased to see me. My mother and sister have been as welcoming as could be imagined. My father received me a little coldly; but his solemn indifference did not continue, and at present I receive good humour from him as well as the rest of the household. I have not had the chance to embrace my brother yet, as he is now in the seminary; he went there eight days before my arrival. He is definitely committed to the priesthood, so the family is now reduced to two. I believe the career will suit him, given that surpassing piety of his, which makes him so proud; so I am not against this development. I am making a round of visits. Those provincial folk open their eyes very wide at a man whom they did not expect to see again so soon and whom they have been gossiping about so recklessly . . .
>
> I am quietly working towards obtaining an annuity from my parents, if only twenty-five *pistoles*. It would always be something, whatever happened. With you being determined to take me to your arms, in whatever shape I return, I shall not care too much if my schemes come to nothing . . .[13]

His parents, who had heard alarming reports about his Paris existence, were half hoping he might have come home for good. However, then the proofs of the history of Greece began to arrive, and this made an excellent impression, so much so that they began to worry on another score – were they keeping him too long from his important work in the metropolis? Diderot, meanwhile, was rather enjoying himself, and was in no hurry to leave. He was still cautiously feeling his way over the money issue and the even more delicate one of Nanette. At length, however, Nanette began to write complaining letters, and at last he plucked up his courage and revealed the true purpose of his visit. The result was a most appalling explosion. There were violent recriminations and threats of disinheritance from his parents, who had formed their own marriage plans for him, and Diderot himself lost his temper completely. He demanded instant payment of his share of the family property and told his father that, if he were not satisfied, he would call the bailiff and have his father arrested. To this his father, in *ancien régime* fashion, promptly retaliated by having Diderot arrested in good earnest and imprisoned in a monastery. (The *lettre de cachet*, it needs to be remembered, was not the exclusive perquisite of the aristocracy.) A severe and choicely worded letter of admonition from Diderot senior to Nanette's mother arrived soon afterwards.

Langres, 1 February 1743

Madame,
If I have postponed writing to you up to now, it is because I thought that the good sense of Mademoiselle your daughter and my own opposition would have served to deter my son.

But judging from the excesses into which he has been led, I feel sure that she cannot approve of his activities. He has passed so brusquely from solicitations to menaces, and from menaces to actions, that I have thought it my duty to take precautions against a folly likely to be fatal to your daughter and to himself. What could she do with a man who has no situation in the world and may perhaps never have one? Has she enough means for both of them? If I am to believe his account, nature has been more prodigal of its favours to her than fortune. No, Madame, I will not allow him to make a woman unhappy or to make himself so.

This inclination of his that I disapprove of has already done him considerable injury, losing him a chosen and most suitable partner. If you do not resolve the situation, your daughter will succeed in ruining him; for you will be aware that disinheritance is the normal consequence of engagements of the kind that he wishes to impose on me.

If Mademoiselle your daughter is as well-brought-up and loves him as much as he believes, she will exhort him to renounce her hand. It is only by this means that he will regain his liberty, for, with the aid of friends, who are outraged, as am I, at his audacity, I have had him put in a place of security: and we shall, I believe, have all the power we need to keep him there until he has changed his views.

A son, for whom I have done everything, threatening to send the bailiff for me, and you allow it!

I would not dare, Madame, to express myself as a less mild and reasonable father might in the same circumstances. But put yourself in my place. Imagine that it was your own daughter acting in such fashion. What would you think? What would you say? What would you do?

If you write to my madman of a son in a suitable manner, I will have the letter conveyed to him, with all the respect that I owe to a right-thinking mother and a virtuous daughter.

Madame,
your very humble and very obedient servant,

DIDEROT[14]

Denis, after some days of incarceration (it is not known how many) escaped by climbing out of a window and made his way by foot to Troyes. From there, in great turmoil of mind, he wrote to Nanette:

My dear friend,
Having suffered unheard-of torments, here I am, a free man. What shall I say to you? My father had the sternness to have me shut up among monks, who treated me with the greatest malice imaginable. I threw myself out of the windows last Sunday night. Since then I have been on foot and have just arrived at the Troyes coach, which will take me to Paris. I have no linen. I have walked thirty miles in appalling weather. I have had a bad time on the journey, for, prevented from following the high-road for fear of pursuit, I have had to lurk about in villages, where I could scarcely find a crust to eat or a drop of wine. Luckily I have some money, which I took care to put by before I revealed my plans. I saved it from the hands of my gaolers by hiding it in my shirt-tails.

If you blame me for the failure of my journey and you show it, I am so full of distress – I have suffered so much, and there are so many more miseries in store for me – that my mind is made up: I will put an end to everything. My death or life will depend on how

you receive me. My father is in such a fury I am sure he really will
disinherit me, as he has threatened to. If I lose you as well, what is
there left to keep me in this world?

I shall not be safe in my old apartment, for no doubt Father Angel
has received orders to have me arrested, and will be only too keen to
obey. Be so good, therefore, as to find me a furnished room, near your
own home or elsewhere . . .

I am yours as much as, and more than ever.

DIDEROT

Troyes, Wednesday.

I forgot to tell you that, to prevent my escaping, they took the futile
precaution of cutting off half my hair.

In the household, I only had one aunt on my side. I took refuge
with her during our quarrels. We shall have to regard the little linen
that I brought with me as lost: but I expect she will send on my books
which I left on her table.[15]

During the month or two after his return to Paris there was a
temporary estrangement between Diderot and Nanette, and he
wrote her a melancholy letter, using the formal "vous" instead of
"tu" and reproaching her for indifference. He had in fact,
suffered a serious collapse. Hearing that he was ill, Nanette sent a
friend to visit him and was told that he was living in a perfect
hovel, half-starving, and altogether miserable. At this, she went
to see him herself and, without more ado, she agreed to marry
him. They had to be very cautious about the wedding, for Diderot
was still a fugitive from justice, and they went through the
ceremony quite privately and at midnight, on 6 November 1743,
in a church which specialised in such clandestine marriages near
Notre Dame. The two then set up home in the rue Saint-Victor,
near the Place Maubert, and were joined there not long after by
Nanette's mother. The fact of the marriage was kept a secret from
Diderot's father for some six years.

2

The Dungeon at Vincennes

In later years Diderot came to be known by the nickname of "the Philosopher", and it is commonly agreed to see in him the supreme exemplar of the breed known as the *philosophe*. During his century the term *philosophe* became both a term of invective and a rallying-cry. According to Diderot's own school of opinion the *philosophe* was a philosopher who had joined the party of humanity. He was a man who not only reasoned but lived by reason and was thus a pre-eminently sociable and civic-minded individual, one who – as the anonymous article PHILOSOPHE in the *Encyclopédie* was to put it – regarded civil society as his "divinity", and to whom Reason was what grace is to the Christian. He was on the side of virtue and decency (*honnêteté*) and differed from the common run of his fellow-citizens only in a superior grasp of logic and general principle.

By contrast, among the orthodox and *bien-pensant*, the term *philosophe* carried a sulphurous aroma: one of its meanings was "misanthrope" and another was "freethinker", and as late as 1740 the *Dictionnaire* of the Académie defined it as "A man who, by libertinism of mind, places himself above the duties and ordinary obligations of civil and Christian existence. It signifies a man who refuses himself nothing and observes no constraint." In the bookselling trade, the term "philosophical books" was used to include pornography.

There had for long been a freethinking tradition in France, and numerous clandestine writings had been in circulation in manuscript form. They were read both in certain aristocratic circles – for instance the group of so-called "Free seekers" that clustered round the Duc de Noailles – and among humbler folk in the more literate professions: teachers, music-masters, copyists,

bookbinders, *colporteurs* and the like. Some of these writings were
by impecunious radicals and garret-dwellers; others were the
secret productions of highly respectable *savants* and members of
the royal Academies. Many of the writings themselves dated back
to the beginning of the century or even earlier, but the flood of
copies had increased rapidly from the 1740s onwards, defeating
all efforts at suppression.

In these subversive writings one can identify a certain loose
orthodoxy or consensus of opinion on certain topics, easily
recognisable as the groundwork of the more elaborate systems of
thinkers later in the century – those of Helvétius and d'Holbach,
for instance – and likewise of Diderot's own philosophical
fantasies. One may summarise it thus:

MATERIALISM. Only the material exists, "soul" being a superfluous
hypothesis; matter has existed from all eternity (thus there is no
need to suppose a Creation); matter is, or may be, self-moving; it
may display the capacity for feeling and thought; the particles of
matter may combine in innumerable different configurations,
producing an infinity of different animate or inanimate forms.

PERCEPTION. All knowledge derives ultimately from the senses; it is
produced in us mechanically, without the aid of volition. Reason is
the fruit of the senses, being rendered possible by the power of
comparing one sense-impression with another; the information
supplied by one sense may conflict, or seem to conflict, with that
supplied by another; nevertheless it is useless to seek for any other
source of knowledge.

DETERMINISM. Every thing in the order of nature is causally
determined; Nature produces all sorts of prodigies, but blindly and
according to purely mechanical laws; the universe being eternal
and uncreated, all possibilities are eventually realised; the moral
life, being as much subject to inexorable laws as are physical
phenomena, can be studied in the same mathematical spirit; the
causal factors in moral behaviour are pleasure and pain, human
behaviour being always ultimately explicable in terms of self-
interest.

NATURE. Moral and social laws are always relative, but there may
be an ultimate appeal to natural law.

RELIGION. Organised Christianity and religion are the enemies of all social progress; the church is a social parasite; a promising path of attack on them lies through comparative religion and scientific bible-study; tolerance is the requisite of all good rulers; an atheist can be as morally good a man as a believer – indeed he is quite likely to be a better one.

Diderot, from these and more orthodox sources, was already beginning to evolve his own philosophic system. His approach was an eclectic one, and in an article ÉCLECTISME in the *Encyclopédie* he would praise the eclectic, who, "from all the philosophies, which he has analysed without partiality or prejudice, makes himself a particular and domestic philosophy that belongs to him." The process would take him some years yet, but one element in it, and imaginatively speaking the most important one, would remain constant: the grand materialistic world-view of Lucretius in the *De rerum natura*. That the senses are the foundation of all belief and the only source of knowledge; that there is a plurality of worlds and an infinite universe; that there are no "final causes"; that the Gods, if Gods there be, take no interest in mankind; and that the chief goods of human existence are a body free from pain and a mind not enslaved by superstitious fear: this was a philosophic vision profoundly appealing to Diderot, and what sounds like Locke or Spinoza in his writing often comes straight from Lucretius.

He had done some reading in the English philosophers, and was impressed by Hobbes and even more so by Shaftesbury, whose enthusiastic Deism and cult of "moral sentiment" were particularly attractive to him. Shaftesbury was not very well known in France, certainly not so much so as Locke or Berkeley, and in the months following his marriage Diderot managed to obtain a commission to translate him. He chose the work most central to Shaftesbury, the *Inquiry Concerning Virtue and Merit*, which had originally been published in 1699; however, as he proceeded, he found himself adapting Shaftesbury's text pretty freely, adding his own interjections and digressions and, in his Notes, drawing opinions from other writings of Shaftesbury's. It was not the last time that he would produce original work in the margins of another writer's text. The resulting book, *Essai sur le mérite et la vertu*, was liable to be considered subversive, so when it appeared in April 1745 it did so without either Shaftesbury's or Diderot's name upon it and under a bogus "Amsterdam" imprint.

The reason why the *Essai* would be thought dangerous was the obvious one, that it advocated a natural morality independent of Revelation. The central and all-important argument in Shaftesbury's *Inquiry* is that anyone who affirms a true, just and benevolent God must have some standard of judgement *independent of the Deity* by which to decide that God is in fact true, just and benevolent. The manoeuvre is a very effective one, with potentially the most radical implications, tacitly turning the Deity himself into a human construct (on the lines of Samuel Butler's "An honest God's the noblest work of man").

That we do in fact possess such an independent standard of ethical judgement, so Shaftesbury's argument runs, is a familiar truth. We possess by nature a faculty for perceiving not merely physical beauty but *moral* beauty. Even a depraved person is not altogether without this faculty, and it takes a systematic course of error to eradicate it completely. Thus a creature may be struck by the beauty or ugliness of intellectual and moral objects before forming any clear notion of a divinity. (Diderot adds, in a note, that many races have never had the idea of a divinity at all.)

But if God is not the originator of the ethical life, asks Shaftesbury, what is his role in it – and more particularly, what kind of a God is favourable to the good life? Not an all-powerful one, he says; for the fear of hell and hope of heaven are not "liberal and generous affections". But certainly a God who is supremely good, for such a God would provide the perfect audience for good deeds. "How shameful it would be to commit a vile action in such company! What satisfaction, on the other hand, to have practised virtue in the presence of our God!"

The main motive of virtue, in fact, says Shaftesbury, is just such applause, whether on the part of God or on that of our fellow-humans. If pleasures could be calculated, nine-tenths of our joys would be found to consist in participation in the happiness of others and desire for their good opinion. Thus virtuous behaviour is in the real interest of each individual, because of the intense pleasure attached to it. "When the social affections make themselves heard, their voice suspends every other sentiment, and the rest of our inclinations are silent. The enchantment of the senses has nothing to compare with this." The only reason why a wicked person would not prefer these joys is because, being wicked, he has never experienced them.

The genial and enthusiastic Shaftesbury, who described Christianity as "a witty and good-natured religion", left a permanent mark on Diderot. He adopted a certain strain of rhapsody about Virtue in which he speaks with the very accents of Shaftesbury; it is one of the aspects of the "I" character ("Diderot-*Moi*"), in the novel *Le Neveu de Rameau (Rameau's Nephew)*, that the Nephew finds invincibly comic. His own utilitarianism was originally inspired by Shaftesbury's mode of proving that "virtue and interest may be found at last to agree", and it was from Shaftesbury that he gained his conception of ethics as a kind of moral spectacle or theatre.

We need not ask ourselves, though, how much, in detail, Diderot went along with Shaftesbury's views, for his own were on the verge of a radical change. At the time of this translation he was still a theist, or wanted to appear as such. Indeed he was more orthodox than Shaftesbury: he piously reminds his readers that Shaftesbury's strictures upon unsociable men should not be thought to apply to religious solitaries and rebukes him for advocating tyrannicide, a crime which has been so solemnly condemned by the Sorbonne. Jacques-André Naigeon, Diderot's atheistical friend of later years, describes the religiosity of these Notes of Diderot's as what doctors call "a perfect crisis", expelling all superstitious matter from his system, a fact proved by his sceptical *Pensées philosophiques (Philosophical Thoughts)*, published in the following year.[1]

For Diderot, the public he imagined himself as addressing, and the one before which he was justifying himself, always included his home circle at Langres. He liked to raise his differences with Langres to the level of a public debate. Thus he prefaced the *Essai* with a dedicatory epistle "To my Brother", a first blow in a long and often acrimonious conflict over religion between Denis and his younger brother Didier-Pierre. Didier-Pierre was as narrowly orthodox and austere as Denis was hedonistic and intellectually adventurous; indeed he was already threatening to become a saint, and Denis, who was fond of his brother, believed that religion was doing him great harm. It was, he thought, teaching his brother intolerance, and making him impossible to live with. He was not the only person to think so; their father later lamented, "Alas! I have two sons. One will certainly be a saint, and I am very much afraid that the other may be damned. But I cannot live with the saint, and I greatly enjoy the time I spend with the damned one." Diderot's dedicatory epistle thus took the form of a manifesto against intolerance – a rather devious one, in which, in exchange for conceding, what Shaftesbury would not have conceded, that there is "no virtue without religion", he bargained for his brother's agreement that of all intellectual vices fanaticism was the worst.

The *Essai* received very respectful reviews in the journals, even on the part of the Jesuit-run *Mémoires de Trévoux*, which might have been expected to look at it askance. Diderot was becoming a "name" in intellectual circles, and his success brought him another invitation from his publisher Briasson, this time to translate the great three-volume *Medical Dictionary* of Robert James, published in Britain in 1743-45. It was the occasion of an act of generosity on Diderot's part, for, badly as he needed the money, he insisted on passing on part of the work to Toussaint and to another of his necessitous friends, the translator and part-time pornographer Marc-Antoine Eidous.[2]

Some time during the first year of their marriage, the Diderots had moved from the Left Bank and found lodgings in the rue Traversière, on the outskirts of Paris out beyond the Bastille. It was here that, in September 1744, they buried the six-weeks-old Angélique, their first child. The move may have had something to do with secrecy, for Nanette was also still living under her maiden name. In the parish burial-register Diderot is described as a "day-labourer".[3]

By May 1746, however, when a second child was born to them, also fated to die in infancy, they had returned to their familiar Left Bank scene and were living in humble lodgings in the rue Saint-Victor, in the parish of Saint-Médard. The parish had been the scene, twenty years earlier, of the episode of the "convul-sionists". A belief had grown then that the body of a saintly Jansenist deacon named François de Pâris could work miracu-lous cures, and for several years from 1728 onwards the graveyard of Saint-Médard had been thronged, day after day, with the sick and with spectators come to watch their convul-sions. The cemetery had eventually been closed by order of the government, but the convulsionist sect had continued to hold meetings behind closed doors – occasions for prophesyings and violent penitential ceremonies, even crucifixions. Diderot had witnessed the scenes in the graveyard soon after his first arrival in Paris, and the work he was next to publish, the *Philosophical Thoughts*, is coloured by his repugnance.

A suburb resounds with outcries: the ashes of one of the elect perform more prodigies there than Jesus Christ performed in the whole of his life. People run, or are carried to the spot, and I follow the crowd. I have no sooner arrived than I hear people exclaiming "Miracle!" I approach, I look, and I see a little lame boy walking with the help of three or four charitable onlookers; and the crowd, awe-struck, cry "Miracle! Miracle!" Where is the miracle, then, you fools? Cannot you see that the rogue has done no more than change one pair of crutches for another?

(LIII)

The *Philosophical Thoughts*, Diderot's first independent work, was intended, or so at least the title would suggest, as a sceptical counterblast to the *Pensées* of Pascal. It is in part a re-working, in manifesto-like form, of ideas from Shafesbury; but from another point of view it can be seen as a kind of résumé or *summa* of freethinking arguments on religion – the ones that, as I have said, had been circulating for half a century in clandestine writings. The book was written very speedily in the spring of 1746 (Diderot's daughter says over Easter, though this sounds far-fetched) and it was distributed in clandestine or bootleg fashion. It made a considerable impact, provoking a whole string of retorts and rebuttals, and it earned the compliment of being condemned to be burned by the Paris *Parlement*, as "presenting to restless and reckless spirits the venom of the most criminal opinions that the depravity of human reason is capable of." Of Diderot's works it was the one that went through most editions in the eighteenth century.

That it should succeed in this way one can well understand, for it is in some ways a brilliant book. It is, for one thing, full of extremely quotable epigrams, in the tradition of Pascal or La Rochefoucauld. For instance: "The thought that there is no God has never frightened anyone, but rather the thought that there might be one, of the kind that people describe"; or "It can be required of me that I look for the truth, but not that I should find it." The book is also, in places, remarkably eloquent. Stylistically, indeed, it is rather a jumble, or perhaps one should say pastiche; and from an intellectual point of view, though for a better reason, it is even more unstable, swivelling confusingly between Theism, Deism and putative Atheism. The reason for this, undoubtedly, is camouflage, for the dangers to a heterodox writer were then very serious indeed.

The *Pensée* that most rings in one's memory is the seventh:

What voices! What outcries! What groans! Who has shut up all these plaintive corpses in these prison cells? What crimes have these poor wretches committed? Some beat their breasts with stones; others tear their bodies with iron hooks; all have regrets, sorrow and death in their eyes. Who condemns them to these torments? . . . *The God whom they have offended* . . . What sort of God is He? *A God full of goodwill.* . . . Would a God full of goodwill find pleasure in bathing in tears? Would such terrors not be a reflection on his clemency? If criminals had to appease the fury of a tyrant, what more could be expected of them than this?

(VII)

Diderot had good reason, from personal experience, for a hatred of monasteries. Not only had he been forcibly incarcerated in one, but his younger sister Angélique had entered one of her own volition and was shortly to die there in a state of religious mania. Diderot always tended to see monasteries in terms of imprisonment, whether self-imprisonment or arbitrary imprisonment by a tyrant; and in the *Philosophical Thoughts* this hatred of incarceration becomes, in some striking lines, the metaphorical basis for a sort of millennial Deism.

> . . . Men have banished Divinity; they have confined it in a sanctuary; the walls of a temple hide it from sight; it has no existence outside. Madmen that you are; destroy these enclosures which so narrow your ideas; set God free; see him wherever he is to be seen, or say that he does not exist.
>
> (XXVI)

Again, as a complement to its impassioned condemnation of claustration and of self-mortification, the *Pensées* offers a defence of the passions:

> People declaim without end against the passions; all the ills of mankind are attributed to them, and it is forgotten that they are also the source of all pleasures. They are an element in the human constitution of which one cannot speak too highly or too lowly. But what annoys me is that everyone merely regards them from their bad side. It would be considered an insult to Reason if one said a word in favour of its rivals. Nevertheless it is only passions, and grand passions, which are able to raise the soul to grand achievements; without them there would be no sublimity, whether in morals or in works; the fine arts would revert to infancy, and virtue would become petty-minded.
>
> (I)
>
> It is the height of absurdity to aim at the destruction of the passions. A fine plan indeed, the religious person's, to torment himself like a madman so as to desire nothing, to love nothing and to feel nothing. He would be a real monster if he succeeded!
>
> (V)

Diderot, as we shall see, was on the whole tolerant in his anticlericalism and in his attitude towards religion generally – more so in some ways than Voltaire. It was always the monastic idea which aroused really passionate hatred in him and captured his imagination. Michel Foucault writes, in *Madness and Civilisation*, "It is no accident that sadism, as an individual phenomenon bearing the name of a man, was born of confinement and, within confinement, that Sade's entire *oeuvre* is dominated by the Fortress, the Cell, the Cellar, the Convent, the inaccessible Island."[4] We shall see how Diderot returned to the theme of claustration later, not however in Sade-like or Gothic-horror style, but in a profound and humane novel, *La Religieuse* (*The Nun*).

The other strong impression that the *Pensées* leaves on us is that, of the various philosophico-religious positions canvassed by Diderot, it is Scepticism that – by far – he makes most persuasive, and indeed seems clearly to take his stand on. "Force a Pyrrhonian to be *sincere*, and you will have a sceptic," runs *Pensée* XXX. Scepticism, argues *Pensée* XXIV, is a school of rigour, scrupulousness and responsibility:

> Scepticism is not for everybody. It presupposes profound and disinterested inquiry. He who is a sceptic merely because he does not know the grounds for belief is no more than an ignoramus. The true sceptic has counted and weighed reasons. But it is no mean task to weigh reasonings. Who among us knows their precise value? Offer a hundred reasons for the same truth, and they will all have their partisans. Every mind has its own telescope. The objection that is a colossus in my eyes disappears for yours; you are unimpressed by an argument which crushes me. If we are divided over intrinsic value, how shall we ever hope to agree over relative value? Tell me, how many moral proofs are needed to counterbalance a metaphysical conclusion? Are my spectacles at fault, or yours? If it is so difficult to weigh reasons, and there are no questions which do not present reasons on both sides, and almost always in equal quantity, why do we rush to conclusions in such a hurry? Where do we get that tone of confident decision?

That Scepticism is, for the moment, his own chosen position is clear from the title of his next work, the unpublished "Promenade du sceptique".

Diderot's friendship with Rousseau had flourished. Rousseau had spent a year in Venice, as secretary to the French ambassador. The appointment had ended in a spectacular quarrel, and on his return to Paris in the autumn of 1744 he had put up, as once before, in a humble lodging-house near the Luxembourg. There he had begun an affair with one of the maids, Thérèse Levasseur. She came from Orléans, lived with her elderly parents, who had come down in the world, and was supporting them on her modest wages. She was shy and affectionate and quite remarkably ignorant; she never really learned to read or to count, and Rousseau had the greatest trouble in teaching her to tell the time. Nevertheless he found the relationship, which was to last the rest of his life, the greatest comfort; and, though his friends were rude about Thérèse, he was inclined to compare his lot very favourably with Diderot's, whose wife Nanette had proved to have a rasping temper. During the following decade Rousseau had five children by Thérèse and despatched each of them to the Foundlings' Hospital, a secret which later returned to plague him.

Rousseau's ambition now was to make his mark as an opera-composer. In the meantime, however, he had made his peace with Mme Dupin, with whom there had been a falling-out, and he was again working for her and Francueil, helping her with her writing and Francueil with his chemical research. (The two even composed a treatise on chemistry together.) This sort of arrangement was becoming fashionable in Paris, and his employers treated him in a flattering manner, so that he did not resent his dependent role.[5]

Mme Dupin's house was at the other end of Paris from Diderot's, but Rousseau and Diderot and another friend, the Lockeian philosopher Etienne de Condillac, formed an arrangement to meet once a week at the Palais Royal and to go and eat at a nearby restaurant, the hotel Panier Fleuri. In his *Confessions* Rousseau writes nostalgically about these little weekly dinners, saying that Diderot must have enjoyed them, "for though he practically never kept appointments, he never missed one of these."[6] Condillac, whose ideas would have some influence on Diderot, was at work on his first book, the *Essay on the Origins of Human Knowledge*, and Diderot, always one to busy himself on his friends' behalf, took it on himself to find a publisher for it.

Recently Diderot had become friendly with the mathematician Jean Le Rond d'Alembert, who was to play an important part in his life. D'Alembert had a curious history. He was the illegitimate

child of the aristocratic *salonnière* Mme de Tencin,[7] who had
abandoned him as a baby, depositing him on the steps of a nearby
church. Eventually his father, an artillery officer named
Destouches, had traced him to the Foundlings' Hospital and had
settled a small annuity on him. He had been brought up by a
foster-parent, a kindly glazier's wife named Madame Rousseau,
whom he came to regard as his "true mother" with whom he
would live till near his fiftieth year.

D'Alembert was four years younger than Diderot, but already
very distinguished in his own field, the author of an important
Treatise on Dynamics (1743) and a member of the Academy of
Sciences, as of various foreign academies. He was physically
slight, with a high falsetto voice: a wit and a brilliant mimic, and a
cooler and more competitive character than Diderot, very clear-
cut and intransigent in his atheism and contemptuous of the
stupidity of the people, "its aimless curiosity, its coarse charity,
its inept and inoffensive goodness, its compassionate harshness."[8] It was a euphoric period in his life. Marmontel, in his
Memoirs, tells us how "After spending his morning working at
algebra and resolving problems in dynamics and astronomy, he
would emerge from the house of the glazier's wife like a pupil
escaped from school and asked only to enjoy himself; and by the
sprightly and amusing turn shown by his luminous, profound,
and solid mind, he made you forget the philosopher and the
scientist to see in him only *l'homme aimable*." By this time, as
Marmontel implies, he lived a busy social life, being an habitué of
the famous *salons* of Madame Geoffrin and Madame du Deffand.
He was not, however, a social climber; indeed he considered that
men of talent tended too much to prostrate themselves before
those who ought by right to be at their own feet. "LIBERTY, TRUTH
and POVERTY" – he was later to write – "are the three words that
men of letters should always keep before their eyes, as a monarch
should keep POSTERITY."[9]

Diderot and Rousseau had plans to produce a periodical, to be
called *Le Persifleur*, and they invited d'Alembert to contribute. The
periodical came to nothing, but before long Diderot and d'Alembert
were to be closely involved as editors of the *Encyclopédie*.

The first stirrings of the *Encyclopédie* occurred when, early in

1745, the bookseller André-François Le Breton formed a plan to bring out a French translation of the *Cyclopaedia, or Universal Dictionary of the Arts and Sciences* of the Scottish encyclopaedist Ephraim Chambers, published in 1728. A quarrel with the translator ensued, and later in the year Le Breton formed a consortium of booksellers to re-launch the project on a more ambitious scale, involving some expansion and rewriting of Chambers's text. At this point he engaged the services of d'Alembert, in some sort of editorial capacity, and a few months later those of Diderot, who joined the payroll in February 1746. For the moment it was merely part-time work; but in the summer of 1747 the chief editor, the *abbé* Gua de Malves, resigned or was dismissed, and Diderot and d'Alembert were appointed to take his place.

Le Breton was one of the leading French bookseller-publishers, with the largest printing-house in Paris; the revised *Encyclopédie* was conceived very lavishly and would represent a very large capital investment. Diderot, who was by temperament a polymath, soon saw immense possibilities in it. He perceived very clearly, as did d'Alembert, the importance of what Chambers had attempted. Such few general encyclopaedias as there had been, apart from his, had been published before the great age of French science and letters, the epoch of Descartes, Bernoulli, Racine and Bossuet.[10] What could be more rewarding, then, as well as publicly useful, than to present this mass of new knowledge and discovery *as a whole*, displaying all its logical and genealogical interconnections? What better opportunity, more-over – though this was not to be spoken so loudly – for the enemies of prejudice and superstition to form themselves into an effective fighting force?

The enterprise was on such a scale that, for good or evil, the eyes of the government and the church were on it from the start; and it was arranged that, to explain and promote the work, Diderot should have an interview with the Chancellor of France himself. D'Aguesseau, the Chancellor, was a venerable and Cato-like dignitary, of immense piety, and he can scarcely have liked all that he had heard of Diderot. However, Diderot's eloquent account of the new project and of its amazing and glorious potentialities seems quite to have dazzled the old gentleman, and he went so far as personally to recommend Diderot as editor-in-chief. A year or two later Diderot drew up a *Prospectus* for the *Encyclopédie*, and from it one can guess at one at least of the arguments he employed upon d'Aguesseau. It was both cunning and patriotic, and ran thus: the best part of *Chambers* had of necessity, and in the nature of things, been drawn from French authors, so what must be the reaction in France if all that was now produced was a mere translation from *Chambers?* "It would excite the indignation of scholars and protests from the public, who would be receiving, under a new and pretentious title, riches that had already been in their possession for many years past." Whether at the Chancellor's behest or not, Diderot was in fact given the post of editor-in-chief, with d'Alembert as a more or less equal collaborator, in charge of the mathematical articles.

The ebullient Diderot and the cautious d'Alembert were not only different in temperament, but were, as time would show, radically different in scientific outlook, yet in the initial planning of the *Encyclopédie* they seem to have seen eye to eye. What, evidently, they needed first to decide upon was some overall system of classification (or "tree of knowledge"), to serve both as a shaping principle and for mnemonic or retrieval purposes. Here they were influenced by Buffon, who, in the recently published first volume of his great *Natural History*, had described the near-impossibility of finding an agreed classification even for the contents of the natural world. For the even vaster field that they were to deal with, a "tree of knowledge" based, like Buffon's, upon *things* (i.e. upon the *objects* of knowledge) seemed to them totally impracticable; thus they opted instead, as Francis Bacon before them, for a system based upon human faculties (that is to say, on the *sources* of knowledge). Of these faculties, *memory, reason* and *imagination* were to be regarded as the most fundamental, and to them would correspond the three great branches of knowledge, History, Philosophy and Poetry, with their various subdivisions –the whole ramification being eventually set out in Diderot's *Prospectus* in the form of an elaborate chart or "Illustrated System of Human Knowledge". The "tree" adopted was fairly close to

Bacon's in *The Advancement of Learning*, but differed from it, significantly, in treating revealed religion as a mere branch of "philosophy".

The *Encyclopédie* would be designed, so Diderot wrote in the *Prospectus*, to serve all the purposes of a library for a professional man on any subject apart from his own. It should also, as a totality, become a permanent "sanctuary" where "men's knowledge shall be secure from time and revolutions." It should be more, however (this was an idea especially dear to Diderot) than just a repository: it should also be an engine of research and a stimulus to invention. By its up-to-date account of the state of knowledge in all its various departments, it should prevent scientists and scholars from wasting their time, by accident or design, in going over old ground. The *Encyclopédie* would thus promote fresh discoveries and "excite genius to open untrodden paths for itself, treating as their stepping-off place the point where great men have stopped." As for the decision to follow *Chambers* and combine an Encyclopaedia with a Dictionary (that is to say, to arrange the contents by letter of the alphabet), it might be thought, said Diderot, that this would destroy "liaison" and be a violation of the "tree of knowledge", but in practice this would not be so. The system of knowledge would be made visible in "the disposition of the materials within each article and by the exactitude and frequency of cross-references."

The next task was to recruit contributors – which, indeed, both d'Alembert, with his academic connections, and Diderot, with his large miscellaneous acquaintance, were well placed to do. They invited their friend Rousseau to write the articles on music. Buffon, though he warmly approved of the *Encyclopédie*, could not be persuaded to contribute on Natural History, but his distinguished colleague Daubenton agreed to do so. Many specialist articles – on naval matters, civil engineering, finance and the like – were assigned to highly-placed government officials. The articles on Ballet and Opera were given to the composer Cahusac, a well enough known name in his day, and the grammatical articles to the eminent philologist César du Marsais. That in his unpublished writings du Marsais was a doctrinaire atheist was no doubt well known to Diderot, but

certainly not to the general public. As regards the tender subject
of theology, for which the doctors of the Sorbonne firmly expected
to be given responsibility, the editors arrived at a compromise.
They assigned a number of the articles to writers of a freethinking
tendency but gave many others to a certain *abbé* Mallet, the Royal
Professor of theology and a man of orthodox, not to say
thoroughly obscurantist, views. (A preposterous article by him,
ARCHE DE NOÉ, discussing the exact internal arrangements of
Noah's ark, has often been taken as covert satire but, it would
appear, was composed in all earnestness; at all events he was a
stout supporter of the revocation of the Edict of Nantes.)
D'Alembert would eulogise him with perhaps suspicious
emphasis at the end of his own "Preliminary Discourse", and his
appointment may reflect some behind-the-scenes bargain with
the Church. D'Alembert himself, naturally undertook the articles
on mathematics and theoretical physics and in fact would write
on quite a variety of other topics. As for Diderot, he would find
himself contributing on almost any subject no one else would
undertake. Thus in the first volume (A–AZY) of the *Encyclopédie*
he would be responsible for long articles on ACIER (steel),
AGRICULTURE, ANIMAL, ART, AUTORITÉ POLITIQUE, ARABES, and
ARGENT (silver) as well as some hundreds of briefer ones of every
possible description – gazetteer items, recipes, definitions of
ethical terms, and so on. Articles by the major contributors, those
of them who did not prefer anonymity, were identified by their
own letter or symbol, Diderot's identifier (when he chose to use it,
which was not always) being an asterisk.

There were two large subject-areas for which he took particular responsibility: these were the description of "arts" (that is to
say of crafts and manufacturing processes), and, especially in
later volumes, the history of philosophy. The description of the
"arts", a subject rather skimped in *Chambers*, was of special
interest to Diderot, and indeed the treatment of it in the
Encyclopédie, and the magnificent engravings illustrating it, are
perhaps the single most characteristic feature of the whole work.
It was also a feature of much socio-political significance. What it
represented, by implication, was a rebuke to court culture and its
attitudes, according to which it was below the dignity of a person

of fashion or standing to know the technical detail of any craft or anything in the way of technical nomenclature. "The men of letters who know the language best," Diderot wrote in the *Prospectus*, "do not know a twentieth part of the words that actually exist." (It was a point that Samuel Johnson was demonstrating at the very same moment in his *Dictionary*.[11]) Further: in the eyes of Diderot, the son of a master cutler, it was a matter of doing justice to a social species, the skilled craftsman, whose role in the national life was absurdly undervalued.

The idea of a "description of the arts" was not, in fact, the *encyclopédistes'* own invention. Indeed such a "Description", sponsored by the Academy of Sciences, had been supposedly in progress, under the direction of the great Réaumur,[12] for forty years or more, though, from either torpor or perfectionism, Réaumur had never brought it near to publication. The main fruit of this official enterprise, so far, had been a series of very fine engravings of machinery and manufacturing processes; and an impression of these plates, or some of them, had found its way illicitly into the hands of Diderot's publishers. Thus, initially, the plan was for Diderot simply to base his written descriptions on these engravings. As he proceeded, however, he found more and more that he needed to visit workshops and interview craftsmen, or commission written briefings from them, and in general to study machines and processes at first hand. On occasion he would get hold of a machine, or a model of it, himself. He also ran up against the problem of trade secrets. The odd truth was, he discovered, that working men tended to believe that whatever they made no secret of would be perfectly well known to everybody, and anything they considered a secret was known by nobody whatever. Thus they regarded Diderot, when he was questioning them, alternatively as an imbecile and as a transcendent genius. His account of his enquiries, though no doubt rather idealised, is impressive:

> We addressed ourselves to the most skilled workers in Paris and the kingdom at large. We took the trouble to visit their workshops, to interrogate them, to write under dictation from them, to follow out their ideas, to define, to identify the terms peculiar to their

profession, to list these, to define them, to converse with those who
had provided us with reports and (an indispensable precaution) to
correct, by long and repeated discussion with one set of workers,
what another set had explained to us imperfectly, obscurely or
wrongly. There are craftsmen who are also men of letters, and we
could name one or two; but they are very rare. Most of those who
practise mechanical arts do it merely to earn their bread and
operate merely by instinct. Among a thousand one will be lucky to
find a dozen who are capable of explaining the tools or machinery
they use, and the things they produce, with any clarity. We know
of workmen who have worked for forty years without
understanding the first thing about their machines. With them we
have had to fulfil the function recommended by Socrates, the
painstaking and delicate one of acting the midwife to people's
intelligence: *obstetrix animorum*.

But there are machines so hard to describe and skills so elusive
that, short of trying the work oneself and operating the machine
with one's own hands and seeing the product with one's own eyes,
they are difficult to describe with any accuracy. Thus it has often
been necessary to get hold of such machines, set them in
operation, and lend one's hand to the work – or as it were, become
an apprentice and produce bad results so as to be able to teach
people how to produce good ones.[13]

Le Breton, whose headquarters were in the rue St Jacques,
provided Diderot with a studio, where he could correspond with
contributors and could store their manuscripts and his own fast-
expanding working library. Jacques Proust, in his *Diderot et
l'Encyclopédie*, gives this rather romantic picture of Diderot at work:

> He was there like the spider in the middle of his web, alert to
> every vibration of the invisible threads stretching across the
> country, sensitive to every gust of wind, quick to seize the smallest
> prey. No French writer, save perhaps Balzac, has had the good
> fortune to be for so long in intimate contact with the most active
> elements of his own society.[14]

The romance had rather quickly gone out of Diderot's marriage.
In the early days the couple had been exceedingly poor, and this
had been a bond between them. Nanette would take pleasure in
denying herself on Diderot's behalf. On days when he was going
to dine in town, she might starve herself or live on bread and

water so that she might give him a good meal the next day. Coffee was too much of a luxury for the home, but she would insist on his having six *sous* a day to buy a cup of coffee at the Café de la Régence, where he would go to watch the chess-players. Nanette had been accustomed to poverty and it did not greatly worry her, though she had qualms on her mother's behalf; and of course there was the question of what would happen if they had a family.

Their trouble, rather, was that they had no intellectual interests in common. Nanette had received only a brief and sketchy convent education; her spelling was always quite wild.[15] She made dogged efforts to read the French classics, but subversive or freethinking writing, such as Diderot was involved in, was outside her experience and alarming to her, and she was suspicious of Diderot's "philosophical" friends.

Two more children, both sons, had been born to them but had died in early years like their predecessors, and it was not till 1753 that Nanette would produce a child, called once again Angélique, who would survive to adult years. At the time of their marriage, out of a jealous fear of possible rivals, Diderot had persuaded his wife and her mother to give up their little millinery business. Thus Nanette was altogether rather isolated; and with the coming of the *Encyclopédie* project, though this meant some financial security,* she was left even more out in the cold.

Nanette was a woman of spirit and very far from negligible: generous and loyal, and sometimes shrewd in her judgements on people. There was, however, a streak of violence in her which made her a terror to servants, and more than once she got into trouble in street-fights. Even in her late fifties she got into a fist-fight with a market-woman – out of chivalrous motives, for the woman was brutally beating a little boy – and she had the woman arrested, though out of charity she finally let the charge drop.

According to her daughter Angélique, she always remained wrapped up in Diderot; and jealousy, for which she very soon had good cause, turned her over the years into a termagant, whose scolding often turned the household into a "hell". Diderot was sorry for her and, though not much given to guilt-feelings,

* See Appendix, Diderot's Finances, pp. 474–5.

somewhat remorseful. He would often tear his hair over their
marriage but kept trying out new tactics: reasoning, self-
amendment, conciliation, resignation and escape. He once even
went to see her confessor, telling him firmly that it was up to him
to remind Nanette of her Christian duties towards her husband –
which indeed the good man rather surprisingly did. To the end
the two retained a certain respect for each other. Diderot's friends
were very rude about her behind his back, as, later, were foreign
visitors and admirers of his, who were inclined to speak of her as
his "Xanthippe"; but when a friend, the *abbé* Morellet, had the
bad taste to joke about her to his face, he gave him a furious
dressing-down.[16] Similarly their daughter Angélique, though she
idolised her father and regarded him as the "consoling angel" of
the household, was greatly enraged, in her own middle age, when
she read a passage in Rousseau's *Confessions* where he referred to
her mother as a "shrew and fishwife" and drew invidious
comparisons between her and that "slut" (as Angélique called
her) Thérèse Levasseur.

> My mother [writes Angélique] was a grumbler and a scold; but
> she was the daughter of a respectable gentleman, who had brought
> his family to ruin. She had been brought up in a convent, and not
> only was she as beautiful as an angel, she had the prudence of one.
> My father would never have had his way with her without
> marriage. My father's fault lay in not educating her for the world,
> out of a jealous wish to keep her in seclusion. I would liken my
> mother's character to a piece of rock-crystal, unpolished and
> bristling with sharp spikes. A very noble and proud soul; a
> frankness incapable of polite hypocrisies; a piety without bigotry
> . . . Loneliness, the petty domesticities to which poverty
> condemned her, distress at my father's infidelities and ignorance of
> the manners of society had soured her temper; so scolding became
> a habit with her.

Nanette's rival, for the space of some five years from 1746
onwards, was Madeleine de Puisieux, the wife of one of Diderot's
collaborators on the *Encyclopédie*.[17] She was seven years younger
than Diderot and decidedly ugly, but she possessed literary
ambitions. Diderot, who was attracted by intellectual women,

was for some time passionately in love with Madeleine de Puisieux. She was chronically hard up, and, according to Diderot's daughter, he wrote the *Philosophical Thoughts* to get money for her.

The affair was well publicised, and when her first book, *Advice to a Woman Friend*, was published in 1749, the rumour spread, to her indignation, that Diderot was the real author, or at least had contributed a good deal to the work. Given his *penchant* for telling authors how to write their books, there may have been a grain of truth in this. In her "Preliminary Discourse", however, she insisted that he had done no more than encourage her and offer to find a publisher for her book, and she gave it him on condition "that my maxims should remain with all their negligences, their contradictions, and all their faults." She added, an eccentric touch, that, since she has decided to be an author, she had better give up all hopes of personal beauty, for this "does not suit with the night-watching demanded by study and application." The book, which is quite lively and caused a mild flutter, purports to present the maxims given to her by an older woman friend during their sojourn together in a convent. It is a kind of manifesto for the emancipated woman, born to a higher destiny than just to "drink, eat, sleep, produce children, play cards, deceive one's lover, husband and confessor and slander one's fellow-women." The doctrine that her worldly-wise friend has taught her is enlightened cynicism: "Be prudent, then, but remember that there is a sort of good reputation which is absolutely necessary to ordinary women but which a woman of exceptional merit is in no need of."[18]

It was for Madame de Puisieux that in 1748 Diderot composed his first novel, the licentious or "philosophic" *Les Bijoux indiscrets (Indiscreet Jewels)*. He had told Madeleine that this sort of writing was quite easy, and, challenged by her, he had set to work to prove it, completing the novel, so we are told, in a fortnight. The novel is in the "oriental" style, popularised by Montesquieu and others, and concerns Mangogul, Sultan of the Congo, and his mistress and bosom friend Mirzoza (a sort of oriental Madeleine de Puisieux). The Sultan suffers acutely from boredom, which even the pleasures of the palace or the conversation of the beautiful and witty Mirzoza cannot always allay. However, by good fortune, a genie gives him a magic ring, which he has only to rub for all the "jewels" in its vicinity (the word *bijou* is slang for the vagina) to begin to speak – to the confusion of their owners and the entertainment and instruction of the Sultan, furnishing excellent new themes for his conversations with Mirzoza. The allegory, as Aram Vartanian has pointed out, is a thoroughly "enlightened" one, showing how "the body, perennially silent, has at last recovered its voice and now dares to speak".[19] In the course of the novel the Sultan turns his ring some thirty-odd times, and from its results Diderot extracts philosophic allegories on a whole range of current topics: sexual ethics, the love-life of Louis XV, French music, French theatre, Cartesian dualism, Newtonian versus Cartesian physics and the growth of the Baconian child-giant "Experiment".

Diderot seems to have borrowed the central device of the speaking *bijou* from an earlier novel, by or attributed to the Comte de Caylus, and his style is broadly modelled on Crébillon's in *The Sofa*, though with an added touch of boldness and grossness. The novel, as one might expect, greatly upset Diderot's nineteenth-century critics and biographers, especially the British ones. John Morley, in his *Diderot and the Encyclopaedists* (1886), could not even bring himself to name it and spoke of it as "the lees of Diderot's strong, careless, sensualised understanding" and as belonging to his "vein of defilement". Even Diderot's friend and biographer Naigeon was embarrassed by it, and reported Diderot as often saying he would gladly sacrifice a finger to suppress this "delirium of his imagination". What has helped to confuse the reputation of *Indiscreet Jewels*, moreover, is the idea that it is pornographic; and indeed it is true that, as a kind of dare, Diderot got his friend Eidous to supply him with a page or two of straight pornography, taken from Aretino, *Fanny Hill* and the like, which he included, concealed in their original English, Spanish and Italian.

We need not doubt that Diderot made those protestations of regret, but what tells against them is that he actually added one or two new chapters to the novel some years after it was first written. The new chapters are, moreover, the best and most inventive portions of the whole work. A brief sketch of one of them, Chapter 18, will give a good idea of Diderot's style and purpose. It is entitled "Travellers" and relates what a traveller, despatched by Mangogul to a far-distant island, has reported to his monarch about the marriage customs there. It was explained to him by an islander that, in his country, church and government took the propagation of the species very seriously and had some admirable laws. "You mean," asks the traveller, "you have the secret, which we lack, of ensuring well-assorted marriages?" Not exactly that, the islander had replied, for – in theory at least – there was much less need for it, Nature having designed his countrymen's "jewels" in a superior way.

Some males in his country, he says, have their jewel in the form of a screw, others in the form of a cylinder, of a polygon and so on, and this makes it necessary that they should mate with a female with a "jewel" of corresponding design (screw-threaded, circular, polygonal or otherwise) Also, as a further precaution – remembering the difference in temperature between, say, a highly sexed girl and a "frozen" sexuagenarian – it is the custom for prospective marriage-partners to take part, naked, in a solemn temple ceremony, in which the temperature of their respective "jewels" is taken with a holy thermometer. To couple with a partner outside one's own band of temperature or possessing the wrongly-shaped "jewel" is to commit incest, a grave offence in their country as in others. If it is not possible to take a bridegroom's temperature, his "jewel" not rising to the occasion, island maidens can approach and attempt the "resurrection of the dead". "We call this performing their devotions," says the islander "and a maiden who is zealous in this duty is said to be pious – she is 'edifying'." "So true is it," he continues, eyeing the traveller fixedly, "that all is opinion and prejudice, and what you call a crime we in our country regard as an action agreeable to the Deity."

This is indecent, and intentionally outrageous, but it is quite wrong to think of it as pornographic. Indeed, leaving aside the indecency, it is the method, and to some extent the outlook, of Samuel Butler's *Erewhon*. There is something deliberately jarring in the tone. Diderot is in earnest as a sexual liberator, and he is mocking the reader – pretending just to be pandering to his "corrupt" tastes – out of rage that the church forbids honest discussion of sex, marriage and eugenics. During reading of the Traveller's report, Mirzoza discreetly leaves the room, but on her return Mangogul rebukes her for her prudery. "I wish you would tell me the use of the hypocrisy which is common to you all, respectable or libertine alike. Is it the things which alarm you? No, for you know about them. Is it words? Truly, it is not worth it. If it is ridiculous to blush at the action, is it not infinitely more so to blush at the expression of it? I really love the islanders described in this precious journal; they call everything by its name. Their language is simpler, and their idea of decent and indecent is much more clear-cut."[20]

The writing of *Indiscreet Jewels* had gone on side by side with some of a very different sort. Diderot always had ambitions as an inventor (later he drew up plans for an encoding machine and a sort of typewriter[21]), and in the *Mercure de France* for October 1747 he published a project for the improvement of barrel-organs. This "Project for a new organ" was quite a practical scheme, its originality lying in making the barrel-pins moveable, so that the instrument could be adapted to any piece of music, and a musician might actually compose upon it. Diderot introduced it with charming enthusiasm and with sanguine visions of benefit to humankind – it would take music out of the jealous hands of experts – and it aroused interest in Britain, earning him a flattering review in the *Gentleman's Magazine*.[22] He published it under his own name in the following year as one of five *Memoirs on Different Subjects in Mathematics* (1748), the other memoirs dealing, respectively, with a method for fixing musical pitch, "a new compass made of the circle and its involute", the theory of tension in cords, and atmospheric resistance to the movement of pendulums. The book, a nicely calculated mixture of theoretical and applied mathematics, received an extremely warm press, the reviewer in the *Mercure de France* describing its author as "a learned musician, an ingenious technician and a profound geometer."[23]

The fact that Diderot's *Philosophical Thoughts* had been burned by the public hangman was not in itself enough to put him in immediate danger. It was a gesture that had grown stale from over-use, for the authorities had used it a dozen times earlier in the century, during their conflict with the Jansenists; thus it was received now in rather *blasé* fashion. "Regularly books were condemned to be burnt by the executioner," writes Alfred Cobban, "and as regularly the publishers produced piles of unwanted remainders to be ceremonially destroyed, and continued to circulate and sell the condemned works as freely as before."[24] None the less, from that time on, Diderot had been a marked man, known to be a freethinker or, as a police informant put it (for by now the police had a dossier on him), "a very dangerous man who speaks of the holy mysteries of our religion with contempt."[25] His personal life also counted against him, and in June 1747 his local parish priest wrote complaining of him to Berryer, the Lieutenant-general of Police.

> M. Diderot is a young man who passed his early years in debauchery. Eventually he attached himself to a young woman without money but of the same social position as his, and he married her without the knowledge of his father. To conceal his so-called marriage he has taken lodgings in my parish at the house of M. Guillotte; his wife goes under her maiden name . . . The remarks that Diderot sometimes makes in this household clearly prove that he is a deist, if no worse. He utters blasphemies against Jesus Christ and the Holy Virgin that I would not venture to put into writing . . . It is true that I have never spoken to this young man and do not know him personally, but I am told that he has a great deal of wit and that his conversation is very amusing. In one of his conversations he admitted to being the author of one of the two works condemned by the *Parlement* and burned about two years ago. I have been informed that for more than a year he has been working on another work still more dangerous to religion.[26]

The work "still more dangerous to religion" was no doubt Diderot's "Promenade du sceptique", and it would appear that the police confronted Diderot over the work and made him promise not to attempt to publish it. In June 1749, however, he brought out a *Letter on the Blind: for the Use of those who can See*, a book that, in its oblique way, was much more likely to do real injury to the religious cause. It was Diderot's first really original production as a philosophical writer, and I shall discuss it and its companion, his *Letter on the Deaf and Dumb*, in the next chapter. The *Letter*, addressed to a woman friend – perhaps Mme de Puisieux or Mme de Prémontval, or maybe some merely imaginary personage – was published anonymously and distributed clandestinely, but word quickly went round as to its authorship. It made a considerable impact. Among other things, it prompted Voltaire, who had perceived a promising recruit, to write to Diderot asking the honour of his acquaintance and inviting him, with lavish flattery, to join him some day soon in a "philosophical repast". As a Deist, he found the *Letter* too bold in places, for instance where Diderot makes the blind mathematician Nicholas Saunderson invoke his being born blind as an argument against God's existence. Nevertheless, he told Diderot, he desired "passionately" to talk with him, "whether you think yourself one of his [God's] works or whether you regard yourself as a necessarily-organised portion of an eternal and necessary matter. Whichever it be, you are a truly estimable part of that great Whole which is beyond my understanding."[27]

It so happened that in this summer of 1749 the French government was in a mood of near panic, the country being thick with rumours of national bankruptcy and sexual scandal in high places. Thus it was decided to make a round-up of anti-government propagandists and of suspicious characters generally – atheists, Jansenists, pornographers or abusers of the King. By now Diderot was an obvious candidate, and on 24 July, at seven-thirty in the morning, he was arrested at his house – to which he and Nanette had lately moved – in the rue de la Vieille Estrapade. The two police officials ransacked his study for documents and led him off to a waiting hackney-coach, to take him to the prison fortress of Vincennes, six miles to the east of Paris.

He pretended to Nanette that he was merely called away on business, but as she looked out of the window she saw a kind of scuffle (a messenger from the printing-house approached the coach-window to hand Diderot a proof-sheet but was hustled away) and with horror she realised the truth. It was an arrest by royal *lettre de cachet*, which meant that no particular charge was specified nor any term to his imprisonment; and for the time being Diderot was placed, for extra security, in the grim-looking central keep of Vincennes. An interrogation by the police chief Berryer[28] followed a week later, at which Diderot learned that he was in custody not merely for the *Letter on the Blind* but for his other works as well, and even for Toussaint's *Treatise on Morals*. For the moment he decided to brazen things out and deny authorship of any of the offending works. However, not knowing what would be the next move, or whether he might not simply be left there to rot, and having anyway an intense horror of claustration, he soon began to suffer badly – indeed according to his friend Condorcet's later account, the confinement almost drove him crazy. On 10 August he sent Berryer an impassioned apologia for his career, adding mournfully that, most probably, "despair will soon finish what my bodily infirmities have greatly advanced," and he wrote to Count d'Argenson, the Director of Publications, in a similar strain. He added, as a sort of bribe, that if he might be released and allowed to continue work on the *Encyclopédie*, d'Argenson should receive the dedication of the great work, which would be "the glory of France and shame of England." His captors were careful not to respond; three days later his nerve broke and he wrote again to Berryer, making a full and even abject submission and declaring to his "worthy protector" Berryer, "what the tedium of prison and all imaginable penalties would never have made me admit to my judge: that the *Pensées*, the *Bijoux* and the *Letter on the Blind* are excesses that slipped out of me, but that I can pledge my honour (for I have some) that they will be the last, and that they are the only ones." He would, he said, even disclose the names of the printers and publishers of his clandestine works, and would tell them that he had done so – on one condition, that Berryer would give his word that he would not proceed against them unless they repeated the offence. It was all, and more than, the authorities needed, for there was nothing Diderot could reveal that they did not already know from their own spies. He was thus forthwith released from the tower and given the freedom of the castle grounds, and Nanette was given permission to come from Paris and join him.[29]

His arrest had naturally made a considerable stir, and on the very day that it took place, his publishers addressed an anxious petition to Count d'Argenson claiming that if Diderot were detained for any length of time, they would be faced with ruin. He was, they said, quite indispensable: "the only man of letters we know capable of so vast an enterprise and who alone holds the key to the whole undertaking." This seems to have been d'Alembert's view, too, and in a letter to a friend (19 September) he was careful to minimise his own share of responsibility. "I never intended to have a hand in it [the *Encyclopédie*] except as regards mathematics and physical astronomy. That is all I am in a position to do, and anyway I have no intention of condemning myself for ten years to the tedium of seven or eight folio volumes."[30]

Meanwhile the news had reached Voltaire – to fortunate effect, for his mistress Mme du Châtelet was a relative of the Governor of Vincennes and she wrote pressing this kinsman, the Marquis du Châtelet, to show kindness to his prisoner. This he was very willing to do; and during the remaining three months of his imprisonment Diderot was treated by him with great courtesy and consideration, and he often dined at du Châtelet's table.

Diderot confidently expected that his father, on hearing of his predicament, would hurry to Paris. In fact, he showed no such inclination; rather his letters suggested that he was half enjoying the lesson his son was receiving. He reminded Denis of his mother's pathetic warnings of his "blindness" and told him that everything that the King thought fit to decree was worthy of great respect and must always be obeyed. Denis's best hope in his present plight, he told him, was to give the public "some Christian work". "This will bring down the blessings of Heaven on your head, and I will also preserve you in my good graces" – a remark in which, a critic has observed, he seems rather to equate himself with the Deity. He asked Diderot whether it was true that he had a wife and children. If so, he hoped Denis would give his sister Denise the pleasure of rearing them and himself of having them before his eyes. As regards Diderot's appeals for money, he expressed sardonic surprise that "a man like you, at work on such immense enterprises, should be in need of it", and anyway, for the last month he had enjoyed the privilege of free board and lodgings. However, he sent him 150 *livres*, and also some writing

materials, urging him to make better use of these latter than in the
past.[31]

On Rousseau the effect was very different, and in his *Confessions*
Rousseau describes his anguish at Diderot's arrest. "My sombre
imagination, which always expects the worst, took alarm. I
pictured him as remaining there for the rest of his life. I nearly
went out of my mind." Their first reunion was an impassioned
affair. "On entering I saw only him," writes Rousseau, "I made a
single leap, a single cry and glued my face to his; I crushed him in
my arms, my tears and sobs doing duty for words." Diderot, on
being released from his embrace, turned to a bystander, exclaiming, "You see, Monsieur, how my friends love me!" It was a
gesture very expressive of him, for he thought any edifying scene
was the better for an audience. Rousseau, though – writing when
estranged from Diderot – made a cutting remark about it later.
Had he been in Diderot's position, he said, this would not have
been the first idea to occur to him.[32]

After that, Rousseau made repeated visits to Vincennes, and
one of these was the occasion of a very famous event. "It is two
leagues from Paris to Vincennes," he writes in the *Confessions*:

> Hardly able to afford a cab, I would, if I was on my own, set out
> on foot at two o'clock in the afternoon and would walk fast to get
> there the sooner . . . Often, quite worn out with heat and fatigue, I
> would have to lie down, unable to stir a yard further. To go more
> slowly, I decided to take a book with me. One day I took the
> *Mercure de France*, and as I walked and read, I came upon the
> question proposed by the Academy of Dijon for their prize essay
> for the following year. It was "Whether the progress of the
> sciences and the arts has contributed to corrupting morals or to
> purifying them?" At the very instant of reading I saw another
> universe and I became another man. . . . By the time I arrived at
> Vincennes I was in a fever bordering on delirium. Diderot
> observed it. I told him the cause, and he urged me to give rein to
> my ideas and to compete for the prize.[33]

Their reports differ as to what followed, and Diderot's own
account tended to vary over the years. It seems clear, though,
that Rousseau asked Diderot which side he should take, and

Diderot said something like, "You will take the side that no one else will." The response helped to encourage Rousseau in the direction he was always to follow as a writer.

One decisive effect of Diderot's imprisonment was that, for whatever reason, it was the end of his relationship with Mme de Puisieux. His daughter's account is that his mistress visited him at Vincennes, wearing a particularly smart get-up, and that when she had left, Diderot, who suspected an assignation, scaled the park wall, followed her, and surprised her with a new lover. This does not sound too convincing, but a decisive rupture certainly took place at that time. Her comment, in the preface to her second book, *Caractères* (1751), was: "I have learned that five years of familiarity with people do not reveal the depths of their heart when they have some advantage in concealing it." As for Diderot, he later recalled saying, after he had begun to perceive faults in her: "Madame, take care; you are disfiguring yourself in my heart. There is an image there which you no longer resemble."[34] In the context of ethics his thoughts would often run on images and statues.

The scandal-sheets were as aware of the ending of their affair as they had been of its beginning, and two years later *La Bigarrure* reported, with relish, what was perhaps Diderot's last sight of his mistress. Passing by Diderot's house with two of her children (so their story ran) the vengeful Mme de Puisieux caught sight of Nanette at the window and shouted up at her, "Look at these two children, Mistress Pieface! They are your husband's. He has not paid you the same compliment!" At this gibe, whether truthful or not, Nanette in sheer rage had practically hurled herself out of the window, and the two had had a fight on the pavement – so violent that they had to be separated "by the measure they use in England to separate fighting dogs . . . three or four good pailsful of water." The writer went on to speculate, sardonically, as to the Philosopher's reflections "on marriage and the characters of women, which Mme Puisieux had just demonstrated so much more 'to the life' than her book did!"

Various rumours and legends, some no doubt emanating from himself, began to spread about Diderot's activities during solitary confinement at Vincennes; how he had smuggled in a volume of Plato, or alternatively of the works of Milton, and had used the margins as writing paper; how he had constructed a pen out of a toothpick and made ink from a mixture of wine and stone-chippings, incising the recipe on the wall for the benefit of future prisoners. It is certain that one of his occupations in the tower was to make notes on the first three volumes of Buffon's *Natural History*, for in September he wrote to the Marquis du Châtelet asking for the notebooks to be returned to him. The most significant fact, though, is that he made a translation of *The Apology of Socrates*, of which the text has survived. It marks the beginning of a self-identification with the imprisoned and martyred Socrates, which later became a cult with him. One may suspect in this some unconscious compensation for his less than heroic behaviour at Vincennes.[35]

3

Letter on the Blind and Letter on the Deaf and Dumb

For Diderot, as for almost all of the "enlightened" thinkers, one philosophical tenet held peculiar authority. This was Locke's dogma that there were no "innate" ideas and that all knowledge was derived from experience.

> Let us then suppose the mind to be, as we say, white paper, void of all characters, without any ideas; how comes it to be furnished? Whence comes it by that vast store which the busy and boundless fancy of man has painted on it with an almost endless variety? Whence has it all the materials of reason and knowledge? To this I answer, in one word, from *experience*.[1]

The Lockean view was aimed, most specifically, against Descartes, who held that there were ideas, for instance those of God, Mind, Body, or the Triangle, whose truth was recognised by the light of reason alone and could thus be called "innate". Locke's *Essay Concerning Human Understanding* thus represented as drastic an overthrowing of Cartesian metaphysics, which were dominant at the Sorbonne, as Newton's *Principia* did of Cartesian physics.

According to Locke's own formulation, the term "experience" should be understood as including not only sensations (as received by sight, touch, smell, etc.) but also reflection (i.e. the operation of the mind upon ideas provided by the senses). However, as popularly discussed, the Lockean doctrine tended to be given in the simplified form, *nihil in intellectu quod non prius in sensu* (nothing in the intellect which was not previously in the senses). "These," said the materialist La Mettrie of his five senses, "are my philosophers". Indeed Condillac, Locke's French disciple, criticised him for regarding reflection as an independent source of knowledge, whereas, according to Condillac, it was merely the channel by which ideas were conveyed from the senses. In his *Traité des sensations* (1754) Condillac gives an imaginary step-by-step depiction of the building-up of a human being's mental life from sense-impressions alone. Employing a fantasy conceivably borrowed from Diderot, he ask us to imagine a statue, endowed successively with the senses of smell, sight, touch, etcetera, and acquiring progressively sensation, pleasures and pains, the faculties of attention and of desire, a sense of its own existence, a sense of the existence of an external world, and so on.

Condillac's statue-come-to-life, a well-sustained if prosaic philosophical vision, was an expansion of Locke from the point of view purely of epistemology. However, *nihil in intellectu quod non prius in sensu* was also a subversive theory, or potentially so, in all sorts of other ways. If God has not stamped any predetermined truths on our mind and we have to build up our being for ourselves out of our own direct dealings with the external world, we shall have less reason to subscribe to the dogmas and "common notions" of our society. For though they may claim to come from God, they may be no more than what our governors find it convenient to have us think. Again, if the senses, which are treated rather condescendingly by Descartes and his follower Malebranche, really are our teachers and the architects of our soul, it would seem they are more deserving of honour; and if the senses, then perhaps, as a corollary, the "sensual" as well. By a very little stretching Lockeism can be made to lend respectability to a philosophy of libertinism.

It was such wider implications in Locke's theory, not just epistemological but also theological, political, ethical, aesthetic and psychological, that attracted Diderot. He put to himself the obviously very pertinent question: what would it be like to be deprived of one of the senses? Might it not perhaps change one's world-picture in quite unexpected and radical ways? And if so, would this not reflect back on, and raise doubts about, the world-picture of people with the full complement of senses? It was to explore these questions that he came to write his *Letter on the Blind: for the Use of those who can see* (1749) and its companion the

Letter on the Deaf and Dumb: for the Use of those who Hear and Speak (1751). The sub-titles are significant: he is implying, with deliberate irony, that the "problems" of people lacking a sense are not problems for them alone and are of use in unsettling prejudices and received ideas generally. The works are conceived in a very free, exploratory and impulsive style. In them, one feels, Diderot has for the first time discovered his own personal mode of philosophising, full of dizzying shifts of perspective, returns upon itself, extravagant analogy-hunting and sidelong glides from metaphysical insights to polemical "scores".

It is worth looking rather closely at the opening lines of *Letter on the Blind*; at first slightly inconsequential-looking, read with attention they reveal the drift of the whole work.

I felt fairly sure, Madame, that the girl born blind whose cataract M. de Réaumur was going to remove, would not tell you what you wanted to know; but I had not guessed that it would be neither her fault nor yours. I appealed to her benefactor myself, and through his closest friends, and by dint of various compliments; but we had no success, and the first removal of the dressing will be performed without you. Persons of the highest distinction have had the honour to share this refusal with the *philosophes*; and, in a word, he wished to part the veil before only a few unimportant sets of eyes. If you are curious to know why that able Academician conducts his experiments so secretly – when, according to you, they could hardly have too many enlightened witnesses – I shall reply that the observations of so celebrated a man are less in need of spectators at the time than of auditors after the event. So, Madame, I have returned to my original plan; and, forced to renounce an experience from which I did not expect much instruction either for you or for myself, but from which no doubt M. de Réaumur will profit much more, I have set to work to philosophise with my friends on the same important topic. How happy I should be if the account of our discussions could be fair compensation for the spectacle which I too rashly promised you!

The very day on which the Prussian surgeon performed the operation on Simoneau's daughter, we went to interrogate the man-born-blind of Puiseaux; he is a man not lacking in good sense; a man who is known to many people, who knows a little chemistry and who has attended, with some success, the lecture-courses on botany at the *Jardin du Roi*. His father lectured on philosophy with applause at the University of Paris.[2]

Diderot, it will be seen, begins by announcing a substitution. The great Academician Réaumur having, for his own good reasons, refused all requests to be allowed to witness his experiment on Simoneau's daughter, Diderot has had to satisfy his curiosity by other means. (There is a flicker of satire here, which we need not dwell on; for Diderot greatly disliked Réaumur, regarding him as the arch-example of the secretive scholar.) However, says Diderot, perhaps the refusal was all for the best; for he had never really believed the spectacle would tell his woman friend much.

What was it to have "told" her? Diderot omits to say, treating it as too obvious to explain – and – indeed at the moment of writing it could well have been. He means an answer to the famous "Molyneux problem", first raised by Locke's friend the English doctor William Molyneux: i.e. if a person blind from birth were to be given the use of his or her eyes and were to be shown a cube and a cylinder, would he or she, simply by looking at them, be able to tell which was which?[3]

His woman friend had evidently, in conventionally "enlightened" fashion, expected Réaumur to have the operation performed in the presence of as many competent observers as possible; but this, suggests Diderot, is to misunderstand the nature of the scientific problem. One would learn less from actually witnessing the restoration of sight than from reading what Réaumur would write about it subsequently; and one would probably gain even more by doing as Diderot and his friends had done, that is to say going to question *another* person blind from birth, one who had *not* had his sight restored but possessed the great compensating advantage (from their point of view) of having a philosophic mind and training. In investigating blindness – this is the implication – one should try inwardness and reflection as much as outward observation and, in a word, attempt to do without eyes.

This *Letter* on blindness has, we perceive, already revealed itself as an allegory, concerned with the paradox of blinding oneself in order to see better. Such emphasis on a *substitution*, moreover, makes a fitting preface to a work preoccupied with how a blind person finds substitutes for eyes.

We should also notice something else. The *Letter* begins rather casually and as if in the middle of a conversation, and this would become a favourite device of Diderot's. His works, as we shall see, frequently take the shape, and sometimes even the title, of a "Contribution" or a "Supplement", presenting themselves as an addition to some work, real or imaginary, that has gone before. It is worth noting that the French verb *suppléer* has a wider sense than the English to "supplement" and can mean not only to "continue" but to "supply what is lacking", or even to "provide a substitute for". Diderot's "supplements" exploit all these possibilities.[4] Indeed, we might think of the various sections of *Letter on the Blind* as a succession of "supplements", standing in a sort of leapfrogging relationship to one another. He himself frequently asks pardon for digression ("I promised you a conversation and cannot keep my word without this indulgence"), but we may think of this as largely strategic, for the structure of the work is, in its own way, really quite firm. It has five sections.

Section 1. The report of interviews by Diderot and friends with a certain "blind man of Puiseaux", who has been blind from birth, showing how radically the ethical and metaphysical outlook of the blind must differ from that of the sighted.

Section 2. General reflections on the problems of thinking and (especially) of *imagining* for people blind from birth.

Section 3. Description of the ingenious solutions to these problems found by the blind English mathematician, and lecturer in optics, Nicholas Saunderson.

Section 4. Saunderson's imaginary deathbed conversation with a minister who is trying to convert him to religion.

Section 5. The "Molyneux problem".

It is important to Diderot's strategy that he should begin with the ethical question. For if it can be shown that the blind will possess a different code of ethics from the sighted, this is already quite a victory for relativism. It is one of the several ways of enforcing the point that the world is not simply "there", as a solid and unquestionable fact, but has to be constructed by each individual as best he or she can. For this purpose he offers a most effective flow of teasing and unsettling speculation. People blind from birth, he surmises, will not know what beauty is and will have to take it on trust and from hearsay; they will be likely to be philosophical materialists; they will not be put in awe by the panoply of civic authority – nor indeed will they be frightened by that favourite sanction of authority, prison. (To the magistrate who threatens him with prison, the young "blind man of Puiseaux" is imagined as replying: "Have I not already been in one for twenty-five years?") They will be immune to physical shame. They are very vulnerable to adultery and may have to accept the practice of holding wives in common. They will have a peculiar aversion to theft. They may have a tendency to inhumanity. (For what difference is there, to a blind person, between a man urinating and a man who, uncomplainingly, is shedding his own blood? Do not we ourselves cease to feel compassion when distance, or the littleness of objects, produces the same effect on us as deprivation of sight?)

To these unsettling speculations the "blind man of Puiseaux" has a striking one of his own to add. Diderot and his friends have been describing the mirror and mirror-reflection to him. He explains these to himself as a sort of raising-in-relief, but he cannot understand how it is that the "other self" formed by the mirror is only available to vision, not to touch. "Your little machine seems to be putting two senses into contradiction," he says. "A more perfect machine would perhaps make them agree, though without the objects having to be real. But perhaps a third and even more perfect machine, a less perfidious one, would make them disappear and allow us to realise our error." It is a most richly sceptical remark, and we feel obscurely that he has made a real score.

But further, and even more important, in this first section Diderot is raising the question: in what sense shall we say that a blind person, when discussing the visible world, knows what he or she is talking about? This is in fact a question deeply troubling to the blind themselves, or at all events to blind writers, as is its corollary, how shall the blind writer know when he or she is plagiarising? When the blind eighteenth-century poet Thomas

Blacklock wrote of "red lightnings" and "Purple Evening", it seemed to his readers an unanswerable question, and perhaps was so even for Blacklock himself, whether this was just borrowed poetic diction, or whether he actually thought lightning was red and the evening sky was purple.[5] Equally Helen Keller, when she was writing about the external scene – but indeed in almost anything she was writing – was "tortured" by the fear of not knowing her own thoughts from those of others. "When I wrote a letter, even to my mother, I was seized with a sudden feeling of terror, and would spell the sentences over and over, to make sure that I had not read them in a book."[6]

Diderot's way of handling this issue, as posed by the blind man of Puiseaux, is polemically most cunning and may be regarded as the master-thought of this whole section.

> Our blind man keeps talking about mirrors. You may be sure that he does not know what the word "mirror" means; nevertheless he will never set a looking-glass facing the wrong way. He speaks as sensibly as we do about the qualities and defects of the organ which he lacks. If he attaches no idea to the terms which he uses, he at least has this advantage over most other people, that he never misuses terms. He speaks so well and so judiciously about things which are absolutely outside his experience that converse with him should do much to weaken the inference we all make – without good reason – from what goes on inside ourselves to what is going on inside others.[7]

The argument, as we perceive, has imperceptibly extended to something more general and far-reaching than blindness. The blind man of Puiseaux, being the admirable intelligent person that he is, can talk most convincingly about things he knows nothing about. Indeed, for all his intelligence, he may himself not fully realise he knows nothing about them; and it is only because we happen to know that he is blind and has been so from birth, that we listen to him with anything but complete trust. What better, or more disturbing, analogy could we ask for to the pronouncements of theologians? Diderot's real target, and the force of his lessons in scepticism, have for a moment revealed themselves.

The next two sections, dealing as they do with a specific problem in psychology and logic, are deliberately less polemical. "How," Diderot asks himself, "does a person blind from birth form an idea of figures, i.e. geometrical shapes?" It is a question that he throws himself into with great zest and sympathetic insight. The heart of the problem, as he sees it, is that a person blind from birth can hardly be said, in the literal or image-making sense, to *imagine*. "For in order to imagine, one needs to colour a background and to separate portions out from this background by supposing them as different in colour." Evidently the blind from birth must evolve some alternative to this system, and Diderot envisages a system based on touch – thinking in "images" being replaced by thinking in reminiscences of touch. If the retrieving of tactile sensations can be made into a regular and

"Palpable arithmetic" machines, as devised by the blind mathematician Nicholas Saunderson. In the second diagram the pins are connected by lengths of silk.

disciplined habit, there might be all the makings there of a mental mechanism equivalent to "imagination". Indeed, some such system is a possibility, as Diderot goes to some length to show, by the ingenious hole-and-pin touch-machines invented by the blind mathematician Nicholas Saunderson to help him in algebraic and geometrical calculations.

It is an honest and serious discussion, yet Diderot's fanciful, speculative and even playful style can be seen to be appropriate. For it is not merely a matter of a sighted writer peering into the experience of the blind-from-birth. It is also a matter of the blind-from-birth peering into, and speculating about, the experience of the sighted; and the latter's speculations, when expressed in *language*, are often metaphorically brilliant. They are brilliant, and they are false, and thus they throw light on the very genesis of language. Hence it is not really a digression, though it might seem to be so, when Diderot leads us from the "happy expressions" which the blind stumble into out of ignorance to the problems of literary expression in general and, by various logical steps, to the reasons why the brilliant but "precious" Marivaux is the French writer most admired by the British!

We come now to the most important section of all, and the most polemical – indeed the one to which, in a sense, the whole work has been leading up. There was an authentic memoir of Nicholas Saunderson appended to his posthumously published *Elements of Algebra* (1740), and up to now Diderot has been relying on it. But now he unfolds an invented scene, a Diderotian "supplement" to Saunderson's biography, in which the dying Saunderson is visited by a clergyman named Holmes, who attempts a death-bed conversion. This kind of device represents in a way Diderot's most original contribution to philosophical writing. One may call it his "supposititious" or "foisting" method. By a feat of dramatic manipulation, not exactly ventriloquism, and something more than the conventional "imaginary conversation", he "takes over" a real-life personage, projecting him into some situation that uniquely enables him to see and utter certain truths. We shall meet the device again in *Le Rêve de d'Alembert* (*D'Alembert's Dream*) where the philosopher d'Alembert dreams and is over-heard talking in his sleep – being thus both observed and observer, and what is more a philosophical observer, hence the ideally chosen spy on his own mental secrets.

Mr Holmes has armed himself for his evangelising task with the favourite Deistic "argument from design", the argument that the marvels of Nature cannot but prove the existence of a benevolent Creator. To this Saunderson replies, with melancholy aptness: "Ah, good sir, let us forget that fine spectacle, which was not created for my benefit. I have been condemned to pass my life in the shadows; and you are speaking of prodigies which mean nothing to me and could only serve as proof for you, and those like you, who are able to see. If you want me to believe in God, you will have to make me touch him."

If for an instant this put-down of Saunderson's appears crude, it grows more and more subtle and unsettling the more one thinks about it. It does so because of its double thrust. For in the first place, Saunderson is clearly right. Arguments for the existence of God drawn from the uplifting "spectacle" of Nature are devised by the sighted for the sighted; it is a sort of argument no one would ever have thought of were it not for the special linguistic privilege attached to metaphors from "seeing": one "sees" the truth, one becomes "enlightened", problems grow "clear" or receive "illumination", etc. The "argument from design" is much more deeply rooted in the visual than one might suppose and is very unlikely to have occurred to the mind of a philosopher or theologian blind from birth.

But then, secondly, as Saunderson points out with rueful cogency, a man born blind (a "monster" in creation as one might say) is hardly the person to whom to extol the marvellous "order" of the universe. Who knows what monsters and botched species may have been necessary to produce the humankind of today? Nor can it be said that monsters are not sometimes still to be found.

And turning to face the minister, Saunderson then adds: "Look at me, Mr Holmes. I have no eyes. What had we done to God, you and I, that one of us should have that organ and the other be denied it?" – "Saunderson spoke these words with such a touching and earnest emphasis that the minister, and the others present, could not but share his sorrow and fell to bitter weeping on his behalf."

It is a wonderfully telling *coup de théâtre*; and time after time, in this way, Diderot has Saunderson make capital out of his own life-situation. The trick is played again most effectively in the following:

> Even if the animal mechanism were as perfect as you claim, and as I would wish to believe, for you are an honourable man and would not wish to deceive me, what has that got to do with a supremely intelligent Being? If this perfection in design astonishes you, it is perhaps because you are in the habit of regarding anything you cannot understand as a miracle. I have so often been an object of wonder to you myself that I am not much impressed by your notion of a miracle. I have been an object of awe to people from all over England, who could not conceive how I could do geometry; you must agree they had a poor conception of general possibilities. Does some phenomenon strike us as beyond our understanding? Then immediately we say "It is the work of God": our vanity is satisfied with nothing less. Could we not put a little less pride into our discourse, and a little more philosophy?[8]

By Diderot's strategy Saunderson is given the moral as well as the intellectual advantage, and his blows against the "argument from design" are proportionally devastating.

A year or so later, and after his spell of imprisonment, Diderot wrote a companion piece to his earlier *Letter*, a *Letter on the Deaf and Dumb: for the Use of those who Hear and Speak*. It came out in February 1751, and a few weeks later he published a second edition, containing some "additions" in answer to objections raised by a woman friend of his named Mlle de la Chaux.[9] The touching story of this young woman, translator of David Hume and one of Diderot's most brilliant and ill-starred Grub Street friends, is told in his short story *This Is Not a Story*. *Letter on the Deaf and Dumb* is written in a somewhat different spirit from its predecessor. For one thing, he seems not so objectively and humanly interested in the psychology of deaf-and-dumbness as in that of blindness, and his handling of it is more purely polemical. For another, the line of argument in this second *Letter* is, partly for reasons of caution, extraordinarily entangled. (Diderot himself called this *Letter* a "labyrinth".) The work is valuable as a completion of Diderot's Lockeian project and is full of striking thoughts, some of its aesthetic speculations strongly influencing Lessing in his *Laokoon*. It does not hang together so well artistically as its companion, however, and I shall treat it more briefly.

Diderot considers the deaf-and-dumb from the point of view of what their own method of communication – that is to say, gesture – can tell us about the nature and working of language. In particular, in the first large section of the book, he calls in the deaf-and-dumb for the light they might bring to a current linguistic controversy about what was called "inversion". The debate was about whether the order of words in French was more or less "natural", than the order in Greek and Latin – or to put it another way, whether French showed few or more "inversions" of natural word-order than the classical tongues. The famous Port-Royal *Logic* of 1660 had asserted, with true *grand siècle* confidence, that the order of words in French was the most natural, because the most logical. (The grammarian Louis le Laboureur even asserted, in his *Advantages of the French Language over Latin* [1669], that "the ancient Romans thought in French before speaking Latin."[10]) However by the time that Diderot was writing, a school of opinion had emerged, led by Charles Batteux, which held exactly the contrary: that the grammar and syntax of French, especially after its strict regularisation in the seventeenth century, were actually a fetter on free and natural expression. It was Greek and Latin which observed natural word-order, an order "founded in reason".[11]

The debate, it must strike the modern reader, offers wonderful opportunities for muddle. For, as one cannot help objecting, what can there be in common between "inversion" in a language like French or English, which is governed by rules of word-succession (e.g. such a rule as that subject must come before verb) and "inversion" in a language like Latin, which has no such rules and allows the user to arrange words in whatever order he thinks most telling? "Inversion" reveals itself as a term as elastic – and, one cannot help thinking, as unfruitful – as the term "natural" itself.

Diderot, in his *Letter on the Deaf and Dumb*, is not really concerned to take sides in this debate, and he broaches it for special and oblique reasons of his own, which take some time to reveal themselves. Let it be supposed, he argues, that there is, or was, some "natural" or "primitive" order in the construction of sentences and one wants to find out how "inversions" or violations of this order have crept in. For this purpose it will not be necessary to "go back to the birth of the world and the origin of language", for one could invite somebody to pretend to be deaf-and-dumb and compelled to converse by means of gestures. By observing the sequence of gestures employed by such a pretended deaf-mute to convey some particular thought, one would be able to establish "the order of ideas which would have seemed best to the first men in communicating their thoughts", and also the order in which they would have *invented* oratorical signs. There would be advantages, says Diderot, in using a pretended deaf-mute (a "mute by convention") rather than a real one, since he or she could function as an observer as well as an object to be observed.[12]

It is this last point, one gradually comes to realise, that is the important one for Diderot. It connects with a remark of his in the *Letter on the Blind*, that more could be learned about the nature of seeing from a blind philosopher than from an uneducated person possessing eyesight. (Diderot's answer to the "Molyneux problem" was that what a person blind from birth would "see", when given the power of sight, was not a question with any fixed answer; all would depend on the person's particular training and aptitude, or otherwise, in drawing logical conclusions.) What is involved here, I would suggest, is the inspiration of this whole Lockean project of Diderot's. He is viewing the deprivation of the senses not as a handicap but as a vast philosophical opportunity, an occasion for truly philosophical guessing. We saw the importance he gives to the "happy expressions" and guesses of genius of the person blind from birth when speculating about the visible world. It is a theme he returns to in *Letter on the Deaf and Dumb*, where he tells how he took a deaf-mute along to see the famous "colour-organ" invented by Père Castel.[13] This was a keyboard instrument like a harpsichord which combined colours in the same fashion as one might combine musical notes, and the deaf-mute made a brilliant guess as to its function. He supposed the inventor must be a deaf-mute like himself who had devised the instrument as a way of *conversing* or writing. "Each nuance of the instrument," the deaf-mute supposed, "was the equivalent of a letter of the alphabet, and with the aid of the keys and the agility of his fingers, he could combine these letters to form words, and sentences, and eventually a whole discourse in colour." Of course we need not suppose that this edifying incident in Père Castel's studio ever actually took place. It has all the air of one of Diderot's philosophical fictions, like the deathbed scene of Saunderson.

From the insights vouchsafed to the blind and to the deaf-and-dumb – this is the point – Diderot is drawing an analogy to the insights the philosopher may attain by deliberately blinding or deafening himself. By blinding himself, and stopping his ears to the customary, the philosopher, according to Diderot's notion, is enabled to make "happy guesses", to see further and understand more deeply. He will be behaving, with all seriousness, as Diderot playfully describes himself as behaving in his early theatregoing days, when, knowing the texts by heart and wanting to study the actors' powers of mime, he would listen with his fingers in his ears. (When his neighbours showed surprise he would remark coldly, "Everyone has his own way of listening."[14]) Legend has it that Democritus blinded himself to enable himself to think more intensely, and he is Diderot's model.[15] It is, we should notice, by no means what stock notions of "enlightenment", as a cult of the eye and the shadow-dispelling light of day, would lead one to expect. What is being adumbrated here is a whole philosophic self-discipline, and Diderot adduces its virtues in a pair of La Fontaine-like apologues. He imagines a group of five people each possessed of only a single sense, and this becomes for him an allegory of prejudice and scholastic over-specialisation; for each of the five treats the other four as mad. It is "an image of what happens at every moment in the world: people have one sense only and pass judgement on everything!" Then by contrast, in his *Additions to the Letter on the Deaf and Dumb*, he imagines five whole sects or factions of the single-sensed: a sect of the eye, of the nose, of the palate, of ears and of hands. The spectacle now becomes the opposite one: that of the many tyrannising over the few.

These sects would all have the same origin, ignorance and self-interest; the spirit of intolerance and persecution will soon have crept among them. The Eyes would be condemned to the Petites-Maisons [lunatic asylum] as visionaries; the Noses would be regarded as imbeciles; the Palates shunned as insupportable, with their caprices and false delicacy; the Ears detested for their curiosity and arrogance; the Hands despised for their materialism; and if some superior Power were to second the honourable and charitable intentions of each party, the entire nation would be exterminated the next instant.[16]

We should not be misled by the playfulness, for this rebuke to the sectarianism or chauvinism of the senses connects with Diderot's deepest purposes. In the two *Letters*, perceptual and epistemological relativism is intended, all the time, as a reinforcement to cultural relativism, which is one of the causes that Diderot did most to serve. Elisabeth de Fontenay's words, in *Diderot: Reason and Resonance* (1982), seem very apt:

The great figures borne by his writings – Rameau's nephew, the Nun, the blind, the deaf-mute, the mad mathematician, the savages, the women – undermine the pretensions of the Western male subject to set himself up as the basis of neutral knowledge and sovereign power. Those figures are insidious traps intended to destabilise the current order unique in its five manifestations: political, metaphysical, religious, ethical and mathematical. . . . Thus do paroxysm and marginality in Diderot constantly militate for universality and equality, for the transformation of subjects into citizens.[17]

One may, in fact, interpret Diderot's "Lockeian" project in these two *Letters* in an even wider sense, relating it to the great allegory of Plato's cave with which I began. As it happens, in a letter to a friend about *Letter on the Deaf and Dumb*, Diderot gives a preliminary sketch of the same allegory.

Plato imagines us all sitting in a cavern, with our back to the light and our faces towards the end of the cave. We can scarcely move our heads, and we can only see what is directly in front of us. Between us and the light, there stands a long wall, above which all sorts of figures come and go, advance, retire and disappear, whilst their shadows are projected on the cavern's end. People die without ever seeing more than these shadows. If a man of intelligence, by some chance, grows suspicious of this illusionary show and, with painful effort and contortion, overcomes the powers who are keeping his head turned and manages to scale the wall and escape from the cave, he had better take care, if he ever returns, to keep his mouth shut as to what he has seen. An excellent lesson for philosophers![18]

In this fiction we see the underlying purpose of Diderot's mature philosophical writing and the justification for its divagation, paradoxes, fantasies and provocative speculations. He is inviting the reader to shut his eyes and ears to what the tyranny of governments, and the even greater tyranny of habit, would *want* him to see and hear.

I have not so far mentioned an essential fact about the *Letter on the Deaf and Dumb*; that it is a satire, at times rather a brutal one, on Charles Batteux.[19] There is some historical background to this. In 1750 the prestigious post of Professor of Greek and Latin Philosophy at the Collège de France fell vacant and was given to Batteux, and this was resented by the *philosophes*, who thought the post should have gone to a philosopher (like Condillac, or Diderot himself) instead of to a mere scholar and rhetorician. Thus the *Letter on the Deaf and Dumb*, written in the form of a Letter to Batteux, is plainly, in part, an act of warfare on behalf of "philosophy"; and the conclusion to which Diderot seems really to be driving, in this first part of the *Letter*, is that the whole issue of "inversion" is meaningless. ("What is inversion for one person will often not be so for another.")

Meanwhile Diderot has been preparing the way for a quite unexpected transition from the realm of grammar to the realm of aesthetics. The Port-Royal view is correct, he concedes: French, as regularised in the reigns of Louis XIII and Louis XIV, is now the most logical and reasonable of languages. But, for this very reason, it is quite unsuited to poetry. Thought and experience occur in complex wholes, but language is by nature sequential, a matter of one word after another; and for most normal purposes a discourse is to be judged by the success with which the elements of such wholes are made to proceed in orderly and logical sequence. Language, in this respect, differs somewhat from gesture; for certain inspired gestures (for instance the handwashing of the sleepwalking Lady Macbeth) pack a rich multiplicity of meaning into a single action. And poetry, so Diderot argues, lies more in the direction of gesture, of pantomine and tableau, than of language as conceived by logicians and grammarians. In poetry a discourse is "no longer merely a concatenation of energetic terms which present a thought with force and nobility, it is also a tissue of hieroglyphs, piled one upon another, which *paint* it. I might say, in this sense, that all poetry is emblematic."[20]

With Diderot's "hieroglyphic" conception of poetry we have made a leap into nineteenth-century aesthetic theory; and in what follows Diderot gives some quite subtle analyses of passages from Racine and Virgil in terms of their gestural and mimetic effect. In passing, moreover, while discussing the sequentiality of language, he formulates something close to Mallarmé's notion of words outstripping meaning – that is to say, attracting a meaning to themselves retrospectively.

It happens sometimes that many ideas are attached to a single expression. If energetic expressions like these were more frequent, instead of language continually trailing behind the intelligence, the quality of ideas rendered all at once could be such that language would be forced to chase after it.[21]

What is more significant, though, is the remark which he makes to Batteux, that, in this work, he is "concerned more to form clouds than to dispel them, and to suspend judgements rather than to judge." Whatever the immediate point of this remark (and teasing Batteux is no doubt part of it) it is expressive of Diderot's whole underlying project as a philosophical writer. It is another version of his ruling notion of the philosopher as one who puts his eyes out in order to see more clearly – not a view one instantly associates with "enlightenment". The young Lessing, who reviewed the *Letter* admiringly in 1751, was particularly struck by his observation. "A short-sighted dogmatist," he wrote, "who dislikes nothing so much as the calling in question of the learned principles which make up his system, will know how to pick a number of holes in this writing of M. Diderot's. Our author is one of those philosophers who give themselves more trouble to make than to dispel clouds. Wherever they let their eyes fall, the supports of the most familiar truths shake; and what we imagine we see quite near is lost in the distance. They conduct us 'through dark paths to the shining throne of truth' while schoolmen, by paths full of fancied light, bring us to the gloomy throne of lies."[22]

4

Birth of the *Encyclopédie*

Diderot was released from Vincennes on 3 November 1749, bound by oath "to do nothing in future which would in the least degree be contrary to religion and sound morals." It meant that work on the *Encyclopédie*, at a standstill for four months, could now at last resume. By now a great deal of material had been written ("enough to fill a room"), and it was growing clearer to Diderot how much need, and how much scope, there would be for him to remodel articles by other contributors, adding a proviso here, an expansion, a generalisation, or a delicate piece of subversion there. As one example we may take his treatment of the article ÂME (soul). He "improved" this article, a fairly orthodox or at least Deistic affair by the *abbé* Yvon, by a long addition, signed with his asterisk, subtly ridiculing the whole vexed question of the physical location of the soul.

It was during this time of intense activity that Diderot got to know the Baron d'Holbach,[1] a rich dilettante of ardently materialist and anti-Christian views. D'Holbach had been born in 1723 in the Palatinate, as Paul Henry Thiry, and had been brought up in Paris by his vastly rich maternal uncle, who had made a fortune by speculation at the time of the great John Law financial "bubble". He had thus inherited a title and great wealth, with fiefs in the Low Countries and Germany, and in due course he would become the head of the whole wealthy d'Holbach-Aine clan, twice marrying within it for dynastic reasons. He had studied law at Leyden university, but on his return to Paris he seems almost immediately to have decided to act as Maecenas to the *philosophique* circle and to devote his life to its cause.

D'Holbach was a secretive man, a devoted worker but a

restless one, continually acquiring and tiring of some new intellectual craze. The attics in his vast mansion were crammed with portfolios, cabinets of specimens and collections of all sorts, gathering dust. He was capricious in a rich man's style, with something cynical and priapic about him, and prone to sardonic misanthropy, but he was capable of delicate acts of charity. Diderot would by turns be amused and shocked by the spectacle of this strange man, who seemed to have to reason himself into doing good.

It was d'Holbach's great service to the *encyclopédistes* to provide them with a *salon*, beginning a series of twice-weekly dinners in his *hôtel* in the rue Royale Saint-Roche (now 8 rue des Moulins), at which he brought his aristocratic friends into contact with scientists and *savants* and with the circle of the *philosophes*. The dinners took place on Thursdays and Sundays – days chosen, one may suppose, so as not to clash with the celebrated Monday and Wednesday receptions of Madame Geoffrin (Monday for painters and artists and Wednesday for men of letters). Diderot was a regular guest from very early days, as were Marmontel and the *abbé* Raynal and, with a little persuasion, Rousseau. There was a legend that Diderot converted d'Holbach to atheism; at all events his coterie gained a reputation as a "synagogue" of atheists, where one was liable to encounter any sort of freethinking opinion. (When, some years later, David Hume was a guest at d'Holbach's, he expressed amazement at having been speaking to an atheist – at which d'Holbach exclaimed: "Never seen an Atheist! Look about you. There are fifteen of them round this table."[2]) It was the only Paris salon run by a man and was essentially a masculine gathering, d'Holbach being a lavish host and possessing a superlative *chef* and a magnificent cellar. Diderot became the acknowledged star of these meetings, and there are many descriptions, more than one by himself, of his dazzling improvisations and ardent tirades at d'Holbach's table. It became the place where, most in the world, he felt at home.

However, d'Holbach was not merely host and patron; he was also an indefatigable writer and translator. He made it his business to popularise German scientific writings, the Germans being in advance of the rest of Europe in certain areas like geology and metallurgy, and his home became a little translation-factory, he and his protégés doing their best to "atheise" the works they translated. He was also the author of freethinking works on his own account, of which his famous *System of Nature* of 1770, a complete system of atheism, materialism and determinism, would provoke a good deal of scandal. He always published anonymously or pseudonymously, passing off his first book, *Christianity Unveiled*, as the work of a dead friend; his writings were conveyed in secrecy to a publisher in Amsterdam. Indeed, for whatever reason, conceivably some form of social pride, he contrived to conceal his writing activities even from most of his friends. They may have guessed at them, but if so they kept their suspicions to themselves.

Diderot found in him an enthusiastic contributor to the *Encyclopédie*, and over the years d'Holbach was to contribute innumerable articles on chemistry, metallurgy, mineralogy and the like. In the Preliminaries to the second volume of the *Encyclopédie* Diderot writes of the special debt owed to this "person whose maternal language is German and who is very well-versed in matters of mineralogy, metallurgy and physics. He has given us a prodigious multitude of articles . . . but has asked that his name should remain unknown. This is what prevents us from revealing to the public the name of this citizen philosopher without self-interest, or ambition, or self-advertisement, who, content with the pleasure of being useful, does not even aspire to the legitimate glory of being seen to be so."

By the end of 1750 the publishers of the *Encyclopédie* felt themselves ready to release Diderot's long-delayed *Prospectus*, of which they circulated as many as 8,000 copies, and to solicit subscriptions. The *Prospectus* claimed, with a certain amount of fantasy, that the *Encyclopédie* was "no longer a work to be done" but was complete. It was to comprise no fewer than eight volumes, plus two of plates, and these volumes would follow "without interruption". Subscribers were to pay 60 *livres* on account and further sums amounting in all to 280 *livres*, and non-subscribers would have to pay 25 *livres* for each volume of text and 172 *livres* for the two plate volumes. The work, so the *Prospectus* euphorically and not too veraciously ran, had been written entirely by experts working within their own particular fields, and the editors' task had been proportionately small. They would consider it sufficient glory for themselves if the public were pleased. On behalf of their colleagues, however, and in the conviction that a perfect encyclopaedia would be the work of centuries, they declared themselves eager to receive corrections, which they would submit to "with docility". The honour would not be for them but for "POSTERITY AND THE BEING WHICH NEVER DIES."

The France to which the *Encyclopédie* was to be addressed had for more than half a century been a battleground of religious conflict, and specifically for a duel between Jesuits and Jansenists. Jansenism was an austerely spiritual movement within the Catholic church, akin in some important ways to Calvinism, with which it broadly agreed in its theories about Grace and the irredeemable corruption of the human will, though in other respects, for instance in regard to church order and discipline, the two were quite alien. Its greatest days, those of Quesnel and "the great Arnauld" and their illustrious converts Pascal and Racine, lay by now in the past, and, under continued persecution, it had developed a superstitious and miracle-mongering tendency. Politically speaking the two religious parties were fairly evenly matched, the Jesuits imposing their authority at Versailles and the Jansenists being predominant in the Paris *Parlement*. It was plain that both parties might be likely to find offence in certain aspects of the *Encyclopédie*, but what was also plain was that there might be opportunities for the *encyclopédistes* to drive a wedge between them.

The first signs of hostility came from the Jesuits. They took Diderot's *Prospectus* as a challenge, and their journal the *Mémoires de Trévoux*,[3] in its issue for January 1751, carried a needling little article on it by the director of the journal, Father Berthier. Berthier, with some irony, claimed that he so much shared Diderot and d'Alembert's admiration for Francis Bacon that he was printing Bacon's "tree of knowledge" side by side with the one in the *Prospectus*, so that readers could compare them. The implication, plainly, was that the *Encyclopédie* had plagiarised it. This was a very unjust aspersion, or so it seemed to Diderot,

since he had been at some pains to acknowledge the debt to
Bacon, and he retaliated in a sarcastic open letter. He praised
Berthier for his well-known kindness to totally obscure writers
("who could not, and should not, attain immortality without
you") and promised to save him the trouble of searching for
further extracts, from such a "dry and difficult" work as the
Encyclopédie, for he would send him some himself. There was a
further exchange between them and a little flurry of letters and
pamphlets from other hands. It was an intimation that the Jesuits
might want a confrontation with the *philosophes* and a sign that the
Encyclopédie was going to be the victim of power-struggles in the
nation at large.

The sample which Diderot had enclosed with his first letter to
Berthier was his own article ART. As used in the eighteenth
century, of course, the term "art" signified something nearer to
"craft" or "technology", an illuminating fact from the point of
view of cultural history. Diderot's treatment of it is a striking
piece of writing, philosophically systematic and at the same time
full of enticing and suggestive paradoxes. In part its aim is to
vindicate the social value of the "mechanical arts" and to put to
shame the snobbery which imagines a social gulf between them
and the "liberal" arts. ("How strangely we judge! We expect
everyone to pass his time in a useful manner, and we disdain
useful men.") From this, however, the article makes a glide to the
intellectual value and beauty of "arts" and machines.

> In what physical or metaphysical system do we find more
> intelligence, discernment, and consistency than in the machines
> for drawing gold or making stockings, and in the frames of the
> braid-makers, the gauze-makers, the drapers, or the silk workers?
> What mathematical demonstration is more complex than the
> mechanism of certain clocks or the different operations to which
> we submit the fibre of hemp or the chrysalis of the silkworm before
> obtaining a thread with which we can weave?[4]

This analogy between a machine and a philosophical system or
argument, with its unobtrusive implication that the soul/body
antithesis is an illusion, is very dear to Diderot, and it connects in
his mind with the whole problem of a "description of the arts".

SYSTÉME FIGURÉ
DES CONNOISSANCES HUMAINES.

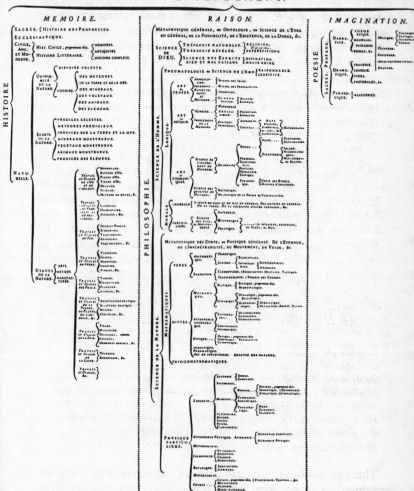

The Système Figuré from the prospectus to the *Encyclopedie*

The problem is partly one of priorities. Sometimes one uses a very complex machine to produce a simple effect, at other times one uses a simple machine to produce a very complex action: to describe the former one will begin by stating its effect, and the latter by describing the machine itself. It is also a problem about nomenclature, for, Diderot argues, the current language of the arts is full of gaps and redundancies and is altogether crying out for reform.

> At times an insignificant difference is enough to make artists invent specific names as a substitute for the generic name. At other times a tool distinctive in its form and its use either has no name or is given the name of another tool with which it has nothing in common. Geometers do not have as many names as they have figures, but in the arts a hammer, a pair of tongs, a bucket, a shovel, etc., have almost as many names as there are arts . . . I am convinced that the most unusual operations and the most complex machines could be explained by a fairly small number of familiar, well-known terms, if it were agreed to use technical terms only when they communicate a distinctive idea . . . It would be desirable if a good logician, well versed in the arts, undertook to describe the elements of a "grammar of the arts".[5]

For Diderot, though, the problem of description extends even further and is in fact inherent in the sequential nature of language. How shall one describe, he asks in another article, BAS (Stockings), that famous example of early industrial technology, the stocking-knitting frame?

> The interdependence of the machine's various parts would seem to require one to talk about them, and illustrate them, all at the same time; and that is impossible – both in prose description, which has to be sequential (i.e. a matter of one thing after another), and in the plates, in which one working part will inevitably obscure the view of another.

Diderot's solution is "a kind of analysis or dissection, dividing the machine up into a number of separate assemblages, showing beneath the picture of each assemblage the parts which are not clearly seen in it, combining these assemblages progressively,

and thus building up the complete machine."[6] What we perceive
is that, in this enormously long article, Diderot is playing with the
fancy of constructing his article as though it were itself a machine.

The article ART was published separately as a pamphlet and
was received, on the whole, with great acclamation. One critic, it
is true, found it too "German" and obscure and asked plaintively,
"M. de Fontenelle, where are you?" That Diderot was too
"German" a writer became a recurring complaint, a fact which
his admirer Goethe, on looking back, found not at all surprising.
"Diderot was sufficiently akin to us; as, indeed, in everything for
which the French blame him, he is a true German."[7]

The Vincennes episode had drawn Diderot and Rousseau closer
together and had led to a general sharing of their friends. In
particular, Rousseau brought Diderot into contact with his other
particular "friend of choice", a young German, Friedrich
Melchior Grimm. It was a momentous introduction, of great
consequence for Diderot's future career. Grimm was the son of a
Lutheran pastor in the imperial city of Ratisbon. At school he had
become the friend of a son of the Comte de Schomberg, and, on
graduating from Leipzig university, he had gained employment
as a tutor in the Schomberg household, coming with the family to
Paris late in 1748 when his friend took up a post in the French
army. There was at this time a little group of German nobles and
princelings in Paris, drawn there partly by the brilliant fortunes
of France's great general, the German-born Maréchal de Saxe,
and Grimm was soon well known within it, giving lessons to the
young hereditary prince of Saxe-Gotha and becoming the
secretary and companion of a nephew of the Maréchal de Saxe,
the Comte de Frise. For such posts he had an all-important
recommendation; unusually for a German, he spoke French
without a trace of foreign accent or idiom. Goethe in his
Autobiography relates ruefully how, during his own years in
Strasbourg, "an evil genius whispered in our ears that all
endeavours by a foreigner to speak French were doomed to
failure. One is tolerated, but is never received into the bosom of
the only church of language. Only a few exceptions were granted.
They named to us a Herr von Grimm."[8]

Grimm was rather an ugly man, with a crooked nose and
protuberant eyes. He was nevertheless a great dandy, with a
penchant for perfumed face-powder. He possessed a cynical tongue
and a nonchalant but despotic manner and was known to his
friends as "Tiran lo Blanc" or "The White Tyrant". In his early
days in Paris he occasionally wrote for the press in the role of
reporter of things German to the French, but before long he
discovered his true vocation, which was as an interpreter of
things French to the Germans – to German princes, in particular –
and to European royalty generally. His friend and employer, the
young and libertine Comte de Frise, gave Grimm use of his *hôtel*,
and Rousseau would be a constant guest there, sitting beside
Grimm at the harpsichord and singing "Italian airs and
barcarolles without pause from morning to night, or rather from
night to morning."[9] The chaplain and tutor to the prince of
Gotha, Emmanuel-Christoph Klüpfel, was another of their
circle, and Rousseau relates a drunken episode when Klüpfel,
who lived with a prostitute, insisted they must all enjoy his
mistress's favours. Grimm stayed with her for hours but,
according to his later claim, did so only to tease his friends and
never laid a finger on her. Rousseau spent so much time with his
German friends that Thérèse began to feel neglected. In return he
introduced Grimm to all his own circle, Diderot among them;
and before long Grimm had become a very confident mover-
about on the social scene, with a mysteriously large and
distinguished acquaintance.

Rousseau, who came to dislike Grimm, accused him of a
parvenu arrogance. He would, according to Rousseau, summon
his servant with a mere shout of "Hey!", as if he did not know his
name, and if he had to give him money, he simply threw it on the
floor. Grimm was subject to grand passions, and there was a
strange episode in 1751 when, in a desperate infatuation with the
actress Marie Fel,[10] he suffered for a week or two a sort of
cataleptic trance and had to be looked after night and day by his
friends Rousseau and the *abbé* Raynal.[11] He none the less came to
be regarded by his friends as peculiarly deep and worldly-wise,
and he became the repository of innumerable personal secrets,
though he would offer none in return. "He is perhaps unique,"

his mistress Mme d'Epinay would write later, "in having the gift of inspiring confidences while giving none."

Between Grimm and Diderot there soon developed a strong alliance. For one thing, and it was an important bond, they had the power to make each other laugh, and they shared a taste for fantastic practical jokes. This was to become the deepest of all Diderot's friendships, but indeed for a time he, Grimm and Rousseau were all very close. It became a fantasy of theirs how they would go on foot to Italy together, with carbines on their shoulders for protection and a purse in common. What would happen, according to Grimm, was that Diderot, who could never hold his tongue, would talk treason and atheism in public, and Rousseau, not Diderot, would be burned by the Inquisition.

It was announced in July 1750 that Rousseau's essay had won the Dijon Academy's prize. Rousseau was ill when the news arrived, so Diderot, who insisted that the essay. must be published, took it on himself to find a publisher for it and saw it through the press. The *Discourse on the Sciences and Arts* came out near the end of the year, and this eloquent diatribe against advanced civilisation and hymn to "ignorance, innocence and poverty" made an extraordinary impression. For months to come, with the attacks on it and Rousseau's replies, it was the centre of attention in the literary journals. "You are raised to the skies," reported Diderot gleefully. "There never was a success like it!"

Rousseau had by this time set up house with Thérèse Levasseur. They had taken lodgings in the rue Grenelle-Saint-Honoré, and Thérèse's parents and various of her brothers and sisters came to live in an apartment two floors above. Thérèse's mother did some housework for them and sometimes acted as Rousseau's amanuensis. She was an insinuating and managing woman, who affected high-society airs, and Rousseau was not really very fond of her, considering her a mischief-maker and intriguer. Her husband, who lived in awe of her, called her "The Chief of Police".

The reception of his *Discourse* had a transforming effect on Rousseau. The work represented only a small part of the "great system" revealed to him on the road to Vincennes, and he took its success, which came at a time when he believed he had not long to live, as a sign that he should devote all his energies to writing – and, by corollary, should reconstruct his whole way of life. He thus resolved to embrace poverty and independence, to "break the fetters of opinion and do with courage whatever seemed good to him without regard to others' opinion." At the moment he was, rather improbably, working as a cashier for a friend of his, Charles-Louis de Francueil, a Receiver-General of Finance, but he decided to give up the post and for the future to support himself by the humble occupation of music-copying. Meanwhile he sold his watch and gave up gold lace and white stockings; a thief (he suspected one of the Levasseur family) completed the transformation by stealing all his best linen. He even made a change in his personal manner. He had always felt awkward and tongue-tied in fashionable society, but now he was to be forced into the public eye. He decided therefore to become bear-like and to despise, or pretend to despise, good manners.

Such is his own account in the *Confessions*, or part of his account. But what he also asserts is that the change in him was, in a way, the mischievous work of Diderot. Somehow, he says, his conversations with Diderot always tended to make him more "satirical and mordant" than was natural to him.[12] No doubt the harsh tone of what he wrote while in Paris was partly "the bile of a man harassed by the turmoil of that great city and soured by the spectacle of its vices"; but it was also, he decided, the effect of Diderot, who urged him to make "hard" remarks and to give his writings "that grim tone and black air that they did not have when he ceased to direct me." In the same spirit, the two disagreed over La Tour's pastel portrait of Rousseau. Diderot considered it too tame and "gentle shepherd"-like, whereas, so Rousseau insisted, it was by far the best likeness of him there had been.

This intuition of Rousseau's about Diderot is suggestive. No doubt, of course, he was wanting an excuse for his own aggressive tendencies; but, for all that, one guesses that he may have been right. It was a characteristic of Diderot to be intrigued by "hardness", picturing it as a quality that he would never possess but that might have its own value and claims. This was to become a major theme for him in his theories and paradoxes about "genius", but it also seems unconsciously to have influenced his friendships. Hardness, one supposes, must have been one of the attractions he found in Grimm, and equally in a later boon companion, the gruff and brutal-mannered Etienne-Noël Damilaville, described by Voltaire as a loyal ally but "a soul of bronze".[13] Further, as we have already seen, Diderot had a marked fondness for speaking through the lips of others. Whatever the cause, he undoubtedly had a major influence on Rousseau's prose style; it was from Diderot, as Rousseau admitted himself, that he caught a certain abrupt and sententious manner.[14]

What is even more important is that, to a degree one can hardly overstate, all of Rousseau's major writings are at bottom a debate with Diderot. This is true of his second *Discourse* (on Inequality), of the *Letter to d'Alembert on Stage-performances*, of the Geneva draft of *The Social Contract* and of the "Confessions of Faith of a Savoyard Vicar" in *Emile*. Thus it is not quite absurd when the historian Michelet writes, in his highly-coloured manner: "Prodigious sybil of the eighteenth century, many others he either made or changed, the great magician Diderot! On a certain day he breathed, and up sprang a man, a man who was to be his opposite: Rousseau."[15]

The first volume of the *Encyclopédie*, covering the letter "A", finally made its appearance in June 1751. Only a month or two before, Diderot had been elected a member of the Berlin Academy. It was one of the very few public honours he was ever to receive, and it made a good effect on the title-page. The title-page epigraph, from Horace, ran: *Tantum series juncturaque pollet / Tantum de medio sumptis accedit honoris!* ("What grace may be added to commonplace matters by the power of order and connection.")[16]

Among its readers there was general agreement on one matter at least, the impressiveness of d'Alembert's "Preliminary Discourse". The full title of the work is *Encyclopédie*, or *Dictionnaire Raisonné des Sciences, Arts et Métiers*, and d'Alembert constructs his "Preliminary Discourse" in two parts, in one of which he explains how the work is to function as an encyclopaedia and in the other, how it is to function as a dictionary. As an encyclopaedia, he says, the aim is to display human knowledge, not in the order in which, historically, it happened to develop, but from a "metaphysical" or eagle's-eye viewpoint known as "encyclopaedic order". The philosophic reader is to be placed on a high vantage-point from which he can survey the vast labyrinth of the sciences and arts simultaneously, can "distinguish the general branches of human knowledge and the points which separate or unite them, and even sometimes glimpse the secret routes which connect them." For this purpose, he says, the editors have based their plan on Bacon's "tree of knowledge" – though in full awareness that, like any other classification, it is arbitrary and they could well have chosen some other. They have not made the mistake – such a snare in the natural sciences, according to Buffon – of expecting too much of classification and spending endless time in dividing the productions of Nature into genera and species, time better spent in studying the productions themselves.

What the ordinary reader, though, as opposed to the philosopher, is likely to be most interested in, says d'Alembert, is not so much "encyclopaedic order" as "dictionary order": and he explains how the *Encyclopédie* is to win the best of both these worlds, by a rational use of cross-references. A truly philosophical cross-reference, sending the reader back to the "tree of knowledge", will serve the purpose of encyclopaedic order at the same time as those of dictionary order.

But further, he explains, when it comes to dictionary order, the actual history of the development of knowledge becomes relevant after all and will influence the way in which the knowledge is transmitted to readers. With this preliminary, he embarks on a grand history of intellectual progress from the Renaissance onwards, culminating in the heroic succession of Bacon, Descartes, Newton and Locke.

There had been nothing in *Chambers* to compare with this ambitious philosophical statement; central to it is d'Alembert's vision of the unity of truth. Just as each science, according to him, is no more than the expansion of a single axiom, so knowledge in general is to be thought of as an uninterrupted series or "great chain" of propositions. "The Universe, for someone who was able to take it in as a whole from a single standpoint, would appear, if one may so put it, as a unitary fact and a single great truth." Of the great chain, however, says d'Alembert, human-kind has discovered only a very few links. In fact, at the point reached so far, we possess only two kinds of *certain* knowledge, and these are so remote from each other as to constitute, as it were, two poles. They are, first, our knowledge of our own existence; and second, the truths of mathematics – or rather "that part of it which deals with the properties of bodies, space and magnitude." Everything lying between these poles is, in varying degrees, still wrapped in obscurity and is to be approached only in a fragmentary and approximative manner. Scientists tend to imagine not a single truth, but a multiplicity of truths in Nature, and this is the surest indication of their present ignorance. "Our wealth in this respect is actually the effect of our poverty."

In a very striking passage in this "Preliminary Discourse" d'Alembert as it were dismantles the universe, stripping it down to its innermost components, impenetrability and space, and then shows how it is to be built up again with the aid, each in its turn, of the various sciences. It represents, as one may say, *par excellence* the mathematician's vision of things ("obscurity invades our ideas of an object," says d'Alembert, "in proportion as we study more of its sensible properties"). A gulf here opens up between d'Alembert and Diderot, who believed that the future lay with the life-sciences; and Diderot's next philosophical work, *On the Interpretation of Nature* (1753), will open with an assault on the overweening pretensions of mathematics.

In other and important ways, none the less, the ethos of the *Encyclopédie*, as revealed in this first volume, was expressive of both the editors, as indeed of their whole circle. It exhibits what, at least to modern eyes, seems a very slighting attitude towards history, which is relegated to the Arts of Memory and is evidently not to be regarded as a serious intellectual discipline. Nor was the balance much redressed when Voltaire came to write the article HISTOIRE for Volume VII, which contains the strange remark that only *three* authentic written records of "ancient" (i.e. pre-classical) history had survived.[17] Again, by deliberate principle, there are no biographical articles – or at least none as such, though the lives of some famous people are smuggled in incidentally, for instance under the name of a place. D'Alembert, in a polemical foreword to Volume III, would say that he and his co-editor had purposely included not the genealogies of great families, but the genealogies of sciences, and had given prominence not to conquerors who had ravaged and laid waste the earth, but to immortal geniuses who had brought it enlightenment. Further – as Edward Gibbon, with some resentment, would find was common in French intellectual circles – there is an audible note of contempt for *savants* and for "mere erudition". The "Preliminary Discourse" has some hard things to say about the "Man of Erudition", who – anyway in the eyes of the Poet and Philosopher – is portrayed as a kind of miser, engaged in a mere joyless and fruitless amassing and hoarding.

What was quite fundamental to the *Encyclopédie*, as observant readers very soon spotted, was the issue of censorship – or rather of the necessity for rigid self-censorship to escape fatal offence to the government or the Sorbonne. Even the intractable d'Alembert, in his "Preliminary Discourse", at one point pays pious tribute to God and to the approved Cartesian theory of the soul/body relationship, only betraying his hypocrisy (as a reviewer pointed out) by his laconic tone.

It was the challenge of outwitting the censorship that, in quite large degree, gave the *Encyclopédie* its character. A variety of ruses were employed: for instance, in describing religious rites or practices, to focus on their puerile or bizarre *externals*, or to ridicule pagan observances in words that would apply all too easily to Christian ones; to state objections to religious dogmas so convincingly that, though ostensibly refuted, they tacitly won the day; to invoke lay figures – a Chinese interlocutor, or the like – to raise objections to religious beliefs which the author of the article dared not raise in his own person; or again to yoke together mutually reductive topics in the same article. In the article ADORER Diderot deals, in the same breath, with the worship of God and the worship of a mistress, and, by a pseudo-naive warning against the adoration of beauty, "which is so often accompanied by capriciousness and injustice", he slyly hints at the unspoken continuation that the ways of God – for instance electing certain humans to salvation, and others to damnation, at birth – seemed quite as bad.

Above all, an orthodox or straight-faced article could be undermined by an insidious cross-reference to some other article which, when consulted, would turn out to correct or contradict it or put it in ironic perspective. Much was said in few words by such a cross-reference as "ANTHROPOPHAGY: see EUCHARIST, COMMUNION, ALTAR, etc." It was, as may be seen, a trick with a good chance of eluding the censor. In practice it was more for this duplicit and strategic purpose than for the seriously philosophical one dear to d'Alembert that cross-references in the *Encyclopédie* came to be put to use. It was a cunning and effective device and the sort of mystification that Diderot greatly enjoyed. Michel Butor, indeed, has described the whole of the *Encyclopédie* as being "a gigantic mystification at the expense of the censors –an entirely *useful* mystification but one in the course of which the moments of heroism and alarm must have been compensated for by some remarkable laughs."[18] This seems right so far as it goes, but it only tells half the story. Diderot certainly loved mystifications, and they were the inspiration of some of his most original and powerful writing; but on the other hand, unlike his friend Grimm, he was not a secretive man, in fact he was vehemently hostile to secretiveness in all its self-interested and privilege-securing forms. Thus, what is quite as characteristic as the game with cross-references is the fact that in a later article (ENCYCLOPÉDIE) Diderot, as we shall see, would deliberately give this game away.

Diderot's own contributions to this first volume were of all sorts, from the briefest dictionary and gazetteer items to extensive articles running sometimes to many thousands of words. The more substantial articles might be compiled from a wide range of sources, and often he would clearly indicate these sources, but also quite often he would not: he was capricious over the matter. He would, in any case, submit the borrowed material to various kinds of stylistic revision and simplification, as well as embroidering it with reflections of his own. The fruit of his magpie method can be seen in an article such as ACIER (Steel), an impressive feat of organisation and clarification, the sources of which range from French, German and English treatises and scholarly transactions to shop-floor information from a Langres cutler (a friend of the Diderot family). Next comes some information on iron-working in antiquity, taken (though with a minor scholarly cavil from Diderot) from an English source, published in the *Philosophical Transactions* of 1693. This is followed by extracts from Réaumur's *The Act of Converting Forged Iron into Steel* (1722), or rather from a résumé of it made by Fontenelle for the Academy of Sciences. There follows a passage from Geoffroy's *Treatise on "Materia Medica"*, and then the most substantial part of the whole article, an account of the making of "natural" steel, taken without acknowledgement from an anonymous work published in Strasbourg in 1737 which is itself a condensation of a book by Swedenborg. Finally come some observations on the different qualities of steel, obtained from the cutler, some reflections by Diderot on the right way to conduct research into steel-making, and an extract from the *Memoirs of the Academy of Sciences* reporting Réaumur's experiments on sparks.

The articles on the history of philosophy and ancient religions had initially been assigned to the *abbé* Yvon[19] and another clerical contributor. Yvon, however, as we shall see, was soon forced to flee the country, and from then on, beginning with ARABES (State of Philosophy among the Ancient Arabs), these became Diderot's province. For this series, by contrast with his technological one, Diderot (as he frankly acknowledged) depended very much on a single source, the *Historia critica philosophiae* by Jacob Brucker. It was an admirable choice, for Brucker's book, published in Leipzig in 1744, was far and away the best in its field and retained some currency as an authority late into the nineteenth century. Brucker was a German Lutheran, of mildly Deistic tendency, who treated Christianity as merely one religion, though the best, among many; and Diderot's method was to condense and refashion Brucker's information in a more polemical and sceptical spirit. Jacques Proust speaks of the "astonishing dialogue" between Diderot and Brucker. "There are only two speakers . . . Brucker the learned and pious historian provides the narrative thread. Diderot listens to him, sometimes mis-hears him, interrupts him when he becomes boring, and enlivens his discourse with witty sallies or grafts his own reveries upon Brucker's reflections."

The first volume of the *Encyclopédie* was received with some acclaim, and despite its high price it sold extremely well. It justified the confidence of the publishers, who had risked raising the print-run from 1,625 to over 2,000. The success caught the attention of a syndicate of British publishers, who made a serious effort to pirate it and had to be bought off. Its critics were respectful too, although, as might be expected, there were complaints of its tendency to impiety, also of its weakness for "declamations". Father Berthier in the *Mémoires de Trévoux* was, at first, judicious and restrained. He pointed out some minor errors and expressed outrage at the radical sentiments in Diderot's unsigned article AUTORITÉ POLITIQUE (Political Authority), but he denied any intention on his own part of wounding "the authors of this greatest of Dictionaries" and prophesied that "it would acquire greater perfection as it went on." On one subject he made some unkind fun, and this was plagiarism. There were, for instance, the gastronomical articles, AMANDE, ASPERGE (Asparagus), AGNEAU (Lamb), ANGÉLIQUE (Angelica) and so on. It had been Diderot's idea to include such articles (there were none in *Chambers*) and, as Berthier gleefully pointed out, they had been lifted wholesale, and sometimes verbatim, from a popular recipe-book, the *Dictionnaire Œconomique* of Father Noël Chomel. The point at issue, of course, was not so much the borrowing, which was not unnatural in an encyclopaedia, as the fact that it had not been acknowledged. In the preface to Volume II, a few months later, Diderot made a nonchalant apology, saying that "when articles borrowed without acknowledgement are otherwise well-designed, the resulting inconvenience seems fairly slight." This provoked further and more ferocious teasing, and in Volume III Diderot felt obliged to apologise more earnestly. After this there were no more recipes. The game of catching the *Encyclopédie* out in plagiarism was, however, one that the *Mémoires de Trévoux* would soon be playing with more openly hostile relish.

It was at this moment, when the *encyclopédistes* were much in the

public eye, that they attempted an audacious and in the end
brilliantly successful *coup*. One of their contributors, the *abbé*
Jean-Marie de Prades,[20] was a student of theology at the
Sorbonne and was at work on a doctoral dissertation; with their
encouragement, he filled his thesis with *philosophique* and
Lockeian doctrines, derived from d'Alembert's "Preliminary
Discourse" and from Diderot's *Philosophical Thoughts*. There was
much praise of "natural religion" and not a word about original
sin, some veiled scepticism about miracles (he compared the
miracles of Jesus Christ with those of Aesculapius), and an
indignant if obscure remark about despotism and social inequality. It was rumoured later, almost certainly untruly, that
Diderot and d'Alembert had written most of the thesis for him,
but it seems likely that they were deliberately using de Prades to
lead the Sorbonne doctors into a trap. If so, they succeeded
beyond all expectation. On 18 November 1751 de Prades
"sustained" his thesis for ten hours and was awarded his degree
with acclamation, receiving warm compliments on his "beautiful
sentiments in favour of religion". As soon as copies began to
circulate in Paris, however, the word spread that his work was not
only heretical but seditious. It was the signal for a violent
scandal.

The first blow was struck when the thesis, and the Sorbonne
doctors who had approved it, were denounced on the floor of the
Paris *Parlement* and the Syndic of the Sorbonne was summoned to
appear before *Parlement* to offer some explanation.

A word is needed on *Parlement*, a highly important institution in
eighteenth-century France and to the eyes of the outsider a
puzzling one, shot through with anomalies. There were in all
thirteen *Parlements*, that of Paris exercising the most influence.
Parlement was the highest judicial body in the land, hearing in its
various "chambers" not only appeal cases but a variety of first-
instance ones, including charges of sedition, forgery and highway
robbery; it also functioned as censor of the theatre and of public
morals generally. Offices in *Parlement* could be bought, were
hereditary, and the higher ones bestowed nobility on their
possessors, who jealously insisted on the dignity of the "nobility of
the robe" as against the "nobility of the sword". Parlementarians

were protocol-mad, and their processional return every
November after their summer recess was one of the great ritual
spectacles of the year. One must not confuse *Parlement* with the
British Parliament, but it had this in common with it: that it
constituted a legal curb on royal prerogative. For it was laid down
that the King's edicts, to be enforceable, had to "registered" by
Parlement, and this gave it the right to criticise royal policy by way
of a "remonstrance". As a result, it was for good or evil the centre
of legalised opposition to absolute monarchy, and through all the
middle years of the century it was in continual conflict with the
throne. The Palais de Justice, the home of the Paris *Parlement*,
was, in the words of Simon Schama, "virtually a miniature city in
itself."[21] Its courtyard swarmed with traders and hawkers of
every kind, among them – for it was outside police jurisdiction –
the sellers of cheap prints and satires directed against the
government.

Between *Parlement*, which was predominantly Jansenist in its
sympathies, and the Jesuits of the Sorbonne there was long-
standing animosity. It dated back to the conflicts of thirty years
ago, when *Parlement* had been forced, much against its will, to
"register" a papal bull, *Unigenitus*,[22] which condemned
Jansenism, as the law of the land. The Sorbonne itself had been
divided over the issue, and a hundred or more of its doctors of
theology had been expelled at the time for protesting or
"appealing" against the bull. Thus the de Prades affair offered
the Parlementarians a golden opportunity to moralise. It was
clear proof, they were able to say, of the sad decadence of the
Sorbonne ever since this purge.

The Syndic of the Sorbonne, seeing no other escape from the
present awful situation, promised the fullest possible enquiry. De
Prades's licence was suspended, and a panel of forty-one doctors
of the Sorbonne was appointed to re-examine the thesis; the
Archbishop of Paris meanwhile issued a *Mandate* condemning the
thesis for its philosophical materialism. The Sorbonne doctors'
report, after many stormy sessions, was published on 1 February
1752 and condemned the thesis not merely as heretical but as part
of a concerted and infamous plot against religion and the state.
"Impiety," it said, "no longer content to dogmatise in private,

has formed a plan to insinuate itself into the very sanctuary of truth." This *volte-face* on the part of the Sorbonne was all that *Parlement* could have wished, and it proceeded to order the arrest of de Prades as guilty of "sentiments worthy of Ravaillac" – at which the *abbé* fled the country and took refuge in Holland.

In the meantime, late in January 1752, the second volume of the *Encyclopédie* had appeared and was seen to contain a long article on CERTITUDE by the *abbé* de Prades, discussing the grounds for belief in miracles. It was liberally laced with quotations from Diderot's *Philosophical Thoughts*, and attached to it was a note by Diderot praising de Prades for his fair-mindedness and love of truth and exhorting him to continue to use his great talents in defence of religion – *a cause so sorely in need of competent defenders*. This bold and teasing gesture was calculated to annoy both religious parties equally, and the King's Jesuit advisers represented to him that his authority was being systematically undermined: religion was "dying before his eyes". It so happened that, at this moment, the King's daughter Henriette was in the last throes of a fatal illness, and the King's confessor suggested that God might save her if the King, as a token of piety, would suppress the *Encyclopédie*. He agreed gladly. By royal decree a ban was placed on the first two volumes of the *Encyclopédie*, and the order went out to seize all the unpublished text and plates.

Here we come up against a circumstance of crucial importance in the history of the *Encyclopédie*. For Lamoignon de Malesherbes,[23] the current Director of Publications – that is to say, the minister responsible for overseeing the book-trade – was a most courageous and enlightened man. This high-minded and most un-courtly aristocrat, clumsy, always shabbily dressed and in private an ardent botanist, with a self-appointed mission to refute Buffon, is one of the heroes of his age. Later he would become one of Louis XVI's wisest advisers, and after the King's flight to Varennes he would insist on returning to France, to act as Louis's defence lawyer; as a result he ended his life on the guillotine. Malesherbes believed passionately in the freedom of the press (he believed in it more, one has to say, than the *encyclopédistes* themselves), and as son of the Chancellor of France he exercised great influence. Thus on this, as on many future occasions, he was able to give Diderot and d'Alembert protection from behind the scenes. It seems, indeed, that on the present occasion he invited Diderot to hide his manuscripts in his (Malesherbes's) own house, as the safest of all hiding-places. For a brief while there was talk of arrest for Diderot, and for a few weeks he may have had to go into hiding, but, largely through Malesherbes's good management, the scare soon died down.

D'Alembert's attitude in this first crisis, as again in later ones, was irascible and intransigent. Earlier he had been irritated by an unfavourable review of his "Preliminary Discourse" in the *Journal des Scavans*, and he now declared to friends that he would not go on with the *Encyclopédie* unless the *Journal*'s editors made him "an authenticated apology, just as I shall dictate it." Further, he said, Diderot and he must be given "enlightened and reasonable censors, not brute beasts in fur, in the pay of our enemies." Malesherbes, however, succeeded in mollifying him; and by May the *Encyclopédie* editors were, positively, being entreated in high quarters to resume. It would, however, be under new and stricter censorship arrangements, according to which every article, whatever its subject, would have to be approved by a theological censor.

Meanwhile the source of the trouble, the de Prades thesis, was driving a wedge ever deeper between the Jesuits and the Jansenists, and not only that, but between the Jansenist clergy and *Parlement*. The clandestine Jansenist periodical, *Nouvelles ecclésiastiques*,[24] was filled with scandalised comment on the affair, and the elderly Bishop of Auxerre,[25] a celebrated battler in the Jansenist cause, issued a weighty Pastoral Instruction, denouncing de Prades and his views – his excessive stress on the senses, his refusal to admit that Man is a fallen creature, his theory of monarchy as a mere matter of contract – but also lamenting the "decay" into which the proud Sorbonne had so evidently fallen. De Prades himself was meanwhile preparing a written defence of his thesis from his refuge in Leyden.

The situation, as Diderot perceived, was a gift to himself and his fellow-*philosophes*, and he hit on a brilliant scheme to exploit it. He would forestall the *Apology* which de Prades was preparing by a supposititious "Continuation" to it, published as if from de Prades' own pen, and would seize this opportunity not only to vindicate "philosophic" principles but to enflame the animosity between Jesuits, Jansenists and *Parlement*. It is not clear to what extent, if any, de Prades was party to the scheme himself or contributed to the "Continuation". He later denied any part in it; but then, by this time, through Voltaire's friendly offices, a place had been found for him at the court of Frederick the Great. (In due course, on Frederick's advice, he would make a formal recantation of his earlier beliefs, securing as a reward a snug benefice in Silesia.)

The Bishop's *Pastoral Instruction* provided the mythical "Diderot/de Prades" with an invincible opening gambit. He was enabled to say to the Sorbonne: "Either my thesis is a tissue of heresies, and you have applauded it; or it is sound and orthodox, and you have most unjustly denounced it; and in either case the Bishop is right – by your treatment of it and of myself you have earned yourself undying shame." But then, Diderot/de Prades continues needlingly, what can the *Parlement* itself think of the Jansenist Bishop's condemnation of the contract theory of monarchy, seeing that, in its recent conflicts with the Crown, it had taken its stance precisely on this theory? Further, does it not seem plain that the Bishop, in un-Christian fashion, is less concerned with warning his own flock against dangerous doctrines (of a kind it is hardly likely they would be tempted by) than with humiliating the Sorbonne? "Is this premeditated design, of discrediting a society of men dedicated to the study and defence of religion, worthy of a Christian, a priest of Jesus Christ and a pontiff of His Church?"

These are beautiful "scores"; and side by side with them runs a powerful and effective defence of the Lockeian philosophic system. But something even more striking develops. For though the *Continuation of the Apology of the Abbé de Prades* is in the nature of a hoax, it modulates in its final pages into a grandly eloquent and impassioned denunciation of the fanaticism of the Jansenists and the hypocrisy of the Jesuits. Buffon regarded these pages, not too absurdly, as one of the most inspired declamations in the language. We have here a good example of how Diderot's imagination was fired by supposititious enterprises – by, that is to say, the prospect of fathering or foisting sentiments upon others.

Two fragments will give just a taste. Diderot/de Prades, alluding to the "convulsionists", addresses the Jansenists thus:

> *O cruels ennemis de Jésus-Christ, ne vous lasserez-vous point de troubler la paix de son Église? n'aurez-vous aucune pitié de l'état où vous l'avez réduite? . . . L'impie a vu dans la capitale du royaume, au milieu d'un peuple affairé, dans un temps où le préjugé n'aveuglait pas, vos tours de force érigés en prodiges divins, vos prestiges regardés, crus et attestés comme des actes du Tout-Puissant, et il a dit:* Un miracle ne prouve rien; il ne suppose que des fourbes adroits et des témoins imbéciles . . . *Malheureux! vous avez réussi au delà de votre espérance. Si le pape, les évêques, les prêtres, les religieux, les simple fidèles, toute l'Église; si ses mystères, ses sacrements, ses temples, ses cérémonies, toute la religion est descendue dans le mépris; c'est votre ouvrage.*
>
> O cruel enemies of Jesus Christ, will you never weary of troubling the peace of his Church? Will you have no compunction for reducing it to its present condition? . . . The impious have seen, in the capital of the kingdom, in the midst of a busy populace, in an epoch when prejudice no longer blinds men's eyes, your conjuring-tricks elevated into divine prodigies, your illusions esteemed, believed and attested as the acts of the Almighty; and they have said to themselves: *A miracle proves nothing: it supposes no more than cunning rascals and imbecile witnesses . . . .* Wretched men! You have succeeded beyond all your hopes. If the Pope, the bishops, priests, monks, nuns, humble believers, indeed the whole Church – if its mysteries, its sacraments, its temples, its ceremonies, and the whole of religion have fallen into contempt – it is your doing.[26]

As for the Jesuits, "who were so ardent to display their zeal only because in fact they possessed none, and were the first to cry out, and so loudly, because, not being offended, they needed all the more to appear so," will they, for the sake of a humble individual, asks Diderot/de Prades scornfully, be likely to "doff the iron mask, which they have worn for so many years that it has, as it were, become their face?"

> *J'ai vu que l'état de tous ces gens était désespéré, et j'ai dit: je les oublierai donc; c'est le conseil de ma religion et de mon intérêt; je me livrerai sans*

relâche au grand ouvrage que j'ai projeté; et je le finirai, si la bonté de Dieu me le
permet, d'une manière à faire rougir, un jour, tous mes persécuteurs. C'est à la
tête d'un pareil ouvrage, que ma défense aura bonne grâce: c'est au devant d'un
traité sur la vérité de la religion, qu'il sera beau de placer l'histoire des injustices
criantes que j'ai souffertes, des calomnies atroces dont on m'a noirci, des noms
odieux qu'on m'a prodigués, des complots impies dont on m'a diffamé, de tous les
maux dont on m'a accusé, et de tous ceux qu'on m'a faits. On l'y trouvera donc,
cette histoire; et mes ennemis seront confondus; et les gens de bien béniront la
Providence qui m'a pris par la main, dans le temps où mes pas incertains erraient
à l'aventure, et qui m'a conduit dans cette terre où la persécution ne me suivra pas.
It is clear the condition of these people is beyond hope, and I have
said to myself, I will forget them. It is what my religion and my
interest suggest. I shall devote myself without rest to the great work
that I have projected; and I shall complete it, if the goodness of God
allows, in a manner that, one day, shall make all my persecutors
blush. It is as the preface to such a work that my apology will make its
best effect. It is at the front of a treatise on the truth of religion that it
will be most fitting to place the story of the crying injustice that I have
suffered, the atrocious calumnies with which I have been blackened,
the odious names I have been given and the impious plots by which I
have been defamed, of all the evils of which I have been accused and
all those which have been done to me. It will be there to see, there,
that story; and my enemies will be confounded, and men of good will
shall bless the Providence which took me by the hand, at the time
when my uncertain steps were wandering astray, and led me to this
country where persecution cannot follow.[27]

5

The Art of Conjecture

In the summer of 1750 Voltaire took refuge from France and began a three-year sojourn at the court of Frederick the Great. It was the beginning of an episode full of malicious comedy, of which, eventually, he would get the worst[1]; but it also represented a decisive turning of his back on Paris, which he would not revisit till his triumphant return in the very last year of his life. It was at this moment that Diderot, by a natural drift of circumstance and character, became the effective director of the *philosophique* movement. Not a world figure like Voltaire (or at least not yet), nor with so brilliant a reputation as d'Alembert, he was, by sheer energy, intellectual abundance, charm, generosity and officiousness, the person who kept things in motion: the one who caused ideas to form, opinions to circulate, and works to get written. The phrase "effective director" is deliberately chosen, for his leadership was not obvious to the outside world. From behind stalking-horses, and by supposititious devices, Diderot could throw himself to brilliant effect into a public affray. But he lacked, and for very deep reasons, what was such a strength to Voltaire, and equally to Rousseau: their marvellous *rapport* with the public and with the notion of a "public". It follows that sometimes he could be clumsy in his dealings with public opinion.

With his friends, though, and among the society of *philosophes*, he attained a dominating position. There was something rare and engaging in his self-forgetfulness and enthusiasm, his amazing knowledgeableness and willingness to be interested in, and if possible have a theory about, absolutely anything; it gave his friends a protective feeling towards him, as towards some admirable freak of nature. These friends, and his enemies too, liked to call him a "dreamer", and not unfairly, for "dreams" was his own favourite word for his philosophical conjectures. They said that when he read a book, he unconsciously rewrote it, seeing not what was in front of him but (very often) an altogether more sublime or original work. He certainly believed in inspiration and prized the experience of being "carried away", but he knew also that there were those who could fake it.[2] He was at the same time intensely sociable and a very zestful lover of life. He was a hearty eater, sometimes an over-eater, paying for it with fearful indigestion, and he was capable of working all night after a drunken champagne supper. He enjoyed a stirring, living scene; he liked boys to be unruly and was warmed by the sight of pregnant women; modern Paris theatre audiences, as compared with those of his youth, struck him as depressingly cold.

As all witnesses agree, he was an unquenchable talker, carelessly pacing the room and tearing off his wig when some topic fired him. The voluble *abbé* de Raynal, himself a conversation-hogger, would get in a fury if the two sat at the same dinner-table. "If he [Diderot] spits or coughs or blows his nose, he is lost," Raynal once threatened grimly to a fellow-guest. It would appear, however, that he could also listen.

He had on occasion been a guest at Madame Geoffrin's Wednesday dinners in the rue Saint-Honoré, but, being a stickler for propriety, she did not really approve of him. She thought him altogether too reckless a talker. Also unmannerly; at table, she would complain – or friends complained on her behalf – he would pinion the arm of the guests on either side of him and deafen them with his talk, as he blithely gobbled down his dinner.[3] He had his reservations about her too, not relishing her passion for scolding friends and telling them how to run their lives. It said a good deal about her, in his view, that she did not like it that Houdon's bust of himself, which she possessed, should be bareheaded and she got a sculptor to give it a marble peruke. Thus the two tended only to meet on neutral ground – which, Diderot told Grimm, "suits us marvellously". The conversational scene which really suited him was the very different one of d'Holbach's *salon*, where he could be himself without constraint.

Throughout his life he suffered, on his own confession, from "a violent desire to discover, to invent, interrupting my sleep by night and pursuing me during the day." For fifty years, he would say sadly, he had waited in vain for the "happy chance" entitling him to call himself a genius. It was, he said, a great pity, for, "being born as communicative as it is possible to be", if he had actually made a discovery he would have passed it on instantly to the first comer.[4] Conversely, an inner voice would always whisper to him that, what someone else could do, he could probably do better. Invariably, he could see how his friend's writings should be written and, with very little encouragement, he would do it for them; he even once did it for Voltaire.[5] Equally, though he could not paint, sculpt or draw, he was desperate to seize the pencil or chisel out of artists' bungling hands. He told the painter Vien how to design his "Mars and Venus",[6] and Vien cheerfully obeyed (as did the composer Grétry when he told him how to set a certain line[7]). The most magnificent images would paint themselves on his mind's eye, and it enraged him that he could not communicate them. Sometimes, indeed, he tried to. Once he got a young art student to make a sculpture under direct dictation from him and was highly pleased with the result.[8] He was careless of his own intellectual property and equally careless of other people's, a trait which sometimes got him into serious trouble. (It went with that habit of his, when carried away in talk, of gripping his interlocutor's body as if it belonged to him.) It was perhaps a kind of complement to this that he was a tireless, and rather humble, self-educator. During three of his very busiest years on the *Encyclopédie* he was attending, three times a week, a lecture course on chemistry given by Rouelle[9] at the Jardin du Roi, taking voluminous notes.

Friendship, for him, was of supreme importance and an imperative duty for mankind; and in his *Letter on the Deaf and Dumb* he praises the law of the ancient Scythians which required all citizens to have at least one friend, allowed them to have two, and forbade them three.[10] He liked to surround all his activities with friendship. Thus his philosophical works tend to take the form of "Letters", or, like *D'Alembert's Dream*, to be woven around the transmogrified figures of friends; his novel *The Nun*, likewise, took its rise in a friendly, if outrageous, practical joke. In his *Salon* review for 1767, discussing a landscape by Vernet, he makes gentle fun of his own propensity:

> It is on behalf of myself and of my friends that I read, that I reflect, that I write, meditate, listen, look and feel. In their absence, my devotion refers everything to them. I dream unceasingly of their happiness ... It is to them that I have consecrated the use of all my senses and of all my faculties; and that is perhaps the reason why, in my imagination and talk, everything gets slightly improved and exaggerated. They sometimes reproach me for this, the ungrateful wretches![11]

Being, and knowing himself to be, an intensely sociable man and a person of generous and tender feeling, he was nevertheless drawn, as a speculation, to imagine a "beauty" in crime. There was here a whole theory or fantasy, pursued with great subtlety and gaiety, about "genius" and its right to despise the warm heart and muddled goodness of the ordinary "man of good will".

A glowing description of Diderot is given by his friend the *abbé* Morellet,[12] author of some *Encyclopédie* articles, FOI (Faith), FATALITÉ, FILS DE DIEU (Son of God) etc. It was just after the de Prades affair; and Morellet, a respectable if freethinking Jesuit, and tutor to the grandson of the King of Poland, found it prudent to conceal his visits to Diderot. He found them, all the same, wonderfully rewarding:

> The conversation of that extraordinary man Diderot, whose talent is as contestable as his sufferings, had great power and great charm; his style of discussion was vivid, supremely honest, subtle without being obscure, varied in its forms, speaking with imagination, fecund in ideas and stimulating ideas in others ... There was never a more easy-going and indulgent man than Diderot; he lent, indeed he positively made a gift of, wit to others. He was eager to make converts, but not so much to atheism as to philosophy and reason.[13]

An old friend of Morellet's, the *abbé* d'Argenteuil, was also making furtive visits to Diderot, having formed the project of converting him. "I shall always remember our mutual embarrassment," says Morellet, "the first time we met at his house, and the excellent spectacle we provided for Diderot, who saw us as two shamefaced libertines meeting face-to-face in a house of ill-fame." Diderot insisted that the two *abbés* have a disputation, on religious toleration – standing benevolently by, his hands tucked in his dressing-gown sleeves, to see fair play. As Morellet implies, though Diderot was an atheist, he was not in general a proselytising one and even retained a certain tenderness towards religious feeling. He was touched by the look on his father's face when he had been at prayer, and he once said that he could never see the *Fête-Dieu* procession without feeling moved.

He was genuinely a tolerant man, on principle invariably, and most of the time in practice, and he was always looking for occasions to preach tolerance. He also liked to let his fantasy run on inspired acts of tolerance and generosity: acts of genius, rivalling the "genius" that some people put into crime. His story was that, for several years, he supported a struggling young writer, and the first fruit of the young man's pen was a satire against himself. It was published (Diderot could have had it suppressed but chose not to), and the young man, to his great amazement, came to bring him the very first copy. "You are a scoundrel," Diderot exclaimed, "and another man would have you thrown out of the window, but I am glad that you knew me better." He told him to take the pamphlet to his (Diderot's) enemy, the Duc d'Orléans; and matters ended with his writing a petition to the duke ("the old Fanatic") himself, thereby earning 50 *louis* for the young man. "The story became known," relates Diderot, "the protector was left looking ridiculous, and the protégé looking very base."[14]

Diderot studied good taste in his behaviour and was full of devices for avoiding *amour propre*. He liked to put down any good deeds of his own to "vanity", the vanity of wanting the praise of friends and fellow-citizens. He insisted, however, on enjoying the spectacle of his own good behaviour. It was, he held, the duty of thinking people to be *exemplary*. He was capable of doing good by stealth, but he attached no special value to this; and if modesty was a virtue in his eyes, humility was most definitely a vice.

He laid claim to all the pleasures and the disadvantages of

volatility. Unlike his friend Grimm's well-regulated soul, so he told
him (2 September 1759), his own was "a hair which the least puff of
wind sets fluttering". In any day he had a hundred physiognomies.
It was a mask that no painter could fix, he said, whether because
there were too many things blended in it or because the impressions
on his soul passed over his face too rapidly.

He was very responsive to flattery and seems to have accepted
it without suspicion – perhaps regarding it, on conscious
principle, as a natural part of friendship. He loved praise, indeed
he bathed in it, and no writer has seen more deeply into the
lengths people will go to obtain praise. Correspondingly, one of
his leading traits was a delighted self-admiration. Few people can
have praised themselves so unabashedly – or, one is inclined to
say, more attractively. This was by no means just a quirk: it was
done deliberately and on philosophic principle. He was proud of
his own goodness of heart and tenderness and enthusiasm. He
was impressed by the wonderful fertility of his own mind. He
loved the beautiful expression of sensibility that, as he could tell,
sometimes passed over his features. These were feelings that, in
his view, only false modesty would wish to conceal. "What is the
difference between a modest man and a vain one?" he once wrote
to his friend, the sculptor Falconet (15 February 1766). "The one
thinks and remains silent. The other speaks." For Diderot self-
admiration was a matter of self-discovery, of amazement at the
admirable qualities that he often found in himself and that works
of art could sometimes help him to find there. "I must have a
good character," he once said about a play by his friend Sedaine,
"for I feel the merit of this work most keenly."[15]

It was his impression (broadly Freudian, one might say) that
every tendency was to be found in the heart: noble, base, healthy,
perverse, exalted, lustful and homicidal. Thus virtue was a
matter of self-censorship. This, he once told Mme Necker, was
the "secret history" of the soul. "It is a dark cavern, inhabited by
all sorts of beneficent and maleficent beasts. The wicked man
opens the cavern door and lets out only the latter. The man of
good will does the opposite."[16]

There was something in Diderot's public style, his vehemence,
his fondness for declamation, his rapt look, that could make him

appear as a sublime simpleton. "Diderot is simplicity itself . . . He always declaims with fervour; he raves; he is *warm*, as warm in matters of conversation as in his books." So wrote an Italian visitor[17]; some, like Marmontel, praised his conversation above his books. "It was above all there [in d'Holbach's *salon*] that, with his sweet and persuasive eloquence, and his face sparkling with the fire of inspiration, Diderot spread enlightenment in everyone's mind, his warmth in everyone's soul. He who knows Diderot only from his books does not know him."[18] This is the Diderot for whom Barbey d'Aurevilly later found a magnificent simile: "He resembles those fountains which, incessantly and powerfully, pour forth a violent torrent through a roaring-lion mouth, and every ear was for him a basin to inundate and fill."[19] On occasion, other observers were less friendly. The critic and dramatist La Harpe, who was later to write with violence against Diderot, recalled visiting him as a young man and receiving an impassioned four-hour dissertation on the new drama. Throughout it, so runs La Harpe's malicious account, Diderot strode restlessly to and fro, sitting down once or twice for rhetorical effect.

> His most familiar action, and what you might call his favourite *tic*, was to shut his eyes as if seeking inspiration. He did it with head raised and arms dangling, and the words tumbling from his mouth recalled the comparison with "flakes of snow" applied so naively by Homer to the worthy Nestor. From this ecstatic utterance and prophetic posture he would emerge with a sudden start. "What reply could there be to that?" he asked, and he hurled his nightcap into the corner of the room, then gravely went to retrieve it, exclaiming oracularly, as he put it on again, "None"![20]

To us, who have read *Rameau's Nephew* and *D'Alembert's Dream*, as these contemporaries had not, this rhapsodic conception of Diderot is only half right, and therefore entirely wrong. There can be no doubt he was an impetuous, ardent, overflowing man; but another self within him observed this Shaftesburian "enthusiast" and man of feeling with utter detachment, as if (to use his own phrase) from the "epicycle of Mercury". Baudelaire put his finger on the matter with great exactitude when he spoke of

Diderot as one who "applied himself, so to speak, to notate and regulate improvisation; one who first of all accepted, and then of deliberate purpose utilised, his enthusiastic, sanguine, turbulent nature."[21] His obsession and great originality as a writer was, precisely, to confront these two opposing elements in his personality, though as a man he did not wish to disown either. His was never a soul divided against itself.

Near the end of 1752, soon after the de Prades affair, Diderot and his friends became involved in a musical controversy, the famous "Guerre des Bouffons". It was a war, ostensibly anyway, over the respective merits of French and Italian music and was sparked off by the visit to Paris of a touring Italian *opera buffa* company, under the direction of a certain Manelli. Their programme opened in August 1752 with Pergolesi's *La Serva padrona*, and over the next year and a half they gave some eleven other *intermezzi* by Italian composers. It was an entertainment very different from the stately productions of the Paris Opéra, a contrast brought home the more vividly in that performances took place between the acts of French operas. Audiences noisily took sides over it. A pro-French faction was formed, which sat under the King's box, and a pro-Italian one, which sat under the Queen's box and soon included many of the leading *philosophes* – Grimm, d'Holbach, Rousseau, d'Alembert, Buffon, Turgot and Diderot himself. Italian music, according to the party of the Queen's corner, was the music of nature and feeling; it was essentially melodic and rhythmically alive, unlike the dragging "plainchant" and tedious declamation of French recitative. It sprang, unlike its French counterpart, from a people and a language designed for music by nature. (French musicians were enslaved by the poets; Italian musicians made poets their servants.) Grimm and Rousseau, if not the rest, already had some knowledge of Italian music; Rousseau, indeed, had written a little pastoral opera, *Le Devin du village (The Village Soothsayer)*, in the Italian style. What lay at the root of the affair, though, was that, for the *philosophes*, the Paris Opéra was as much an affair of state, a symbol of monarchical self-aggrandisement and chauvinism, as a mere musical institution. It passed, so Rousseau was to make Saint-Preux say in *La*

Nouvelle Héloïse, for "the most imposing, the most pleasurable, and the most magnificent spectacle ever invented by human art," and it was "a sovereign court which judged in its own case without appeal."[22] Criticism of it thus had all the attractions and some of the dangers of sedition.

By November a war of pamphlets had broken out. D'Holbach championed the Italians in *A Letter to a Lady of a Certain Age,* and early in January 1753 Grimm published a little fantasy in mock-Biblical prose entitled *The Little Prophet of Boehmischbroda.* It tells how, by angelic agency, a penniless student of Prague is transported through the air, from his freezing garret to the opera-house in Paris, and told he has been chosen to announce harsh truths to a vain and presumptuous people. The spectacle there baffles and bores him unspeakably, until he is attracted to the Queen's corner, where the *philosophes* and wits gather "and are rarely bored, because they rarely listen", being too much absorbed in their own conversation. Here the Angel mournfully tells the "little prophet" how he sent the French the great Rameau, to cure them of their infatuation with the uninspired Lully, and sent them, furthermore, his "servant Fel",[23] to show them what real singing is. But these miracles have failed, and he has now, out of his mercy, vouchsafed them one miracle more, causing his humble "servant Manelli" to shed his clogs and quit his native mud to bring to France the music of Pergolesi. If this, too, fails, it is decreed that the French shall have no music at all, neither old nor new, nor any serious drama, and will spend all their hours at the Opéra Comique, "which is neither opera nor comic". The Voice ceases, and the "little prophet" weeps loudly over the fate of the French, receiving a box on the ears for his pains, which wakes him from his dream.

Grimm's tract caught on and ran through a number of printings; meanwhile the patriots of the King's corner rallied, with extravagant eulogies, round a new French lyric tragedy by Mondonville, entitled *Tithonus and Aurora.* Pamphlets flew, and among them a reply to *The Little Prophet* from Diderot, in which he offered himself as a peacemaker. He has read all their little writings, he tells the pamphleteers, "and the only thing they could have taught me, if I had needed to learn it, is that you have a great deal of wit and an even greater amount of malice." If they do not want just to show off but seriously to adjudicate between French and Italian music, then why, he asks, do they not perform a simple experiment? They should take an acknowledged master-piece of French music, Lully's *Armide* (even Rameau, Lully's rival, allowed its famous monologue "At last it is in my power" to be sublime), and, without prejudice, make a bar-by-bar compari-son of three scenes from it (the last three of the second Act) with three similar scenes in Terradellas's *Sesostris*. If they would accept this honourable challenge, he said, the face of the combat would change: reasons would succeed personalities, and enlightenment supersede "prophecies". What he also implied, though he did not say as much, was that Terradellas would come out an easy victor.

The war proceeded briskly for the rest of the year. The Parisians were fond of such cultural dog-fights. (There had been one a few years earlier, between the Lully-ists and the Rameau-ists, and there was to be another later on between the Gluck-ists and the Piccini-ists.) These controversies always contained a large element of game; and it was so in the present case, until, in November 1753, Rousseau published a *Letter on French Music*. It was a most savage affair, bitterly attacking French opera, French orchestras and every other element in French musical life. Diderot, in his *Letter on the Deaf and Dumb*, had argued that the French language, precisely because of its vaunted "clarity", was not well suited to poetry; and Rousseau, invoking this view of Diderot's, claimed that it was even less suited to music. Indeed, he argued, because of the "didactic" order of the French sentence, combined with a certain accentless and "dragging" quality in the language as pronounced, France not only had never had, but never could have, a music of its own ("and if they have one, it will be the worse for them!"). Here, he said, was the explanation for the mania of French musicians for abstruse harmonic science – for fugues, counter-fugues, *basses contraintes* and the like. It was not even possible, he said, to *explain* the beauties of music in French; hence he would not take up Diderot's challenge regarding Terradellas and his *Sesostris*. Nevertheless he would offer a few words on Lully; and hereupon he fell on the much-prized monologue in *Armide* and tore it to shreds. He could find in it no "measure", no "character", no melody, no expressiveness – nothing but "wiredrawn" sounds, and trills and inappropriate ornaments, "even more ridiculous in such a tragic context than they generally are in French music."

Rousseau's *Letter* was evidently intended to cause trouble, and it did so on a great scale – so much so that, according to his own account, he came in danger of banishment or the Bastille, and the orchestra of the Opéra formed a plot to assassinate him. (He was, in fact, roughly handled when he appeared in the auditorium, and was burned in effigy in the opera-house courtyard.) The incident came at a moment of national crisis; for, during the summer, the King had dispersed the Paris Parlementarians by *lettre de cachet* and he was now attempting to dissolve the Great Chamber of *Parlement* and replace it by a Royal Chamber of his own devising. In this tense situation the distraction caused by the *Letter*, or so Rousseau liked to claim, helped saved the country from a revolution.[24]

It also had a further consequence, for it poisoned relations between the *encyclopédistes* and the composer Rameau. Up to now the *philosophes* had been warm champions of Rameau's genius. Grimm, on his arrival in France, had been an extravagant admirer; Diderot had praised Rameau highly in his *Memoirs on Different Subjects in Mathematics*, and indeed he seems to have helped him with the writing of one of his treatises; and d'Alembert had published a popular exposition of Rameau's musical theories.[25] (Rousseau's own musical articles in the *Encyclopédie* were largely, if rather inaccurately, based on these theories.) The *Letter on French Music*, with its gibes at "Gothic" musical pedantry, was, however, plainly designed to annoy Rameau; he was indeed greatly enraged, and retaliated in a series of tracts exposing the musical "errors" in the *Encyclopédie*. The effect was to throw both Diderot and d'Alembert into the anti-Rameau camp and to leave a general legacy of ill-feeling.

Rousseau's intervention, coming from the author of a highly praised French opera, was the sort of paradox he most loved. For in fact the performance of his *The Village Soothsayer* before Louis XV at Fontainebleau (18 October 1752) had been a brilliant success.

All next day, so a courtier told Rousseau, the monarch was humming its airs, "with the worst voice in the kingdom", and he asked to see Rousseau, with the intention of offering him a pension. This had put Rousseau in a quandary, for, despite the "Roman air" he assumed at court, the prospect of a royal audience terrified him – if for no other reason, because of his bladder-disease, which made him need to urinate every other minute. Anyway, as he told himself, a pension was a threat to his intellectual independence. He thus decided, as the best way out, to make a hurried escape from Fontainebleau, excusing it on the grounds of ill-health. Two evenings later in Paris, however, as he was entering a friend's house, a figure beckoned to him from a nearby cab. It was Diderot, who made him climb in and gave him a tremendous lecture for refusing the royal pension. It was Rousseau's right, Diderot told him, to be disinterested on his own account, but absolutely not when it came to Thérèse and her mother. The two friends argued for hours. It was their first real quarrel and, as Rousseau wrote, it was to be the pattern of all their later ones: "he telling me what he claimed I should do, and I defending myself because I believed I ought not to do it."[26]

Beneath this dispute of theirs, and later ones, there lay a serious philosophical difference. Diderot, as a Shaftesburian moralist, held that it mattered what other people thought of one's conduct – indeed, in a sense, this was all that mattered, private judgements of right and wrong being merely internalisations of public opinion. Rousseau, on the contrary, held that the only judgement that counted was one's own, and he made, or was soon to make, a distinction between "love of self " and *amour propre* – "love of self " being innocent, and indeed the one truly natural passion, but *amour propre*, an ignoble desire for the good opinion of others, being a vice. It was a difference of opinion between them which went with different attitudes towards self-approval. Both firmly rejected the Augustinian Doctrine, revived with such force in the previous century by Pascal and La Rochefoucauld, that love of self and self-approval were the root of all evil; but beyond that, their attitudes diverged widely. Diderot loved to discover admirable qualities in himself, whereas Rousseau took the grimmer view that one simply *had* to think well of oneself. ("What can one be pleased with in life, if one is not pleased with the only man one can never be separated from?"[27]) For Rousseau, then, self-approval was a necessity rather than a pleasure; but, possessing it, he felt he had no need of Diderot's anxious lectures. It was nothing to him, or rather it was an annoyance to him, to be told he was putting himself in the wrong in the world's eyes.

Volume III of the *Encyclopédie* (CHA-CON) came out in November 1753; and at almost the same moment Diderot published a philosophical treatise entitled *On the Interpretation of Nature*. This strange little work (like his earlier *Philosophic Thoughts*, it consists of a series of numbered reflections) is clearly meant as some sort of theoretical complement to the *Encyclopédie*. Its title is most probably inspired by Bacon, for Diderot the great exemplar of experimental science, who wrote a *Cogitata et visa de interpretatione naturae*. The book has been described as an eighteenth-century *Discours de la méthode*, but if so, it is a very unmethodical one. What it represents, more precisely, is a rumination on the place of "conjecture" in science.

The immediate occasion of the book seems to have been an attack recently made by Buffon on the pretensions of mathematics. Buffon's words, in the First Discourse of his *Natural History*, were striking. "There are many kinds of truth," he had written, "and customarily placed in the first order are those of mathematics, which are, however, only truths of definition . . . There is no more in that science than we have put into it. And the truths which are drawn from it can only be different expressions under which the suppositions which we have made are presented." In astronomy and optics, the fields explored by Newton, mathematics was the perfect ally to physics; but there were very few other parts of natural science in which it could contribute so much. In most cases the mathematical approach was to "make suppositions which are always contrary to nature"; its method was to "strip the object of most of its qualities and to make of it an abstract entity which has no resemblance to an actual being."[28]

Diderot, in his opening reflections, is embroidering on Buffon's theme. Mathematics are from beginning to end, he writes, "an

affair of conventions like a game. The subject-matter of a
mathematician has no more existence in nature than that of a
games-player." Mathematicians are fond of accusing other
thinkers of "metaphysics", but increasingly chemists and
physicists and naturalists are inclined to throw the same insult
back at them. In fact, says Diderot, science stands on the
threshold of a revolution. Mathematics, in all its grandeur and
inutility, is about to be dethroned and its work to come to an end,
at the point to which Bernoulli, Euler, Clairaut, Maupertuis and
d'Alembert have brought it. These great mathematicians will
have "set up the pillars of Hercules, beyond which there will be
no going."[29]

That mathematics might be an exhausted science was quite a
prevalent view at the time when Diderot was writing. It was
shared by Buffon and Voltaire and was later voiced even by the
great mathematician Lagrange. But Diderot is also commenting
on a piece of social history. For a generation or so mathematics
had been the fashionable science, and (Le Guay de Prémontval's
working models perhaps give a hint of this) it had brought with it
a vogue for useless experiment – the sort of experiment that
produced no new knowledge and merely served to confirm known
physical laws. Thus what Diderot is heralding is not merely a
shift from mathematics to the natural sciences but a new and
more creative role for experiment. The French word *expérience*
means both "experience" and "experiment", and Diderot
develops a conception of *expérience* in science that embraces both
meanings. There is the "experiment" sense, in which *expérience* is
to be distinguished from mere "observation" and will require
some sort of laboratory – and by corollary, money. This prompts
Diderot to play with the notion that the rich should choose *this*
way of ruining themselves in preference to other less reputable
ones. But on the other hand there is the "experience" sense; the
experience and lifelong practice of skilled mechanics, which may
provide them with an insight, a flair or guiding spirit almost like
Socrates's *daimon*. It may give them the talent for seizing truth by
its "hairy side", where the philosophers can only get hold of its
"bald side". "They have seen Nature at work so often and at such
close quarters that they can guess with sureness what course she

will take when the fancy takes them to 'provoke' her by the most bizarre experiments."

The subject of "experiment" thus leads Diderot on to the central concern of his book, which is "conjecture". What the skilled mechanic may possess, and the experimental philosopher may lack, he says, is a gift of inspired conjecture or divination, a way of "sniffing out" new procedures and new conclusions. The question is, can this gift be passed on? If it is to be so, it will require its possessor to scrutinise his own thought-processes, his instinctive habit of looking for oppositions and analogies – in a word, "all the extravagances that have ever passed through his head. I say extravagances, for what other name shall we give to such a chain of conjectures, based on oppositions or resemblances so remote that the dreams of the sick-bed could not seem more bizarre or disconnected."[30]

This is Diderot's cue to introduce a series of seven "conjectures" (in the first edition his word was "dreams") of his own – in biology, physics, chemistry and technology. The first (XXXII) is on the mysterious phenomenon known as the "mole" (or false birth) in obstetrics. The next is on terrestrial magnetism and whether, on the assumption that the earth has a vitrified core, such magnetism is caused by atmospheric friction at the poles. The third is on the use of electricity in chemical processes, the fourth on whether the air is an electrical substance, the fifth on the harmonics of vibration in solid bodies, the sixth on the impossibility of accelerating natural processes, and the last on a workshop secret in steel-making. These speculations, some quite sketchy, others worked out in considerable detail, are offered to some extent for their own sake, but, more importantly, as specimens in the art of conjecture.

We catch sight here of Diderot's fundamental strategy in the book, which is to offer himself as an object-lesson in the very topics he is discussing. The intention is visible in the opening words of the book, in which he says that, since his topic is "Nature" (i.e. the real world) as opposed to some philosophic abstraction, he will put himself in Nature's hands and let his thoughts flow from his pen as they will – "for in this way they will better picture the movements and march of my mind." The plan is, as against the orderly method of a Descartes or a d'Alembert, to plunge headlong in: to write a book *about* scientific conjecture in the same spirit, and with the same audacity mitigated by self-criticism, as one would pursue any actual scientific speculation. Thus, by the time we reach Diderot's seven "conjectures", we have been loudly warned, as we shall go on being warned, of the precarious, the "extravagant", the possibly quite futile nature of the whole conjectural process; but we have also been persuaded to see it as being what, with all its defects, "Nature" herself dictates. The art of thinking, in science as elsewhere, is to win the favours of this recalcitrant deity "Nature" who is so fond of going veiled and playing deceptive tricks.

Conjecture – the *interpretation* of nature – has of necessity, Diderot argues, to obey different rules from mere "observation". "One of the chief differences of the observer of nature from her interpreter is that the latter begins at the point where the senses and instruments of the former break down." Nevertheless, as Diderot comes round to showing, conjecture has its rules too. There is, for instance, the simple rule that experiment must be allowed its autonomy. If you furiously question the results of an experiment when they do not please you, then you must question them equally furiously when they do. Nature is not to be believed at her first utterance. Again, there is the rule of *inversion*. Precisely because conjecture is forced to work with hints and analogies and with what may turn out to be "chimeras that the heated mind mistakes for true visions", one should never finally give up a conjecture that has proved fruitless without trying its *opposite*.

Moreover, Diderot finally argues, there is a point where "philosophy" (or as we would now say, "science") must give way entirely to conjecture – or at least would do so, he adds mock-piously, were it not for the wholesome restraint of religion. For "philosophy" assumes that Nature is constant; but what if it were in flux? What if we needed to bring *time* into our definition of Nature and re-define her, forgetting all mythological verbiage, as merely "the present general result, or the successive general results, of the combination of elements"? Our natural history would then be merely the incomplete history of a single moment; and "conjecture" would come into its own. It might be forced to envisage an endless process of transformation, in which species were as perishable as individuals and whatever is logically possible would at some point become actual. It would have to picture certain natural elements, existent from all eternity, as at some point coming together to form the animal "Man", developing in succession movement, sensation, ideas, thought, reflection, conscience, sentiments, passions, signs, gestures, sounds, articulated sounds, language, laws, sciences and arts, and this in turn being followed by a prolonged "withering-away" (*dépérissement*) during which all these faculties would desert the human animal and it would disappear from nature for ever or reappear under some quite other form.

This grand evolutionary vista constitutes the climax of the book – one could even regard it as its *raison d'être* – and what it brings home to the reader is the intensely positive and creative nature of Diderot's scepticism, scepticism and conjecture being for him almost synonymous and together justifying a vision of unbounded possibilities. It is his fable of Plato's cave, and of what may lie outside the cave, all over again. In his version of "enlightenment", which is a very different one from d'Alembert's or Voltaire's, darkness plays quite as big a part as light, and he imagines the philosopher as pondering problems within his own "night". Conjecture is, for him, a sort of wilful going blindfold – a thought hinted at in the Lucretian epigraph to this book, *Quae sunt in luce tuemur/E tenebris* ("Things shine more brightly to an observer/ who is in the dark").[31]

A few months after his book appeared, Diderot brought out a revised edition, to which he attached a curious and riddling dedication, semi-ironically warning the reader against materialism and Spinozism. It begins with the words, "Young man, take and read" – a temerarious parody of the words of God, "*Tolle, lege*," which led to Saint Augustine's conversion.[32]

Young man, take and read. If you can get to the end of this book, you will not be incapable of understanding a better one. As I am concerned less to instruct you than to exercise your mind, it matters to me very little whether you accept or reject my ideas, so long as they at least receive your full attention. A cleverer person

than myself will teach you to know the forces of nature; it will be
enough for me if I make you try your own. Adieu.

   P.S. One more word, before I leave you. Never forget that *nature is
not God*; that a *man* is not a *machine*; that a *hypothesis* is not a *fact*; and be
assured that you will not have understood me, wherever you
think you find something in my book contrary to these principles.

The opening sentence brought Diderot in for a good deal of
unkind teasing; and in general the book was not very well
received, only the assiduous Grimm describing it in his journal as
a masterpiece and a work too "holy" to profane by quotation.
The general complaint was that it was obscure, indeed was an
essay in deliberate obfuscation. "The author is perhaps a very
great genius," wrote Elie Fréron in the *Année littéraire*, "but the
star is always covered with clouds of impenetrable metaphysics."
It was not an altogether unfair reaction, since, for all its
suggestiveness and the impressive sweep of its final pages, there is
something uncertain and makeshift about the book, as if it had
not quite found its proper form. Michel Butor has called it
Diderot's "masterpiece, in the medieval craftsman's sense" in the
art of self-censorship,[33] and this probably gets somewhere near
the truth. It is a book full of swervings and forestallings of
criticism, and gives the impression of being caught up in its own
stratagems.

   One question that *On the Interpretation of Nature* raises for us is
the nature of Diderot's relationship to d'Alembert. What could
d'Alembert have thought of the denigration of mathematics, his
own speciality, as an exhausted science? Did he take it as a
personal attack, as he might well have done? For if Diderot was
sceptical towards mathematics, d'Alembert was quite extreme in
his devotion to it, as the true key to science and the only home of
clear and demonstrable truths. He was a purist, a positivist and a
simplifier, regarding it as the ambition of a scientist, in any given
field, to reduce the number of scientific principles to the smallest
possible number. The model among the physical sciences was, for
him, theoretical physics, which he held to be an essentially
deductive science, not dependent upon experiment, and his
bugbear was "metaphysics", in which he included such concepts
as "forces", "power" and "causes". The proper subject-matter of

physics, he held, was not causes but *effects*, for they alone were measurable.[34]

D'Alembert was at heart suspicious of "conjecture". It was a favourite refrain of his that certain grand hypotheses – for instance Descartes' famous vortices – might explain observed phenomena very brilliantly but would serve to explain different phenomena equally well, perhaps even better. Equally, such "approximate" sciences as chemistry and physiology were uncongenial to him, and privately he rather looked down on them, as he did on experiment in general. When he was teased about his ignorance of physical facts commonly known to much humbler men, he would reply airily that "there would always be time for him to learn such interesting things."

Thus the gulf between d'Alembert and Diderot was huge and would eventually help to alienate them. Nevertheless, it is probably wrong to assume that in 1753 the two friends were at each other's throat. D'Alembert's public response to Diderot's book was markedly friendly and generous, and in the article ÉLASTICITÉ in the *Encyclopédie*, he went out of his way to make a case for the kind of scientific "conjecture" which honestly proclaimed itself as such and could, as he said, "be so happy and fecund". "Such are those which M. Diderot proposes on the causes of elasticity in his *On the Interpretation of Nature*, a work full of profound and philosophical reflections."

Evidently, if theirs was a partnership of opposites (and this was plainly the case) they could well have regarded it as an advantage. Indeed, when one looks at what they achieved together, one may agree that it was. It was enormously to the advantage of the *Encyclopédie* that d'Alembert had full control of the articles on theoretical physics and astronomy and could impose his own coherent outlook on them. But it was also greatly to the *Encyclopédie*'s profit that the placing of the chemical articles rested in Diderot's hands; for he was able to foresee what d'Alembert was ill-fitted to imagine, the enormous leap forward that would be taken in chemistry over the next thirty years, a period culminating in Lavoisier. He assigned the leading chemical articles to Gabriel-François Venel (1723–75), a disciple of Rouelle. Venel was a vigorous champion of the speculative, intuitive and non-mathematical approach, insisting that, where as in physics one was studying ideal abstractions, in chemistry one was studying real bodies, in all their concreteness and complexity; this would increasingly be Diderot's own doctrine.

It is worth adding that, for Diderot, the great Rouelle himself, whose impressive and wildly eccentric lectures on chemistry he attended, became to some extent his ideal and model of the scientific genius. "He embarked on a subject, but soon he got distracted from it by a crowd of fresh ideas," Diderot would write of him later. "He applied his experiments to the general system of the world; he embraced the phenomena equally of Nature and of the arts and linked them by the subtlest analogies. He lost himself, one got lost with him, and one never returned to the particular subject of the day's demonstration without amazement at the distance one had travelled."[35]

Some time in the early 1750s, as seems to have been agreed even at the time, Paris entered on an especially brilliant period. This was the more so because of the gloomy and furtive atmosphere at Versailles. The King was becoming a prisoner of the *dévot* party and was increasingly unpopular in the country at large. It was rumoured that he was speculating in grain and was deliberately starving the French people for his own profit, also that he was exploiting poverty and starvation to stock a harem of under-age girls. Whatever the truth of these allegations, he rarely now set foot in Paris, preferring to go by a roundabout route even when moving from one royal residence to another.

Thus the eyes of the world were on Paris and its writers and thinkers. ("In the shameful eclipse of sovereign authority," writes Michelet, "people admire the sovereignty of the mind.") It became the ambition of European princes to be up-to-date with French intellectual developments and, if possible, to acquire their own stable of *philosophes*. Thus when Catherine the Great came to the throne in 1762 she issued glittering invitations to d'Alembert, Diderot, Voltaire and others. Equally, for French intellectuals, it became a temptation, if a rather dangerous one, to woo and admonish European despots and imagine they could win them over to "enlightened" views.

It is significant that during the summer of 1753 Grimm acquired control of a manuscript journal or news-letter entitled the *Correspondance littéraire*, which had been started a few years earlier by Grimm's friend the *abbé* de Raynal, a tireless founder of periodicals; it provided a running report on the cultural life of Paris, intended for the eyes of foreign princes. The journal came out once a fortnight, being despatched through diplomatic channels, and had a very select list of subscribers, never more than fifteen or so. Among them, in these early days, were the Queen of Sweden, the King of Poland, the Duchess of Saxe-Gotha, the Duc des Deux Ponts and the hereditary Princess of Hesse-Darmstadt. Copies of the journal were treated as very precious and confidential, and Goethe relates what a vast privilege was made of it when, some years later, the Prince of Saxe-Gotha allowed him to read Diderot's *Jacques the Fatalist* in the *Correspondance littéraire*, though even then forbidding him to make a copy.[36]

Here was a real sphere of influence, and, quite naturally, Grimm called on Diderot for help and advice. Before long the journal's pages were full of Diderot's opinions and doings, and he would contribute reviews and articles. It became, indeed, a sort of publicity-organ for him, since Grimm's references to him were always lavishly euologistic, and, as he admitted himself, he identified with all of Diderot's views. "You are my friend, you are my master," he was to tell him, in the pages of his journal. "You show me what I think, and you confirm me in thinking it."[37]

As Diderot and Grimm grew in intimacy, a coolness developed between Grimm and Rousseau, who had originally brought them together. Rousseau thought Grimm too much of a social climber; also he suspected, rightly, that Mme Levasseur came to Grimm and Diderot with tales about him and his impracticality over money. (Later it would appear that, unknown to Rousseau, Diderot and Grimm actually gave Thérèse and her mother a small allowance.) It was not only a personal, but an ideological falling-out, and, now that Rousseau had acquired confidence in his own philosophy, he began to resist the whole *Encyclopédie* coterie.

This was revealed in a grotesque little episode that took place

early in 1754. A certain *abbé* Petit, a country priest from
Normandy and immensely vain amateur author, had got into
conversation with Diderot in the Luxembourg gardens, complaining of intellectual loneliness and describing his literary
hopes. He had written a madrigal some seven hundred lines in
length. Diderot had quailed at this; but it turned out he had also
written a tragedy, and Diderot arranged for him to give a reading
of it at d'Holbach's house in the rue Royale. The reading, which
took place on Shrove Tuesday (3 February 1754), soon developed
into a joke at the *abbé*'s expense. From his first words, a ludicrous
preface on the art of drama, the whole company, apart from
Rousseau, was in a high state of suppressed laughter and,
unkindly, was egging the poor man on. At last Rousseau sprang
up ("like a madman", said Diderot) and, grabbing the manuscript from the horrified author's hands, hurled it on the floor.
"Your play is worthless, your disquisition on drama is absurd,"
he exclaimed. "All these gentlemen are making fun of you. You
should go home and do an honest *curé*'s duty in your village." The
amazed *abbé*, far from thanking Rousseau for his admonition,
responded with the most furious abuse, and the two nearly came
to blows, after which Rousseau left the house in a rage.[38]

None of this friction had, so far, affected Rousseau's friendship
with Diderot himself. The Dijon Academy had announced a new
prize-essay competition. It was on the subject "What is the origin
of inequality among men, and is it sanctioned by natural law?",
and with Diderot's encouragement he had entered, with the essay
which became his *Second Discourse*. It was the work that, Rousseau
later said, was more to Diderot's taste than all his other writings
and for which he gave him the most useful advice. Diderot in fact
provided some active collaboration. It was he who suggested to
Rousseau the satirical picture, meant in some sense as a satire on
himself, of the philosopher whom Reason has schooled in the art
of not feeling for others. "One can safely cut the throat of one of
his fellow-men under his window; he has only to put his fingers in
his ears . . ."[39] It was one of those "harsh" passages which,
Rousseau later said, Diderot had "abused his confidence" by
making him write.

Rousseau left the manuscript with Diderot when he paid a visit to Geneva in the summer of 1754, though during this stay in his native town he showed his growing independence of the *philosophes* by being re-admitted into the Genevan church. He even contemplated returning to live in Geneva, and he might actually have done so if Voltaire had not got there first. Nevertheless, on his return to Paris, it was once again Diderot's company that he depended on. He was often ill at this period, and when he was, Diderot's visits gave him the most comfort.

At this period Diderot's influence on Rousseau, or rather Rousseau's use of Diderot as symbolic antagonist, was at its height. It was to Diderot, for instance, that Rousseau originally owed one of the leading conceptions in his own political thinking: the theory of the General Will, as being the true basis of law and the criterion of justice and injustice for the individual citizen. The theory was important to Diderot's social thinking and gave it a certain totalitarian tinge. It prompted him, for instance, to support the practice of vivisection on condemned criminals, on the grounds of its potential benefit to humanity (though on condition that, if the victim survived the experiment, he should have won his right to freedom). Rousseau explicitly acknowledged, in his article ÉCONOMIE POLITIQUE in the *Encyclopédie*, that he owed the "grand and luminous principle" of the General Will to Diderot; though, what is equally important, much of his own later political thought derives from his disagreement with Diderot over how to interpret this concept.

While in Geneva, Rousseau had made a sketch of what was to become his *Contrat social*, and the first substantial chapter of it took the form of a systematic refutation of Diderot's way of depicting the "General Will". In his article LOI NATURELLE Diderot imagines a violent man, so tormented by destructive passions that life would be a burden to him, and who addresses his fellow-humans thus:

> I am aware that I carry terror and disturbance into the midst of the human race; but either I must be unhappy, or I must cause unhappiness to others.
>
> Do not reproach me with this abominable predilection; it is not voluntary. It is the voice of Nature, which never speaks so clearly

and forcefully in me as when it is speaking in my favour. (But is it only in *my* heart that she speaks so loudly? O mankind, I appeal to you! Who is there among you who, being on his deathbed, would not purchase further life at the expense of other men's if he could do it undetected?)

Nevertheless I am a man of fairness and sincerity. If my happiness demands that I should rid myself of all existences that stand in my way, it is only right that any individual, whoever he may be, should have an equal right to get rid of me if I am in his way. Reason requires this, and I consent to it.

"What shall we say in answer to our violent-minded reasoner," asks Diderot, "before we strangle him?" First, he says, it is to be noted that the violent man has made an important admission: that we have a duty to *reason* about everything. This implies that anyone who refuses to use his reason, or to recognise truth when reason elicits it, is renouncing his human status and deserves to be treated like a wild beast. On this understanding, then, mankind might try various answers to the violent man: for instance that his proposed bargain may be fair in itself, but he has no right to impose it arbitrarily upon others; that he only possesses one life, but by putting it at risk is claiming mastery over an infinity of lives; that what he is exposing to hazard may not be equal in value to what he is forcing us to risk by the same hazard; and that his "court of law" is therefore most probably not competent to try the case.

But if we deprive the individual of the right to define right and wrong, Diderot asks, to whom or what shall we address this great question? Why, to the General Will. "Individual wills are suspect . . . but the general will is always good; it has never been wrong, and it never will be wrong." The General Will of the species is the rule of conduct for one individual *vis-à-vis* another in the same society, of an individual *vis-à-vis* the society of which he or she is a member, and of the society of which he is a member *vis-à-vis* other societies. (And if animals could vote in a general assembly, it would be up to mankind to summon them to such an assembly, and cases of natural law should be pleaded no longer before *humanity* but before *animality*.)

It is one of Diderot's most brilliant articles; and, for Rousseau, in the present state of his outlook, it seemed to bring to a focus all that was wrong with the *philosophique* attitude. All such imaginary founding of social life in rational debate, he wrote, is a fatal fallacy. Man is not by nature a reasoning animal, and he becomes one only by joining society – which is to say at the expense of his happiness and virtue. As all observation goes to show, "general society", far from being a blessing as the *philosophes* would hold, is an unmitigated evil; it offers encouragement to the basest passions and gives the strong endless scope to tyrannise the weak. Diderot's account of his "violent man" is very convincing, wrote Rousseau. To judge from the behaviour of warring nation states, this is just how such a man *would* speak. But the answers that Diderot would give him are worthless. For the violent man could always reply: "It is not a matter of teaching me what justice is, but of showing me why it is in my interest to be just"; and anyway we have no right to expect sound reasoning from someone so recently recruited to sociality. The truth is, Rousseau argued, the *philosophes* imagined things exactly the wrong way round. Their cosmopolitanism and boasted "love of the human species" would be quite meaningless to Diderot's "violent man", and indeed, anyway, are just an excuse for loving nobody in particular. Thus it is only by establishing happy *little* republics that men can ever rise to the conception of a larger one. The only effective answer to Diderot's violent man will be, not words, but example: "showing in a perfected art the cure for the harm that art has inflicted on nature in its beginnings."[40]

6

A Circle
with Man at its Centre

Diderot, though so confirmed a Parisian, did not look on himself as a refugee from his native Langres and continued to think of his home background with affection. He enjoyed the notion of being thought a great man there; also he was eager to prove to his father, and more particularly to his brother, the great principle that an atheist could be a man of virtue and good will. His mind would often run on the River Marne, his "sad and tortuous compatriot",[1] whose waters, through endless windings, connected Paris with Langres.

By now Diderot's father and his sister Denise had long been reconciled to his marriage. At some stage, while the marriage was still a secret or a semi-secret, Diderot had been receiving disagreeable letters from his father, who had heard bad rumours about his life with "two women". It had made him adopt a simple solution. He had packed Nanette off in a coach to Langres, sending a message: "She left yesterday, she will arrive in three days; you can say what you like to her and can send her back when you are tired of her." The move had been the greatest success. Nanette had arrived to a decidedly frosty reception; but "next morning, as soon as she got up," writes her daughter, "she went to see her father-in-law and behaved to him as if to her own father," and she had then proceeded, being always a fanatically hard worker, to make herself thoroughly useful about the house. The old man had been charmed with her, as had Denise, and they had insisted on keeping her for three months.[2]

There was thus now a good deal of contact and correspondence between the rue de la Vieille Estrapade and Langres. From time to time, too, Diderot would perform commissions for Langres friends. In the early days of 1753 he went to great lengths to help a neighbour and close friend of the Diderots, Nicolas Caroillon, to secure the reversion of a lucrative post in the tax-farming service, as *entreposeur de tabac* (bonded warehouse-keeper for tobacco). It meant, as such things generally did, the offer of bribes, as well as the use of influential contacts. Diderot solicited help from Buffon and from the economist and court physician du Quesnay, and even made an approach to Madame de Pompadour.

In September 1753, at the age of 43, Nanette gave birth to a daughter, the last of their four children and the only one to survive to adult years. They named her Marie-Angélique, after her paternal grandmother; and in due course she and Diderot were to become intensely devoted. It is from her conversations with him that we learn such facts as are known about his early life. Almost at once a marriage was arranged, or at least projected, between the newly-born Angélique and one of Nicolas Caroillon's sons, and twenty years later the marriage would take place.

It was thus not as a prodigal or black sheep that, late in September 1754, Diderot made a return visit to his parental home. It was his first since his disastrous stay twelve years before, but the furies of that time seem to have left no grudge either on his or his father's part, and the two were reunited in great good humour. Denis's devout and cantankerous brother was away from home, which of course may have helped matters. His father made a nice *mot* at Denis's expense: "My son, we have both made a lot of noise in the world; the difference is, the noise from your implement has ruined your own peace, whereas the noise from mine merely ruins other people's."

There would have been a good deal of hospitable coming and going in the parental house in the Place Chambeau. Diderot, in his *Conversations of a Father with his Family*, imagines them as visited in one evening by the local Prior, a notary, a retired engineer and a hat-maker. Diderot's father enjoyed a reputation as a sage or Solomon, and the hat-maker had come to him for advice on a question of conscience. The discussion, as depicted in Diderot's sketch, becomes a little allegory of two conflicting theories of ethics, his own and his father's, and the need for both to exist. The Diderots had a web of family connections in the Langres neighbourhood, with relatives in the local magistracy and clergy as well as in the tanning, apothecary and bookselling trades. Thus Diderot was taken on an extensive round of visits, and was made to stand as godfather to another of Caroillon's sons.

Also, apart from the visits and the gossip, there was a question on which he seriously wanted his father's advice. Recently he had decided to demand a better contract from his publishers, and this was the sort of matter to interest Diderot senior, who was an excellent businessman. He threw himself into it with zest, and with his aid and that of a local attorney friend, Diderot drew up some new proposals. There was even talk of Denis's father coming up to Paris to help in the negotiations.

On Diderot's return to Paris, as was his way, he did not get round to writing home for a month or two, and then, in compensation, he wrote at enormous length. This engaging letter (6 January 1755) tells much about Diderot as a son. As one can see from it, he liked to play up to his reputation as a licensed sinner and brand for the burning. Thus, part of his letter is jovial and mock-salacious chaff about the charms of his father's devout female friends: how, when they went to see a certain Madame de Montessu in her monastery, he ought to have posed as a visiting foreign doctor and made a proper inspection of her "infirmities", if "infirmities" was the word.

> She is the most amiable, the most lively, the most witty, the least infirm and the least crucified of the brides of Christ whom I have the honour to know. Saving the respect I owe to Mme de Montessu, I believe my precisionist of a wife would do very well in her place, and Mme de Montessu would do very well in the place of my precisionist of a wife. As for me, I would imitate Adam; I would close my eyes and accept whatever it pleased God to place at my side; and then . . . and then, when I had had enough on that side, I would turn over.[3]

According to the same licence, however, having been the receiver of so many parental sermons in the past, he retaliated with some sermons of his own. One was on tolerance, and the grossly intolerant attitude of two young Capucin monks he had be- friended on his way home; another, addressed specifically to his father (it was to be his "New Year's gift") was on his father's sin in destroying his health and spirits by gloomy all-night vigils and prayers for the dead when he could be succouring the living and needy. ("Woe to your children, if they ever regretted money spent to satisfy the goodness of your heart in this world and assure your destiny in the next.") Was his father's life useful? Then his most meritworthy act would be to prolong it. Was it not useful, or not sufficiently so? Then he was in danger of dying before it had become so. His prime duty was to live, whether to become better or to be good for longer.

It also emerges from the letter that Diderot actually pictured himself as retiring to Langres on completing the *Encyclopédie*. What a pleasant prospect it would be, he told his father, to live beside him, and "bring, as well as a reputation fairly won, a somewhat more substantial and solid mark of the good use I have made of my time, of the life that I owe to you and the education that you gave me. Don't you agree, dear Father? Would it not make a charming future?"

Some casks of wine had arrived from Langres, sent by Denise; and in return, wrote Diderot, his circle in Langres would shortly receive a chest. It would contain several copies of the latest volume of the *Encyclopédie*, edifying manuals for his friends' children ("our little bishop" and "our little capucin"), some stockings, a skull-cap, velvet for a skirt, a muff for Denise, ribbon-knots for the notary's wife and slippers for the *petites racines* ("little blessings").

As for the contract, he reported, he had had a meeting with his publishers soon after his return, at which every one of his proposals had been rebuffed, and "we all put so much heat and so little reason into this first interview that I thought we would probably never meet again." A few days later the publishers had sent him a proposal of their own, which had not been much to his liking, and Nanette had persuaded him not to reply for the moment, pretending to be indifferent. The publishers adopted the same tactic, and he told his father, "I don't know how, during the wait, I didn't lose my patience and tell them to go to the devil . . . Had I had a little more confidence in my colleagues, that is what I would have done." (This last sentence is significant;

evidently Diderot, rightly or wrongly, had begun to suspect d'Alembert of a wish to supplant him.) It seemed like a total *impasse*. Then, out of the blue, and by a mixture of threats and diplomacy, d'Alembert and another friend managed to get the whole affair settled in his favour. It meant a substantial improvement in his finances, enabling the Diderots to move to a new and larger apartment.

The Diderots' new lodgings were in the rue Taranne, on a corner with the rue St Benoît, near Saint-Germain-des-Prés. It was in the heart of the Latin Quarter; Sorbonnists in their *soutanes* were much in evidence in the narrow and pavementless streets. The Diderots occupied the fourth floor, and in later years Diderot would rent the floor above as a study, but in these early days it was occupied by poor working men and their families. The wives, who always seemed to be ill, were a great object of concern for the charitable Nanette, who would be upstairs ten times a day to look after their needs. Almost as soon as Angélique could walk, she would be sent up to them with bowls of broth and fruit, the children would be invited down to play with her, and Nanette would give them cast-off clothes and pockets-full of goodies – they would also receive ferocious scoldings if they misbehaved. Angélique, on the other hand, would get her ears boxed if she said the least word to offend them.[4]

As has been said, Diderot regarded it as a crime against one's fellow-men to withhold useful knowledge from them. How many times, he lamented, did a craftsman or artisan know some technique that other craftsmen, in other trades, could have made use of if only they had known of it. One needed an "artisan Monarch" who would bring the mechanical arts together in an Academy.

Inspired by such thoughts – and by others equally dear to him – he published in 1755 one of his very oddest writings, entitled *The History and Secret of Painting in Wax*. A year or two earlier the Comte de Caylus,[5] a well-known amateur of the arts, had exhibited a painting of Minerva, with a claim to have rediscovered the lost art of encaustic painting. Diderot disliked the Comte de Caylus, regarding him as the quintessential meddling "connoisseur".

What is more, he had heard the painter Bachelier[6] speak with scorn of de Caylus's "discovery". Bachelier told Diderot and others that he had himself hit on something very like it years before. It amounted to very little: merely a new and unsatisfactory painting medium, composed of wax dissolved in turpentine and not involving any firing process – which is what the term "encaustic" implies. Now, however, spurred by de Caylus, Bachelier had experimented further and had arrived at a new technique, according to which the artist, working with a sort of alkaline "soap", fixed and hardened his canvas by heating before the fire. The process offered many advantages, among them an admirably hard and indestructible paint-surface, and Bachelier felt able to claim that he had rediscovered the "encaustic" painting described by Pliny.

It was not Bachelier's intention to publicise his discovery, though he allowed a fellow-artist named Odiot to buy the secret from him; however, Diderot, from a curious mixture of motives, decided that he would divulge it. He published an anonymous pamphlet in which he disentangled the rival claims of de Caylus and Bachelier, reconstructed Bachelier's thought-processes in the way that they should, logically, have occurred (not the same as the way they actually occurred), gave a detailed account of the process, in his best "Description of the arts" manner, and drew some philosophical conclusions. "How many discoveries that *touch* one another in nature and the arts and are separated by such great intervals in time and in our minds! They have to wait for some trivial event, like a candle-end falling into a painter's saucer or the reading of a passage in Pliny, before they can unfold and cause fools to say 'What, is that all there is to it?' "[7]

Diderot's enterprise in this pamphlet was an equivocal one, a sort of experiment in ethics, for he was, after all, trespassing against a friend of his. Accordingly he composed it impetuously, as if to silence any guilt-feelings, proceeding afterwards to add some self-mocking footnotes. "That is a terribly long and knotted sentence, which everyone will criticise. If it were the only one, I should correct it." "I think I may have made this up." "What a very silly and ill-judged joke . . ." The footnotes, he said, were a soberer judgement on himself passed in retrospect; and now he came to think of it, it was an excellent way to write, and others would do well to imitate it. This little *History*, with its insistence on divulgation, its "twice-over" method in writing, and its mystification (for, in some obscure way, he is plainly teasing Bachelier), strikes one as peculiarly Diderotesque.

With moments of idleness and disinclination to answer letters, and sporadic complaints at his contributors' sloth or impracticality, Diderot laboured on with devotion at the *Encyclopédie*. The work had achieved the greatest success, encouraging further famous and highly-placed persons to contribute to it (among them Turgot, Montesquieu and, in due course, Necker), as well as inspiring various rival enterprises abroad. By this time, moreover, he and d'Alembert had acquired an invaluable collaborator, the Chevalier de Jaucourt.[8] Jaucourt, born in 1704, came from a grand aristocratic family in Burgundy, which had converted to Protestantism in the sixteenth century. He himself had studied in Geneva and, briefly, at Cambridge (about which he was very scathing) and had later studied medicine in Leyden under the great Boerhaave. It was, in his family's eyes, an odd career for a member of the *noblesse d'épée*, but he was altogether a despiser of privilege and a most public-spirited man, wide in his culture, latitudinarian in religion and a committed believer in "enlightenment" and civil liberty. The great calamity of his life was that the manuscript of a vast medical dictionary, compiled by him, had been lost at sea. This was perhaps why he offered his services to the *Encyclopédie*. At all events, when the editors announced his recruitment, in the "Advertisement" to Volume II, they described his articles as "the precious debris of an immense work which perished in a storm and of which he did not want the remains to be useless to his country." He was a born compiler, paying three or four secretaries out of his own pocket and ready and eager to produce articles not just on medicine but on practically any topic. He was by no means a genius, and Diderot and d'Alembert regarded him with a mixture of amazement, gratitude and mild mockery. As time went on, though, he became, apart from Diderot himself, the chief mainstay of the *Encyclopédie*. It is calculated that, of the 60,660 articles in its seventeen volumes 17,050, or 28 per cent, were written by de Jaucourt.

The fifth volume of the *Encyclopédie* came out in November 1755, containing, among many other articles by Diderot, a long and remarkable one entitled ENCYCLOPÉDIE. It can be seen as a sort of counterpart to d'Alembert's "Preliminary Discourse" and is worth close attention, as Diderot's personal account of the ambitions, methods, pains and constraints of encylopaedism.

It is, says Diderot, the very moment to undertake an encyclopaedia. The opportunity is a grand one; Reason is in the ascendant, philosophy is making vast strides, men are beginning to shake off the yoke of authority and custom. Nevertheless this enterprise must be planned and conducted in a fashion never yet attempted. It must be no vain monument, erected for the glory of a monarch; for royal projects are conceived not for utility but for dignity and honour, and just for that reason they never get done. Again, it must not be a mere repository, a sterile compendium. It must be of the moment. Its writers must sense the present mind of the nation – must try, even, to outstrip it and to write as if for future generations. All this will entail, among other things, the work being done *quickly*, unlike the stately progress of national projects in the past.

It will also mean employing very numerous contributors, with all the problems and agonies this entails. They should, says Diderot, be men of letters and "artists", living dispersed, each with his own private occupation, and linked only by the general interest of mankind and sentiments of reciprocal benevolence. *Dispersed*, because no existing society or academy has the range of knowledge required; and to form one, and devote time to formal meetings and rituals, would be the surest way never to get finished (witness the Académie, which took sixty years to produce a mere dictionary). *Motivated by general benevolence*, because this is the most active and sustaining motive: "people grow warm, they undertake for their colleagues and friends what they would never undertake for any other reason. *Drawing on the help of "artists"* (i.e. craftsmen), because there are many "precious" and knowledgeable men among them, though, for reasons of social status, the doors of academies are shut to them. What or where a contributor is should be of no concern. "What is required is a citizen of the world, belonging to no country, to no sect, to no rank, reporting things of the day as if two thousand years in the past and those of the place they live in as if two thousand leagues distant."

What next must be asked is, how shall the encyclopaedia be arranged? The word "encyclopaedia" itself means literally "circle of knowledge"; and very little thought is needed, he says, to see that, like all circles, it begins and ends nowhere. The universe merely offers us individual entities and logically speaking can be described from an infinity of different points of view. Thus any system of knowledge or scheme of classification must, in the nature of things, be arbitrary; but indeed if this were not so and there could be such a thing as a non-arbitrary system of knowledge, how would it profit us? What would be the difference between studying this system or "great book" and studying the universe direct? One consideration had weighed with him and his fellow-editor: that it is the presence of human beings which makes the existence of other beings interesting. Banish Man, the thinking and observing being, from the surface of the earth, and the spectacle of Nature grows sad and silent. Why not, then, place Man in the *Encyclopédie* where he is placed in the universe – at the centre, with all lines beginning from and ending in him?

This Man-centred ordering once adopted, there remained, writes Diderot, four further problems of arrangement. First, on what principle should space be apportioned as between articles? This was, he said, a more or less unanswerable question – above all in a first edition. It was so even in theory: for "which kind of material shall serve as a module? Shall it be the most noble, the most useful, the most important, the most extensive?" But it proved to be so even more in practice, for workmen made the most wildly diverse estimates of the scope of their "art", and scholars and *savants* were not much better. It meant that the *Encyclopédie*, at least in its first edition, could not avoid being a sort of monstrosity.

Here we are swollen and exorbitant, there meagre, small, paltry, dry and emaciated . . . We are alternately dwarfs and giants, colossi and pygmies, straight and well-proportioned, and crooked,

hump-backed, limping and deformed. Add to these oddities a style
of discourse sometimes abstract, obscure or *recherché*, more often
careless, long-winded and slack, and you have to compare the
entire work to the *monster* in poetic theory, or something even more
hideous.[9]

Secondly, how should material be distributed within a given
branch of knowledge? This, he said, was a problem more
amenable to reason. Within a given subject area it should be
possible to form a fully intelligible tree of knowledge, all the way
from axioms, which would be its roots, to particular items, which
would represent the leaves and foliage. To put it another way:
encyclopaedic order would function like an atlas; particular
"orders" would function like maps; the dictionary arrangement
would supply local detail, of both the visible and the intelligible
worlds; and cross-references would function as "itineraries"
between those two worlds.

Thirdly – for the work was a dictionary as well as an
encyclopaedia – in what order should one introduce different
senses of the same word? This was a problem specifically for the
editor and called for a delicate combination of system and
flexibility, the aim being to soften (one could never hope to
eradicate) grotesque collocations.

Fourthly and finally there was the arrangement of headings
within the same meaning of a word. Here logic and principle were
of the essence, for an article should form a single uninterrupted
argument; and there was a method that he pressed on contributors, for it mimicked the actual process of scientific discovery.

It is to start from individual and particular phenomena, to ascend
to more extended and less specific knowledge, and from this to an
even broader kind, until one arrives at the knowledge of axioms
. . . for in any sphere of knowledge, one has not covered all the
ground till one has arrived at a principle which one can neither
prove, define, clarify, obscure or deny without losing part of the
daylight already won and taking a step backwards into the
shadows.[10]

Diderot's strategy in this article is unconventional and
reckless. He makes a point of stressing the terrible faults in the

Encyclopédie and speaks of "gross errors" in one of his own contributions. One weakness that he and d'Alembert have only lately recognised is that they neglected the subject of *language* – as distinct from *grammar*, which has been well treated. It is a fault so serious, "casting weakness on the whole work", that he sets to work to remedy it in this very article, and there follows a twelve-page dissertation on language in his most dashing and innovative style. At the heart of it is the problem of "radicals". One might have hoped, he says – and it is what a perfect encyclopaedia or system of knowledge would have to assume – that language was a seamless fabric, in which every word was definable in terms of other words; but this is prevented by those knots or blanks in the web known as "radicals" – indefinable terms, playing the same part in language as axioms do in general science. How does one establish which terms really are radicals? There may be a purely philosophical answer to this problem, he says; but for present purposes he offers a "technical" one, showing that there is a partial escape from it in the use of a dead language (Latin or Greek) as a fixed point of reference.

As often is the case, Diderot is eager to make capital out of frankness; and it is partly from this motive, as well as a general objection to secrecy, that he even gives away the devious game he and his friends have played with cross-references. In an encyclo-paedia, he says unblushingly, cross-references can be used not only to connect notions but to sow dissension among them. "They may secretly attack, unsettle and overthrow absurd opinions which one would not dare to insult openly."

> There should be great scope for ingenuity and infinite advantage for the authors in this latter sort of cross-reference. From it the work as a whole should acquire an inner force and a secret efficacy, the silent results of which will necessarily be felt with the passage of time. Whenever, for instance, a national prejudice seems to merit honour, it will be necessary, in the article specially devoted to it, to discuss it respectfully and to give it its due panoply of probability and persuasiveness. But by supplying cross-references from it to articles where solid principles support diametrically opposite truths, we can throw down the whole edifice of mud and scatter the idle heap of dust.[11]

A wave of enthusiasm for virtue seizes Diderot, and he waxes oratorical. The *Encyclopédie* may neglect mere biography, but it cannot, he says, afford to neglect noble examples. Virtues, like vices, have their own physiognomy, their own system of signs and symptoms, and they need to be studied in effigy. He is touching here on a contentious issue. For throughout the *ancien régime* only monarchs enjoyed the right to an effigy in a public place, but soon there was to develop an almost idolatrous cult of busts and statues of great men, and especially of *philosophes*, as objects of private veneration.[12] In the same spirit, in 1758, the Académie would offer a prize for eloquence to eulogists of "great men" – not just of monarchs and heroes but exemplars of any kind of civic virtue.

The eulogy and the statue, argues Diderot, represent a public pact or contract, compelling the man of virtue to remain virtuous, lest he should deliberately ruin his own effigy. "We cannot erect too many of these statues in our work nor in our public places, inviting us to virtue on those pedestals where at present we and our children see displayed the debauches of the pagan gods." Nor is it only the dead who deserve eulogies. "It would be a great injustice to grant them only to the cold and insensible ashes of men who can no longer hear them." The eulogy of a man of good will is the sweetest and most fit reward for another man of good will. "O Rousseau," (the name leaps to Diderot's lips) "Rousseau, my dear and worthy friend, I have never had the strength to resist praising you! My taste for truth and love of virtue have grown in the doing of it."[13]

Diderot's article ENCYCLOPÉDIE, with all its admissions of error, is lavish in its tributes to the encyclopaedists and their high virtue. In the same month as it appeared, however, their complacency received a little tweak, in the form of a stage burlesque. It was entitled *The Circle; or, the Originals* and was staged in Lunéville at the court-theatre of Stanislas Lescinzski, the Duke of Lorraine. Stanislas was a sometime king of Poland and father to the present queen of France, and at the end of the War of the Polish Succession (1733–36), as compensation for his lost throne, he had been installed as titular ruler of Lorraine, this province, to all intents and purposes, now becoming a part of France. Stanislas was, in a modest way, an intellectual, who had engaged in a polemic with Rousseau, and his court at Lunéville tended to be a focus for anti-*philosophique* sentiment. As for the author of *The Circle*, the young Charles Palissot,[14] he was a renegade from the *philosophique* camp and a protégé of the highly influential Comte de Stainville – soon, as Duc de Choiseul, to become Louis XV's chief minister. The play formed part of the celebrations on the erecting of a statue to Louis XV in the public square at Nancy.

The Circle is really a skit on *salon* intellectuals in general. It features a vain poet, who has invented a new genre of play which arouses laughter and tears at the same moment; a middle-aged *femme savante*, who is a learned geometer, a physicist or an expert on the fine arts according to whom she has been talking to the night before (she is writing an article on FLUXIONS for the *Encyclopédie*); a dilettante financier; an up-to-date quack doctor; and a philosopher (evidently meant for Rousseau) who has decried civilisation, poured scorn on his public and pretended to despise money, and – now that the world is beginning to laugh at him – is finding life uncomfortable. Would it not be better, he is asked, to return to common sense? "But what advantage would I find in thinking like everyone else?" replies the Philosopher indignantly. "No, Monsieur, no; I will not compromise the honour of philosophy in such a way."

Palissot's play was a mild affair. All the same it succeeded in offending Duke Stanislas and in greatly enraging d'Alembert, who took it as an intolerable insult to himself and his friends, the more so for receiving semi-official backing. He wrote angrily to a friend at Stanislas's court, attempting to have Palissot disgraced and expelled from the Academy of Nancy, and it took a chivalrous letter from Rousseau, the chief victim of the play, to save him. A few years later Palissot, taking his revenge, would satirise the *encyclopédistes* again and to much more damaging effect, in his play *Les Philosophes*, staged in that most "establishment" of milieux, the *Comédie Française*.[15]

7

The "Letter to Landois"

I earlier described Diderot's philosophical position as Scepticism, and this remains the best description of his later outlook, for his deepest instinct was, always, to distrust what tradition, prejudice, laziness or the powers-that-be offered as a picture of the world. Might not the world be quite otherwise? Did not a rebellious inner voice keep murmuring that it was so? This does not mean, however, that he arrived at no firm philosophical commitment. By the 1750s he had formed quite a rounded and well-worked-out system, of which the main features were materialism, atheism and determinism. These were doctrines – especially the atheism – that of course had to be somewhat cloaked in his published writings and in the *Encyclopédie*; but he could and did expound them freely within the d'Holbach circle and they won him some disciples there.

There is sometimes said to be a glaring inconsistency between Diderot's determinism and his enthusiasm for "virtue", and indeed he occasionally sighed over the discrepancy himself. On a closer look at his system, however, the objection begins to look much less solid. A good way of approaching his system is through one of his most striking occasional writings, his "Letter to Landois" of 1756.

Paul Landois was an unsuccessful playwright and hack writer, who contributed a few articles on painting to the *Encyclopédie*, and in the summer of 1756 he wrote Diderot a letter of furious complaint: against Diderot's criminal slowness in paying him for one of his articles, his failing to put in a word on his behalf with Voltaire, his silence over a manuscript that Landois had sent him, and the malignant way in which not only Diderot but the world in general seemed determined to conspire against him. The letter (not the first such that Landois had written to Diderot) has not survived, but its tone was evidently a mixture of misanthropy and cynicism, and made jibes at the hypocrisy of "virtue".

Diderot, in a way we have seen him do before, saw in the letter an occasion for a statement of principle, and he sent Landois a weighty rejoinder – which for all we know was never posted, but which was published in Grimm's *Correspondance littéraire* for 1 July 1756.[1] It told Landois, essentially, that to nurse grievances, and likewise to go in for his brand of cynicism, was a kind of moral stupidity. It was simply petty, whereas a true ethical philosophy might be bleak but would at least take large views. He told Landois he would answer, first, as a "preacher", and secondly as a philosopher. As a preacher his sermon would run thus. Virtue is not an enemy to the passions, its role is merely to help us make the best use of them. One has to choose which passion to listen to, and if the "virtuous" choice inflicts some pain at first, it will soon become second nature; and the rewards, rewards for one's own *self-esteem*, will be amazing! For what is a virtuous man? It is a man vain with that particular kind of vanity. "Everything we do, we actually do for our own sake. We may appear to be sacrificing ourselves, when we are merely satisfying ourselves." (Woe to Landois if he did not have a fund of good actions to be vain of, to intoxicate him with the sweet smell of self-approval.)

Conversely, the greatest objection to "bad" behaviour is that it, too, will soon become second nature. "Do not forget that a bad action never goes unpunished. I say *never*, because the first bad deed we commit disposes us towards a second, and that second towards a third and thus we advance towards the scorn of our fellow-humans, which is the greatest of all evils and pains." Nor does it make sense to say, that, if disgraced in one social group, one can always go away and be virtuous elsewhere. Ceasing to be wicked is not just a matter of saying "I want to." "The crease is taken," writes Diderot. "The cloth will keep it for ever."

So much for the didactic answer. Now, says Diderot, he will quit the tone of the preacher for that of the philosopher. If one looks at the matter closely, one will see that the word "liberty" is a meaningless one. There are not, nor could there be any, free beings, and we are merely what befits the general order of things:

we are the product of education, organisation and the universal chain of events. One cannot conceive of a creature acting without a motive, and our motives come not from within us but from outside and as part of a larger causal system. Thus the idea that we *will* freely and act freely is a phantom, a matter of confusing the *voluntary* with the *free*.

But if there is no freewill, it follows that there is no action deserving of praise or blame, no vice, no virtue, nothing calling for reward or punishment. From a philosophical point of view, we should not speak of vice and virtue but rather of beneficence and maleficence. The maleficent man is a man whom we have to destroy, not punish; and, similarly, to be beneficent is a form of good luck, not virtue. However, if human beings are not free, they can nevertheless be modified, whether by exhortation, example, education, pleasure or pain. (This is the justification for, among other things, public executions.) Thus what the spectacle of life should teach us is a philosophy full of pity and fellow-feeling, one which inclines us strongly towards the good but no more makes us angry with the wicked than we would be with a hurricane for blowing dust in our face.

There is, strictly speaking, only one kind of cause (all causes are physical) and only one kind of necessity – the same for all of us, however different we may claim to be or really are. This thought should reconcile us to the human race and to ourselves and makes nonsense of misanthropy. Reproach no one, repent of nothing: these are the first steps in wisdom. For after all, he asks Landois, is there one among the whole of mankind who has given him a hundredth part of the pain he has given himself? "Is it the malice of mankind that makes you sad, uneasy, melancholy, abusive, restless and moribund?" Again, why should he speak of nature and fortune as conspiring against him? "My friend, you think too much of yourself, you give yourself too much importance in the universe. Save for one or two people who love you, who pity you or who make excuses for you, all is tranquil around you, and you may sleep soundly."

Most of the main elements in Diderot's formal philosophy come into play in the "Letter". One feature, though, needs a little filling out; this is the distinction between "voluntary" and "free".

We can best clarify it by a look at Diderot's *Encyclopédie* article on VOLONTÉ (Will). This article is plainly his answer to the kind of theistic conception of the will which makes it out to be a grandly rational and spiritual faculty (the nearest we get, according to Descartes, to sharing the greatness of God).[2] For Diderot, by contrast, willing is not really a rational activity at all; for one is helpless not to will, it is imposed upon one from outside and as part of the causal system governing the world. Of course, human beings make choices; but since they do not choose *what* it is that they shall wish or desire (indeed they may even have trouble in discovering what it is), the act of choice is a banal little event (like, shall we say, the "on" or "off" position of a switch). The actual assent or choosing of a man asleep, says Diderot, is no different from that of a waking one, that of a fool from that of a wise man, that of a man with fever from that of one in good health. It is an account that puts one in mind of Schopenhauer's memorable description of the "spectator" role of the intellect in situations of choice. "It [the intellect] awaits the real decision just as passively and with the same intense curiosity as if it were that of a foreign will . . . The intellect can do nothing more than bring out clearly and fully the nature of the motives; it cannot determine the will itself; for the will is quite inaccessible to it and . . . cannot be investigated."[3]

As for the discrepancy between Diderot's determinism and his advocacy of moral effort and "virtue", it is at least not an inadvertence, for in the "Letter to Landois" he deliberately brings it to the fore. He is saying that the term "virtue" belongs in one kind of discourse but not in another: the term is very important in didactic discourse, but it is out of place in strictly philosophical discussion. This seems an acceptable manoeuvre, and in the "Letter to Landois" it strikes one as very effective. Indeed, for a man determined to remain both a moralist and a philosopher, Diderot's system is cunningly designed and has some powerful advantages. All the various elements in it work together to discredit egotism. Its drift is that, though the moral life is enormously important, one should not consider one's own part in it important. Wide views of social utility should replace the drama of the solitary soul and its wrestlings with God.

8

Diderot and the Theatre

Diderot's publisher Le Breton had a little country house and farm near the village of Massy, just south of Paris, to which he would sometimes invite his authors; in the summer of 1756 Diderot, exhausted by his labours on the *Encyclopédie*, went there for a few weeks rest and holiday. While there, or so it would appear, he happened to come on a copy of Goldoni's comedies and read *Il Vero amico (The True Friend)*. The play is about a man who, having fallen in love with his friend's fiancée, shows the world just how nobly a true friend and man of virtue can act. Diderot considered it very feeble, but the theme appealed to him, and the question occurred to him whether he could not do better with it himself. It was thus that he became a dramatist, and also a theoretician of the drama. It was an episode which, as it oddly turned out, would have extensive repercussions in theatrical history, though for Diderot himself it brought more trouble than pleasure.

To the play that he sketched out in the following few weeks he gave the title *Le Fils naturel (The Natural Son)*. This is rather misleading, for though he makes the hero illegitimate (which he is not in Goldoni) the drama is not really about bastardy. For all the earlier part of his play, indeed, Diderot follows the Goldoni play remarkably closely. As in Goldoni, Diderot's hero, the austere and melancholy man of virtue Dorval, is staying in the house of his bosom-friend Clairville, has fallen in love with Clairville's ingenuous young fiancée Rosalie and has in turn been fallen in love with by Clairville's sister Constance. He decides to flee the household; but the unsuspecting Clairville, mystified by Rosalie's sudden coolness, and knowing her respect for Dorval's wisdom and virtue, insists, in the name of friendship, that Dorval shall go to Rosalie and find out what is troubling her. Dorval, in agony, complies. It is a fatal step, for Rosalie, under his questioning, tacitly reveals an answering passion and she proceeds to write to him, confessing her love. He is beginning a reply ("I love you, and I flee . . . alas, far too late!") when he is summoned to rescue his friend from the hands of ruffians. Meanwhile Constance enters, finds his half-written letter, and jumps to the conclusion that it is addressed to her . . .

All the foregoing, in outline, is pure Goldoni, and the borrowing extends, to a lesser degree, to some of the later steps by which Dorval, by reckless and secret acts of generosity, succeeds in rescuing his friend's marriage. In other respects, in their later scenes, the plots of the two plays diverge. Diderot's tearful and lengthy *dénouement* depends on the announced return of Rosalie's father (Lysimond) from the West Indies, his servant's recital of their cruel sufferings when their ship was captured by the British, and the final appearance of Lysimond himself, who turns out to be Dorval's long-lost father. By contrast the father in *Il Vero amico*, a comic miser based closely on Molière's Harpagon, is a central character throughout (and indeed his love-scene with his money-box is the best thing in Goldoni's play).

Goldoni's is a brisk, well-engineered and, to modern readers, thoroughly empty play. It is, at all events, a farce (though he was inclined to resent the description): a mildly cynical entertainment with not the slightest pretensions to a message or even, except in the case of the miserly Ottavio, to anything one would seriously call character-drawing. As for what Diderot made out of it: to be frank, there can be few readers today who would not call it preposterous, and one could if one wanted make very unkind fun of it. The pomposity, the self-righteousness, the sheer gorgeous absurdity of Diderot's self-declared paragon of "virtue", certainly take some believing. To give the flavour of Dorval, let me quote just one of his remarks. Constance, who would like him as a husband, is rebuking him for his wish to retire from the world and his over-anxious scruples over begetting children. His reply begins: "Constance, I am not a stranger to that inclination, so widespread and so sweet, which leads all creatures onwards and brings them to perpetuate their species . . ."

More worthwhile, though, than poking fun at Diderot's play is to think oneself into his motives; and in some sense the key to his play is fairly plainly not Goldoni but Rousseau. "Virtue" was a cult word for Diderot as much as for Rousseau, but there is distinct wildness in his conception of the deeds that might be performed on virtue's heroic stage – for instance that, like Dorval, one might nobly decide to *argue* one's lover and beloved into transferring her affections from oneself to one's best friend! But further, the Virtue that is paraded in this play strikes one as being, not the sanguine and Shaftesburian quality natural to Diderot, but the austere version of Rousseau, that stern and Utopian virtue which inspired Robespierre and would flourish round the guillotine. The play is, indeed, meant as a critique of Rousseauesque virtue, and its climax comes in the fourth Act where, in place of Goldoni's swift repartee, we have a weighty debate between Constance and Dorval, on the question, is it right for Dorval to embrace a childless solitude? "Only the wicked man lives alone," says Constance. He ought rather to stay among his fellow-men, cultivate the social virtues and pass on his moral excellences to children? It is this debate, one feels, that represents for Diderot the *raison d'être* of his theatrical enterprise. He was made to suffer severely for his plagiarism of Goldoni, but his fault was not quite what it appeared. He was not attempting to steal Goldoni's clothes – indeed Goldoni was too well-known a dramatist for anyone to get away with this. It was, rather, sheer impetuousness and presumption, traits which, on the whole, had been a strength to him on the *Encyclopédie*. He had jumped to the conclusion that he could quite easily annex the art of the theatre and put it to better and more philosophical purposes.

The first draft of *The Natural Son* was shown to Grimm and other friends, who helped revise it, and in February 1757 it was published – not, however, on its own, but with an elaborate "framing" fiction of extraordinary ingenuity. The genius that seems conspicuously absent from Diderot's play emerges in this surrounding fiction.

Preceding the text of the play he provided an Introduction written in the person of the well-known encyclopaedist

"Diderot". "The sixth volume of the *Encyclopédie* had just appeared," it runs, "and I had gone to the country in search of repose and health, when an event, as interesting for its circumstances as for the people concerned, became the wonder and topic of conversation of the whole district. All spoke of a certain man of rare qualities who had had, on one and the same day, the strange fortune to risk his life on a friend's behalf and the courage to sacrifice to this same friend his own passion, fortune and liberty."[1] Diderot feels he must meet this hero and does so, finding him a man deeply marked by sorrow, though momentarily transfigured and even gay when he speaks of virtue. His name is Dorval, and he relates to "Diderot" the strange events and misunderstandings that once overtook himself, his family and his beloved friend Clairville. "Diderot" says that it is so moving a story that someone ought to write a play about it, and Dorval replies that this is exactly what his aged father Lysimond had said. Lysimond, who never ceased to thank heaven for his own and his children's rescue from their past dangers, had urged Dorval to perpetuate these moving events in a drama. It would not be a stage play, not a play at all in the theatrical sense, but rather a ritual commemoration, by which they, and after them their descendants, might at stated times "renew themselves", using as a stage the house in Saint-Germain-en-Laye[2] where their destiny had first been enacted. He would, he had said, even be ready to act in it himself.

Dorval had duly written such a drama, but alas their father had died before it could be staged. However, so he tells "Diderot", the other protagonists are planning to perform it on the following Sunday, each playing the same part that he or she had done in real life. There would be no audience, but as a favour "Diderot" would be welcome to watch them from hiding.

He does so, and what he witnesses corresponds in every detail to the real-life Diderot's play *The Natural Son*. Or rather (for reasons "Diderot" promises to explain to the reader later) he witnesses the whole of the drama except for the last scene.

So ends the Introduction, and there follows the text of *The Natural Son*. The framing fiction or "novel" then resumes. "Diderot" now explains to us how he came to be prevented from seeing the last scene of Dorval's play. Dorval's father having died, his part had had to be taken by a family friend; and at the sight of him, wearing the very prison-rags worn by Lysimond during his captivity among the British, the whole company had burst into tears and had been unable to continue.

"Diderot" was much moved by the commemorative play, but, he tells us, even more so by the irruption of real-life feeling which eventually halted it. The performance left him tearful, but also mystified, realising there were complicated puzzles here about the relationship of art to life. He calls on Dorval a few days later, to thank him for the "delicious and cruel" evening that he owed to him, and asking to be lent a copy of the play, which he returns covered with pencilled queries and annotations. The two men's friendship flourishes, and during the following days, both being passionate nature-lovers, they roam the countryside discussing realism and the theatre. "Diderot" plays the interlocutor; and at his questioning Dorval outlines a whole programme for a new and reformed theatre.

It is a call for a new simplicity, a return to the "natural". Dorval imagines a new theatrical genre, to be called *tragédie domestique et bourgeoise*, and a new style of acting, according to which actors, instead of addressing the audience in *Comédie Française* fashion, should turn and face, and even touch, one another and behave at all times as if there were no one observing them. He also requires a new freedom in stage-grouping, opening up vast new potentialities for the *tableau* (which is a higher form of art than the *coup de théâtre*), and for *pantomime*; and he dreams of a continuously-changing décor.

But of course, in all this, it is crucial that we are listening to the opinions of an imaginary personage – Dorval – a character in a play. Who better placed than a fiction to discourse on the relationship of fiction to reality? He is giving us the most privileged and "inside" view imaginable.

Dorval insists that what he has himself written is, for good or evil, *not* a play, since it had to obey the rule of fact and of what-actually-happened; and this enables him to clarify what a play is and how it would be different. "Diderot" has criticised one of Rosalie's speeches as too grandiose for an *ingénue*, and in reply

Dorval shows him the manuscript, where those very words have been written in by Rosalie herself. "Diderot" mentions a striking *coup de théâtre* in the play. Did not Dorval say he despised *coups de théâtre*; why then did he resort to one? Because, says Dorval, that is how things actually happened. It would have made for a better play if they had happened otherwise.

Diderot's ploy, as we see, is a fantastic but cunning one. He has found a way to draw critical lessons and generalisations from his own play while at the same time disowning responsibility for it. In these ingenious, indeed over-ingenious, "Conversations" we have the germ of certain of his later masterpieces – for instance the dazzling pages in his *Salon* of 1767 in which, in imagination, he steps across the frame of Joseph Vernet's landscape-paintings and takes a country walk within them, discussing the relative claims of natural beauty and the beauty of art. But further, as we shall see, it offers a clue to his whole conception of fiction.

The published text of the play and the "Conversations" made a very gratifying stir. "I cannot express to you," Elie Fréron told his readers in the *Année littéraire*, "with what warmth the Public received this play, which has never been performed . . . It was for some time the topic of all the conversations, and almost all the eulogies, of Paris."[3] Actually, though one would not have guessed it from these words, Fréron was a devoted enemy of the *philosophes*; and, to his glee, he soon discovered Diderot's plagiarism from Goldoni. His first thought, on doing so, was to publish a mock letter of complaint as if from Goldoni, but this was forbidden by Malesherbes as constituting "a falsehood worse than all the plagiarisms in the world". He therefore adopted a more devious and, in fact, horribly effective tactic. In his issue for 30 June 1757 he printed a detailed synopsis of Diderot's play. It began "Act I. Dorval enters, alone; at first he walks about pensively. At last, after some motions which reveal the trouble in his soul, he takes the honourable decision to leave the house where he is staying. He calls out loudly: *Charles! Charles!* . . ." This was followed by a thorough and very sensible critique of the play, Fréron remarking politely that, from all he heard of Monsieur Diderot, he would be the last person to resent "just, honest and respectful criticism". Then in his issue for 12 July he offered his readers a critical essay on Goldoni and, with straight face, prefaced it with a synopsis of the first two acts of Goldoni's *Il vero amico* – in exactly the same words, barring the names, as the one of *The Natural Son!* ("Act I. *Florindo* enters, alone; at first he walks about pensively. At last, after some motions which reveal the trouble in his soul, he takes the honourable decision to leave the house where he is staying. He calls out loudly: *Trivella! Trivella!* . . ." etc.)

Michelet describes Fréron as "very learned, dull and heavy, a gross Breton from Quimper." He was, however, a shrewd, well-informed and independent-minded man. Like Diderot, he had suffered a spell in the prison of Vincennes, and his periodicals would from time to time get suppressed, for scandal or sedition. All the same, for twenty years or more, he was the most formidable of all the enemies of the *philosophes*. He had the support of the *dévot* party, including the Queen of France and her father Stanislas, the Duke of Lorraine, and for some years already he had been skirmishing with Voltaire, who had tried at first to win him over but came to detest him heartily and would savage him (under the name of "*Frelon*" or "Wasp") in his comedy *L'Ecossaise* (1760). D'Alembert had blocked his election to the Berlin Academy, threatening his own resignation if he were to be elected, and Fréron had, in retaliation, poured scorn on d'Alembert's speech of reception at the French Academy. Thus this attack on Diderot did not come out of the blue.

Nevertheless Diderot, caught in the toils of his own mystification, was exceedingly galled by this trick of Fréron's over *The Natural Son*; and though friends rallied round, and Grimm defended him in the *Correspondance littéraire*, he nearly gave up his theatrical projects in disgust. He was not a man to give up easily, though; and eventually his *Le Père de famille* (*A Father and His Family*) got written, and with it a long discourse on *Dramatic Poetry* in which he put his theories into systematic form. They were published together in 1761; and in the discourse, which is addressed to Grimm, Diderot brazens out his borrowings from Goldoni as best he can. Goldoni's farce, he says, is a tissue of borrowings from Molière's *L'Avare* and Corneille's *Le Vrai ami*, and he has done no more than follow suit. He took over part of *Il Vero amico* "as a property that belonged to me" and thought he could make better use of. "I wish there were a dozen such thefts to reproach me with, and [he adds ruefully] I don't know if *A Father and His Family* will have gained much by being entirely mine."

A Father and His Family is about a young man of good family and his struggles to persuade his father, a man of good heart but narrow and conventional views, to agree to his making an "unworldly" marriage. It is a more workable play than *The Natural Son*, and at the opening of Act I and again at the opening of Act II, Diderot has made quite effective use of the *tableau* and of multiple stage-action (features very dear to him) to render the cross-currents of feeling within the family. Honesty compels one to say, though, that, like its predecessor, the play is a dreadfully wooden affair. It was, nevertheless, performed by the *Comédie Française* in 1761, with moderate success, and on its revival in 1769 it was received with great enthusiasm. According to Beaumarchais, it was this revival of *A Father and His Family* that sent him back to serious drama. From then on, for nearly a century, it formed part of the repertoire of the Comédie Française, and in Germany it fared even better, coming to be regarded as a masterpiece and inspiring the young Schiller's *bürgerlich* comedy *Kabale und Liebe*. It was also twice adapted, again with success, for the English stage: by Sophia Lee in *The Chapter of Accidents*, first performed in 1780, and by John Burgoyne in *The Heiress* (1786).

Nor can one exactly deny that Diderot, in his way, had made a real innovation in stagecraft. When the young Chateaubriand was first taken to the theatre, in Saint-Malo, they were doing *A Father and His Family*. He was, no doubt, expecting something on the lines of *Le Cid* or *Tartuffe*, and he found the whole affair quite baffling.

> I saw two men walking up and down the stage and talking to each other, with everybody looking at them. I took them for managers of a puppet-show, chatting outside the home of the Old Woman who Lived in a Shoe while they waited for the audience to arrive. The only thing that surprised me was that they should discuss

their business so loudly and that they should be listened to in silence. My astonishment grew when other characters coming on to the stage started waving their arms about and weeping, and everybody took to crying out of sympathy. The curtain fell without my having understood a word of all this . . . such was the first impression I obtained of the art of Sophocles and Molière.[4]

The influence of Diderot's actual plays, however, is nothing to that of his *Discourse* and "Conversations", or rather, of the plays and theoretical writings combined. From the beginning, they made the strongest possible impact on Lessing, who claimed that his taste had been formed by Diderot. Lessing hastened to make a German translation of *The Natural Son* and the "Conversations", and when he came to write a theatrical periodical, the *Hamburgische Dramaturgie*, he drew continually on Diderot's theories and made propaganda for *A Father and His Family*. He even, broad-mindedly, quoted to his readers the long conversation on the theatre in *Les Bijoux indiscrets*, exclaiming "What clarity, what good sense in this Diderot! But all these truths were then thrown to the wind." When one considers that Lessing's own plays, from *Minna von Barnhelm* onwards, are strongly coloured by Diderot, one has to say that Diderot achieved all the influence he might have hoped for, and became one of the founding fathers of the German national drama.

9

"Only the wicked man lives alone"

Rousseau was growing more and more out of sympathy with the d'Holbach circle, and indeed with Paris generally. He was, he told himself, sick of the "salons and fountains and tiresome people who wanted to show them off," of the "pamphlets and clavichords and card-games and stupid *bon-mots*, the little tellers of tales and the givers of great suppers." He pined for a country existence, where he could walk half the day and could write in peace of mind. The thought occurred to him that he might return to Geneva, but Voltaire had now settled there and this meant it would be Paris all over again: the same chatter, the same manners, the same cynicism. Geneva was somehow too small to hold both Rousseau and Voltaire.

At last, though, quite unexpectedly, a perfect solution to his problem was offered by a friend of Grimm's named Louise de La Live d'Epinay.[1] She was the wife of La Live d'Epinay, one of France's forty farmers-general. They had a grand country mansion, La Chevrette, near Montmorency, ten miles to the north of Paris. There was, however, trouble between her and her husband, who was unfaithful and a spendthrift, indeed distinctly crooked financially. The two were estranged, and for some years she had been the lover of Rousseau's friend Dupin de Francueil,[2] but more recently she had begun an affair with Grimm. Rousseau had got to know her through Francueil, and from time to time he had been invited to her country home. He had performed in private theatricals there, and on one occasion he had written a play for her little private theatre.

Mme d'Epinay was, in her friends' eyes, an appealing character. She was small, vivid and fragile-looking, with great lustrous eyes. Voltaire, who came to know her in Geneva, was greatly smitten with her, calling her "an eagle in a cage of gauze". She was trusting and easily led and rather unsure of herself, having come in, one way or another, for a good deal of unkind gossip. It was known that, though unawares, she had contracted a venereal disease from her husband and passed it on to her lover Francueil; also there were rumours that she had behaved dishonestly over an inheritance, furthering her husband's interests by illicitly destroying a document. She was a romantic and liked to picture herself as a character in a novel. Rousseau fascinated her, and she believed him a genius, though she was well aware of his prickliness. She liked to address him as her "dear Bear".

One day, walking on her estate, they had passed a cottage known as the Hermitage. It was empty and dilapidated, but Rousseau, unthinkingly, had said it was the sweetest of spots, the sweetest of homes, and "made for him". At this, unknown to him, Mme d'Epinay had set to work to have it refurbished, and when the work was completed, she offered it to him as a home. He hesitated, but she used her powers of persuasion on Thérèse and her mother, who were all for the scheme. Thus, at length, the decision was taken, and on 9 April 1756 she collected the three in her carriage and installed them in the cottage. So old and frail was Mme Levasseur that she had to be carried to the door in a chair. It was understood that Rousseau, though Mme d'Epinay's guest, should retain his cherished independence and not be forced into the social round at La Chevrette. When, however, there was no house-party at the big house, it was expected that he should visit and offer Mme d'Epinay his companionship. The whole arrangement provoked gloomy prophecies among Diderot's circle. They said he would be driven back to Paris by sheer boredom, or, alternatively, he would grow introspective and mad.

All went well for Rousseau during his first few months at the Hermitage, and he found the liberty and solitude as delicious as he could have hoped. He had expected to occupy himself with philosophical projects, of which he had several on hand. To his surprise, however – for he had said hard things in the past about sentimental fiction – he found himself writing a novel, his *Julie, or the New Héloïse*. It was a Richardsonian novel-in-letters, telling of ideal love, remorse and renunciation, and he composed it in unplanned fashion on his day-long forest walks.

Mme d'Epinay adopted a policy of pretending to leave him alone but in fact continually cosseting him, and she conspired with Thérèse's mother to subsidise his existence without his knowing it. He adopted a regular routine, copying music in the morning, taking long walks in the afternoon (alone, for Thérèse did not much enjoy walking), and writing in the evening. As agreed, he shunned La Chevrette when there were guests staying but at quieter times he would dine with Mme d'Epinay, and they would play chess or go for walks together. His constant refrain to her was how he wished Diderot were there, how he kept wondering when, or if ever, he would see him. It was not, he said, that he doubted his friend's good intentions; but it was a long way from his door to Rousseau's and all too many people to waylay him. "It will be hopeless if he actually arranges to come, for he will plan it a hundred times and I shall not see him once. He is a man who needs to be kidnapped and forced to do what in fact he wants to do." Mme d'Epinay did her best to console Rousseau, telling him he put too much anxiety into his friendships; and in fact Diderot would occasionally come to the Hermitage, in company with other friends. The *abbé* Morellet recalled day-long visits there with Diderot, when they all sat under the chestnut-trees listening while Rousseau read from his novel.

Mme d'Epinay only used La Chevrette during the summer months, and when winter approached she urged Rousseau not to risk spending it there – if for no other reason because of Mme Levasseur, now in her eighties and alarmed at the prospect of winter in so isolated a cottage. Rousseau, however, was scornful of Mme Levasseur's fears. As a gesture, he borrowed a musket and some pistols and acquired a watch-dog, but he set his mind firmly against returning to Paris, telling Mme d'Epinay he was "determined, whatever happened" to stay and that she must not oppose him, as contradiction upset him "mortally". His siege-preparations amused his journalist friend Alexandre Delyre, who wrote threatening that he and Diderot would come and take the place by storm. It proved a bitterly cold winter, but all the same an enjoyable one for Rousseau, and he would look back on this as the last really peaceful interval in his life.

The year which followed was certainly catastrophic. Trouble began when, in the middle of February 1757, Diderot sent him his play *The Natural Son*. In reading it Rousseau came upon Constance's words "Only the wicked man lives alone," and was instantly convinced that the remark was aimed at himself. Indeed, one senses, he may have been right; for, in this scene, Dorval's whole self-portrait, the "austere virtue", the loneliness, the "untutored manners" that he attributes to himself, is extremely reminiscent of Rousseau. He was bitterly stung and wrote Diderot a letter of reproach – a gentle one, according to his own account, but the letter has not survived – rebuking his friend not only for this cruel blow but for neglecting him generally.

Diderot's reply was rather breezy. What with the bad weather and illness in his family, he told Rousseau, it was impossible for him to come to Montmorency. Thus Rousseau ought to come to Paris and ought to stay with him for a night or two, when they could discuss his novel and one or two other important concerns.

> I am very glad you liked my work and that it moved you! You are of a different opinion from me about hermits. However much good you say about them, you are the only one in the world that I will think well of. In fact there is more to say on that score, if one could speak of it without your getting angry. An eighty-year-old woman! etc . . .
> *Thursday*
> I beg your pardon for what I said to you about the solitude you are living in. I had not spoken to you about it till then. Forget what I said, and trust me not to speak of it again.
>   Adieu, Citizen! [Rousseau liked to sign his works "Jean-Jacques Rousseau, Citizen of Geneva."] All the same, a hermit is a strange sort of citizen.[3]

Rousseau was much offended by this letter and sent Diderot a sharp reply (also now lost), refusing to go to Paris, now or ever. He gave vent to his griefs in a letter to Mme d'Epinay, in Paris.

> My dear Friend, I shall suffocate if I do not pour out my troubles

in the bosom of friendship. Diderot has written me a letter which has pierced me to the soul. He seems to say that it is a mercy he does not regard me as a criminal, and that *there would be much more to say on that score* – those are his words; and do you know why? Because Mme Levasseur is with me. But my God, what more could he say if she were not? I took them out of the street, she and her husband, at an age when they were no longer able to earn a living; she was my servant only for three months, and for ten years I have fed her with bread from my own mouth. I have brought her into wholesome fresh air and a situation where she wants for nothing. For her sake I have given up my own native land. She is entirely her own mistress and can go and come just as she wishes. I take as much care of her as if she were my mother. But all this goes for nothing, and I am no better than a criminal if I do not also sacrifice my happiness to her and go and die of despair in Paris for her amusement. Alas, the poor Woman desires no such thing, she does not complain, she is very contented. But I see what is at the bottom of it: Grimm will never be satisfied until he has stolen from me all the friends I found for him. Philosophers of the great city, if those are your virtues, I am happy to be a sinner. I was happy in my retreat, solitude does not worry me; I am not afraid of poverty; the world can forget me if it wishes; I bear my ills with patience. But to love and to find only ungrateful hearts, that I cannot bear! Forgive me, my dear Friend; my heart is overborne with sorrows and my eyes full of unshed tears. If I could see you for a moment and weep, I would feel better! But I will never set foot in Paris again; that is decided once and for all.

I forgot to say that there are even jokes in the Philosopher's letter. He is becoming a barbarian, cheerfully: he is growing *civilised*, it would appear . . . [4]

Diderot bounced back to Rousseau's letter with vigour. " 'I will not go to Paris. I will never go again. This time, I have made up my mind.' This simply cannot be the voice of reason," he wrote to him (14 March 1757). They absolutely needed to discuss Rousseau's novel, and also another affair (a commission Rousseau had received from d'Holbach).

It is necessary. You will not come to Paris. Well then, on Saturday morning, whatever the weather, I will set out for the Hermitage. I will go on foot. My problems have not allowed me to go sooner; my fortune does not allow me to go in any other fashion; and I need to take revenge for all the trouble you have caused me over the last four years.

However much pain my letter gave you, I do not repent writing it. You are too pleased with your own reply.

You will not reproach heaven for having given you friends; may heaven pardon you for not making better use of them.

I am still worried on Mme Levasseur's behalf, and I shall go on being so until I see you. (Let me whisper that making her read your letter to me could have been a very inhuman sophism.) But at present she owes her life to you, so I will hold my tongue.

I hear that the Scholar [i.e. Mme d'Epinay's ten-year-old son] has written to you saying there are twenty paupers on the "*rampart*" [a place of public resort] dying of cold and hunger for want of your halfpenny. It's a sample of our gossip, and if you heard the rest, you would enjoy it too.

It is better to be dead than to be a scoundrel; but woe to him who is alive and has no duties to enslave him.[5]

Mme d'Epinay tried to play the peacemaker, but this second letter enraged Rousseau even more, and he composed a furious response, begging Diderot not to come on the Saturday, as "it had all the appearance that it might be their last interview."[6] He sent it, and Diderot's letters, to Mme d'Epinay in Paris, asking her to read and judge between the two of them. He had, he told her, explained to Mme Levasseur that his friends thought it best she should go back to Paris; and now she was complaining of a plot to get rid of her. "You see," he told Mme d'Epinay, "that I cannot avoid being a Monster now. I am one in Diderot's eyes if Mme Levasseur stays, and I am one in her eyes if she is not allowed to stay."[7]

On studying the letters, Mme d'Epinay decided that Rousseau was quite in the wrong and told him so. Diderot, she said, had made him an apology, and it was up to him to accept it. She refused to pass on his new letter to Diderot, promising to send her son to him merely to say that Rousseau asked him not to come on Saturday because of the bad weather. At this Rousseau gave in, though remarking maliciously that she must not expect to have put Diderot off. "He would be very annoyed if the weather turned out fine. Anger will give him leisure and strength where friendship fails to. He will wear himself out, trudging here to repeat his accusations, and will return to Paris ill, and the world will call me a villain."[8]

The message that Mme d'Epinay actually sent to Diderot was somewhat different. It was that Rousseau would be coming to Paris himself on the Saturday, so that Diderot need not stir. Accordingly Diderot waited in, and when Rousseau did not arrive, it was his turn to get angry.

[21 or 22 March 1757]

Madame d'Epinai told me on Friday, by the way of her son, that you would be coming on Saturday, so there was no point in my coming to the Hermitage. It would have been such a good thing for you to come, and I was so sure you would, that I waited for you all day. It is not hard to guess why an honourable and truthful woman should have decided on this little lie. I understand. You would have abused me, you would have shut your door to me, and the idea was to spare you behaviour that would have distressed me and would have made you blush. My friend, believe me, do not live cooped up with injustice, it is a bad house-mate. Once and for all, ask yourself, "Who was it who took care of me when I was ill? Who supported me when I was attacked? Who has taken such interest in my glory? Who has taken such pleasure in my success?" Answer yourself sincerely, and recognise who it is that loves you. If you have written something unworthy about me to Madame d'Epinai, so much the worse for you . . . Oh, Rousseau, you are growing wicked, unjust, cruel, ferocious, and it makes me weep.

If a visit would not upset you, write and tell me so, and I will come and see you and embrace you and talk about your work with you. It is not possible to write to you about it, it would take too long. You know I only have Wednesdays and Saturdays free, the rest are given over to chemistry.[9]

Rousseau's reply (23 or 24 March) was a long rehearsal of their quarrel, showing that at every step he had been the injured party and Diderot the aggressor. As for bringing Mme d'Epinay into it, he would have suffocated without someone to talk to. Anyway Diderot seemed so proud of his behaviour, he ought to be pleased to have an audience. "Indeed she is a great support to you, and if I did not know her motive I would think her as unjust as you."

But the issue between them, insisted Rousseau, was about the heart, and the heart alone.

> You speak of the services you have done me; and I have not forgotten them. But you are mistaken all the same. Many people have done me services, but for all that they were not friends . . . All your eagerness, all your zeal to obtain me things I wouldn't know what to do with, counts for very little with me. All I ask is friendship, and that is the one thing I am denied. . . . Hard, unfeeling man: two tears shed in my bosom would have been worth more than the world's throne; but you refuse me them and are contented to wring them from me. Well, you can keep all the rest: I want nothing else from you.[10]

All through this last letter Rousseau is going through the motions of estrangement, but at bottom, evidently, it is a plea for reconciliation. Indeed his friend Delyre, amused but considering the quarrel bad publicity for the *philosophes*, told Rousseau (31 March) that he and Diderot were playing at "the sublime of friendship". It was the behaviour of lovers: "searing reproaches, bitter asperities, remorse, reversals of feeling, in a word whatever will cement and redouble their union."

It was indeed not long before the two were reconciled and Diderot had visited the Hermitage, being received with open arms. Soon afterwards Fréron published his attack on Diderot, accusing him of plagiarism. It was a moment, so Rousseau put it to himself, to make a public demonstration of loyalty, and he broke his vow and went to stay a night or two with Diderot in Paris. They read *La Nouvelle Héloïse*; Diderot's comment was that it was too "leafy". But it seemed that, for the moment, all was well between the friends. It annoyed Diderot, though – or at least it did so when he thought about it later – that when he wanted to discuss his own new play, Rousseau had yawned, saying it was getting very late and high time to go to bed.

Meanwhile, there had been an unexpected development in Rousseau's life. Mme d'Epinay had a sister-in-law, a few years younger than herself, named Sophie, Comtesse d'Houdetot. She was often at La Chevrette, where from time to time Rousseau had encountered her. Her husband, a *capitaine de gendarmerie*, was on active service in the army. The marriage was, in fact, unhappy, and the great love of her life was the Marquis de Saint-Lambert, an army officer and prominent member of the d'Holbach circle. He had a property near La Chevrette, at a little place called Eaubonne, and during her husband's absence she had rented a house nearby. Saint-Lambert was a friend of Rousseau's, and when he, too, went away on military service, he had encouraged Sophie to see Rousseau and had invited Rousseau, in somewhat vague terms, to look after her.

The Comtesse was a lively, dashing, emancipated young woman, with a minor talent for versifying. It was rumoured that she was the author of a mildly scandalous "Hymn to Breasts", and she did not positively deny it. She was impressed and intrigued by Rousseau, and one day in early May 1757 she came to the Hermitage, in riding costume, to pay him a call. As a result, Rousseau – for the first time in his life, or so he claimed – fell passionately in love.

It was a fraught and in some ways unequal affair. Rousseau bombarded Sophie with letters and notes of assignation, sometimes leaving messages for her in the crook of a tree or, if necessary, even – a bizarre stroke – sending them by way of Thérèse. In the early stages he was inclined to play the moralist and to inveigh against irregular unions, such as hers with Saint-Lambert. Soon, though, they were wandering hand-in-hand in the forest or embracing and rhapsodising ardently about love – Sophie about hers for Saint-Lambert, and Rousseau about his for Sophie. To Thérèse's annoyance, Sophie was continually calling at the Hermitage to take Rousseau off, and he would sometimes even spend the night in her house. Sentimentally speaking Sophie was carried away almost as much as Rousseau, but from a physical point of view the passion was all on his side. He was in the habit of masturbation and would sometimes arrive at their rendezvous limp from solitary orgasms. Altogether it was a time of the most intense disturbance for him, and was eventually to leave him a physical legacy in the form of a hernia.

In the midst of all this, to the alarm of Rousseau and the Comtesse, Saint-Lambert returned unexpectedly to Paris. The affair had by this time been much gossiped about in their circle.

Thus Rousseau, fearing exposure, resorted to a ruse. He concocted a formal and innocent-sounding letter to Sophie (addressing her as "Madame") which she might show to her lover. The scare died down for a moment, but late in August, on a visit by Rousseau to Eaubonne, Sophie told him that Saint-Lambert "knew everything". It was in fact another false scare, and it seems that Saint-Lambert still did not suspect the truth; but by now Sophie was seriously frightened, and she told Rousseau she must put a stop to their affair.

The blow shook him profoundly. At first he blamed Thérèse and he threw a violent scene, accusing her and her mother of betraying him. Thérèse, however – whether truthfully or otherwise – stoutly denied it, insisting that his betrayer was Mme d'Epinay. Mme d'Epinay, she said, had been spying on him for some time and was continually cajoling or bullying her into showing her his private mail. At this Rousseau's feelings swung violently round. He began to picture Mme d'Epinay as a jealous and vengeful woman, frustrated by the spectacle of his idyll with Sophie; and when, on 31 August 1757, he received one of Mme d'Epinay's little notes, asking why she had not seen him of late, he sent her a reply which astonished and terrified her. "I cannot say anything to you yet," he wrote. "I shall wait till I am better informed, as I shall be sooner or later. Meanwhile be sure that outraged innocence will find a defender ardent enough to give some remorse to the Calumniators, whoever they may be." Several further exchanges between them followed during the day (it is known among Rousseau biographers as the "day of the five notes"), and Rousseau brought his accusations out into the open, whereupon Mme d'Epinay vehemently, and perhaps sincerely, protested her innocence. He professed to believe her, and, according to his account, they even spent an affectionate evening together at La Chevrette. But it was plain, at least from his point of view, and before long from hers also, that their friendship was in ruins.

In this quandary (but here we only have Diderot's word for it, and there are problems about his account) Rousseau asked for advice from Diderot, who counselled him to distance himself from Sophie and to write to Saint-Lambert frankly confessing the truth. Rousseau promised to do this, and at a subsequent meeting he thanked Diderot for his excellent advice, which could only have come from a friend with a feeling heart, and which had put him at peace with himself.

What, however, Rousseau actually did (and here we are on firm ground again) was very different. He decided that attack was the best defence and wrote Saint-Lambert (15 September 1757) a long letter of astonishing, if maybe not altogether conscious, hypocrisy. It complained that, since Saint-Lambert's return to the army, Sophie had grown inexplicably cold and reserved towards Rousseau. Why was this, he asked? Was it at Saint-Lambert's own direction? Did Saint-Lambert suspect that Rousseau, out of misplaced moral scruple, wanted to separate the lovers? If so, he need not fear. It was true, he could not approve of their irregular relationship, but he would consider it a crime against friendship to try to interfere. "No, no, the bosom of Jean Jacques Rousseau does not enclose the heart of a traitor." Saint-Lambert replied with the greatest friendliness, admitting that Rousseau had guessed right and apologising for such ignoble fears.[11]

Rousseau, nevertheless, was by now feeling desperately at odds with the world; and it added to his discomfort that, at this moment, Grimm, who had been at the battlefront in Germany as an *aide-de-camp*, reappeared at La Chevrette. Rousseau got the feeling that, with his imperious manner and blank stares, Grimm was deliberately trying to make the great house unbearable to him – also that, with sermons about the duties of friendship and boasts that he himself had never lost a friend, he was setting up as Rousseau's judge. Nor could he doubt that Grimm, when in Paris, would be discussing him with Diderot: thus he might be poisoning Diderot's mind.

A few weeks after the "day of the five notes" Mme d'Epinay summoned Rousseau to La Chevrette to tell him that she was seriously ill. The doctors had diagnosed her as consumptive, and she would have to go to Geneva, to be treated by the celebrated Dr Tronchin. She added lightly, "Maybe you will come too, dear Bear?", to which Rousseau replied, equally casually, that invalids like himself made poor nurses.

The news about Mme d'Epinay soon reached Diderot. Up to now he had disapproved of all he had heard of her, so much so that he had refused to meet her and had warned Grimm earnestly against her. Nevertheless, he had to acknowledge, she had treated Rousseau with extraordinary generosity; and Rousseau's own recent behaviour towards her must, he felt sure, look to the world like gross ingratitude. He imagined that Rousseau must be desperate to clear his name; and this latest turn of events, so he felt impelled to tell him, provided a heaven-sent opportunity – he must offer to accompany his ailing friend to Geneva. His letter to Rousseau (it is undated, but belongs to the last days of October 1757) turns on the ethical issue that most profoundly divided them: have others the right to judge us? Diderot held that, in some sense, they had.

I am fated to love you and to give you pain. I hear that Madame d'Epinai is going to Geneva but I do not hear that you are going with her. My friend, if you feel well-disposed towards Mme d'Epinai, it is up to you to go with her; and if you feel ill-disposed, it is even more urgent to go. If you feel weighed down by too many obligations to her, here is the chance to repay some of them and relieve your conscience. Will you ever find another such opportunity to show your gratitude? She is going to a country where she will feel as if dropped from the clouds. She is ill, she will need amusements and distractions. True, it is winter! Well, consider, my friend. Perhaps your own health is a stronger objection than I imagine. But are you worse at present than you were a month ago or will be next spring? Would the journey be any easier three months from now than it is today? As for me, I confess that if the carriage-journey would be too much for me, I would take a stick and follow her on foot. And then, are you not afraid that people will misinterpret your conduct? You will be suspected of ingratitude or some other secret motive. Of course I know that, whatever you choose to do, you will have the approval of your own conscience; but is that enough? Can you afford to neglect, up to a certain point at least, the approval of others? At all events, my friend, I am writing this letter as what I owe to myself and to you. If you do not like it, throw it in the fire and let it be between us as if it had never been written. I salute you, love you and embrace you.[12]

Rousseau read the letter with rage. It stung him in a dozen ways, far more than Diderot was in a position to know. At heart he realised that, officious and tactless as the letter might be, Diderot's intentions were friendly; but he found it impossible to admit it to himself, and his mind leaped to sinister interpretations. The hated Grimm must, he decided, be behind the letter – if not Mme d'Epinay herself. The phrase about a "secret motive" must refer to Sophie d'Houdetot. Moreover Mme d'Epinay's "illness", so Thérèse told him the servants were saying, was no illness but a pregnancy by Grimm. He dashed off a reply, telling Diderot he was a fool to give advice on subjects he knew nothing about, "and what is worse I can see that your advice does not come from you." He then rushed over to La Chevrette, where he found Mme d'Epinay with Grimm, and insisted on reading both letters to them. As he describes it in the *Confessions* it was a kind of challenge, and "at this unexpected audacity in a man ordinarily so timid, I saw them both stunned, dumbfounded and left mute. Above all, I saw that arrogant man Grimm lower his eyes; but in the same instant, in the depths of his heart, he vowed my destruction."[13]

In fact, caught in this appalling dilemma, Rousseau proceeded straight to his own destruction. He wrote to (of all people) Mme d'Epinay's lover Grimm (26 October 1757), asking him what he ought to do – should he go to Geneva? was it right for him to continue living at the Hermitage? – going on to complain of his "two years of slavery" to Mme d'Epinay, his folly in ever letting himself be "dragged" to the Hermitage, the slights that poverty exposed him to, and the obstinate refusal of people to recognise that he was "a being apart" not to be judged by their rules. Grimm sent him a brief and non-committal reply, and when Rousseau asked for further explanation, he wrote again in dire terms. He said that, having read Rousseau's "horrible apologia", he at last understood the principles of his "monstrous system" and he hoped never to see him again in his life. Rousseau, thunderstruck, was reduced to returning the letter to Grimm, saying that "it did not apply to him."

Meanwhile he wrote a much briefer but harsh note to Mme d'Epinay in Geneva, accusing her of being in a "league" against him and of employing Diderot to gain from him what she could not obtain in her own person. "I find in all this an air of Tyranny and intrigue which has put me in a bad humour." Her reply took several weeks to reach him but was almost as crushing as Grimm's. She could hardly believe, she said, that his letter really came from him and was intended for her, and she had no intention of responding. "I feel pity for you; and if these are your sober thoughts, your conduct makes me quite afraid for you."[14] A further frigid exchange of notes took place a few weeks later. Rousseau wrote asking Mme d'Epinay whether, seeing that "their friendship was now extinguished", he ought to stay on at the Hermitage until the spring, as his friends advised – to which she answered that she did not consult her friends as to her own duties and had nothing to say as regards his.

For much of this time Rousseau was writing almost daily to the Comtesse d'Houdetot, and her advice to him was to be reconciled with Diderot, at whatever cost to his dignity. It was in fact what he himself most wanted in the world, and he did not really think it would be too difficult. He might have written some unkind things to Diderot, he told her, "but that is how we are used to treating each other, and we love each other none the less." It worried him, though, that no word came from Diderot, and even more that Grimm might have shown Diderot his own disastrous letter. Perhaps the best plan would be, he suggested to her, for her to write to Diderot herself, and perhaps even let him see one of Rousseau's own anxious letters to her. If she did so, "I think he would have pity on so tormented a heart and would be disarmed more easily."[15]

She did in fact try to bring the two friends together and wrote to Diderot, whom she had never met, suggesting she should bring him to the Hermitage in her own carriage. He wriggled out of the offer, with some awkwardness, and Rousseau told her she had bungled things and should have carried him off by force. Growing desperate, Rousseau then sent Thérèse to see Diderot; and on 15 November or thereabouts Diderot wrote him a long-awaited letter. It was in the affectionately hectoring and take-it-or-leave-it style he tended to adopt with Rousseau. All through, he acted in a very human, concerned, and, perhaps, clumsy way, but

Rousseau was much too glad to receive the letter to quarrel with
its tone.

"It is certain that you have no friends left apart from me,"
wrote Diderot, "but it is certain that you do still have me."

I have said the same frankly to everyone who asked; and here is
my analogy – a mistress whose faults I know very well but from
whom I cannot wean my heart. Once and for all, my friend, let me
speak openly to you. You imagined a conspiracy between your
friends to send you to Geneva; the notion is quite false. Everyone
has discussed this journey according to his or her own particular
lights. You believed I had taken it on myself to speak on their
behalf; that is not the case. I felt I owed you some advice and
preferred to risk giving you advice you would not take than to fail
to give you advice you ought to take. Like a prudent man, I wrote
you a letter for your own eyes alone, which you passed on to
Grimm and to Madame d'Epinay; and the fruit of that
indiscretion was embarrassments, reticences amounting to minor
lies, ambiguities, cunning questions and devious answers. For after
all, I had to keep the silence that I promised you, and all your
wrongs towards me could not dispense me from my given word to
you. Another mistake; you write me a reply and you read it to
Madame d'Epinay, and you fail to notice that it contained things
that would offend her – about her showing discontentment and her
services not being appreciated and I don't know what else. And
how shall we describe your letter as regards myself? It was a bitter
piece of irony, a harsh and scornful telling-off, the reprimand of a
stern teacher to his pupil . . . For God's sake, my friend, let your
heart direct your head, and then you will always do the best
possible; but do not let your head talk sophistry to your heart.
Every time that happens, you will do the wrong thing and you will
neither please others nor yourself. What would happen to us if I
let the roughness with which you wrote to me make me decide not
to discuss your affairs with you again until you asked me? – But let
me say this, my friend. I have had quite enough of all these
vexations. I can see nothing but pettiness and meanness in them
and cannot conceive how they could ever arise, let alone continue,
among people with a little good sense, strength of mind and
dignity. Why are you leaving the Hermitage? If there is some
practical problem, I will say no more. But any other motive for
leaving would be bad, unless it be the danger you might run in the
coming season. Pay attention to what I am saying about this.

Your going to live in Montmorency will give a bad appearance. Well, if I am meddling in your affairs again without enough knowledge of the facts, what of it? Nothing. Am I not your friend? Have I not the right to tell you everything that enters my head? Have I not the right to make mistakes? Is it not my duty to tell you what I think it is proper and decent to do? Adieu, my friend. I have loved you for a long time. I still love you. If part of your trouble lies in not knowing my feelings towards you, you may stop worrying. They are what they have always been.[16]

Three weeks later, that is to say early in December 1757, Diderot went to see Rousseau at the Hermitage. Rousseau felt it as a deliverance and made the most of the occasion. ("I had a full heart; I poured it out to him.") He talked openly about what Diderot "knew only too well", his "fatal and mad" passion for Sophie d'Houdetot – though for her sake, as he told himself, he did not admit that he had actually declared love to her. He also took the chance to complain of Mme d'Epinay's "unworthy manoeuvres", and Thérèse backed this story up; but, to his fury, when it came to the turn of Thérèse's mother, she said she "knew nothing about it" and more or less gave them both the lie. It was an ugly moment; but despite it, Rousseau felt their reunion had been all that he had hoped.[17]

On Diderot, however, it had a very different effect. Rousseau's vengeful fury against Mme d'Epinay and Grimm alarmed him, and altogether he was appalled by Rousseau's state of mind. According to his story, at this (or some other) meeting, he accused Rousseau of having tried to sow dissension between Sophie and Saint-Lambert. Rousseau denied it and took out of his pocket a letter from Sophie which – to his confusion – proved precisely that. Diderot then reproached him for his falsity over the letter to Saint-Lambert, and he replied that he "knew human character" and "what was good with one person was bad with another."

Whatever passed at this December meeting, so differently interpreted by them, it seems to have made Diderot take fright and, in his heart, to give Rousseau up for lost: it was to be their last encounter.[18] In later pages we shall see how, in their estrangement, they would eventually harden their hearts against each other.

10

Cacouacs

From the earliest days of the *Encylopédie* Voltaire had perceived
the work's full significance and had felt the itch, or the duty, to
have some connection with it. It was, for one thing, a matter of
solidarity, his cry being always that the *philosophes* must act as a
brotherhood, a "close-knit battalion". When d'Alembert's
"Preliminary Discourse" appeared he praised it as "superior to
Descartes' *Discourse on Method* ", and in the second edition of his
Age of Louis XIV he paid a public compliment to the *encyclopédistes*
as "a society of *savants* full of talent and enlightenment" – though
admittedly rather a two-edged compliment, for he spoke of them
as compilers and custodians rather than as creators. The
previous century, he wrote, had "pushed the sciences and arts as
far as they could go", and it was the task of the present century to
"assemble these achievements in a single *corpus* and transmit it to
posterity".[1] By this time he was in correspondence with
d'Alembert, and he wrote him in September 1752: "You and M.
Diderot are creating a perfect work which shall be the glory of
France and the humiliation of all those who have persecuted you.
Paris is swarming with scribblers; but when it comes to eloquent
philosophers, I know only of you and him."[2]

The letter was a veiled hint that he might be willing to write for
the *Encyclopédie*, and d'Alembert was not slow to follow this up. In
the "Advertisement" to Volume IV the editors were thus able to
announce an important *coup*: that the great Voltaire had supplied
articles on ELOQUENCE, ÉLÉGANCE, ESPRIT (Wit), and LITTÉRATURE
and was giving hope of further contributions. "The *Encyclopédie*, by
the justice which it has done him and will always continue to do
him, should be worthy of the interest he is willing to take in it." For
the moment, as the titles make plain, it had been decided to

confine Voltaire to innocuous and belle-lettristic topics, and he lamented to his friend Mme du Deffand that he was doing them very badly.

Collaboration, indeed, caused him to moderate his enthusiasm, and during the mid-1750s he sometimes wrote commiseratingly to d'Alembert about the terrible problems and the shocking defects of the *Encyclopédie*. "What I hear about the articles on theology and metaphysics makes my heart bleed," he wrote. "It is very cruel to have to print the opposite of what you believe."[3] D'Alembert replied that, with theological censors and the dubious blessing of royal *privilège*, he defied anyone to do better; also in less conspicuous articles the damage was repaired. Voltaire also reported various complaints he had heard from others, in his new home in Geneva – for instance at the "rambling declamations and trivial moralisings", where what was wanted was "method, truths, definitions and examples". What stuck in his throat especially was a pawky article on FEMME (Woman), by Desmahis. "I can scarcely credit your allowing such an article in so serious a work," he told d'Alembert (13 December 1756). "It seems to have been written by Gil Blas's lackey."[4] D'Alembert did not really disagree and came round before long to speaking of the *Encyclopédie* as "a monument to what we wanted, and were not able, to achieve".

That Voltaire should have chosen Geneva as his home was, of course, a momentous fact, at least for the Genevans. It was also at first sight a puzzling one, seeing that he was, if anything, more hostile to Calvinism than he was to Catholicism; moreover, his consuming passion in life, private theatricals, was a pastime forbidden in the republic. However, he was hoping to reform the Genevans in these and other ways; and it was under his influence and with similar hopes in mind, or so it would seem, that the idea came to d'Alembert to write a substantial article on GENEVA for the *Encyclopédie*. This was somewhat against the policy of the *Encyclopédie*, in which articles on places were normally kept quite dry and brief; but he could see tempting polemical opportunities. To gather material, he proposed a visit to Voltaire at his Genevan home Les Délices and received a response in Voltaire's most flowery and laid-on-thick style.

You would need to be terribly philosophical to accept the
wretched hovels which remain to us in my miserable hermitage;
they are fit at the most for a savage like Jean-Jacques, and I think
that you have not yet reached his degree of Iroquois wisdom. If,
however, you could extend virtue thus far, you would do an
infinite honour to my Alpine caves by deigning to sleep in them.[5]

This three weeks' stay of d'Alembert's in Geneva, which took
place in August 1756, attracted a good deal of publicity, and the
wit-combats of the two philosophers became a sort of local
spectacle. Voltaire introduced him to one or two members of the
Council of Geneva and also to a large group of pastors, one of
whom, Jacob Vernes, drew up for d'Alembert's benefit an
exposition of the Genevan constitution. Voltaire himself, despite
his sulphurous reputation, believed he was welcome among his
neighbours; he managed to convince d'Alembert that
"enlightenment" was fast taking hold in the republic and that the
clergy, or anyway the more intellectual portion of them, were
turning their back on Calvin. By implication, if not in so many
words, he told d'Alembert what he should write in his article,
including a defence of the theatre; his influence, as things turned
out, was to get the *Encyclopédie* into serious trouble.

Meanwhile, as time went on, Voltaire felt tempted to play a
bolder part in the *Encyclopédie*. He asked for, and obtained, the
commission to write on the meatier topics of IDOLE and IMAGINA-
TION; and then a new scheme occurred to him. The part of the
Encyclopédie that lay nearest his heart, and that had, so he felt,
been handled most deplorably, was Theology, and to remedy this
in future volumes he formed the plan of procuring articles, of a
less mealy-mouthed kind, from a "heretic" Swiss pastor of his
aquaintance named Polier de Bottens. These could embody his
own opinions and could be published without signature, thus
obeying his motto, "Strike and conceal your hand." Polier was
only too willing to oblige, and d'Alembert fell in with the scheme,
privately promising himself to tone the articles down if they
overstepped the mark.

With every year criticism of the *Encyclopédie* had grown more
vociferous, and it constituted a further danger for the *encyclopédistes* that, since 1756, France had been at war. It was a war

which had involved a startling diplomatic realignment; for France's old ally Frederick the Great had made a pact with her enemy, Britain, and France herself had formed an alliance, a fateful one, with her traditional enemy Austria. It meant that the *encyclopédistes* were in a vulnerable position. For one thing, there were many texts in the *Encyclopédie* exalting the civic virtues above the military ones and the broad sympathies of the "citizen of the world" above narrower loyalties to nation and *corps*. Further, as their critics were not slow to point out, they had strong links with France's enemy Frederick, d'Alembert receiving a pension from him and Voltaire being his intimate friend.

Despite this, since the de Prades affair, there had been no actual crisis in the affairs of the *Encyclopédie*, and both d'Alembert and Diderot were feeling a certain confidence in the forthcoming Volume VII. They believed it would be the best yet and with the least of what Voltaire called "twaddle". This was a comfort to Diderot, for whom 1757 had been a galling year. However, in the last weeks of this year, when his troubles with Rousseau were at their height, events converged to create an alarming new crisis, no less than d'Alembert's deciding to quit..

The train of events began when, in October 1757, the seventh volume duly appeared, containing d'Alembert's article GENEVA. This oddly tactless article was bound to be very needling to any Genevan reader and especially to any pastor. It had praise for Genevan democracy and for one or two other aspects of Genevan enlightenment, but it lectured the republic sharply on its attitude towards the theatre, it endorsed Voltaire's opinion that Calvin had possessed "an atrocious soul", and it reported, with enthusiasm, that many Genevan pastors, perhaps most, were out-and-out Socinians, "rejecting revelation and everything known as mysteries and imagining that the first principle of true religion was to propose nothing which shocked reason." The Genevan pastors, led by Jacob Vernes, were amazed and highly incensed (it was, indeed, still quite a serious charge to brand someone, and especially a minister, as a Socinian), and they hastily formed a committee to draft a Declaration of Orthodoxy and to seek some redress. There was even talk of an official complaint to the French government; meanwhile the eminent Dr

Tronchin, in his role as secretary to the pastors' committee, wrote to d'Alembert politely asking for a retraction. The whole affair was widely reported in France and elsewhere, and things began to look awkward for Diderot and his friends. D'Alembert, however, was quite unyielding and tacitly implied by his tone that the protests were hypocritical nonsense. It was a difficult situation for Diderot, who had had nothing at all to do with the offending article and was furious at d'Alembert's indiscretion; however, when Tronchin, who was a friend of his, also wrote to complain, he told Tronchin he hoped his colleague d'Alembert would not be condemned for "a careless word". Indeed, since no apology seemed to be coming from d'Alembert, he offered to apologise to the pastors in his own name.

It may seem surprising that so cautious a man as d'Alembert should, for once, have acted so recklessly, but the truth was he was growing sick of his whole position on the *Encyclopédie*. One may guess at various reasons for this, but one obvious one is simply that he detested criticism. It cannot be said that, as a body, the *philosophes* were very philosophical in the face of criticism. They were inclined to put it down to unprincipled malice and would react very testily, each in his own way: Voltaire with gleeful vengefulness, Diderot with self-righteous indignation and d'Alembert with petulant haughtiness. Nor were they squeamish in the means they resorted to to suppress it. For d'Alembert, though, criticism was more even than an annoyance: it was an outrage to all civilised values, and he could see no reason why he should put up with it.

It was thus too much for his patience when, in the midst of the GENEVA affray, and on top of the normal castigation in the religious press, new and virulent attacks on the *Encyclopédie*, some serious and some satirical, began to rain in. Of the latter kind was the *Little Letters on Great Philosophers* by Charles Palissot.[6] Palissot was still smarting at d'Alembert's machinations against him at the time of *The Circle*, and his *Little Letters* were thus a thorough act of reprisal. They attacked the *encyclopédistes* for "servilely" following Bacon, made fun of their sensitivity to criticism, and accused them of becoming a "church"; also, in passing, they twitted d'Alembert for accepting a pension from France's enemy

Frederick the Great. Fréron loyally praised the letters, which were not actually all that brilliant, as the equal of Pascal's *Lettres provinciales (Provincial Letters)*.

Worse, because wittier, was a series of articles in the *Mercure de France* on a newly-discovered savage tribe known as "Cacouacs", who lived near the 48th degree of latitude north (the latitude of Paris) and were more ferocious by far than the Carib Indians. A "Useful Warning" against them was included in the October number, and in the December one there was an extended "New Memoir" on them, by an anonymous author (he was a government-supported journalist named Nicolas Moreau) who claimed to have been living with them, first as a prisoner and then as a brother and a potential leader. The Cacouacs, the author wrote, do not believe in absolute truth, and regard ethics as purely a matter of convention; nevertheless, surprisingly, the words "Truth" and "Virtue" are continually on their lips. They do not recognise parental authority or the claims of patriotism, and they are very warlike; but a neighbouring nation has found an infallible weapon against them, the *whistle*. ("The enemy trumpet animates them, the whistle makes them flee.") During his stay, he relates, a venerable old man came to him bringing a mysterious book, saying, "Young man, take and read!"; then, on a later occasion, he brought a set of sacred coffers, equally mysterious, with the first seven letters of the alphabet picked out on them in diamonds, and containing the most sublime jumble of objects. Under their influence he had had a series of mystic visions, leading to a supreme vision of his own excellence. Meanwhile he found that he, and his companions, had grown sixty feet high.

The teasing, evidently, was more at Diderot's expense than at d'Alembert's, though geometry was mocked, in passing, as "a queen carrying her head in the clouds". However, the sobriquet "Cacouacs" caught on; further "Cacouac" pamphlets appeared, and the name was soon on everyone's lips. What is more, or so d'Alembert was convinced, the original article had been directly inspired by the government. For him, it was the last straw, and he let it be known he was withdrawing from the *Encyclopédie*.

The news reached the ears of Voltaire, who was greatly

alarmed and wrote twice within a week, insisting that d'Alembert must neither retract over the GENEVA article (it would "dishonour him for ever") nor think of resigning; but d'Alembert, for the moment, was not to be moved. "I do not know whether the *Encyclopédie* will be continued," he wrote to Voltaire on 11 January 1758, "what is certain is that it will not be continued by me. I have just indicated to M. de Malesherbes and the booksellers that they can find a replacement." It was, he said, a matter of all the "insults and vexations" the work had brought on him and Diderot, the "hateful and even infamous satires" and the "intolerable inquisitions" of censors; but there were also good practical reasons for prudence. If attacks were authorised today, there would no doubt be more tomorrow. It could be a case of "piling up faggots at the seventh volume, so as to cast us on the fire at the eighth."

Fréron, seizing the opportunity, reported the "Cacouacs" attack in his *Année littéraire*, naming d'Alembert as the geometer it satirised, and at this d'Alembert wrote to Malesherbes demanding reprisals. This was too much for Malesherbes, who replied frostily and sent their mutual friend Morellet to d'Alembert to explain his own principles as regards free speech, which required freedom for such as Fréron as well as for such as d'Alembert. Morellet, however, found himself talking to deaf ears. "The philosopher merely raged and blasphemed, as was his bad habit."[7]

Throughout this time Voltaire was in a state of high excitement, sending letters in all directions. From one point of view he regarded the affair with glee, seeing a chance to "lead them [the Genevans] a fine dance" and make them "drink the cup to the dregs". From another and more responsible aspect, however, it disturbed him, and, as the month of January went on, his advice changed and changed again. D'Alembert and his colleague, he wrote, must on no account resign; then, they must at all costs resign, and do so together – it would be "cowardice" to do otherwise. Several times he wrote to Diderot, and when he received no reply he flew into a rage, complaining bitterly to friends of Diderot's "impertinence" and writing once again, this time to demand the return of his manuscripts.

Diderot, meanwhile, remained very calm, though he told his father and sister his health must be "like iron" to have stood up to such harassments. He felt, evidently, in no great hurry to respond to Voltaire, regarding him as a mischief-maker and as partly responsible for the present imbroglio. At last, though, on 19 February 1758, he wrote him a full, most robust and resolute reply.

I ask your pardon, *Monsieur* and *cher maître,* for not replying before. Whatever you may have thought, it was no more than negligence.

You say we have been treated odiously, and you are right. You believe I have been indignant on this account, and I am. Your advice is that we ought to quit the *Encyclopédie* altogether, or that we should go and continue in another country, or that we should obtain justice and liberty in this one.

That is all very splendid, but the project of completing it in a foreign country is a chimera. Our colleagues' employers are the booksellers, their manuscripts are not our property, and even if they were, there is nothing we could do with them in the absence of the plates. To give the work up would be to turn our backs on the enemy and do just what the rascals who persecute us most desire.

So what is to be done? Why, what befits men of courage: to despise our enemies, to combat them and take advantage, as we have already done, of the imbecility of our censors. Ought we, on account of two miserable pamphlets, to forget what we owe to ourselves and to the public? Have we the right to disappoint four thousand subscribers, and do we owe no obligation to our publishers? If d'Alembert resumes work and we finish the task, shall we not have had our revenge? Ah! my dear master, where is the philosopher? Where is he who compared himself to Boccalini's traveller? Silenced by the noise of a few cicadas!

I do not know what has been going on in his [d'Alembert's] head; but unless he is thinking of quitting not just the *Encyclopédie* but the country, he has taken a foolish step . . . The reign of mathematics is over. Taste has changed. It is now the hour of natural history and *belles-lettres.* At his age d'Alembert will not plunge into the study of natural history, and he will find it difficult to produce a work of literature worthy of so famous a name. A few *Encyclopédie* articles would have sustained him with dignity during and even after the publication. There is a point there that he has not considered and that no one will perhaps dare to mention to him, but which he will hear from me; for I was born to tell the truth to my friends, and sometimes even to strangers, which is more honourable than wise.

Another person would secretly have rejoiced in d'Alembert's desertion: he would have seen in it honour, money and peace of mind for himself. As for me, though, it causes me despair, and I shall neglect no chance of retaining him. This is the moment to show my attachment to him, and I shall not fail either him or myself. But, for God's sake, do not work against me. I know your power over him, and it will be no use my proving to him he is wrong, if you tell him he is in the right.

After all that, you will suppose I feel deeply attached to the *Encyclopédie*, and you will be quite wrong. My *cher maître*, I have passed my fortieth year, and I am weary of harassment. My cry, from morning to night, is peace! peace! Not a day passes but I am tempted to choose obscurity and go to die a tranquil death on my own home soil. A day comes when all our ashes will mingle. When the time comes, what will it matter to me to have been Voltaire or Diderot, or for it to be your three syllables that survive rather than my three? . . .

Farewell, my *cher maître*; keep well and continue to love me.

Do not be angry with me, and above all do not go on asking for your papers back; for I would return them, and I would never forget the injury. I do not even have the articles; they are in d'Alembert's hands, as you very well know.[8]

Voltaire was ruffled by Diderot's letter and he vented his spleen to his friend the Comte d'Argental. That he, who had concerned himself so ardently over the *Encyclopédie*, he who could expect a reply from Frederick the Great within a week, should be made to wait two months for a letter! That a great man like Diderot should trouble his head over a paltry set of booksellers (men who should be awaiting orders in his ante-chamber)! That he should be so blind to the obvious: the need for a strategic withdrawal, or a removal of the whole enterprise to Switzerland! "I love M. Diderot, I respect him and I am angry."

The fact was, as this last rueful sentence implies, Voltaire felt himself bested by Diderot, and he had the greatness to admit it to himself. It was a turning-point, and henceforth his attitude would be clear. Whatever Diderot's misjudgements, whatever his limitations as a writer (for he thought him much the inferior of d'Alembert), he was a great man, a *necessary* man, and was to be humoured in all his weaknesses, even the not answering of letters. "Everything is in the sphere of activity of his genius," he would write in November 1759. "He passes from the heights of metaphysics to the weaver's loom, and from thence to the theatre. What a shame for a genius like his to be laden with stupid fetters and that a troop of guinea-fowl should have contrived to chain an eagle!"[9] His customary names for him became "Plato-Diderot" or "Diderot-Socrates" ("I embrace in Plato, in Diagoras, our great brother Diderot"), and he would write a little play, *Socrate*, in his honour, depicting him as the wise and serene Socrates, persecuted and made to drink hemlock by "the high-priest of Ceres" and his venal followers, and as a man henpecked – a bold allusion to Nanette – by his loving but uncomprehending wife Xanthippe.

There was, indeed, on both sides, a statesmanlike decision to put the "cause" before all private feelings. Personally speaking, Diderot was no idolater of Voltaire. He thought him a meddler, a faithless intriguer, a petty and spiteful foe. Voltaire was, for him – with a touch of irony he habitually referred to him as "de Voltaire" – "that malicious and extraordinary child of *Les Délices*,"[10] that "illustrious brigand of the Lake." He was a man who had outlived his best talents: "The sixty-year-old Voltaire is the parrot of the Voltaire of thirty."[11] Maybe, indeed, he had never really been *supreme* in anything: "That man comes only second in all the genres."[12] For all that, he was, beyond question, the great man of the century, one whose name and works would live a hundred thousand years and would make his detractors look small. Moreover, Diderot would say, how could one not admire this "bizarre" man, "who becomes generous and gay at an age when the rest of us grow avaricious and glum?" When Voltaire misbehaved and "rolled on a dunghill", Diderot was to tell his friend Naigeon, he felt the urge to sponge and clean him and treat him tenderly, as an antiquary cleans a soiled bronze.[13]

D'Alembert may have expected that his defection would prompt a wholesale exodus of contributors. In fact only one or two followed his example; and at last, after some months of diplomacy by Diderot and others, he reluctantly withdrew his resignation, agreeing that he should at last complete his mathematical articles. Voltaire, with less reluctance, also resumed work on his articles; indeed he asked Diderot whether he would care for more contributions from him. Diderot took some time to reply, but when he did so, it was with all the enthusiasm that could be desired. "Do I want articles from you, *Monsieur* and *cher maître*? Could there be the faintest doubt of it? Would one not travel to Geneva and beg them at your very knees, if nothing less would serve?"[14]

It was still Rousseau's belief that Diderot and he were friends. Delyre had written to him that Diderot spoke of him with kindness and seemed worried lest he might be in want. Thus in the early days of 1758, hearing the alarming rumours, Rousseau had written to Diderot, telling him of his fears of another Vincennes, and begging him to resign along with d'Alembert. His anxious letter, however, received no answer. This, so he wrote to Sophie d'Houdetot (13 February), told him more than all the rest and he began to fear that their friendship was at an end. "I shall never cease to love him," he wrote to her, "but I shall never see him again."

By now he had left the Hermitage and had moved with Thérèse to a rented cottage in Montmorency, despatching the aged Mme Levasseur back to Paris. He was at work on a long "Letter" to d'Alembert, intended to combat d'Alembert's GENEVA article and its plea for a theatre in Geneva. It was written as if in sorrow rather than anger. What good, his "Letter" asked, could a theatre do for his beloved birthplace, compared with the infinite harm it might easily cause? For that matter, what good did the theatre ever achieve, for all the imposing claims that were made for it? It did nothing to change morals or manners, merely appealed to the spectators' already-formed prejudices. Reason had no influence in the theatre. People went there not as an act of social solidarity but, on the contrary, to isolate themselves. Tragic pity was a self-indulgent and sterile emotion, and the triumph of virtue on the stage (virtue for all the world but himself) was just what a wicked man would most want to see. Brilliant, paradoxical, perverse, Rousseau's *Letter on Stage-*

Performances was, among other things, a personal apologia, and a challenge to the d'Holbach circle. Molière, he argues, failed to understand his own play, *Le Misanthrope*. Its hero, the gloomy and intolerant Alceste, is *entirely in the right*, and the worldly "good sense" of Alceste's friends, a set of men much like the *philosophes*, is just an excuse for baseness.

In Rousseau's eyes, the cause of his break with Diderot was clear. It lay not so much with Diderot himself as with the circle he moved in. Thus he decided to make one last effort at *rapprochement*, writing to his friend (2 March) to appeal, this time, not to his heart but his reason. Diderot believed him a "wicked man", the letter ran (he was still, even now, brooding on *The Natural Son*), but would a wicked man flee the company of other humans, as he had done? "The wicked man may plan his crimes in solitude, but it is in society that he would have to execute them." Might it not be that Diderot relied too much on his own good nature? Could he not have been exploited by cunning sycophants, people who entrapped him, not by crude flattery, but by "the bait of feigned sincerity"? "What a fate for the best of men to be led astray by his own generous spirit and serve as an innocent instrument of the perfidy of wicked men!"[15] He composed the letter in tears, or so Thérèse later remembered it; but once again Diderot made no reply.

Then, in April, Saint-Lambert returned from Germany and happened to meet Diderot. The two talked about Rousseau, and Diderot, for whatever reason, spoke as though Saint-Lambert knew about Rousseau's passion for Sophie d'Houdetot. According to his later account he did so fully believing that Rousseau, on his advice, had already written to Saint-Lambert to make a full confession. This, however, does not quite square with the facts; for one of the things Diderot had learned at their last meeting, or so it would seem, was that Rousseau had written no such letter. Thus it may be that Diderot was somewhat to blame, and more so than he would later admit or like to remember; though his crime, one supposes, was at most a blunder. The results, however, were serious. Saint-Lambert, reflecting on the pious letter that Rousseau had sent him, was furious, declaring "one could only answer it with a stick." He confronted Sophie with the story, and she, in turn, wrote reproachfully to Rousseau (6 May) telling him that, through his and his friends' indiscretion, her lover knew the truth about their affair and, to her terror, had come close to breaking with her. She had managed to convince him of her innocence, and had even allayed his first anger against Rousseau, but, she said, she "owed it to her reputation" never to see Jean-Jacques again.

For Rousseau this could have only one explanation: Diderot had deliberately betrayed him. The truth seemed inescapable to him; and then something happened to confirm it. Saint-Lambert generously came to visit him, and they discussed recent events in amicable fashion; but from something Saint-Lambert let drop to Thérèse – a secret that Rousseau had told only to Diderot – he became even more convinced of his friend's perfidy. There was nothing left for it, he decided, but a final break; and, in the present state of their relations, it ought to be as public as possible. Accordingly, in the proofs of his *Letter on Stage-Performances*, he added a paragraph to the Preface. It apologised for the defects of his style and continued: "Living alone I had no one to show it to. I used to have a severe and judicious Aristarchus [i.e. critic]; I have him no longer, and I do not want him any longer; but I shall never cease to regret him, and he is even more a loss to my heart than to my writings."[16] A footnote added a quotation from *Ecclesiastes* condemning those who disclosed their friends' secrets.

Rousseau half hoped that such a solemn declaration, which did not actually name Diderot, would be counted an act of courage. Actually it earned him much odium. Saint-Lambert, to whom he sent a copy of the *Letter*, returned it saying the book had fallen out of his hands at this public insult to a man whom, in Saint-Lambert's presence, Rousseau had accused of, at the most, a little weakness. He asked Rousseau from now on to forget his existence, and in turn he would forget Rousseau as a person, remembering only his talents.

As for Diderot, Rousseau's public insult offended him beyond measure. As a rule, he was inclined to forget injuries and wrongs, and – perhaps for this reason – he occasionally recorded really grave ones in a private *aide-mémoire*, which he stowed away in the back drawer of his desk. He drew up such a document not long afterwards, listing in detail Rousseau's "Seven Rascalities".

1. He wrote a letter to Mme d'Epinay that was a prodigy of ingratitude.

2. He had once planned to retire to Geneva himself, but when Mme d'Epinay's health made it necessary for her to go there, he did not even offer to accompany her.

3. He was accusing her of being the worst of women at the same moment that he was on his knees to her, asking pardon for his wrongs.

4. He spoke of Grimm as the deepest of villains, and at the same moment he was asking him to be the judge of his conduct towards Mme d'Epinay.

5. He accused Mme d'Epinay, at a time when he was living on her charity, of plotting to separate Saint-Lambert and the Comtesse d'Houdetot and of trying to bribe Thérèse Levasseur to act as informer on himself.

6. He fell in love with Mme d'Houdetot and tried to make trouble between her and Saint-Lambert.

7. He deceived me disgracefully over his behaviour towards Saint-Lambert.

It went on:

I have lived with that man for fifteen years. Of all the tokens of friendship one person can give another, there is none that he has not received from me, and he has never given a single one back. It has occasionally made him ashamed. From time to time I have worn myself out over his writings, and he half admits as much, but only half. He does not say what he owes to my care, to my advice, to our conversations, and his last work is partly an attack on me . . . He says critical things about sentimental comedy (*comédie larmoyante*), because that is my genre. He poses as a man of religion, because I am not one. He drags the theatre in the mud because I have said I am fond of it. He says he used to believe one could be an upright person without religion but that he has learned better – this because, being despised by all who know him, it would suit him that they should be considered scoundrels. From this it follows that this false man is as vain as Satan, ungrateful, cruel, hypocritical and wicked. All his apostasies, from Catholicism to Protestantism and from Protestantism back to

Catholicism, without real belief in anything, prove it only too clearly.

There is one thing in his behaviour towards me that has always offended me: this is the slighting manner in which he treated me in front of others, and the marks of admiration and docility he gave me when we were alone. He fed off me, he used my ideas, and he pretended to despise me.

Truly that man is a monster.[17]

The *Encyclopédie's* troubles were by no means over. In July 1758, a friend of Diderot's, the freethinking philosopher Helvétius, published a treatise *De l'Esprit* (*On Mind*), which provoked a violent scandal. He claimed in his book to be studying ethics as an "experimental science", much as if it were physics; and his neo-Lockeian theme was, broadly, that all ideas spring from physical sensations and indeed are no more than feeling and sensation under a more or less complex disguise, and by corollary that pleasure, and the desire of pleasure, is the sole principle of human thought and actions. Virtue is a matter of fortunate temperament; moral choices are effects and not causes; and "liberty" (the liberty of the will) is a meaningless word. These views, which have a loose family likeness to Diderot's, outraged Church, court and *Parlement* almost equally. Helvétius was a mild, ingenuous and philanthropic man, and the uproar came as quite a surprise to him. Fortunately for him he was rich and had influential friends at court, including the chief minister Choiseul and the Queen, and he hastened to make an abject submission. It took a rather odd form. The second edition of the book carried not only a humble retraction by himself, professing full adherence to Christian dogma, but also a "charge" by the Archbishop of Paris,[18] in which the Archbishop declared that his "pastoral bowels" had been wrung by this monstrous book and he wished for the tears of Jeremiah to appease such an outrage to Divine Majesty. It was, he wrote, the fruit of an "arrogant and profane philosophy", of which Paris was the well-head and which was spreading throughout the country through a thousand channels – in works of ethics, in natural science, in political theory, in travel-books, *jeux d'esprit* and plays.

The scandal of *De l'Esprit* had thus rebounded on the

Encyclopédie, and the more so since it was widely rumoured that Diderot was the real author. The Archbishop was in perpetual feud with the Jansenists, but on one matter they were agreed: that there existed a deliberate, cunning and well-organised conspiracy against religion and authority and that Diderot could be regarded as its ringleader. This became the theme of a new and formidable *anti-philosophique* organ, *Legitimate Prejudices against the Encyclopédie*. The work, by the Jansenist Abraham de Chaumeix,[19] would run to several volumes and went in for much close detective work on the *Encyclopédie*'s concealed impieties and traps for the unwary.

During 1758, as the result of d'Alembert's hesitations and changes of front, work on the *Encyclopédie* was often at a standstill, and this meant that Diderot had leisure to finish his new play, *A Father and His Family*. Of course, it had to pass the censors; and his name, at the moment, made censors extremely nervous. Thus, to protect their own skin, they demanded the most pettifogging changes, nearly managing to drive Diderot wild. "I saw the man yesterday," a friend wrote to Malesherbes, "and he was in so violent a despair we were afraid he might throw himself out of the window."[20] One change, especially, the omission of a very innocuous stage prayer, he simply could not stomach. The prayer was liked by Saint-Lambert, he told Malesherbes, it was approved by his wife Nanette, "a good woman who lacks neither sense nor taste", and another friend considered it a stroke of genius.[21] In the end he left it unaltered, and nobody took the least notice.

A Father and His Family was published in 1758, together with the essay *On Dramatic Poetry*, in which, more systematically this time, Diderot expounded his programme for a new drama: a theatre of truth and Nature, related, in its use of pantomime and tableau, to the art of painting. Both the play and the essay represented an attack on the *Comédie Française* and its conventions. He sent a copy of the play to an actress acquaintance of his, Mme Riccoboni, and she explained to him where it would not work in the theatre. Actors could not perform sitting down, they would not be heard if they turned their faces away from the audience, and so on. To this his reply was that what needed changing was not the play but the French theatre. "Your rules have made you wooden, and the more they multiply, the more automaton-like you become." Every day the theatre, that prized possession of an absolutist state, grew – like the state itself – more null, more glacially formal, more moribund. Indeed Diderot could scarcely bear to go, and he yearned for the days, not so very distant, when theatres were "places of tumult".

The coolest heads grew very warm on entering, and men of good sense shared, in varying degrees, in the transports of the mad. The cry on one side was "Make way for a lady!", on another "Haut les bras, monsieur *l'abbé*!", or "Off with your hat!"; and everywhere "Quiet there! Quiet the cabal!" People were on their feet, they jostled, they were out of their mind. Now, I know of no disposition more favourable to a poet. The play would begin haltingly, with continual interruptions; but if there was a fine passage, then the uproar was incredible, encore after encore was demanded. All was enthusiasm for author, actor and actress. The excitement spread from the stalls to the amphitheatre, from the amphitheatre to the boxes. People arrived warm and went away intoxicated – some going in search of girls, others into society. It was like a departing storm; hours later one still heard the murmur of its thunder.[22]

In the fourth chapter of his *Discourse* Diderot advocated a *genre* he called "philosophic drama". A promising subject for it, he wrote, might be the death of Socrates: Socrates manacled and on his prison bed, sleeping the sleep of the just; the arrival of his sorrowing friends; his trial; the speech on immortality; his last sight of his wife and children, etc. What a challenge to genius, wrote Diderot! What would he not give for the skill to achieve it, to catch the philosopher's character: firm, simple, tranquil, serene, exalted, at every moment bringing a smile to the lips and tears to the eye. In a later chapter, on "Pantomime", he sketched the play in more detail, supplying stage-directions, and asked: why could not such a succession of tableaux have all the grandeur of a painting by Poussin? For Diderot, Socrates, the incarnation of persecuted virtue, was by now a cult. It involved not only memories of the prison of Vincennes, but more recent tribula-tions. ("For ten years, for *thirty*," he would write to Malesherbes,

"I have drunk bitterness from an overflowing cup.") At some stage he acquired an intaglio ring, bearing the head of Socrates, and sealed his letters with it. Voltaire knew how to please him when he nicknamed him "Diderot-Socrates", and Rousseau how to score off his old friend, writing in *Emile* that "one could wish no easier death than that of Socrates."[23]

It thus naturally warmed Diderot's heart when in November 1758 his Genevan friend, the pastor Jacob Vernes, wrote encouraging him actually to compose a *Death of Socrates*. He told Vernes that, for all his incapacity, he might just possibly attempt it: it would be his farewell to the drama. Were he to do so, he would preface the text with a discourse attempting something equally demanding: i.e. to prove to mankind that, all things considered, it could do no better for its own happiness than to practise virtue. The problem, he said, was one he had often wrestled with before, but never to his own satisfaction: "I tremble at the thought that, if Virtue did not emerge triumphant, I would, as it were, have produced an apologia for vice." If he were a bachelor and a man of means, he told Vernes, he would leave his fortune to the writer who, in the eyes of a town like Geneva, could be said to have put the proposition beyond doubt. What would he not give to feel innocent, to be sure of his own virtue, himself? How he pitied their mutual friend Rousseau, "alone amid crime and remorse and with deep waters at his side." How serene and free from ills, by contrast, was the man with a clear conscience.

> Ah! monsieur, stretch that man out on straw, in the depths of a gaol. Load him with chains. Pile torment upon torment on his limbs. You may draw some groans from him, but you will not prevent him being what he would most wish to be. Strip him of everything, cause him to die at the corner of the street, with his back against a kerb-stone, and you will not prevent him from dying happy.[24]

It was a dream that Diderot never ceased to nurse – that he could put it beyond doubt, by some syllogism, that virtue was the best policy – but he always gave himself the same warning, that he had better not try, for he might end up proving the opposite. A commitment to "virtue", a commitment he earnestly desired, was always beset for him by questioning and adversarial voices.

As his enemies were not slow to point out, there already existed a play by Goldoni with the same title as Diderot's, *The Father of a Family (Il Padre di famiglia)*. On this occasion the resemblance went no further than the title; nevertheless, to help clear the air, it was arranged that French translations of *Il Padre di famiglia* and *Il Vero Amico*, by two friends of Diderot's, should be published simultaneously with his new play. This led to a baffling and foolish little imbroglio. For at some point in the publishing process both translations were found to have been furnished (nobody quite knew by whom) with an ironic and obscurely insulting dedication: in the case of *Le Véritable Ami* to the "Comtesse de * * *" and in that of *Le Père de famille* to "the Princesse de * * *." Also, in continuation of the joke, the volumes were described as to be purchased from "Bleichnarr", a name that, being translated into French, comes out as *Pâle sot*, i.e. "pale fool". It was thus a dig at the satirist Palissot, and he was further insulted, though not by name, in a bawdy Latin epigraph. For anyone in the know, the whole contrivance was plainly aimed at the Comtesse de la Marck and the Princesse de Robecq, two well-connected ladies known to be intimate with Palissot and, like him, sworn enemies of the *philosophique* clan. The two ladies were furious and wrote to Malesherbes, demanding instant redress. Since the translations had passed through the hands of Diderot and Grimm, strong suspicion fell on Diderot, and in the end he called on the Comtesse and made some kind of written confession, which she then tore up. The truth was, as only came out much later, the real culprit was Grimm, and Diderot had generously covered up for him.

The whole confusing little episode of the dedications (there were further twists to it) greatly annoyed Malesherbes, more indeed than any other during his time in office. It was also ill-judged from another point of view, for the Comtesse de la Marck and the Princesse de Robecq were dangerous enemies and had much influence with the King's chief minister, the Duc de Choiseul. Up to now Choiseul, an intelligent and sceptical man of

the world and a friend of Voltaire, had looked kindly on the
Encyclopédie. This, the second year of the Seven Years' War was,
however, a very fraught moment for him politically, requiring the
most delicate manoeuvring between *Parlement* and the opposing
dévot party at Versailles. Thus it would seem (this anyway is
Michelet's interpretation) that he now decided to sacrifice the
Encyclopédie, as a sop to the *Parlementaire* faction. At all events,
early in the New Year – just when d'Alembert had rejoined his
colleague and Diderot was sanguinely declaring the *Encyclopédie*
to be "reborn" – circumstances suddenly closed in on them. On
23 January 1759 the Advocate-General Omer Joly de Fleury
delivered a furious diatribe in *Parlement* against both the
Encyclopédie and Helvétius's *De l'Esprit*. As a result the sale of the
Encyclopédie was suspended, and a commission, composed entirely
of Jansenists, was set up to examine its activities. Its report was
violently adverse; and on 8 March the news came that, by royal
decree, the *Encyclopédie* had been suppressed and its *privilège*
withdrawn.

Here, clearly, was a supreme crisis, and Diderot responded to
it with great vigour and courage. The answer was plain, in his
eyes: *privilège* or no *privilège*, and whatever the personal peril, they
must continue and finish the *Encyclopédie*. It was a matter of public
duty and of sheer self-respect. It might mean working in secret,
perhaps for years; and the completed work might have to be
published outside France. He told the publishers of his attitude,
and a day was fixed for Diderot, d'Alembert and one or two more
colleagues to meet the publishers for discussion over dinner.
Grimm had by now gone to Geneva to join Mme d'Epinay, and
Diderot sent him a vivid account of the grand confrontation.

We sat down at four in the evening. Everyone was in high spirits.
We drank, we laughed, we ate; and as the evening wore on we
embarked on the great affair. I explained my plan for completing
the manuscript. I can't tell you with what surprise and impatience
my dear colleague [d'Alembert] listened to me. He broke out with
that puerile impetuousness you know so well; he spoke of the
booksellers as if they were lackeys, of the whole idea of continuing
the work as madness, and, in the course of this, said disagreeable
things to me which I thought it best to swallow.

The more unreasonably and violently he raved, the more indulgence and calm I displayed. It is plain the *Encyclopédie* has no more determined enemy than that man . . .

And our friend the Baron, you will say; how did he behave during the discussion? He fidgeted in his seat. I was afraid every moment that d'Alembert's stupid talk would send him over the edge and he would burst out. However he kept himself in check, and I was impressed by his discretion. As for the Chevalier, he did not say a word but looked down at his plate as if stunned. D'Alembert, having stuttered, sworn and pirouetted, went away, and I have had no word of him since.

When we were free of that little madman we reviewed the great question. We examined it from all angles, came to various agreements and gave one another encouragement. We swore we would see the enterprise to its end. We agreed to speak as freely in the succeeding volumes as in the early ones, even if it meant publishing in Holland. And so we parted.[25]

One of the subjects discussed with the booksellers was Diderot's own pay, and a new contract was agreed, by which, for his work on the remaining seven volumes, he could expect to receive 25,000 *livres*. (See *Appendix*, pp. 474–5.) It was a handsome enough arrangement in his view, though not to Voltaire's who, when he learned the figure, thought it pitiable. There was also some discussion of security, and it was agreed that for safety's sake Diderot should be left out of direct dealings with contributors. Soon he was able to tell the absent Grimm that the Baron was once again ferreting in his library, innumerable copyists were once more "groaning" under Jaucourt's sway, and, for the time being, his own door would be bolted against all visitors from six in the morning till two in the afternoon.

Diderot and Statues

Diderot, who sometimes lost his head over his private concerns, faced the crises of the *Encyclopédie*, including the crucial one of 1759, with great courage and clear-headedness. We might even call his conduct heroic. Something has not been mentioned yet, however, which may a little help explain his optimism and resilience. He had, some three years before, begun a most rewarding and inspiring love-affair. His mistress was named Sophie Volland. She was then thirty-nine, thus three years or so younger than himself. Her father, a financier and Inspector-general of the Royal Farms, had died three or four years earlier, and she was living with her mother in the rue des Vieux-Augustins, a favourite quarter for the financial *élite*. (Her father had also bought the *seigneurie* of a country estate at Isle-sur-Marne.)

Her baptismal names were Louise-Henriette.[1] Thus "Sophie" ("Wisdom") was a courtesy-name and may perhaps have been bestowed by Diderot (it was a cult name at the time). She was an intellectual, or at least an intelligent reader of books, and Diderot found, and was attracted by, something mannish in her personality ("my Sophie is man and woman, as she chooses"), also a kind of downrightness and abruptness. She was, Diderot told her, "a trifle baroque". "The rest may rub against you as they will, they will never soften your natural asperity, and I am very glad of it. I prefer your angular and knotty surface to the dreary polish of the worldly."[2] About her appearance not much is known, save that she wore spectacles and, according to Diderot, had "a dry little paw" (*une menotte sèche*).[3] She remains rather shadowy to us, for no letter from her, or description of her by another hand, has survived. To Diderot she seemed, to a puzzling degree for a woman of her age, enslaved to her mother. (Diderot's biographer André Billy suggests she may have been under a cloud as the result of some earlier affair.) Thus they concealed their liaison from her mother, at least for a time. Diderot would go to visit her by the back stairs, or the porter of a friend of his, living near the Volland mansion, would tell him when the coast was clear for a meeting in the Palais Royal gardens. In May 1759 Sophie's mother took them by surprise in Sophie's room and there was some kind of showdown, after which Diderot wrote Mme Volland an enormous letter, of (he said) "inconceivable violence". To his perplexity, she did not even bother to open it for a day or two and then responded to it very mildly, encouraging him to "be the happiness of her daughter and herself". Poor Nanette soon discovered the affair and became intensely jealous; thus Sophie's letters had to be transmitted through a third party, and there could be no question of the two women meeting.

Diderot's affair with Sophie was to be an ardent and long-lasting one, and he felt that it made his emotional life complete. He had, he told her, "erected a statue" in Sophie's heart, which he hoped he would never cause to crumble. They – Diderot, Sophie and Grimm – were "three beautiful souls", Sophie's "the most beautiful woman's soul", Grimm's "the most beautiful man's soul", in the world.[4] It was, for Diderot, a monumental grouping of a kind to inspire mankind. He was indeed a most wilful man in his emotional life, relentlessly fixing ideal roles on those he loved, though ardently loyal to his idea of them once fixed. It was not a question of naivety, for he was an acute observer of humanity, more a matter of philosophical determination. Near the end of his life he suffered a change of heart towards Grimm, but there was to be none, so far as is known, between him and Sophie.

The great bond between Diderot and Sophie was letter-writing. It was a difficulty for them both how Sophie's letters should reach him, for he could not very well receive them at home. Fortunately, in the following year he became friendly with a certain Etienne-Noël Damilaville,[5] a friend and disciple of Voltaire, who worked in the bureau of the new poll-tax, the *Vingtième*. His post gave him the right to frank letters, and it was a privilege he was very ready to use on his friends' behalf. He agreed to do so for Diderot, and in addition to provide him with an accommodation address. It was the perfect solution to the lovers' problem.

Damilaville, an ex-army officer, was a curmudgeonly and rough-mannered character, but of a type Diderot tended to be drawn to. He would regularly make his way at evening to Damilaville's office in the quai des Miramionnes, and, if he found no letter from Sophie, he might, in consolation, spend the rest of the evening with the misanthropic Damilaville and his mistress, in their lodgings in the Ile de la Cité.

Diderot's letters to Sophie, some of them hugely long, have an extraordinarily living quality. It was agreed between them that she was a "man", to whom anything and everything could be said, and that he should open his mind to her with philosophical completeness. It was his plan, he said, "to tell you, without order, without reflection, without sequence, everything which takes place in the space that I fill and outside that space; in the spot where I am and the one where others are moving." He numbered his letters to her, and the earliest to have survived is no. 135, which I shall quote in full. He was in a mood of mild melancholy when writing it, exhausted by the strains of the *Encyclopédie*, missing Grimm and apprehensive about Sophie herself, who was unwell (she suffered from some kind of chronic abscess on her bosom) and was soon to be taken off by her mother to Isle-sur-Marne – for how long neither of them could tell. His friend d'Holbach thought him quite ill and in need of distraction and he had been taking him on pleasure-jaunts. Most recently they and their friend the Baron de Gleichen[6] had been to visit the palace at Marly.[7] This letter (to my mind an enchanting one) will have to stand as a representative of many:

10 May 1759
This Friday morning.

We left for Marly at eight o'clock yesterday. We arrived at half past ten. We ordered a grand dinner, and we wandered in the gardens, where what struck me was the contrast between a delicate art in the berceaux and bosquets and the wildness of nature in a massive glade of great trees dominating them and forming the background. The pavilions, standing each on its own and half buried, in a forest seemed to be the homes of different subaltern genies whose master occupied the one in the middle. It gives the whole scene a fairy-like air which pleased me. There should not be too many statues in a garden, and this one seems to me a little over-populated.

We should regard statues as beings who love solitude and seek it – poets, philosophers and lovers – and these creatures are not common. Such beautiful statues, hidden in the remotest spots and distant from one another, statues which call to me, that I seek out or that I encounter, that arrest me and with which I have long conversations – no more, no others.

I passed these objects with wandering feet and a soul full of melancholy. The other strode on, and the Baron Gleychen and I followed slowly. I felt happy to be with that man. It was as if our hearts were sharing a secret feeling. It is amazing how sensitive souls can understand one another almost without speech. A stray word, a distraction, a vague and rambling reflection, a mild regret, a distant look – one's tone of voice, and way of walking, of looking and attending and staying silent, all reveal the one to the other. We did not say much, we felt a great deal; both of us were sorrowful but he more to be pitied than me.[8] From time to time I turned my eyes towards the town; his often fastened on the ground. He was searching for something that no longer existed. We came upon a piece of work which struck me with its simplicity and force and the sublimity of the whole idea. It was a centaur with a child on its back. The child grasped the beast's ferocious head in its little hands and was leading it by a hair. You needed to see the centaur's face, the turn of its head, its languid expression, its awe of the tyrannical child. It looked at the child as if it were afraid to move. Another piece gave me even more pleasure: an old faun, touched at the sight of the new-born infant lying in its arms. The statue of Agrippina does not come up to its reputation, or perhaps I was badly placed to judge it.

We split our walk in two. We explored the lower grounds before dinner. We dined with great appetite. Our Baron was unbelievably mad. There's something original in his whole tone and his ideas. Imagine a satyr, gay, piquant, indecent and lusty, amidst a soft, chaste, and delicate group of figures. This is how he was with us. He would not have embarrassed or offended my Sophie, for my Sophie is man or woman as she chooses. He would not have offended or embarrassed my friend Grimm, for he has a free imagination, and is only offended by a word if it is used out of place. Oh the regret we felt for that friend! Oh how sweet the interval when our souls opened and we began describing and praising our absent friends! How warm our words were, how warm were our feelings and our ideas. What enthusiasm! How happily we spoke of them! How happy would they have been to hear us! Oh my Grimm, who shall repeat how I spoke of you! It was a long dinner, but it did not seem long. Then we explored the upper grounds. I observed that of all the waters, the loveliest were the ones that flowed or fell ceaselessly and had not been made by human hand.

We spoke of art, of poetry, of philosophy and love; of the grandeur and the vanity of our undertakings, and the longing for, the gnawing worm of, immortality. Of men, and gods and kings; of space and time; of death and life. Through this concert one could hear, all the time, our Baron's discordant voice. The wind rose and dusk began to fall, chilling us and sending us back to our carriage.

The Baron de Gleychen has travelled a good deal. It was he who paid our fare home. He told us about the state Inquisitors of Venice, who always walk between the confessor and the executioner. Also about the barbarity of the Sicilian court, who gave to the monks an ancient triumphal chariot, with its bas-reliefs and horses, for them to melt down for bell-metal. This was apropos of a cascade at Marly which has been destroyed and whose marbles are now decorating chapels at Saint-Sulpice. I did not speak much. I listened and dreamed. We arrived at our friend's door between eight and nine. I rested there till ten.

I have slept with lassitude and pain. Yes, my friend with pain. I augur badly of the future. Your mother's soul is sealed with the seven seals of the Apocalypse. On her forehead is mystery written. At Marly I saw two sphinxes, and they reminded me of her. She has promised us, and herself as well, more than she knows how to perform. But I take consolation; I live in the faith that nothing can separate our two souls. We have said it, we have written it, we have sworn it so often; let it be true just for this once. If it is not, Sophie, the fault will not be mine.

M. de Saint-Lambert invited the Baron and me to Epinay, to spend some time with Mme d'Houdetot. I refused, and I did right, don't you think? Woe to the man who seeks distractions, for he will find them. He will be cured of his distress, and I want to keep mine till the end of time. I am afraid to come and see you. I must, though. Fate treats us as if pain were needed by us if our bond is to be lasting. Adieu, my friend. Send me a word, if you will, through Lanau. By the way, take care how you handle your sister. Do not talk to her about us except when you cannot stifle your feelings, or she asks you yourself. To our friends, even the tenderest of them, the whole affair cannot mean all that much. How to listen to lovers and to pity is a skill that has to be learned. She does not possess it yet, and may she never need to learn it. I kiss the ring that you wore.[9]

It is a letter much concerned with statues, and this leads us to a large subject, Diderot's attitude to statues, which in a way represents a key to his whole ethical outlook. Virtue, as he saw it, was not natural to man; one arrived at virtue only by a laborious sculptor-like effort, erecting a statue or effigy of oneself in the minds and hearts of others. But once erected, the statue would remain. It became a safeguard and warning to the sculptor himself, and only he could destroy it. By a similar process of thought, in his discourse *On Dramatic Poetry* Diderot asks how an ordinary fallible reader, with all his accidental quirks and prejudices, can become a just critic, and he answers: by the effort to construct, in imagination, the statue of a just critic.[10]

Virtue for Diderot was an effortful form of art, not entirely remote from hypocrisy – which was less of a sin than it was often considered. Of course someone might simply refuse all this effortful statue-building and cheerfully proclaim himself "madman, impertinent, ignoramus, idler, glutton and buffoon", and what then? This is the question which Diderot will explore in the person of the Nephew, whose words these are, in his novel *Rameau's Nephew*.

Statues, in the nature of things, symbolise reputation. Their function is to be exemplary, with the rigidity and impassivity of the ideal. It might be proper to kneel to them, and many are the reverent tirades addressed by Diderot to statues – "O sages of Greece and Rome, when I meet your statues in some solitary forest byway and they halt my step . . . when I feel the divine enthusiasm escaping from your cold marble and passing into me . . ." etc.[11] He feels, on the other hand, an impulse to grant statues human rights, for instance the right to solitude. He instinctively longed, moreover, to have personal relations with them – to overcome their aloofness and drag them into the living world. In his *Letter on the Blind* he imagines how much statues might mean to the blind, more perhaps even than to the sighted; how there could be touch-statues, and that they might even be a substitute for lovers. One thinks, too, of the role of the statue in *D'Alembert's Dream*: how, pounded in a mortar and mixed with humus, it is imagined as converted into living flesh, thereby supporting the doctrine of materialism. He hazarded once that the great stone figures on the roofs of palaces might be meant to represent those palaces' true guests[12]; and when, in the *Salon* for 1763, he reviewed Falconet's great marble group "Pygmalion and Galathea", he was enraptured by the joyousness of the subject, a statue coming to life. He wished Pygmalion could have been shown differently, not just gazing at Galathea but touching her.[13]

I shall add one more instance of the significance of statues for him which may be entitled "The King of Denmark's hat". At d'Holbach's, in July 1762, Diderot would be introduced to a Frenchman just returned from Copenhagen, where he had seen the King of Denmark at the unveiling of a statue to himself. At the King's arrival, so the traveller told them, "five or six hundred thousand voices were raised, crying as one person 'Long live our king! Long live our master, our friend, our father!' " At this the King, in a transport of joy, opened the carriage door, leaped into the crowd and hurled his hat into the air, crying "Long live my people! Long live my friends. Long live my children!" and kissing all who were standing by. "How rare and beautiful a spectacle," wrote Diderot to Sophie. It brought tears to his eyes to write. *There* was the happiness he envied the masters of this world, "to cause the ecstasy of an immense people, to see it and to share it"; it was enough to make one die of pleasure. And the King's hat? Who had retrieved it? If it had been himself, he would not have exchanged it for a hat of gold. How he would love to show it to his children, and they to theirs, till the end of time. How often they would repeat and commemorate the moment when he first took possession of it![14]

There is a lot of Diderot here. The dionysiac scene and the series of substitutes – the King, the statue of the King, the King as statue to his subjects, the sacred relic and the commemorative ritual – epitomise both his theory of ethics and his theory of drama.

*

Diderot's dearest hopes still lay in playwriting, but he found it easier to plan plays than to write them. There was *The Kentish Judge* (or, *The Sheriff*); *Madame de Linan*; *The Unlucky Man: or, Consequences of a Grand Passion*; *The Death of Socrates*; and *The Way of the World: or, How We All Live Now*, which, he told Grimm, unless he was mistaken, would be the strongest "machine" ever to reach the stage. "Thirteen or fourteen characters and not a shred of probity in any of them, except for a kept woman – intended by nature to be a charming creature, but necessity, circumstances, the world and the devil . . ." The idea had come to him in a "mental debauch, a violent effervescence", but where would he find the time or the concentration actually to write it? He had tried dictating it to Sophie and her sister, with hopeless results. It might be better, he told Grimm, if he passed on the great conception to someone else.[15]

In June 1759 he was "encyclopaedising like a galley-slave" and working on *The Kentish Judge*, his head full of "priests, executioners, victims . . . spectres of all kinds",[16] when he received the news of his father's death. The old man had been ailing for a year, but the end had been sudden and quite peaceful; he had been chatting cheerfully with his children Denise and Didier-Pierre, had leaned back in his chair, and the whole thing was over. Diderot was shaken and, for a moment, talked of "the curse of heaven" that he had seen neither his mother nor his father die. His mood, however, soon changed to pleasurable melancholy. His father had left what seemed an admirable will, a testament just like the old cutler, full of delicate thought towards his children and dependants. All debts, even questionable ones, were to be paid; Denise was to give Blind Thomas two *sous*, six *deniers* a week, as during his own lifetime, to say a prayer at his and his father's tomb; and Denis and his brother were asked to give Denise, who had cared for him with such devotion in his illness, some little financial advantage, to be agreed between themselves. The intention was obvious. The father, who knew very well how his children quarrelled, had laid a little plot to bring them into harmony; and Denis, as elder brother, decided to show how a philosopher and loving son could do his father's bidding.

He set out for Langres on 25 July. Mme Volland had actually
lent him her carriage, and the plan was that on his way home
from Langres he should collect her at her country estate at Isle
and accompany her back to Paris. On the morning of his
departure Nanette threw the most dreadful quarrel, and he
arrived at Langres feeling more dead than alive: the old
maidservant Hélène said he looked as if come to join his father in
the tomb. Two days later he wrote to Nanette, reasoning with her
as best he could. There was, he insisted, no one in the world
dearer to him than herself and their daughter. "I am not perfect,
and you are not perfect either. We are thrown together, not to
reproach each other's faults with bitterness but to support each
other. You hold the happiness of all three of us in your hands. You
sent me on my journey with a heart bursting with sorrow . . . and
if you managed to send me to my tomb, how would it profit
you?"[17]

His father had left a substantial inheritance: various valuable
contracts, vineyards, a quantity of grain, farm-rents and three
houses. After division among the three children it would, Diderot
calculated, bring him in about as much again as he was already
earning. It would not spell riches, but it would give him and
Nanette modest financial security. The details of the division had
been left to them, and Diderot's brother had been busy and
punctilious in preparing the figures and documents.

Before Denis's arrival, Didier-Pierre and Denise had decided
that they had better live apart, and Denis had to admit to himself
that they were, perhaps, just not born to get on – the one so
honourable but inflexible, so suspicious and silent over intimate
matters, the other so boisterous and irascible, not caring what she
said. Didier-Pierre, as a busy cleric, liked to fill the house with his
clerical acquaintances, which meant endless labour for Denise.
Anyway, she complained, her brother's friends were such an
appalling crew.

But the truth was, she and the *abbé* set a lot of store on Denis's
visit and were half hoping he might somehow manage to reconcile
them. It was a task he was very glad to attempt. Part of the
trouble, he found, was that his brother was jealous of Denise: he
was convinced that Denis was fonder of her than of himself, which

of course was quite true. Diderot did his best to soothe him, telling him, as he reported to Sophie, the kind of white lies that deceive those who want to be deceived. Anyway, he added, were he to love Denise a thousand times more than he did, he would love justice and equity more.

Over the actual inheritance they all behaved very well and came to an arrangement which involved, to some extent, a common purse. The two younger children were to collect all annual incomings and it should be left to them to fix the figure of Denis's share. Denis also hit on a solution to their domestic problem: a friend of Denise's who had fallen on hard times, should come and live with them and take charge of the housekeeping, and Denise should pay Didier-Pierre a rent on her and her friend's behalf. The proposal went down very well; and, emboldened, Denis offered himself as mediator in any future quarrel, and Didier-Pierre, as graciously as he could, accepted. All, for the moment, was harmony, and the three signed their legal agreement with tears and protestations of good will.

Then there was a relapse. The *abbé* came home one day to find Denis's bags packed, and he burst into the bitterest recriminations. They had not told him Denis was going; they never told him anything; they did not love him, everything went to prove it. He grew speechless with misery and rage, and Denis, embracing him and offering comforting words, trembled for Denise's future. The servants brought dinner, but the three could not bring themselves to eat and remained stricken silent in their armchairs – Denis holding his face in his hands, Denise pretending to yawn, and Didier-Pierre squirming restlessly. It took the most passionate appeals from Denis to restore them to reasonableness. They at last sat down to their meal, now grown quite cold, and over it Denis gave them a fine sermon. "I don't know what I said," he wrote to Sophie (16 August), "but the end of it was, they stretched their hands across the table, clasped each other's and squeezed them, with tears in their eyes. They frankly admitted their faults, asked a thousand pardons of me and smothered me in embraces."[18]

Diderot left Langres in a very different mood from when he arrived, indeed in the highest spirits. He had at this moment much to buoy him up. There was the comfort of self-approval, as an elder son who had shown himself worthy of his father. There was the hope of seeing Sophie again and the intriguing prospect of a *tête-à-tête* with her mother. No less important, he would soon be reunited with Grimm, his soul-mate, his inspirer and his best audience. He began a vast journal-letter to Sophie – a little in the style, before its day, of Sterne's *Sentimental Journey* – and added a further instalment at each staging-post. Here he was in Guémont (he wrote) twelve leagues from Langres, writing with the local *curé*'s pen and ink, the only ones in the parish. It was with the very same pen, used by him to tell Sophie he loved her to madness, that the *curé* used to scrawl his sermons, "damning his poor idiots for listening to their hearts, which preach better than he does." . . . But here was his fricassee of chicken, growing cold while he wrote. His humble hosts were impatient. . . . Excellent fricassee, excellent water! . . . Ah! if Sophie could only see him eat. His poor hosts were too ashamed to tell him there was no dessert. They took him for some great man, or at least for some rich prelate; and it was true, he had a chaise and horses, all he needed was a lackey . . . "By the way, country cats do not dare to eat off plates. They must be born to crime. They have an air of stealing their food, even when they are being given it. There are human beings like that. Where was I? Oh yes, the delicious water! Your health, Sophie! – Madame, may I? – Yes . . ."[18]

The first news to greet Diderot on his return to Paris was that a further royal edict ordered the publishers of the *Encyclopédie* to reimburse their subscribers with the unearned portion of their advance. As it turned out, though, with Malesherbes's help, the publishers had secured a compromise, allowing them to treat the unearned money as a credit against the plate volumes. Meanwhile Pope Clement XIII, on 3 September, issued a brief instructing any of the faithful who possessed a copy of the damnable work to take it to their bishop or to an Inquisitor to be burned. Diderot was beyond taking alarm and was soon working long hours at the *Encyclopédie* in his "shop". It was, he told Grimm, his sole occupation, the "author" being dead in him till Grimm should return to resurrect him.

During his two days with Sophie's mother, Diderot had

worked his charm to the utmost, and rather successfully, or so he believed. Inexplicably, though, now they were back in Paris, she would scarcely allow him to see Sophie. Or perhaps, he wondered anxiously, it was Sophie herself who was avoiding him. On the rare occasions he was allowed to see her and her sister she would sit sad and silent or go out of the room to weep. The family was due, in a week or two, to go off to Isle, and Sophie seemed convinced that she would die there and would never see Diderot again. Left alone, they would sit holding hands; but when he told her to lean on him, she would say mournfully, "My friend, you must not let yourself get used to that." Altogether, the Volland family seemed full of mysteries. He began to suspect some kind of incestuous and lesbian attachment between Sophie and her young married sister Mme Le Gendre. It made him jealous and at the same time intensely curious. When the sisters shared a bed, he asked Sophie, did their bosoms touch? "I should very much like to know that."[18]

The Baron d'Holbach had recently acquired a country house called Grandval, some twelve miles south-east of Paris, and he kept pressing Diderot to come and stay there. The house was legally speaking the property of d'Holbach's mother-in-law Madame d'Aine. She was in fact his mother-in-law twice over, for on the death of his first wife Geneviève, in 1754, he had married Geneviève's sister Charlotte-Suzanne. This Mme d'Aine, the widow of a royal official, was an eccentric and bawdy-tongued old lady whom Diderot greatly relished. He was loath to leave Paris while Sophie was still there, but he made a brief visit to Grandval, where he completed a *Salon* review. He then returned to Paris for one more vain effort to see Sophie, after which he set off for Grandval for a longer stay. Nanette, he wrote to Sophie, opened her eyes when she saw how many books and clothes he was taking. "She cannot imagine me bearing separation from you for longer than a week."[19] From now on, for some years to come, he would be spending long summer or autumn visits at Grandval, and in Nanette's eyes they represented, perhaps, the lesser of two evils.

At the d'Holbachs' insistence, Diderot treated Grandval as a second home and as a workplace. He would get up at six and spend the whole morning in his room, working undisturbed. The Baron might knock at his door to bid him good-morning but would go away again at once unless encouraged to stay and talk. At half-past one Diderot joined the rest of the household for conversation or a game of *tric-trac*; then came dinner, as sumptuous or even more so than in the rue Royale. Round about three or four o'clock they would take their sticks and go walking, the women in one party and the Baron and Diderot another. The two men were ardent landscape-lovers and would sometimes walk for several hours, discussing "history, politics, chemistry, literature, natural philosophy or ethics". In the evening there would be more cards, perhaps some music from the Baroness, supper, conversation, and by half-past eleven they were all asleep in bed ("or ought to be").

One of the fixtures at Grandval was a melancholy Scotsman named Hoop. He was only in his late thirties, perhaps, but was so wrinkled, so bent, so dried-up that they called him "Father" Hoop. He had been a medical student in Edinburgh and had travelled for a firm of exporters to Spain, China and other distant parts. There was some romantic story of how a brother of his had nearly brought their family to ruin and Hoop had rescued it at the expense of his own career and happiness. At all events his favourite theme was that life was an intolerable burden. "That's why I give you the room opening on to the moat," said Mme d'Aine one day; to which the Baron added, "But maybe you don't like the idea of drowning. If the water is too cold for you, Father Hoop, we two can always fight a duel." "With the greatest pleasure, my friend," replied Hoop, "but only on the understanding that you kill me." They went on to talk of a certain famous swindler, M. de St Germain, and his elixir of life which, so he claimed, had begun his rejuvenation at the age of a hundred and sixty. If he could take an hour off his life, they speculated, by a careful doubling and redoubling of the dose he ought to be able to take off a year, or ten years, or make his way back to his mother's womb. "If I ever reached there," said Father Hoop, "I assure you they would never get me out again."[20] Diderot interjected that death, according to sound materialist views, had nothing absolute about it. The only difference between death and life was that at present one lived in the mass and in twenty years time one would be living dispersed and in detail. Thus, he said, the lookout for Father Hoop was even worse than he feared. It was the sort of conversation that he liked to start, and the friends would go on from fantasy to fantasy.

Early in October 1759 Grimm and Mme d'Epinay returned from Geneva, and Grimm hurried on to Grandval. Between him and Diderot it was a most impassioned reunion. "We were at dessert when he was announced," wrote Diderot to Sophie:

> I ran to him. I leaped to his arms. He sat down; he made a bad
> meal of it, I suspect. As for me, I could not open my teeth, either
> to eat or to speak. He was beside me. I held his hand and looked
> at him ... I don't know how the Baron, who is a little jealous and
> perhaps had been somewhat ignored, regarded it ... They all
> treated us like a lover and mistress and left us alone in the *salon* –
> even the Baron did. How did that man find the delicacy to realise
> even he was *de trop*? Our meeting must have made an
> extraordinary impression on him.[21]

Diderot accompanied Grimm back to Paris for a day or two, and they went to dine with their friend Montamy[22] in his apartment in the Palais Royal. Diderot was in an exalted mood and held forth in a kind of rapture. "I was full of the tenderness you inspired me with when I appeared among the guests," he told Sophie. "It shone in my eyes, it gave warmth to my words, it dictated my movements, it showed itself in everything. I seemed to them extraordinary, inspired, divine: Grimm could not open his eyes or his ears wide enough."[23]

He had an appointment the same evening to meet d'Alembert in the Palais Royal gardens, and, half-reluctantly, he left Montamy's table to keep it. It was their first encounter since his visit to Langres, and it proved, in a way, decisive. They began diplomatically. D'Alembert inquired politely after Diderot's family and about his inheritance and gently fished for information about the *Encyclopédie*. Had Diderot been badly held up in his work by his father's death? Was he making much progress? ("Very much," said Diderot calmly.) It was time, said d'Alembert, that he himself got back to work. "Whenever it suits you," replied Diderot coolly. He was, however, (said d'Alembert) still bargaining with the publishers; and the truth was, he confessed, he was short of money. With France at war with Prussia, his pension from Berlin had been cut off; and even the Académie seemed not to be paying its dues. If the publishers really wanted him back, he said, it was up to them – surely Diderot must agree? – to pay him in a decent fashion?

At this Diderot began a sweeping denunciation of d'Alembert's whole conduct from their first troubles till now. The publishers, he said, had actually been quite generous to d'Alembert; and they would no doubt be as well-disposed now, had he not made such a nuisance of himself six months ago. D'Alembert had insisted on reprinting his *Encyclopédie* articles, for his own glory. It had been against the publishers' interests, but they had gone along with him; and then, when it came to a second edition he had given the book elsewhere. He had resigned ostentatiously, not caring that he might be throwing an army of printers out of work. He seemed to think that, as a philosopher, he had the right to treat mere business people with contempt. He should ask himself, though: were the publishers his friends, or were they merely business acquaintances? If they were friends, his conduct towards them was horrible; if just business associates, then they had kept their side of the bargain, and he could have no complaint against them. The onslaught continued, and in the end d'Alembert, a little sheepishly, agreed to a compromise. He would go on with his articles, but that would be all. There was to be no more editing on his part, no more prefaces. "Above all, no more prefaces!" agreed Diderot devoutly.[24] It was not unknown for Diderot's friends to receive such browbeatings, and the two parted, ostensibly anyway, as good friends. It was, all the same, the end of their partnership and of all closeness between them. When they met, in the future, it would be as amiable strangers, and a year or two might go by without their paths crossing.

Diderot returned to Grandval for another two or three weeks, and an account of another day's doings there will help to give the flavour of the place. Diderot, the Baron and Father Hoop had gone a twelve- or fifteen-mile walk along the banks of the Marne, returning exhausted. They joined the ladies in the *salon*, settling themselves in front of the fire. "Well, philosopher," asked Mme d'Aine, "how are you getting on with your work?" "I am on to the Arabs and the Saracens," replied Diderot. "That's Mahomet, isn't it – women's best friend?" "Yes, and the greatest of all enemies to Reason." "That's not a very polite remark." "Madame, it's not a remark, it's a fact . . ." . . . "The Arabs," said Diderot, giving Mme d'Aine the benefit of his current article, "only discovered writing just before the *hegira*." (MME D'AINE: "What sort of animal is that?") "Before that time they were a race of gross idolaters. Anyone gifted by nature with eloquence could do what he liked with them. Those whom they dignified by the name of *chated* became pastors, astrologers, musicians, poets, physicians, legislators and priests . . ."

MME D'AINE: No news from Paris. My box-edgings will never get planted this autumn. That Belize [d'Holbach's steward] is an imbecile.

DIDEROT: It was a certain Moramere who invented the Arabic alphabet . . .

MME D'AINE (to her chambermaid): Mademoiselle Anselme!

MLLE ANSELME: Madame?

MME D'AINE: You have the ugliest bum anyone ever saw!

MME D'HOLBACH: Really, Mama, you must be mad!

MME D'AINE: Yes, Mademoiselle, an absolutely frightful bum . . .

MLLE ANSELME: It makes no difference to me. I don't have to look at it.

MME D'AINE: . . . so black, so wrinkled, so scrawny, so dried-up, tiny and leathery.

DIDEROT: There was no sect the Mohammedans hated so much as the Christians. Nevertheless the men of learning summoned to the court by the last of the Abbasids were Christian. The people made no objection.

FATHER HOOP: That was because they were happy under that government. I would like to say to princes, "Have a large army at your command, and then you can have universal toleration . . . Overturn those asylums of ignorance, superstition and uselessness . . ."

MME D'AINE: By the way, is the little God-botherer from Sussy coming to supper? If he comes, do spare his blushes, my son. How can you expect him to say his mass, after laughing at your filthy talk?

D'HOLBACH: Well, let him not say it!

MME D'AINE: It's not as easy for him not to say it as for you not to hear it.

D'HOLBACH: Well, I suppose I might have to one day.

MME D'AINE: I hope you will. He's a good little man. I like his hearty laugh.

"So you see, my dear, how we pass the time," wrote Diderot to Sophie. "We had gorged ourselves, the women especially, and were all ready to talk nonsense, and to perform it, when the dear little priest himself appeared. . . . He is no hater of women. Mme de St Aubin was at a table, leaning on her elbows, and he plumped himself down in front of her. He's a friend of the whole household. Mme d'Aine, tempted by his posture and the size of his rump, took a chair and moved it close to him."

"*Abbé*, hold steady," she cried, and with a leap she had bestridden the *abbé*, one leg on one side and the other on the other. She dug in her heels and urged her mount on with voice and fingers, while he neighed and reared and kicked. The lady's petticoats rolled up, both in front and behind, till she was practically bare, and her steed was nearly bare in places too. We laughed, and so did the lady. She laughed louder and louder, holding her sides; till all at once she was stretching right over the *abbé*, crying, "Have pity on me, have pity, I can't hold out, it will all have to go! *Abbé*, hold still!" And the *abbé*, who had not realised what was happening, halted and received a deluge of warm water; it poured all over him, right into his shoes and inside his breeches. It was his turn to cry out. "Help, help, I'm drowning!" he yelled, and we all fell about with laughter on the sofas. Meanwhile Mme d'Aine, still in the saddle, called her chambermaid: "Anselme, Anselme, get me off this priest! *Abbé*, my dear little *abbé*, don't worry, not a drop has been lost."

The *abbé* kept his temper and behaved very well. Poor Mlle Anselme was a sight. She is innocence, shamefacedness and timidity in person. She opened her eyes wide at the great pond on the floor exclaiming: "Oh! but Madame . . ." MME D'AINE: "Oh, indeed! It's mine, it's the *abbé's*, it's both. What a relief! Fetch me some shoes, fetch some stockings, some petticoats, some linen. . ."

Mme d'Aine is a woman of honour. The little priest is poor, and the very next day she ordered him a complete new outfit. What do you think of that, my city ladies? For us, the ill-bred inhabitants of

Grandval, it is all we need to keep us amused from one day to the
next.[25]

Despite the ban on the *Encyclopédie*, its enemies were still busy,
and in November of 1759 they adopted a new line of attack.
Fréron, in his *Année littéraire*, published a letter from Pierre Patte,
a discharged employee of the *Encyclopédie*, alleging that the
Encyclopédie's plates were plagiarised. They were, said Patte, not
based on original drawings, but merely on impressions, which
Diderot had acquired by bribery, from some plates prepared
from Réaumur on behalf of the Academy of Sciences. How much
truth, if any, there was in this accusation is somewhat obscure.
Undoubtedly the publishers of the *Encyclopédie* did possess some
proofs of the Academy plates, indeed they admitted as much
themselves; and what is more, certain of Diderot's descriptions,
in the early volumes, seem to correspond more closely to the
Academy plates. At all events the publishers denied any evil
intent and offered to submit to an inspection; a deputation of
Academicians, after examining their stock of drawings and
plates, absolved them of fraud. What most galled Diderot was
Patte's implication, certainly false, that he had made no visits to
workshops and that his descriptions were merely cooked up in the
office.

A more severe blow was to follow. This was the staging by the
Comédie Française of a play, *The Philosophers*, by Diderot's old
enemy Charles Palissot. The play, modelled on Molière's *L'Ecole
des femmes*, was a satire on the theories of Helvétius and on the
philosophes generally, but above all a savage lampoon on the works
and character of Diderot. It represented him as a knave, a
pretentious charlatan, an enemy of common morality and above
all a dangerous anti-patriot. It seems that Palissot's play had the
backing of the King's own chief minister, Choiseul, and was to
some extent forced on the *Comédie Francqise* through his
influence. The story goes that it was read to the company by
Fréron, who was then a friend of Palissot's, though later they
became bitter enemies, and when some of the actors objected to
the play (among them the great Clairon) he told them truculently
that they might as well accept it with grace, since *they would have to*

anyway.[26] The play made a great hit. It received its première on 2 May 1760, and, according to report, there was such a crowd at the theatre as had never been seen.

The central character of Palissot's play is Cidalise, the wealthy widow of a magistrate, who has fallen under the influence of a rascally gang of *philosophes* and has been persuaded by them to believe herself a philosopher and a genius. She has even written a book, though it is really largely the work of the *philosophes* Valère and Dortidius. Her daughter Rosalie is engaged to be married to Damis, a worthy young man but no philosopher, and Cidalise, in justice to her new-found role, has decided to break the engagement and to give Rosalie in marriage to Valère.

Valère is, of course, only after Rosalie's money, and we see him give his servant Frontin a lecture in the new ethics, according to which virtue no longer is placed on a steep rock but is now identified with self-interest. Frontin meanwhile is trying unsuccessfully to pick Valère's pocket. (Does not philosophy hold that all goods are to be held in common?)

Valère has managed to pass Frontin off on Cidalise as a secretary and a man of learning, and she asks him to take down a Preface to her great treatise. She is lost for an opening phrase, but at last, in triumph, hits on the Diderotesque words "Young man, take and read!"[27] Frontin is all encouragement. Nothing, he tells her, could be at once so sublime and so modest.

There follows a long scene between Cidalise and Damis. She explains how, thanks to the lessons of Dortidius (Diderot) and such "divine" men, she has been raised above the vulgar prejudices of family affection and has adopted Humanity as her fatherland. Damis replies that he hears too many scoundrels invoking "Humanity". He suspects them of loving the human race as a way of loving no one in particular.

Next we see Cidalise among her admirers, who are lavish with compliments on her supreme genius. "Is there any news?" she asks Dortidius. "I do not trouble myself with Kings and their quarrels," he replies. "What is the outcome of a siege or a battle to me? The true sage is a cosmopolitan, and nothing can trouble his serenity." Cidalise's bookseller joins them, hawking the masterpieces of the day: *Indiscreet Jewels*, *Letter on the Deaf and*

Dumb, On the Interpretation of Nature, A Father and His Family (he is
not sure if she will like that, for few do). He also has Rousseau's
Second Discourse, and Cidalise is greatly taken with this last and
has visions of their all returning to a state of nature.

We now reach the great *coup de théâtre* of the piece. Damis has a
valet called Crispin. He is the lover of Rosalie's maid Marton and
has in earlier days been amanuensis to a bizarre and prickly sage,
who, out of dislike of mankind, has taken refuge in the woods.
Marton has stolen from Frontin an incriminating letter, revealing
the philosophers' plot to befool Cidalise, and they arrange that
Crispin shall bring it to Cidalise's eyes.

It is accordingly announced that a "philosopher" wishes to see
Cidalise. Enter Crispin on all fours, with a bunch of lettuce
protruding from his pocket – the very epitome of Rousseau's
Second Discourse. He addresses Cidalise:

> A taste for philosophy, seizing my mind, has led,
> To my choosing, as you observe, the state of
>   quadruped.
> My body, on these four pillars, moves with a stabler
>   gait,
> And I see fewer fools . . .

Cidalise is impressed, wondering whether perhaps she ought
not to follow this new four-footed *philosophique* fashion; but then
Frontin and the philosophers enter. It is the cue for Crispin to get
to his feet, show the letter and unmask them in all their rascality.

As will be seen, the real victim of Palissot's satire was not
Rousseau but Diderot. (When a bookseller sent Rousseau a copy
of the play, possibly at Palissot's own request, he indignantly
returned the "horrible" present, telling him he made a great
mistake if he thought he would enjoy seeing his old friend
libelled.) As for Diderot, he refused to go and see or even to read
the play; he adopted a tone of injured contempt towards it and to
the several imitations that it spawned.[28] "Six months ago," he
would write to Sophie later, with feeling, "everyone was cackling
with laughter at *The Philosophers*, and what has become of it by

now? It lies at the bottom of the abyss which gapes for all productions without morals or genius."[29]

Diderot's friends confidently expected that Voltaire, never one to overlook an insult to the "cause", would take reprisals. However, the awkward fact was that Palissot was a protégé of his and had once spent some hero-worshipping days under his roof. He thus compromised by writing Palissot a letter of only mild reproof. It praised Palissot's wit and asked with mock indignation why he himself had not been chastised in the play (had he not done his poor best to be a "philosopher"?). It blamed Palissot, however, for slandering such honourable men. "I do not know M. Diderot at all, I have never cast eyes on him. I only know that he has been unfortunate and persecuted: that reason alone should have caused the pen to drop from your hand."[30] Further letters followed, and the correspondence was published; Diderot and his friends thought Voltaire's behaviour rather shabby.

But what the Palissot episode also suggested to Voltaire was that Diderot must be made an Academician. It became quite an obsession with him for some months, and he wrote about it to a dozen different correspondents. "What a fine retort it would be to the infamy of Palissot!" he told his friend the Comte d'Argental (9 July 1760). In such a good cause, so he argued, Diderot could afford to pay visits to pious people and convince them of his religious orthodoxy. Maybe it might even be wise for him to deny authorship of his more contentious books. He wrote to Diderot himself about the plan, and, forgetting his good resolutions, became enraged when he received no response. As for Diderot, who thought the scheme quite wild, he was distinctly ungrateful. "Apropos of de Voltaire," he wrote to Sophie, "he complains bitterly of my silence. He says it would at least be polite to thank one's advocate. But who the devil asked him to plead my cause? And who the devil has told him he has done it the right way? The whole thing, he says, has caused him the most grievous pain. My dear, you couldn't pluck a hair from that man's head without his deafening Heaven with his groans."[31]

Another of Diderot's champions took a more drastic revenge on Palissot and published a pamphlet entitled *The Vision of Charles Palissot*: a scurrilous affair, in which Palissot's patroness, the dying Princesse de Robecq, was mocked for rising from her sickbed to attend the play. Great offence was taken at it in government circles and, despite his vehement denials, it was for a time ascribed to Diderot. In fact it was written by the caustic *abbé* Morellet – Voltaire liked to call him "*Mords-les*" ("Bite 'em!") – and it earned him some weeks in the Bastille. He was supplied with every comfort there, and, as he wrote complacently later, it established his credit for ever with the *philosophes*. It was, indeed, the making of his career.

Among the circle of Diderot and his friends, for some years, had been the elderly and eccentric Marquis de Croismare.[32] He had served for a time in the army, though without much taste for it, and had earned the Croix de St Louis. Then he had married and had retired to his estates in Normandy to live the life of a country gentleman. His wife had been a Protestant, but the Marquis, who was, at least intermittently, a moderately devout Catholic, had succeeded in converting her. However, in 1742 she had died, and at this the grief-stricken Marquis had come to Paris to find distraction. In a short time he had acquired a wide acquaintance-ship among the *philosophes*, and as a result he had become a freethinker and *esprit fort*. He was, indeed, a most impressionable and volatile man, always with some new ruling passion: at different times it was painting, music, book-collecting, print-collecting, chocolate-making, and the art of cooking omelettes. For weeks he would disappear, living among the garret-dwellers and down-and-outs of Paris, to get to know their way of life, and making many friends in the process. Everyone was fond of the Marquis, who was a gallant, tender-hearted and ebullient man. Diderot thought his wit the most delicate and unmalicious he had ever known: it was, he said, like brandy-flames, "running all over my head without burning a hair". However, in the autumn of 1758, de Croismare had paid a visit on business to his country estate near Caen and, coming under the influence of his friend the local *curé*, he had suffered a reconversion to religion. As a result, he showed every intention of staying in Normandy.

Grimm and Diderot were greatly put out by this desertion, and some time early in 1760 they formed a bizarre plot to lure their friend back to Paris. A year or two before de Croismare, in his chivalrous way, had become concerned on behalf of a nun who was demanding to be released from her vows.[33] She was by now in her forties and, it would seem, she had received very cruel treatment; her parents, determined to get her off their hands, had forced her to choose between entering a convent or being sent to a house of correction. According to her own belief she was illegitimate and the daughter of a highly-placed lady, this being partly the reason for her parents' malignity. The affair had, in the first place, been handled by the religious authorities, then, in 1757, she had managed to have it brought before *Parlement*; at this point de Croismare had intervened, energetically lobbying various Parlementary friends. Neither he nor her other supporters had had any success, however, and the unfortunate woman had been ordered to return to her convent at Longchamps (where she would in fact remain until the Revolution).

The idea that now came to Grimm and Diderot was to forge a supposititious letter from this nun to de Croismare, announcing that she had escaped from her convent and was in desperate straits – alone in Paris, a refugee, and estranged from her parents– and begging the Marquis to help her. The notion was that, given the Marquis's Quixotism, the letter might bring him hurrying back to Paris. Further letters were also planned, including a memoir by the young nun relating the harrowing story of her life. Diderot was the official scribe, but Mme d'Epinay and perhaps others lent a hand in the writing; and before sending the letters were tried out on Nanette, who sometimes advised them to tone them down. The writing sessions were conducted amid gales of laughter.

The joke or mystification, however, took an awkward turn. The Marquis (or so all the evidence suggests) was completely taken in, and he wrote back instantly, not proposing to come to Paris but offering the unfortunate nun "Suzanne" a post and place of refuge in his own household in Normandy. The conspirators went ahead, however, and to add to the pathos it was made out that Suzanne had been ill and very near to death, though she was slowly recovering. The fiction was that Suzanne had a friend and benefactor, a certain Madame Madin, living at Versailles; and soon quite a correspondence developed between the Marquis, Suzanne and Suzanne's supposed benefactor.

For Diderot and Grimm, always addicted to mystifications, this developed into their most elaborate exploit. An "idea of genius", and a further twist to the logic of the plot, came to these "children of Belial" (Grimm's words), and they wrote to de Croismare, in the name of Mme Madin, asking if he had some reliable friend in Paris whom Mme Madin might visit, to concert further steps on the nun's behalf. The hope was that de Croismare would nominate Grimm and would write to Grimm begging for aid and advice, a delicious redoubling of the "horrible conspiracy"; and eventually this is what de Croismare did. The plot thus succeeded beyond expectation and became more than they had bargained for. At every new pathetic detail or revelation the chivalrous Marquis grew more concerned and heart-stricken. Soon it was clear to his friends that there was only one decent way out; and by agreement "Suzanne" was given a return of fever and made to die a peaceful death in Mme Madin's arms.

This, as has been said, was the account of the affair given ten years later by Grimm in the *Correspondance littéraire*,[34] where he printed the whole sequence of letters and asserted that, when the truth was finally revealed to the Marquis, he laughed heartily and bore not the slightest malice. It would be prudent, though, not to accept Grimm's story without question; for one thing, it represents a curious indifference on de Croismare's part to the fate of the real nun. Also, the story contains various oddities and minor self-contradictions – and there would, after all, be nothing to stop it being a further mystification. The truth could not impossibly be that the Marquis quickly saw through the plot and thus was fooling Diderot and his friends, or again that the friends, together with the Marquis, were really fooling Diderot – a suspicion that at one point entered Diderot's mind.

We may leave this teasing problem for the moment for a different and very curious reflection concerning Diderot and the art of fiction. For it was during this same year, 1760, when he and his friends were gaily devising the nun's mock-deathbed, that Diderot became a passionate champion of Richardson's novels –

and above all of the deathbed scene in *Clarissa*. He considered Richardson was a moral genius, superior to Montaigne or La Rochefoucauld because he showed ethics in action. He pictured his novels as producing a hundred good deeds every day and was in danger, he wrote, of making a liking for Richardson a condition of friendship. But what amazed and overwhelmed him even more was Richardson's hypnotic illusionism, which turned the reader into a child at its first stage-play, crying "Don't trust him! He means to deceive you." "If you go there, you are lost!"[35] One day he was reading the famous deathbed scene in a friend's presence but could bear it no further and got to his feet and – to his friend's alarm – uttered the most piteous outcries against Clarissa's unfeeling family. We have here a paradox, and evidently a very fruitful one so far as Diderot is concerned. For though "Suzanne" might be dead, a major work of fiction, with Richardson's encouragement, had been born, the disturbing and profoundly original novel *La Religieuse (The Nun)*.

It so happened that about this same period the Jansenist *convulsionnaires* had once again been practising crucifixion. The explorer La Condamine had witnessed a crucifixion on Good Friday (securing one of the nails as a memento), and Grimm had published a brief report by him in the *Correspondance littéraire*. "Yes, Monsieur, I have seen what I wanted to see," La Condamine wrote.

Sister Françoise (55 years of age) was fixed to a cross in my presence, with four square nails. She hung there more than three hours. She suffered a good deal, especially in the right hand. I saw her shudder and grind her teeth with pain as they drew the nails out. Sister Marie (22 years of age), her proselyte, found it all very difficult to face. She wept and said frankly that she was afraid. Finally she made up her mind; but the fourth nail was too much for her, and they did not drive it right in. She read the Passion-story in a loud voice as she hung there, but her strength began to fail, and she nearly fainted, crying "Take me down quickly!" She had been on the cross twenty or twenty-five minutes. They took her out of the room for she had colic. She returned in quarter of an hour or so. They bathed her feet and hands with the miracle- working water of saint Pâris and this resource was more comfort to her than hammers and nails.[36]

These and other such reports were fresh in Diderot's mind when he began work on "Suzanne's" autobiographical memoir. The mystification, begun in fun, touched some of his intensest feelings and most deeply grounded theories, and the memoir, which was never sent to the Marquis, turned imperceptibly into a complex work of art. The novel represents, in a sense, the story implicit in Diderot's *Philosophical Thoughts* ("What voices! What outcries! What groans!"). "I am at my *Nun*," he wrote to a friend on 1 August 1760, "but it expands under my pen, and I don't know when I shall reach land."[37]

During September 1760 Diderot went to stay with Mme d'Epinay at La Chevrette, taking with him the growing manuscript of his novel. Soon he is writing to Sophie vividly and voluminously about the "sweet and innocent" and solitary few days that he, Mme d'Epinay and Grimm enjoyed there – days "when we have been entertained and occupied, have thought thoughts, have received improvement and admiration and love *and have told one another so.*" He was coming to feel, so he told Sophie, that Mme d'Epinay and he were made for one another. They understood each other without the need for words. "We condemn or approve things by a flicker of the eye."[38] Sometimes they even took sides against Grimm. For example, a friend argued that though strict probity was required among friends, it was a "dupery" to apply the same standard with people one did not know: they were outraged at this doctrine, but Grimm seemed all too ready to go along with it.

At moments Diderot felt sorry for Mme d'Epinay, who was so deeply, and a little forlornly, in love. Grimm had recently obtained a diplomatic post, something he had been wanting for many years. He was now representative in France of the free city of Frankfurt, and with this and his post with the Duc d'Orléans and the *Correspondance littéraire* he was very busy and bustling, often away at Versailles and inclined to be neglectful of his mistress. Once, when he had broken an appointment with her, she made touching excuses to Diderot: Grimm had so much on his mind, it was as bad for him as it was for her, etc. Diderot made no comment. "Why don't you say anything, Philosopher?" she asked. "Do you think he may not love me any more?" "What the devil was I to answer?" wrote Diderot to Sophie. "One cannot tell her the truth. One simply has to lie and leave her with her illusions. The moment of opening her eyes might be the last moment of her life."[39]

Monday 15 September was the day of the annual fête at La Chevrette, when the villagers and tradesmen's wives came to do honour to their lord and lady (as in *The Marriage of Figaro*), and there was an influx of visitors to the great house. Diderot had planned to escape to Paris but changed his mind when he saw his friends' reproachful looks, and that afternoon in the d'Epinays' "gloomy and magnificent *salon*", he took part in a charming scene. It was the sort of exemplary *tableau* that appealed to Diderot and that he had devised in *A Father and His Family*.

Near the window overlooking the gardens Grimm was having his portrait painted, and Mme d'Epinay was leaning on the back of the chair of the person doing the painting.

A draughtsman seated lower, on a stool, was doing his profile in chalk. It is a charming profile: no woman could resist wondering if it is a likeness.

Saint-Lambert sat in the corner reading the latest pamphlet.

I was playing chess with Mme d'Houdetot.

The good Mme Esclavelles, Mme d'Epinay's aged mother, had all the children round her knee and was chatting with them and their tutors.

Two of the sisters of the person painting my friend were doing embroidery, one in her hands and one on a frame.

And the third played a piece by Scarlatti on the clavichord.[40]

One of Mme d'Epinay's visitors was the Neapolitan *abbé* Ferdinando Galiani.[41] He was then thirty-three, the nephew of a Cardinal and a secretary in the Neapolitan embassy. This tiny, mercurial and somewhat *louche* figure was learned in a virtuoso-like way and famous for his fables and his pantomimic brilliance in telling them. Philosophically he was an extreme cynic, declaring "Be damned to our neighbour. There are no such things as neighbours," and admitting in politics only the purest Machiavellianism, "unmixed, raw and in all its force and harshness". Nietzsche wrote of him as "the profoundest, most sharp-sighted and perhaps also the dirtiest man of his century."[42]

For a moment Galiani's dry-eyed humour grated on Diderot. "The *abbé* Galiani greatly displeased me," he told Sophie. "He confessed he had never wept in his whole lifetime, and the loss of his father, his brothers, his sisters and his mistresses had not caused him to shed a single tear. Mme d'Epinay, I have the feeling, was as shocked as I was."[43] The repulsion did not last, and Diderot soon developed a kind of cult of Galiani, as an original and "a treasure for rainy days".

At Grandval, the following month, a dispute arose about the claims of "genius" as against those of "method", and Galiani told a fable about the cuckoo (method) and the nightingale (genius) and how they held a singing-contest before a donkey (i.e. Galiani himself). "How you would have laughed," Diderot told Sophie, "to see him stretch up his neck and pipe as the nightingale, throw out his chest and sound gruff as the cuckoo, and lay his ears back to mimic the imbecile gravity of the donkey – and all without the faintest effort. He is all pantomime, from his head to his feet."[44]

At La Chevrette, as at Grandval and the rue Royale, the conversation was often sparked off by some paradox of Diderot's. He reported one, "rather strong for our little stomachs", that he had floated at table. It was that he could not help admiring human nature even when, as sometimes, it was "atrocious".

> For example, I said, they condemn a man to death for hanging seditious posters, and the day after his execution even worse ones appear on the walls. Or a thief is executed, and in the crowd around the gallows other thieves pick pockets, risking the retribution directly before their eyes. What contempt for death and for life! If the wicked did not have such energy for crime, the good would not have the same energy for virtue. . . If Tarquin does not dare rape Lucrece, Scaevola will not put his wrist in the flames.[45]

There were some swans on the lake at La Chevrette, who annoyed Diderot by the officious clamour they made when he came near; he thought they had a very nasty look in their eye ("proud, stupid and evil-intentioned, three qualities that often go together"). He decided to tease them, rushing about and ambushing them on one side of their "empire" and then another; but in his excitement he tripped over the key to a manhole and cut a terrible gash in his instep. It put him out of action for some days, and his friends seized the opportunity to have his portrait painted. The affair was arranged, again, as a sort of *tableau*, Diderot and Mme d'Epinay being painted before each other's eyes. Diderot was a great admirer of Mme d'Epinay's looks and he wrote excitedly about her portrait to Sophie, who could be trusted not to take such a thing amiss. "She is depicted with bosom half bare," he told her, "some curls loose over her throat and shoulders and the rest tied in a blue ribbon across her forehead. Her lips are half open: you can feel her breathing. Her eyes are full of languor. It is the very image of tenderness and pleasure."[46]

As for his own portrait, by a quite unknown artist named Garand, he was enraptured with it. "I have never been done well," he was to write later, "save by a poor devil called Garand, who hit me off as a fool occasionally hits off a *bon mot*. I am depicted bareheaded, in my dressing-gown, sitting in a chair, my right arm supporting the left, and the left arm supporting my head. My eyes have a faraway look." (This was his idea of the "meditation" posture *par excellence*.) "On this canvas," he tells Sophie, "you can see me meditating. I am alive, I am breathing, I am all animation. There is thought behind that brow."[47]

The urge possessed him to reach out, through Sophie, to Sophie's sister, the stately and grave-mannered "Uranie". (The nickname means "goddess of heavenly love".) He did not know what he wanted of her but needed to make his presence felt. He would send her teasing and flirtatious reproofs, he would pass harsh judgements on her (she was "unjust and vain", an *allumeuse* or prick-tease, a perverse man-hater), and every now and then he would burst out to Sophie with sexual jealousy.

> I have become so touchy, so unjust, so jealous. You tell me so much good of her [Uranie] and get so angry when anyone makes a

criticism, that . . . I had better not go on! I am ashamed of what goes on inside me, but I can't stop it. Your mother says that your sister is a lover of women, and there is no doubt she loves you a great deal; and then there was that nun she had such a *penchant* for, and that tender and caressing way she has of leaning on you, and those fingers so closely entwined with yours!

Adieu. I am a madman; would you want me to be otherwise? Adieu. Adieu – must I keep on uttering that gloomy word?[48]

He was commuting between La Chevrette and Paris and returned home in the first days of October, intending after a few days to go on to Grandval. He found Nanette ill, however, and in such a rage against him that he dared not ask her how she was and had to rely on their daughter Angélique's report. His relations with Nanette were in one of their worst patches at this period, and he described them with great frankness to Sophie. The trouble was his fault, as he knew, but at the same time not altogether his fault, and he was getting resigned to the situation; he no longer felt the urge to punch himself or beat his head against the wall. All the same, he asked himself, could anyone's health hope to stand up to the life she led? "Never going out, working every moment, living on nothing and complaining night and day. Bronze itself could not withstand it."

On 9 October 1760 he set out for Grandval, for a stay of several weeks. It turned out to be one of the richest, most varied and most diverting of all his country-house sojourns, and more and more, for Sophie's benefit, he enjoyed playing the novelistic observer. One of the things that had most amazed him in Richardson was that every one of his huge cast of characters seemed to have his or her own tone and mode of thinking, and not only that, a tone that altered as their circumstances changed. It occurred to him that he might do the same. He told Sophie how, though he has never met the Vollands' friend the *abbé* Marin, he can imagine him in perfect detail: his little round balding head, his wrinkled but still pink cheeks and so on. If he had the time, he said, he would be able to paint the whole *tableau*: the *abbé*, Sophie, her sister and their mother. "And your conversation, could I not do that too? Could I not make you three each speak in the style I know, and the *abbé* in the style I choose for him?"[49]

He was, as always, at work on the *Encyclopédie* – so far as he was able, for, he complained, his colleagues seemed determined to starve him of material – but he was also, we may assume, continuing *The Nun*. What we notice is that he produced this novel, and all his fiction, in a manner very different from his vociferous dealings with the theatre. "Above all, make it a law to yourself not to throw a single detail down on paper until your plan is in its final form," he wrote in *On Dramatic Poetry*.[50] It sounds like good advice for a dramatist, and was, indeed, the practice of Racine, but in Diderot's own case it strikes one as entirely the wrong theory. Indeed, he seems to have come to realise this himself. There is an undated letter of self-description in which he writes: "I only talk well to myself, or to others when I forget they are there. The faster I write, the better I do it."[51] Thus *The Nun* grew under his hand in a manner quite unforeseen. The work went on silently, very privately, almost one might say absent-mindedly. His most expansive comment on it comes in an undated letter to Mme d'Epinay, perhaps written after his return to Grandval.

I have come back. I set to work on *The Nun*, and I was still at it at three o'clock in the morning. I am going like the wind. It is no longer a letter, it is a book. There will be things both true and pathetic in it, and I ought to be able to make them strong but I do not give myself enough time. I let my thoughts run free; I don't know how to restrain them.[52]

12

The Nun

With hindsight, one is inclined to view the early history of the European novel from the point of view of the direction that the form eventually took. The potentialities of the novel-form would have seemed somewhat different at the time. If I put the point in terms of the English novel, this will not take us too far from Diderot, for his chief inspirations as a novelist were Richardson and Sterne.

To a contemporary of Defoe, Sterne and Richardson a basic choice would have seemed to be offered: the choice between, on the one hand, a conception of the novel as *deception*, as falsehood dressed up as truth and leaving a margin of possibility that it might in fact turn out to be truth; and on the other hand a conception of the novel as *illusion* – or, as one may express it, illusion unambiguously acknowledged as such.

Plainly, any novel (one, say, like *Tom Jones*) that has an elaborately contrived plot is bound to belong in the second category, the novel of "accepted illusion". It is a genre which entails a certain fundamental contract with the reader, according to which the novelist should, as it were, be continually nursing the reader and looking after his or her comfort. Over the years the genre would develop a whole conventional narrative rhythm, with dramas and lulls, suspenses and aftermaths, pauses for reminiscence and endings that are like deathbeds. What is developed is a form of mimicry of time, according to which reflections, character-descriptions, exposition, pauses and re-introducions of characters have an understood relation to the pace of events and help in depicting that pace. By a natural turn of logic, moreover, one way in which such a novel – that is to say an object so remote from common experience as an elaborately plotted tale – will aspire to be praised is for its "lifelikeness". It was, and still is, a very fruitful genre, and over the years and through the genius of Jane Austen, Dickens and George Eliot and kindred writers it came to seem to be the only genre and to constitute "the novel" itself.

This, of course, was an error, and what I have called the *novel as deception* offered equally rich possibilities. The "novel as deception" works by never formally and finally severing its ties with real life, including the real life of the reader. The possibility is always left open that the work may turn out to be a genuine document, written by a real Pamela or Moll Flanders or Cavalier, or perhaps a piece of "secret history". It may indeed, make such lavish use of genuine documents that readers do not suspect it of being a novel; but then this is to defeat its own artistic end. For in this genre the point is continually to exploit the reader's uncertainty. Novels of this school will develop quite different conventions from those of the "accepted illusion" kind. In the nature of things, they will have to simulate artlessness and eschew the more familiar devices of the professional story-teller. Further, since the author has absconded, passing on the responsibility for the narrative to "real life", a quite different, more demanding and bewildering, role is imposed upon the reader. In this kind of fiction the author can be expected to be hiding his or her intentions much more effectively than in the novel of accepted illusion; and then there exists, for the reader, always the possibility that there is no "author" anyway. Faced with this double difficulty, the reader may grow uneasy – may hedge himself around with caution as in a difficult real-life situation. Or he may simply flounder, as, for instance, readers have so often floundered about Defoe's *Roxana*. (Shall they regard it as a very moral, or as a very immoral, tale?) But more valuably, in the case of a scrupulous reader, he or she may be placed in a tender and vulnerable position, which it will be open to the *novelist of deception* to practise upon in all sorts of ethical and philosophical ways.

Nor is this the only form that the *novel as deception* may take. Richardson discovered another very potent form when he had the idea of writing what is simultaneously a novel and a behaviour-manual. This, again, entails a double or ambivalent relationship with the reader. The reader's interest in a behaviour-manual is, *in theory*, educational, a matter of learning how to behave in such-and-such circumstances. It is, that is to say, a practical and real-life activity on the reader's part, a direct invitation to apply the story to his or her actual life. Richardson is inviting him, and quite sincerely, to study Pamela's letters and Grandison's conduct as a model and guide, and the fiction is *in theory* subordinate to this end. The novelist is thus able to play upon the reader in a false-dealing manner, as it were, appealing under this exemplary front to the reader's credulity, emotionality and, perhaps, even prurience. It produces a very different kind or novel, evolving quite different conventions, from one of the "accepted illusion" kind.

But then a further and even wider consideration arises; for it would seem that the novel-as-deception lies close to the novel-of-undeception. The writer who conceives of the novel as falsehood is liable also to be the writer who is tempted to blow the gaff: to frustrate the reader's desire for a "romance" and remind the reader that a "narrator" may be a real-life author – perhaps a teasing, bored or angry one. One can perceive a logical affinity between this Sternian kind of novel and the Richardsonian or Defoean kind. The writer who can throw his or her genius into "practising" on the reader may equally be tempted to triumph over the reader by showing the whole business to be a fraud and a confidence-trick. The three cases, the pretended document, the pretended behaviour-manual and the novel that blows the gaff, share the same underlying decision, that of never finally severing the link with the outside world.

These two great genres, the novel-of-accepted-illusion and the novel-as-deception (and undeception) seemed at first, and perhaps were, equally rich in artistic potential. However, as I have said, it was the former genre – the novel of Fielding, Jane Austen, George Eliot and Dickens – which triumphed, and this has a distorting effect on one's picture of the past. It has meant that the idea of pretending that your novel may be a real-life document, "true confession" or "secret history", now tends to look naive or primitive, as if belonging to the pre-history of the novel, while the novel-as-undeception, the novel which disrupts narrator–reader relations, has, on being rediscovered in the twentieth century, come to be seen as *avant-garde*.

Diderot, as novelist, belongs entirely to the novel-as-deception school. In his novels, as in his philosophic fantasies (like his *Letter on the Blind, D'Alembert's Dream* and *Supplement to Bougainville's Voyage*), the "fiction" always remains embedded, to very subtle effect, in its real-life matrix. This is, indeed, just what one would expect, given his bent towards the "supposititious" and towards "mystifications". (He entitles one of his short stories "Mystification", and another "This Is Not a Story".) What is striking, moreover, is that he produced a masterpiece in each of two separate veins of the novel-as-deception. *The Nun* is a masterpiece of the fraudulent "true confession" type, and *Jacques the Fatalist* is a masterpiece of narrator–reader disruption (asking – in emulation of Jacques with his own master– "who shall be master, novelist or reader?"). But indeed *The Nun*, with its final blowing-of-the-gaff, is a masterpiece in both genres: the novel-as-deception and the novel-as-undeception.

What one discovers in this first novel of Diderot's, possibly with a shock of surprise, is that it exhibits hardly a trace of sentimentality. This, indeed, proves true of all his novels and stories. The art of fiction evokes in him a salutary and impressive coldness, a detachment in the manner of Stendhal, and with it various other very un-Richardsonian qualities, like swiftness, incisiveness and economy. The note is struck very early in the novel, in the incident of the heroine's nosebleed. Having successfully staged a refusal to take her vows, she is returning home with her implacable mother. They face each other in silence in the carriage, and then, writes Suzanne:

> I do not know what was going on inside me, but suddenly I threw myself at her feet and laid my head in her lap. I could not speak but sobbed and choked. She repelled me harshly. I did not get up. My nose began to bleed. I seized one of her hands, against her will, and bathing it with my tears and the blood streaming from me, I pressed it to my mouth and kissed it, saying: "You are still my mother, I am still your child!" She replied, pushing me away more roughly and pulling back her hand: "Get up, wretched child, get up!" I obeyed and sat down, hiding my face in my coif. There

was so much firmness and authority in her voice that I felt I
needed to hide from her. My tears and the blood from my nose
mingled together, running down my arms, till, without my
realising, I was covered in them. From something my mother said,
I gathered they had dirtied her dress and that she was displeased.[1]

The verisimilitude of that nosebleed belongs to nineteenth-
century and not to eighteenth-century fiction.

It is this coldness which upset the critic Barbey d'Aurevilly,
who, in his *Goethe and Diderot* (1880), was eager to depict Diderot
as a man of warmth and "fire", as against the "reptilian" frigidity
of Goethe. *The Nun*, wrote the royalist and Catholic d'Aurevilly,
was a novel no one now would read, "were it not for its ignobly
libertine details which, for corrupted minds, give a spice of
cantharides to this cold book, which the hatred, always faintly
simmering in Diderot's pusillanimous soul, was unable to
warm."[2] It is a reaction worth pondering, and for one thing
because Barbey d'Aurevilly reacted to Diderot with passion – in
this he was rather rare among critics – and drew a portrait of him
on heroic lines.

It is a point of significance that, until quite recently, *The Nun*,
like *Indiscreet Jewels*, was regarded as a pornographic novel. (It
was actually banned in 1824, and again in 1826, no doubt partly
for that reason – and as late as 1968 Mme de Gaulle forced the
Ministry of Information to ban the film of it by Jacques Rivette.)
One was simply not supposed to depict lesbianism, as Diderot
does in the later pages of *The Nun*; and a cold and objective
treatment of it was liable to appear to readers as an especially
unpleasant kind of libertinism, and evidently did so to
d'Aurevilly. Anyway, leaving aside the matter of lesbianism,
there was quite a school of titillating fiction about convent life,
with titles like *Venus in the Cloister; or, a Nun in her Shift*, and this is a
fact very relevant to Diderot's complex purposes in *The Nun*. But
furthermore *Indiscreet Jewels* really is a cold novel, rather
jarringly so. Thus it is not too hard to see how *The Nun* could have
been misread and not seen for the heartfelt and impassioned work
that it is, one that is made all the more poignant by its refusal of
sentimentality.

This matter of "coldness" touches on something central to

Diderot's intellectual life. He was, as we have seen, very ready to proclaim himself a sentimentalist and believed that virtue tended to be of the party of the sentimentalists. On the other hand – the thought could not be suppressed – sentimentality seemed to go hand-in-hand with mediocrity and to be, as it were, the antithesis of "genius". The issue was summed up in an anecdote about an encounter he had with the playwright Michel-Jean Sedaine. He believed Sedaine to be a disciple of his, with all the right ideas about the drama, and was greatly excited by a successful performance of Sedaine's *A Philosopher Without Knowing It*. He rushed half across Paris to congratulate the author, arriving, according to Sedaine's account, "all out of breath, sweating, and exclaiming, with tears in his eyes, 'Victory, my friend, victory!' " – to which Sedaine's only reply was, "M. Diderot, how beautiful you look!"[3] In this, Diderot said, one saw all the difference between the sentimentalist and the "observer and man of genius". It was a favourite story with him and helped to inspire one of his most influential writings, his *Paradox of the Actor*, where he argues that the actor of genius portrays emotions so powerfully precisely because he feels none of them.

When writing fiction, Diderot seems instinctively to have fallen into a "genius" tone. This must not be misunderstood. He was emphatically *not* the actor who feels nothing; indeed he could become, towards his own fiction, the same enthusiastic, naively credulous reader as Richardson created for himself. He later told a story of how, at the time of writing *The Nun*, a friend of his called on him and found him in floods of tears. "What on earth is the matter?" exclaimed his friend. "What a state you are in!" "I will tell you what is the matter," replied Diderot. "I am breaking my heart over a story I am telling to myself."[4] For all this, though, the actual tone of *The Nun* shows that very marked "coldness" that separates his fiction, in a striking manner, from most of the rest of his work. It is at bottom the same unmistakable but somehow unclassifiable quality – not "bleak", not "savage", not "amoral" – which has disconcerted readers of *Rameau's Nephew*. Diderot, both by experience and by instinct, was a self-censorer. He was a compunctious man and saw a good deal of virtue, as well as necessity, in self-censorship and respect for certain common prejudices. In writing fiction, however, it seems to come naturally to him to forget all such compunction.

The Nun falls into four broad sections. First we read of the young Suzanne Simonin's family unhappiness, her entry into her first convent (the Sainte Marie), her realisation that she has no religious vocation and her bold public refusal to take vows. Next comes the callous and punitive treatment she receives on her return home, her discovery of her bastardy, her more or less forcible despatch to the convent of Longchamps and her long sequence of vicissitudes there: her friendship with the saintly Mother de Moni, her unwilling taking of vows, her ferocious victimisation at the hands of Mother de Moni's successor, and her decision to take legal steps to cancel her vows, bringing on her an even more appalling series of persecutions. The third section concerns her removal to the convent of Sainte-Eutrope outside Paris, her exposure to a new form of persecution there, at the hands of its lesbian Prioress, and her eventual escape from the convent with a rascally Benedictine monk. Finally (I am describing the novel in the shape it took in the *Correspondance littéraire* in 1780–82) a "Preface to the Preceding Work", revealing the hoax or "horrible conspiracy" out of which the novel has sprung and giving the text of the letters exchanged between the imaginary "Suzanne" and the real-life Marquis de Croismare.

When, now an old man, Diderot came to offer *The Nun* to Henri Meister, Grimm's successor on the *Correspondance littéraire*, he wrote: "I do not believe anyone has ever written a more terrifying satire on convents."[5] The word "satire" will need some glossing, but plainly the work is a polemic. It is not, however, a polemic against religion as such, nor is it much concerned with the Jesuit-versus-Jansenist controversy. It is not even, initially, a wholesale attack on the conventual system, though it certainly becomes one. The focus of his actual plot is very precise, it is the crime and outrage to the human soul of forcing the religious life on someone with no vocation for it; and neither Diderot nor his protagonist Suzanne (a tenacious and inflexible character) ever lose hold of this issue. To "crime" and "outrage", though, the reader is asked to add "danger". For the paradox, very clearly understood by Suzanne herself, is that whereas she lacks all vocation for the religious life, she has a definite natural talent for it; and altogether she is a formidable and disruptive personage.

For this, among other reasons, the Mother de Moni episode, and its placement, are crucial to the novel's strategy. For the humane, far-seeing and truly spiritual Mother de Moni represents the very best that the conventual system can offer, and her relationship with Suzanne underlines a tragic irony: that, in the convent system, such superior virtues may be as dangerous as, or even more dangerous than, the common vices – worldliness, intolerance, herd-instinct and lust for cruelty – of the monastic life. Suzanne herself comes to realise that her contact with the noble and inspiring Mother de Moni was "fatal". "I cannot say enough good of her," she writes to the Marquis. "But it is her goodness that was my undoing." It is her feeling for Mother de Moni that, against not just instinct but the certain knowledge that she is doing wrong, persuades her to take religious vows. Again, of course, it is jealousy of Mother de Moni and irritation at Suzanne's cult of her memory, that provoke such hostility in her ferocious successor. This "fatality" is not an innocent accident, for their relationship, and Mother de Moni's relationship with all her chosen flock, is (it is Suzanne's own word) a "seduction". For some of the novices, to receive consolation from Mother de Moni becomes a craze and a morbid addiction. "She did not intend to seduce; but certainly that is what she did. One came from her presence with a heart on fire and joy and ecstasy painted on one's face. One wept such sweet tears!" "Seduction" is a strong word. It is one that the reader is expected to remember; and later Diderot, by a number of cunning touches, suggests the parallel between this spiritual seduction and the physical seduction attempted by the Prioress of Sainte-Eutrope.

We remember, too, that it is through her friendship with Mother de Moni that Suzanne finds that she herself has a "genius" for the spiritual life. Suzanne is made to reflect what dire use she could have made of this rare gift, what a gift it would have been in the hands of a hypocrite or a fanatic. The wise Mother de Moni makes a chilling remark, which Suzanne often has cause to remember: "Among all these creatures you see around me – so docile, so innocent, so sweet – well, my child, there is hardly one, no, not one, whom I could not turn into a wild beast." Her words prove all too true, and under the influence of her successor the inhabitants of Longchamps in fact become "wild beasts", pursuing the hapless Suzanne with insane vindictiveness. The whole place, indeed, for a time goes mad.

Nor is the "fatality" only on one side. Innocent victim though she is, neither now nor later can Suzanne be said to be harmless to her fellows. If Mother de Moni is "fatal" to Suzanne, Suzanne is fatal to Mother de Moni, dispossessing her of her "genius" and hastening her end.

All these ironies, so subtly drawn out by Diderot, are directed towards a single conclusion: that the root of the trouble is not "fate" or original sin but a profoundly, an irremediably, vicious human institution. Its vices can be detected at work even in so mild and enlightened a régime as that of Mother de Moni; thus the horrors that are to come, so runs the logic of the narrative, need not take us by suprise.

These horrors and persecutions fall into two separate sequences. The *donnée* of the novel, as we know, is the real-life nun Marguerite Delamarre and specifically her effort to repudiate her vows; and the moment when the same idea occurs to Suzanne is a turning-point in the novel. Up to this moment she has been a doomed figure. In her rebellion against Mother de Moni's successor she succeeds in destroying her own character, making herself hard, horrible and legalistic; and the rebellion, anyway, is bound to be hopeless. The only real possibilities for her in the long run are an unsustainable hypocrisy, madness or suicide. Indeed the only reason for not committing suicide, she reflects with a last flicker of obstinacy, is that everyone seems to *want* her to commit it.

As soon as she thinks of repudiating her vows, however, her strength of character returns; it helps to give force to all that follows – that crescendo of hardly conceivable malignities (though, in fact, they can all be paralleled in contemporary records) – that they fall on no passive victim but on a most courageous, resourceful, obstinate and even "violent" woman (so at least she describes herself).

On the day of her arrival at the rich and worldly convent of Longchamps Suzanne is persuaded to perform at the clavichord, and ("without irony", she tells the Marquis) she finds herself singing Telaire's great air from Rameau's *Castor and Pollux* bidding farewell to the sun, "Sad attire, pale torch-flames, day more terrible than night itself." It is a telling stroke. Diderot himself, in recommending his novel to Meister, said that it would be a gift to painters. Indeed, indirectly, it would inspire Delacroix; for his sensational "L'Amende Honorable" illustrates a scene from Maturin's *Melmoth the Wanderer* – the victimised monk Moncada being dragged from his cell into the presence of the Bishop – which Maturin had filched directly from Diderot.

The nocturnal *tableaux* which follow – the nuns being ordered to step on the prostrate Suzanne's body, their dressing her in a shroud and laying her out on a bier, their leading her to a mock-execution, and so on – make an extraordinary sequence. One especially is most moving. The Archdeacon is completing his public inquisition, during which Suzanne has answered every question about her sufferings firmly but laconically. He asks her if she wants to accuse anyone in particular. She replies "No," and he dismisses her to her cell. On a sudden instinct, though, she turns back, falls down before him, and, displaying her bruised head, her bloodstained feet, her fleshless arms and filthy clothes, says simply: "You see!"

Many strands in the novel come together here. Such a charge of emotion and indignation has built up in us that Diderot can risk enlarging his book into a universal statement.

We need to stand back for a moment and form a clear idea of Diderot's strategy. A passage in his *Essays on Painting*, where he discusses painterly composition, is helpful here.

A man is giving a friend an interesting reading. Without conscious thought on either's part, the reader disposes himself in the manner he finds most appropriate, and the listener does the same. If it is Robbé reading, he will have the air of a fanatic: he will not look at his text but will be gazing into the air. If I am the listener, I will have a serious look; my right hand will move to my chin, to prop my drooping head, and my left hand will reach for my right elbow, to support the weight of both head and arm. This is not how I would listen to Voltaire.

Add a third character to the scene, and he will submit to the law of the two former: it is a combined system of three interests.[6]

A "combined system of three interests" is precisely what we find in Suzanne's narration, working, implicitly, at three different levels: she has been telling the story of her wrongs for its own sake, she has been telling it for the special benefit of the Marquis, and she (or Diderot) is telling it, over the Marquis's head, to the world at large. Now Diderot dares to make all this explicit. He causes Suzanne to raise, to the Marquis, the very issue of credibility that will have troubled the reader– could one person have suffered the whole imaginable repertory of evils in the conventual system? Is this not more like some insane fantasy? – and her answer is a good one. Given our sense of something unique and challenging in Suzanne's personality, a sort of lightning-conductor quality, we find ourselves happy to accept it.

> The more I reflect, the more I persuade myself that what is happening to me has never happened up till now and will perhaps never happen again. Just once (and pray God that it be the first and last time) it has pleased Providence, whose ways are not to be fathomed, to assemble upon one unfortunate creature all the mass of cruelties otherwise distributed – in its unsearchable decrees – among the infinite multitude of wretches who have preceded her in the cloister and who are to come after.[7]

The Suzanne who was stoical and laconic to her clerical inquisitor now unlooses her tongue and makes unashamed and imperious appeal to the Marquis's feelings. "Monsieur le Marquis, beware lest a fatal moment come when you wear your eyes out weeping over my fate. You might then be wrung with remorse, but this would not help me return from the abyss where I had fallen; it would have closed for ever over a castaway." And finally, gathering strength from the story of her own defeat (for it is at this point that she learns that her legal suit has failed) she is made to deliver what the reader is now most willing to hear, a searing and magnificent tirade against the whole convent system. The structure of feeling that has been built up almost requires that Diderot's voice should now mingle with Suzanne's.

What need has the Bridegroom of so many foolish virgins? Or the
human species of so many victims? Shall we never feel the need to
close up those gulfs where future races fall to their destruction? All
the formal prayers made there, are they worth one farthing given
in fellow-feeling to the poor? Does God, who created Man for
society, approve of his being immured? Can God, who created him
so inconstant and so frail, encourage him in such a reckless thing
as vows? . . . etc.[8]

When, unexpectedly, Suzanne is at last released from her
sufferings at Longchamps and is transferred to a new convent,
that of Sainte-Eutrope, she finds that Providence has played a
fresh trick on her, plunging her into a quite new dilemma. In this
Sainte-Eutrope episode, in weight and extent a balance to the
Longchamps section, there is not only a shift to a new evil of the
cloister, a sexual one, but also a shift in our sympathies. For the
real victim in the new episode is not Suzanne but the Prioress,
a figure only driven to tragedy by the convent system.

There was a principle which would loom large for Diderot as
an art-theorist and amateur physiologist. It was that there was a
"system" in deformity, so that an expert need only see a pair of
feet to say that they belonged to a hunchback, or a woman's
throat and shoulders to say that she had lost her eyesight in
childhood. From an aesthetic point of view the implication was
that an artist ought to forget academic rules of "correctness", for
"Nature does nothing that is incorrect," and should study,
rather, the "secret liaison" and "necessary concatenation" of
natural phenomena. "Every form, beautiful or ugly, has its cause,
and of all creatures that exist there is not one which is not as it has
to be." One is reminded of this theory when it comes to Diderot's
moving portrait of the lesbian Mother Superior. "Her head is
never still on her shoulders," writes Suzanne; ". . . there is always
something astray in her dress; her face is attractive on the whole;
her eyes, of which one, the right one, is higher and larger than the
other, are *distraits* and full of fire . . . The unsymmetry of her
features expresses all the disconnectedness of her character."
When, later, Suzanne gives the charming picture of the Mother
Superior's *levée*, she notes that her tender, shining black eyes "are
always only half-open", a neat symbolic suggestion that she does

not want to see what she is doing. Diderot is evidently treating the Mother Superior, very compassionately but "scientifically", as a "system of deformity", with a "skew" running visibly right through her moral as through her physical makeup.

In this new episode, Diderot's novel, so full of surprises, has a further and even bolder surprise in store. For the reader finds that a trick, of a most disturbing kind, has been played on himself or herself. Throughout this new episode the possibility looms for the reader that the book is a titillating or pornographic convent-romance, a steamier variation on the story of a nun breaking her vows because she has a lover. (Indeed Suzanne is eventually rescued by a "lover".) Suzanne's way of reporting her Superior's sexual advances is erotic in itself. She is caught up in her own innocent amazement and describes it excitedly and excitingly.

> After this, as soon as a nun had committed any fault, I interceded for her, and I was sure to obtain her pardon in exchange for some innocent favour; it was always a kiss on the forehead or on the neck or on the eyes or on the cheeks or on the mouth or on the hands or on the bosom or on the arms but most often on the mouth . . . She declared I had sweet breath, white teeth and fresh and rosy lips.[9]

Though Suzanne now much less often addresses herself directly to the Marquis, the reader is soon speculating on the effect of all this on that ardent and impressionable man; and of course all the more so when it comes to the heated if semi-comic scene of the Prioress's first successful seduction of Suzanne (if "seduction" is the word; in any event, when she first achieves an orgasm in Suzanne's arms). Evidently it is to Suzanne's advantage to involve the Marquis's feelings, by any means almost; indeed in a "postscript" to her narration Suzanne frankly admits she may half-consciously have been manipulating him. "Is it because we believe men less sensitive to the painting of our distress than to the image of our charms, and that we promise ourselves it will be easier to seduce them than to stir their pity?"[10]

The obliquities and calculation in Suzanne's narration to the Marquis are a most important element in the novel; nevertheless they are only, in a sense, an adjunct to something even more

essential: the obliquities in Diderot's relationship with the
reader. For, from the beginning, what the Prioress of Sainte-
Eutrope finds sexually exciting in Suzanne is not just her beauty
but her past sufferings. The great erotic thrill that she promises
herself is to hear Suzanne tell her story; and eventually she stage-
manages this event in the most voluptuous style, entwining her
whole body with the story-teller's. It is to be, as she says herself, a
supreme indulgence: the two of them will weep delicious tears,
and "perhaps we shall be happy in the middle of the story of your
sufferings. Who knows where tender compassion may lead
us. . . ?" Suzanne begins, and the reader is treated to a *louche*
parody of his own emotions – you might say, the emotions of any
person of good will – in reading of the same events earlier.

So I began my story more or less as I have been writing it for your
eye. I cannot tell you the effect it had on her, the sighs she
breathed, the tears she shed, the indignation she voiced against
my cruel parents, against the terrible girls at Sainte-Marie and the
ones at Longchamps. I would be very sorry if they suffered the
tiniest portion of the evils that she wished them; I would not
myself want to pull a single hair from the head of my most cruel
enemy. From time to time she interrupted me and got up and
walked about and then returned to her place. At another time she
raised her hands and her eyes to heaven, then she buried her head
between my knees. When I spoke of the scene in the dungeon, of
my exorcism, of my *amende honorable*, she practically cried out.
When I reached the end of my story I fell silent, and for some
minutes she lay with her body stretched out on her bed, her face
hidden in the coverlet and her arms across her head. I said: "Dear
Mother, I beg your pardon for causing you such pain; I warned
you, but you would persist . . .", but her only reply was: "The
wicked creatures! The horrible creatures! Only in convents could
people be so lost to human feeling . . . But how could that frail
health have borne so many torments? How were those little limbs
not all broken? How was that delicate machine not wrecked? How
were those bright eyes not dimmed for ever by tears? The cruel
creatures! To bind those arms with cords! . . .", and she took my
arms and kissed them. "To have drowned those eyes with
tears. . . !", and she kissed them . . .[11]

The Prioress's reactions grow more and more orgiastic, and, for a second time, she has an orgasm while in the uncomprehending Suzanne's arms.

This ambush for the reader is a marvellously audacious stroke on Diderot's part, and there is a natural progression, an advance into scepticism, from this episode onwards to the final blowing-of-the-gaff about the de Croismare hoax in the "Preface to the Preceding Work". The novel is revealed as what Stanley Fish calls a "self-consuming artifact" and raises doubts about "innocence" of all kinds, but especially the innocence of those who tell stories and those who listen to them.

We seem to be at the heart of Diderot's way of looking at the world, both as philosopher and as artist. His scepticism is certainly very profound, but it would be a mistake to think of it as pure negativity (expressing "the nothingness of all things"), or for that matter as pessimism, in a La Rochefoucauldian vein; it does not feel like pessimism, let alone cynicism. Suzanne's sufferings, after all, remain a harrowing and all-too-believable possibility that an enlightened society might do something to prevent. Nor is the reader of such horrors being asked to give up generous emotion and indignation; he or she is merely being asked to look more deeply into the lengths to which he can push his questioning and the bottomlessness of the abyss in ourselves into which he asks us to peer.

13

The "Menagerie"

One effect of the great falling-out with Rousseau was that Diderot, who had refused to know Mme d'Epinay, had quite changed in his feelings towards her. He had asked to be introduced to her, and the two had greatly taken to each other.

Mme d'Epinay's return from Geneva in 1759 was an anxious moment for her. For one thing her husband, the farmer-general, was doing his best to bankrupt himself; he would squander 20,000 francs on a day's hunting and lavished vast sums on his mistress. Diderot, who disliked what he knew of him, said that he was "a man who has consumed two millions without saying a single good thing or doing a single good deed."[1] But apart from this, Mme d'Epinay's wish now was to feel she was starting a new life, free from scandal. Thus this approach from Diderot was a boost to her self-confidence. She found him altogether enchanting and his conversation amazing. He had, she said, "given her soul a shake" and enabled her to enjoy the world again.[2]

During her stay in Geneva she had occupied herself writing an autobiographical novel, *The Memoirs of Madame de Montbrillant*.[3] It was an amalgam of fact, semi-fiction and pure invention and told the story of her childhood, her friendships with the *philosophes* and the sufferings of her married life. A good deal of the earlier portions is given over to the heroine's struggles to escape the genial bullying and "despotism" of her self-appointed friend "Desbarres", modelled on the historian and novelist Charles Duclos. Her friends and lovers were recognisably depicted in it, though under invented names, her first lover, Francueil, appearing as "de Formeuse" and Grimm as "Volx". It also told, with some severity, the story of Rousseau ("René") and the Hermitage, in the course of which the fascinating René gradually reveals himself as an incurable quarreller, a hypocrite and a traitor. The novel represented, in a sense, her apologia and a coming-to-terms with her past and was not intended for publication. Intellectually speaking, its hero was Diderot ("Garnier"), whose ideas and *mots* dominate the set-piece scenes of salon conversation.

Diderot, for all his tribulations, had not given up hope of public acceptance as a writer, and, to his elation, the Comédie Française, which had turned down his first play, showed a gratifying interest in *A Father and His Family*, which had several performances in February 1761. He was able to report to Voltaire that, despite bad casting and a hostile *cabal*, it had made a modest success. According to his friend Damilaville, a voice was heard from the stalls exclaiming, "What a reply to *The Philosophers*!" It was, said Diderot, "the word I was waiting for."[4]

It was not just persecution-mania on his part to imagine a *cabal* against himself, but such hostility did not arouse a lust for battle in him, as it did with Voltaire; nor, out of wisdom as well as vanity, was he willing to let it poison his life. Nevertheless, at this period especially, it ran a good deal in his thoughts, connecting in his mind with a vision of the literary scene as a menagerie. The term "menagerie" had originated with Mme de Tencin,[5] who applied it mockingly to her own fashionable and aristocratic *salon*, but for Diderot and others it tended to evoke the hangers-on of tax-farmers and their mistresses: a swarm of paid writers and parasites who made and unmade reputations.

The tax-farmers were, at this time, an immensely influential group in France. With their thirty thousand or so employees, many of them armed and with a right of entry into private dwellings, they were, in Simon Schama's words, "a state within a state. Half a business and finance corporation, half a government."[6] They came in for much abuse and were stock figures for invective; nevertheless, being the most lavish spenders in the kingdom, they were also much courted and altogether lived in a very brilliant style.

Their foible was patronage of the arts and sciences, and the plight of their protégés was once feelingly described by the *abbé* Raynal:

> Here the fashionable thing is to have writers in your employment. Wit has been for some time so much the rage in Paris that the house of even the most humble financier is filled with academicians or with men who aspire to that rank. Yet, in spite of this craze for wit and learning, the financier remains as stupid as ever, the writer as poor as ever. The part the latter has to play is truly agonising. If he wants to retain his post, he is obliged to applaud the dreary talk of his master and the bad taste of his master's wife; to think like the former and talk the latter; to endure the arrogance of the one and the whims of the other; to ingratiate himself with the time-servers or habitués of the household. In short, he has to flatter everyone, even the humblest servants – the doorkeeper, so that he can have access to the house at mealtimes; the footman so that he is not ignored at table when he asks for wine, and lastly the chambermaid, because the fate of a book depends on the opinion she forms of it as she reads it aloud while her mistress is at her dressing-table.[7]

Diderot had a Grub Street friend, the *abbé* Joseph Delaporte, once an ally of Fréron but now his enemy and rival, from whom, during the summer of 1761, Diderot received an inside account of a rich scandal within the tax-farming circle. It concerned the financier Louis-Auguste Bertin de Blagny, a sometime tax-farmer, now enjoying a sinecure as "Treasurer of the Casual Parts". Bertin was a member of the Academy of Inscriptions (elected more for his money than for his learning, so his enemies claimed) and he supported a little entourage of needy writers. Diderot had no reason to be fond of him, for Bertin was the author, or anyway the inspirer, of the skit on himself, *The Wooden Philosophers*.

For some fifteen years Bertin had been the protector of the *Comédie Française* actress Pauline Hus.[8] (It is worth noting that she was one of the cast of Palissot's play *The Philosophers*.) They would spend the summer months in a villa near Passy, but this summer Bertin suspected her, with good reason, of having an affair with the handsome young manager of the Passy spa. He therefore laid a trap for them. Returning home unexpectedly, during one of their assignations, he pretended to notice nothing and spent the evening with his mistress in their normal fashion, dining and playing cards, knowing all the time that his rival had taken refuge on the roof. The unfortunate seducer, having starved and shivered all night on the tiles, made his escape next morning, at the point of the sword; within a few hours, so Diderot retailed to Sophie (12 September 1761), Mlle Hus was on her way back to Paris, in a cab piled high with her belongings, the house at Passy was being stripped, and the Bertin–Hus affair was at an end.

The story of Bertin and Hus now merges, in Diderot's letters, into that of another long-standing affair, between the Comte de Lauragai and the actress Mlle Sophie Arnould. The rich and slightly crazed Comte de Lauragai[9] was one of the more famous dilettantes of his day, and his liaison with the engaging and witty Sophie Arnould[10] one of its best-known love-affairs. For some reason, though, just at this moment, the lovers had fallen out. The Count left Paris to visit Voltaire, it being one of his manias that Voltaire thought him a playwright of genius, and in his absence Mlle Arnould wrote to break off the affair, sending him back not only all his gifts but also their two children.

Diderot did not actually know Sophie, but he was charmed by all he had heard of her, and he naturally blamed the crack-brained Lauragai. Then it came out that, as soon as Sophie had dismissed Lauragai, she had taken the now available (and immensely rich) Bertin de Blagny as her lover. Diderot was disgusted – "the slut," he exclaimed. He told Sophie Volland that the news had upset him more than he could say. "That woman has two children by him [de Lauragai]. He is the man of her choice. There was never any constraint, any concern for appearances, any of the conventional motives for an engagement. If ever there were a sacrament, this was one." Also, he continued, he had just heard of another "sluttishness": the world seemed to be full of it. Bertin had let Mlle Hus keep everything she had had from him, more than that, he had asked for a list of her debts, so that he could pay them; and the grasping creature had blown them up to a quite exorbitant figure. "I don't know why I should tell you these miseries," sighed Diderot.[11]

He had in fact good personal reason to be reflecting on these "miseries". For it was in the *salons* of such as Bertin, and at their lavish tables, that the Palissots and Poinsinets throve and that literary reputations were made and unmade – his own included. He was at the turning-point of his own career, nearly at the end of his labours on the *Encyclopédie*, a semi-success as a dramatist, and as a philosopher a mixture of martyr and butt. Could he be said to have received his due? And given the way success was manufactured, was it even reasonable to expect one's "due"? It was a time to consider rewards and to ask what he was living the literary and *philosophique* life for.

So thinking, he went at the end of September 1761, as he had done before, on a visit to the Le Bretons at Massy. Recently he had been spending half his days in Le Breton's workshop, revising the proofs of the final text-volumes of the *Encyclopédie*. He was tired and not in the best of spirits, the more so in that lately he had had a ferocious quarrel with Nanette. He knew, too, that his days of forced labour were not yet over, for Angélique was growing up and would soon be in need of a dowry. He was thus in a mood to wonder, not too cheerfully, about his future. Nevertheless the letter he wrote to Sophie from the Le Bretons (2 October 1761) is a blithe and very charming one: shorn of a sentence or two at beginning and end, it reads:

. . . I passed two days at Massy with the husband and wife. We went for a walk. Madame Le Breton is a thousand times madder than befits her age, her piety and her character. I would very much like to know what that woman was like in her youth. She was very thick with a certain Madame de la Martelière. So, if the old proverb be true, enough said. You know, or maybe you do not know, that I sometimes amuse myself by playing the role of the passionate lover towards her. She does not misunderstand it, nor does her husband, and it gives a pleasant and gay tone to the conversation.

It is beginning to get cold. Yesterday we sat around a beautiful fire. It was made from the staves of an old barrel. The one with the bung in it displayed its opening to us all aflame. The extravagant old creature said to me: "Philosopher, you have been soliciting my favours for a long time now. Here's your moment! Go and purge yourself there [indicating the bung-hole] and I am yours."

There is a cœnobite, a very happy personage, in the corner of the farmyard. He drinks, he eats; he grows fatter visibly. He does not go out very often. I cannot tell you whether he spends much of his time in reflection. I think he belongs to the sect of Epicurus. His gaiety upon leaving his cell gives the best possible impression of his way of employing his time. We went to see him twice a day. I can assure you he bothered himself very little with us. When he first arrived he was very young and had no name. I baptised him Antony, or Dom Antonio.[12] He is fed and looked after by the farmer's wife. He is not difficult to please. I do not mean that he does not do a lot of grunting, but this is not so much from bad temper as because it is what his temperament demands. If the rest of his history interests you, I will inform myself. I am not inquisitive. I enjoy people, without troubling to know who they are, or where they come from. Once, when I showed my hostess I was surprised by her changeableness of mood, she gave me a rather curious reply. "My theory," she said, "is that there are no religious people, there are only hypocrites. It makes no difference going down on your knees, or praying, or keeping vigils, or fasting, or piously joining your hands, or raising your heart or your eyes to heaven: Nature does not change. One remains what one is. A man may be dressed in a blue coat, wear a shoulder-knot on his shoulder, hang a long sword at his side and stick plumes in his hat. But it's no use – all that looking fierce and lifting up his head and frowning terribly; he is still a coward pretending to be a man of spirit. When I am reserved, serious and demure, it means I am not *me*. I have a church air, a 'great-world' air, a counting-house air and a mistress air. There you have my *life of grimace*. As for my real life, my true face, my natural style, I don't indulge it very often, but it's a different matter altogether. It doesn't last long; but for the moment I talk all sorts of nonsense; and I only stop because I seem to hear my mother saying 'Now, my girl!' Then I hold my tongue, and I am back behind the veil. When I am *me* with other people, I almost always repent later in church. All the same, the people I like most are the ones I'm most able to be my disgraceful natural self with. When people *press in on me*, I'm as proper and goody-goody as a stuffed prune."

Little Count Lauragai has left Mademoiselle Arnou. Instead of living in bliss on the bosom of one of the most loveable girls in the world, he lets his stupid vanity take hold of him and send him careering from Paris to Montbard [home of the naturalist Buffon] and from Montbard to Geneva [home of Voltaire]. He has gone there with a sheaf of splendid verse, all written by somebody else, and he will sit writing it out again at Voltaire's side, to convince him it is his own. He's a strange creature. He has acquired two young chemists. One day, he gets up at four o'clock in the morning. He goes and wakes them in their attics. He puts them in his carriage. The six horses have brought them to Sèvres before they have opened their eyes. He shows them into a little house. When they are installed there, he says to them: "Sirs, here you are. I need a discovery. You are not to leave until it has been made. Goodbye: I will be back in a week. You have got all you need here: retorts, stoves, and charcoal. Food will be provided. Get to work."

So saying, he shuts the door on them and is gone. He returns. The discovery has been made. It is explained to him, and in the very same instant he believes he has made it himself. He congratulates himself. He couldn't be more proud of his achievement, even standing there before those poor devils it really belongs to – whom he treats like idiots and starves into the bargain. What he is saying is, really: "You have genius and no money, I have money and I want some genius. Let us come to an understanding, you shall have breeches to wear, and I shall have glory."

I shall not be leaving Paris this autumn. One annoyance follows upon another. I am ruining my eyesight over plates, all spotted with numerals and letters, and, amidst all this weary labour, there is the bitter thought that the fruit of it all will be abuse, persecution, torment and insults. A charming prospect, don't you agree? Friend Grimm may make his fine speeches, but that is the truth of it; and I cannot live on dreams any longer. – A delicious meal; a book to one's taste; a solitary walk in the cool of evening; a conversation in which one opens one's heart and pours forth all one's sensibility; a strong emotion, of the kind that brings tears to the eyes, flutters the heart, chokes one's voice and ravishes one's soul with ectasy – whether at the story of some generous deed or from one's own tender feelings; health, gaiety, liberty, idleness, ease. *Those* are the true happiness, I shall never know any other.[13]

Running through this letter are at least three separate themes which obscurely hang together in Diderot's mind and make one. We might spell them out thus:

One is oneself, and at heart only oneself, and had better remember it. All the rest of existence is a lying performance and a "life of grimace"; and perhaps there is no escaping the life of grimace, but the spirit can have no home or happiness there.

Or on the contrary, maybe if one tried hard enough, or had the right temperament (if one were the Comte de Lauragai, say) one could tell lies to oneself perfectly successfully. The art is in really *wanting* to believe them.

But then again, consider the pig Dom Antonio. Dom Antonio pays no attention to public opinion and gets on with the serious business of enjoying life; and when he grunts, it is not out of any complaint against the running of the universe, but out of sheer self-importance. This pig seems to have made an excellent and philosophical adjustment to life.

Or again, we might simply label the themes, for convenience, as "Being oneself", "Wanting to be a genius" and "The rewards of life".

All the themes running through Diderot's letter to Sophie bear on a question that, at this particular period, Diderot had much reason to ask himself: "What has my life been for?" After fifteen years of gruelling labour and the most fearful vicissitudes – organised vilification, defection by collaborators, suppression and threats of arrest and so on – he had brought the text volumes of the *Encyclopédie* to completion. With mixed success, he had published some philosophical treatises and two plays – the plays, in particular, having brought him as much obloquy as praise. So what, it seems a good moment to ask, has he been doing it all *for*? The answer "To spread enlightenment" misses the real point of the question, which is, rather, What has he been doing it all for *in terms of personal satisfaction*? The question is a natural one, you might say, to a needy author when being shown the comforts of a publisher's life. But Diderot was never an envious man, and the question puzzles him in a wider way; the more he considers it, the more it seems to reveal itself as a genuinely open one – not to be asked in a spirit of resentment or pessimism, but impartially, philosophically, even light-heartedly. The complexities and philosophic reversals and fascinating ironies it enfolds begin to seem inexhaustible.

For, a first possibility, was he doing it all for money? If so, he was a fool. An editor's meagre rewards might just suffice for himself; but it will not be too long, he tells Sophie, before his daughter Angélique will be reaching puberty (and entering her own "life of grimace"), and where will her dowry come from? Not from the *Encyclopédie*. Some more plays, some more imaginary marriages, may be needed from his pen to finance a real one.

Can it be, then, that he is doing it for the pleasure of it, and for happiness? This least of all. For happiness, true enjoyment of life, is a thing of the moment and is offered to all for the asking. It is a matter of the senses and the heart, and . . . Here the professional Man of Feeling takes over Diderot's pen.

Can he have been doing it for glory? If so, for all his friend Grimm may say about fame and laurels, he had better give up the idea and not feed himself any longer with vain fancies; for the reality will not be glory but just more persecution and abuse of the kind there has been so much of already.

Could he then, perhaps, have been doing it out of a more secret hope, that he might be allowed to consider himself a "genius"? One would certainly endure much for the sake of that. One sees what the Comte de Lauragais is ready to do to be *reputed* a genius, and no doubt his way is wonderfully absurd. Or is it so absurd? It is such a beautifully direct way as almost *to amount to genius*. One says to oneself, "I could never have done that!", and is not that what one says about works of genius? (It is precisely what Rameau the nephew says: "I have never heard them play the overture to *Les Indes galantes*, I have never heard them sing *Profonds abîmes du Ténare* or *Nuit, éternelle nuit*, without saying to myself wretchedly, "There's what you'll never achieve yourself, however long you live.)"[14]

Plainly the Comte de Lauragai is not "being himself", indeed he is being exactly the opposite of himself, in that he is dressing himself in stolen garments; but here another possibility opens up. For the Count (he is a favourite butt of Diderot's at this time) wants not just to be thought a genius by others, but to believe it himself; indeed he seems actually to be able to do so. This, too, one could regard, with some awe, as a kind of genius.

Already the concepts "being oneself" and "wanting to be a genius" can be seen as entering into a sort of game or system of exchange.

Then we must look more closely at the pig Dom Antonio. For to
the pleasures of gluttony the hedonist Dom Antonio adds the
pleasures of self-approval. When Dom Antonio grunts so loudly it
is not out of ill-humour but out of self-confidence and because it
befits his character. It is reminiscent of what, Diderot tells
Sophie in an earlier letter, he most likes in the naturalist Buffon –
the unabashed and ringing tones in which the great man pays
compliments to his own talents. (Would it be a cruel chore for
Buffon, as Director of the Académie, to have to produce so many
official eulogies? Well yes it would, he tells Diderot, but it has to
be done. "So I'll praise them, I'll praise them very well, and I
shall be applauded. Could any subject be barren to a man of real
eloquence?"[15]) To grunt as complacently as this seems as if it
might be a sign of greatness. The Nephew in *Rameau's Nephew*
dreams enviously of *snoring* like a great man. The admirer of
Diderot's great novel will have the feeling of entering familiar
territory.

14

Rameau's Nephew

The novel *Rameau's Nephew* takes as its imaginary moment in time the April of the year 1761, and it would appear that Diderot began the writing of it not long after. One can, indeed, fix this imaginary date quite precisely with regard to certain details, like the operas currently in performance at the Opéra, the age of Diderot's daughter and the date of death of Rameau the Nephew's wife. On the other hand, the controversies and vendettas which figure in the novel sometimes date back a decade or so, and in successive expansions and revisions (for he went on working at the novel for the rest of his life) he drew on events and preoccupations belonging to later years. As to when he began to write the novel, the truth is we have no definite evidence at all. Diderot, who once described himself as "born as communicative as it is possible to be", never once refers to this, his masterpiece, and, at least so far as we know, never showed it to anyone.

There was such a person as Rameau's nephew. He was called Jean-François Rameau and was born in Dijon some time about 1716. He was the son of a musician, though a less distinguished one than his uncle, and himself became a not very successful composer. A set of *New Keyboard Pieces* by him has been lost and is only known to us through a review by Fréron. Like his uncle, he was fond of giving his pieces fantastic titles, and there was one called "The Encyclopaedia". According to Fréron it was fairly bizarre and ended with a grotesque and very noisy *chute*.

With his extravagant theories, his chronic poverty and his love of music and subversive jokes, Rameau the Nephew was a well-known figure on the Paris scene, and descriptions of him by friends tally closely with Diderot's fictional portrait. Diderot almost certainly knew him, for he quotes a saying of Rameau's in his *Salon* for 1767, and Rameau, in his epic poem *The Raméïde*, mentions "the wise Denis" as one of his friends.

According to his old schoolfriend, the writer Jacques Cazotte, Jean-François Rameau was a baffled genius.

> Rameau's sallies were *instructive* sallies . . . They were not *bons mots*; they were remarks that seemed to spring from the most perfect understanding of the human heart. His appearance, which was truly burlesque, gave an extraordinary piquancy to his jokes, which were all the more unexpected since he normally played the part of a madman. This person, born a musician like his uncle, never plumbed the depths of the art, but he was born full of song and had a strange facility for finding, quite impromptu, an agreeable and expressive setting for any words that you gave him . . . He was horribly and comically ugly and very often a bore, for his genius inspired him only on rare occasions; but if the verve came to him, he could make you laugh till you cried . . . That strange man nursed a passion for glory and never found any way of attaining it.[1]

His friend Piron remembered him making fun of his uncle, yet draping himself in his great name; and another friend[2] describes a favourite theory of his, that the aim of all great feats, whether of genius or heroism, was *mastication*. All that showy sort of thing, he would say (with "a very picturesque motion of the jaws") had one aim and one result alone: to put something between one's teeth.

Let us remind ourselves of the action of Diderot's novel *Rameau's Nephew*. One day at the Café de la Régence, near the Palais Royal, the philosopher (we will call him Diderot-*Moi*) is accosted by a raffish and dishevelled-looking acquaintance, a nephew of the great composer Jean-Philippe Rameau. This Rameau the Nephew, so Diderot-*Moi* tells us, is one of the strangest creatures in all France, a mixture of nobility and baseness, of good sense and madness. "The ideas of decency and indecency must have got extraordinarily confused in his head, for he displays the good qualities that Nature has given him without ostentation and the bad ones without shame." Also, he is never the same twice running; one month he is pale and as thin as a rake, like a man in the last throes of consumption; the next he will be as sleek as a regular diner-out or a Bernardine monk; one day he

NEVEU DE RAMEAU

Rameau's Nephew

will be in rags, slinking along like a beggar, the next day curled
and powdered and strutting like a man of fashion. He lives from
day to day; and if he sleeps in a stable, as is sometimes his lot, you
may see the remains of his bedding in his hair. "I do not really
care for such characters," remarks Diderot-*Moi* primly, "though
some people grow quite friendly with them."[3] Still, he says, they
are amusing to meet once a year. They liven things up, they jolt
people out of set attitudes. They have a queer way of bringing
truth out into the open. Thus Rameau has his patrons, if only for
his entertainment-value. With malicious relish Diderot-*Moi* tells
us how he once saw Rameau in a well-to-do household, where he
had a standing invitation to dinner – on the condition, that he did
not speak at table without permission.

He kept quiet and ate with fury: it was excellent to see him in this
state of bondage. If he felt tempted to break his contract and
opened his mouth, his fellow-diners would all cry: "Oh, Rameau!"

At this his eyes would blaze with rage, and he fell back even more furiously on his food.[4]

The Café de la Régence is a haunt for chess-players, and the two fall into a discussion of the famous players around them. Rameau affects to despise these: only two of them have any genuine talent, he says. "You seem very hard to please," remarks Diderot-*Moi*. "Yes I am," says Rameau, "when it comes to chess and women and poetry and oratory and music – all that sort of nonsense. For what is the use of *mediocrity* in such things?" "But," counters Diderot-*Moi*, "do there not have to be a hundred mediocrities to produce one of that sublime breed, the *genius*?" Rameau reacts churlishly to this pious tribute to "genius". It puts him in mind of his odious "genius" uncle, who never did a thing for him or, so far as he can hear, for anyone else either. There you have a typical man of genius, he says, good at one thing and one thing only and perfectly unaware of what it means to be a citizen or a father or a mother or a brother or a relation or a friend. Why – says Rameau, warming to the theme – probably all the evil in the world has come about through men of genius. A minister of the crown once proved to him that, for the sake of the public good, children with the stamp of genius on them ought to be stifled at birth. "All the same," replies Diderot-*Moi*, "enemies of genius like your minister would reckon to be geniuses themselves." "They might secretly think it, yes," says Rameau, "but I'm certain they would never admit it." "You seem to have acquired a terrible hatred of genius," says Diderot-*Moi*, "yet I remember a time when what made you despair was just to be an ordinary man-in-the-street. You will never be happy if you let the 'for' and the 'against' upset you equally . . ."[5]

The conversation comes round to Rameau's own affairs. He has just suffered an appalling set-back in his career. He had found his way into a most admirable *niche*, a household where he was fed, clothed and fêted to his heart's content on the strength of his impeccable qualification – as ignoramus, fool, lunatic, idler, crook and glutton. Nobody could have enjoyed a better situation or been more suited to it; and by his own act he has lost it! He has had the unforgivable folly to, for once, *not* be a fool – to make an intelligent joke and show a little taste, wit and reason. For this, he has very justly been thrown out into the street and stripped of all his pay and perquisites.

This painful train of thought leads Rameau, in an effort to salvage his self-esteem, to expound the great contribution to human thought and enlightenment by which he originally secured his enviable place in Eden. It is the science of *parasitism*. For Diderot-*Moi*'s benefit he examines the many branches and divisions of this science: posture, voice, facial expression, measure, reserve and timing. Meanwhile, in a wild pantomime, he impersonates the rival parasites (very much his inferior in talent) who infested the same desirable household, and he goes on to enact the higher-level parasitism of their hosts. It is the world envisioned as parasitism, with himself as its interpreter and seer. But he has to admit there are certain geniuses of parasitism whose work leaves him feeling humbled. There is, for instance, the great Bouret[6] who, to ingratiate himself with a high minister of the Crown, alienated the affections of his own pet dog, had a mask made in the likeness of the minister and, by feeding and fondling the dog while wearing the mask and beating it at other times, taught the dog to fear him and to rush towards the minister as to a long-lost master. "The mask! The mask!" exclaims Rameau reverently. "I would give one of my fingers to have thought of the mask."

The philosopher Diderot-*Moi*, throughout this disquisition, and indeed throughout the rest of the dialogue, adopts the stance of the *honnête homme* or man of good will, in turn intrigued, amused, unwillingly impressed and disgusted by his shameless interlocutor. For a while, when Rameau is extolling the beauty of great crime, Diderot-*Moi* becomes, not too surprisingly, positively terrified, though by the end of their conversation he has recovered his composure, and they part with ironic good will.

Evidently, the novelist Diderot has decided to explore what he is aware of in himself as a double identity. On one side there is the enlightened *honnête homme*, who believes in the citizenly virtues and the common pleasures of life, and also in those greater pleasures which spring from altruism (being inclined to make speeches about these latter). And then there is the hostile *alter ego*, spokesman of "baseness" but also of the temptations of "genius" and the dangerous and cynical doctrines that go with genius: altogether a most formidable inward critic, continually whispering treasonable and seemingly unanswerable objections to the *honnête* outlook on life. The enterprise in the novel *Rameau's Nephew* is to give these two portions of himself independent life and to compel the insidious critic to be no longer a whisperer but to come out into the open and defend his position. Rameau – it is a suggestive touch – has a stentorian voice.

We should notice that Diderot-*Moi*, in this very unlike the real-life Diderot, makes no pretensions to "genius"; and as a debater he is definitely outmatched by Rameau, though he achieves some malicious personal "scores". He comes out as a somewhat Pharisaic and not too impressive figure, who has to reassure himself with the thought of Rameau's "baseness". At one point, though, he halts Rameau and makes an honest avowal of his own ethical theories. They are not too far from the theories expressed by the real-life Diderot in that letter to Sophie written from Le Breton's.

> I do not despise pleasures of the senses; I have a palate myself, and it relishes delicate dishes and a delicious wine; I have a heart and have eyes, and I love to see a pretty woman, I love to feel the firm contours of her bosom, to press her lips to mine, to drink pleasure from her look and expire with pleasure in her arms. Sometimes when I am with friends a little debauch, even a rather wild one, does not offend me; but I will not conceal from you that what is a thousand times sweeter to me is to have succoured the unfortunate, to have settled a painful feud, to have given helpful advice, read a delightful book, strolled with a man or woman dear to my heart, been an instructive father to my children, written a page to be proud of, fulfilled the duties of my estate, spoken sweet and tender words to my beloved, earning her embrace.[7]

It is a recognisable caricature of one side of Diderot himself, a side he was very ready to question and expose to irony but which he would never disown.

The philosophic systems of the two speakers are of course quite different; they are different not only in content, but in kind.

Diderot-*Moi*'s is an assemblage of conclusions – good solid beliefs
which an "enlightened" thinker might honourably hold.
Rameau's on the other hand, we begin to find, is a form of
intellectual motion, one to which, for intrinsic reasons, there can
be no conclusion. He proves, if not the truth of Diderot-*Moi*'s
remark, "You will never be happy if you let the 'for' and the
'against' upset you equally," at least that for every "for" there is
an "against" which leads on to a new and different "for".

The novel is called, and is, a satire, and as such its central joke
may be said to run thus: *One would need to stoop incredibly low* to
consort with scoundrels like Palissot, Fréron, Poinsinet and their
like, as well as their corrupt patrons the Bertins and the Huses,
and so be able to report on them at first hand; and here is a man,
Rameau the Nephew, willing and eager to stoop in just such a
way, even to put his whole genius into it. Already we glimpse the
beauty of Diderot's vicarious revenge on his enemies, a revenge
that, as a *philosophe* and man of self-respect, it would be
unbecoming to take in his own person. Rameau's unbridled
scurrility towards the Palissots and the Frérons (the
"menagerie") can be represented as shocking to the right-
thinking Diderot-*Moi*, or at any rate he need not be held to have
complicity in it.

Rameau, moreover, possesses a special talent (perhaps his only
real talent), a gift for pantomime. He is, that is to say, an expert
on the outward show and husk of human behaviour; and such a
gift is a great aid in projecting oneself into the lives and thoughts
of the Palissots and the Bertins, creatures who are *nothing but*
outward show and husk, mere automata operated by the springs
of interest and vanity. Rameau sets up as an expert on the
postures and "positions" taken up by mankind, a *practising*
expert; and his report from the Bertin–Hus inferno (which, being
expelled from it, he paints as a lost paradise) provides the *Dunciad*
aspect, as it were, of Diderot's novel. The difference between
Rameau and Diderot-*Moi* comes out as strongly here as any-
where else. Diderot-*Moi* himself likes complacently to think of the
world as a pantomime ("The pantomime of crooks is what makes
the world go round"), but for him, and as he supposes for
Rameau too, the pantomime is to be enjoyed as a spectacle: one

will observe it from some remote vantage-point or, as Montaigne puts it, "perched on the epicycle of Mercury". Rameau will have none of this holier-than-thou aloofness. If he is such an expert on "positions", he says, it is because he has not been too proud to take them.

But we must now remind ourselves of the significance of the novel's title. This is a novel about a man who, being the nephew of a famous figure and a genius, has had his life overshadowed by the concept of "genius" and by the tormenting question, "Am I a genius?" Rameau the Nephew is plainly obsessed with the subject, so that it underlies almost everything he says and directs almost every twist and turn of his tortuous and compelling arguments. It is true, he declares early on that he has no genius. "Yes, yes, I am mediocre, and it makes me angry." But we are not inclined to believe him sincere. Or rather, we realise that he cannot possibly rest in that proposition, any more than in any other proposition, and will move on – the hope that leads him on in this case being, perhaps, that frankness on this scale may actually amount to genius. At any point, with endless resourcefulness, Rameau can find a way to postpone the fatal question, "Am I a genius?"

Diderot has here found a way of raising, in fictional form, a profound truth: that once the subject of "genius" has been raised (and in the Nephew's case it has been raised inescapably, from his birth, by the inheritance of a famous name) it is not really possible, or at all events not truly human, to decide once and for all that one does not possess it. What one will say to oneself, rather, is that there are many different kinds of genius, and "genius" may lie in finding a new one. For Rameau the prospect of, after all, discovering himself to be a genius lurks round every corner; or rather, there is always some further corner round which he may take refuge from the avenging thought that he is not a genius. He will not be pinned down by Diderot-*Moi*'s broad-minded cliché that many things can be forgiven to genius and that, in the perspective of history, it does not matter that Racine was a bad citizen, a bad friend, a bad lover; that his vices will be forgotten, while his *Phèdre* and *Athalie* will endure. Those are the platitudes that men of good will love to utter, wanting "genius" to be neatly labelled or fixed for public admiration like a public statue; they are the notions of those who have never themselves tasted the fatal ambition. For one of the truths that Rameau has grasped, and is in continual flight from, is that they might erect a statue to you, and *still* you might not believe yourself a "genius". To believe it you need your own self-approval and this is what, however hard you chase it, or even – as one might say – however much genius you put into chasing it, you will never attain.

We may label Rameau in certain traditional ways. Philosophically speaking he is a Sceptic, instantly able to spot the weak points or self-contradiction in any proposition put forward by Diderot-*Moi*, and more particularly by himself. He shows in a high degree the conviction I have attributed to the real-life Diderot: that things might simply be totally different, not in the least what custom or the powers-that-be would have people think.

Further, ethically speaking, he is a Cynic; or rather, a complete and systematic cynic is what he makes his best effort to be, but the enterprise proves frustratingly difficult. It proves difficult, for one reason, because scepticism is a very doubtful ally to cynicism, which is, after all, a kind of faith. The presumptions of cynicism are one of the things that the novel *Rameau's Nephew* looks at with scepticism.

It is plain that the cynical and pantomimical *abbé* Galiani has made some contribution to the *persona* of Rameau the Nephew. (Diderot-*Moi* says at one point that the follies of Rameau, the tales of Galiani and the extravaganzas of Rabelais have sometimes made him "dream profoundly" and have furnished him with a store of comic masks which he fits on to the faces of grave personages.[8]) Thus I am reminded of a striking passage in Nietzsche's *Beyond Good and Evil*. The study of the "average" human being, writes Nietzsche, is the "most unpleasant and malodorous" part of a philosopher's duties. Nevertheless it has to be done; and fortunately there is a short cut to it, in the shape of *cynics* – that is to say those who frankly declare their own animality and "commonness". Cynicism, he says, is the only form in which common souls can come close to honesty, "and the higher man must prick up his ears at every cynicism, whether coarse or refined ... There are even cases in which fascination mingles with disgust; namely where, by a caprice of nature, such an indiscreet goat or monkey is touched with genius, as in the case of the *abbé* Galiani."

Nietzsche puts the case for cynicism admirably here, and what he goes on to say has some relevance for us too.

> Whenever anyone seeks and *wants* to see only hunger, sexual desire and vanity, as though these were the actual and sole motives of human action; in brief, whenever anyone speaks "badly" of man –but does not speak *ill* of him – the lover of knowledge should listen carefully and with diligence, as indeed he should in general lend an ear whenever anyone speaks without indignation. For the indignant man may indeed stand higher, morally speaking, than the laughing and self-satisfied satyr, but in every other sense he is the more commonplace, less interesting, less instructive case.[9]

This contrast of the cynic and the less interesting "indignant moralist" hits off the confrontation of Rameau and Diderot-*Moi* very neatly.

Rameau claims not only to be a cynic but to be very advanced in his cynicism. He has, for instance, had a thought of genius about how a cynic may make advantageous use of the classics. The classic moralists, like La Bruyère and Molière, are regarded as one of the glories of French culture and – so Rameau gleefully points out – rightly so, if, like himself, you know the way to read and profit from them.

> I learn from them everything one must do and everything one must not say. Thus, when I read Molière's *L'Avare [The Miser]* I tell myself, "Be a miser if you like, but be sure not to speak like a miser." When I read *Tartuffe*, I say to myself, "Be a hypocrite if you choose, but do not speak like a hypocrite." Cling to the vices which suit you, but do not have the tone and the appearance that go with them, for fear that they make you a laughing-stock and subject for comedy. Now, in order to avoid such a tone and such an appearance, you have to *know* them; and these authors have given excellent pictures of them. . . . I am not one of those who despise the moralists.[10]

This subversion of the *grand siècle* inheritance seems to have been one of the master-thoughts of the French eighteenth century, and we meet it again in Laclos' novel *Les Liaisons dangereuses (Dangerous Acquaintances)*, where Mme de Merteuil tells Valmond how she learned to be a libertine by studying the severest moralists. Rameau, however, in his fertile way, elaborates it into half-a-dozen further enticing paradoxes – such as that the advantage of his reading-method is that it is *systematic* and a way of doing on principle what other men only do by instinct . . . For he might well *want* to be a laughing-stock (it is the shortest way to a great man's heart), but whereas other men become laughing-stocks in spite of themselves, he will be one only when he so chooses.

Nevertheless – and this is his cross – for all Rameau's vaunting, and for all his brilliant sophistry, cynicism lets him down. In its outlook on life cynicism opts for the rock bottom, as being a place perhaps not very comfortable but at least secure. But, so Diderot's novel continually makes us ask, is it really so secure? What happens if you take cynicism literally, as a serious philosophy, and actually try to live by it? The answer is quite unexpected. There *is* no rock bottom. It is impossible to take your stand on cynical certainties, for they shift and give way under your feet, and you find yourself not standing on a rock but pursuing an ever-retreating, ever-changing, shadow.

As a cynic one may take one's stand on the "average" human's "average" desires – on food, wine, sex and soft beds – regarding them as the solid goods, the goods that do not let you down: the *only* goods, if people would be frank enough to admit it. This is the "mastication" theory of the real-life Rameau, but for Diderot's Rameau it is a chimera and a deception. For, for him, with his obsession with genius, these goods lose all substance almost before they have been proclaimed and are revealed as mere tokens; their real value is as proofs that you are "great" enough and a "genius" enough to secure them. It is only the conventional, or conventionally unconventional, Diderot-*Moi*, not the intellectually adventurous Rameau, who knows how to be a hedonist.

Cynicism may suggest to you again (it suggests it to Rameau's Nephew) that to declare yourself *dishonest* and a total hypocrite is a superior and ultimate form of honesty. But nothing of the kind. Total dishonesty is not so easily achieved, and honesty has a way of breaking in unawares. To claim to have achieved it is itself a hypocrisy, and there is no more ultimacy in this second-degree honesty than in the first.

The same, or something similar, is true of self-abasement. If the ordinary satisfactions of vanity are denied to one, one may seek food for one's vanity in humiliation, that is to say in the perfection of one's own self-abasement. This, according to the great authority La Rochefoucauld, is one of the innumerable ruses and disguises to which *amour propre* may resort. In its desperation to survive, *amour propre* may even go over to its enemies.

> . . . it can live on nothing, it makes do equally well with things and with the lack of them; it even joins the faction of those who make war upon it; it enters into their schemes, and, what is amazing, it joins them in hating itself, it conspires its own destruction, it works for its own ruin. The truth is, all it is concerned with is *existing*, and so long as it can exist, it will cheerfully be its own enemy.[11]

The Nephew certainly essays such a going-over-to-the-enemy, eagerly wooing his enemies' judgement on himself as "Rameau the mad, the impertinent, the ignorant, the idle, the gluttonous, the buffoonish, the big-headed." Also he will claim that his over-riding concern is at all costs to *exist*; but this claim will prove as slippery, and as little offer a resting-place, as any other. For one thing, human flesh is not strong enough for perfect self-abasement. To Rameau's account of his recent catastrophe, his expulsion from the Hus–Bertin household, Diderot-*Moi*'s malicious response is that he had better go back to Hus and throw himself at her feet, crying "Pardon, Madame, it was all a mistake. I promise not to show common-sense again as long as I live!" While Diderot-*Moi* is speaking thus, Rameau performs a beauti-ful pantomime of this very scene; but he has to admit that – humiliatingly – he could not perform it in actual fact. "I, Rameau, nephew of the man they call the great Rameau, whom one sees in the Palais Royal gardens walking upright, with his arms swinging free, now that Carmontelle has drawn him bent-backed, with his hands hidden under coat-tails! . . . No, Monsieur, it just cannot be."[12] It is a matter of simple human weakness. Self-humiliation is only acceptable if one *wants* to perform it, and it so happens that today he is plagued by an absurd self-respect which prevents it. Today he does not want to "kiss Hus's arse", though he knows quite well that some other day he will be perfectly happy to do so. One cannot will oneself to will things. "I am very ready to be abject, but I want to be so of my own free will."[13]

The passage is intended to tell us, among other things, something about pantomime. In pantomime, Rameau can cheerfully sink to any depths required, just as in pantomime, and without any actual instruments, he can rise to his uncle's musical heights and give, if not a superlative performance, at least a superlative performance of a performance ("You see, we too know how to place a tritone, and a *quinte superflue*"). Pantomime, we perceive, is as painless a road to genius as the one found out by the Comte de Lauragai, who simply stole it from others.

In actuality, though, and as a living and suffering mortal, Rameau finds himself brought to a stop by certain unexpected obstacles. He believes himself to have killed shame, but he finds that shame has an odd capacity for survival and redeployment. It is a shame to him that he should have been fool enough to, for once, *not* be a fool. It puts him to shame that, with all his dedication, he has failed to become a really successful parasite or pimp. To put it more generally, he is ashamed to find himself hindered by shame.

There is a logical problem here that has not been much studied outside the pages of Diderot, and the thinker who comes nearest to doing so is Hegel. It is all part of the bizarre history of this novel that, as has been mentioned, it first reached the reading public in 1805 (more than twenty years after Diderot's death) in a German translation by Goethe, made from a clandestine copy of a manuscript in St Petersburg, and that it first appeared in French in 1821, not in Diderot's own words, but in a mangled translation from Goethe! Now it so happened that, at the moment Goethe's translation appeared, Hegel was at work on his *The Phenomenology of Spirit*, and he made use of a passage from Diderot's novel, using the Nephew, whom Goethe had referred to as a "self-estranged soul", as an exemplar of "The World of Self-Alienated Spirit".

There is, according to Hegel, a stage in the coming to self-consciousness of Spirit, which requires that Spirit, in the shape of "the disrupted consciousness", should embrace ignobility and "baseness", or rather should experience the emptiness of the distinction between "noble" and "ignoble". In speaking about itself, it must shamelessly express "the perversion of every Notion and reality, the universal deception of itself and others (for the shamelessness which gives utterance to this deception is just for this reason the greatest truth)". This kind of talk, says Hegel, quoting *Rameau's Nephew*, is "the madness of the musician [i.e. the Nephew] who heaped and mixed together thirty arias, Italian, French, tragic, comic, of every sort; now with a deep bass he descended into hell, then, contracting his throat, he rent the vault of heaven with a falsetto tone, frantic and soothed, imperious and mocking, by turns." It is a kind of talk or performance which, to what Hegel calls the "tranquil" or "honourable" consciousness, the consciousness which sees the Good and the True as residing in harmony (he is of course referring to Diderot-*Moi*) seems like pure madness. But in truth, says Hegel, what is really to be found in such Rameau-esque shamelessness and discordant notes is "a strain of reconciliation" and "in their subversive depths the all-powerful note which restores Spirit to itself."[14]

We cannot force *Rameau's Nephew* as a whole into Hegel's system, nor does Hegel attempt to do so; nevertheless the instinct that drew him to Diderot's novel was a good and profound one. Indeed quite often, and not just where there is direct quotation, the *Phenomenology* seems to read like a commentary on Diderot's book. It is hard to read Hegel's description of the Sceptic, and his twofold consciousness of the Unchangeable and the protean Changeable, and not think of Rameau:

> It [the sceptical self-consciousness] affirms the nullity of ethical principles, and lets its conduct be governed by those very principles. Its deeds and its words always belie one another, and equally it has the doubly contradictory consciousness of unchangeableness and sameness, and of utter contingency and

non-identity with itself . . . Point out likeness or identity to it, and
it will point out unlikeness or non-identity; and when it is now
confronted with what it has just asserted, it turns round and
points out likeness or identity . . . it is merely the contradictory
movement in which one opposite does not come to rest in its
opposite, but in it only produces itself afresh as an opposite.[15]

The feature that Hegel seizes on in Rameau is his wild
changeableness and fragmentation; and this is something that
the novel itself insists on from its very first words, that is to say its
epigraph. According to the quotation from Horace, Rameau is a
man "born under the capricious malice of all the Vertumnuses"
(Vertumnus being the god who presides over seasons and the
weather, and mutability generally). He is the epitome of
changeableness and inconsistency, a fact which Diderot-*Moi*
harps on continually, and which indeed we are given plenty of
opportunity to witness. Nevertheless we must also remember the
very last words of the novel and Rameau's parting shot to

Carmontelle's print of the musician Jean Philippe Rameau (erroneously
named in the caption)

Diderot-*Moi*: "Is it not true that I am always the same?" To this Diderot-*Moi* can only return a rueful "Alas, unfortunately, yes!" Changeableness, we must accept, is Rameau's way of life, his *unchanging* way of life.

Let us consider, too, with Hegel in mind, that intriguing remark of Rameau's, thrown off so casually: "I, Rameau, nephew of the man they call 'The great Rameau', whom one sees in the Palais Royal gardens walking upright, with his arms swinging free, now that Carmontelle has drawn him bent-backed, with his hands hidden under coat-tails." He is referring to a well-known print of Carmontelle's which immortalised the composer as he was wont to appear on his daily stroll: a spindle-shanked and hollow-stomached man, with his hands tucked behind him to give him aplomb and to disguise his stoop; and his point is that the very making of this famous print has meant that the great Rameau will henceforth not resemble it. Far from wanting to look like his portrait, the great Rameau now finds himself throwing out his chest and strutting like a prince. It is a neat and most beautiful example of the Hegelian dialectic, of which Hegel writes that "The negative itself perishes along with the positive whose negative it is."

Let me try to summarise the philosophical and logical discovery that this extraordinary novel has managed to present. It is that moral concepts can be used, as mathematicians say, "recursively". "Fool", "genius", "parasite", "honest", "performance" and "shame" are all terms that may be used to manipulate the very sentences in which they themselves occur. One may have a "genius" for passing oneself off as a genius, one may think it the acme of honesty to admit one's dishonesty, one may feel shame at experiencing shame, one may give a performance of a performance; and, alas, that is not the end of it, there is further and infinite regress in prospect. The pattern is drawn out by the Nephew with particular completeness in his pronouncement about the "Fool".

There is no better role with great people than that of the "fool". For many years there was an official royal fool; on the other hand, there never was an official royal sage. I am Bertin's fool and many other people's fool, perhaps yours at this moment; or maybe you are mine. A wise man would not have a fool. So he who has a fool is not wise; and if he is not wise, he is a fool; and perhaps, if he is a king, he is his own fool's fool.[15]

One might perhaps think of this as a completed circle, but in fact the king being his fool's fool is not the end of it, and the process of thought that Diderot has envisaged is endless. It is an alarming discovery; and to have invented a character, Rameau's nephew, who *lives* this discovery is a claim to greatness that no one will ever deny to Diderot.

Denis Diderot, drawn
from life by Jean-
Baptiste Greuze not
later than 1767
(*The Pierpont Morgan
Library, New York*)

The Keep of the
Château de Vincennes,
where Diderot was
imprisoned in 1749
(*Mary Evans Picture
Library*)

Detail from the Plan de Turgot of 1739
(*Photograph by Bany Cotton*)

"Convulsionists"
in the
Graveyard of
St-Medard
(*Mary Evans
Picture Library*)

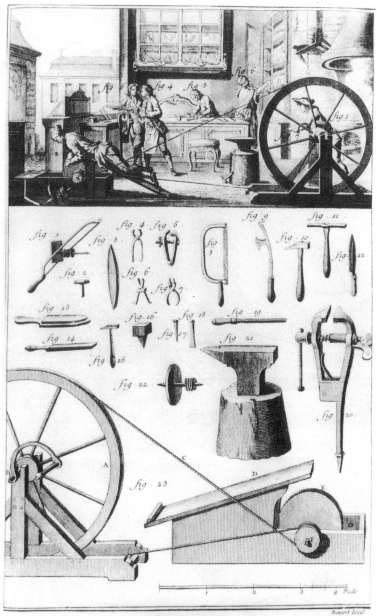

Coutelier.

Plate from the *Encyclopédie* showing work in a cutlery

Jean Le Rond d'Alembert,
after a pastel by
Maurice Quentin de La Tour
(*Mary Evans Picture Library*)

Melchior Grimm in 1758,
by Carmontelle

Left
Jean-Jacques Rousseau
(*Mary Evans Picture Library*)

Below
Mme d'Epinay,
after a portrait by
Jean-Etienne Liotard
(*Mary Evans
Picture Library*)

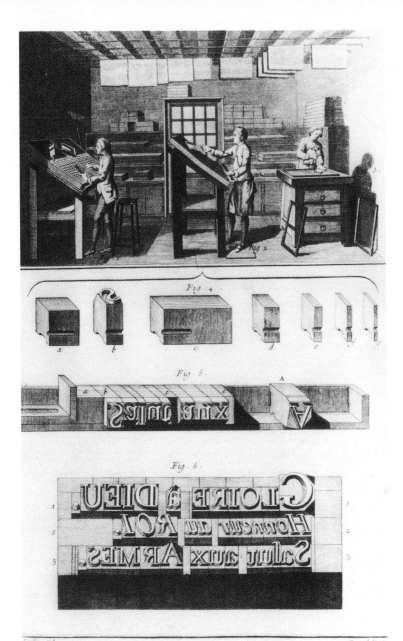

Plate from the *Encyclopédie*, showing work in a print shop

Romantic landscape by Joseph Vernet (*Courtauld Institute*)

Etienne-Maurice Falconet's statue of Peter the Great, St Petersburg

Portrait of Diderot
by Michel Van Loo, 1767
(*Louvre*)

Bust of Diderot
by Jean-Baptiste Pigalle, 1777
(*Louvre*)

The Private and the Public

During the August of 1761, working ten hours a day for twenty-five days in his workshop at Le Breton's, Diderot revised the final text volumes of the *Encyclopédie*. (In all, there would be seventeen volumes of text and eleven of plates.) It left him exhausted, and as he found, there had been a price to pay for his absence; for his daughter Angélique, left alone with her mother for all these days, seemed to him to have deteriorated. "She lisps and simpers and grimaces," he told Sophie. "She has learned to exploit her moods and her tears and sulks and whimpers over nothing. Her head is stuffed with idiotic riddles. Uranie or her sister could have made something remarkable of her, but her mother holds on to her and will not let me have the shaping of her. Ah well: she will be like a hundred thousand others, and if she gets a stupid husband, as it is a hundred thousand to one she will, it will mean she is less discontented."[1] Angélique's upbringing was a great bone of contention between Denis and Nanette. He wanted to bring her up on natural and "enlightened" lines and held that children should not be shielded from the truth. He would sometimes lecture Sophie's sister "Uranie" for wanting to "put her children's eyes out", that is to say for presenting ignorance as a virtue.

The child's upbringing was not the only source of friction between the Diderots. Nanette wore everyone down, herself included, with her compulsive nagging; and from time to time, as earlier, there would be a crisis. "Since the last domestic storm we eat our meals separately," Diderot wrote to Sophie on 22 September 1761. "I have mine in my study. When we only see each other in passing, let us hope we shall not have time or occasion to quarrel. Oh cruel life!"[2]

The rift on this occasion was not very long-lasting, and they were soon on speaking terms again. Indeed, they found themselves sharing a joke. One of their neighbours, a young widow, came to dinner, and when Diderot asked her teasingly, did she not have any lovers, she replied that, as a matter of fact, she had two. But one was so very humble, so very respectful, she would really have to get rid of him – "One does need a *little* fun" – and as for the other, at least he knew what he wanted, and she would keep him on just for a while. "Then I will do what one does with nasty insects, squash them on the spot where they stung you, to make it better." At this the pious Nanette laughed uproariously. "Even virtuous women," remarked Diderot to Sophie, "are not too displeased at the thought of a little vice."[3]

The reconciliation prospered. Early next month, a few days before his birthday, Diderot announced that he was going to Grandval, at which Nanette's face fell, as did Angélique's. It turned out they had prepared all sorts of birthday celebrations. Angélique had rehearsed a long harangue, and Nanette had in secret arranged a dinner-party. Hearing this he cancelled his plans; and the party, according to his own wry account, proved a brilliant success.

> Madame had invited all her woman friends. I was very gay. I drank, I ate, I did the honours in fine style. After dinner I played cards, never once deserted the party and saw everybody off at eleven or twelve. I was charming – and if you only knew with whom! What physiognomies, what people, what talk, what screams![4]

Nanette praised him afterwards for his excellent behaviour, revealing – he had ruefully to admit to himself – what she might have been fearing.

During the following year Nanette fell seriously ill with some ailment of the dysentery type. She was a bad invalid and bullied their maid Janneton so furiously from her bed that Diderot felt sure she would leave. From moment to moment Nanette would convince herself she was dying and in the night she would cry out so loudly that their neighbours imagined she must be in labour. "She groans, she weeps, she cries out," Diderot told Sophie (19

September 1762), "she throws her arm about like a pastor preaching the Passion." Diderot was in fact a good and attentive nurse, and by the end of October Nanette was out of danger, but so enfeebled that she grew quite gentle and pathetic, weeping half the day like a child. It frightened Diderot more than all the rest: "One must be very ill when one loses one's character." Over the next year or two she would fall ill again once or twice, so seriously that there were fears for her life, and in her weakened state she finally gave in over Angélique's education and allowed Diderot to take charge of it.

It was at about the same time that Grimm convinced himself that he was going blind (as indeed he eventually did, but not till many years later). Diderot was much distressed, also half thrilled at the prospect of being his white stick and guide-dog. Grimm, he told Sophie, "is as unhappy as any stone and locks up the trouble in his heart." Diderot wrote him a long letter – "such a letter!" – and, meeting him at Mme d'Epinay's, he had kissed his eyes. "Do not be jealous," he told Sophie. "Yes, I kissed them a hundred times as if they were yours: those beautiful eyes, once clear as the heavens, and now darkening."[5]

It so happened that just then affairs at Grandval and in the rue Royale had fallen into confusion. Someone told d'Holbach that Mme d'Epinay suspected her lover Grimm of having an affair with his wife; and when d'Holbach had questioned his wife, she said yes, Mme d'Epinay had been giving her very strange looks and indeed she and a friend of hers, Mme de Maux, had passed one or two quite barbed remarks. But of course, she said, the whole thing was complete nonsense. The Baron, believing her, was incensed and decided to break with Mme d'Epinay, whereupon Grimm said haughtily that if he did so, their own fifteen-years-old friendship would be at an end.

In Diderot's eyes this business was a great disaster. "What a treat for the evil-minded, if the gossip once spread," he remarked to Sophie. "The talk would be: 'Ah well, those *philosophes*, what else would you expect?'" He partly blamed d'Holbach: "That Baron does not feel the value of a friend." He blamed Grimm too, slightly, and had a serious talk with him, saying that, though of course he knew Grimm was perfectly innocent, he took too little care about appearances. If he [Diderot] had been in Mme d'Epinay's shoes, he told him, he would have torn his eyes out long ago. Grimm would have none of this. "He is so grave, so wise," Diderot lamented to Sophie. "He finds us petty and childish."[6]

Next, the Baron received an anonymous letter to the effect that the writer and journalist Jean-Baptiste Suard, a frequent house- guest of the d'Holbachs, had fallen in love with Mme d'Holbach. This, so the Baroness said when he challenged her, was also quite true. Indeed, she told him, in her innocent or mock-innocent way, it was a great nuisance to her. Suard was so lugubrious, so full of sighs and tears; she did not like seeing people cry; she would ask him to turn his head away the next time he felt inclined to weep.

Nor was this all. When Mme d'Holbach's doctor had pre-scribed horse-exercise for her, another friend of theirs, Georges Le Roy, a notorious libertine, had volunteered to squire her and, so it appeared, had declared a violent passion for her. When she rebuffed him, he accused her of having another lover.

Diderot lectured and sermonised his friends, but without much effect. "What a transformation," he told Sophie. A fortnight ago all had been harmony in the rue Royale. "There were laughter and kisses, and people said whatever came into their head." If one felt inclined to kiss a woman, and her husband or lover happened to be sitting in between, one asked him to move his head. "Now everyone is serious; they hold aloof; they make little bows and forced compliments on coming in and going out. They listen but they scarcely speak, because no one knows what to say or dares say what he knows . . . I see all this and am consumed with annoyance and boredom." The famous *salonnière* Mme Geoffrin, a devotee of Molièresque "good sense", came to call in the rue Royale but soon retreated. "Madame, you are not leaving?" asked one of the guests; to which her reply was, "There is no one here today!"[7]

It was all, finally, too much for Diderot. For a moment he was overcome with suspicions, deciding – so he told Sophie – that all of them, Grimm included, were as false as hell. Grimm, very likely, had *invented* his eye-illness so that he too could be prescribed riding and could keep Mme d'Holbach company. Maybe Mme d'Epinay, not relishing a future with a blind lover, had found this subtle way of getting rid of him. The doctor himself was probably madly in love with Mme d'Holbach; and even the *abbé* Galiani, in his sly way, had his eyes on her.

The suspicions were a mere fling of Diderot's imagination, not serious hypotheses. He no more doubted Grimm's honour, he hastened to tell Sophie, than he did his own. All the same, he said, what a "stupefaction" he would fall into, what cries to heaven he would raise, should he ever come to believe his friend and idol false.

For the present he decided there was nothing to do but stand aside "with his fingers in his ears". Moreover he was much needed at home, now that Nanette was ill. He therefore tried the experiment of seclusion. The truth was he had been overtaken by a curious obsession. On several occasions at this period he had written mysteriously to Sophie and her sister of an "important question" that was "tyrannising" him. There was a "truth" that he was on the track of which, if found, might cover him with glory, or alternatively, load him with ridicule. At all events, it preoccupied him continually. It got in the way of his most essential duties and gave him sleepless nights. If it had been any other question, he told the sisters, and not this very special one, he would have trusted his proofs and slept peacefully. But as it was, the wretched affair gave him *souleurs* (attacks of panic), and he found himself going over the proofs again and yet again. "It is a terrible thing to back one's own judgement against the multitude's, especially when the multitude is all of the same opinion." But then, did not an outsider, a "Goth", sometimes discover what all the experts had missed? For that matter, did not erroneous theories and sophisms sometimes reveal more genius than valid ones? And anyway, despite the *souleurs*, the thing gave him such golden visions. "Illusory or real, what a beautiful dream I shall owe to it! I have erected an immense château on the point of this needle." And why indeed must he be so eager to bring the matter to a test? Could he not emulate the traveller from Cairo who found a piece of painted glass and for three months had the pleasure of believing it the Queen of Alexandria's opal?[8]

It may surprise the reader to learn what Diderot's "important question" was. He believed he had squared the circle! He was, of course, by no means the only such believer at this time. The Academy of Sciences was pestered by memoirs on this subject and in 1775 it would refuse to receive any more. (It was not till 1882, though, that Lindemann showed that a purely geometrical construction for quadrature, using only ruler and compasses, was impossible.) The drafts of what Diderot called his "cyclometry" have survived, and, according to J. Mayer, his reasoning in them is much clumsier than in his other mathematical writings.[9] It is significant, too, that in his *Salon* review for 1767 he would write ironically of people who "reject the glory which is offered, to chase after the one that flees". The philosopher, he writes, "wants to be a poet, the poet to be a philosopher; the geometer [he is thinking of d'Alembert] aspires to be a man of letters, and the man of letters busies himself with squaring the circle and knows very well his own absurdity."[10]

None the less, occasionally during the rest of his life, Diderot would become a recluse for a few days or weeks, live in night-cap and dressing-gown all day, and return to his "cyclometry". Once or twice, indeed, against the advice of friends, he came near to publishing his discovery, though significantly he never actually did so. It is an instance of how the "public", that imaginary assembly and judge, was a fascination to him and could throw him off his balance.

Not long after Mme d'Epinay's return from Geneva, her husband suffered the fate that, for long, he had been inviting. Towards the end of the Seven Years' War the country's finances were in a worse than usual state of chaos and, as a measure of reform, La Live d'Epinay, together with several others, was, in January 1762, dismissed from his post as farmer-general. The disgrace made no great impression on him, though it did on Mme d'Epinay, who at first pictured them as facing total ruin; and in fact, according to the odd customs of France, d'Epinay was allowed to retain a half-interest in the incoming farmer-general's *charge*. It meant, however, the end of any pretence of married life on their part; and it meant further that Mme d'Epinay would have to live in more modest style. She made plans to let La Chevrette and to move into a much smaller house in the vicinity, named La Briche. Meanwhile, for the rest of the winter of 1762, she set up with her daughter Pauline in a cottage in the Paris suburbs. She made it a test of loyalty who would visit her there in these reduced circumstances. The d'Holbachs passed it sufficiently for the recent rift to be healed, but the really faithful visitors and comforters were Grimm and Diderot. Diderot taught her *tric-trac*, and the three spent cheerful evenings gambling and quarrelling round the *tric-trac* board. It was an ambition of Mme d'Epinay's that she should, eventually, set up a "philosophic" *salon*. In the meantime, continuing her *Memoirs of Mme de Montbrillant*, she composed one or two brilliant *pastiches* of dinner-party discussions, embodying the views, and sometimes the actual words, of Diderot, Grimm, Saint-Lambert and others.

In February 1763 France and Britain signed a peace treaty, and at once Paris was invaded by British visitors. The country was, indeed, going through a phase of Anglomania. "Our opinions, our fashions, even our games, were adopted in France," writes Gibbon in his *Autobiography*. "A ray of national glory illuminated each individual, and every Englishman was supposed to be born a patriot and a philosopher."[11] Friends of David Hume wrote to him that he was "worshipped" in Paris, and when in October he arrived there, as secretary to Lord Hertford the new ambassador, he found this hardly an exaggeration. He was presented to Louis XV, had a long conversation about his *History* with Madame de Pompadour and was soon a regular guest at the leading *salons*, d'Holbach's included. Altogether, as Horace Walpole reported without enthusiasm, Hume was "fashion itself, although his French is almost as unintelligible as his English."[12]

It had been much the same with Laurence Sterne, who had found his way to France the previous year, while the two countries were still at war. Very soon, he reported, he was "Shandying away" in bad French in various grand households, including those of the Duc d'Orléans and the Prince de Conti, and d'Holbach had told him to treat his *hôtel* in the rue Royale as his own.[13] In turn, Sterne wrote to his friend David Garrick, telling him he was "much expected" in Paris and was a constant topic of conversation. The Garricks' reception, when they reached the city in September 1763, was, indeed, particularly brilliant. There was an elegant supper-party for them at the embassy. Garrick was introduced to d'Alembert and Marmontel, the great actress Madame Clairon recited Racine in his honour, and he gave them the Dagger scene in *Macbeth*, the Curse in *Lear* and "the falling asleep in Sir John Bute".[14] After this, he reported to George Colman, he was stared at in the theatres and "talk'd of by Gentle & Simple".[15] The Garricks went on to Italy and Germany, but on their return next year Garrick became an habitué at d'Holbach's twice-weekly dinners.

The squabbles in the d'Holbach circle had by now been composed, or at least well hidden away, and the impression made on these distinguished foreigners was all that Diderot could have wished. What struck the British was the easiness, the geniality of French intellectual life. "What makes these men truly entertaining and desirable," Sterne wrote to a friend, "is, that they have the art, notwithstanding their wits, of living together without biting or scratching – an infinitude of gaity [*sic*] & civility reigns among them – & wh. is no small art, Every man leaves the Room with a better Opinion of his own Talents than when he entered."[16] Hume's reaction was very similar. "The Men of Letters here are very agreeable," he wrote to the Revd. Hugh Blair, "all of them Men of the World, living in entire or almost entire Harmony among themselves & quite irreproachable in their Morals." He added implausibly, and no doubt teasingly, that it would give his clerical friend "great satisfaction to find that there is not a single Deist among them."[17] Only Horace Walpole, who detested philosophy and disliked being lectured, took against the Holbachic set. They were "so overbearing and so underbred", so liable to bully him with absurd scientific theories. "Nonsense for nonsense," he wrote to his friend George Selwyn, he preferred the Jesuits, [18] and he took refuge with the *philosophe*-hating Madame du Deffand.

Diderot and David Hume took to each other almost at once. Hume, with his plump cheeks and rosy benevolence, put Diderot in mind – as he was not slow to tell him – of a well-fed Bernardine monk. Theirs was a friendship in citizen-of-the-world style, a sort of philanthropic freemasonry. Hume, hearing that Rousseau was in poverty, decided to organise a subscription on his behalf, and Diderot, despite his estrangement, was all eagerness. He would, in turn, ask favours of Hume on behalf of protégés of his own, in the name of "the fraternity that Nature has established between all men". "One gets nothing for nothing in this world," ran a letter of his to Hume in 1769, introducing an American medical student. "One has to pay for one's vices, but also for one's virtues, and do not imagine that you are an exception. People will want to see you, and to boast that they have seen you. So have the goodness to open your door and vouchsafe your rotund and laughing Bernardine visage to a young Pennsylvanian, who has sworn not to cross the seas again without doing you homage."[19]

Diderot's friendship with Sterne evidently prospered too, for within a month or two he was employing Sterne to buy him books – Tillotson's sermons, the *Works* of Chaucer, Pope, Cibber and Locke — from his English booksellers. Sterne in addition, and momentously, made him a present of the first six volumes of *Tristram Shandy*. "I am reading the maddest, the wisest, the gayest of all books," Diderot told Sophie in September 1762.[20] Sterne's novel was a revelation to him and later volumes were to be the direct inspiration of his own *Jacques the Fatalist*.

Meanwhile a friend of Sterne's in Paris, an Irish writer named Elizabeth Griffiths, showed him her adaptation of Diderot's *The Natural Son*, and he considered, but decided against, sending it to Garrick. "It has too much sentiment in it (at least for me), the speeches too long, and savour too much of *preaching* – this may be a second reason it is not to my taste – 'Tis all love, love, love throughout, without much separation of character; so I fear it wouldn't do for your stage, and perhaps for the very reason which recommends it to a French one."[21]

The influence of David Garrick on Diderot was more complicated but almost equally profound. Garrick had long been famous in France, at least by reputation, and as far back as 1758 Diderot was citing him in a long theatrical homily he wrote for his friend, Madame Riccoboni. How absurd, he said, Garrick would have found the "accursed" rules of the *Comédie Française*, prescribing how high hands might be raised or how far necks be turned. Would Garrick have worried in the least whether the audience saw him full face or in profile or whether his action was "decent" or not? Garrick, he told her, had once claimed that anything whatever could be conveyed by wordless dumb-show, and when the company protested, he had taken up a cushion, exclaiming "Sirs, I am this child's father."

> Upon which he opens a window, takes his cushion, tosses it in the air, kisses it, caresses it and imitates all the fooleries of a father playing with his child. But there came a moment when the cushion, or rather the child, slipped out of his hands and fell through the window. Then Garrick began to mime the father's despair . . . The spectators were seized with such consternation and horror that most could not bear it and had to leave the room.[22]

Evidently Garrick repeated this performance for the benefit of his friends in Paris, for Diderot refers to it again, as one who has seen it, in a letter to another actress, his young protégée Marie-Madeleine Jodin. Actors, he told her, should study the potentialities of silence. "I wish you could have seen Garrick play the part of a father who has let his child fall into a well [*sic*]. There is no maxim that our poets have more forgotten than that the great sorrows are mute."[23]

Equally significant for Diderot was that Garrick could turn on such performances at will. What kind of man, he asked himself, could, in cold blood and at a moment's notice, harrow the souls of his spectators with such merciless success? His answer is suggested by his comment on a bust of Garrick by Lemoine, in the *Salon* of 1765. "It is Roscius commanding his eyes, his forehead, his cheeks, his mouth, and all the muscles of his face, or rather of his soul, which adopts the passion which is required of it and in turn disposes the whole body."[24] A great actor must, he is implying, be an exceedingly masterful individual, one who can dictate to his own soul.

All of Diderot's thoughts about Garrick would eventually, as we shall see, come to a focus in 1769, in a review of a book entitled *Garrick; or English Actors*.[25] It is here that Diderot first sketched the theory, later elaborated in *The Paradox of the Actor*, that the actor of genius, far from acting from his heart and feelings, is a kind of monster of insensibility.

Another visitor to Paris remains to be mentioned. In June 1763 Leopold Mozart, with his two infant prodigies, the seven-year-old Wolfgang Amadeus and Wolfgang's sister Nannerl, had set out from Salzburg on a grand European tour; on 18 November they arrived in Paris. They had come furnished with letters of introduction from several ambassadors and other grand personages, but, as Leopold reported to his Salzburg landlord Lorenz Hagenauer, none of these recommendations had the slightest effect. The only one that proved of value was from a Frankfurt merchant's wife to a certain Monsieur Grimm. This M. Grimm was secretary to the Duc d'Orléans. He was "a man of learning and a great friend of humanity", and he had "done everything", arranged for their first concert, disposing of three hundred and twenty tickets, and paying Leopold eighty *louis d'or* on his own account. "In addition he paid for the lighting, as more than sixty large candles were burnt." Now he was arranging a second concert. "So you see what a man can do who has good sense and a kind heart. He comes from Regensburg, but he has been in Paris for over fifteen years and knows how to launch everything in the right way."[26]

At Christmas-time, through Grimm's management, the Mozarts were invited for a fortnight to Versailles. Wolfgang was much petted by the Queen and the princesses and performed the amazing musical feats and circus-tricks that were already becoming famous: he improvised entrancingly for an hour at a time, devised an accompaniment to a song that he did not even know and played unseen on a keyboard which had been covered with a cloth. He also composed four sonatas for piano and violin. Two of these he dedicated to the kindly royal princess, Madame Victoire, and the other two to the Comtesse de Tesse, a lady-in-waiting to the Dauphine, and Grimm undertook the writing of the dedications – though the Comtesse refused the one to herself as altogether too flattering, and it had to be toned down. Carmontelle produced at this time the charming and well-known watercolour of the Mozart family at the *clavecin*, and Grimm had it engraved and put on sale.

The visit, from a worldly point of view, was a dazzling success, and Grimm was quick to report its triumph, with a flick of rebuke to the unmusical French. "I do not despair of that child turning my head if I hear him often again . . . I am no longer astonished that Saint Paul lost his senses after his strange vision. The children of M. Mozart have excited admiration among all those who have seen them. The Emperor and Empress have laden them with kindnesses, and they received the same reception at the courts of Munich and Mannheim. It is a pity that people know so little about music in this country."[27] This was an episode in which the resourceful Grimm showed to great advantage. As we shall see, though, it was to have a bitter sequel, when Mozart made a return visit to Paris fifteen years later and met with the "white tyrant" side of Grimm's nature.

In July 1762 Catherine II had, by dubious means, come to the throne of Russia, and one of her earliest activities as Empress was to try to acquire some resident *philosophes*. Glowing invitations were made to Voltaire; d'Alembert was offered, but refused, the post of tutor to the Grand Duke Paul; and soon a flowery message was despatched to Diderot, by way of Voltaire, pressing him to complete the *Encyclopédie* on Russian soil. What a chance, wrote Voltaire gleefully, to demolish *l'infâme*. "Do you not consider her proposition the most enormous slap one could give to the cheek of an Omer [i.e. Joly de Fleury]?"[28]

Diderot replied, promply this time, saying he would go neither to Petersburg nor to Frederick's Berlin. And the reason?' "That at the very moment of writing, fresh volumes of the *Encyclopédie* are being printed and I have the proofs before me on my desk – but hush, not a word!" In any event, what these would-be helpers did not seem to realise was that the manuscripts of the *Encyclopédie* belonged not to their authors but to the publishers. And then, he told Voltaire, what he liked about his colleagues was that what united them was not so much hatred of *l'infâme* as benevolence and a love of the true, the good and the beautiful – a kind of Trinity worth rather more than their enemies' one! Thus, wrapping himself up in his own virtue, he urged his "great brother" to live to defend more Jean Calases, and bade him farewell with the cheerful valediction: "Adieu, sublime, *honnête* and dear Antichrist."[29]

That there were dangers in Diderot's employment, and unexpected ones at that, he had reason to realise once again in September 1761. For some four years he had given work as a copyist to a penniless intellectual named Glénat. He would visit him and talk with him by the hour in his hovel ("about as big as my hand", Diderot told Sophie, but with a dozen excellent books on the shelf), and he had admired the philosophical cheerfulness of this poor devil, "eating his crust with appetite and from time to time caressing his woman-friend on the wretched truckle-bed that filled two-thirds of the room." He would feed Glénat when he came to the rue Taranne, opened his purse to him, and would find him employment among his friends.

Then he discovered that Glénat was a police spy and had passed on one of his friends' manuscripts to the police authorities. What is more, Glénat had been personally planted on him by Antoine de Sartine, the Lieutenant of Police, who was a friend of Diderot's from college days and had naturally been looked upon by him in the light of a protector. He went to confront Glénat; who took the matter very coolly, telling Diderot that he had no need to worry so long as he gave him nothing "reprehensible" to copy. Sartine, when he next saw him, was equally unabashed, and when Diderot fulminated against the ungrateful "scoundrel", he said no, not at all, Glénat was an excellent fellow who could not have done otherwise. "You need such people," Diderot agreed. "You use them. You pay them. But they cannot but be dirt in your eyes"; at which Sartine burst out laughing. Diderot told Sophie mournfully that the poor devils with ragged stockings and the "look of poverty and decency", who used to flow through his house, might have to find the door shut on them.

It was at about this time, if indeed it happened at all, that the *Encyclopédie* acquired a new admirer, no less than Louis XV. The story is related by Voltaire, who got it, he said, from one of the King's servants. Louis was supping at the *Petit Trianon*, when the conversation turned upon gunpowder. The Duc de Nivernois said it was absurd that they killed partridges every day at Versailles and frequently killed human beings, or had themselves killed by them, on the frontiers of France, yet none of them understood the means they were doing it with. "Alas, it is the same with everything in the world," replied Mme de Pompadour. "I don't know what the rouge I use is made of, and I should be hard put to it if someone asked me how my silk stockings were made." "It is a pity," said another courtier, the Duc de la Vallière, "that Your Majesty confiscated our *Encyclopédies*, which cost us a hundred *pistoles* a volume. We would soon have found the answers there." The King defended the confiscation; he had, he said, been told that the *Encyclopédie* was a most frightful affair, a danger to the whole nation. Still, he was ready to give it a trial; and he sent three of his footmen to fetch the volumes. They were an instant success: the Duc de la Vallière found the formula for cartridge-powder, and Mme de Pompadour learned the difference between Spanish rouge and the Paris variety and was enraptured by Diderot's account of the stocking-machine. "What a beautiful book," she exclaimed. "Sire, have you confiscated this store of useful things to enjoy it alone and be the only *savant* in the kingdom?" The rest of the company, wrote Voltaire, fell on the volumes "like the daughters of Lycomedes on Ulysses' jewels." Those involved in law-suits found the answer to their legal problems, and the King read all about the rights of the Crown. "I don't know why they told me so much ill of this excellent book," said the King. It was pure envy, said the Duc de Nivernois, and the Comte de Coigny told the King to thank God for causing such men as the *Encyclopédie*'s editors to be born in his country. "Still," protested the King, "they say there are many faults in it." "Sire," replied the Comte de Coigny, "at your supper two of the ragoûts were uneatable, yet we ate well all the same. Ought we to have thrown the whole meal out of the window because of two bad ragoûts?"[30]

Even now, despite all his disclaimers, Diderot still invested literary hopes in the *Encyclopédie*. He reported to Sophie that the eighth volume, which would contain some four hundred articles from his own pen, would be "full of charming things, of all hues".[31] There was, however, a shock in store for him, more shattering than any he had yet received. Some time during October 1764 he happened to want to consult his own article SARRASINS. It was the one he was working on at Grandval and which was now printed and awaiting publication as part of the final ten volumes. To his horror, he found the article bowdlerised and mutilated; and when he anxiously consulted other, similarly controversial, articles, he discovered the same to be true of them. The fact, as very soon became plain, was that Le Breton, out of sheer pusillanimity and commercial prudence, had decided to censor and emasculate the *Encyclopédie* behind Diderot's back, removing anything that might cause trouble. He and his printing-house overseer had worked in complete secrecy, and had moreover deliberately destroyed the authors' original manuscript so that the damage could not be repaired.

It was a staggering blow, extinguishing Diderot's last spark of pleasure in his undertaking, to which he had given twenty years, and for some days it put him into an absolute frenzy. He wept with anger in Le Breton's presence and wept for grief in his own home. Whenever he remembered this event in later years, it frightened him to think to what fearful resentment a mild man – for this was how he regarded himself – could be driven. He had a furious confrontation with Le Breton. Then he summoned Grimm back from the country by express messenger, and the two discussed the situation from all angles. There seemed, however, no remedy. Le Breton's fellow-printer Briasson, when Diderot told him the story, implored him not to make the news public, for it would kill the work dead. But anyway, as Le Breton had no doubt calculated, for Diderot to publicise the matter would be to put himself in jeopardy. It would be to admit that work on the *Encyclopédie* had been continuing, in defiance of the royal prohibition, and it would probably mean that he would have to flee the country. In the end, therefore, Diderot took the only rational course and bowed to circumstances, forcing himself to continue work as if nothing had happened. With the strength of mind he could show in real emergencies, he said not a word to any of his contributors, and the only compensation he allowed himself, a meagre one, was to write Le Breton a letter on 12 November such as he should never forget.

Le Breton, he wrote, had performed "an atrocity without parallel" in the history of publishing. "With the aid of a stupid beast of burden you have massacred the work of twenty honourable men who had given up their time, their talents and their days and nights for the pure love of truth and the public good." And for what? The moment the work was published, the contributors would utter "loud cries" at what they found, and others would join in the chorus. The disgrace would be appalling. "Our work will be derided as a flat and miserable rhapsody. Voltaire will look for us and not find us." Le Breton had brought certain ruin on his associates and an infamy on himself that nothing would ever expunge. He would, Diderot told Le Breton, continue his duties as editor. He would even continue to come to Le Breton's premises, though the prospect made him shudder, but he would treat Le Breton as if he were invisible and hoped Le Breton would do the same for him. As for the remaining articles, Le Breton might do his worst with them; he would not look at the results, for it had made him suffer too much the first time. It had taken away his appetite and destroyed his sleep. He had been "wounded till the grave".[32]

16

Diderot as Art Critic

With all pleasure in the *Encyclopédie* finally extinguished; with some success – but of an equivocal kind – as a dramatist; and with two masterpieces of fiction in his desk-drawer, reserved for his eye alone; Diderot's literary situation in the mid-1760s did not look very satisfactory. However, it had one important compensation, for a few years back he had discovered a new and rewarding literary outlet as resident art critic for the *Correspondance littéraire*. It had become his task, from 1759 onwards, to review the great recurring event of the Paris art scene, the biennial *Salon* exhibition in the Louvre.

He was not an ignoramus when he set up as an art-critic. Through Grimm, he had had the run of the Duc d'Orléans's old-master collection, and he was familiar with many other private collections and had some notion of the history of art. Nevertheless, as he told Grimm, his new task called for a thorough-going self-education.

With such a man as Diderot no experience is likely to be wasted, let alone such an all-absorbing one as editing the *Encyclopédie*. Thus it was as an encyclopaedist, and according to his own conception of that role, that Diderot faced his new challenge. As a good encyclopaedist, he worked the whole subject out, so far as possible, from first principles. He was also concerned, in proper Baconian fashion, to locate fine art in the map or genealogy of human activities. This meant, in the first place, distinguishing all its different aspects: what a painting or a sculpture is, what are the conditions of its production, what an artist is, what a spectator of art is, what an art critic is, what is the role of taste, of technique and of the genres and the hierarchy of genres. In all that he would write about art, these questions would never be far from the surface.

Again, as with the mechanical arts, he saw the prime importance of a well-functioning vocabulary. The *Encyclopédie*'s articles on the fine arts, by the painter Watelet and others, were in fact assiduous in defining artistic terms, and Diderot took great pains to master these. He also coined one or two valuable ones of his own. Describing a fleecy-looking painting of Cupids by Fragonard, he spoke of it as *cotonneux* ("cottony"). "This word has perhaps not been used before," writes Diderot, "but it serves its purpose very well."[1] The word was picked up by his admirer Stendhal when he, in turn, became a *Salon* reviewer in the 1820s.[2]

As, in the earlier days of the *Encyclopédie*, he had frequented workshops and factories, so now he frequented artists' studios, and he became friendly with many, one might almost say with most, of the leading French artists of the day. La Tour, Chardin, Greuze, Michel Van Loo, Casanove, Joseph Vernet and the sculptors Pigalle and Falconet all welcomed him, and, talkative as he was, he was skilful in questioning them. He thus in time gained an excellent grasp of "studio" technicalities, as well as the gossip, traditions and aesthetic trends of the Paris art scene. He developed a particularly valuable friendship with Chardin, who for some years had been charged with the hanging of the Salon exhibitions and talked to him freely about the secrets of this task.

He took pride, with some reason, in the thoroughness of his self-training as critic, and in the Preamble to the *Salon* of 1765 he thanked Grimm for it.

If I have any thought-out notions on painting and sculpture, it is to you, my friend, that I owe them . . . It is the task you set me that has fixed my eyes upon a canvas and set me moving round a marble. I have given my impression the time to arrive and enter. I have opened my soul to its effects, I have let myself be penetrated by them. I have noted the verdict of the old and the thoughts of children, the judgement of the man of letters and the comments of the People; and if I happen to have wounded an artist, it will often have been with the weapon he sharpened for me himself. I have interrogated and have understood the nature of fine drawing and of truth to nature; I have grasped the magic of light and shade; I have fathomed the notion of colour; I know how to judge the handling of flesh. In solitude I have meditated on what I have seen and heard; and those terms of art "unity", "variety", "contrast", "symmetry", "ordonnance", "composition", "characteristics", "expressions" – so familiar on my lips, so vague in my mind – have been defined and pinned down.[3]

In his *Salon* reviews he was writing for readers, that is to say Grimm's foreign clientele, who would not be visiting the exhibition themselves. Thus it was up to him not only to pass judgement on works of art, but to record and describe them in some detail. It meant he needed to visit the exhibition a number of times, sometimes spending as long as seven hours at a time there. One may presume he made rough notes on the spot. Also, for the 1765 exhibition, and perhaps for others, he received some assistance from a young painter named La Rue, who supplied Diderot with his own notes and comments. Mainly, though, he would do the descriptions of paintings from memory and in the privacy of his own study. (He would mentally project the paintings on his study wall.) His powers of visual recall seem to have been prodigious. He claimed to be able to visualise in detail pictures he had seen only once, twenty years before.[4]

Diderot would write his *Salons* in bursts of continuous activity, sometimes working night and day. They give us a clear idea, more so perhaps than any other of his writings, of the form that reflection took with him: the abundant rush of ideas, the lateral swervings, the extempore fantasies and glimpses of new laws, and the blithe turnings-back upon himself in irony. With certain differences, this must have been how he talked. It is also, one reflects, rather how Coleridge must have talked. It brings home to us, then, our good fortune that Diderot, unlike Coleridge, should have hit on an art-form (the *Salon*) in which he could re-create, could "stage", his whole reflective process.

Diderot had a happy feeling towards his *Salon* reviewing, as a release, an invitation to shine and a challenge to all his powers. His friends had a stock joke about him, that he was an arch-dreamer who could see a hundred brilliant things in a work but not the ones that actually happened to be there. There was a good deal of truth in this, but when one considers his art criticism the joke begins to look thin. For he taught himself to see and recall paintings with remarkable minuteness and faithfulness, and his analyses are often a triumph of seeing what is there. For one thing, he developed a great and easy mastery of the "line": that "simple, true, unique line of liaison" which snakes its way through a composition and "directs both the person looking at a painting and the one who wants to describe it." It was, significantly, painting rather than sculpture that excited him as a critic. For all his preoccupation with statues and monuments, he admitted to finding them difficult to judge as art. They were somehow too edifying; "Marble does not laugh." What attracted him in painting was its demiurgic quality, the way it created worlds out of nothing or out of the "chaos" of the palette.

It was as an art critic, too, that he found good use for his habit of improving other people's works. The re-designing of an artist's work became one of his favourite critical ploys, as when he explained how the grouping of the sculptor Falconet's great "Pygmalion" could have been made even more appealing.[5] Several major artists assured him, and he believed them, that he was almost the only man of letters whose ideas could pass straight on to a canvas. This power had come from long practice and discipline, so he believed. Little by little, he had learned to imagine "the attitudes, groupings, passions, expressions, movement, depth, perspective and planes" that art could make use of.

What grows plain is that he demanded a thoroughly active role for the critic. He wanted to be alive and doing in front of a work of art and to throw himself into the critical act – or at least the first and spontaneous part of it – with zest and abandonment. It became for him part of the logic of criticism that the critic should not attempt to efface himself – should on the contrary insist on his own presence, though not in a self-regarding fashion. The question besetting Diderot's mind was what relationship, and how many different kinds of relationship, a critic might stand in towards a work of art; and in these *Salon* writings he continually invented new relationships, new ploys and new fictions.

Stendhal was later to mock at the "great" artists, "forgotten" figures like Carle Van Loo and Fragonard, whom Diderot had made much of in his *Salons*.[6] His remark brings out how completely, for a time, eighteenth-century French painting went into eclipse; and, on the whole, the artists whom Diderot made most of – Chardin, Greuze, Joseph Vernet, Loutherbourg, and the sculptor Falconet – rate highly again today. His equal passion for Greuze and for Chardin, at first sight rather a surprising combination of tastes, gives a good idea of his catholicity of appreciation.

For Chardin, Diderot's admiration was boundless. This painter, above all others, it seemed to him, raised the question of "handling" (*faire*). The "magic" of Chardin's "handling" was peculiar to him, wrote Diderot, and in this one point he was as far above Greuze as sky is above earth. But further, Chardin raised basic questions about the nature of paint and painting themselves. It helps in understanding Diderot's comments on Chardin if one reads them in the light of an admirable passage in the *Salon* of 1765 describing the compromises and falsities that lie at the heart of painting.

> What the musician offers you is actual sounds, but what the painter grinds on his palette is not flesh, blood, wool, sunlight, atmosphere, but "earths", gums, calcined bones, crushed stones and metallic limes. Hence the impossibility of rendering the imperceptible reflections of objects one upon another. For the painter, there are warring colours which can never be reconciled one with the other. Hence an individual palette, a "handling", a technique peculiar to each painter. And what is that technique? It is the art of concealing a certain number of dissonances, of finding cunning means to elude the great difficulties of art. Hence the need for a certain selection of objects and colours. But even after this selection, however well made, the finest and most harmonious painting is no more than a tissue of falsities, one disguising another.[7]

Implicitly the paradox of Chardin, for Diderot, is that this most "true", most divinely natural, of artists – a painter seemingly without personal mannerism – is precisely the one supremely adept in all these compromises and duplicities. It is Chardin for whom, against all experience, there are no "friendly" and "hostile" colours. "Sunlight itself is not better in reconciling the disparates in what it lights."

One understands nothing of this magic. There are thick layers of colour applied one upon another and of which the effect transpires from below to above. At other times one would say it was a vapour blown on the canvas; at others again, a light foam thrown there . . . Approach, and everything grows confused, flattens and disappears. Stand back, and everything creates and reproduces itself.[8]

The questions raised by Chardin's art, for Diderot, amount to philosophical ones and put him in mind of Berkleyan idealism. "If it is true, as philosophers say, that there is nothing real in our sensations," he says to Chardin, "let these philosophers tell me what difference there is for them, when a few feet away from your paintings, between the Creator and yourself."[9]

Diderot writes of Chardin, always, in the same moved, wondering and grateful tone. "One stops in front of a Chardin by instinct," he writes in the *Salon* of 1767, "as a weary traveller goes and sits down, half unaware of doing so, in the spot which offers him a seat among verdure, silence, waters, shade and coolness."[10]

Counterpoised with his love of Chardin is his huge enthusiasm for Greuze, a painter who might be regarded, at first sight, as almost his antithesis. Greuze was a great discovery for Diderot. "That Greuze is decidedly my man," he wrote in the *Salon* of 1763, reviewing Greuze's "Filial Piety". "To begin with, the genre pleases me. It is moral painting. What? Has the brush not devoted itself long enough, too long even, to debauch and vice?" That there could be a "moral" school of painting came to him as a surprise, and rather naturally so, considering his tendency to adduce a "beauty" in crime. "One makes only tranquil and frigid paintings out of virtue," he was writing to Sophie only the year before. "It is passion and vice that animate the composition of the painter, the poet and the musician."

It was clear to him, as indeed it was to others, that Greuze's scenes of peasant life were intended as a blow against the "hierarchy of the genres". They were a gesture not so much of defiance as of subversion, for Greuze was treating peasant subjects, not in the manner of the Dutch genre-painters, but in the heightening style of a "history-painter", with a Poussinesque tautness of composition and structural unity. "This painter," as Diderot remarks, "excels above all in the ordering of his scene." This intention of Greuze's, indeed, helps account for a certain strained and overwrought quality in paintings like "Filial Piety", which, to a modern viewer, seem to be drawing attention rather too consciously to their own composition.

From another point of view, however, Greuze's is a style of painting far removed from Poussin and close to the theatre, especially to the *drame bourgeois* of which Diderot was the theoretician. Far from the "timeless" quality of classical history-painting, this was an art focused very insistently on time and the moment – or, as Diderot has it, on the present moment and the one just before. A Greuze canvas of this type is a *tableau*, a moment of silence as in a play; and moreover it is meant to be read as a story. Greuze, Diderot wrote in a later *Salon*[11], "is the first among us who had the idea of giving morality [*moeurs*] to art and concatenating events upon which it would be easy to write a novel." In his analysis of "Filial Piety" he patiently teases out Greuze's dramatic and anecdotal idea, and, as we can feel, with admirable success. This really is the kind of labour that Greuze wishes the beholder to perform. In the painting (it is one of those long frieze-like or "planimetric" compositions Greuze specialised in) a paralysed old man lies outstretched at full length in his armchair, amid the loving attentions of his family. "The old man's fine head is so touching," writes Diderot, "he has such difficulty in speaking, his voice is so feeble, his looks are so tender, his complexion is so pale, that one would need to have no entrails not to feel moved." Every detail in the painting, Diderot insists, is dramatically relevant, even including the great sheet hung up to dry which serves as the background. "This sheet is a fine stroke of imagination both as subject-matter and as art, and you can rest assured he has not failed of 'largeness' in the handling of it."

In the painting, a young man – one guesses him to be the old man's son-in-law – is offering the old man something to eat, while his daughter lifts him to re-arrange his bolster. Critics have complained, says Diderot, that it would be more appropriate for the young man to do the physical labour of lifting and the girl the traditional feminine duty of offering food; also that it is unnatural that every single figure in the painting should have his or her gaze riveted on the old man. Which only goes to show, says Diderot, what an instinct critics have for the banal and the uninteresting. The point of Greuze's painting is to represent a *special* moment, a happy and unrepeatable accident of circumstance:

> By chance it so happened that day that it was his son-in-law who brought him food, and the good man, touched by the fact, signified his gratitude in so vivid, so moved, a fashion that it interrupted all other occupations and fixed the attention of the whole family.
>
> They say that the bolster is too new-looking and should show some signs of use . . . Perhaps . . . That the heads in this scene are the same as in his "Village Betrothal" and "Peasant Reading to his Children". Agreed; but what if he were following the history of the same family? . . . That . . . A thousand devils take those critics, and me first of all! This painting is beautiful, most beautiful, and woe to him who can look at it unmoved . . . The background, the furnishings, the clothes are of the greatest finish; and then, that man draws like an angel. His colour is beautiful and strong, though however not yet that of Chardin . . . Consequently the painting draws spectators in a crowd, and one cannot get near it.

Diderot, who got to know Greuze in 1759, became closely involved with him during his spectacular rise to fame and served as his confidant and propagandist. Greuze became in his imagination one of his "genius" figures. "If he [Greuze] encounters a head which he finds striking," he wrote in the *Salon* for 1765, "he will willingly go on his knees to the owner to come to his studio. He is a ceaseless observer, in streets, in churches, in markets, at the theatre and in public assemblies. If his mind is running on a subject, he becomes obsessed by it, it pursues him everywhere. It even affects his character. He takes the character of his picture: he is brusque, gentle, insinuating, caustic, *galant*, sad, gay, cold, serious or mad, according to the nature of his current project."[12]

Like most of the world, Diderot was soon to find Greuze a ruthlessly ambitious and egotistical man. Greuze had greatly annoyed the Académie by his arrogance, and when, in 1769, as his long-overdue *morceau de réception*, he submitted a history-painting ("Severus and Caracalla"), it was criticised savagely, and he suffered the humiliation of being "received" merely as a genre-painter. By this time Diderot's friendship with him had cooled; moreover Diderot had never had any faith in the long-meditated "Severus and Caracalla", guessing the subject had long ago gone dead on Greuze. Nevertheless he felt the urge to go and see him and do what he could to soothe his wounded vanity. Then he thought better of it, for he realised that Greuze, who believed there was a conspiracy against him, might imagine he was part of it and had merely come to gloat.

Diderot's *Salon* of 1765 came accompanied by some *Essays on Painting*. He gave them idiosyncratic titles – "My bizarre thoughts on drawing," "All I have ever understood about chiaroscuro," "Paragraph on composition (or so I hope)," etc. – but in fact they add up to a coherent and richly suggestive little treatise. He is particularly rewarding on composition and on the related subject of crowds. For Diderot, who disbelieved in "unities" and preferred to speak of "systems" – a concept always important to him philosophically – a crowd, whether in life or in a painting, was above all a "system": it was to be understood quasi-politically, as a polity or an economy. Consider a crowd at the first moment of a tumult, he writes:

> The energy of each individual is being exercised in all its violence; and as no pair of individuals possess it in exactly the same degree, it is here as with the leaves of a tree – no two are of exactly the same green, no two of these individuals display the same action or position.
> Then consider the same mass in the moment of repose, when each participant will have sacrificed part (though as little as possible) of his own privilege; there will be the same diversity in what they have sacrificed, and hence the same diversity of actions and positions. And the moment of tumult and the moment of repose have this in common, that in them each individual reveals what he is.[13]

It was in the handling of crowds, wrote Diderot with some reason, that the academic painter, with his eternal pyramid-design and meaningless "contrasts", showed all his weakness. "The only true contrast is one that springs from the very heart of the action, or from the diversity of organs or interests."

One of Diderot's favourite fictions as a critic is that a given painting is not a painting at all but a piece of the real world: an apparently playful or *belle-lettristic* device that became extremely fruitful in his hands. In his account of Greuze's "Young Girl Mourning Her Dead Bird" he not merely reconstructs the whole narrative supposedly folded up within it,[14] he composes a lengthy sentimental dialogue between himself and the young girl, in which he wrests her secret from her (for her mourning is not just for the dead bird) and gives her consolation. Not inaptly, he intends to convey by this that didactic painting of this kind is offering itself for something more than detached contemplation. It invites, it even demands, an act of fantasising to complete its effect.

A related fiction of Diderot's, very prominent in the *Salon* of 1767, is that he can step into a canvas and move about within it freely, seeing views not visible to a beholder stationed in front of it. He exploits this in a great set-piece on seven landscapes by Joseph Vernet, where he relates three long imaginary expeditions that he and some companions make within them. As Michael Fried has shown in his *Absorption and Theatricality* (1980) this bold ploy is, once again, a perceptive act of criticism. Diderot is in fact responding to a central originality in Vernet's art: a desire to incorporate a whole sequence of different vantage-points within the same canvas, "each of which competes with all the others for the beholder's attention and in a sense for his imagined presence at that spot." The result is to call into question the beholder's fixed position in front of the canvas. His firm foothold there "dissolves as it were beneath his feet", just as it is dissolved in Diderot's fantasy.[15]

There is, however, more to the matter. For one thing, the fact that Diderot is willing to intrude upon a painted landscape relates to his detestation of the breed of the "connoisseur", who insists on staying outside a painting. "Ideal beauty strikes all men; beauty of 'handling' [*faire*] is all that arrests the connoisseur. If it sets him dreaming, it will be about art and the artist, not about the thing itself. He always remains outside the scene, he never enters into it."[16]

Further, this same willingness is for Diderot an act of discrimination. One is tempted to intrude upon a painting exactly because, or in so far as, it does not seem inclined to intrude upon oneself (to say "look at me!") and has the self-sufficiency and autonomy of a natural object. We are brought back to Diderot's theories about the stage; and in fact these theories strike one as more convincing, or rather as revealing their deeper meaning, in the context of painting. It is here that one grasps the full force of his doctrine that performers must behave as if they were unobserved (the "fourth wall" theory, as it came to be called later). Diderot puts the point thus, in a letter to Sophie Volland: "If, when one is painting a picture, one supposes the presence of spectators, all is lost. The painter steps out of his canvas, as the actor who speaks to the *parterre* steps out of the stage-scene."[17] In his writings about painting, "theatricality" is always a word of condemnation or vituperation – and here, so Michael Fried has argued, is the heart of his campaign against the rococo. "That man," writes Diderot of Boucher (it is an admirable put-down) "only takes up the brush to show me tits and buttocks. Now, I am more than happy to see such things, but I cannot have somebody pointing them out to me."[18] Again, in a discourse on "Mannerism" in painting, he writes: "Any personage [in painting] who seems to be saying to you, 'See how well I weep, how well I get angry, how well I supplicate,' is false and mannered."[19]

This *Salon* of 1767 is, it should be added, a remarkable literary invention, a fiction or parable artfully constructed round that Italian journey of which Diderot and Grimm have dreamed so often but know now that they will never make. In his Preamble Diderot tells Grimm not to hope that the present *Salon* review will be "as rich, as varied, as wise, as mad, as fertile" as its predecessors; all things wear out. Perhaps, indeed, it need not have been so if he could have found a new form for his review – if, say, he had been to Italy, returning with his imagination refreshed and fired by the Old Masters. But they will never go to

Italy. Never will they embrace in the Pantheon, that "ancient, silent and sacred abode", under whose sombre vault their souls could dare speak "of all those mysteries of our life which officious decency forbids should be confessed."[20]

As we detect, there are ironies playing round this Italian journey, and when we reach the two great set-pieces of this *Salon* on Joseph Vernet and on Hubert Robert, we realise that paintings are being equated with journeys – journeys in space, like Vernet's romantic landscapes, and journeys in time, like Hubert Robert's studies of ruins. In his pages on Vernet Diderot adopts a pleasant fiction: that, having written the word "Vernet" at the top of his page and been about to write his review, he was invited by friends to stay in the country, in a château near the sea, where the resident tutor, an *abbé*, invited him to come walking with his two young charges and be shown the splendours of the surrounding countryside. As they walk in this sublime and mountainous landscape they argue about the relative merits and rights of art and nature and about how, if Vernet teaches one to look at Nature better, Nature for her part may teach one to look at Vernet better. All this time, of course, the walkers have been following the contours of one of Vernet's *Salon* paintings, and not only that, but, in Vernet-like style, they have been seeing the view from the several different viewpoints established within the canvas. Thus fiction has been folded within fiction and paradox within paradox, a double confusing of art and nature. It is a "supposititious" device of great brilliance, closely related to the one by which, in the *Conversations on "The Natural Son"*, one of the characters in the play (Dorval) is invited to discuss the play, and canvass the conflicting claims of art and life, from his privileged "inside" position.

The device can also have another function, for by means of it Diderot is able to re-enact the impulses that are felt by the beholder of a painting. They are by no means all of them "pure". Aesthetic response is, and can hardly help being, full of distracting human passions, temptations and self-indulgences; and, Diderot implies, wisdom lies not in trying to ban these but in giving them their head and working through them to a balanced judgement.

One such passion or temptation is the "philosophic" one. Refreshed after his inspiring first day's outing and the healthful sleep that ensued, the fictional Diderot wakes up in a very philosophical mood. "Here," he says to himself, reclining in his armchair and apostrophising the admirable landscape before his eyes – but is the reader to take this to be a real landscape or a painted one? – "here is the real life, the true habitat for man. All the false attractions of society have not extinguished the taste for it." "Diderot's" mood every moment grows more rapt. "Where am I at present? What are these objects round me? I do not know, I have no idea. What do I lack? Nothing. What do I desire? Nothing. If there is God, this is how he must be; He enjoys *himself*."[21] It is altogether a delicious reverie, with only one objection to it, that his eye and mind are neither on a real landscape, nor on a painted one, but on himself; and a moment later it is shattered, when one of Vernet's washerwomen arouses him with the sound of her paddle. Some people, it seems, have work to do. He is not put out. He reflects that, if it is good to exist after the fashion of God, it is also good to do so after the manner of men and women, and this is the cue for another response to landscape-painting, the erotic one. In his reverie, as he beholds the beautiful effect made by a certain clump of trees ("thrusting up just *there*!"), the thought, "Vernet must at all costs come and paint this scene – he might even improve on it" – mingles with the thought, "If only she could be here, could appear to me, if I could see once more her great eyes, and she would lay her hand softly on my brow and smile at me."[22]

The same enactment of a beholder's response, the same seesawing between art and nature, is taken even further when Diderot comes to Hubert Robert's paintings of ruins. His theme is now travel: travel in place – Robert has just made that Italian journey that Grimm and himself failed of – and travel in time. Ruins (the work of time) are a subject that, for all his wonderful talent, Diderot believes the young Robert does not yet really understand. (What a cruel fate for him to be hung next to Vernet!) How does one paint ruins? Diderot gives him not a lecture but an object lesson and there and then proceeds to think the thought "ruins".

How old the world is! I walk between two eternities . . . What is
my fleeting existence in comparison with that decaying rock, that
valley digging its channel ever deeper, that forest soon to totter
and those great masses above my head already preparing to fall? I
see the marble of tombs crumbling into dust, and yet I want not to
die . . . A torrent sweeps whole nations, one tumbling upon
another, into the common pit; I, I alone, imagine myself halting at
the brink and dividing the flood that flows round me![23]

But if ruins suggest time and mortality, they also, by their
remoteness, suggest freedom, confessional intimacy and licence.
It is here, among ruins, that he would, in imagination, summon
his friend or encounter his mistress; here, under these shadowy
arcades, a betrayed woman will return to sate her bitterness, then
rub the tears from her cheeks and return among mankind, who
will not guess that she has been weeping.

If he had lost his mistress or were parted from her, it is among
such ruins – Diderot's swelling reverie continues – that he would
come to converse with her and enjoy the same "intoxication"
they had so often shared. "My heart will race at once; I shall seek
for, I shall find, the same voluptuous distraction. [He seems to be
imagining some kind of orgasm.] You will be there in that very
place until the sweet languor, the sweet lassitude of pleasure, has
passed. On my return, men will notice my joy but will never guess
the cause."[24]

Freedom, licence, erotic secrecy and a place safe from shame:
these, for Diderot, are all part of the message of ruins. He allows
such thoughts to run their course, and in doing so they bring their
own reaction, and self-censorship re-awakes, as it is proper that it
should. "O censor, installed in the depths of my heart, you have
followed me even here. I was trying to silence your reproach, and
it speaks here even more loudly. We must flee from these
abodes."

As will have been seen, Diderot did not believe in restraint, in
the sense of stifling any thought – it being his conviction that
thoughts, if allowed to run their course, had a natural capacity for
righting themselves. On the other hand he saw the need for
self-censorship in one's communications with others. It was an
issue very relevant to the visual arts; and a titillating painting in

the *Salon* of 1767, Baudoin's "The Bride Preparing for Bed",
provoked from him a long, powerful and subtle defence of self-
censorship. Artists who desire continuing fame, his argument
runs, will be well advised to choose decent subjects; for indecent
works, however magnificent, are likely eventually to get
destroyed, if not by superstition and pettifogging scruple, then by
virtue and probity. It is not that such works are necessarily evil,
but that they are, as it were, too much for humanity – a fact
revealed by obscene *graffiti*. "Those who people our public
gardens with images of prostitution hardly know what they are
doing. With how many filthy inscriptions is the statue of the
'Venus of the Beautiful Buttocks' scribbled over in the thickets of
Versailles; how many dissolute actions are confessed in those
inscriptions, how many insults made by debauch against its own
idols, insults which reveal 'lost' imaginations."[25] It is a theme we
shall meet again in the remarkable last pages of *D'Alembert's
Dream*.

Catherine the Great's Librarian

In August 1765 d'Holbach went on a visit to England, spending some days with the Garricks and – it may be assumed – meeting various friends of his old companion from Leyden days, John Wilkes, at present in exile in Italy. Diderot suspected, so he told Sophie, that amid his good fortune the baron was bored and restless. "Run, run, my friend," he apostrophised him; "run as far as you will; you will not escape from yourself."[1] If indeed this was d'Holbach's motive (but it was not so entirely), the trip effected a cure. England, the home of liberty and constitutionalism, the Utopia so lauded by Voltaire and Montesquieu, proved greatly overrated, and the baron was soon passionately longing to be back in Paris. The truth was, almost everything English was disappointing: the great of the land were impossibly haughty, the common people were brutal; the buildings were bizarre and Gothic; English gardens, with their affectation of naturalness, were even worse than the prim French ones; English dinner-parties were insufferably formal; English universities were dens of idleness; and the sanctimonious gloom of English concerts was quite crushing, reminding him of "the seven processions of Egyptians round the mausoleum of Osiris". As for the famous British constitution, with its vaunted tripartite division of powers, it was a fraud, and the British monarch gained as much through corruption as the French one ever did by despotism.

D'Holbach, however – though Diderot perhaps had not realised it – had had a further and secret purpose in coming to England, connected with clandestine publication. D'Holbach had decided that the time had come for a bolder campaign in the *philosophique* cause and a concerted programme for publishing "dangerous" texts.

I spoke earlier (pp. 23–25) of certain freethinking texts which had been in circulation in France, in manuscript form, since the beginning of the century, and one of the most influential of these was the *Testament* of the *curé* Jean Meslier.[2] In this voluminous and impressive work a disillusioned cleric disavowed the Christian doctrines that he had preached all his life in favour of materialism, Lockeian "sensualism" and (to all intents and purposes) atheism. Voltaire was a great admirer of the work and published an *Extract* from it (admittedly toning it down and giving it a Deistic tinge) in 1762. "Jean Meslier ought to convert the earth," he wrote to d'Alembert. "Why is his gospel in so few hands? How lukewarm you are in Paris!" Voltaire's venture had, perhaps, served as a challenge to the by no means lukewarm d'Holbach. The dissemination of such texts as Jean Meslier's was what his life had been a preparation for. Also, the mid-1760s seemed a propitious time, for the enemies of *philosophie* were on the defensive. Ever since France's humiliation in the Seven Years' War, the Crown had been in bad odour. For a time the chaos in the country had been extreme – so much so that Malesherbes, with a look forward to the dramatic measures of 1788, had suggested summoning the States-General. But further, by a quite dramatic turn of fortune, the Jesuits had quite suddenly been disgraced; their schools had been closed, and, in 1764, their very Society had been dissolved. It was extraordinary, d'Alembert wrote to Voltaire (8 September 1762), in his ruthless manner, with how little fuss the whole thing had taken place and these "vermin" had been destroyed.

One of d'Holbach's aims in coming to London, accordingly, was to make contact with British printers, and likewise with emissaries of the Dutch publisher Marc-Michel Rey, who specialised in the clandestine trade. Then there were arrangements to be made for clandestine books, when printed, to be smuggled into France. Works produced in Holland might have to come via London and be brought to Paris in ones and twos. They might be brought, perhaps, in the luggage of friends or business acquaintances of d'Holbach's, disguised by false bindings or hidden in false-bottomed suitcases. Meanwhile, in his own baggage, d'Holbach was bringing home copies of classic texts by English

freethinkers – Toland, Clarke, Hobbes and the like – with a view
to their translation.

He returned from his six-weeks stay full of plans and greatly
relieved to be back among his compatriots. (Light-minded and
"mad" they might be, but worth a hundred times more than the
"surly pedants" across the Channel.) His helpers were set to
work; and over the next five years, before the appearance of his
own *magnum opus*, *The System of Nature*, there would issue an
absolute torrent of freethinking works from the "factory" in the
rue Royale. They would include some of the most revered of the
clandestine French manuscripts and several works from
d'Holbach's own pen. A few titles will give the flavour: *Antiquity
Unveiled*, *Portable Theology*, *Priests Unmasked*, *The Philosophic Soldier*,
Sacred Contagion (or The Natural History of Superstition), *Religious
Cruelty*, *Essay on Prejudices*, *Hell Destroyed*, *A Critical History of Jesus
Christ*. Diderot, who was closely in touch with all this activity,
would write to Sophie, with a flicker of irony, that it was "raining
bombs in the House of the Lord". "Every day when I get up, I
look out of the window to see if the great whore of Babylon is not
already pacing the streets, her great cup in her hand."[3] He would
also comment, not very kindly, on d'Holbach's abilities as a
translator. Having in the past had to "wash d'Holbach's filthy
rags", he wrote feelingly. The baron, he told Sophie, had an
ingenious stratagem: when a new religious work in some foreign
tongue came out, he would set to work one of his drudges, who
would translate it very tediously, killing it stone dead. Unfortunately, however – though he did not intend it – it was just what
the baron himself did, when translating works that he admired
and wanted to promote.

On d'Holbach's own *System of Nature*, which was to become a
very famous "materialist" text, Diderot's influence would be
pervasive – though more so in detail than in the book's basic
argument, for d'Holbach was a "reductionist" in a way that, as
we shall see, Diderot was not. D'Holbach's central postulate is
that Man is a purely physical being. Physical man is Man acting
under the impulsion of causes that our senses reveal to us; moral
man is Man acting through physical causes that are not directly
revealed to us (partly because of our own prejudices). Everything

in the universe is in motion (it is its "essence" to be so), and self-love or self-conservation ("gravitation towards oneself") is in the moral sphere what Newton's "force of inertia" is in the physical one.

The work would bear the mark of innumerable conversations between the two friends, and d'Holbach, who knew himself to be no stylist, would on occasion get Diderot to supply him with a purple passage. The concluding paean to Nature ("O Nature! Sovereign of all beings! And you her adorable daughters Virtue, Reason and Truth, be for ever our sole divinities," etc.) is believed to be Diderot's work.

D'Holbach, by this time, had found himself an ideal fellow-worker and protégé. This was a young man named Jacques-André Naigeon, son of a mustard-manufacturer; he had been an art-student but had turned philosopher and was a most fanatical and single-minded atheist. The introduction had originally come from Diderot, who had got to know Naigeon in 1765 (or perhaps before), and in a short while he became d'Holbach's housemate and intimate friend. He joined in all the baron's publishing exploits; he translated, adapted and edited under his direction; and, as was sometimes necessary, he would correct blunders and contradictions in the baron's own writings. In addition he took charge of the business of clandestine distribution, employing his younger brother to re-copy d'Holbach's holographs, to conceal their author's identity, and to serve as a channel of transmission to Holland.

Naigeon was not only an atheist but, unlike Diderot, a tirelessly proselytising one. His enemies were rude about him. La Harpe wrote a poem saying he combined the gravity of a scholar with the airs and *coiffure* of a *petit-maître* and claimed that he aped Diderot, repeating his views and copying his mannerisms. Even Diderot's friends called him "insufferably vain", and d'Holbach himself complained of his being so *proud* of not believing in God. He had nevertheless, the merit of integrity. The vividest story about him dates from his later years. One day, at the height of the Terror, his friends were alarmed to see him so troubled and shaken, and they feared he might have found his name on a list of victims. "It is worse than that," he cried. "What, then?" "That monster Robespierre has just decreed a Supreme Being."[4]

Naigeon's ruling passion, after atheism, was the collecting of fine books. He had no sense of humour, as Diderot was well aware, for, as we shall see, a story of his, *The Two Friends from Bourbonne*, originated in a hoax played upon the credulous Naigeon. For all this, Diderot took an affectionate interest in the vehement "misotheist", the "little hurricane, Naigeon", and he, for his part, became as wholesale a devotee of Diderot's philosophy as Grimm himself. Eventually Diderot appointed Naigeon as his literary executor, a step that did a good deal to shape his posthumous reputation.

It will help convey the tone within this close-knit little group, as also Diderot's state of mind regarding their secretive activities, to consider a letter of Diderot's to an unnamed correspondent (most likely Sophie) some time about the middle of 1769. He is reporting an argument between himself and his friends during a summer expedition. D'Holbach, Naigeon and he, together with Suard and the *abbé* Bergier,[5] had gone on a picnic to Saint-Cloud, and the conversation had got on to Helvétius and his shameless retraction during the trouble over *De l'Esprit*. Diderot said how much he would admire a man who, summoned before a tribunal, would stoutly defend his authorship of a "dangerous" work, saying "Yes, I wrote it. Those are my views. I shall not unsay them."

He was not thinking of himself in this, he told Sophie, if she were worrying; his days for "follies" of that kind were over, he did not have enough confidence in his own opinions to defend them to the death. Nevertheless that afternoon, thinking of the matter as an abstract question, he had felt impelled to testify, and his friends could tease him if they wished. Which of course they did, very ribaldly – as he meant them to.

> It was a foolish, gay, altogether excellent day. That temperamental Naigeon is such an acquisition. How they made fun of me, because I insisted on being burnt! The thin-skinned Naigeon is still trembling, I don't doubt, and I would forgive him, were he as stout as the towers of Notre-Dame . . . Never was an important question treated in gayer fashion and with less pedantry: we laughed like children.[6]

The fact that Diderot can make a joke, and an excellent joke, of his hankerings after martyrdom and a Socrates-like deathbed, is important in understanding him. Rousseau could be irresponsible, as when propounding utterly perverse paradoxes; Voltaire, especially in old age, could be outrageously irresponsible, unable to resist gratuitous mischief; but Diderot strikes one as having a streak of even profounder irresponsibility.

"Ah! How beautiful those days were in France, when all seemed hope for her. Why did violence have to be used to achieve what Time, in its peaceful progress, must have given us soon?" So wrote Mme Suard[7] after the Revolution, remembering the 1760s. She was partly thinking, we may suppose, of the philosophic *salons* of Paris; and certainly, for free and enlightened discussion of national problems and easy intellectual commerces between the sexes, they had, it was generally agreed, no rival in Europe, though on the other hand plenty of imitators. It was characteristic that, together with some backbiting malice, the holders of these *salons* showed a certain solidarity and made a point of respecting one another's "day". Mondays and Wednesdays were agreed to belong to Mme Geoffrin, Tuesdays to Helvétius, and Thursdays and Sundays to d'Holbach.

Thus when, in 1765, Mme Necker decided to set up her own *salon*, she took advice and decided she would receive on Fridays. She was then twenty-nine, the daughter of a Swiss pastor. As Suzanne Curchod she had been wooed, and rejected, by Edward Gibbon and had subsequently married the Genevan banker Jacques Necker. She was not a born hostess, being somewhat starchy and "improving" in manner; nevertheless before long she had attracted quite a distinguished circle. The malicious said the real purpose of her *salon* was to promote her husband's career, and certainly it did much for it and was a factor in his rise to power as France's Controller-General. He contributed nothing much to the conversation, however, preferring to suck his thumb in impressive fashion.

One of the first acquisitions to the *salon* was Diderot, who reported to Sophie (1765) that "a Madame Neckre [*sic*], a pretty woman and *bel esprit*," was "in love with him" and quite persecuting him to attend her receptions.[8] He became a regular attendant, anyway for a time, and helped her to recruit other well-known *philosophes*. Writing of these gatherings later, Mme Necker gives a nice glimpse of him in his citizen-of-the-world guise. On being introduced to a new member of her circle, the ex-colonial administrator Dubucq, his greeting was simply: "Embrace me; it is one *honnête homme* embracing another. I am Diderot."[9]

Though a believer herself, Mme Necker welcomed the free-thinkers to her table, saying "I have friends who are atheists. Why not? They are friends one pities." On one occasion, the dinner-table conversation, led by Diderot and Grimm, became too much for her, and, to everyone's alarm, she burst into tears. When the two friends went next morning to apologise, they were however, pardoned with good grace.

By the early 1760s the break between Rousseau and such *philosophique* circles was complete. The year or two following the great "Hermitage" crisis of 1757 had in fact proved the climax of Rousseau's writing career, and the works he produced at this period were a clear repudiation of "philosophic" principles. "Julie devout is a lesson for philosophers," he wrote to a friend about *La Nouvelle Héloïse*; "and the atheist Wolmar is one for the intolerant."[10] In *Emile* he is more direct. It is declared there that even fanaticism, in the long run, is less fatal to humankind than the "philosophic mind".

Equally it was open war by now between Rousseau and Voltaire. Rousseau had written to Voltaire in 1760 saying Voltaire had inflicted grievous wrongs on himself, his one-time disciple and admirer: he had ruined Geneva, making it impossible for Rousseau to live, or even to die, in his own country. "In short," he wrote, "I hate you."[11] Voltaire, astonished, took the line that Rousseau had simply gone out of his mind – which was "a pity". D'Alembert agreed with him. He commented with characteristic coolness that "Jean-Jacques is a sick man of great intelligence, but intelligent only when he is suffering from fever. One must neither cure him nor outrage him."[12]

In truth, Voltaire was nursing much rage against Rousseau. For one thing he realised that Rousseau had been trying, in his

Letter Upon Stage-Performances, to make trouble for him in Geneva, where even private theatricals – by now his great passion in life – were forbidden by law. Eventually, therefore, he took his revenge, and it was a most savage one. In December 1764 a pamphlet was published – it was anonymous but it is generally regarded now as by Voltaire – entitled *Sentiments of the Citizens,* attacking Rousseau with the utmost ferocity. It described him as "a man who, disguised as a mountebank, drags with him from village to village, from mountain to mountain, the unfortunate woman whose mother he brought to her death and whose children he exposed at the door of the Foundlings' Hospital."[13] This publishing of his most closely guarded secret was devastating to Rousseau. It shook his hold on life and made him feel the need to re-think his whole conception of himself. He had for some time been considering writing his autobiography and had been assembling material for it, but now, suddenly, he saw that such a work – a uniquely unsparing portrait of himself, and of his enemies – must become the very object of his existence. His *Confessions* took clear shape in his mind.

Rousseau felt himself surrounded by enemies, but among their number he did not, so far, include Diderot. His words about him in the Preface to his *Letter on Stage-Performances* had been, "I shall never cease to regret him, and he is even more a loss to my heart than to my writings." A dozen passages in the *Confessions* that he was now writing suggest that the words were sincere. There would come a time when he would see Diderot as the blackest of villains, but for the moment he remembered their old friendship with tenderness, considering him "less wicked than indiscreet and weak". If anything, it was Diderot who thought of himself as the injured party, and he observed Rousseau's public doings critically. "He is an *excessive* man," he told Sophie apropos of *Emile,* "a man tossed from atheism to the baptism of church-bells. Who knows where he will stop?"[14] Nevertheless early in 1765, through a mutual acquaintance of theirs named François-Louis d'Escherny, he made overtures for a reconciliation. D'Escherny was asked to convey a message from him to Rousseau that he admitted he might have done Rousseau a wrong, but if so, it had been from no evil motive, but simply through thoughtlessness and because of a misunderstanding. Rousseau, however, was quite immovable. He told d'Escherny he could not imagine what Diderot was wanting after seven years of silence. He asked nothing from Diderot and was very far from wishing him ill. "I know how to respect the rights of friendship even when extinguished. Only I never rekindle; it is my most inviolable maxim."[15]

The year 1765 was for Rousseau a succession of persecutions and wanderings. His house in Môtiers was stoned, and he was insulted and threatened in the street; having taken refuge on the Ile de Saint Pierre, he was expelled by the Bernese authorities. As his troubles intensified, so did the concern of the benevolent Hume, and he now offered to help Rousseau find asylum in England. It seemed to Rousseau, in his bewildering situation, to be his best hope, and in the last days of the year, defying the ban on his presence in France, he came to join Hume in Paris. He established himself in the Temple, under the protection of its *Grand-Prieur*, Prince de Conti, and each morning he would hold a sort of *levée*, dressed in his squirrel-fur hat and Armenian robes. It was a moment of glory for him, but he sent no word to Diderot, nor did Diderot really expect it. "For three days Rousseau has been in Paris. I do not suppose he will visit me," he wrote sadly to Sophie (20 December 1765). "But I will not conceal that it would give me great pleasure, and that I should be very glad to see how he would justify his conduct towards me."[16] On the evening before their departure for England, Hume paid a call to d'Holbach, who warned him, or so it was said later, that Hume was "nursing a viper in his bosom".

Grimm's eyes were set, and had been for some years, on a diplomatic post, perhaps as the envoy of some German court. He had made a beginning in 1759, when the free city of Frankfurt had appointed him their representative in Paris. This had ended in near-disaster, for some indiscreet private correspondence of his had fallen into official hands and he had been forced to resign; indeed, without help from the Dauphin it seems he might have been expelled from France as a spy and enemy alien. This setback, however, had not dampened his ambition. He had come to be on close terms of friendship with "the great Caroline", Landgravine of Hesse-Darmstadt, patroness of the garden-cult and of the religion of friendship.[17] The whole royal family of Hesse would look to him for advice, and he busied himself with marriage-plans for the Landgravine's three daughters. Another princely friend, with whom he was almost equally intimate, was the Duchess Louise-Dorothea of Saxe-Gotha. He would visit her humble court, would write to her in lavish compliment as "the sovereign of his heart" and was continually performing services for her and for the royal family, sending them books, wigs, the latest engravings and useful information of all sorts. It is worth adding that he helped his (and Rousseau's) old friend Klüpfel (see p. 80), who was now a court official in Gotha, in founding the famous *Almanach de Gotha*, the great authority on precedence and the bedside book of princes.[18] In these royal contacts his great asset and stepping-stone was, of course, the *Correspondance littéraire*. "After all, it is an advantage of no small significance," he was to write to the Landgravine Caroline, "to have the right to speak twice a month to all there is by way of enlightened great princes and princesses in Europe."[19] In 1764 his journal won him the greatest of all his royal conquests, when, by delicate diplomacy, he persuaded Catherine the Great to become a subscriber and was encouraged to correspond with her privately. As time went on, he was often called abroad on errands for his royal patrons, and in his absence Mme d'Epinay and Diderot would "look after the shop", that is to say keep the *Correspondance Littéraire* going. Mme d'Epinay was a very prolific contributor to the *Correspondance Littéraire*, providing essays, theatre reviews, book reviews articles on politics, philosophy and economics, and light verse; and sometimes, when she and Diderot had been left in charge, the "workshop" would be set up on her own premises in the rue Sainte Anne. The journal was, indeed, her main foothold in the literary life. Her educational dialogues, the *Conversations with Emilie* (1781), made their first appearance there, and she used it to circulate the letters she received from Voltaire and the *abbé* Galiani.

As Diderot's daughter grew up, it began to be a worry to him how he would provide her with a dowry. The thought occurred to him, since his work on the *Encyclopédie* was nearly over, that he might sell his library. He made one or two tentative moves in that direction. Meanwhile, however, Grimm had had an inspiration, and in February 1765 he wrote to Catherine the Great's Chamberlain, General Betzki,[20] asking whether the Empress might not feel disposed to buy Diderot's library. Betzki replied promptly and with enthusiasm. Her Majesty's "compassionate heart", he wrote, had been wrung at the thought of such a sacrifice, and, to encourage such a great and worthy man, she was eager to purchase the library, and at the price (15,000 *livres*) that Grimm had stipulated, but on one condition, that Diderot should remain the "depository" of the books till further notice, and not only that, but should receive a salary of a hundred *pistoles* a year as her "librarian".[21]

The startled Diderot asked the French authorities whether he might accept, and was told, in flattering terms, that he could; and Voltaire, for his part, asked Diderot to receive his "transports of joy". "Would one have suspected, fifty years ago, that one day the Scythians would so nobly recompense, in Paris, the virtue, knowledge and philosophy so unworthily treated among us ourselves?"[22] For Diderot, it was a sign of approval such as he had despaired of ever receiving.

In the spring of 1766 a second mark of favour followed. It had been the ambition of the Empress Elizabeth of Russia to erect a grand monument to her father Peter the Great, and Catherine, who decided to fulfil this plan, instructed General Betzki to find a suitable sculptor. He wrote to Prince Gallitzin,[23] the Russian ambassador in Paris, and Gallitzin, who was a friend of Diderot's, asked him for his advice. Diderot at once, and most energetically, recommended his friend Etienne-Maurice Falconet,[24] whose work had been one of the great sensations of the *Salon* of 1765. It was in some ways a surprising and bold choice, for up to now Falconet's *forte* as a sculptor had been for the delicate and the intimate, not for the heroic. He was in fact, and with great success, Director of Sculpture for the porcelain factory at Sèvres. However, Diderot's choice was approved, being helped by the fact that Falconet had underbid his rivals in regard to fees.

No commission could have been more to Diderot's taste. For

not only was he to fix the terms of the appointment, it was also expected that he should give the sculptor the benefit of his own artistic advice. This was something he was infinitely ready to do, the designing of imaginary monuments being one of his very favourite occupations. It was in this way, and thanks to Diderot's good judgement, that St Petersburg gained its prodigious monument, the "Bronze Horseman" later celebrated in Pushkin's poem.

Nevertheless, Falconet was not a man to let Diderot, or anyone else, dictate artistic ideas to him – anyway on such an occasion as this, which was the great opportunity of his career. In fact the simple and marvellous design of his statue, the Tsar on a rearing steed, galloping up a steep rock, with one protective hand extended over his city, came to him almost at once. He remembered later how he had done a pencil sketch of it "on a table-corner" in Diderot's study and how his friend had been impressed. Soon afterwards Diderot was able to tell Falconet that the Empress approved of the conception too – as how could she not? "It is grand, it is simple, it is violent, it is imperious, it characterises the Hero."[25] All the same – interpreting the statue, perhaps rightly, as an allegory of "enlightenment" – he suggested some improvements. Could not Falconet surround his horseman with allegorical figures, representing "Barbarism defeated", "Love of the People" and "The Russian nation"? Falconet, however, tactfully excused himself, saying that his hero was "self-sufficient"; he was himself "at once subject and attribute".

A third mark of favour from Catherine soon followed. Diderot's salary as her "librarian" did not actually get paid, and when the fact came to her ears, she told him, via Betzki, that, to ensure the good running of the library, he must accept five years' stipend in advance. At this, Diderot's gratitude quite carried him away. "Great Princess," he wrote to her via Betzki (29 November 1766), "I prostrate myself at your feet. I stretch out my arms to you, I would wish to speak, but paralysis grips my soul." His friends embrace him, he tells her, his wife weeps tears of joy. It seems he hardly knows where or what he is. "A noble enthusiasm kindles in me." (He had recently been reading Ossian.) "My fingers reach of their own accord for an ancient lyre of which Philosophy severed the strings. I unhook it from the wall, and, bareheaded and with my chest uncovered, as is my habit, I feel myself impelled to song." The Ode that follows pays tribute to the "great soul", another Antonine, who deigned to seek out and succour a lowly stranger, "ignored even by his own master and suffering his stern fate without a murmur."[26] Diderot was now embarked on a cult of Catherine which, for good or evil, would colour the rest of his days.

On 10 November 1765 Diderot wrote Sophie that exultant letter quoted in the Introduction (p. 3), telling her of his *Salon* review for that year and the fortnight of seclusion and "obstinate toil" it had cost him, and of Grimm's extravagant praise of it. "He swears upon his soul . . . that no one else under the sun could have performed, or ever will perform, such a feat, and frankly I have the secret vanity to believe so too." It is appropriate here to give some more thought to this letter. Shall we take it at its face-value, and believe Diderot when he says that, in writing this *Salon*, his *amour propre* felt no need of public rewards – that it would not even insist on praise from his own circle of friends, so long as one soul, one ideal friend, esteemed him at his true worth?

It is an important question for us, and I am inclined to think that Diderot is sincere. The tone of the letter is attractive and somehow "right". He is often at his best and most in command of himself when, as here, he is in full flood of self-praise. (It is otherwise when he is imagining himself a victim.) Also, he was quite correct in thinking that this *Salon* review of 1765 was one of his best and richest pieces of writing. He was very capable of talking for effect, but one gets the feeling that, in this happy moment, he was reading himself rightly. If so, it is important. For the *Salon* review in general character belongs with *Rameau's Nephew*, with *D'Alembert's Dream* and with the rest of Diderot's truly original works, the group that he was inclined to think of as his "mad" writings. One observes one obvious fact about them: in every case there were very good reasons why Diderot could never have thought of publishing them. As he himself says, it would have been impossible to publish the *Salons*, because of their genial or hectoring familiarity, their *brusquerie* towards struggling

artists. But, then, no more would it have been possible to publish
Rameau's Nephew, The Nun or *D'Alembert's Dream* – and for a similar
reason, the fantastic and presumptuous licence that they take
with living people. The truth seems to be that Diderot, having
decided, after the alarming affair of *Letter on the Blind*, to publish
no more "dangerous" works, had come to see attractions, and as
it were a potential new art-form, in the "unpublishable" work.

It was, most likely, much about this time that he began another
such "unpublishable" work, the entrancing *Jacques the Fatalist*. It
is an admiring imitation of Sterne, and one can hazard a guess as
to when he started work on it; for in the summer of 1765 David
Garrick sent d'Holbach a copy of Books VII and VIII of *Tristram
Shandy*, and a passage in chapter 19 of Book VIII, in which
Corporal Trim gives his views on predestination, was clearly the
direct inspiration of Diderot's novel:

> King William was of an opinion, an' please your honour, quoth
> Trim, that every thing was predestined for us in this world;
> insomuch, that he would often say to his soldiers, that "every ball
> had its billet." He was a great man, said my uncle Toby – And I
> believe, continued Trim, to this day, that the shot which disabled
> me at the battle of Landen, was pointed at my knee for no other
> purpose, but to take me out of his service, and place me in your
> honour's, where I should be taken so much better care of in my
> old age – It shall never, Trim, be construed otherwise, said my
> uncle Toby.
>
> The heart, both of the master and the man, were alike subject to
> sudden overflowings; – a short silence ensued.
>
> Beside, said the corporal, resuming the discourse – but in a
> gayer accent – if it had not been for that single shot, I had never,
> an' please your honour, been in love –

Here, it seems obvious, is the source for Diderot's Spinozan-
minded servant-hero Jacques; and the business of Trim's
wounded knee is taken over more or less unaltered.

We know nothing much more about the composition of *Jacques
the Fatalist*, except that by September 1771 some kind of draft
existed and Diderot gave a two-hour reading from it to a friend.[27]
There is reason to think that he went on adding to it and revising
it for many years to come.

The issue of "closet" writing, writing done with no public in view, is significant, for, soon after the November 1765 letter to Sophie, Diderot became involved with his friend Falconet in a vast and year-long correspondence on the subject of posthumous fame. It arose from some fireside conversations between the two in the rue Taranne, in which they discussed "whether it is the thought of posterity that inspires the best actions and the best works." Diderot said that it was. Falconet disagreed; that is to say, he denied that it was so in his own case. As an artist, he said, he scarcely gave a thought to posterity: what mattered to him was his own self-approval, the approval of critics and friends, and maybe the imaginary approval of Raphael. As long as his "Pygmalion"[28] pleased its owner, he would pay much for it not to be destroyed; otherwise, so far as he cared, it could "go to the devil". Evidently part of the point of the thing was that Falconet was a statuary, that is to say a producer of vehicles of posthumous fame. Now posthumous fame is, in the nature of things, the only kind that unpublished and "unpublishable" works can aspire to, so we might easily assume that, in the recesses of Diderot's mind, this is what the debate with Falconet was all about. I think, though, that this would be to jump to a false conclusion.

At all events, the dispute excited the two friends. They began to leave little notes to each other, continuing their discussion where they left it the night before; and then in December 1765 Diderot sent Falconet a full-scale letter on the subject, the first of many. It is a subtle and engaging piece, worth quoting nearly in full.

You believe that posterity will love me, and this pleases you; and you believe much more that it will love yourself, but this does not interest you. But how can you set store on a good on another's behalf that you despise on your own. If it pleases you to have as a friend . . . I will not go on. I was going to offer a sophism which would have spoilt a reason of *sentiment*.

Since it is sweet to hear, at night, a distant concert of flutes, whose scattered sounds my imagination, helped by my discerning ear, succeeds in assembling into a connected melody – one that charms all the more because, in good part, it is my own creation –I must conclude that a concert near at hand would be well worth hearing. But will you believe me, my friend, when I say it is not this nearby concert which enthralls me but the other one? The sphere in which we are admired, the length of time in which we live and hear ourselves praised, the number of those who give us our well-deserved eulogy in person, all that is too little for our ambitious soul. We do not feel ourselves sufficiently rewarded, perhaps, by the genuflections of an existing world; we want to see people yet unborn upon their knees, beside those already kneeling. Only so limitless a crowd of worshippers can satisfy a mind whose impulses are always towards the infinite. You will say that such claims are often more than there is merit to justify; and you will be right. But should we not see such claims as an oblique compliment to our contemporaries? Are we not really saying to them: "You consider me a marvellous man, you have told me so yourself, and posterity will never dare contradict such enlightened characters"?

So you see, my friend, I admit it is all nonsense; all such poor crazed creatures as me are as absurd as one another. Yes, but (shall I confess it?) when I look into my heart. I find there the very feeling I am mocking; my heart, more vain than philosophic, can hear at this very moment certain faint notes from that far-distant concert. *O curas hominum! O quantum est in rebus inane!* Very true. But confine happiness to the meagre allotment called reality and tell me what it is worth. Since there are a hundred imaginary pains, which yet cause real suffering, let these poor madmen, in compensation, invent a hundred chimerical pleasures. My friend, let us not try to lay these ghosts, which, near us or further off, will never cease to haunt us.

What a chance for eloquence! How my head was warming to the theme, had there been time to let it. But I must leave you, to go to the people who (without flattery) are not worth as much as you, and on business that will not concern posterity.

Truly, posterity would be an ungrateful wretch if it forgot me altogether, seeing how often I remember it.

My friend, let me make myself quite clear. I am not interested in posterity on behalf of the dead. I am interested in its praise, legitimately presumed and guaranteed unanimously by contemporaries, as a present pleasure for the living: a pleasure just as real as the praise you know that some contemporary is giving you but which you cannot hear, since he is not in the room.

Eulogy in the hand, paid in hard cash, is what we get from our contemporaries; presumed eulogy, eulogy on a credit basis, is the kind we hear from a distance and is that of posterity.

My friend, why will you accept only the half of what is due to you?

It is not myself or Peter or Paul or John praising us. It is good
taste, and good taste is an abstract being which does not die: it
speaks, uninterruptedly, through an endless succession of tongues.
That immortal voice will, no doubt, fall silent for you when you
cease to exist; but you hear it at present, and it is immortal in
spite of you, and it will go on its way, crying "Falconet,
Falconet!"[29]

It will be seen that what has tempted Diderot is a nice paradox,
one very logical for a materialist who firmly holds that there is no
life after death. Nothing could be more absurd than for such a
man to speak, as sages sometimes do, of enjoying reputation in his
tomb; but could he not, by an act of creative imagination, enjoy it
now? His letter turns upon pleasure (why deny oneself the
pleasure of posthumous fame?), love (Falconet had performed a
loving act, in wanting future fame for his friend, and this merits
some return) and expansiveness (the philosopher's vision rushes
out to fill up all time and space). It is an admirable *jeu d'esprit*, no
doubt with strong feeling behind it; but one does not detect in it,
or in the rest of the correspondence, any special reference to his
"unpublishable" works. What Diderot demands from posterity is
praise, not understanding – praise of the same brand as provided
by his contemporaries. It does not seem that he is expressing a
longing, whether eager or desperate, for some eventual audience
for *Rameau's Nephew*.

This first letter is actually the best thing in the whole
sprawling, rewarding, sometimes infuriating correspondence.
Diderot intended it as his last word on the subject, but at his
friend's goading the correspondence continued and swelled to
enormous proportions. Falconet was a contentious fellow, one of
those harsh and quirky characters whom Diderot was drawn to,
and he enjoyed the idea of pitting himself against a famous writer.
He adduced all the many things one could say against
posthumous fame: how it was prey to accident, fraud and
imbecility; how the reputation of lost "great" works of art, like
the frescoes of Polygnotus at Delphi, was manufactured by
ignorant men of letters who simply repeated what previous ones
had said. As a practising artist himself, he said, he had only to
read the eulogy by Pausanias of those frescoes to perceive that

they must have been very bad indeed: "no order, no *vraisemblance*, no perspective, no harmony, and hence no interest."

This criticism, of course, provides a fatal temptation to Diderot, with his passion for mental painting; and he demonstrates how, from the plodding words of Pausanias, he can reconstruct Polygnotus's work as the superlative masterpiece it must have been. Falconet is sceptical. Diderot writes to him all one day and night, and Falconet replies at the same length, causing Diderot to beg him to stop, for it is killing him. In all this logic-chopping and jousting with classical texts, though, Diderot's supple paradox about posterity gets somewhat lost, or rather becomes rigidified.

At much the same period as the Falconet correspondence, Diderot began one of a different kind with a young actress named Marie-Madeleine Jodin. She was the daughter of a clockmaker, of Swiss Protestant origins, who had written pamphlets on the design of watch-escapements and had engaged in controversy with the astronomer Lalande. He had become friendly with Diderot, and at his death in 1761 Diderot and Nanette had taken a kindly interest in his widow and daughter.

At the date of Diderot's first letter to her (21 August 1765) Marie-Madeleine was with a troupe of French actors in Warsaw. She played "Queens and character-roles" and modelled herself on the great Clairon. Her mother, a neighbour of the Diderots, had recently been robbed of half her possessions. Diderot and Nanette had insisted that for the time being the poor woman should take her meals with them, and Diderot urged Marie-Madeleine to send her mother money and in general to play the part of a good daughter. He tells her he is going to "judge her" by how she behaves now.

Diderot adopted this stern, painful-truth-telling, hectoring, tone in all his letters to her – and, we may suppose, with deliberate purpose, for she was a wild character. At the age of nine she had been induced by her parents to declare herself a convert from Protestantism, for the sake of the *pension* atached to such conversions, and it had embittered her against religion. During the remaining years of her girlhood she was expelled from no less than six convents, and for a time after this both she and her mother had lived by prostitution, till their family made complaints of them to the authorities, who confined them for a time in the Salpêtrière prison. More recently, in her theatre company in Warsaw, she had given the Director of her troupe "a lesson in manners" by spitting in his face.

Diderot, who knew of her wretched youth, felt a good deal of pity for her; he would tell her she had a good heart but "the worst head in the world". He tried to arrange work for her in St Petersburg, but this fell through. In the meantime she deserted her company in Poland and went to Dresden, where she acquired a wealthy lover, the Danish envoy the Comte Werner de Schulemburg. When she returned to France, to join a theatre company in Bordeaux, de Schulemburg followed her. It meant that, for the first time, she was in funds, and she asked Diderot to look after her savings for her, which he agreed to do with enthusiasm, telling her unflatteringly: "Detach yourself promptly from that money, which is certainly in the most unsafe hands I know of – your own."[30] He went to great trouble over her money-affairs, as also over her mother's hopelessly muddled ones, and he sent her further stringent lectures when she quarrelled with de Schulemburg. Then, however, she got herself into further trouble. In her reckless way, she chose to make fun of a religious procession and was arrested for it and sent to prison, obtaining her release only through her lover's bribes. It was the same offence as, three years earlier, had brought hideous punishment on the young La Barre – a judicial atrocity memorably denounced by Voltaire. The escapade tried Diderot's patience, and he told Sophie (11 September 1769) he would have been "enraged" had he been interested in Marie-Madeleine beyond a certain point. His surviving letters to her end at this point, but the two seem to have remained in contact, and Jodin, retiring from the stage at the age of thirty-three, was to make a new life for herself in Paris, as a *philosophe* and a feminist.[31]

Diderot, evidently, had decided that the way to help her was by tough criticism, and his letters to her became a complete miniature treatise on acting and conduct: on how to behave on the stage and off it – two questions that, as he treats them, turn out to be much the same. She should shun the mirror; perform as if no audience were watching and even, sometimes, have the courage to turn her back on it; eschew gesture; make a special study of "tranquil" and silent effects. They are his known theatrical doctrines, and in these letters to Mlle Jodin we see most clearly their ethical drift. He is telling her, as it were, that what is wrong with her acting is wrong with her life.

18

"Is he good? Is he wicked ?"

The title of this chapter is taken from a short play that Diderot wrote in his old age, the one really effective piece that he ever wrote for the stage.[1] It concerns a man who enjoys doing things for others but likes to do them his own way, for which reason he is not always thanked.

It was no empty boast of Diderot's that he gave up half his existence to other people's concerns. His study was always knee-deep in other writers' plays, pamphlets, treatises, epic poems and the like which he had been asked to pronounce upon, and which, after procrastination, he would in fact criticise and blue-pencil with great thoroughness – if indeed he did not re-write them for their authors. Then there was the *Correspondance littéraire*. Increasingly, as Grimm's avocations took him more often abroad, Diderot, with Mme d'Epinay's help, would find himself standing in for him as editor, compelled to keep up with all the new publications and the latest operas and plays – a task that would make him groan.

Equally, with his benevolent officiousness and enormous acquaintance, he was, as we have seen, the person whom others depended on to pull strings for them. The role did not displease him, and he felt he had a certain genius for it, though sometimes the beneficiaries were not too content when they discovered his methods.

There was the time in 1765 when he was plaguing the Navy Department on behalf of the young widow of a naval officer, Mme Dubois, trying to persuade them to extend her pension in favour of her child – the child that, as he told Sophie mysteriously, "I had by a woman I have never met, by agency of the Holy Ghost."[2]

Or there was the "Story of the Portraits". When his friend Prince Gallitzin, the Russian ambassador, left Paris in 1768, he broke with his current mistress Mlle Dornet, a dancer at the Opéra, and, meeting the beautiful young Comtesse de Schmettau at a watering-place, he paid court to her and married her. He then began to regret having presented Mlle Dornet with certain portraits, and he asked Diderot if he could think of some way to recover them. Diderot considered and recalled that Mlle Dornet, as well as being extremely mercenary, was a confirmed hypochondriac, and it suggested to him a fantastic plan. Another friend of his, a young bankers' agent named Desbrosses, should be introduced to her – at the house of a mutual acquaintance of theirs, a German woman painter named Mme Therbouche – in the guise of a Turkish doctor and chiromancer, and he should warn her of the medical danger of preserving any souvenirs of the past, whether furniture, jewels, letters or portraits. They were liable to emit impalpable "simulacra", he was to tell her, with injurious effect on the retina.

The scheme seems actually to have been put into effect, or at any rate the first meeting ("Our mystification is going ahead," Diderot wrote to Sophie on 1 October 1768), and matters would no doubt have proceeded further, only their host Mme Therbouche suddenly decided to quit France. From the start, however, the real *raison d'être* of the plot was its story-value (Diderot told Sophie he would reserve it to amuse them in "the dead seasons"), and a year later fate gave this abortive frolic a grim but apt conclusion. Desbrosses, threatened with exposure of an extraordinary financial fraud or "mystification", came to see Diderot, discussing with him with the utmost calmness his plan to commit suicide, and went home and blew his brains out. Diderot used the story – an *opera buffa* plot with a macabre ending – as the basis for a playlet or story-in-dialogue entitled *Mystification*.

Even Mme Geoffrin, who considered Diderot a dreamer and a disorderly fellow, acknowledged that he had talents as a fixer, and she asked him to help her get out of the hands of a "man from Gisors" who was pestering her about his late wife's will. She had wanted to help the wife's family, who were contesting the "man

from Gisors's" right to a certain sedan-chair, but nothing she
could do, not even offering to pay the value of the wretched chair
herself, would stop him besieging her with letters and threats.
"So here is the lady of the rue St Honoré toiling up to my garret,"
wrote Diderot to Sophie (26 October 1768), "collapsing into a
chair and spreading out her papers." It was slightly awkward for
Diderot, since the man from Gisors was one of Sophie's relatives,
but he took on the assignment and began to relish its intricacies,
asking Sophie to frighten her relative with fantastic prospects of
retribution if he did not respond well to Diderot's "decent but
firm" letter.

Diderot saw it as part of his role as a philosopher and man of
feeling to intervene in his friends' moral life. In *Woman in the
Eighteenth Century* (1862), by the Goncourt brothers, there is a
tirade about that portentous new figure of the French eighteenth
century, the lay "director of conscience". In any house of note,
the Goncourts write, some "saint of the *Encyclopédie*" will have
installed himself as a fixture, coming between a wife and her
husband: lecturing, scolding her, "penetrating her sentiments",
reading her letters, interfering in her children's education and
taking her reputation into his hands.[3] They cite Charles Duclos
and Mme d'Epinay, and they might with some aptness have cited
Diderot and Sophie's sister "Uranie" (Mme Le Gendre).

For much of the time in the early 1760s Uranie lived in Paris,
while Sophie, willingly or otherwise, remained with her mother in
Isle. It gave Diderot a feeling of responsibility for Sophie's sister,
and he would lecture her on ethics, be nice to her disagreeable
husband, call in famous doctors when she was ill, and report on
all her doings to Sophie. Uranie, in her teasing way, was keeping
two would-be lovers on a string: an engineer named Guillaume
Viallet, and Viallet's superior in the Department of Highways,
named Perronet. Diderot spotted that she was receiving letters
from Viallet on the quiet. It was at the time that, at his direction,
the whole Volland family was reading Richardson and taking
sides heatedly over his characters; Diderot quoted *Clarissa* to
them, as a warning of the fatal folly of secret correspondences.

Time passed. Diderot got to know and to form a high opinion of
Viallet. He pulled strings for him on behalf of his career and

commissioned him to illustrate slate-making in the plate-volumes of the *Encyclopédie*. Eventually in 1767, believing him now cured of his passion for Uranie, Diderot – unprompted – offered him Angélique's hand in marriage. The event, he told him, could not take place for four years, when Angélique would be eighteen, and, he explained, he would himself regard it as a firm commitment but would not expect Viallet to do so.

At first Viallet was flattered by the offer, then he began to have second thoughts. The four years seemed very long to him; also his passion for Uranie had flared up again. He composed complicated letters to Diderot, who did not reply, and finally he wrote, withdrawing from the engagement.

Diderot's reaction was decidedly unorthodox. It made him decide that now, if ever, was the time to save Uranie's soul. Assuming the rights of a director of conscience, he lectured her furiously; as he later described it, he "descended into her heart, showed her its emptiness and how it was the source of all the wretchedness of her life, her neglect of her duties and the mortal boredom of her days." He painted a glowing picture of Viallet's talents and virtues and told her that, though it might be a crime, she had better stop tormenting him and sleep with him. "For God's sake, Madame, commit this one wrong that will save you from a thousand more!" According to him, she wavered, then she declared with unction that it was impossible – she was a virtuous woman – adding casually that, as a matter of fact, Viallet did not attract her physically.

Then Viallet, in one of his many letters to Diderot, made fun of his gesture in offering Angélique's hand; at this Diderot, no doubt feeling a little foolish, decided he must teach Viallet a lesson and despatched to him one of those epic lambastings that sometimes flowed from his pen. He defended his own conduct in minute detail, showed how Viallet had behaved like a lunatic, a would-be Lovelace and a futile sophist, and stigmatised Uranie as an "unbridled" and "infernal" coquette. What was one to do, he asked with a madman like Viallet and a "tuft of down" like Uranie? All the same, he confessed, he could not stop loving and serving them. It was, he said self-admiringly, how he was made. "At the first moment I jump to the roof; the next moment I am myself, that is to say a frank, gentle, just, indulgent, *honnête* and beneficent man. Continue this eulogy if you like, for it is not complete. It has said nothing about my intelligence."

Diderot, naturally, remained intensely aware of his obligations to Catherine the Great; and he found a way to repay them. She was acquiring art-objects on a lavish scale, and he volunteered to act as her agent on the art-market. Others were helping her in the same way, among them Diderot's friend Prince Gallitzin, the Russian ambassador; indeed the two friends would sometimes go on picture-buying expeditions together. They were on such an expedition in May 1768, on the day before Gallitzin, much against his will, was leaving Paris to take up a new appointment in The Hague. The friends had tacitly agreed not to say goodbyes, but, as they were examining the paintings, their eyes met and filled with tears. According to Diderot's account, envious French art-collectors were heartily glad when Gallitzin left French soil.

In the early months of 1768 an opportunity arose, with the death of Louis-Jean Gaignat, owner of a very famous collection of paintings and books. Diderot at once put out feelers to the executors and heirs, and he wrote to Falconet asking him to inform the Empress – guessing, rightly, that she might want to buy the two collections *en bloc*. The matter would need diplomacy if he were not to make enemies. "Ah! if the prince were only here," he lamented, "how we would have manoeuvred." Catherine responded with enthusiasm, and though he did not manage to secure all he wanted, he was able to buy her, as he reported, "Five of the most beautiful paintings there are in France" – a Murillo, three Gerard Dous and a J. B. Van Loo.

Three years later, at the expense of huge effort, he brought off a much greater *coup*, and secured, to the fury of rival French collectors and of Horace Walpole, more or less the whole of the great collection of the connoisseur Pierre Crozat, that is to say the portion of it in the possession of the Baron de Thiers. This contained, among other items, two Raphaels, a Sebastiano del Piombo, a Fra Bartolomeo, a Giorgione, three Titians, five Van Dycks, five Rubens sketches, three Rembrandts, a Jan Steen, a Poussin, two Watteaus and a Chardin. In virtue of these and other purchases one can regard Diderot as, to quite a considerable degree, the founder of the Hermitage collection.

The friend in need, the prop, the confessor, the puller of strings: Diderot was all of these things, as he would have been the first to insist (the contrast with Rousseau is extreme). But was he "responsible"? Opinions differed about this, and perhaps still do differ. We may consider his stormy relationship with Mme Therbouche, of whom I spoke earlier (p. 311). Anna-Dorothea Therbouche, a self-taught German painter in her forties, arrived in France at the beginning of 1767. She had been determined, according to Diderot's account, to "make a noise in France", and in fact was not long in winning membership of the Academy of Fine Art. Diderot quickly got to know her. He admired her independence of mind and liked the way she insisted on painting the male nude: it showed, he thought, a very proper attitude to modesty. ("Why should vice have the exclusive privilege of undressing a man?") The friendship flourished, and, no doubt at Diderot's instigation, his friend Prince Gallitzin installed her in a house left at his disposal by the sculptor Falconet.

Her career, though, ran into difficulties. A "Jupiter Metamorphosed into Pan surprising Antiope Asleep", submitted by her for the *Salon* exhibition, was rejected as indecent. Diderot arrived at her studio just as the bad news had arrived and found her tearing her hair and brandishing a knife, undecided whether to use it on her painting or on herself. In his usual generous way he took much trouble, though to no avail, to try to get the decision reversed; and before long he found himself looking after her generally – securing patrons for her, criticising her paintings, advising her about self-promotion and – for she was wildly extravagant – helping to stave off her creditors.

Eventually it was decided that she should paint his portrait. She did the head, and then it became a question of his neck and upper chest, but, she complained, his clothes rather hid them. Accordingly he went behind her screen and reappeared "in Academy model style", that is to say stark naked. Mme Therbouche was very approving. "I would not have dared to propose it," she said, "but you have done well, and I thank you."

She went on with her painting, and meanwhile (according to Diderot in his *Salon* review), they "chatted with a simplicity and innocence worthy of the first centuries." There was indeed, he confessed, a problem; "For since the sin of Adam one cannot control all the parts of one's body as one can one's arm; there are some parts that show willingness when the son of Adam does not wish it and none when the son of Adam would greatly like it." However, should circumstances have called for it, he had an answer ready. It was what Diogenes had said to the young wrestler: "My son, do not be afraid, I am not so wicked as *that!*"

There was no affair between Diderot and Mme Therbouche (it amused him to consider their friendship as a parable of innocence) but of course gossip insisted otherwise. Thus the "poor philosopher" was faced with a cruel choice; should he abandon her to her fate, or should he injure her reputation further by remaining her friend? Conscious of his rectitude, he decided on the second, saved her from the debtor's prison on twenty occasions and in time was nearly driven mad by her prodigality and vanity; all the reward he got, when she finally beat a retreat from France, was that she told the world he had ruined her career, forcing her to leave just when success was about to dawn. Diderot related the story in his *Salon* of 1767, and how the "unworthy Prussian" had given the poor philosopher a good lesson. "But he will not profit from it," he wrote. "He will remain good and stupid, as God has made him."

Diderot, then, very much liked to pose for his statue as the most serviceable, self-sacrificing and forbearing of men. He had, for that matter, very definite ideas on the subject of his actual physical appearance. When his friend the painter Michel Van Loo made him a present of the wonderfully attractive portrait of him now in the Louvre, Nanette told Denis it made him look like an aged coquette, and he thought she was quite right. It depicted him as too young, he told his *Salon* readers, too smiling and simpering and full of airs, a Secretary of State not an author; also it dressed him in a style which would have spelled ruin to any half-starved author. What would his grandchildren say, when they compared his grave writings with this effeminate old *beau*? He was, he would like them to know, a man who in a day had a hundred different physiognomies – serene, sad, contemplative, tender, violent and impassioned – but this was not one of them. "I had a large brow, very lively eyes, rather massive features, a head altogether in the style of an ancient orator's, with a *bonhomie* verging on the stupid and the rusticity of a bygone age."

But if he enjoyed penning his own self-portrait, he had, on the other hand, begun to fret at the role implied by his nickname "The Philosopher": that is to say, a being made a sort of circus-turn or public monument of, a curiosity every visitor to Paris had to be shown. It was to a large extent the work of Grimm, and near the end of 1768 Diderot decided to put his foot down. Grimm had the young prince of Saxe-Gotha, the future Ernest II, in tow and sent Diderot his instructions – how he was to visit the Prince, dine with him, take him to see Mlle Biheron's famous anatomical waxworks, and so on – and Diderot refused. He told Grimm that he was sick of such "ridiculous parades". It was a painful thing to have to do, he told Sophie (4 November 1768), but it would be worth it in the long run.

He had, however, not reckoned with his friend. He received such a series of icy notes from Grimm, who promised "never to importune him again with any mark of interest", that he fell quite into despair. Grimm, Diderot lamented to Sophie, talked to him as he did to his valet when he was in a bad mood. He could not imagine himself doing the same to Grimm, under any provocation. "It must mean that I have a feeling for him which is not returned," and the pain of it was killing him. "I only have him in the world, is that not enough?"

Grimm won. They were perfectly reconciled in a week or two, and the young Prince came to visit Diderot, incognito, in the rue Taranne. Next day the Prince and he were introduced formally at d'Holbach's, and Diderot amused himself by pretending that they had never met. "I played my part like an angel," he wrote cheerfully to Sophie.

As in Britain in the 1840s, so in France in the 1760s one of the burning topics of the day was the corn-laws. For centuries the grain trade in France had been subject to a mass of confusing regulations, preventing any easy movement of grain from one part of France to another. Bread-supply was held to be a state responsibility, and the export of grain to foreign countries was a criminal offence. From the late 1750s, however, the group known as the Physiocrats, founded by the King's physician François Quesnay, had been campaigning for free trade in grain. The name "Physiocracy" means "The Rule of Nature", and the leading doctrines of the school were that all true wealth was derived from the soil and that, as a corollary, all internal customs barriers, excises and export restrictions should be swept away and, with them, France's whole elaborate national tax system, to be replaced by a single property tax. Acknowledge the primacy of agriculture, and give cultivators free play in the national and international market, so the argument ran, and the result will be prosperity and social harmony – a self-regulating harmony between country and town and between "productive" cultivator and "unproductive" manufacturer.

Quesnay and his disciples, among them Mirabeau the elder and Turgot, found the government ready to listen to their views, and in 1763–64 the experiment was actually tried: first, restrictions on the internal trade in grain were removed, then, in a decree phrased very much in Physiocratic language, the curbs on the export of grain – with the proviso, deplored by the Quesnay school, that exports must be carried in French vessels. The result was chaos. The harvest of 1765 was a relatively poor one, and very soon there were riots, street-demonstrations against the King and his chief Minister, assaults on merchants and engrossers and a general clamour for a restoration of the old regulations. The Paris *Parlement*, always spoiling for a fight with the King, threw its weight against the new system, and eventually some provincial *Parlements* defiantly suspended freedom of export on their own initiative. By the autumn of 1768 free trade in grain was as good as non-existent in the greater part of France.

Diderot, who had published articles by Quesnay (on FERMIERS and CÉRÉALES) in the *Encyclopédie*, could be said to have been an early promoter of Physiocratic doctrines. In fact he had briefly become a convinced disciple of one of Quesnay's closest associates, Le Mercier de la Rivière, and had helped to despatch him to Russia as economic adviser to Catherine the Great – an appointment which had turned out very badly, for Catherine had considered him impossibly arrogant ("He thought we went on all fours"). However, one evening at Mme Necker's in the autumn of 1768, Diderot heard the *abbé* Galiani preaching against the Physiocrats, and he underwent an instant conversion. "At last, the *abbé* Galiani has explained himself," he wrote excitedly to Sophie (22 November).

> Either nothing can ever be proved in politics, or exportation is madness. I swear to you, my dear friend, that up to now no one has said the first word on this question. I begged him on my knees to publish his ideas . . . Here is just one of his principles. What does it mean to sell corn? – It means exchanging corn for money? – *Not in the very least*. It means exchanging corn for corn. And at present, could you ever, to your own advantage, exchange the corn you have for the corn people sell you? He showed us all the branches of this law; and they are immense.

Diderot had a genius for encouragement; and it was at his urging, over the next six months or so, that Galiani composed his famous *Dialogues on the Corn-Trade*, a very dazzling polemic against the Physiocrats. The *Dialogues* are set, initially, in the *salon* of "Mme * * *", and the speakers are the ingenuous and philanthropic "Marquis de Roquemaure" (loosely based on the Marquis de Croismare), a "Président de * * *", and the "Chevalier de Zanobi" (a thinly-disguised portrait of Galiani himself). The work is a masterpiece of wit and applied reason and in its "realism" and profound cynicism seems to have some influence on Diderot's own later outlook.

Diderot also had a talent for bringing labour and trouble on himself, and it is illustrated once again here. For in the following year, as the result of a diplomatic indiscretion, Galiani got himself recalled to Naples. It was a crushing blow to him, for Paris was his spiritual home: he ceased to exist, he would say, he "belonged merely to the vegetable kingdom", when parted from his French friends. Thus he completed his gay *Dialogues* "weeping", and on his departure in June, he had to leave his manuscript in the hands of Diderot and Mme d'Epinay, for them to edit and see through the press. It meant a lot of work for Diderot and much delicate negotiation, for in the present tense state of national affairs Galiani's book was a dangerous commodity. The censor caused difficulties, and before the book could appear, the government had already commissioned the *abbé* Morellet to produce a refutation. Meanwhile Galiani, a very tetchy author, kept plaguing Diderot with remonstrances at the delay. All was still in suspense in December 1769, when the Comptroller-General, Mayon d'Invau, was squeezed out of office and replaced by the *abbé* Teray, a strong opponent of free trade, and this effectively removed all obstacle to the book's publication. "It needed the dismissal of a Comptroller, and practically the overturning of the State, for my little book to appear," remarked Galiani, with relish.

The book made a great impression, and the self-important Morellet, though a friend both of Galiani and of Diderot, lost no time in producing his refutation, writing so furiously that he rubbed all the skin off his little finger. Sartine invited Diderot to act as censor for it – a cunning stroke, for, given his known principles, Diderot could hardly call for the book to be suppressed. Nor did he, though he reported that it was "hard, dry, full of spleen and poor in ideas" and could do Morellet's reputation no good.

The issues went on working in his mind, however, and in a month or two he found himself composing a lengthy "Apologia for the *abbé* Galiani" – a refutation of Morellet's refutation. Its drift, for much of the time, is that what Morellet lacked was a sense for the concrete. He gives Morellet a lesson on the real-life mechanism of a famine, a phenomenon he had had some first-hand experience of, telling him that, if one wants to calculate accurately, "one must lay aside general views and enter into all the detail of fears, greed and hope."

What this brings home to us is how strongly Galiani was always able to influence Diderot's imagination. In a striking passage in the eighth of Galiani's *Dialogues*, Galiani's *alter ego* the Chevalier de Zanobi gets on to the subject of the personal character of the Physiocrats. (By a subtle stroke, he seizes a moment to do so when Roquemaure is out of the room, for the paradox he now explores might well have distressed the kind-hearted Marquis.) Why does Zanobi rate the writings of the Physiocrats so low, asks his interlocutor the President? "Because," answers Zanobi disconcertingly, "they are the work of men of good will."

> ... Believe me: do not fear the rascally or the wicked; sooner or later they are unmasked. Fear the deluded man of good will; he is on good terms with his own conscience, he desires the good, and everyone trusts him ... But unfortunately he is mistaken as to the means of procuring it for us.
>
> THE PRESIDENT: So from what you say, you would rather have us governed by wicked men than by good ones?
>
> ZANOBI: I don't say that; but I want to explain how hard it is to find a great man. A great man has to combine extreme and opposite qualities, almost impossible to reconcile; he must have the ardent will for good of the man of virtue, together with the calm and – as you might say – the indifference of the wicked.

In his *Apologia*, Diderot picks this passage up. "You do not agree with this view of Galiani's?" he asks Morellet. "Upon my word I, if anyone, ought not to. And yet I go along with him here. For let us ask ourselves, with our hand on our heart, whether our natural ardour, plus a conviction of desiring the good of mankind, has not caused us to make many blunders – ones we would not have committed had we possessed more enlightenment, no less honour and a cooler head." It was at much this same moment that Diderot was sketching his *Paradox of the Actor*, with its insistence on the "coldness" and insensibility necessary to the great actor and to "genius" generally, and Galiani, we can see, has contributed something, perhaps a good deal, to the shaping of its argument.

In a different way, Diderot's imagination also still ran on his old friend d'Alembert. Their personal relations, since the split in 1759, had been tenuous. When, in the summer of 1765, d'Alembert fell seriously ill and there were fears for his life, Diderot had visited his sickbed and, as he told Sophie, they had had a "very tender" meeting, but it was their first encounter for a long time. Intellectually and ideologically, however, the

differences in their outlook had continued to grow in significance
for him. In 1761 he had reviewed two "Memoirs" recently
published by d'Alembert, one on "Probability", and the other, a
set of sceptical reflections on Inoculation, also much concerned
with probability and the computation of risks. Diderot found
d'Alembert's doubts and reservations about inoculation subtle
but too detached and not at the height of this subject – for it was
an intensely burning one in France just at this moment.[4]
D'Alembert's was not, he held, the behaviour of a good citizen.
But what also figured as significant for Diderot was d'Alembert's
whole approach towards probability. Curiously, brilliant
mathematician though he was, d'Alembert had a rather shaky
grasp of probability theory, a fact that Diderot found it not
difficult to demonstrate. D'Alembert fell indeed into the most
elementary snare, that of supposing that one toss of a coin
somehow influences the result of a succeeding one. It would seem
as though, with his passion for clear-cut answers, he found the
mathematics of probability too untidy; and Diderot took his two
"Memoirs" as symptomatic of a faulty general approach to
science. D'Alembert, he argued, treated the whole issue of
probability too abstractly: he had not envisaged, for instance, the
real-life situation of a gambler. Mathematicians made poor
gamblers, for the same reason that, ultimately, they made bad
scientists and philosophers: they had an insufficient grasp of the
concrete and failed to observe "a subtle current in things, only
revealed to the close observer."

This was not Diderot's last word on the subject. He continued
to conduct an imaginary debate with d'Alembert; and in 1769 it
inspired one of his most inventive and original works, a
philosophical fantasy woven round d'Alembert and his friend or
mistress Julie de l'Espinasse.

At this juncture there had been an important change in
d'Alembert's life. He had, till early middle age, led a rather
sexless existence; but in 1760 or thereabouts he had become
friendly with a young *protégée* and house-companion of Mme du
Deffand, Julie de l'Espinasse, and in a little while this had
become a very passionate attachment. The result, indirectly, was
a furious rift with Mme du Deffand herself. She discovered – this

was in 1764 – that visitors to her "evenings", before appearing in her drawing-room, were spending some time with Julie in her own apartment. To the blind and jealous Deffand this was an unforgivable piece of rivalry or treachery; there came an explosion of temper, Julie was banished, and in sympathy d'Alembert had broken off relations with his old patroness. As a result of this upheaval, Julie, helped by d'Alembert, set up her own *salon* in her modest lodgings in the rue Saint-Dominique nearby, and Mme Deffand's remaining *philosophique* friends, such as Turgot and Condorcet, transferred their allegiance to it. By all accounts Julie was a brilliant intellectual hostess, and many Académie elections would be plotted under her roof. Shortly after her removal, however, she fell dangerously ill with smallpox. She was tenderly nursed through it by d'Alembert; and not long afterwards he had finally deserted his lodgings with his beloved foster-mother and set up house with Julie.

In the summer of 1769 Diderot was all alone in Paris, slaving over various tedious chores. All his friends seemed to have deserted the city, and Nanette and Angélique had gone for some weeks to Sèvres, where a friend of Diderot's, a jeweller named Belle, had lent them an apartment in his country mansion. It was scorching hot, he was groaning at the galley-slave existence of a man of letters, and as a relief he amused himself composing some fanciful philosophical dialogues, set in the d'Alembert and l'Espinasse *ménage*. In the first dialogue, he reported to Sophie, d'Alembert and he chat "gaily and even fairly clearly, despite the dryness and obscurity of the subject". This dialogue, moreover, had been followed by another much longer one, entitled *D'Alembert's Dream*. The interlocutors are d'Alembert dreaming; d'Alembert's friend Mlle de l'Espinasse; and Diderot's own friend and physician Dr Bordeu. Diderot hardly knew Julie de l'Espinasse, but it was his habit, as we have seen, to make free with real-life personages for fictional ends.

Eleven days later he told Sophie that the fancy had taken him to add even a third brief dialogue. It was one which would make Sophie's prim sister Mme de Blacy's[5] hair stand on end, for which reason she would never see it; and he defied Sophie to guess what was in it. (No doubt he was planning to read it to her.) The piece of writing, he told her, could not be "more profound or more mad".

The "dry and obscure" subject discussed by "Diderot" and "d'Alembert" in the opening conversation is ontology, and in particular the nature of matter. This topic was much in Diderot's mind, for among the freethinking works published by d'Holbach the previous year had been a translation, in which he and Naigeon had taken a hand, of that classic document of materialism, Lucretius's *De Rerum natura*, and also one of Toland's materialistic *Letters to Serena*.[6]

Diderot was a doctrinaire materialist. D'Alembert was a much more cautious one – perhaps not a materialist at all, for he rejected Spinoza's version of the doctrine – and at all events it was not the sort of issue he felt it vital to take a stand upon. The purpose of Diderot's three dialogues (from now on I will refer to the whole work as *D'Alembert's Dream*) was accordingly, to elaborate his own materialist position – and a very extraordinary and fantastic method he adopted.

But, even more to the point, he found a way to present, in all its symbolic significance, the conflict between his and d'Alembert's approaches towards science and the world. This brings us back to their amicable exchange, at the time of Diderot's *On the Interpretation of Nature*, over "conjectures" and "dreams" in science. In *D'Alembert's Dream* one perceives a most beautiful joke on Diderot's part. In imagination he not only puts himself in d'Alembert's shoes, but intrudes himself into the very recesses of his friend's sleeping consciousness, compelling him to re-enact one of his own "conjectures" or "dreams". It is the supreme example of Diderot's "supposititious" method.

It is also, of course, a rich, or flagrant, example of Diderot's presumptuousness: the same invasive familiarity which made him commandeer people's bodies when talking to them, take liberties with other people's mental properties, or (as in the *salons*) make free with their personal lives and their good names. At one point, it is true, he toyed with the idea of giving his characters the respectable names of "Democritus", "Leucippus" and "Hippocrates". To have named them in this way, he told Sophie, would have given the thing more "nobleness of tone", but it would have done so at the expense of "richness of substance". The specificity of real-life names was in fact all-important to him, for one thing because it offered him the opportunity for ruses. One sees this in the fact that, in *D'Alembert's Dream*, Diderot depicts d'Alembert as having a "Dr Bordeu" as his physician. This is a telling, if somewhat private, joke, for in real life d'Alembert's physician was not Théophile de Bordeu but a certain Michel Bouvard, an arch-enemy of Bordeu, who indeed had succeeded in getting Bordeu struck off the register of Parisian physicians. The two doctors were poles apart theoretically and ideologically, Bouvard being a medical "interventionist" and an implacable enemy of inoculation, whilst Bordeu, the author of the article CRISES in the *Encyclopédie*, was an exponent of the waiting or "expectative" method and a believer in instinct and genius – or, as he put it, "that sort of enthusiasm so little known among theoreticians". Diderot was a friend and admirer of Bordeu, indeed much influenced by his ideas. He had been, in particular, struck by a passage in Bordeu's *Anatomical Researches on Glands* (1752), in which he described bodily organs as being, like a swarm of bees, an alliance of separate and possibly contesting interests. That in his fiction he should give such a man as physician to the over-cautious d'Alembert – to d'Alembert the sceptic towards inoculation – was a subtle didactic stroke.

This use of real-life characters was thus no mere matter of verisimilitude. Diderot had met Julie de l'Espinasse for the first and perhaps only time, at the bedside of d'Alembert during his illness in 1765, and it is this recollection, evidently, which suggested his picture of her in *D'Alembert's Dream*, where she sits all night at the philosopher's bedside writing down his sleeping pronouncements. The *épatant* and scandalous paradoxes he puts into Julie's mouth are not meant to evoke her as a real-life person (rather they may in some sense have been meant to evoke Sophie), and his presumptuousness did not go unrebuked. Someone, possibly Suard, tactlessly informed Julie about Diderot's work and her role in it, and she was furious, It was, she said, most ungentlemanly behaviour with possibly dangerous consequences; he really ought to forbid himself to talk, or encourage others to talk, about women he did not know.

D'Alembert was equally incensed and demanded, "imperiously", that Diderot destroy the work. Indeed, if we are to believe him, he did so; for we find him writing sadly, some time later, of trying to reconstruct his "broken statue" from a few surviving fragments. It was an act of heroism if he did destroy it, for it was his favourite among his own writings. Fortunately, though, by some mysterious means or other, a copy of the original survived.

19

D'Alembert's Dream

D'Alembert's Dream is one of Diderot's most inventive fictions, a fantastic mock-Socratic dialogue which, as has been said, takes as its theme the theory of materialism. We need to ponder this term "materialism", for it is sometimes used misleadingly. It was first coined in the early eighteenth century, and was popularised by Voltaire, and what people often mean by it would be better called "scandalous materialism", that is to say materialism with subversive intent. No doubt it was "materialism" when Lucretius wrote that mind (*animus*) and soul (*anima*) are both composed of matter, but it did not cause scandal; he was, indeed, a scandalous writer, but not for what he said about "spirit" and "matter". Scandalous materialism really came in with Descartes – that is to say as a reaction against Descartes and the extreme antithesis that he proclaimed between soul and body. No one before Descartes had made matter or the body seem so desacralised and dead – nor so eerily so, for not only did he represent animals, for lack of a soul, as mere hydraulic mechanisms, he likened them to *automata*, or machines deliberately designed to simulate life and to deceive.

Cartesian dualism, quickly adopted by orthodox opinion in the Church and the Sorbonne, is an intensely powerful, intensely disturbing concept, and the only way of combating it seems, at first sight, to be some equally dramatic and extreme monism. For instance that of Spinoza, who claimed that matter and spirit (and God and nature) were one and the same; or that of La Mettrie in his *Man the Machine*, where he argues that Descartes was quite right in regarding animals as mere machines and only erred in not recognising that the same was true of human beings. Whether Spinoza should be called a "materialist" or not is a puzzling question; but there is no doubt that Spinozism and La-Mettrie-ism were deliberately scandalous and politically as well as religiously subversive doctrines. (One of the implications of La Mettrie's theories was that the functions of priests and magistrates would be better performed by doctors, i.e. by specialists on the human machine.)

In short, the debate about "materialism", in the sense it acquired for the eighteenth and nineteenth centuries, was no calmly speculative difference of opinion over the nature and constitution of matter. (Did it consist of particles or was it infinitely divisible? Was it inert or possessed of motion?) Nor was it a question of some supposed "tradition" of thought going back to Epicurus and Democritus (though of course they were convenient names to invoke). It was, rather – like much of philosophy ever since – a life-and-death struggle to escape from the Cartesian world-view.

The struggle, of necessity, encouraged speculations and conjectures about the nature of matter. "Materialists" were attracted by Toland's theory that the particles of matter were inherently self-moving, and by that of Maupertuis, that all matter had a capability of feeling and intelligence. These were both speculations that Diderot dallied with and half-espoused and at all events found very useful polemically in the attack on Descartes's "dead" universe. But if one reads D'Alembert's Dream, responding to its plot, as one would with any work of fiction, rather than literal-mindedly searching it for evidence of his "beliefs", one will perceive that it is combating Descartes from a quite different angle and in an altogether more cogent and searching manner.

It has been Diderot's fate, especially in the nineteenth century, that it was felt necessary to apologise for his materialism as somehow blinkering or narrowing, or alternatively to defend it – on the grounds that he triumphed in spite of it. One can detect defensiveness even in Lionel Trilling's "The Fate of Pleasure" (Beyond Culture, 1966) where he writes of Diderot as "the most uncompromising of materialists, as he was the most subtle and delicate". There is a muddle here which helps to obscure what D'Alembert's Dream is actually expressing, which is an attack on the Cartesian idea of the self. If we consider the famous materialist slogans of a later day, for instance Cabanis's "The brain secretes thoughts as the liver does bile," or Jacob Moleshott's "No thought without phosphorus," we shall see that their outrage lies in the implication that there is no grandly-privileged unitary self, "Subject" or thinking "I", on the Cartesian pattern, making use of the brain; and it is to put in question and dismantle the idea of such a self that Diderot sets himself so resourcefully in *D'Alembert's Dream*.

In the conversation with which *D'Alembert's Dream* opens (we enter it, in the Diderotesque fashion, in mid-stream) "Diderot", we gather, has been trying to induce "d'Alembert" to come out against the dualist ontology of Descartes. Actually, "d'Alembert" is in many ways a Cartesian, also he believes metaphysical questions largely a waste of time. Still, he is certainly not a theist, and he is ready to humour "Diderot". What is imagined is such a scene as must often have taken place between the real-life Diderot and d'Alembert, in the first days of their friendship, when Diderot would press his conjectures or "dreams" on his too soberly rational colleague. The ensuing work, the three-part *D'Alembert's Dream*, is an exploration of philosophical materialism – that is to say of the real, as opposed to the reputed and merely conventional, difficulties of the materialist position – presented in the form of a fantastic "reprisal" by the "dreamer" on his cautious colleague.

"D'Alembert" freely admits that a dualism of "spirit" and "matter", *à la* Descartes, is impossible to swallow. What sense can one make of an entity (spirit) which is supposed to exist somewhere but corresponds to no particular point in space, which differs fundamentally from matter and yet is intimately united with it, and which accompanies and moves matter without itself moving? On the other hand, he asks, what alternative is there? "Diderot" wants to replace this incomprehensible "spirit" by "sensibility"; but if, as he seems to hold, sensibility is an essential quality of all matter, would this not imply that stone can feel? "And why not?" replies "Diderot". But in that case, asks "d'Alembert", what in "Diderot's" eyes would be the difference between marble and flesh or between a statue and a man? "Very little," says "Diderot". "One can make marble out of flesh, and flesh out of marble." "Still," says "d'Alembert", they are not the same thing. And no more, says "Diderot", is what physicists call *vis viva* (active force) the same as what they call *vis mortua* (the latent or "dead" force that a stationary object exerts on the surface it is resting on). "D'Alembert", knowing "Diderot", guesses where this is leading. Does "Diderot" want to argue that, if there is something you can call a "latent force", there could equally well be "latent" sensibility, a merely *potential* capacity for feeling? "Exactly so," replies "Diderot". But, says "d'Alembert", it is easy to see how latent force can turn into active force, but how can latent sensibility turn into active? By a very simple process, replies "Diderot": it happens every time you eat. By eating you remove the obstacles impeding the active sensibility of the food; you make flesh of it, you animalise it, you render it capable of feeling. "I take that statue," he continues. "I pound it up in a mortar. (D'ALEMBERT: "Go gently; it is one of Falconet's masterpieces!" DIDEROT: "He will not mind; he sets very little store by present appreciation and none at all by the future kind."[1]) . . . I mix it with humus . . . I let it putrefy for a year, for two years, for a century . . . Then I plant peas and beans and cauliflowers in it . . . The plants feed on the soil; and I feed on the plants."

"D'Alembert", whether convinced or not, finds this transition from insentience to sentience rather appealing. Still, he objects, to be sensitive is not the same as to *think*. Upon which "Diderot", with cheerful effrontery, describes the coming-into-being of that most eminent exponent of thinking, d'Alembert himself. This masterly flight of rhetoric mimes in its cadences and cyclical rhythm a whole materialist ontology and cosmogony.

DIDEROT: Before going a step further, allow me to tell you the history of one of the greatest geometers of Europe. What was this marvellous being at the outset? Nothing.

D'ALEMBERT: How do you mean, nothing? Nothing can be made of nothing.

DIDEROT: You take me too literally. I mean that before his mother, the beautiful and wicked canoness Tencin, had reached the age of puberty, before the soldier La Touche was adolescent, the molecules which were to form the first rudiments of my geometer lay dispersed inside their two youthful and delicate frames: they filtered with their lymph, they circulated with their blood, until at last they found their way to the reservoirs destined for their coalition, the testicles and ovaries of his mother and father. Behold the rare germ formed; behold it, as common opinion will have it, carried by the Fallopian tubes into the womb; see it attached to the womb by a long pedicle; see it growing and attaining the condition of the foetus; see the moment come for its emergence from its dark prison; see it born and exposed on the steps of the church of Saint-Jean-le-Rond, which gives it its name; see it rescued from the Foundlings' Home, attached to the breast of the good glazier's wife, Madame Rousseau, see it suckled and grown big in body and mind: a man of letters, a technician, a geometer. How has this been brought about? By *eating* and other such purely mechanical operations. Here in four words is the general formula: "Eat, digest, distil in *vasi licito, et fiat homo secundum artem*." And a scientist in the Académie, to demonstrate the formation of a man or an animal, would need to employ only purely material agents, showing the way they produce, in succession, a feeling being, a thinking being, a being solving the problem of the precession of the equinoxes, a sublime being, a marvellous being, a being ageing, decaying, dying, dissolved and restored to the vegetative earth.[2]

One glimpses at once the ingenious and deliberately outrageous strategies that are going to be employed in *D'Alembert's Dream*. In a quite unexpected and fantastic sense, the work is to be an argument *ad hominem*. Extreme liberties are to be taken with "d'Alembert" himself, beginning with this raking up of the scandalous history of his birth, the first of a whole series of "invasions", but a very expressive one, for Diderotian materialism can be seen, from a certain point of view, as a matter of blowing "the gaff", a "scandalous" exposure of the pretensions of human consciousness. By cunning rhetoric, in "Diderot's" *résumé* of his friend's life-history, the expected proportions of biography are overturned. The great man's progress from babe-in-arms to "man of letters, technician, geometer" is telescoped into a half-sentence, becoming the briefest of episodes, a mere speck, compared with the long unconscious and vegetative before and after. It is just such cosmic vistas and dizzying revisions of scale that, in the second part of the work, "d'Alembert" himself is going to be made to dream.

The fictitious "d'Alembert" is not offended by this making free with his biological history. He congratulates "Diderot" in fact, for telling it in terms of *epigenesis*, that is to say the accretion and subsequent dispersal of distinct parts, and not of *preformation* – that is of all future generations being already contained, one within another, in the testicles and ovaries of Adam and Eve.

Still, "D'Alembert" objects, "Diderot" has not yet explained the step onwards from feeling to thinking. So "Diderot" sketches a theory – with a fanciful analogy from keyboard instruments – to explain how matter, from its own resources, and merely assuming the persistence of vibrations, could evolve memory, and memory in turn could develop into intelligence. "D'Alembert" finds this ingenious but asks: since a keyboard instrument presupposes a musician, has not "Diderot" slipped back into dualism? Would not the musician be the equivalent of a Cartesian soul? No, says "Diderot", that would be to take analogies too literally. In what he is envisaging, the living being is both musician and instrument, both played upon and playing.

So if the *clavecin* could eat and procreate, "d'Alembert" suggests flippantly, we might hope to see it producing a family of "living and resounding" baby *clavecins*. And why not, replies "Diderot". What would be so strange in this, considering the phenomenon of the *egg*? By purely physical processes (here "Diderot's" prose falls again into a cyclical rhythm) the egg, from being an inert mass, becomes an embryo, develops into a chick, begins to walk, fly, get angry, complain, suffer and desire. Will "d'Alembert" say – like Descartes, desperate to defend the uniqueness of Man – that the chick is no more than an automaton? "Why, children would laugh at you, and philosophers would reply that, if the chick is a machine, you are another."

Warming to his task, "Diderot" demonstrates how his *clavecin* could learn to socialise, develop language, handle syllogisms, and, perhaps, experience the same solipsistic doubts – maybe he is the only *clavecin* in the world? – as humans do. "D'Alembert" hints that "Diderot" sets a perilously high value on analogy; but

"Diderot" is firm that, with all its dangerous seductions, it is by analogy that science, like poetry, has to proceed. Upon this, the sleepy and sceptical "d'Alembert" bids his friend a cheerful good night. "Well, you may laugh," says "Diderot". "But you will dream about this conversation all night on your pillow."

"Diderot" is quite right. Their conversation comes back to "d'Alembert" in his dreams, and he has a most terrible night. He makes such an outcry in his sleep that Julie decides she must stay by his bedside; and, for occupation, she tries to take down the strange things he says. At last, growing quite alarmed, she summons the doctor, who takes "d'Alembert's" pulse and examines Julie's notes. All is well, he concludes: the patient is neither ill nor mad. Indeed he claims to be able to follow the sleeping geometer's train of thought, and is even, to Julie's amazement, able by conjecture to fill in some of the gaps.

The beauty of this invention of Diderot's, the sleeping philosopher and his waking witnesses, is wonderfully rich. For, according to Diderot's view of things, science could not ask for a more perfect scenario. To begin with: here is a human specimen exposed to the eye of science in its sleeping and vegetative, its most "material", state and the one most likely to offer support to the materialist hypothesis. It is, as it were, an Académie demonstration or Rembrandt "Anatomy Lesson" – but with the ineffable advantage that the demonstrator is the patient himself, and moreover a philosopher and man of giant intellect. We are reminded of Diderot's claim in his *Letter on the Blind* that more could be learned about the nature of seeing from a blind philosopher than from an uneducated person with the gift of sight; for a sleeping philosopher is, for the moment, a blind one. We are reminded, too, of the paradox, several times broached in the two *Letters*, about shutting one's eyes or ears to see or hear better. Diderot briefly toyed with the idea of calling his protagonist not "d'Alembert" but "Democritus", and it is not hard to see why; for was it not related of Democritus that he put out his own eyes to be able to think more intensely?[3]

The significance of Diderot's philosopher, sleeping and talking in his sleep, extends further. The phrase used in the

"Conversation" is crucial: there is no limit to the "ideas awoken, in a connected chain, in the philosopher *who meditates or who listens to himself* in silence and obscurity." "Diderot" is listening, at two removes, to his own ideas, as they propagate in this necessary and quasi-mechanical way. The Lockeian or Condillac-style "association of ideas" is demonstrated in this ideal laboratory experiment.

Then it is a further rich irony that the sleeping "d'Alembert" is, as sleepers tend to be, in a state of loosened connection with his own identity. It makes it possible for "Diderot", the advocate of conjecture or, as he likes to call it, "dreaming", as a scientific procedure, to invade "d'Alembert's" consciousness and force this sober rationalist to dream some of his ("Diderot's") own scientific "dreams". It is a new and even more adventurous Diderotian "supposititition" or foisting of oneself upon another.

So we come to "d'Alembert's" dream or nightmare. What is obsessing him on his pillow is, precisely, the question of personal identity. For once you reject the concept of a "soul", Diderot is implying, you are faced with some awkward problems about human identity. Indeed, you may have to admit that the whole concept of human identity is suspect and may be in need of thorough dismantling. "D'Alembert", in the very first words of his nocturnal soliloquy, is wrestling with this issue. If a living being is built up "epigenetically", by the accretion of distinct parts – he asks himself, baffled – how can it come to have a single identity?

> A point that is alive . . . No, I am wrong. *Nothing at all* at first, and then a point that is alive . . . To this point another living point is added, and then another, and from these successive additions there results a single being. For surely I am *one*? I can hardly doubt it . . . (He feels himself all over.) But how has that unity been created? – Listen, good philosopher [in his dreaming, unbeknown to Julie, he is still arguing with "Diderot"]: I can see an aggregate, a knot of little feeling beings; but as for a whole! a unified system, a "he" conscious of his own unity, no, I simply cannot see it.[4]

At this, in his dream, "d'Alembert" hears the siren voice of

"Diderot", offering a solution. Whereas an aggregate of inert and dead molecules remains a mere aggregate, this voice suggests, it may be otherwise with living molecules, and when they come together, it may be that they compose a unity. As a drop of mercury melts into another drop of mercury, so, by an exchange of sensibility, a live molecule forms a unity, a *continuity*, with another. There is a special kind of a unity peculiar to animate beings.

"D'Alembert" listens, half-convinced, and has an inspiration: a swarm of bees! Someone who had never seen a swarm of bees before would certainly take it for a unity, a single animal, a creature with five or six hundred heads and twice as many wings; and who is to say he is wrong?

Julie asks Doctor Bordeu what he thinks of this, and he replies that it is at least a "beautiful dream", and he believes he can guess how it went on. "D'Alembert", a man of logic even when asleep, would have continued to himself thus: No, after all, that will not quite do – the swarm of bees, if we are to be literal, is *not* an animal. But is there not a rider to this? For, though a swarm may not be an animal, an animal, so medical knowledge tells us, is a swarm. We, who think of ourself as an individual, as a unitary member of our species, are in fact a swarm or society; our bodily organs are so many independent animals, held in a "sympathy, a unity, a general identity" only by the law of "continuity".

Julie is astonished, for "Bordeu" has reproduced "d'Alembert's" train of thought almost word for word. It is important to catch Diderot's drift here. For if the "association of ideas" theory is correct and ideas propagate themselves *necessarily*, in a "great chain", then it should be possible for one speaker to anticipate another. This business of anticipating and completing a discourse by conjecture represents the right philosophical approach to Nature. The scientific mind, we are to understand, is the one that, by instinct and practice, has learned to take just such anticipatory leaps. Soon, to her surprise, Julie will show such talent herself, and Bordeu and she will have a sort of competition in anticipating each other's ideas. The little exchange between Julie and Bordeu here makes the general point and at the same time gently mocks it. "Now I can tell the whole world," says Julie, referring to "Bordeu's" inspired guesses, "that there is no difference between a waking doctor and a dreaming philosopher." She means it admiringly, but it is a reversible remark, as the sardonic "Bordeu" underlines in his mock-rueful retort, "One had always guessed it" (i.e. doctors are terrible dreamers too).

We have not heard the last of "d'Alembert's" swarm of bees, for it has opened up another vista for him. What happens if one tries to cut the swarm? Say that one imagined the bees as very tiny? In that case, one could cut the swarm with a pair of scissors without injuring or even touching the bees. The swarm would be a polyp – each time you cut it, you would produce a new individual – and polyps raise new and staggering questions about identity.

"D'Alembert" continues his imaginary conversation with "Diderot". So his friend can picture all sorts and varieties of polyps? Even perhaps human ones? ... "But no," he tells himself, "Nature does not offer us those." ("Bordeu" remarks drily that "d'Alembert" cannot have heard of Siamese twins.) But say that human polyps really were to be found, so "d'Alembert's" reverie continues, what amazing possibilities it would open up . . . eugenics on a scientific scale, whole provinces, perhaps, raised from the remains of a single human! Not such an absurd idea either, comments Bordeu; for if human do not proliferate by division in that way, it could be said that species do. "D'Alembert" is thinking the same. He imagines himself, microscope in hand, repeating the famous experiments of the scientist John Needham, who claimed to breed tiny living eel-like creatures out of vegetable matter. He sees a universe in fermentation, whole species coming into being and dying in the twinkling of an eye, like those fleeting generations in Needham's test-tube. Small things are to be compared with large in this way, "d'Alembert" reflects, since in the universe, because it *is* the universe – that is to say, there is nothing outside it to measure it against – scale and succession have no absolute value. "The world begins and ends without cease; at each moment it is at its beginning and at its end."

These cosmic speculations and visions are very dizzying, and, as it were in an earth-bound reaction against them, "d'Alembert" has a wet dream – to the commotion of the innocent-minded Julie, who cannot understand what has come over him. It fills "d'Alembert" with euphoria. He demands that his sperm, with its promise of future generations, shall be put in a flask and taken straight to Dr Needham. The innocent Julie asks "Bordeu" if this sounds like madness to him, and he replies, with *louche* wit, "Undoubtedly, with you at his side." It is perhaps not too surprising if the real-life d'Alembert and Julie de l'Espinasse looked askance at this work of Diderot's!

The thought of his own sperm sets "d'Alembert's" dreaming mind running on the generative fermentation of the universe, a universe in flux, producing ever-new combinations and transformations and in which all separate identities are dissolved or prove illusory. "Julie" is inclined to consider such speculative "follies" as useless, only suitable to the sleeper, but "Bordeu" gets her to revise her opinion and to see that the most "certain" of truths she can imagine, for instance the truth of her own identity, is by no means sure. She begins to perceive the value of these questionings. What is more, she discovers a talent for them. The vibrations of that original "Conversation" have, we see, not only persisted but propagated themselves. "D'Alembert's" dream has become a collaboration. It is now the work not of one but of four "dreamers": "Diderot", the propounder of themes and conjectures; "d'Alembert", the abstract rationalist; "Bordeu", the embodiment of observation, experience and flair and a realist and *louche* joker besides; and "Julie", the neophyte gifted with intuition.

We begin to see further into Diderot's plot in this work. Its goal is not only the conversion of "d'Alembert", it is also, and even more importantly, the emancipation of the conventional-minded "Julie". Her emancipator is to be Bordeu, or rather a fictional "Bordeu" constructed – like Rameau the Nephew – with strong hints from the real one. At the bedside of "d'Alembert" he shows to the full the well-known "wait and watch" and non-interventionist approach of the real-life Bordeu; but the crisis he is watching and waiting for and by subtle means advancing is not the recovery of "d'Alembert", who is not ill, but the liberation of Julie from her prejudices. "Bordeu's" flirtatious and libidinous manner, one perceives, is all part of the technique. Indecent jokes and all – the jokes that at first pass right over "Julie" but then begin to produce a response – are a way of coaxing her to think the thoughts and ask the questions that do not normally get aired: in a word, to "listen to herself" and let conjecture and analogy take her wherever they want. Diderot's handling of this is extremely subtle, witness the brilliant little sequence in which "Bordeu", intent on expounding his genetic theories, proposes to take "Julie" herself and her formation as his "laboratory" specimen. He tells her that, in studying the formation of any animal, it is too late if we study the developed structure: thus he must strip "Julie" of her beautiful exterior and return to a moment when she was "no more than a soft, fibrous, formless, vermicular substance, more resembling the bulb and root of a plant than an animal." There is a faint erotic overtone to the remark, as there is to "Julie's" response: "If it was the custom to walk naked in the streets, I would neither be the first nor the last to conform. So do whatever you want with me, as long as you instruct me."

"D'Alembert" has meanwhile begun to talk in his sleep again, still wrestling with the meaning (or meaninglessness) of his own so-called "identity". He embarks on a scornful tirade against the whole concept of the "individual". In the universe there are no inviolable boundaries, he declares, and everything has a share of everything else: "Every animal is more or less man, every mineral is more or less plant. . . . And yet you speak of individuals, wretched philosophers!" There is, he dreams, one great individual only, the All; all other things being no more "individuals" than the parts of a machine. Change the All, and you will change yourself. He ("d'Alembert") is an effect not a cause, and he is called a "man" not a "monster" simply because men are common and monsters are rare.

But by now, through "Bordeu's" Socratic midwifery, "Julie" is as much puzzled as "d'Alembert" by the problem of identity, and a thought comes to her mind: the spider! The spider spins his web out of himself and can retract it. The web thus is the spider and at the same time is not, somewhat as a swarm of bees is at once a confederation and a single "animal". Exactly! replies Bordeu. Moreover she has guessed something that medical science will confirm: that the human creature, with its limbs and organs, develops in spider's-web-like fashion, by the proliferation of a web of filaments from a primordial genetic bundle. Each part of the web, each "paw" of the spider, will possess its own "interest" and volition, while a spider-like sensorium or command-centre – situated perhaps in the meninx – receives and processes their messages and does its best to impose some order on them.

"Bordeu" and "Julie" are now launched on a wild sea of conjectures. Could there be a spider-like god somewhere in the universe: a god with merely fallible powers of control and foresight, who has been born and will age and die? Or again, who shall dominate in the human organism: shall it be the extremities, the spider's "paws", thus causing anarchy; or shall it be the centre, which will lead to despotism? A parallel is adumbrated – despotic intellect versus the diaphragm, the "genius" versus the "mediocre" creature of feeling, "Bordeu" versus "Julie". Prompted by "d'Alembert" their thoughts turn to monsters. What is a "monster"? Since it is merely a rare rather than a common form, one must rid one's mind of prejudice against monsters. "Julie" falls silent for a spell and then announces an idea more "mad" than usual. It is that perhaps man is a "monstrous" woman, or woman a "monstrous" man. She would have thought of that sooner, comments "Bordeu", had she known, as doctors do, that the sex organs of men and women are essentially the same, merely differently adapted.

To think of monsters is to be brought back, with renewed perplexity, to the theme of identity. For what shall be thought of the Siamese twins reported in the *Gazette de France*, [5] who had only one life between two, so that when one was alive and active the other would be dead, and vice-versa (realising, as it were, the fable of Castor and Pollux)? Should one think of them as two deprived creatures, or as a single creature doubly endowed – enjoying, potentially, a double memory and a double imagination?

"D'Alembert" wakes up and joins their conversation, posing

the classical question: how is it that, since not a single molecule in his body is the same as when he was a child, he nevertheless remains the same individual? It comes about through memory, answers "Bordeu", and also because of the slowness of normal human change. If he were to pass in a flash from youth to decrepit old age – from a vigorous young genius to a dotard who could not understand "his own" books – he would simply *not* be the same individual, either for himself or for others.

The reply is, we reflect, doubly apt; for "d'Alembert" has just suffered exactly such a sudden break of continuity, i.e. from his sleeping self to his quite different waking one. "Julie" and "Bordeu" tell him that he has been discoursing on the same problem all night, and he is at once all curiosity to hear what thoughts were expressed on the subject by his sleeping self. Now we have a fifth character in the debate, for the initial four have been joined by the waking "d'Alembert". The drift is clear. When thinking is done so collaboratively, as it were by a "necessary" process, indifferent to who is doing the thinking, we shall feel less inclined to adopt Descartes's argument, "I think, therefore I exist." It will encourage us to picture ourselves as, inextricably, a part of Nature, not a privileged intruder on the natural scene.

Diderot's writings themselves, as we have seen, tended to be created "epigenetically" and by accretion, rather than by "preformation" or the unfolding of a primordial germ. So the "Dream" adds to itself a "Continuation" or supplement. "Dr Bordeu" leaves to attend his other patient but returns to dine *tête-à-tête* with "Julie", "d'Alembert" having gone out to dine elsewhere, and, as soon as the servants have left them alone, "Julie" volunteers the question that, all through their discussions of monsters, has been hovering in the air – i.e. what does "Bordeu" think of "mixture of species"? By this phrase she means not only crossings of animal species, a topic much in the news in France at this time, but also bestiality. It is, by conventional standards, as "shocking" a topic as could be imagined for a respectable woman, especially when *tête-à-tête* with a man, and it is "Bordeu's" triumph to have brought her so far that she can calmly raise it. It is, moreover, a topic with special relevance to the work in hand, for what word would better describe the monstrous conjunctions of ideas in *D'Alembert's Dream* than "miscegenation"? One asks oneself, have some of these monstrous crossings proved fertile? It is the crisis in "Julie's" education that "Bordeu", in accordance with his "waiting" technique, has long been working towards.

"Bordeu" has a clear-cut answer ready for her question. In his view, he tells her, it brings up all the stupidity of the existing laws and prejudices regarding sexual behaviour. However, if he is going to tell her his mind, she must promise not to let those very prejudices make her think ill of him. This she duly promises, though begging him, out of respect for her weakness, to cover what he says with "gauze" – "just a little gauze".

So he proceeds – answering her question obliquely. Does she agree that rigid chastity and continence are not really virtues, as they are often claimed to be, and can sometimes actually be harmful to health? "Julie" does. Then would it not be possible, for somewhat similar reasons, and adopting for the moment a strictly utilitarian attitude, to argue a case for masturbation? She tacitly agrees to this too, though, she says, it is not a doctrine to preach to children. "It is not a doctrine to *preach* at all," replies "Bordeu". "I would not take my hat off in the street to a man suspected of practising my doctrine [i.e. of taking a professional fee for such opinions]; I would be happy for him to be called infamous. But we are talking now without witnesses, and what we say can affect nobody."

This prompts "Julie", covering her face with her hands, to say she can guess what "Bordeu" will answer to her original question, and "Bordeu" replies that she will have guessed right: yes, he is ready to make out a case for bestiality. "You are a monster," says "Julie", affecting conventional modesty. "Do not blame me," replies "Bordeu". "You must blame Nature or society."

Here we have reached the heart of "Bordeu's" position and the position which this work of Diderot's is in one sense designed to embody. One half of it is that there should be no thoughts that one dare not think. The utmost boldness in thought befits humanity; and to teach this saving truth to others, a task which calls for all one's tact and heuristic skill, is what a philosopher exists for. "Bordeu's" discourse in these last pages is a parable on this theme. Certain of his patients have clearly benefited from his clearing his own mind, and thus being able to help them clear theirs, of a blanket prejudice against masturbation. Thus there *could* be similar benefit in freeing the mind of prejudice against bestiality; though he does not claim to know of one and lets the discussion of it run off into jokes and fantasy. (Could we, perhaps, save our brother humans from the indignity of slavery by breeding goat-servants, goat-lackeys. . . ?)

The other half of the position concerns publication, and is pragmatic. When it comes to publishing one's more "dangerous" thoughts a further set of considerations must come into play: "delicacies, reasons of circumstance, prudences on behalf of society and on one's own behalf." There are a thousand ways of being misunderstood; and those misunderstandings can in fact be dangerous, for others as well as oneself, as any person of decent feeling knows.

"Bordeu's" theory is in some ways close to Kant's, in his famous manifesto "What is Enlightenment?", where he says that "enlightenment" means Man's "quitting his self-inflicted nonage". But Kant goes on to say that a thinking man, in his professional capacity, is bound to pay lip-service to the opinions that his employers require of him, while in his capacity as a man of letters he has a corresponding duty, indeed an urgent "call", to publish his true opinions. "Bordeu's" position has a certain air of paradox, but it strikes one that Kant's does so as well, and of the two paradoxes one might even prefer "Bordeu's".

20

Angélique

In March 1770 a son of the Diderot's' lifelong friends the Caroillons – he was known as Abel-François Caroillon de Vandeul – asked for Angélique's hand in marriage and was accepted. The Caroillons were a fairly well-to-do family in Langres and financially ambitious, Vandeul and his brothers already having a stake in one or two manufacturing enterprises. At present, though, he was in search of a "place" under the Crown, and Diderot set to work to press his claims with highly-placed friends, among them the banker Necker. He told Vandeul's mother that he would "employ all my protectors, great and small, to procure your son an honourable estate."

Angélique was only sixteen, and, at Diderot's insistence, it was agreed that the marriage should not take place for three years. Meanwhile, with some altercation, steps were taken to draw up a marriage-contract. As a result of Catherine's munificence, Diderot was able to give Angélique a substantial dowry. To his irritation, though, he found Caroillon a tough and devious bargainer.

Angélique's education was now, for Diderot, an absorbing preoccupation. It was a time of great closeness between them. He was inordinately proud of her, lectured her during their walks on "enlightenment" and ethics and persuaded himself she showed a talent for philosophical argument. He attached much importance to her sex-education, and, towards this end, he sent her to receive anatomy lessons from the famous Mlle Biheron, who made wax models of the human body, exhibiting them in a little private museum. Mlle Biheron was an old friend and ex-neighbour of his, and he greatly admired her enterprise, which, to his feminist way of thinking, was a thoroughly "enlightened" one and an excellent model for his daughter.

He was very eager that Angélique should be musical, both for its own sake, and also as a social accomplishment. He had given her a harpsichord and provided her with a music-master, a young Alsatian named Anton Bemetzrieder, a shy and prickly character but, in Diderot's view, an inspired teacher. Bemetzrieder had composed some "Lessons on the Harpsichord" in dialogue form, and Diderot, in his usual enthusiastic way, quite took charge of them, polishing up the dialogues (perhaps, though he denied it, completely rewriting them) and finding a publisher for the work. The book made Bemetzrieder's reputation, and Angélique's progress certainly did him credit. Diderot's friend the composer Philidor, having heard her improvise for half an hour, told him that "she had nothing to learn in that quarter."

Diderot had theories about music, as he had about most things, and had accumulated a mass of notes on the subject. Thus it was an excitement to him when, in December 1770, he met the great English musicologist Charles Burney. The meeting took place at d'Holbach's. Burney, for his part, had long wanted to know Diderot, and the two fell into each other's arms as if old friends. Next day Burney called at the rue Taranne, and the two had a most animated conversation, which lasted the whole morning. Diderot was all enthusiasm for Burney's projected book, on *The Present State of Music in France and Italy*, and when the conversation came round to ancient music, he fetched out a great sheaf of notes and thrust them into Burney's hands—just in case, as he said, Burney might find some use for them. Then he had Angélique play for Burney. Burney noted: "She is mistress of modulation and has good finger-technique but she does not observe strict time." In his book he mentions her as "one of the finest harpsichord-players in Paris."[1]

Angélique's life was opening out. In the following June, with her mother and Naigeon, she went to a masked ball at Prince Gallitzins's, where she danced all night and consumed thirteen ices. She was, in fact, in demand. Her father was friendly with the Comtesse de Forbach, a sometime actress and morganatic wife of the Duc des Deux Ponts. He would attend her *salon* in the rue Royale, and, when she asked for his opinion of the "Plan of Education" she had drawn up for the royal children, he had responded with a "Plan" of his own. The Countess made much of Angélique. She invited her to her dinners and receptions and had plans to marry her to a protégé of hers, a young German painter named Mannlich. Angélique was earning quite a reputation as a conversationalist. Mannlich, in his memoirs, recalls a visit to the rue Taranne, and how the loquacious Diderot was unable, or unwilling, to put a word in while Angélique was in the room.[2]

Diderot's relationship with Sophie was no longer a romantic passion, though it was still part of the groundwork of his life. In an odd way it had become an attachment to the whole Volland family, and he generally addressed his letters nowadays to the sister and mother as well as to Sophie herself. For a year or two, moreover, he had developed an interest in another woman friend, Jeanne-Catherine de Maux. She was the natural daughter of a *Comédie Française* actor and had been married at the age of twelve, some years later becoming the mistress of Diderot's friend Damilaville. Diderot thought her amusing and charming, though, so he once told Sophie (he did not conceal the friendship from Sophie) she was an example of what was wrong with the frivolous French – she not only liked Boucher's paintings, which was pardonable, but considered him the greatest painter in the world. When Damilaville was struck down by cancer in 1768, Diderot in some sense felt himself to have "inherited" Mme de Maux and began to take a serious interest in her. Every now and then he would write her something approaching a love-letter.

Thus when, in the summer of 1770, he decided to pay a visit to his sister in Langres, it was with the knowledge that Mme de Maux, and her daughter Mme de Pruneveaux, who had been ill after a pregnancy, would be taking the waters in the nearby spa of Bourbonne-les-Bains. Diderot knew Bourbonne, for his father had been there twice for his health, and he thought it a dreary hole, without promenade or public gardens or anything in the way of entertainments. The women were complaining woefully of boredom, and Diderot and Grimm were proposing to come and bring them some relief.

On 2 August 1770, therefore, the two friends set off for Champagne together. The plan was that Grimm should spend a night under Denise's roof, then should join the women for a few days in Bourbonne, after which Diderot would take over his duties and would divide his time as best he could between the two places. Denise, who had not met Grimm before, was greatly smitten with him, and it became a stock joke among them all that the two should marry.

For Denise, troubled by the friction between her brothers, it was the great opportunity for a reconciliation, and this was Diderot's wish too. Earlier in the same year he had made fresh overtures, telling Denise she should bring Didier-Pierre to Paris, when the two brothers would speak, or not speak, about their differences, as pleased Didier-Pierre best. Could he be such a man of sin, Denis had written, seeing that he was loved and honoured "by priests, by *curés*, by vicars-general, by monks, by Sorbonne doctors and by bishops"? Didier-Pierre, however, wanted something more definite. Before they could meet, he had declared, he must have a written pledge from Denis never to write against religion again. Diderot was half inclined to consent, and a local cleric, a certain Canon Gauchat, had agreed to act as a go-between. The dispute became public and was causing quite a stir in Langres.

At Bourbonne, meanwhile, Mme de Maux and her daughter were joined by Grimm and acquired a youngish admirer named Foissy, *écuyer* to the Duc de Chartres. They had, moreover, found a relief from their boredom and were composing stories. This gave Diderot, when he arrived in Bourbonne, the idea of an enjoyable "mystification" – not too remote from the one that had given birth to *The Nun*. It so happened that, not long before, Naigeon had sent the two women a newly published story by Saint-Lambert, entitled *The Two Friends: a Tale of the Iroquois*. It was a pallid and sentimental piece in the "noble savage" genre, full of outpourings about friendship. (Friendship was a fashionable topic for writers that year.) Thus it was agreed among them that Diderot should write a *Two Friends* of his own – a story about two smugglers, Félix and Olivier – as a kind of critique of, or counterblast to, Saint-Lambert's and that Mme de Pruneveaux should pass it off to Naigeon as an account of real-life events in the Bourbonne countryside. The story took him only a few hours to write and is a passionate but quite unsentimental one. It is a tale not of tearful speechmaking about friendship but of *unspoken* friendship, and a study of the "natural man", not as virtuous exemplar, but as criminal, or at least what conventional opinion branded as criminal.

The gullible Naigeon rose to the bait. He was highly impressed by this first-hand report from the heart of the smuggling country and wrote asking to be told what happened to the hero Félix after his friend's arrest and death. So a second part, too, got written, and then some further supplements: one in which the focus moves from the "two friends" themselves to the process, a shabby one, by which public opinion gets to work on their reputation, and another reflecting generally on the nature of fiction. The style of this story, which would so much impress writers of the German *Sturm und Drang*, puzzled Diderot's friends when they came to read it. It was hard for them to recognise the "warm" Diderot in its abrupt, incisive and deliberately "cold" style, and they thought it on the whole "detestable".[3]

The five formed a cheerful party – Grimm, as usual, performing the role of impresario or stage-manager. (Diderot's *The Two Friends* was, among other things, a sly tribute to their own friendship.) Grimm had to leave after a few days but kept in touch from Paris, and Diderot shuttled between Langres and Bourbonne. It was, he told himself, his duty to be taking notes on his surroundings. What would "the dear Baron", what would his friend Roux, the chemist, say if he could not answer their questions about Bourbonne and its waters? How should he not offer a "useful page" to those unfortunates who came to drink them? Also, as he remembered, this was the spot from which his father had come home to die. In a tender mood, he composed a *Journey to Bourbonne*, a charming mixture of topography, medicine, anecdote and philosophical parable.

It related, among other things, a *contretemps* during his stay, and how, through benevolent officiousness, he nearly managed to ruin his own reputation. Among the invalids at the spa had been a tax-official from Dijon, an apoplectic, named de Propriac. A friend of Diderot's, knowing de Propriac to be ill, had his eyes on the succession to his "place", and, Diderot, hearing the sick man had had a fit and was dying or dead, wrote off at once to alert his friend. The same evening, however, he was called in, as a man of skill in such matters, to help console M. de Propriac's widow. Indeed, so he believed, he had some success, persuading the distraught woman to give way to her tears and to begin facing the future. To his horror, though, she told him she was planning to leave at once for Paris, to solicit the succession to her husband's post for one of her relatives. What could she, or the world, think, reflected Diderot aghast, when she discovered there was a rival in the field, and that Diderot had recommended him? A man who could worm secrets out of a grief-stricken woman for his own ends – that is how Diderot must appear! In panic, he and his two women friends rushed round to the post office, to see if they could retrieve his letter, and by a mercy they were just in time.

The affair brought home to him a truth, or a collection of truths, about the precariousness of the universe and the contingency of reputation. For some strong characters, a clear conscience was enough, perhaps, but he could see it was not for such as himself. "I need also to appear to others as what I am."[4] In the next few weeks he began an affectionate family reminiscence, *Conversation of a Father with His Family*, which is a parable on this issue, and during the following year or so he would write two more short stories, *This Is Not a Story* and *On the Inconsistency of Public Opinion Regarding Our Private Actions*, exploring the whole intractable subject of "reputation".

In Langres, meanwhile, neither Canon Gauchat nor half-a-dozen other emissaries had made any impression on Didier-Pierre. He refused for the moment to see Denis, and he demanded of him not just a pledge not to write any more against religion, but a published retraction of what he had written already. It confirmed Denis in his worst fears; he really thought his brother must be mad, and as he said goodbye to Denise he gloomily imagined the "void" in which he was leaving her.

There was a further twist to the story of his summer expedition. On his way back to Paris, by arrangement, he rejoined his two women friends, who were staying a night or two in Châlons, accompanied by Foissy, who had insisted on escorting them home. It was all very entertaining, as before, and Diderot began to set great hopes on Mme de Maux, when the truth dawned on him. The assiduous Foissy, whom he had imagined as interested in the daughter, was in fact pursuing the mother, and what is more was receiving encouragement.

It was quite a blow to Diderot. The thing was a signal, he supposed, that he was too old for adventures with women; and several times over the next few weeks he wrote about it ruefully to Grimm. His tone changed from letter to letter: he was "not suffering"; he was suffering and felt grossly ill-treated; he had been given a new heart, "as hard as a pebble", and would like the old one back, and so on. Then he found his line, and it was a very characteristic one. He took up the cudgels for Foissy. Foissy, he told Mme de Maux when he went to see her, was an admirable character, most gentle, considerate, and straightforward. She had no right at all to make a fool of him. She had aroused his desires, so it was up to her to satisfy them. ("Desires?" Mme de Maux had exclaimed, in mock amazement. "Yes, desires!" She looked smug at this.) As for Diderot himself, he told her, she seemed to expect him to dance attendance on her as much as ever, and this would have to stop. She should always have a right to his friendship, but he must take back possession of his time. At this Mme de Maux wept, and soon he was anxiously trying to comfort her. The trouble with her, he told Grimm, was that she wanted to think herself a "marvellous" woman, whereas she was only an ordinary one – no worse than the rest of humanity, but no better.[5]

There was no permanent rift between them, and by December he was zestfully helping her daughter to organise a birthday celebration for Mme de Maux. They were to convert one of the rooms in her daughter's lodgings into a temple of Friendship, and she was to find her daughter as priestess at the altar, reciting verses in praise of that sacred friendship "which kindles the dry tree and bears on its forehead the motto '*Winter and summer*', on its breast '*Both near and far*', and on the hem of its garments '*In good times and in evil*'."[6]

It was now that Diderot, reflecting on the factotum-like role he seemed called on to play in life, sketched a little drama entitled "The Play and the Prologue", dedicating it to Mme de Maux as an answer to her accusations of neglect. "Madame," ran the dedication, "this piece was the work of a day. It took less time to compose it than to transcribe it . . . The author will be content with its success if your friend can disprove the forgetfulness of which you gently suspect him. Forget you! He? Never, never. . . !"

The play is set in the house of a "Mme de Malves", where her great friend "Mme de Chépy" is – much like Mme de Pruneveaux and her mother – arranging a play in honour of her birthday. She sends a lackey to fetch the poet "M. Hardouin", an old flame of hers and the indispensable man to compose such an offering. However, to her displeasure, he at first refuses. He says he cannot write on demand, and anyway he is tired to death and desperately busy. He is helping "Mme Servin" in a bothersome affair, over the ownership of a sedan-chair – also, to complicate matters, he is involved with the opposing party. Nobody will leave him in peace. "If I hear a knock at the door, I am afraid to open it. If I go out, I pull my hat down over my face. If people ask me to visit them, I blench."

Hardouin, nevertheless, lets himself be overpersuaded by Mme de Chépy; and within a single distracting day at Mme de Malves's he not only tricks another poet into writing a play for him (it turns out to be the play we are witnessing), but solves Mme Servin's problem with great finesse, and likewise the problem of the beautiful Mme Bertrand, the young widow of a naval officer, who wants to have her pension prolonged in favour of her son Binbin. Hardouin's method is a bold one: he explains to an official from the Navy Office that Binbin is really his own son, on hearing which the beaming official falls over himself to help him. The infallible route to success, soliloquises Hardouin, is the *personal* approach. Had he told the official he had no personal interest in Mme Bertrand, it was purely a matter of principle and he hoped the official would do nothing against his conscience, he would have been told frostily that the thing was "quite impossible" . . . All the same, when he reveals his system to Mme Bertrand, she seems not at all grateful. "I am born, I believe," ruminates Hardouin mournfully, "to do nothing that suits me, to do everything that pleases others, and to content nobody, nobody at all, not even myself."

This Beaumarchais-like little play – which Beaumarchais himself, we are told, saw performed among Diderot's friends, with Diderot in the role of Hardouin – was later expanded by Diderot into the four-act comedy, *Is He Good, Is He Wicked?*

In the June of this same year, 1770, Rousseau re-appeared in Paris, taking up residence in his old lodgings in the rue Plâtrière. The interim had been a time of appalling havoc for him. Not long after his arrival in England in 1766 he had been overtaken by wild persecution-mania, convinced that Hume, in concert with his French friends, had brought him to England to ruin and dishonour him. A wealthy friend of Hume's had provided Rousseau and Thérèse with a house at Wootton in Derbyshire, and from there in the June of 1766 he had written Hume a terrifying letter, telling him that his treachery had been discovered. The placid Hume, thunderstruck and convulsed with indignation, had written instantly to d'Holbach, declaring that Rousseau was "the blackest scoundrel the world had ever seen", and the story had promptly run round Paris – whereupon Hume had felt impelled to publish a *Succinct Account* of the quarrel and of his wrongs. The scandal was enormous, and all this publicity had of course only worsened Rousseau's condition, causing him to see spies and conspiracies everywhere. Ten months later he and Thérèse made a final pitiable exodus from England, walking – from poverty or out of fear of recognition it would seem – all the way from Spalding in Lincolnshire to Dover.

Back in France, Rousseau, who was still a proscribed man, moved from temporary refuge to refuge. For security reasons he took the name of "Renou", passing Thérèse off as his sister; but in Bourgoin, in a mood of compunction towards Thérèse, he "married" her, in a wedding-ceremony conducted by himself. Thoughts of emigration – to America or Greece – entered his mind, and he even contemplated returning to Wootton. Then, on the night of 9 November 1768, while going through his papers, he discovered that the letters from the time of the "Hermitage" affair were mysteriously missing. They had no doubt, he told himself, been stolen; and in a flash he "pierced the dark mystery" of the conspiracy surrounding him. It must date back to that fatal

year of 1756–57 and must have been the work of Grimm, Mme
d'Epinay and Diderot. With this new "revelation" in mind, he
determined to return to Paris, so that he could confront his
enemies.

His presence in Paris created a great stir. Several times, when
he appeared at the Café de la Régence, a great crowd gathered;
and he received a warning from the authorities to be more
discreet. His life, as he planned it, was from now on to be one of
perfect simplicity and virtuous poverty, and in token of this he
resumed his old profession of music-copier. Meanwhile, he was
continuing his *Confessions*. Under the terms of an agreement with
the authorities, he was not permitted to publish them; but as an
alternative, over the ensuing winter he gave readings from them
in various aristocratic households. One of these sessions lasted
from nine in the morning till three o'clock the next morning, and,
according to a participant, when Rousseau came to the passage
describing how he abandoned his children, his listeners, at first
embarrassed, were reduced to tears by his visible grief.

As no doubt Rousseau intended, the news of these readings
alarmed Diderot and Mme d'Epinay, who wondered what he
might say about them; and eventually, in June 1771, Mme
d'Epinay managed to persuade her friend Sartine, the
Lieutenant-General of Police, to have the readings stopped.

It was about this time that, with Diderot's help, she was
revising her *Memoirs of Madame de Montbrillant*. According to a
theory first put forward by Frederika Macdonald[7] in 1906 the two
friends' purpose in this was to blacken Rousseau's character and
whitewash their own behaviour at the time of the "Hermitage"
affair. The facts do not really bear this out, for the revisions,
which were very thorough, affected all parts of the vast manuscript, not just the passages concerning Rousseau. Moreover the
portrait of him in the first version was already very damning, so
that the few harsh touches added in the revision need suggest no
sinister motive.

What is true, though, is that from this time on Rousseau and
Diderot were unbalanced in their imaginings about each other.
With Rousseau it had been a matter of sudden "revelation". The
truth had dawned on him that the friend he had been finding

excuses for had been in fact the worst of all his enemies. With Diderot the process was more gradual, but no less sure. He imagined Rousseau, in writing his *Confessions*, as calculating that by admitting certain crimes of his own he earned the licence to blacken other innocent people's name to all eternity. For Diderot, given his hankerings for fair reputation, there could hardly be a wickeder scheme.

Each New Year the whole Diderot circle assembled at d'Holbach's house in Paris for the Feast of the Kings, at which the guest who found a bean in his cake was named monarch for the day. In the year 1770 the honour fell to Diderot, and, according to Grimm's report in the *Correspondance littéraire*, he did not leave his subjects to languish but, before they had even risen from the table, he had delivered them a code of laws in verse. He had a definite talent for verse, and his "code Denis" is an elegant piece. It begins:

> *Dans ses états, à tout ce qui respire*
> *Un souverain prétend donner la loi;*
> *C'est le contraire en mon empire:*
> *Le sujet règne sur le roi.*

> [Most princes, in their own realms, desire
> A right of rule over everything;
> It is different in my empire;
> There the subject rules over the king.]

His simple programme of laws resembles Rabelais's *Fay ce que vouldras*. It decrees that his subjects shall each be happy in his or her own way, paying homage to both the god of wine and the god of love.

> For such is our good pleasure: given this
> seventeen hundred and seventieth year of our Saviour.
>   Signed: DENIS, without lands or château,
>   King by grace of the *gâteau*.[8]

The following New Year, by chance or design, the bean fell to Diderot again, and he composed a *ballade* blaming Fate for her imbecility in crowning the least worthy. But the year after that it fell to him for a third time, and on this occasion, as a prelude to his perpetual abdication, he composed a more elaborate piece, entitled "Les Eleuthéromanes" (i.e. "Maniacs for freedom"). It was in the form of a dithyrambic ode and was accordingly in a vein of licensed fury. His mind was running much upon tyrants – such as that other Denis, the infamous Dionysius of Syracuse – and with some reason, for during the previous year France seemed to have taken a step towards tyranny. Louis XV, exasperated by continual friction with the Paris *Parlement*, had stripped it of its judicial authority and replaced it by "superior councils" of his own appointing. (They were nicknamed "Maupeou's *Parlement*", after the name of his new chief minister.) It was a major crisis, and caused the patriotic Malesherbes, in his capacity as President of the Cour des Aides, to issue a "remonstrance", saying it was time to summon "an assembly of the nation".

In Diderot's poem *strophe, antistrophe* and *epode* represent three distinct personages, three Furies, who take turns to torment a guilty tyrant on his throne, filling his mind with fears by day and dreams of bloodshed and revolution by night. In vain does this tyrant cite the "pact" by which his subjects became slaves. Who wrote the words of this pact, ask the Furies; in what forest or cave was it signed? The child of Nature, they declare, abhors slavery and repugns it in his very heart. "Liberty is his wish; his cry is 'Liberty!'" He will say, like the denizen of the woods, "Nature makes neither servant nor master. I wish not to give, nor be given, laws."

> And for want of a rope his hands will knot
> The guts of the priest to strangle kings.[9]

When this festive poem, an exercise in hyperbole, was published in the Year IV (1795–96), it was seized on with outraged zest by the enemies of the Revolution, and for many years afterwards it would earn Diderot a reputation as an arch-Jacobin.

By the standards of his day, being nearly sixty in 1772, Diderot was already an old man. Even seven years before, Horace Walpole had described him as "a very lively old man, and a great talker."[10] He was, nevertheless, producing some of his most joyous and adventurous writing. It was now that he sketched the admirable *Paradox of the Actor*, a dialogue about the art of acting in which the first of the two speakers argues that what characterises a great actor is not some superior power of feeling but an exceptional and total lack of feeling. "No feeling!" expostulates the second speaker. "None," replies the first. "It is extreme sensibility which makes a mediocre actor; mediocre sensibility which makes the multitude of bad actors; and a total lack of sensibility which produces sublime actors. The art of the great actor, so this "First Speaker" argues, lies not in feeling but in rendering the external signs of feeling. He states his paradox in this crude form, for shock effect, and then restates it more soberly, admitting that a great actress like La Clairon would have felt the passions of the character she portrays *once*. But, "the struggle over, and having once been raised to the heights of her 'phantom', she regains full self-control and can repeat herself without emotion."

The *Paradox* has been debated and contested by a whole succession of famous actors, among them Talma, Coquelin, Henry Irving and Jouvet, but in fact it extends beyond acting to "genius" in general. Not only great actors, but great poets and all "great imitators of nature", are, says the "First Speaker", "the least 'feeling' people in the world." The "feeling man" is too much at the mercy of his diaphragm to be a great king, a great politician, a great magistrate, a man of true judgement, or a profound observer.

The *Paradox of the Actor* was a favourite work of Diderot's, and he kept on revising it. But it is worth insisting that it only reveals its meaning if we take note that it is a dramatic fiction. The "First Speaker", as he explains himself, is a professed "man of feeling", the kind of man who cannot tell a pathetic story without stammering with emotion and losing his head; and his vision of the "genius" as a monster of cool judgement and insensibility is only valid, to the extent that it *is* valid, on the lips of such a "warm" character as himself. He recounts how he once heard his friend the dramatist Marmontel propound a similar view, contrasting the "mediocre" man of feeling with the insensible "genius", and how, if he had had the presence of mind, he would have told him he was too much of the "genius" school to say such things and should leave the appreciation of "genius" to others. But then presence of mind is what the man of feeling so fatally lacks; "he loses his head and only recovers it at the bottom of the stairs." (Diderot is the source of the expression *esprit d'escalier*.)[11] It is the special perquisite of the "man of feeling", says the "First Speaker", and a reason for warm self-congratulation on his part, to be a generous appreciator of the qualities he lacks. One has, that is to say, to bargain for the right to say certain things. This is a master-idea in Diderot's writing, and perhaps his profoundest insight.

It was, altogether, a fruitful and inspiring time for Diderot, now that at last, after so many weary years, he was freed from the *Encyclopédie*. For one thing, through the bounty of Catherine, he could now be accounted a wordly success. Mme Geoffrin, characteristically, had recognised the change and, a year before, to repay him for his help over the sedan-chair affair, insisted on redecorating his study. Gone were the kitchen table and common cane-seated chair, and in their place were a bureau and ormolu clock and marquetry bookcase of her choosing. She had also made him give up his old comfortable dressing-gown, which used to double as penwiper and duster, in favour of a magnificent scarlet one; and, in some famous "Regrets over My Old Dressing-Gown", he had pretended to foresee dire consequences for his moral welfare. "O Diogenes, if you saw your disciple under the costly mantle of Aristippus, how you would laugh! I have quitted the tub where I was monarch to serve under a tyrant." Well, it must be so he, said. He intended to remain, even in his scarlet robes, the tender-hearted philosopher with "the good round back".[12]

Meanwhile, his freedom tasted sweet. His friend Mme d'Epinay, writing from the suburban village of Boulogne, gave Galiani a most cheering report on him. "The Philosopher has come to spend two days here . . . He is among us more talkative, more inspired, more radiant than ever. He sees everything through rose-tinted spectacles."[13] He was, nevertheless, sometimes a prey to melancholy, for Angélique would soon be married, and he dreaded the prospect of a home life without her. The whole situation as regards her marriage was in fact becoming fraught; Nanette had set her face against Vandeul, perhaps because of his rumoured irreligion, and was making all sorts of difficulties about the wedding, refusing to allow any of Diderot's friends, even Grimm, to be invited to the ceremony. All through Angélique's girlhood, Diderot wrote gloomily to Grimm (8 September 1772), Nanette had done her best to prevent her from knowing his friends, and she was keeping this up to the last.[14]

The wedding ceremony took place on 9 September at the church of Saint-Sulpice, in the presence of one or two of the Caroillon family, of Diderot's sister Denise and of Nanette's widowed sister Mme Billard, who had come to live with them in the rue Taranne. Angélique stumbled over her responses; and, Diderot told Grimm, the only one to keep her head was Nanette. "She loves her daughter. Tell me how so much hardness comes to be joined to genuine feeling."[15]

He had once told Vandeul's mother that Nanette, though "very good, very humane and very beneficent", was not so adaptable as himself, with whom "Satan with all his horns" could have lived in harmony, but that this need not cause trouble, since the children were going to have a separate establishment. For a few weeks, though, after the wedding, the situation became thoroughly painful. Nanette refused to visit the newly-married couple and received them very dourly when they came to the rue Taranne. Diderot felt in despair. She was killing him with her ill-humour, he told Grimm, and was killing herself too. For a day or two he was reduced to not speaking, but this brought on one of her "attacks", which meant he had to rush to her rescue. "I have no child any longer. I am alone, and my loneliness is unbearable,"[16] he lamented to his sister. His sole consolation, he told her, was to visit "the nest of these young birds", bringing them "the feather or blade of straw that is lacking". He gave them a silver coffee-pot and a pair of silver candlesticks, a handsome pottery ewer and some panel-friezes for their doors. He fussed so continually over them, indeed, that they began to grow irritated. Then he suddenly realised what his trouble was; he was not only lonely, he was jealous. The discovery of this "fine platitude", he told Grimm, quite cleared his mind; it made him laugh and cheered his spirits greatly.

There was a further consequence to Angélique's marriage, however: it brought about a final rift between Diderot and his brother. Didier-Pierre had greatly disapproved of Angélique's fiancé. He was, he declared, a man without religion – the young man's own mother had admitted as much to him. Indeed he was exactly the sort of son-in-law Diderot might have been expected to choose, and he (Didier-Pierre) would have nothing to do with the wedding. Diderot wrote to him, asking him at least to give his niece his blessing, and Angélique added some lines of her own, pleading with him to conduct the wedding ceremony. His reply was the harshest possible rebuff. "I declare to you that I do not approve of your marriage with M. Caroillon; that if it takes place, I shall regard you as a young woman without religion; that you are not, and never again will be, my niece, and that the door of my house will be shut to you and to M. Caroillon, as it is to your father, from the same motive of religion."[17]

Diderot, even now, kept his temper, and after the wedding he sent Didier-Pierre a tough and didactic, but still brotherly, reply. His brother, he wrote, must be feeling thoroughly ashamed of his villainous letter. It was monstrous to urge his niece to hate her own father (for that is what it amounted to), and simply absurd to suspect that all they wanted of him was to be remembered in his will.

Do not deceive yourself; there is not a single decent citizen in your town who does not blame you. One needs to be very strong-minded to be content with one's own self-approval. But if you search the depths of your heart, you will see that you do not even enjoy that. So, once and for all, try to stop being false with

yourself and appearing mad in other people's eyes. Adieu, *abbé*! Do
not think I hate you in the very least. I hate no one, not even
ingrates; I sometimes make them, and the fact that I make them
does not discourage me from making more. We will await you
with open arms. You will return to us when you will; when you
have finally stopped tormenting yourself . . . Your brother and
friend,

DIDEROT[18]

The embittered Didier-Pierre replied as rancorously as ever; and,
at this, Diderot lost all patience and despatched to him a
scorching denunciation, some five thousand words long, accusing
him of being a bad priest, a bad Christian, a bad citizen, a bad
son, a bad brother, a bad uncle and a bad man. Even to this the
abbé responded, raking up old family grievances and twitting
Diderot, with heavy irony, over Angélique's anatomy lessons –
such an "infallible" method of teaching a young woman modesty!
Diderot returned the letter unopened, writing on the cover that
he would have opened it had he hoped to "find his brother"
inside.

21

The Stories

The world is not short of admirers of Diderot as novelist. It is curious, therefore, that his short stories have been left a little in the shade. It was not always so. Balzac thought Diderot's *Ceci n'est pas un conte (This Is Not a Story)* "one of the grandest fragments of the history of the human heart"; he said that it "sweated truth in every sentence". And Diderot's *Les Deux Amis de Bourbonne (The Two Friends from Bourbonne)*, with its impetuous abruptness of style and its romanticisation of the outlaw, helped set Schiller on a new path as a writer; Goethe, thinking of the same story, depicts Diderot as providing a programme for young writers in general. "His children of nature pleased us very much, his brave poachers and smugglers enchanted us."[1] It became the thing for Goethe's friends to praise Diderot at the expense of the "genteel" French tradition and to claim him for their own.

The Germans were right that, as a novelist and story-teller, Diderot was not writing for a French audience. But the truth is, he was – deliberately – not writing for an audience at all: the idea of an audience inhibited him, stifling his originality. The fact is of much significance; and one of its consequences was that, in compensation, he evolved a theory of fiction, and a subject-matter for fiction, profoundly concerned with *audiences* – both the audiences for our conduct and the audiences for our stories.

Diderot's masters in fiction, as we have seen, were Richardson, the "counterfeiter" and exponent of immediacy, hypnotic illusion and vicarious participation, and Sterne, the great disrupter of fictional illusion and of author-reader relations. However, at the time of writing *The Nun*, Diderot had not yet read Sterne, so that his extreme scepticism towards narrative truth was all his own, part of an endeavour to re-think the basic principles of fiction that becomes quite explicit in his stories. There were, in all, five of these,[2] all written in the years 1770–72, and they are closely related, evidently representing some kind of concerted experiment. The first two, which we have already met, were *The Two Friends from Bourbonne* and *Conversation of a Father and His Family*. There followed, though not necessarily in that order, *This Is Not a Story*, *On the Inconsistency of Public Opinion Regarding Our Private Actions* and *Supplement to Bougainville's "Voyage"*, this last a fictitious addition to the explorer Bougainville's *Voyage Round the World*. What is more, as he worked on these last three stories ("story" is perhaps not the *mot juste* for the *Supplement*, but it will do for the moment) they formed themselves into a connected trilogy. Readers have been rather slow to recognise this, or at least see its importance, though it is obvious when one is alerted to it, and was in fact stated explicitly in the *Correspondance littéraire* when these three pieces appeared there.[3] "The story that you are about to read is by M. Diderot," runs an editorial note to *This Is Not a Story*. "It will be followed by several others by the same author. Not till the end of the final story will one see the moral and secret purpose underlying them."[4] To that "moral and secret purpose" I shall come in a moment.

Diderot's theory of fiction may be put quite concisely. Fiction, for him, signified not a story, but the spectacle of somebody telling a story. The point is made in the opening lines of his (paradoxically entitled) *This Is Not a Story*:

> When one tells a story, there has to be someone to listen; and if the story runs to any length, it is rare for the story-teller not to be interrupted by his listener. That is why (if you are wondering) in the story which you are about to read (which is not a story, or if it is, then a bad one) I have introduced a personage who plays as it were the role of listener.[5]

How Diderot imagined "the spectacle of somebody telling a story" is made clearer in that passage from his *Essay on Painting* which I quoted earlier (pp.226–7), in which he describes the "combined system of these interests".[6]

The word "system" is significant here, for – as was mentioned earlier in connection with *The Nun* (pp.228–9) – the world presented itself to Diderot not as a collection of independent entities or transcendent unities but as an interlocking of different "systems" or polities. The thought, which is essentially a necessitarian one, applied for him equally to politics proper, to physiology – the organs of a body constituting a system of warring interests – and to aesthetics. In a review of the painter Watelet's didactic poem *L'Art de peindre* (1760), he wrote that "ensemble" can never be destroyed, "either in nature, where everything is necessary, or in art, when art knows how to introduce necessity into its productions". Similarly, in a discussion of the works of Vien in the Salon of 1767, he outlines a system according to which there must be less or more animation in a painting according to the weight, gravity, age, etc. of the personages portrayed. (Animation befits atoms, repose befits worlds.) In the same spirit, he once described to Sophie how the royal palace of Versailles "gave the law" governing all the gradations of visible grandeur.[7]

This ruling notion is very relevant to Diderot's own fiction. The "system" of a fiction of his will involve at the very least three interacting, and possibly conflicting, "interests": those of the story-teller, of a listener, and of ourself as reader. (Usually there will be more; there are more in several of the stories under discussion.) It is a method very effective in suggesting the relativity of any fictional statement or thesis. It keeps alive the possibility that with other listeners or parties to the discourse the whole face of things might change. The novelist Michel Butor has put the point very well where he imagines a portraitist painting the spectacle of someone giving a reading:

> If the painter presented the person reading frontally, as if speaking directly to us, we should have no means of knowing that his posture was merely one among many possible postures; but if, on the contrary, he also includes a portrait of the primary spectator, he shows us by this that we constitute a third party on the scene; he gives an oblique view of the reader or reciter which allows us to see him in depth . . . The depicted interlocutor gives us a parallax allowing us to calculate where we stand in regard to the speaker.[8]

What is also entailed, and again very important in Diderot's eyes, is that a fiction will never be finally separable from its matrix in real life, including the real life of the reader. He is continually concerned with the margins or "frames" of his stories, unsettling any comfortable sense that they *are* safely "framed". For instance, at the beginning of *This Is Not a Story*, we come in at the tail-end of someone else's piece of story-telling. Equally, in his trilogy, he deliberately mixes up real-life personages (Gardeil, Mlle de la Chaux, etc.) with invented ones (Desroches, Mme de la Carlière, etc.), and in the third, the *Supplement to Bougainville's "Voyage"*, he puts invented sentiments into the mouths of characters in an already existing piece of writing by Bougainville.

As for the paradox of a novelist asserting "This is not a story," it can have three possible meanings. It can mean, "This is not a *conventional* story, obeying the timeworn formulae of fiction-writers"; or it can mean, "This is not an invention, it actually happened"; and thirdly, since a certain kind of fiction tries to make the reader say to himself "This must be true; no one could have *invented* a detail like that," it can mean, "Trust no novelist, including the present one – for novelists love to pretend they are not writing a story." Diderot requires us to understand it in all three senses; and for him it represents in summary form every possibility open to a fiction-writer.

Diderot, spurred into fiction-writing as he was in such an apparently casual manner, found a freedom in it denied him in his more public writings. His approach to fiction was, accordingly, always intensely experimental, but certainly not just for the sheer pleasure of experiment. For reflection on the nature of fiction led him to find new and urgent things for fiction to say. Let us consider his trilogy. Its central theme is announced in that meteorological discussion that frames the second and third stories. Two speakers are out walking on a foggy day, and the question that concerns them is whether, and if so when and by what means, the fog will clear and "points of blue" or starlight begin to pierce the murk. It is, as the reader gradually realises, a most apt and subtle simile for the question already implicitly posed in *This Is Not a Story* and canvassed explicitly and passionately in *On the Inconsistency of Public Opinion*: i.e. have "reputation" and "public opinion" any validity at all? Three tragic love-stories, three "cases", have been presented to us. The first, that of the self-sacrificing Tanié, who endures a dog's life to support his scheming mistress Mme Reymer and then is coolly destroyed by her, is followed by its mirror-reversal, that of the hack-writer Gardeil who lets his gentle and hapless victim, Mlle de la Chaux, wear out her health and good looks by slaving for him and then tells her she is no further use to him; and then, in the next tale, we are presented with a case (that of the Chevalier Desroches and Mme de la Carlière) which subsumes these two previous tales and seems to be interpretable in the light of either or both, unsettling any certainties that, as representatives of "public opinion", we readers may have formed.

The theme was adumbrated at the end of *This Is Not a Story*. Were we right to pass such a final judgement on Gardeil as we were inclined to?

> . . . someone may perhaps tell me that it is much too hasty to pass judgement on a man on the strength of a single action; . . . that one may be inconstant in love, and even be quite unscrupulous when it comes to women, without being a total scoundrel or villain; . . . that there are enough men in our homes or streets who richly deserve the name of rascal without inventing imaginary crimes which would multiply their number to infinity.[9]

These doubts are silenced for the moment with a light question: would you, after all that has been said, and "putting your hand on your heart", choose Gardeil for your friend? They return, though, and with bewildering effect, in *On the Inconsistency of Public Opinion*.

The story features a woman, the aristocratic Mme de la Carlière, who suffers – and frankly admits to suffering – from a morbid hypersensitivity as regards her own "honour" but who falls in love with the fascinating Desroches, a man with a reputation for light-mindedness and Don Juanism. Diderot, in this story, lays a trap for the reader. When we come to Mme de la Carlière's great oration to her lover on the eve of their marriage, we are almost bound to be carried away. "Give me the greatest mark of confidence that self-respecting woman ever asked of a man of honour: *refuse me*, refuse me if you think I put too high a price on myself." These words, and her grandly conceived appeal, win the reader's heart. Thus, when exposed in the ensuing pages to a long and cruel re-appraisal of Mme de la Carlière, and of her exorbitant self-righteousness when she finds herself betrayed, the reader is left wondering whether common ethics, or ordinary human sympathies, are fitted to cope with such issues at all.

Diderot's interlocutory method is, of course, crucial to the stories' effect. The "listener" in *This Is Not a Story* and the first of the two speakers in *On the Inconsistency* are conventional cynics, in contrast to the altogether profounder scepticism of the story-teller himself. The "listener" generalises with conventional misanthropy, and similarly the first speaker in *On the Inconsistency* jumps to trite conclusions (Desroches is a "madman") and assumes a trite and worldly-wise fictional plot (Desroches will simply fall for a designing woman), for which he is rebuked by his interlocutor. Cynicism, we see, is in itself a kind of security – one can always, as it were, fall back on cynicism – and the task of the narrator (as it is of Diderot himself) is to unsettle that security as much as any other.

The moral of *On the Inconsistency of Public Opinion* is clear. Mme de la Carlière has chosen to be judged by public opinion – that is to say by a "tribunal" of friends and relations rather than by the impartial eye of God or conscience – and she must take the consequences. It is a poignant tale, for the consequences are dire. Public opinion, as it turns out (we see it again in *The Two Friends from Bourbonne*) is a hopeless tribunal, weak, venal and feather-headed, swayed by herd-instinct, as the narrator's interlocutor admits to having been, and by instant emotion, as the reader convicts himself of having been. If a just judgement on such as Desroches and Mme de la Carlière is ever to emerge, it will not be thanks to the "public" but to some impersonal and weather-like natural process and clearing of fog.

But on the other hand, what other tribunal is there? No man is strong enough to content himself with his own good opinion, nor would he be right to do so. Virtue is a social matter; it is, anyway for an atheist, essentially a matter of other people's opinion. (We may imagine Diderot as, in imagination, addressing Rousseau, with whom he had quarrelled over just this issue.) Hence the two opening stories of Diderot's trilogy seem to be posing a total dilemma. It remains for the concluding story, *Supplement to Bougainville's "Voyage"*, to suggest that there may be a rational answer to it after all. It could be that the inconsistency of public opinion and the havoc and tragedy it brings are the fruit of something more basic – an error regarding sexual ethics, or the "attaching of moral ideas to certain physical actions which do not admit of them".

The *Supplement* arose as a kind of afterthought to a review that Diderot wrote of Bougainville's book when it appeared in 1771, and it is one of the richest examples of his supposititious or "foisting" technique. He takes over Bougainville's *Voyage*, shamelessly rewriting and falsifying it where necessary, and foists upon it the speeches and arguments that, for the "enlightened" reader, cry out so urgently to be spoken.

The author of the *Voyage* itself, the mathematician and explorer Louis-Antoine de Bougainville (1729–1814) began a circumnavigation of the globe at Nantes on 15 November 1766, and his ship *La Boudeuse* and its companion *L'Etoile* reached home again in the spring of 1769. His book, with its glowing report of sexual freedom in Tahiti, gave a great boost to what in Diderot's text is referred to as the "Tahiti fable". Bougainville was not in fact the originator of the fable, for one of his companions on the voyage, the naturalist Philibert Commerson, had already published an even more rapturous account of this sexual "Utopia".[10] He was, moreover, not really a "primitivist" in the full sense: he gave a very bleak picture of the "state of nature" as exhibited by the Pecherais of Tierra del Fuego, and he was a fierce critic of Rousseau. His admirable book was a godsend to Diderot, who saw it, not only as intensely sympathetic, but as ripe for appropriation.

Bougainville described how, during the first joyous reception of himself and his crew in Tahiti, one old man, his host's father – a magnificent figure despite his great age, with scarcely a wrinkle on his sinewy body – stood aloof.

> He hardly seemed to notice our arrival. He withdrew as if unaware of our caresses, exhibiting neither fear, not surprise, nor curiosity. Far from taking part in the species of ecstasy the sight of

us caused among his fellow-islanders, his sombre and reflective air seemed to proclaim fear that his happy days, spent in the bosom of repose, would be marred by the arrival of a new race.[11]

The passage gave Diderot the cue for the great "Old Man's Farewell", an oration as magnificent in eloquence as it is cunning in its dramatic irony.

Lévi-Strauss, in a striking passage in *Tristes tropiques*, attacks Diderot for being the crude "primitivist" and apologist of the "natural man" that Rousseau has been wrongly accused of being. Diderot's (or rather the Tahitian Orou's) "brief history of almost all our woe" – "Once there was a natural man: inside that man there was installed an artificial man, and within the cave a civil war began which lasted the whole of his life" – is, says Lévi-Strauss, absurd. "He who says 'man', says 'language', and he who says 'language' says 'society'. The Polynesians of Bougainville did not live in society any less than us."[12]

In a sense, of course, Lévi-Strauss is perfectly right; but this is to take Diderot's book for what it is not and to miss its elaborate ruses and ironies. Diderot's complex polemical strategy in this *Supplement*, as in many of his best writings, involves a succession of supplements, designed to revise and sometimes to subvert one another. Notably at two points, the reader finds a polemical trick has been played upon him. The first is a game played over Utopian satire. The reader is drawn enjoyably into the reversal of values by which, in Diderot's Tahiti, chastity is considered a deep reproach, if not a crime, and it is the grossest failure of good manners on the visiting Chaplain's part to refuse to sleep with his host Orou's daughters – or for that matter, with his wife. (This is, as it were, the *Erewhon* game, and the game played by Voltaire in the Eldorado scenes in *Candide*.) But then, as guest and host grow more intimate, Orou reveals a secret. This sexual Utopianism is no mere Arcadian reversal of European *mores*, but rather a cunning eugenic calculation. The European visitors, inferior as they are in almost all respects, possess one advantage, as the Tahitians have realised – a superior intelligence. Tahitian wives and daughters are therefore under orders to get themselves pregnant by them, to "harvest the seed of a race superior to our own". "This was the one thing we were able to gain from you and your friends," says Orou to the Chaplain. "For you see, savages as we are, we can be calculating too."

The second piece of subversion comes in the concluding conversation between "A" and "B", when "B" begins to push the contrast between Europe and Tahiti to extremes, in a way that is not so much romantic-primitivist as misanthropic. As he represents it, humankind is faced with a choice between two evils: either a civilised life in which, through male chauvinism, property-mania and social injustice, the sexual act becomes a source of infinite woe; or a savage life which is sunk in "mediocrity", benumbing indolence and unenlightenment. With a final *reductio ad absurdum*, he caricatures his position beyond all mistaking. He asserts that only two places on earth are suited to human beings: Tahiti, where they have the wisdom not to trouble their heads with enlightenment, and Venice, where they are too cowed to do so. His extravagance gives the game away, and we realise we have been the victims of one more polemical ploy.

There follows a palinode, expressing a sober and unfanatical view which we are safe in taking as Diderot's own. "So what shall we do?" asks "A": to which "B" 's answer is, "What we must do is to speak against insane laws till they are reformed, but in the meantime obey them."[13] The doctrine that Diderot is underwriting is not primitivism at all, but a more cogent, serious and humane one: that it is madness to create institutions that go against the grain of life and set humans at war with their own selves. It is a doctrine running through not just the *Supplement* but the whole of the trilogy, and, persuaded by his chastened tone, we are disposed to listen to the claim to which, all the time, these stories have been moving: that, if the fog of prejudice would clear, and sexual customs and laws cease to put humans at odds with themselves, tragedies of the kind that overtake Gardeil, la Chaux, Desroches and de la Carlière might simply prove unnecessary.

22

Diderot in Russia

Ever since Catherine the Great's first intrusion into Diderot's life, the suggestion had been raised that he might go to Russia to present his thanks in person. He disliked travel, considering it valuable only to the very young. The world, he said, was like a house, and it was stupid to be wandering in the attics and the basement when one could be enjoying the living-rooms. It is true he had cherished the fantasy of an Italian journey, but the furthest he had ever actually travelled was the homeward route to Langres. When Falconet went to St Petersburg in 1766, Diderot made a "solemn vow" that one day he would visit him there and would "prostrate himself at the feet of his great benefactress, letting her see the tears of feeling and gratitude flow from his eyes."[1] However, for many plausible reasons, it could not be just at present.

Nevertheless, Catherine was very pressing, sending him repeated invitations through Grimm and others. And by the early 1770s there were many incentives for the journey. It would be an excitement for him to see the paintings he had bought for Catherine in their new home, and even more to see what his protégé Falconet was making of the monument to Peter the Great. Every few months he would send Falconet hortatory messages: "Work, my friend, work with all your force! Above all, give us a beautiful horse, for they say that this is where you will fail."[2] Further, Catherine had never given up on the idea that one day a new *Encyclopédie* might be created on Russian soil.

Meanwhile, one by one, his excuses for not going dropped away. The *Encyclopédie* had finally been published, and Angélique was safely married. Even more to the point, Grimm had plans to go to Russia in the summer of 1773. His friendship with the

Landgravine of Hesse-Darmstadt had flourished. It was she who had assisted, and paid for, him to become a Baron of the Holy Roman Empire, a title which Diderot would disrespectfully elevate to "Marquis". Grimm had accompanied her son on his travels in England in 1771. Being a specialist in royal marriage-brokering, he had made all sorts of marriage-plans for her daughters, recently achieving his masterpiece in this line, the betrothal of the Princess Wilhelmina of Hesse-Darmstadt to the Grand Duke Paul of Russia. The arrangement was that he should collect the young prince at Darmstadt, join the rest of the Hesse royal family in Berlin, where they would be the guests of Frederick the Great, and from there take them on to St Petersburg. If Diderot was ever to go to Russia, this summer, as he realised, was the golden moment.

It was part of Grimm's vision of things that Diderot should come and join him in Berlin and be introduced to Frederick the Great. Diderot, however, was profoundly suspicious of Frederick. He had rebuffed earlier overtures from the King and pictured him as planning, once he was in Berlin, to humiliate him and take his revenge. Thus he sidled out of Grimm's scheme and arranged instead, as a first step on the road to Russia, to go to The Hague to stay with his friend Prince Gallitzin, who was now Catherine's representative in the Netherlands. There he was to meet another Russian acquaintance, Alexis Narishkin, and it was understood that Narishkin would take Diderot on to St Petersburg in his own carriage.

Diderot was now in his sixtieth year. The journey was a solemn step for him, and he drew up a document appointing Naigeon as his literary executor in case he should die in the course of it. His wife and child were directed to give all his manuscripts to Naigeon, "who will, for a man whom he has tenderly loved and who has paid him well in return, take the care of arranging, revising and publishing everything which, in his view, will harm neither my memory nor any person's tranquillity." One of the excitements of his expedition would be, of course, his reunion with Falconet and Marie-Ann Collot. He was a great admirer of Marie-Anne Collot, as she was of him: it was at this time that, on commission from Catherine, she was making, from memory, the charming, smiling head of Diderot now in the Hermitage collection. He wrote to the two, picturing the moment when he knocked on their door in St Petersburg and hurled himself into their arms. How they would stammer, "It's you!" "Yes, it's me!" "You at last!" (Woe betide one so long parted from his friends who, if he could manage to speak at all, would not stammer!) Nanette agreed to his going, he told them, for she would not want him to die an ingrate; and if had to die, he might as well fatten the St Petersburg worms as those of Paris.[3]

News of his impending journey soon spread. Some of his friends were alarmed, as Nanette and Angélique had been, for it was a hazardous undertaking for a man of his age. Some were critical, being suspicious of such eagerness to pay court to a despot, and others were amused at the prospect. According to the *abbé* Galiani, Diderot would probably simply forget to come back, time and space being for him what they were for God: "He imagines himself omnipresent and eternal."[4] It was a pity, said another friend, that they would learn nothing about Russia either from Diderot or from Grimm, "because one will tell us of what he has not seen and the other will not tell us what he has seen."[5]

On his last night home, talking with a visitor, Diderot got rather carried away, tearfully describing his agonies at deserting his wife and daughter and theirs at parting from him. The three of them, he said, had sat down to a farewell meal but had been able neither to speak nor to eat. . . . No, he really believed he could not go, he would not have the "abominable courage" to do so. It was an impressive performance, spoilt (so the visitor recounted) when Nanette came in and, with hands on hips, loudly berated him. "What's this? Still chattering here when you ought to be upstairs packing? It's always the same: so long as you are making fine phrases, everything else can go hang. That's what comes of going out to supper, when you promised and promised . . . But everyone has claims on you except us. Ah, what a man! what a man!"[6]

Nevertheless, after Diderot had actually departed on his journey, Angélique pined greatly for him, and Nanette hardly knew what to do with herself. "Since M. Diderot has gone to The Hague," Angélique's husband wrote to his mother, "she does nothing but shift the furniture backwards and forwards, change her maids and complain of the terrible characters she meets everywhere."[7]

Diderot reached The Hague on 15 June 1773. He was in an elated mood, enjoying his freedom and a sense of unlimited possibilities. He had soon made innumerable acquaintances. Gallitzin took him to Leyden, where he was lionised by the professors, and Mme d'Epinay reported him as "mad about the Dutch doctors". He was collecting materials for a treatise on physiology, and he drew on these Dutch friends for help. In a letter to Falconet, he had spoken of staying with the Gallitzins for a fortnight – no more – "the lightest push" might shoot him straight on to Russia and to Falconet's welcoming arms. However, the fortnight stretched into three months.

Social life at The Hague itself, dominated as it was by the embassies, was stiff and reserved. Gallitzin and his German wife were, however, most affectionate hosts. He lived among them, said Diderot, "as with a good brother and a good sister". The quietness suited him; he read and wrote and made little jaunts to the seaside. He had never seen the sea before and found its vastness and monotony conducive to dreaming. He was much taken with Holland. "The better I get to know this country", he wrote to Sophie and her sister (22 July 1773), "the more I like it."

> The soles, the fresh herrings, the turbots, the perch, and
> everything they call "waterfish" are the best fellows in the world.
> The walks are charming. I don't know if the women are really so
> well-behaved; but with their great straw-hats, their downcast eyes,
> and those enormous neckerchiefs on their bosom, they have all the
> air of returning from Benediction or going to confession.
>
> The men have good sense; they understand their own business
> very well; they are full of republican spirit, from the highest to the
> lowest. I heard a saddle-and-harness maker say: "I must hurry
> and take my child out of the convent. I'm afraid she may be
> catching those sneaking 'monarchy' ways."

Several of his best writings were composed during this cheerful time; it was now, for instance, that he enlarged a brief review of a book on acting into his memorable *Paradox of the Actor*. He also, through a Dutch friend, proposed to the publisher Marc-Michel Rey a collected edition of his own works, to include some of the newly written ones, and to serve as a corrective to the recent pirated collection, which saddled him with various spurious works. Negotiations, however, did not for the moment get far, for Rey, he complained, seemed "to want his manuscripts for nothing".

One of Diderot's new Dutch friends was the amiable Franz Hemsterhuis, known as the "Dutch Plato". Hemsterhuis had recently published, in French, a *Letter on Man*, designed to "combat by Reason the fashionable philosophy of the day: scepticism, materialism and atheism", and Diderot, reading his copy pen in hand, filled its margins with improvements to Hemsterhuis's French and corrections of his theistic fallacies. As it happened, his host Gallitzin had recently overseen the publishing of Helvétius's posthumous treatise *On Man*, an example of what Hemsterhuis called "the fashionable philosophy of the day" and so inflammatory that no publisher in France had dared to touch it. Diderot, reading it for the first time, was shocked by the inadequacy of Helvétius's "self-interest" theory of Man, and he began an extensive critique of the book, which would overflow from the margins of his copy to form a complete little treatise.

His *Commentary on Hemsterhuis* and his *Refutation of Helvétius*, being rejoinders to such utterly opposed theories, give us a good twofold perspective on Diderot's own philosophical system. The *Refutation*, a very striking piece of writing, is an attack on what struck Diderot in this new work, even more than in Helvétius's earlier one, as the absurd meagreness of its reductionism. It was one thing to say, as any materialist and determinist must, that physical sensation and the quest for pleasure and flight from pain are the basis of all the phenomena of life, but quite another, and wilfully paradoxical, to argue that therefore all pleasures and pains are really of the same kind, just physical phenomena in disguise.

Is it really true that physical pain and pleasure, which are perhaps the sole principle of animal behaviour, are also the sole principle of human conduct?

No doubt we need to be organised as we are, and to have the faculty of sensation, to be capable of action; but it seems to me that these are essential and primordial conditions, a mere *sine qua non*, and that the direct and immediate motives of our aversions and desires are something quite other.

Helvétius's error, in short, is to treat as *causes* what are merely *preconditions*. "I am a man," says Diderot, "and I need causes proper to man." Helvétius, though he is writing about "Man", is not ready to recognise a "human" sphere. He is a taker of short cuts; he is the kind of writer who draws false conclusions from true premises – unlike the genius Rousseau, who draws true conclusions from false premises. He is right in holding that human diversity is – far more than orthodox opinion would like to admit – the product of chance and education; but he becomes ridiculous when he denies all species-differences among men. Only obstinate paradox, surely, could maintain that Leibnitz, who dons a dressing-gown and devotes thirty years of his life to geometry, is really only dreaming of sleeping with women, getting a good "place" and filling a coffer with gold.

At last, on 20 August 1773, Diderot and Narishkin set off for Russia. In their carriage, Diderot talked stupendously, rapidly converting Narishkin into a disciple. He also read and wrote enormously, preparing "Memoirs" with which to instruct or amuse Catherine and taking advice from his young companion as to topics that might appeal to her. At Leipzig, where word of his coming had gone before him, Diderot preached atheism publicly at his room door, amidst a crowd of professors and merchants, and his convert Narishkin did the same with a group of students. At the inn in Riga he composed a bawdy poem about the chambermaid, and later in the journey he wrote a poem for Narishkin, contesting Narishkin's Stoical motto, "Suffer in silence, or end it all." Diderot himself, so the poem ran, intended not to suffer in silence under Fortune's blows but to "cry out like the devil". Early on in the journey, and again at Narva, Diderot suffered violent attacks of colic, and the second was so severe that he half considered telling Narishkin to abandon him. The gentle Narishkin fell ill too, and was sometimes so "broken" that Diderot, so he said later, thought he might have to "leave him dead in the hedge or bring him back to his country an imbecile".

They reached St Petersburg on 8 October, but Diderot had a shock in store for him. His joyous reunion with Falconet and Marie-Ann Collot, and the home from home with which Falconet was to provide him, proved illusory. Falconet's son had turned up in St Petersburg unexpectedly and had been given the spare bedroom; thus Diderot was told rather coolly that unfortunately there would be no room for him. The news, for a moment, threw him considerably. However, he called for pen and ink and dashed off a letter to Narishkin, and within a few hours his problem had been solved. Narishkin was all eagerness for Diderot to stay with himself; a carriage came to collect him and he was installed in his Russian friend's grand mansion in the Place Saint-Isaac, where he would remain for the rest of his stay. He sent a heart-rending letter to Nanette about this *contretemps*, but within a week or so he was finding excuses for Falconet, and soon he was paying friendly visits to Falconet's studio. Nanette, by contrast, could find no words bad enough for him.

Diderot had arrived on the very eve of the royal wedding between the Grand Duke Paul and the Princess Wilhelmina. However, he had nothing but his travelling-clothes, for his bags were still in the customs, and he had lost his wig on the journey: it was thus out of the question for him to attend the wedding ceremony or, for the moment, to make his appearance at court. Grimm, too, was nowhere to be seen, being busy with the Hesse-Darmstadt party. Diderot, nevertheless, was in high spirits and reported his adventures to Nanette with zest. He was not sure whether to dramatise his sufferings or to plume himself on his resilience, as compared with his young companion; accordingly he did both. In another letter a few days later, in philosophical vein, he told her his life had reached the moment for retirement, and he would leave it to Grimm to make a noise in the world. "Nothing is more absurd than a hectic old age." All the same, he wrote, since he had proved so valiant a traveller, ought he to come home "stupidly" by the same route as he set out? Would he not do better to go by the Great Wall of China, make a little salaam to Morocco, see Carthage and the long-sighed-for Italy?

> You will say it is not worth rambling so far to find one's last sleep, and you will be right. You will say I should come back as soon as possible and by the shortest route; and you will be right, and that is what I shall do . . . Adieu, *ma bonne*, and adieu again. Look after your health, look after your happiness; do things and then undo them; shift everything about at home, unshift it, and shift it all over again, and all will be well. I love you, I respect you, and I kiss you from my heart.[8]

It was a week or so before he could be presented to Catherine. Their first meeting was at a masked ball; he had gone to it, as he went everywhere, in his philosopher's black suit, a behaviour which provoked some covert sniggers. The visit of this famous man of letters was, indeed, not very welcome to Catherine's courtiers. They were a philistine lot; when Catherine had set up a classical theatre, she had had to impose fines for non-attendance. Also, there was a party among them, including Catherine's ex-lover Orlov and her chancellor Panin, who disliked her growing friendliness towards the French. The court was, moreover, absolutely riven by faction, and the Grand Duke Paul, who detested his mother, was deep in plots against her. Thus Diderot would find that many doors were closed against him.

All really depended on his reception by Catherine herself, and this proved brilliant even beyond expectation. This statuesque, commanding, sharp-eyed woman was all charm and flattering *camaraderie* with him, and Diderot found himself invited to visit her every day in her private apartments, between the hours of three and six. It was a signal and unprecedented honour, which did not endear him to the rest of the court, and he took her more or less at her word; over the ensuing months he would present himself at her door at least three times a week. He was not a good timekeeper and, according to Grimm, would sometimes come late or stay on long beyond his allotted time, still discoursing blithely and provoking glares from the Empress's secretaries. The *tableau* of philosopher and prince appealed to Diderot profoundly, and he was ruffled when Grimm said to him complacently: "Do you realise that, if you see the Empress every day after dinner, I see her every evening?"

Meanwhile he fulfilled one of his chief purposes in coming to Russia: that is, to inspect Falconet's great statue. The plaster model had been completed three years before, though the figure had not yet been cast, and an enormous lump of granite, fished out of a Karelian bog, had been transported ceremonially to St Petersburg to serve as its base. Falconet, on very bad terms by now with General Betzki and with Catherine, also enraged at the ignorant criticisms of the St Petersburgers, was determined to stay on till his statue had been erected. He was thus in an anxious mood when Diderot came to see him and – such was Diderot's account as well as his own – he positively trembled while his friend studied the statue in silence. Diderot's verdict was rapturous. He embraced Falconet, told him he had produced a masterwork, and wrote him an open letter, intended for publication, declaring he would never pronounce on sculpture again if this work was not "sublime". In this letter he pointed out, with his usual perceptiveness, the subtle antithetical relationship of horse and rider. "The Hero and the Horse make together a beautiful Centaur, the human and thinking part of which contrasts marvellously, in its tranquillity, with the fiery and animal part."[9]

Diderot pictured his position in Russia as one who had been sent for, across Europe, to instruct a monarch or act the part of Socrates to Catherine's Alcibiades. It was a dream-like fulfilment of his fantasies; for he believed, as did other "enlightened" thinkers, that social progress had to be handed down from above and that reformers had to secure the ears of the great. "To whom should a philosopher address himself forcefully," he had written in *Pages Against a Tyrant* (1769), "if not to a sovereign?" No such service had been asked of Voltaire by Frederick the Great, who had merely wanted Voltaire to amuse him and to correct, and praise, his French verses. It would appear that Catherine had wider views.

Soon after her accession, Catherine had begun to drop word of a vastly ambitious plan, no less than to provide Russia with a codified system of law. For this purpose she proposed to summon a legislative commission, drawn from every corner of her Empire, and she herself had drawn up a lengthy *Nakaz* or "Instruction" as an agenda for it – a collection of proposals on law and government, culled from Montesquieu and the penal reformer Beccaria. To all appearances, therefore, she was a philosophic monarch *par excellence*; "enlightened" thinkers, Voltaire and Diderot among them, had been suitably impressed. Voltaire wrote to her (26 February 1769) that Lycurgus and Solon would have been proud to sign her *Nakaz*. His lavish praise of her, Catherine said later, was what "made her the fashion".

Her commission had actually met, moreover, and held a number of sessions, first in Moscow and later in St Petersburg. Its members had found themselves baffled, however, as to what exactly was expected of them, and eventually, at the end of 1768, they had obtained permission to disperse. By this time Russia was at war with Turkey and involved in a crisis in Poland, which Catherine was succeeding in reducing to a vassal state, and the era of Catherine's "legislatomania" appeared to be over. But in Diderot's eyes it was merely suspended, and he pictured it as his task to remind her of her stupendous opportunities. It was too late in the day, he believed, to write a legal code for France, with her jungle of customary laws, but not too late for Russia, still a half-barbarous country. It was too late for France to abolish the privileges of the aristocracy and clergy, for by now so many indisputable property-rights were bound up with them, but it might be achieved in Russia by a resolute monarch.

As for himself, what he might most helpfully do, he decided, was to perform the functions of a philosopher before Catherine's very eyes, offering his impromptu meditations on law and empire as a kind of object-lesson in how to work out questions from first principles. She was welcome, he told her, to laugh at the reveries of a philosopher, "a poor devil who plays at politics in his garret", for no doubt nothing was easier than to run an empire with one's head on a pillow and it was quite another thing to be a ruler and grapple with awkward realities. It was agreed between them that at each of their afternoon sessions, he should present a paper or "memoir", which he would read to her and which would serve as a starting-point for discussion. In one of these "memoirs"[10] he described his own normal method of writing: how he would ask himself if he was the man to tackle a given problem; if it seemed to him that he was, how he would meditate on it night and day – at home, in the street and in crowded drawing-rooms; would dash down headings pell-mell; would then withdraw his mind from the subject for a spell; and finally would begin the writing proper, putting his first "tumultuous" thoughts into decent order. Having done this, and only then, he would find out what others had written on the same subject and perhaps borrow from them, or alternatively tear up his own work.

Catherine, flatteringly, had insisted that, in the privacy of the Hermitage, they could forget ceremony and the formalities usually due to a monarch. It was an invitation he was all too ready to respond to, and Catherine, though she found him very winning, came to wonder what she had brought on herself. "Your Diderot is a most extraordinary man," she wrote to her friend Mme Geoffrin. "I emerge from my conversations with him with my thighs bruised and quite black and blue. I have had to put a table between him and me to keep myself and my limbs out of the range of his gesticulation."[11] They would argue volubly and heatedly. "You have a hot head, and I have one too," she told Diderot. "We interrupt each other, we do not hear what the other one says, and so we say stupid things." DIDEROT: "With this difference, that when I interrupt your Majesty, I commit a great impertinence." CATHERINE: "No, between men there is no such thing as impertinence."[12]

In some sense, Catherine evidently took their conversations seriously, for she took the trouble to answer, point by point and sometimes at considerable length, a statistical questionnaire drawn up by Diderot, the topics ranging from the Russian social system and fiscal policy to the cultivation of wine, oil, hemp, tobacco, timber, salt meat, mulberry-trees, bees, furs, leather and "Muscovite rhubarb". The backbiting La Harpe later called it an outrage on Diderot's part to have put some of the bald questions that he did, but clearly Catherine did not regard it so, and Diderot was impressed by her knowledgeability. I will quote a snatch from their exchanges.

DIDEROT: One hears that efforts have been made to establish a
stud-farm in Russia, but they have not been a success.
CATHERINE: That is a false rumour. Everywhere that the attempt
has been made, it has succeeded. We mount our own cavalry, and
every year the King of Prussia buys horses from us for his.
DIDEROT: What can cause things to go wrong on a stud-farm?
CATHERINE: Negligence.
DIDEROT: Do you have schools of veterinary medicine?
CATHERINE: Heaven preserve us from them.

Diderot's attitude towards Catherine was, in fact, a complex
affair. He praised her to her face, as he had previously praised her
to others, with the greatest effrontery and lavishness, almost in
the style of the old flatterer Voltaire. If asked about her by his
compatriots, so he told her, he would say that she united the soul
of a Roman matron with the seductiveness of a Cleopatra, she
combined force with sweetness and dignity with affability. "My
friends!" he imagined himself saying to them, "picture that
woman on the throne of France! What an empire, what a terrible
empire, she would make of it, and how quickly!"[13] His
enthusiasm was no doubt sincere (long after his return to Paris he
would still be hymning Catherine's praises), but there was
calculation in it too, of a philosophical kind. We come back to his
general theory of ethics as a matter of statue-making. "One leads
men by statues, children by words," he wrote in one of his
"memoirs" for Catherine. "One does not break one's statue; one
does not renounce one's eulogy."[14] If it was so with private
individuals, it ought to be so even more for those in the public eye.
Was not one of his reasons for coming to Russia the wish to
inspect the great statue, the "bronze horseman", that Falconet
was creating? To lavish praise on Catherine and erect a "statue"
to her, to remind her continually that she had all Europe, not to
mention posterity, as an appreciative audience, was a way of
binding her to enlightened policies.

It was also part of Diderot's strategy to assume, or pretend to
assume, that Catherine, as a fellow-*philosophe* – Catherine who
insisted on doffing ceremony and royal protocol in the company
of another intellectual – would relish criticism, and he had come
to Russia forearmed with a radical criticism, one felt as keenly by

her admirers as by her enemies: the hopes and promises of her reign had once been high, no less than the expectations of a root-and-branch social and political reform, but what, so far at least, had been the realities . . . a war with Turkey and a remarkably ruthless partition of Poland? Diderot was determined to pose this challenge, and his method of doing so is to be seen in his "memoir" for Catherine "On the Morality of Princes". It is a suggestive and brilliant little piece and, in its devious way, extremely bold – the boldness beginning with its epigraph, where we find the phrase "the morality of princes in all its atrocity". Its line of argument is that princes cannot be expected to observe the same moral code as private individuals. Above private individuals and citizens there is placed a public tribunal, to protect them in their weakness; and if this were not so, they would need to behave towards their fellow-men like robber barons, nor could they be blamed for so doing. Above the heads of princes, though, there was no such respectworthy tribunal. It might indeed be expected, says Diderot wryly, that God would simply supply one; but then, to any mortal monarch, the divine monarch's idea of justice or government would seem a perfect disgrace.

> Jupiter sometimes seems to me a great joker. He hears noises from earth, he wakes up, he opens his trapdoor, he says: "Hail on Scythia, plague in Asia, war in Germany, famine in Poland, a volcano in Portugal, a revolt in Spain, destitution in France." That said, he shuts his trapdoor again, lays his head on his pillow, and goes back to sleep. That's what he calls governing the world.[15]

As a consequence of God's defection, princes are condemned to remain in a state of nature and act like wolf and tiger. Thus it may be right for princes, as it certainly is not for their subjects, to interfere in the affairs of other princes – even to imitate the dog in La Fontaine's fable, who, finding himself unable to protect his master's dinner, which he is carrying, decides he might as well eat a share of it himself.[16] It is not that all princes are alike, or that there are not princes with benevolent intentions, rather that one bad prince can force the hand of all the rest. When Catherine invaded Poland,[17] he told her, she had not *wanted* to help dismember that country. What no doubt she would have preferred – what indeed would have been much more to her profit – was to have done as France's neighbours did after the revocation of the Edict of Nantes and attract disaffected Poles to her own country. But "The truth is, a just prince can do nothing that he wants." As a critique of Catherine's policies, Diderot's sophistical and half-ironic defence of *Realpolitik* was decidedly ingenious, leaving her with no very comfortable escape-route.

In that reference to immigrants, moreover, we glimpse one of the messages Diderot most wanted to convey to Catherine. Russia was still a half-barbarous society, divided between an arrogant and luxurious nobility and an arrogant and uncouth peasantry. The whole appearance of St Petersburg had offended him. It looked to him like a barracks or cantonment dotted here and there with palaces. To be civilised, he decided, it required to be filled in, connected, joined up. To put it another way, what it needed was a Third Estate. In his "Memoirs for Catherine" his watchword became "*Serrez vos sujets*," "Squeeze your subjects together."[18] If St Petersburg had to be the capital – though Moscow was better placed for this purpose – the way to render it lively and prosperous was by linking its isolated palaces by smaller private houses such as you would find in Paris: homes for workpeople of all kinds, wheelwrights, carpenters, masons, rope-makers, etc. And how would they be recruited? By the freeing of serfs – whether by an immediate emancipation or a progressive annual enfranchisement – and by the inviting in of immigrants. "By this means, all unnoticed, a Third Estate would grow."[19]

Another of his watchwords was "Make streets." He imagined this mainly as a natural process; but if compulsion were necessary, Catherine should not hesitate to apply it. Inmates of foundlings' homes should be apprenticed to mechanical trades, and workshops should be found for them in the capital, with a prohibition against their moving elsewhere. "There is the store from which I would obtain my streets, streets with a mixture of all sorts of social conditions."[20] Diderot's vision was to some degree totalitarian, as is clear in another and extraordinary suggestion.

If, he told Catherine, he had been the ruler in the year 1760, when the Russians had occupied Berlin, he would have forcibly removed the whole population of the city, together with its tools and its manufactures, to Russia. "I would not have made slaves of them. On the contrary, I needed a Third Estate, and this would have produced one."[21]

The other great theme of Diderot's homilies was despotism. It was, he said, a vice seductive to all rulers, enlightened ones included. Habituation to despotism was the greatest threat of all to the human spirit, and one of the gravest misfortunes that could befall a free nation was to enjoy enlightened and benevolent despotism for three successive reigns. Here was the importance of a Third Estate and "squeezing her subjects together"; for what a despot longed for was a society of isolated individuals, "subjects but no nation". Catherine herself was not immune to the temptations of despotism – no ruler was; thus her great concern must be to protect herself against herself. On his way to Russia he had already composed a "memoir" for Catherine, retailing the history of the *Parlements* of France and the final suppression of the Paris *Parlement* in 1771, under Chancellor Maupeou. This last event haunted Diderot's mind. In his eyes, it had revealed France to the world as an oriental tyranny and a nation of slaves. *Parlement* had been "Gothic in its customs, opposed to all good reform, a slave to protocol, intolerant, bigoted, jealous of priests and foe to the *philosophes*"[22]; nevertheless, suppressing it had been a national disaster. Even a phantasm of liberty was better than none at all. Catherine, he said, should learn from this history and give Russia a representative body that would be genuinely what the *Parlement* had only fitfully and chimerically seemed to be, and she should alienate to it a certain portion of her own prerogative, in such fashion that it could never be reclaimed. She should reconvene her "commission" and render it a permanent elective institution, a "depository" of laws. (He had in mind, evidently, something on the lines of the future American Supreme Court.)

Often their talk turned on Frederick the Great, who was at present Catherine's ally and, in Diderot's eyes, a very far from benevolent despot. In truth, Diderot detested Frederick, believing him to be a bully and sadist who committed an unpardonable sin in a monarch; he despised his own subjects. He had no respect for his subjects' self-esteem, not even that wholesome and salutary vanity on which, according to Diderot's ideas, all human self-improvement depended. With some relish, he imagined Frederick paying for this propensity with his life. "Man can bear evil," he told Catherine, "but he cannot bear evil and contempt. Sooner or later a bitter sarcasm is repaid by the stab of a *poignard* – and a mortal stab, for in such a case only a fool will offer merely to wound."[23]

In all this, Diderot was at pains to define the philosopher's role and how his "stammerings" might be made profitable. If the philosopher had a duty towards sovereigns – waiting for the fiftieth ruler, the good one, who would profit from his labours – he also had a duty towards the "people". It was for him to open the eyes of the populace to their "inalienable rights" and to remind them that they were stronger than monarchs – so that if they went to the slaughterhouse, it was because they let themselves be led there. On the other hand, it was not his role to foment revolution. Bloody rebellions against despotism would in the long run come about of their own accord and according to a law of nature. It was in the aftermath of a revolution that the philosopher would become the man of the hour.

Diderot interpreted his role in Russia in a venturesome way. It was audacious to lecture Catherine on her own proclivities to despotism, but it was even more so to write, in his "Historical Essay" on *Parlement*, such blistering criticisms of his own country. They were a kind of expression of his trust in Catherine, for, as he well knew, they could have got him into very serious trouble had they reached the ears of the French government. Thus it was to his great alarm that, soon after his arrival in Russia, the French ambassador, Durand de Distroff, decided he must be put to work as a diplomatic agent. He was to speak to Catherine about France's wish for "an intimate union" with Russia and should take her a document, drafted in the Embassy, offering France's good offices in ending Russia's long-standing war with Turkey. The mission, Distroff told Diderot, was what France expected of him, given his extraordinary popularity with the Empress.

He refused at first point blank, saying it would land him in the Bastille as soon as he once set foot back in France. However, by threats or flattery he was induced to consent; and he composed in connection with this mission a "memoir" for Catherine entitled "The Reverie of Denis the Philosopher". It was a strange document, which, if Distroff had seen it, would have alarmed him exceedingly. It mentioned the decrepitude of Louis XV, alluded to the failings of his heir, the future Louis XVI, hinted that the French offer was probably entirely cynical, and was less than polite about Russia's own foreign policy. The three "wolves" – Russia, Austria and Prussia – it said, had just partitioned Poland, and France would be very happy to see the wolves turn and rend one another, especially if Austria, officially France's ally, were to get a mauling in the process. The refrain of his "memoir" is that he, Diderot, is not just a child repeating his lesson but his own man speaking the truth as he sees it ("for one must be a true man before being a good citizen or a good patriot"). "I know very well that this paper could be the ruin of me and all my posterity. But what I know even better is to whom I have the honour of speaking, and the holiness of the sanctuary in which I lay my thoughts."[24]

Whatever Catherine thought of Diderot's "memoir", she was furious at Distroff, whom anyway she considered an idiot, and she threw the diplomatic document that Diderot brought her on the fire. She pretended not to blame Diderot himself, and this may have been sincere.

It was a curious time for Diderot. After the first few exciting weeks, he fell into his "hermit" mood and would spend long hours alone, reading and writing on Catherine's behalf. One's impression is that at Catherine's court he was so turned in upon himself, so much obsessed by the Socratic tableau of ruler and philosopher, that he did not actually *see* much at all. One might add, did not hear much either; at least it seems that Catherine largely succeeded in concealing from him that she had Pugachev's rebellion, a most formidable peasant revolt, on her hands. In his usual style, Diderot was assiduous in collecting data about Russia, went to some lengths to procure fossils, mineral specimens and the like, and also made a collection of traditional

Russian songs; but he was not, one feels, much inclined to look about him.

He did not even see much of Grimm, who was preoccupied with his own royal charge, the Princess's young brother; Grimm was, Diderot said, "the satellite of a planet which he is obliged to follow". For some of the time, anyway, Diderot was confined to his room, suffering from colic or what he called "the malady of the Neva". Grimm and he were elected to the Russian Academy of Sciences, but he only appeared there once, on the actual occasion of his reception, at which he read a questionnaire about mines and minerals in Siberia.[25] The questionnaire was replied to at the session of 2 December 1773, but Diderot was not informed. He told himself that he was homesick – Grimm thought him quite far gone in this "Swiss malady" – and when, in November, the court for a week or two moved from the capital to Tsarskoye-Selo (the Versailles of St Petersburg), he made excuses not to go with it. For all this, he found himself incapable of writing home. "I am too far from my friends to chat with them. I have tried twenty times . . . " Even his letters to Sophie and her sister became very brief.

It may have contributed to his mood that, as he perhaps sensed, he was the object of much ill-natured gossip. On such visits as he made to great houses in St Petersburg he tended to insist loudly on his atheism, and this sometimes caused offence and led to backbiting. (Not that it mattered, he told a friend, for he only sought the approval of the "mistress of the house", i.e. Catherine, and cared nothing for her "valets".) Frederick the Great, likewise, was spreading disagreeable tales about him – how he was boring the Russians with his verbosity and so on – and these got back to St Petersburg. It would seem, too, that at some point in his stay the Russian courtiers, envious of his favour, staged a practical joke on him. A Russian philosopher came up to him, in the presence of Catherine and the rest of the court, and solemnly announced the nonsense formula "Sir, $a + bn = x$. Therefore God exists. Reply." Diderot was for a moment nonplussed, and this story, with embellishments, was repeated with relish in Berlin.[26] The Swedish ambassador Baron de Nolcken, who was greatly taken with Diderot, finding him one of the most amazing and lovable characters he had ever met, said Diderot had been exposed to "the most venomous jealousy" and thought he would be wise to get out of Russia before he suffered serious hurt.

The true beneficiary of the trip to Russia was in fact Grimm. Like Diderot, though with less *éclat*, he had seen Catherine in private every day, and she had evidently found him a man after her own heart: a practical man, a man of the world, with a rich fund of cynicism, a serviceable man who understood the workings of courts and could be depended upon to perform discreet commissions. They had "chattered like blind magpies", reported Grimm in triumph to Mme Geoffrin. It was the beginning of a long and close friendship.

In Diderot's eyes, however, all was redeemed by the continued and dazzling favour of Catherine herself. Indeed his conversations with her, and his ingenious stratagems to manipulate a Prince, represent an amazing, even grotesque scene. For him it was theatre with a serious purpose; for her, at heart, one must suppose, it may have been theatre pure and simple. For, limitless as was Catherine's thirst for praise, the effects of her reign would on balance be thoroughly reactionary. Her passion for founding public institutions (schools, colleges, orphanages and the like), and for seizing this chance to have artists depict her as "the mother of her people", was only equalled by the speed with which she lost interest once they were founded. Also her reign saw a vast extension of serfdom. Thus, we may surmise, she did not really feel the need for advice – let alone criticism and wholesome reminders that she was a "despot" – and it was unrealistic of Diderot to have supposed differently.

What was Catherine actually thinking herself, at the time? There were to be reasons, as we shall see, why she eventually became hostile towards Diderot, or rather towards his memory. Thus we cannot take what she would say about his visit at this later stage quite at its face value. All the same, it deserves to be quoted.

I frequently had long conversations with him, but with more curiosity than profit. Had I placed faith in him, every institution in my empire would have been overturned; legislation, administration, politics and finances would all have been changed for the purpose of substituting some impracticable theories.

However, as I listened more than talked, any one, being present, would have supposed him to be the commanding pedagogue and myself the humble scholar. Probably he was of that opinion himself, for, after some time, finding that he had not wrought in my government any of those great innovations which he had advised, he exhibited his surprise by a sort of haughty discontent.

Then, speaking to him freely, I said: "Monsieur Diderot, I have listened with the greatest pleasure to all that your brilliant genius has inspired you with; but all your grand principles, which I understand very well, though they will make fine books, would make sad work in actual practice. You forget, in all your plans for reformation, the difference between our two positions: you work only upon paper, which submits to everything; it is also altogether obedient and pliable, and opposes no obstacles, either to your imagination or to your pen; whereas I, a poor Empress, work upon human nature, which is, on the contrary, irritable and easily offended."

I am satisfied that, from that time, he pitied me, and looked on me as one possessed only of a narrow and ordinary mind. From that moment he spoke to me only on literary subjects, and politics disappeared from our conversations.[27]

Diderot was due to leave Russia in February 1774, and Grimm, still eager for the chance to present him to Frederick the Great, urged him to go home via Berlin, but Diderot was not to be persuaded. Grimm wrote about him with pique to the Prussian envoy: "No one has less credit over him [Diderot] than I, for one has to treat him like a child, and scold and shout, and I am not the man to encroach on anyone's natural liberty, even a child's."[28] The King of Sweden, through de Nolcken, made efforts to peruade Diderot to visit him on his homeward journey, and Voltaire wrote to Catherine plaintively of his longing to see Diderot at Ferney, but it was all to no avail. Diderot was resolved to return direct to The Hague, though beyond that all was unclear. There were commissions he had promised to perform for Catherine in Holland, in particular to oversee the publishing in French of the *Plans and Statutes* of her philanthropic institutions, but how long this would take, and how else he would occupy himself, he was unable to decide.

His farewells with the Empress were on a high note of enthusiasm. Catherine asked him what she could do for him, and he replied, "Nothing, for you have done everything already. Nevertheless, here are my demands," and he took out a document, headed "Peace Treaty between a great sovereign and a philosopher." "Give it to me," she said. "I will sign it without reading it." "No Madame," said Diderot, "that will not do. Though it is true, your fellow-monarchs have often enough broken treaties even after having read them. But have the goodness to listen. 'Article 1: no gold, so that the praises I shall give your Majesty shall not seem to be paid for . . . 'etc."[29] He asked to be given a memento of her – something that she used every day, like her breakfast cup and saucer – but she said he would break these and then regret it, and instead she gave him a cameo ring engraved with her portrait. A brand-new English coach was provided for his journey, constructed so that he could lie in it at full length, and a member of Catherine's staff, a Greek named Bala, was instructed to accompany him safely back to Holland. The French Embassy had continued to make use of him, for in his baggage, for the benefit of the Foreign Ministry, was a map of the Black Sea, heaven knows how procured, marking the site of Russian fortresses still to be built at the mouth of the Don.

"He would stop neither to sleep nor to eat. He regarded his carriage as a house." So wrote Angélique in her *Memoir*, describing her father's impetuous return from Russia to The Hague. The "English coach" broke down on the bridge at Mittau, and as he and Bala crossed the frozen Dwina, to the sound of cracking and heaving ice-floes, they were convinced that they would drown. The amiable Bala told him he had been most heroic, and Diderot wrote a poem entitled "Crossing the Dwina on the Ice".[30] He was in a confused mood, elated and at the same time, as one can sense, profoundly shaken by his Russian experience. As at other such disturbed times, he resorted to his dressing-gown, using it as an excuse for paying no visits in the course of his journey. On reaching Hamburg (30 March 1774) he sent the composer C. P. E. Bach, whose keyboard pieces Angélique had spent many hours upon, a grandiose note:

> I am French. My name is Diderot. I enjoy a certain reputation in my own country as a man of letters; I am the author of various plays, among which *A Father and His Family* may perhaps not be unknown to you.
>
> I have just come by post-chaise from Petersburg with a dressing-gown under my fur-coat and with no clothes; otherwise I would not have failed to pay my respects to a man as famous as Emmanuel.
>
> I beg him to send me some sonatas for the harpsichord, if he has some that are still unpublished. He will have the kindness to indicate the price, which I will pay to the person bringing them. The sole observation that he will allow me to make, is that I have more reputation than fortune, an unfortunate condition which I share with many men of genius, without the same right to the title.[31]

Bach obligingly offered him several pieces, and Diderot wrote again, urging him to put a copyist ("two if necessary") to work. "Monsieur Emmanuel, I count on your promise. It is not enough to be a genius, one must also keep one's word punctually."

On his arrival back in The Hague he was for some days very exhausted, sleeping inordinately and unable to work. Before long, though, he was back at his desk, pursuing endless writing projects. He was continuing his *Journey through Holland* and revising his *Refutation of Helvétius*; and he was re-reading Catherine's famous *Nakaz* (the "Instruction" to her Legislative Commission) in order – as he had promised her – to write a commentary on it.

While he was in Russia, Catherine had continued to speak, in warm if vague terms, of subsidising him to produce a new *Encyclopédie*; moreover, if he understood her rightly, she was now reconciled to its being done on French soil. In his present state of mind it seemed to him an invitation he could hardly refuse and a noble and useful occupation for his last years. Writing to Nanette a day or two after his arrival at The Hague, he spoke of the matter as almost settled and described the large sums that Catherine would advance. Nanette was to preserve "profound silence" over the whole affair, and above all not mention it to Angélique and

Vandeul; but it would mean, he told her, a change in their way of life, and she should prepare for a move to more suitable lodgings.

His Dutch admirers thought him changed since his Russian trip: more discreet and "careful to avoid religion and other sacred topics".[32] None the less, it was at this time that he composed a gentle polemic against religion, his *Conversation with the Maréchale de * * **. The tract evokes some friendly disputes he had had a year or two before, with the Duchesse de Broglie, wife of the famous Marshal; but it may also have been coloured by some current bickerings about religion with his hostess in The Hague ... "Are you not Monsieur Diderot?" the *Conversation* begins.

DIDEROT: Yes, madame.
THE MARÉCHALE: So you are the man who believes in nothing?
D: Precisely.
M: Yet your morality is the same as a believer's?
D: Why not, if one is an *honnête homme*?
M: And do you practise that morality?
D: I do my best.
M: What! You do not steal, you do not murder, you do not pillage?
D: Very rarely.[33]

"Diderot" then proceeds, with much mildness and charm, to prove to the Maréchale that the reasons that she and her like bring in support of religion are at bottom purely prudential and utilitarian. And indeed, he argues, utility is an excellent criterion in human affairs – but an atheist has a sounder insight into it than a believer.

The Maréchale, an admirable wife and mother but no intellectual, finds "Diderot" too much for her. "I do not know how to answer you," she says, "and yet you do not convince me."

D: I did not intend to convince you. Religion is like marriage. Marriage, which causes misery to so many, has brought happiness to you and the Maréchal; you have done very well to marry. Religion, which has made, still makes and will continue to make men bad, has made you better than ever; you do very well to cling on to it. It is sweet to you to imagine beside you and above your

head a great and powerful being, who sees you walking the earth;
the idea steadies your footsteps. Continue, madame, to enjoy this
august guarantor of your thoughts, this spectator, this sublime
model for your actions.

M: You seem to have no mania for proselytism.

D: *Absolutely not.*[34]

He was pleased with this little piece and offered it to a Dutch
publisher, but to his surprise, in this supposed home of tolerance,
it was refused as being too inflammatory.

Meanwhile Marc-Michel Rey showed an interest, rather more
eager than on Diderot's previous visit, in publishing a complete
collection of his works, and he began selecting and revising. But
then a letter arrived from Russia, announcing that the matter of
the *Encyclopédie* was "all settled" and he might expect a formal
offer in a matter of days; at this, the excited Diderot put aside his
Collected Works. "The two enterprises cannot go on side-by-
side," he wrote to St Petersburg, "so let us do the *Encyclopédie* and
leave some good soul to collect my own poor rags when I am
dead."[35] The first step, evidently, would be to find helpers, and
by early June he had formed the nucleus of a new editorial team.

Then vagueness and uncertainty returned. The printing of the
Plans and Statutes went as sluggishly as he had feared, making him
resolve never again to have dealings with the "boorish, idle,
greedy and ignorant" Dutch publishers. More important, weeks
passed and the momentous invitation concerning the new
Encyclopédie never came, and it began to dawn on Diderot that it
probably never would.

It was time, and more than time, for him to be on his way
home, the more so in that some obscure rift seems to have
developed between him and his hosts. He had been at work on his
"Observations" on Catherine's *Nakaz*, an explosive document in
some ways, and he got it into his head that Gallitzin had stolen a
copy (fortunately not the only one) from his baggage – "like a
highway robber" as his friend Naigeon later expressed it.

Grimm arrived in Holland, shepherding the two sons of a
Russian general, and it was decided that, as soon as he was free to
do so, he should keep Diderot company for at least part of the way
home to Paris. More confusion and postponements ensued, but at

last in mid-October the two friends set off, travelling together as far as Brussels. From there, Diderot went on alone by public coach to Senlis, where Nanette and Angélique had come to meet him. Angélique found him thin and greatly aged, though as gay, affectionate and warm-hearted as ever. His greeting to Nanette was: "Wife, count my belongings! You will have no reason to scold me, I have lost not so much as a single handkerchief."

It remains, as a last word on his Russian escapade, to say something about his "Observations" on Catherine's *Nakaz*,[36] for they put his attitude to the Empress in a new light. "I will whisper to you," he wrote to Mme Necker (6 September 1774) "that our philosophers who know despotism best have only seen it through the neck of a bottle. What a difference between a tiger painted by Oudry and a tiger in the forest!"[37]

Throughout these numbered "Observations" his ploy is the one he used while at Catherine's court; to pretend, flatteringly, that, like any good *philosophe*, she will relish blunt, even impertinent, criticism. With this as his pretext, he works through her text article by article, returning time and again to the theme of her "despotism". The Empress of Russia, he writes [II], is "certainly a despot". She is so from sheer force of circumstances and training, but she is also more of a despot than she realises. The wording of her "Instruction" here and there betrays her: "One comes across lines in it where, unawares, she re-assumes the sceptre that she laid down at the beginning."[38] His final "Observation" goes even further: "I see the name of 'despot' abdicated, but the thing itself retained, and despotism merely re-named 'monarchy'."

But if Catherine is a despot, he writes, she is by nature most certainly not a tyrant. The great question therefore is: does she in her heart mean to preserve despotism, and pass it on to her successors, or does she sincerely wish to renounce it? If the latter, her path is clear. She must make a solemn and written abdication of it, witnessed by the whole nation, and must collaborate with her own people to ensure the "certain destruction" of any successor who should try to revive it. She must publicly acknowledge that "there is no true sovereign other than the

nation, and there can be no true legislator other than the people."
Thus the first item in her new code, when it is drawn up, should
run "We the people, and we the sovereign of this people, swear
conjointly these laws, by which we are to be judged equally"; and
the second item should establish an independent "repository" of
the laws (one fitter for its purpose than the French *Parlement*). "If,
upon reading what I have just written, and listening to her own
conscience, her [Catherine's] heart jumps for joy, it means she no
longer wishes for slaves; if she shudders, if her blood retires, if she
grows pale, she has believed herself to be better than she is."[39]
These are audacious words, and Catherine found them so when
she eventually read them.

To continue: despotism, writes Diderot, is a poison blinding
rulers as well as subjects to the advantages of liberty, causing
them to live in constant terror of rebellion. "It is very necessary,"
runs Catherine's article 263, "to seek and prevent the causes
which have so often occasioned revolts of serfs against their
masters." Diderot comments tartly: "There is an excellent
method to prevent the revolts of serfs against their masters. It is to
have no serfs."

To an article by Catherine on national defence, he replies with
a homily against standing armies. They are, he says, a menace
equally to free states and to tyrannies: they are used by despots to
enslave free citizens, and by the enslaved to change one tyrant for
another. Only a country where all men are soldiers and trained in
arms can hope to be free. (It is advice he was to repeat in 1778 to
the American rebels.)

Catherine's great privilege, he argues, is to be ruling a country
at a stage when it is still not too late to abolish social privilege.
Legislation is the key. An article in Catherine's *Nakaz* reads: "it is
for legislation to follow the spirit of the nation." On the contrary,
comments Diderot: it is for legislation to *make* the spirit of the
nation. This profound faith in legislation follows logically from
Diderot's theory of ethics, in which virtue belongs to the realm of
artifice, and from his determinism, according to which human
beings, by the very fact of not possessing free will, are the more
malleable by external influences – such as, for instance, laws and
penalties. One cannot, he argues, make public executions and the

ritual attending them too horrific. Laws can achieve everything, and ethics are properly the fruit of laws and not vice-versa. By corollary, all judge-made law is to be condemned, and the proceedings of law-courts should never be printed. "They form in the end a counter-authority to the law."

In all societies, writes Diderot (389–91), there are three distinct codes, the civil code, the religious code and the code of nature, and it is the great task of a legislator to see that the first two do not contradict – indeed that they model themselves upon – the third. Nothing is more desolating to a human than to find himself bound by mutually conflicting codes, a situation in which he can be neither a citizen, a believer nor even a man. It is for rulers to remember that civil life is a mere consequence of the inhospitability of Nature. (Suppose Nature more generous and overflowing, and civil life would dissolve on the instant.) Accordingly, the sanction for law and government is to be looked for, not in some imaginary social contract, nor in patriotism ("It is impossible to love a country which does not love us"), but in happiness. " 'I want to be happy' is the first article of a code, prior to all legislation and any religious system"(37).

In the end, Diderot did not send his "Observations" to Catherine and locked them up, with so much else, in his desk-drawer. It was perhaps as well, for when his daughter sent them to Russia after his death, Catherine – who perhaps did not read much beyond the opening paragraphs – was enraged beyond measure. "That piece is real babble," she exploded to Grimm in November 1785. "One finds in it neither knowledge of things, nor prudence, nor clairvoyance . . . What can one say on reading the 'Observations' of a philosopher who, all his life it would appear, was in need of a keeper!"[40]

23

Diderot in Old Age

Diderot had come home to a changed France. Louis XV had died in May 1774, and the new King, overawed at the task that had fallen on him, had put himself in the hands of the cynical septuagenarian Maurepas, summoned back from a twenty-year exile, and of a dedicated reformer, the great Anne-Robert-Jacques Turgot. It meant a clean sweep of the previous administration: Maupeou and his colleague Terray had been dismissed, "Maupeou's *Parlement*" had been dissolved, and *Parlement* proper had been restored to its rights.

The high-minded and stiff-necked Turgot was an erstwhile *encyclopédiste* and a doctrinaire Physiocrat; thus people spoke of his rise to power as Controller-General as a triumph for "philosophy". It was, so wrote one commentator, the fruit of a long-term plan by "the Voltaires, Diderots and d'Alemberts" and represented, "though quietly and without revolution, the greatest blow against religion since, perhaps, the days of Clovis."[1]

It was an altered France in another sense also. For it could be said that the *philosophique* battle had been won, in the sense that the *philosophes* had gained social acceptance and were by now a party in the state. For one thing, they had breached the walls of the Académie and indeed were bidding fair to capture it. Tireless canvassing in the *salons* of Madame Necker and Julie de l'Espinasse had achieved their purpose, and half the elections to the Académie in recent years – for instance of Saint-Lambert (1770), Condillac (1768), the journal-editor Arnaud (1771) and the eulogist Thomas (1767), – had been of *philosophes* or their associates. D'Alembert, an Academician since 1754, had become Perpetual Secretary of the Académie in 1772 and a most energetic one, promoting the "cause" by every means in his power. It meant that, from now on, a quarrel between *philosophes* and the Sorbonne would be a struggle between two established bodies of the clerisy. Further, most of the leading liberal intellectuals had, in one way or another, acquired "places" and dignities under the Crown; for by this period the royal gift of "places" and sinecures had been parcelled out among a large assortment of nobles and ministers, by no means all of them in tune with the taste of the court. Even Naigeon, who was inclined to speak slightingly of "titles, dignities and cordons", had got himself appointed *garde-magasin du roi*, a post which gave him free royal quarters and would later bring him a pension. Diderot was the exception among his friends in possessing no such "place".

He regarded the new regime as, all things considered, the best hope for the country. Though by now a sceptic as regards Physiocracy, he had much respect for Turgot as a man, and, as he wrote to Catherine (17 December 1774), France had suffered so much under "bloodsuckers" and corrupt lawyers that he defied intellectuals to do worse. "At least they are just, well-informed and disinterested; and experience will perhaps rub off a little of their school-dogmatism and 'system-mania'."[2]

His own private instincts at this moment were, however, for a kind of withdrawal – not just from politics but from social life generally. All through the first winter of his return, ignoring the reproaches of his friends, he hid himself away. It was a prolonged "dressing-gown" period. He had gone back to his "cyclometry" (squaring the circle) and to mathematics generally. At some stage he showed his cyclometric writings to his friend Condorcet, who was tactful but pointed out some slips and errors, which he remedied as best he could. After this, he decided not to seek further criticism. If he showed his work to the public at all, he told himself defensively, it must simply take its chance. Would it matter so very much if he had made a fallacy? It would not be the first in his career. Also, "sophisms" could sometimes show more sagacity than genuine discoveries.

It was during the same winter that he produced designs – somewhat shadowy ones, it would appear – for a kind of typewriter, "designed for philosophers and all those tempted to compromise in speaking the truth", also a portable encoding and decoding machine "for the use of politicians". The *Correspondance littéraire* for April 1775 reported him as saying that any skilled workman could set up this latter machine, and it would take no more than half an hour to learn to use it. The journal remarked diplomatically, "If our philosopher's imagination has not out-stripped his calculations, this discovery would be no less useful than it is novel and singular."

He had half-a-dozen other projects as well. He was acting as a sort of ghost-writer to his friend the *abbé* Raynal, supplying him with disquisitions and declamations for a new edition of his voluminous *Histoire des deux Indes* (*History of the Two Indies*). Also he was making large additions to a work begun a year or two before, a compilation entitled *Elements of Physiology*. It was organised on the pattern of the *Elementa physiologiae corporis humani* of the Swiss physiologist Haller, and to all appearances it was not intended for publication, but he would go on adding to it for the rest of his life.

This fascinating work takes to its utmost extreme what we may call the "Bordeu" element in Diderot's thinking – that de-centring approach to life and the human organism which coloured his *Letter on the Blind* and which dominated *D'Alembert's Dream*. The thought returns, time and time again, that what we lazily think of as a unity is actually a polity of autonomous entities. An animal is made up of animals. "What is an animal, a plant? A co-ordination of infinitely active molecules, a conca-tenation of little living molecules which everything conspires to separate."[3] All the solid parts of the body are composed of fibres, and each of these fibres is an assemblage of other fibres, *ad infinitum*; so that so-called "unities" are no more than sheaves or bundles. It is because sensations come in bundles that they can be compared and judgements can be formed.

From this it follows, as Diderot sees it, that we need not posit dualism of soul and body. The human being is at one and the same time a book (a set of inscriptions on the waxy living substance of the brain) and a reader of that book: it is a book reading itself. We need to remember how much – so much more than it is convenient to admit – our lives are lived *for* us. In a favourite analogy, Diderot evokes the preoccupied philosopher (as it might be, himself or d'Alembert) who negotiates crowds and streets and staircases with perfect unconscious competence – better, indeed, than if he were paying attention. "It is night-time at mid-day in the streets, profound night, for him who meditates profoundly. The eye guides us. We are the blind man, the eye is the blind-dog who guides us."[4]

Diderot's sojourn in Russia had, in fact, left a permanent mark on him and had given him a definite bent towards seclusion. He would spend half or more of his week alone in Belle's house at Sèvres, working on these projects. In his new mood, and no doubt as a symptom of age, he was becoming less assiduous at d'Holbach's dinners and tended to find them more of a strain, complaining – not very seriously – that the other guests were "a scurvy lot" and he could never get a word in. He did not feel at home in Paris any longer, he would say. There were too many of what Nanette called "itchy" people, wanting to be scratched.

It is not clear how often he was seeing Sophie now. Her mother had died in 1772, at the age of eighty or so, and upon this the château at Isle-sur-Marne had been sold. "Uranie" had also died and Sophie and her surviving sister, Mme de Blacy, had set up home together in Paris, in the rue Montmartre. Angélique, who had got to know and admire Sophie, went often to visit her there.

The two sisters had been left well-off and lived in some style, employing five servants – among them the now-elderly "Clairet" who had been such a friend to Diderot when the affair was still a romantic secret. As a consequence of the move to Paris, there was no special need for Diderot and Sophie to write; at all events a letter he sent her from The Hague, on his return from Russia, is the last to have survived. There would be occasional, unrevealing, mentions of her in Angélique's letters and in Denise's, none in Diderot's. Always rather a shadowy figure to us, Sophie now more or less disappears from our view, till her death a month or two before Diderot's own.

Diderot's great preoccupation, when he was back in Paris, was Angélique and her husband. He now got on much better with Vandeul, who was a man of tact. "They love and fear each other, respectively," was the account of Vandeul's brother and partner des Tillières. Diderot would usually have his dinner at the

Vandeuls' house – which served the brothers as their business headquarters – and sometimes also his supper. He by now had two grandchildren, Marie-Anne ("Minette"), born in 1773, while he was on his way to Russia, and Denis-Simon ("Fanfan"), born the following year. Angélique herself seemed to be ill half the time – she was "the poorest specimen", Diderot told Denise – but the children thrived, and he was mad about them. It was decided that they should be persons of learning, and one of their uncles, a few years later, reported them admiringly as "speaking Italian and Latin". We get glimpses not only of Diderot but of his wife in the brother's letters home.

> He [Diderot] dines and sups with us for nearly all of the four days and has never come with greater pleasure. *Maman* Diderot is a little jealous but all the same not really angry, as it means she does not have to cook for him . . .
>
>   Madame Diderot stays at home and is as touchy as ever. At the moment she is much upset at the death of her little dog, who had been blind for three months. Madame Billard sat on him and broke his back legs. Since then, she and Madame Diderot have been on bad terms.[5]

As the brothers' business ventures expanded, Diderot redoubled his efforts on their behalf, and over the next few years he would solicit favours for them – timber-concessions, leases of royal forges and the like – from his many acquaintances among the great. He applied not only to Turgot, but to Turgot's great adversary Necker; to Sartine, and to Trudaine de Montigny, the Intendant-General for Finance. With Sartine he was frank: "As regards my children, though I believe wealth a greater threat to happiness than a modest mediocrity, I want them to be rich; yes, Monsieur, very rich!"[6] In 1779, taking up an old promise of Catherine the Great's, he asked her for money to help Vandeul clinch some speculative transaction, and she gave him 2,000 roubles (about £400 in terms of English currency at the time).

It made a great change in Diderot's life that Grimm, his taskmaster and boon companion, now spent most of his time abroad, having handed over the *Correspondence littéraire* to a young friend named Henri Meister. Grimm was much in demand. On his way back from Russia in 1774 he had spent some days in Warsaw at the court of King Stanislaus of Poland, and Stanislaus had been vastly impressed by him, writing proudly to his friend Mme Geoffrin that he really believed he himself had won Grimm's approval. "There you have a man," he wrote to her again in October, "whose head is not turned by caresses, and whose modesty, on the other hand, has preserved him, from *philosophique* arrogance. It is incredible how few of them escape that!"[7]

The court of Hesse-Darmstadt, about this time, offered him a post, and hearing this the court of Saxe-Gotha made him a better offer, so that he was appointed their representative in France, and became that of Saxe-Weimar into the bargain. For all this, in the summer of 1776 he set off again for Russia, there to attend the wedding of the Archduke Paul, who was re-marrying. This time he stayed at Catherine's court for a whole year, being appointed one of her State Councillors and rewarded, when he left, with a pension of 2,000 roubles. Catherine found him altogether congenial, though even she would sometimes tease him about his passion for princes. He was growing more reactionary in his views, inclining to mock at the *philosophes* as "capucins" and unworldly "system-makers", and this tone suited Catherine very well. He was also master of a most inventive style of flattery. We get a taste of it in a long, facetious document he wrote for her, a "Lamentation of Jeremiah the Prophet" reproaching her, in mock-Biblical style, for killing him with her goodness.[8] Mme d'Epinay, who thought Grimm "drunk" with his Russian triumphs, spoke sadly of him. His friends, too, were ironical about his passion for court-life. When he complained of ill-health, the *abbé* Galiani told him disrespectfully: "The *cholera morbus* is the effect of the sufferings you inflict on your abdomen by too many and too low bows."[9]

Diderot, who was feeling his own age and the age of all his friends, missed Grimm greatly, and he used what urgings he could to make him come home. He had heard, he wrote to Grimm teasingly in August 1776, that their bellies had developed in opposite directions: Grimm's lean "barefoot Augustine" had become a plump Bernardine, whilst his own dwindling stomach had done the reverse. Grimm's, he told him, was a sight he was eager to see. "Goodbye, my friend, my friend of so many years.

We have lost Roux, we thought we had lost the Baron. Mlle d'Espinasse is no more; Mme Geoffrin may be gone by tomorrow. Make haste home, if you want to find anyone left."[10]

Another letter, in October 1776, returned to the theme of Grimm's "full-moon belly", the news of which had caused such astonishment to his friends in Paris.

> As for me, my friend, I am sending my heavy luggage on in advance. My teeth totter; my eyes refuse service after nightfall; and my legs have grown very lazy, endlessly multiplying the need for sticks. However, I am gay. I detect neither improvement nor deterioration in the upper vessel of the alembic: I distil phlegm sometimes, and sometimes spirits of wine. I still do not know the time, and, as before, I confuse days, weeks, years and months. Thus, no diminution in my conformity to the eternal. Add that, though my legs bend under me and my back takes the shape of a tortoise, I still carry my augur's rod upright. Thus all is well.[11]

In November 1777 Grimm returned at last to Paris. It was a propitious moment for his career. France was about to enter the American War of Independence, and Grimm, whose star was in the ascendant, would be offered employment by the French Foreign Ministry, as an intermediary with the American high command. Thomas Jefferson, during his own days as ambassador in Paris, would remember him as "the oracle of society" and "the pleasantest and most conversible member of the diplomatic corps. . . . A man of good fancy, acuteness, irony, cunning and egoism. No heart, not much of any science, yet enough of every one to speak its language."[12]

We catch sight of Grimm at this moment, also, in a different context, as the sometime patron and impresario of Mozart. It is a revealing episode. In March 1778 Mozart, now twenty-two years old, paid a return visit to Paris, the scene of his childhood triumphs. He brought his mother with him, and it was taken for granted that, as before, they should be under the wing of the family's great patron and "sworn friend", Grimm. What soon emerged, however, was that, for Grimm, the child prodigy had been one thing and the adult Wolfgang was quite another. He did not see Mozart cut out to make a success in Paris and confessed as much to Mozart's father Leopold. Wolfgang, he wrote to him, was *zu treuherzig* (too trusting), too little interested in success, to make his way in France. To make an impression there one had to be "artful, enterprising, daring".

> In this country the great public knows nothing about music. Everything depends on names, and only very few are equipped to judge the actual merit of a work. The public is at the moment ridiculously divided between Piccini and Gluck, and the musical debate one hears all round one is pitiable. Your son will find it hard to succeed between those two factions.[13]

Mozart evidently sensed his fall in Grimm's esteem, for he wrote irritably about him, and his managing ways, to his father. "I don't know how it is," he quoted his mother as saying, "but he [Grimm] seems quite changed."[14] In fact the whole of Paris seemed changed. The French were not nearly so courteous as they had been fifteen years before: they treated musicians like servants, they made him wait about for hours in their freezing ante-rooms, and they chattered all through his performance. The complaints greatly worried his father, who anxiously implored him not to play any "impudent prank" on their great benefactor.

Then, on 3 July 1778, Mozart's mother died, and upon hearing the news Grimm and Mme d'Epinay insisted on Mozart's moving to their own lodgings in the rue de la Chaussée d'Antin. The kindness came too late, perhaps. At all events Mozart continued to feel himself slighted and patronised – by Grimm, if not by Mme d'Epinay, who behaved with more delicacy. His room was the sick-bay, he complained, and completely bare of furniture. Grimm made too much of his hospitality (three or four other friends in Paris would have done as much or more for him). He made too much, too, of a loan of 15 *louis*. Further, far from standing aloof from the Piccini-Gluck "war", as he pretended, he was ardently of the Piccini faction and always pestering Mozart to go off to Piccini's "miserable" operas. He spoke about Mozart to no one, or if he did so, spoke disparagingly. "Grimm may be able to help *children*, but not grown-up people," Mozart told his father bitterly.

At last, in September, matters rose to a crisis. Mozart, disappointed at his reception in France, decided to leave – upon which Grimm, who still felt responsible for him, made instant arrangements for his journey. This did not suit Mozart, and he told Grimm, rather truculently, that he would stay on in Paris a further day or two, at another friend's house. At this, according to his account, Grimm's eyes "sparkled with rage". He told Mozart that if he did any such thing, he (Grimm) would "never look at him again as long as he lived" and Mozart "must never come near him, for he would be his worst enemy".[15]

The early editions of La Rochefoucauld's famous *Maxims* contain a frontispiece entitled "The Love of Truth", depicting a Mephistophelean-looking Cupid removing the mask of Virtue from a bust of Seneca. La Rochefoucauld was here reaffirming a long-established tradition: Seneca, tutor and abettor of the infamous Nero, Seneca the philosopher and Stoic despiser of worldly goods who became one of the richest men in Rome, had, even before La Rochefoucauld, become the classic exemplar of a certain type of hypocrite, the sage who preached one thing and did another. This was how the young Diderot had thought of Seneca. In a scorching note to his translation of Shaftesbury, he castigated this "wise and ignoble" philosopher as "more attentive to heaping up riches than to doing his perilous duty". "The reader may think I treat this philosopher a little harshly," he wrote then, "but after reading Tacitus it is not possible to think better of him."[16]

He had reason to remember this thirty years later, for one of the undertakings to issue from d'Holbach's "factory" was a translation of the *Works* of Seneca by a certain Lagrange, a tutor in d'Holbach's household. Lagrange had died with his task unfinished, whereupon it had been agreed that Naigeon should put it into final shape. It was planned, though, that the edition should end with a "Life" of Seneca; and Diderot, who over the years had come to change his mind about Seneca, was persuaded by Naigeon and d'Holbach to undertake it.

He pictured himself, in the first place, as producing quite a brief memoir, but as he worked on it, it turned into a full-scale

Frontispiece from early editions of the *Maxims* of La Rochefoucauld

treatise, the first time in many years that he was producing a book for publication. As a project it had an affinity with his "cyclometry"; for to rehabilitate the archetypical hypocrite Seneca, to go against the world's opinion in such a spectacular way, would have all the fascination of the impossible and, if successful, would ensure kudos in proportion. But underlying the scheme there were also some thoughts connected with Rousseau.

When Diderot began his *Essay*, Rousseau was still alive, dwelling with Thérèse in seclusion in the Paris suburb of Ménilmontant. He had hoped that the readings from his *Confessions* would have brought about some kind of public exoneration and acknowledgement of his wrongs. Their failure to do so had led to a crisis of obsession, prompting him to write a dialogue, *Rousseau juge de Jean-Jacques*, in which, in the person of an imaginary "Rousseau", he himself exonerates Jean-Jacques from the world's accusations. He had decided to entrust the work to God himself, and attempted, on Christmas Eve 1776, to place it on the high altar of Notre-Dame. When he found the chancel-gates locked, he took it as a sign that even God had rejected him.

There followed a time of appeasement and calm. He took a vow to read no more books, spent his days botanising in the lanes and fields near Ménilmontant and began composing music again. In a last work, *Rêveries du promeneur solitaire (Reveries of a Solitary Walker)*, he depicts himself as a solitary wanderer, quietly meditating on his ill-starred but innocent life. "So here I am alone on the earth," it begins, "having no longer any brother, neighbour, friend or company apart from myself." The "conspiracy" against him, he has decided, is beyond his powers to unravel, and he must give up hope of justification, not only during this life but even after death.

Diderot, for his part, had not ceased to brood on that "bargain" of which he suspected Rousseau, according to which, at the expense of somewhat blackening himself, Rousseau planned to rob the innocent of their fair name for ever. Rousseau, it seemed all too possible, wanted to spoil that pleasure of which Diderot had written so fervently in his letters to Falconet – of enjoying the imagined praise of posterity *now*. If that was what he intended, it was monstrous; but might there not be a way to counter it? What if he, Diderot, should, as it were, impersonate posterity – should, in his "Life" of Seneca, be the friend who, in pure disinterestedness, would wipe the mud from a great man's effigy? What better proof that the hope of posthumous good name was not just an empty illusion?

So once more Diderot plunged into seclusion. He set to work, all through the summer and winter of 1777–78, on a vast reading-programme, in preparation for what became a large-scale *Essay on the Life of Seneca the Philosopher, on his Writings, and on the Reigns of Claudius and Seneca*. He was working fourteen hours a day and, according to his daughter, he was shortening his life in the process; still, in the dedicatory epistle, addressed to "monsieur N***" (i.e. Naigeon), he spoke cheerfully of the work as "the fruit of my labour, or I should say of my leisure, during one of the sweetest intervals of my life."

It was, one cannot help thinking, always a bad sign when the naturally sociable Diderot withdrew into solitude. It would mean he was secretly wrestling with that imaginary monster "the public". In all his truly original writing he evaded the need to address a "public", by incorporating an audience, or a multiplicity of audiences, into the fiction itself. By contrast, in the *Essay on the Life of Seneca,* as in his plays twenty years before, he was striving to speak to the public direct. The result is disastrous. The first and historical part of the *Essay* strikes the reader as, in the main, empty rodomontade, a string of resounding sentiments aiming not at conviction but at applause. He fumes, he apostrophises, he utters ringing rebukes and challenges to imaginary enemies. He declaims noisily about "virtue" and "constancy" and against "corruption" and the calumniating of the dead – "Where do we acquire it," he exclaims rhetorically, "we who have nothing to gain or lose from the great of antiquity, this strange mania for decrying their virtues?"[17] It gives us a strange feeling, as if this language of "virtue" were one he has never properly understood.

While Diderot was still at work on his *Essay,* Rousseau died. His death set up a powerful wave of feeling in his favour, and his tomb, on a lake-island at Ermenonville, would soon become a place of pilgrimage. We do not know with what feelings Diderot heard the news of his old friend's death, but it did not quiet his suspicions, and at one point in his *Essay* he more or less brought them out into the open. It is in a footnote to a passage about the quaestor Suilius, the most virulent of Seneca's enemies and detractors. "One must, it seems to me," he wrote, "have some cruel repugnance against believing men of good will, to listen to the accusations of a Suilius, a professional informer, a corrupt fanatic and convicted criminal," adding in a footnote that he will mention what a man of well-known probity and enlightenment once said to him. "If, by an oddity not quite without example," said this man, "there should ever appear a work in which honourable people were pitilessly vilified by an artful villain who, to give plausibility to his unjust and cruel accusations, painted himself in odious colours . . . my eyes would never soil themselves by reading it. I protest I would prefer his invectives to his eulogy." "And I likewise," another had replied. "But I do not think that such a man has ever existed, or ever will exist."[18]

Evidently, what Diderot wants to depict in the person of Seneca is the sage in the market-place and the compromises any idealist must make once he enters the life of action and practical politics. It is, as has been said, as if he were contrasting Socrates, the ideal model, with Seneca, his "deformation" in the real world.[19] Some interpret him also as reflecting, ruefully, on his own role at Catherine's court, though, if Russia is a subtext in the *Essay*, the reference never becomes explicit.

If we sense the influence of his Russian experience at all it is in his stirring outburst, near the end of the book, on the American revolution and its lessons for European tyrants. He hails the new nation born in 1776 as, perhaps, a novelty in the world's affairs, "resisting, at least for some centuries, the decree pronounced against all things in this world, that they should have their birth, their flowering, their decrepitude and their end."

> May the earth swallow up that one of their provinces which is powerful enough, and mad enough, to seek one day the means to subjugate the others! May there never be born in one of them, or if so may he die at once, under the executioner's axe or the dagger of a Brutus, the citizen powerful enough, and enough an enemy to his own happiness, to form the project of becoming its master!
>
> May they realise that the general good never comes about except by necessity; and that it is times of prosperity, not times of adversity, which are fatal to governments . . .
>
> May they realise that virtue often hatches the seed of tyranny . . .
>
> Let each of them [the Americans] have – in his house, at the bottom of his field, or beside his loom or his plough – his musket, his sword, and his bayonet.
>
> Let them all be soldiers.
>
> Let them realise that, when circumstances allow for deliberation, the old will have good advice; but in moments of crisis youth commonly knows better than age.

Diderot's defence of Seneca's conduct, as critics pointed out at the time, is really very weak. He argues that Seneca simply could not prevent riches being thrust upon him, that the hypocritical letter to the Senate he wrote for Nero, explaining away the murder of Nero's mother Agrippina, was mere convention – and at least the letter helped to restore order. Another very "crawling" production, Seneca's "Consolation to Polybius", Diderot explains as a forgery and, at the same time, not very logically, imagines excuses for it. Eventually he falls back on a blanket argument: that we do not need the example of Seneca to teach us what we already know, that it is easier to give good advice than to follow it. This claim – that preaching can be of value, even without practice – is the one that Diderot really has it at heart to make, together with the companion claim that, in the case of a writer who writes as well as Seneca, we can *know* that he was not an evil man.

Much will depend, then, on what Diderot goes on to say about these writings of Seneca's, and how he can persuade us of their qualities; and here, to one's relief, he is altogether more effective. He adopts a very Diderotesque scheme, weaving together direct quotation or report from Seneca, remarks by himself, and strings of maxims which could be by one or the other. In other words, he *insinuates* himself into Seneca's text, in a way which should by now be familiar to us. As he puts it, he sometimes hides behind Seneca and sometimes stands in front of him, offering his own body as protection against the censor's arrows. Out of this there emerges, gradually, an acute critique both of Seneca and of Stoicism, its theme being that Seneca, the so-called "Stoic sage", had too much of the natural man in him to have been a true Stoic, and that moreover Stoicism was a superstition and a persecuting religion like any other. As a counter to Stoicism, he offers a hedonistic and Utilitarian credo of his own, in the form of a paradox – one that he has hinted at in other works but spells out most clearly here.

> Strictly speaking, there is only one duty: to be happy; and there is only one virtue: justice. . . . To be happy, one needs to be free: happiness is not made for him who acknowledges any other master than his duty.
> QUERY: But does this not make duty a tyrant? And if I have to be a slave, what does it matter what master I choose?
> ANSWER: It matters a great deal. For emancipation from *this* master can only bring evil fortune. With the fetter of *this* duty one breaks all other fetters.[20]

It is not for nothing that Diderot was writing at the time of the American Declaration of Independence.

When Diderot's *Essay* came out in the last days of December 1778, it received, on the whole, a severely hostile press. The review in the *Année littéraire*, now run by Fréron's son Stanislaus, spread to two numbers and was very crushing.[21] It attacked Diderot's pompous style – "M. Diderot knows no other style than that of the ode or epic" – and accused him of "blowing up to five hundred pages an essay that needed less than a hundred if pruned of its irrelevancies." Also, it asked, could one – after all Diderot's eulogies – name a single occasion when Seneca had opposed a bad action of Nero's? The *Journal de Paris* said the author seemed to "have wished no kind of bizarrerie to be lacking", and the *Journal de littérature* called his veiled attack on Rousseau "a cowardly insult".

Diderot's reaction, apart from replying to his critics, was to set to work on a new version of the *Essay*, a version half as long again, even less critical of Seneca and considerably more forthright about Rousseau. It took him many months, in failing health, and when Naigeon read the new work, now entitled *Essay on the Reigns of Claudius and Nero*, he was made distinctly anxious by it and drew up a long list of criticisms. Diderot, however, refused to read them. "I have done my best," he told him (28 July 1780), "and that is all I can say. Tiredness and boredom have never produced anything good, and I am tired and bored. . . . It must appear as it is."[22] He arranged through friends in high places for the work to be given "tacit permission". This entailed submission to a censor, who insisted on certain cuts, among them a too transparent allusion to Louis XV in Diderot's portrait of Claudius. In secret, however, Diderot also made arrangements to publish the uncut version at a printing-house in Bouillon, outside French territory. This would prove a slow and delicate business, taking the best part of two years, but – rather extraordinarily – it would be done with the connivance of Le Noir, the new Lieutenant of Police, who agreed that the parcels of illicit copies might enter France addressed to himself.

One of the leading traits in Diderot's outlook was an attraction to the limitless – a vision of boundless possibilities of all sorts, whether for the individual mind or for the human species. He was the least "classical" of thinkers and critics, the notion of "limits" being replaced for him by certain powerful conceptions of self-regulation and internal necessity. Nothing brings the point home more forcibly than his friendship, during his last years, with the writer Joseph Joubert.[23]

Arriving in Paris from his native Périgord in 1778, the young Joubert was taken up by various well-known writers of the day, and above all by Diderot, who treated him with great kindness and, in a short space, had him at work on an aspiring treatise on "Universal Benevolence". It was to be – the wording is evidently Diderot's – a work on "the mind's perspectives, and whether it could do without them. Whether the same breadth that renders the mind capable of conceiving a great idea does not inevitably produce a desire for limitless glory. Whether *vast thoughts* and *far-reaching hope* are not naturally and indissolubly linked."[24] How far he got with it is not clear, perhaps not very far, but the work gives us a vivid sense of Diderot's influence, and an even vivider idea of how that influence might work in reverse. For this was the same Joubert who, as a *pensée*-writer and Christian Platonist, eventually developed almost a mania for limits and nursed, as he would say, "the accursed ambition of putting a whole book into a page, a whole page into a sentence, and that sentence into a single word." His notebook comments on Diderot twenty or thirty years later are full of a strong and half-affectionate hostility, as if to reassure himself of his escape. Diderot, he wrote, had been mad. He had not been mad as a man, but he had had "mad opinions", though he was less pernicious than Rousseau, since no one could possibly take his follies and "ingenious crotchets" for wisdom.

In the same year as Diderot got to know Joubert he had a chance encounter – at Sèvres pehaps, or at Grandval – with a young admirer named Garat, who published a memorable account of the meeting. It is the best evocation we have of Diderot in old age, and it deserves to be quoted in full.

A little while ago the need came over me, as it does to others, to put black on white, or in other words to write a book. I sought

solitude to pursue and give shape to my reveries. A friend lent me
an apartment in a charming house in a charming countryside, fit
to render the one who could appreciate it a poet or a philosopher.
Scarcely had I arrived when I learned that M. Diderot had a
bedroom in the same house. It is no exaggeration to say that my
heart beat violently, and all my dreams of prose and verse
vanished at the thought of meeting this great man, whose genius I
had so often admired. At dawn I entered his room. He seemed no
more surprised at the sight of me than at the light of day. He
spared me any need to stammer out the reason for my visit; he
guessed it from my rapt demeanour. Likewise he spared me long
detours in a conversation fated to arrive at the subject of verse and
prose. At the first mention of these he got up, fixing me with his
gaze, and it was plain that he no longer saw me at all. He began to
speak, but so softly and fast that, though I was beside him and
even touching him, I found it hard to follow. It became clear to
me very soon that my sole role in this scene would be to listen in
silence and wonder, and I had no objection. Gradually his voice
grew clearer and louder. At first almost motionless, he now
became animated, gesticulating freely. He had never met me
before, but as we stood he folded me in his arms, and when we sat,
he smacked my thigh as though it were his own. If in the rapid
transitions of his discourse the word "laws" was mentioned, he
drew me up a plan of legislation; if "theatre", he gave me a choice
of five or six *drames* or tragedies. On the subject of stage *tableaux*
and the need to be shown dramatic scenes rather than listen to
dialogue, he reminded me that Tacitus was the greatest painter of
scenes in antiquity, and he translated or recited to me his *Annals*
and his *Histories*. But what a terrible thing, he exclaimed, that the
barbarians should have buried so many of his masterpieces under
the ruins of so many masterpieces of architecture! Here he waxed
sorrowful over so many beauties lost for ever, mourning them as if
he had known them . . . But wait, what if the excavations at
Herculaneum should reveal lost books from the *Histories* and the
Annals! The hope made him quite radiant. Still, how often, he
reminded me, have clumsy hands destroyed masterpieces in the
very act of rescuing them from tombs! Hereupon he held forth like
an Italian engineer on proper and safe techniques in excavation.
Then, his imagination running to the ruins of ancient Italy, he
recalled how the arts, good taste and politeness of Athens had
softened the terrible virtues of the conquerors of the world. He
transported himself to the happy days of Laeliuses and Scipios,

when even vanquished nations took pleasure in the Triumphs of
their victors. He performed a whole scene from Terence for me.
He recited, or almost sang, several odes by Horace. He ended by
singing me, in good earnest, a song full of grace and wit,
improvised by him at a supper-party, and reciting me a very
agreeable comedy, of which, he told me, he had had a single copy
printed, to save the trouble of copying.

A lot of people came in then, and the sound of shifting chairs
woke him out of his trance and his monologue. At this, he caught
sight of me among the others and approached me, as someone he
must have had a pleasant meeting with on some other occasion.
He remembered that we had had a most interesting conversation,
all about law and the theatre and history, and that I was a most
instructive talker. He hoped I would not let our valuable
acquaintanceship drop. As we parted, he kissed me twice on the
forehead and unclasped his hand from mine with genuine
sadness.[25]

Garat's piece was published in the *Mercure* (15 February 1779).
Diderot was not offended. There was no doubt much truth in it,
he said, and if it made people say he was an "original", did it
matter so terribly? Was it such a fault to have kept "a few edges"
and not be rubbed smooth like the other pebbles on the beach?

Diderot, as we know, thought it right to cherish "posterity".
Thus he had a pleasant surprise when, in 1780, he heard that the
town council of Langres wanted to honour their famous fellow-
citizen and, as they said, hold him up as a model for posterity.
The idea had been born when a local magnate had offered the
municipality a copy of the *Encyclopédie*, to be kept in the Hôtel de
Ville and made available to local readers. This had given the
council the further idea of commissioning a portrait of Diderot, to
be hung above his great work, and the mayor wrote to him, saying
that this act of homage, though it could not compete with the
flattering attentions of "a great princess", would encourage the
Langrois in the study of *belles lettres*, and teach them that "with
constancy and firmness one can triumph over cabals and
envy."[26] Diderot was enchanted, and improved on the scheme by
offering them a bust of himself by his friend Houdon. It was
welcomed with acclamation; and on 1 May 1781 the mayor of

Langres was able to tell him how a party of "the most distinguished citizens" had partaken of a "frugal repast" in his honour, at which Houdon's bust, placed at the head of the table, had attracted all eyes. After the meal – the menu has survived and is quite staggering – the bust was taken in procession to the Council Chamber, to be placed on top of the wall-cupboard housing the *Encyclopédie*. (Didier-Pierre, who refused to attend the feast, found an excuse a little while later to come and take a look at his brother's likeness.)

A month or two later Diderot, who had received very few honours in his life, learned of a further one: he had been elected, together with Buffon, as an honorary member of the Society of Antiquaries of Scotland. He replied to the society, in excellent English, telling them that their letter "came very seasonably to make me amends for past sufferings, and to give me firmness against those to come."[27]

At about the same period, and no doubt encouraged by these tokens of acceptance, Diderot at last decided to gather his writings together and put them into order, and he embarked on a systematic programme of copying. (It may be, indeed, that he was still hoping that some publisher would undertake a collected edition.) He used the services of an admirably efficient copyist named Roland Girbal (one of Henri Meister's employees) and commissioned him to take on as many helpers as he found necessary. In the case of some of his writings, including published ones, he now had no copy, having lost them or considering it more prudent not to keep them on the premises, and it was part of Girbal's duties to track them down. Indeed even now – for there were still dangers – Girbal advised him not to keep the whole mass of manuscripts at the rue Taranne.

There was a need for three copies: one, in fulfilment of a promise to Catherine, to be sent to Russia after his death; one for Angélique and her husband; and one for himself. With, sometimes, as many as four copyists at work it was an expensive business, and in October 1781 we find him brusquely dunning his friend the dramatist Sedaine for repayment of an ancient loan. "If you can return me the money without trouble to yourself, so much the better. If it does mean trouble, then take trouble . . . Do for me what I would not fail to do for you. If you cannot find it in your own purse, then search for it in friends. I am sick of begging from my children and do not want to go on plunging them and me into debt. If you can do this between now and St Martin's day you will oblige me more than I ever obliged you."[28]

It would seem that the American Revolution made a profound impression on Diderot and somewhat radicalised his political views. The fact is plain in what he had been writing for his friend Raynal's *History of the Two Indies*. This massive work, a résumé and radical critique of European colonisation, in both Asia and the New World (the "two Indies" of his title), has a role almost as central to the *philosophique* movement as the *Encyclopédie* itself. For more than thirty years its author, the *abbé* Raynal (1713–96), had been, as his eulogist Garat would put it, "the great master of ceremonies of the literary household". Raynal was an ex-Jesuit, a genial, burly, heavy-featured fellow with a thick meridional accent. He was a great diner-out and a vociferous talker on every kind of political and economic topic, carrying with him a fat book of "anecdotes" to refresh his memory. For some, indeed, he talked too much, or too informatively. Horace Walpole, who did not like to be lectured, complained, "There never was such an impertinent and tiresome old gossip."[29] Once at a Paris dinner-party, to stem Raynal's flow, he pointed to his ears pretending to be deaf, for which he believed Raynal never forgave him. Raynal's great *forte*, or one of them, was to create employment for his needy fellow-writers and bring them into contact with those who could help them: financiers, aristocrats, highly-placed government officials and the like. Thus, though he wrote much of the *History of the Two Indies* himself, he also employed a number of helpers; among them, in the case of the first edition, were Rousseau's friend Delyre, a journalist named Pechmeja and possibly Diderot himself. He was already a man of wealth – it was whispered that, despite his philanthropic views, he had investments in the slave-trade – and he paid his collaborators handsomely.

The original purpose of the work had been to recommend a more rational colonial policy for France, after her disasters in the

Seven Years' War. The tone of the first edition was progressive
and "enlightened", but constructive, hymning the benefits of
commerce and the useful arts, attacking superstition, monopoly
and feudal restrictions, and condemning slavery and the slave-
trade. The book was a vast repository of statistics, anecdote and
sociological fact and fable. It was impressive from its sheer energy
and abundance, though Turgot complained that in it "the most
opposed paradoxes [are] put forward with the same warmth. He
is sometimes a rigorist like Richardson, sometimes immoral like
Helvétius, sometimes an enthusiast for soft and tender virtues,
sometimes for debauch, treats slavery as abominable and wants
slaves."[30]

This first edition came out in Holland in 1770 and was officially
denied entry into France, but in practice it managed to circulate
there fairly freely. A second edition was put in hand; and whether
or not Diderot had contributed to the first edition, he was
certainly closely involved in this second. Two acquaintances who
called on him, in the year 1772, found him with shining eyes and a
"prophetic" air, and he told them, with a laugh, that he was
"doing some Raynal".[31] He found Raynal a demanding
employer and complained loudly to Grimm of his exactions:
"Your devil of an *abbé* is a Fury of whom I am tired of being, and
causing you to be, the Orestes. For God's sake why will he not
leave us in peace?"[32]

Even more important was Diderot's involvement in the third
edition. It was one of the tasks over which, in the late 1770s, he
was labouring in seclusion, and his contributions, eventually,
amounted to nearly a fifth of the text. They included a lengthy
and cogent "Apostrophe to Louis XVI", advising him to
renounce royal extravagance, impose equality of taxation and
abolish the legal privileges of nobles and clergy, etc.; a pathetic
funeral oration for Sterne's friend Eliza Draper[33]; and a sceptical
comparison between "China as depicted by its panegyrists" and
(the same facts shown in a soberer light) "China as seen by its
detractors". These were solid pieces, but side-by-side with them
were many merely hortatory ones, in Diderot's most vehement
and declamatory style.

He would say to Raynal, according to his own account: "My

dear *abbé*, aren't you afraid that all these digressions, however eloquent, may not spoil your work?" "No, no," Raynal would say, "just do what I tell you." "Won't people dismiss it as 'rhetoric'?" "*What* people? Great men's valets? . . . I know a little more about public taste than you do . . . Woe to the author no one speaks evil of."[34]

In their overall effect his additions quite transformed Raynal's work. The professed purpose of the *History* had been to advance colonialism, rendering it more humane and efficient. The message of his interpolations was, rather, that colonialism, in its very nature, was a crime; it brought its victims none of the famed benefits of "civilisation", and it brutalised all those who engaged in it. It was for instance – so his argument ran – exactly through their colonising endeavours that the Dutch has lost their republican virtue; and in a fiery piece of rhetoric he urged the Africans of the Cape to shun their approach.

> Flee, unhappy Hottentots! Flee! Hide yourselves deep in your forests. The wild beasts who inhabit there are less to be feared than the monsters under whose rule you will fall . . . Or if you feel the courage for it, take up your hatchets, bend your bows and rain down poisoned arrows on these intruders. May none remain to bring the news back to their fellow-countrymen.
>
> But alas, you are too trusting. . . ![35]

Over the years, these declamations were to acquire considerable significance. For Raynal's *History*, and especially this edition of 1780, was one of the most discussed and important books of the late eighteenth century – it was for instance an influence on the young Napoleon – and indeed, of all the *philosophes* surviving at the outbreak of the French Revolution, Raynal's would be the most honoured name. But the truth is that, both now and later, and whether for praise or for blame, the parts of the book that really stuck in readers' minds were the ones by Diderot.

It was noticed at the time that Raynal himself, in the third edition, showed signs of a change of views and seemed to be siding with Britain against the American rebels. It made an odd contrast with what Diderot was writing for him, and some of

Raynal's critics even hinted at English bribes. The truth was probably different and was rather that, for Raynal, a little inconsistency here and there in his book hardly counted. What mattered for him was to be in the limelight and to figure as a political hero and martyr. In this he had his wish. The book, as before, was published abroad; but this time, with some boldness, he put his own name, and what is more his portrait, on the title-page. The work was read and discussed all over Europe; smuggled copies soon found their way into France; and eventually, in May 1781, *Parlement* condemned it to be burned and Raynal was threatened with arrest and had to take refuge abroad. The experience of exile would turn out to be highly enjoyable, for he would find himself lionised wherever he went. When Gibbon met him in Lausanne in 1785, he thought fame had gone to his head. "You would imagine that he alone was the Monarch and legislator of the world."[36]

For Diderot his collaboration on Raynal's book had a consequence of a different but momentous kind – no less than a thorough disenchantment with his so-long-adored friend Grimm. In March 1781, during the first stir over the new edition of Raynal's *History*, Grimm met Raynal at the home of the Swiss hostess Germaine de Vermenoux. There were political overtones to this encounter, for Mme de Vermenoux, like Grimm, was a friend of the Neckers, and just then Necker's position, as Turgot's successor as Controller-General, was under fierce attack, one of the accusations against him being that he had helped Raynal to circulate his unpatriotic book. This was causing the Neckers, or at all events Mme Necker, to want to distance themselves from Raynal. "Nobody has seen with more distress than Mme Necker," Meister wrote in the *Correspondance littéraire* in April, "the indiscretion, and one might say the madness, with which the *abbé* Raynal has so needlessly endangered the happiness and repose of his old age."

Grimm thus saw it as a moment to score off Raynal. He put to him a mock-Scholastic dilemma: "Either you believe the people you attack cannot revenge themselves on you, in which case it is cowardly to attack them; or you believe that they can take revenge, and are likely to, in which case it is folly to expose yourself to their resentment." Raynal, for once, made no reply.

A day or two later, Grimm and Diderot were at the Vandeuls', and Grimm spoke scornfully about Raynal's book. He poked fun at its "declamations", saying its title "History" was a misnomer; and he triumphantly recounted his recent "score" off Raynal. Angélique was impressed, but Diderot, though he, like Raynal, said nothing at the time, was profoundly outraged; and back in the rue Taranne he wrote Grimm a long, most furious and bitter letter, taking this put-down of his to Raynal as an index of his general degeneration. The feelings had been building up in Diderot for some time, half-consciously at least, and his letter was written to unburden himself and (it may be guessed from its final sentences) was not one he had any real intention of sending. At all events it was never sent, so that – this is how Diderot would have put it to himself – Grimm would never know how completely he had destroyed his "statue" in his friend's heart. It is a memorable outburst: a mixture of genuine moral indignation, wounded vanity – for Grimm had been hitting at himself as much as at Raynal – and lacerating sadness. He was registering the loss both of a friend – a lover might even be the better word – and of an illusion.

The letter – then or later given the heading "Letter of Apologia for the *abbé* Raynal" – begins with a direct rebuttal of Grimm's "dilemma". It was *not* cowardice to attack someone who could not defend himself, so long as he deserved it; it was *not* madness to attack someone who might take revenge – contempt for vengeance, in the cause of virtue, innocence and truth, was an act of generosity. The men of genius and virtue who, in the past, had attacked "sceptred criminals" and "sacred impostors" were not counting the consequences, they were merely thinking of the task in hand.

The People say: "Live first, then philosophise." But the man who has put on the mantle of Socrates, and who loves truth and virtue better than life, will say "Philosophise first, then live." "If he can . . .," you say. That makes you laugh? Ah, my friend, I see what it is: your soul has grown lean in St Petersburg and Potsdam, at the keyholes and in the antechambers of the great.[37]

Has Grimm, asks Diderot, had the "puerile vanity" to take the rebukes to kings and courtiers in the *History* as aimed at himself? If so, it was as absurd as if he (Diderot) had ranked himself among the Sages.

> I felt very sorry for you, when you said to me in St Petersburg, "Do you realise that, if you see the Empress every day after dinner, I see her every evening?" My friend, I do not recognise you any longer. You have, perhaps without knowing it, become one of the best-concealed but most [word missing] of anti-*philosophes*. You live with us, but you hate us.[38]

Ever since Grimm, a born man of letters, had exchanged his profession for a hanger-on of the great, Diderot tells him, his taste has deteriorated. He depreciates what he once admired and eulogises what he once despised; he mocks at eloquent and courageous writers as mere "declaimers". (This hit of Grimm's had gone home.) Was Demosthenes no more than a "declaimer" in his *Philippics*, asks Diderot? Why was Jean-Jacques truly eloquent and Linguet [a recent enemy of the *philosophes*[39]] truly just a "declaimer"?

> It is because I feel the former to be true, even when he says what is false, and the other, having no principles, to be false even when saying what is true. Rousseau is only lying in his first line; Linguet is a liar from the first line to the last.
>
> My friend, you have gangrene. Perhaps it has not progressed too far to be incurable. What you need to do, I think, is some soliloquising. It is not what I may have the courage to say to you, it is what you say to yourself, that will cure you.
>
> I will cease to live sooner than not love you, but I should never have become your friend if you had spoken at Jean-Jacques', where I first met you, as you spoke yesterday . . .[40]

Should he send Grimm this letter, he asks himself? "Yes. But when? When I respect you enough to believe you would read it without resentment. Farewell, this 25 March 1781."[41]

Two months later he added a postscript.

Under my window I hear them hawking the news of the *abbé's*
[Raynal's] condemnation. I am reading it. I have read it. May
there fall on the head of those wretches and of the old imbecile[42]
whom they have served the ignominy and curses that once fell on
the head of the Athenians who made Socrates drink hemlock. My
friend, one is not capable of heroic actions, if one condemns them;
and one only condemns them because one is not capable of
them.[43]

Was Diderot, the self-professed disciple of Socrates, capable of
"heroic actions"? This painful question, it is easy to see, was one
of the reasons, if by no means the only one, why the Grimm affair
was so bitter to him. The falling-out had cast long shadows over
his own life, and it was not for nothing that once again the name of
Rousseau rose to haunt him. For had not Rousseau been willing
to publish under his own name and to suffer for his opinions? Had
not Raynal, for that matter, even proved eager to suffer for what
were *not* his opinions! These were disturbing questions for a man
who consigned his writings to his desk-drawer, or at most offered
them to a few crowned heads, and whose only recent publicly-
acknowledged work (his *Seneca*) had been a defence of compromise and expediency.

That, with all his many virtues, Diderot was not born to be a
hero – a Brutus, a Socrates – was a truth that he was half aware of.
For one thing, as we have seen (p. 294), he was capable of
joking hilariously at his own passion for martyrdom. Still, it was
too dear a daydream to give up altogether. Further, it had not so
often been tested. Since the time of Vincennes, at least, if he had
been exposed to serious dangers, he had also had powerful
protectors. The position of a well-known man of letters in the
France of Louis XV, and more especially that of Louis XVI, was
altogether different from that of a penniless garret-writer or a
humble printer.

The truth of this was to be illustrated vividly when, in the last
months of 1781, it seemed as if the story of Vincennes might be
about to repeat itself. One of the Paris journals began a virulent
campaign against Diderot, making brutal fun of him as a parasite
of Catherine the Great and speaking of him, quite falsely, and no

doubt to get him into trouble, as author of a recently-published atheistical work, the *New Philosophical Thoughts*. Then, in May 1782, some of the copies of the uncensored text of the *Essay on the Reigns of Claudius and Nero* were seized on their way to Paris, and there was talk of "a violent storm against the new Tacitus". It was known that the King was incensed against Diderot for his aspersions on his grandfather Louis XV, and he was reported variously as saying that Diderot must "be severely scolded, though not otherwise harmed" or that he should be sent to the Bastille.

For a week or two Diderot was distinctly alarmed, and his enemies, such as the critic La Harpe, no doubt heard the news with relish. It so happened that, just then, Catherine's son the Grand-Duke Paul of Russia was on a visit to Paris, travelling under the name of "The Count of the North". He attended the Académie, where La Harpe, who was his accredited Paris "correspondent",[44] delivered two fulsome speeches in his honour; he also paid a personal visit to d'Alembert: but, influenced by La Harpe, he paid Diderot no such attention. Diderot, however, felt he must pay his respects, out of duty to Catherine, and accordingly he waylaid the Grand-Duke at Sunday mass. It turned out an ungracious encounter. "So it's you? *You*, at mass!" exclaimed the Grand-Duke. "Yes, monsieur le Comte; and sometimes Epicurus was to be seen at the foot of the altar." (At about this period someone, in Diderot's presence, praised the Grand-Duke and his gracious manners. "Never believe it," said Diderot. "Open his shirt, and you will see fur.")

There followed an invitation to call on the Grand-Duchess, which turned out very chillily. Diderot told her he was in danger of being sent to the Bastille. "And why is that?" asked the Grand-Duchess. "Because, in my *Life of Seneca*, I wrote like a free man and a philosopher." The Grand-Duchess, who had read the book, replied frigidly, "You should not have written it," and with that he was dismissed."

Diderot was not sent to the Bastille. It was indeed true that the King had told the Keeper of the Seals, de Miromesnil, that he ought to be punished, though he did not specify how. But neither de Miromesnil, who was a liberal and a follower of Turgot, nor the Lieutenant of Police Le Noir – who was, anyway, compromised by the help he had given to Diderot earlier – took the King's command seriously. Some gesture was required, of course. So they summoned Diderot to appear before them, to take part in a mock-ceremony of official reprobation, de Miromesnil delivering a solemn homily, and Diderot responding with well-acted confusion, falling to his knees, declaring that "he deserved to be chastised for the misdeeds of his old age even more than for earlier extravagances," and begging the magistrate to "deign to receive his confession and act of repentance." A letter to Le Noir, written soon afterwards, kept up the comedy:

> The more I consider your régime, the more I see that it is justified by *error* [i.e. the social benefits of religious illusion] and that it constitutes a guarantee of our person and property. When I was young, I occupied the fourth floor; I wrote foolish things, and I was imprisoned in Vincennes for my *Indiscreet Jewels*. Having acquired fortune and celebrity I have come down to the first floor, where, I confess, I have produced even more dangerous works. I have been given a good and gentle lesson for this and am corrected for the rest of my life.[45]

The message of this farcical repetition of the terrors of Vincennes seemed to be that Diderot was not cut out for the heroic stage. If so, he could comfort himself that there were many other parts he knew how to play. "It is incredible how many roles I play in my life," he once exclaimed to Sophie.[46] If he had hankerings to be Socrates, it was as someone who knew that in everyday life he was Diogenes, or a disciple of Diogenes. This was a theme he often came back to in his letters to Sophie; though in the early days of their love he told her that as age overtook him the Diogenes would give way to a sylph or an angel of the annunciation – anyway something more edifying and less suitable to her. But he also sometimes liked to cast himself as the Fool. As a New Year's Day offering to Mme de Maux in 1778, when he was sixty-four, he sent her some charming verses entitled "My Portrait and my Horoscope", in which he warns her that she will still have this "spoiled child of Nature", this fellow with the cap and bells, on her hands, "swollen with old sighs, and burnt with old desires", to his eightieth year.

> But when, on the lid of my sarcophage,
> The great Athene, with tearful eye,
> Points out, in her sorrow, to passers-by
> The graven motto, "Here lies a Sage,"
>
> Do not go staining my memory
> Or giving the tear-stained Goddess the lie,
> Do not start laughing, I beg you, or cry
> "Here lies a Fool." Keep my secret for me.

Diderot was now sixty-seven, an old man, with a heart and chest ailment which made walking and climbing stairs a painful effort. The Baron was ill too, with violent attacks of gout and nephritis, so that there were fewer dinner-parties in the rue Royale. Diderot wrote to Angélique (28 July 1781) that he saw, "with a certain satisfaction", that all his relationships were falling apart.

> I only go to Boulogne [i.e. to see Mme de Maux] when I am summoned there. I shall not go to Sèvres any more. They have given my little bedroom to Madame la Bauche [his landlord Belle's niece] and have stowed me in a garret which looks out onto the courtyard, as bare and gloomy as an ancient prison. I see no more of Madame Duclos these days. The Baron went to Contrexéville without saying goodbye, and Grimm has done much the same. I would have believed him in Paris still if I had not heard by chance that he was roaming Germany.

He told Angélique that "she would not lose" by his growing solitude.[47]

It was a compensation that life with Nanette was growing easier. He told Angélique of a promising development. Nanette had bought a copy of *Gil Blas*, to replace one that Angélique had borrowed from a friend of theirs and had lost, and on casually dipping into it she had found it absorbing. "The effect, I noticed, lasted all day," Diderot wrote to Angélique.

So I have become her Reader. I administer three pinches of *Gil Blas* every day: one in the morning, one after dinner and one in the evening. When we have seen the end of *Gil Blas* we shall go on to *The Devil on Two Sticks* and *The Bachelor of Salamanca* and other cheering works of the same class. A few years and a few hundred such readings will complete the cure. If I was sure of success, I should not complain at the labour. What amuses me is that she treats everyone who visits her to a repeat of what I have just read her, so conversation doubles the effect of the remedy. I have always spoken of novels as frivolous productions, but I have finally discovered they are good for the vapours. I will give Dr Tronchin the formula the next time I see him. *Prescription*: eight to ten pages of Scarron's *Roman comique*; four chapters of *Don Quixote*; a well-chosen paragraph from Rabelais; infuse in a reasonable quantity of *Jacques the Fatalist* or *Manon Lescaut*, and vary these drugs as one varies herbs, substituting others of roughly the same qualities, as necessary.[48]

Nanette and her sister Mme Billard went to Sèvres this September, leaving Diderot, who had rather lost his liking for Belle's house, to look after himself in Paris. It was the year of the *Salon* exhibition, and he had agreed to review it – perhaps not too wisely, for he was not in very good health. His *Salon* review was brief and perfunctory, and Meister, introducing it in the *Correspondance littéraire*, spoke of it as "the last effort of his pen". It was not quite that, but he was, as he was aware, in decline. It is roughly of this period that Angélique is speaking in her *Memoir* of her father:

He began to complain altogether of his health. He found his mind exhausted. He said he had no more ideas; he felt tired all the time; it was a labour for him to get dressed. His teeth did not hurt him, he said, but if he pulled them they just gently came out, like pins. He ate less. He went out less. For as much as three or four years he was aware of an inward "destruction", though strangers had no idea of it, for he talked with all his old fire and sweetness.[49]

Sometimes he would complain that he was quite worn out and had no more ideas. Angélique would urge him to go on, as his writing gave her much pleasure, and he would say that he went on "scribbling" just for her sake.

*

In April 1783 the long-ailing Mme d'Epinay died, in her house in the Chaussée d'Antin; and in October of the same year d'Alembert died also. His last years had been melancholy. As early as 1768 he had suffered from failing powers and had had to acknowledge that his days as a mathematician were over. Julie de l'Espinassse had died in 1776, leaving him, in his own words, with a "terrible void" – made worse by the fact that, on going through her papers, he discovered that, unknown to him, she had been obsessed, to the point of self-destruction, with two affairs with younger lovers. He was famous, much-sought-after, but desolate, and he made a "bad" death, declaring, with his habitual honesty, "People with courage are happy. I have none."

Then, on 22 February 1784, in her sixty-eighth year, Sophie Volland died. The cause of death is not known; and indeed, from our point of view, she died as unobtrusively as she had lived. By her will she had left Diderot "seven little volumes of Montaigne's *Essays*, bound in red morocco, and a ring which I call my 'Pauline'." Sometime before her death she had retrieved her letters to Diderot and had destroyed them; but she had preserved his letters to her, and after her death Angélique was able to persuade her sister Mme de Blacy to surrender them.

Five days later Diderot suffered a stroke. He had been talking to Angélique, when he stumbled over a phrase. He tried it again and stumbled once more. Exclaiming "An apoplexy," he got up to look at himself in the mirror and calmly drew Angélique's attention to his mouth, which was slightly twisted, and to one of his hands, which was paralysed. "He went into his bedroom," writes Angélique, "lay down, kissed my mother and bid her a farewell, kissed me and bid me farewell too also, explained to us where to find some books that did not belong to him, and relapsed into silence. Of all of us, only he kept his head; the rest of us lost ours completely." Doctors were summoned and applied blisters to his back and legs, and at one in the morning he got up and sat in his armchair, murmuring, as they kept plying him with emetics, "You use very nasty things to keep me alive."

He passed three days and nights like this, in a very sober and rational delirium. He discoursed on Greek and Latin epitaphs and translated them for me, held forth on tragedy, and recalled beautiful lines from Horace and Virgil and recited them. He kept talking the whole night through; he would ask the time, decide it was time for bed, lie down in all his clothes and get up again five minutes later. On the fourth day his delirium ceased, and with it all recollection of what had taken place. Two of the blisters closed up, though the one on his right leg remained open and suppurating for the next two months. He seemed to be restored to health.[50]

It was altogether a harrowing time for Angélique; for only a week or two after her father's attack her daughter, the ten-year-old "Minette", died. The event overwhelmed her with grief and misery, and in a sense she never really recovered her spirits. The memory of the brilliant Minette would become a cult with her. She commissioned a bust of her (no doubt from Minette's godfather, the famous sculptor Pigalle) so that she could look on her day and night. Nine years or so later, in a letter to Henri Meister, she would relate a long and poignant dream about Minette, in which Minette was serving as a kind of messenger between herself on earth and her father and Sophie Volland in the Elysian Fields.

Diderot, despite recovery, was obviously failing: his legs and thighs were severely swollen and dropsical, requiring painful remedies, and there were days when he could hardly walk. It was the moment for the *bien-pensant* in his family circle, and especially those in Langres – Denise, Didier-Pierre and Angélique's mother-in-law Mme Caroillon – to give anxious thoughts to his salvation. Someone alerted the *curé* of Saint-Sulpice, a certain Jean-Joseph de Tersac, and he came several times to the rue Taranne. Tersac was a rigorist, well-known for having refused Christian burial to Voltaire's remains, and high hopes began to be placed on his visits. Vandeul wrote home to Denise, telling her how, to their "great satisfaction", Tersac had "insinuated himself" into the Diderots' home and had "won the esteem both of Monsieur and Madame". It was all very promising, he told her, but it would require patience, for the sick man's mind had been weakened by his illness; he no longer had the same "firmness and warmth".[51] (In writing this, Vandeul could conceivably have been trying to protect Diderot – since Diderot's brother Didier-Pierre had been threatening to come to Paris, to attempt the conversion of which he had so signally failed up to now.)

In all this, Nanette, though she encouraged the *curé's* visits, behaved with remarkable, and characteristic, integrity.

> My father [writes Angélique in her *Memoir*] received the *curé* with the greatest friendliness. He praised his charities and kept speaking of the good actions he had done and had still to do. He recommended some of the poor of the parish to him, and the *curé* gave them assistance. He came to see my father two or three times a week, but they did not get on to intimate matters: they discussed theological questions only as they might have done any other topic, as befits men of the world. My father did not seek such topics but was ready to discuss them if they arose. One day, the two finding that they agreed so much over practical ethics, the *curé* ventured to suggest that if my father would publish his ethical maxims, together with a little retraction of his other works, it would do immense good in the world. "You may well be right," answered my father, "but you must agree it would be an impudent lie."
>
> My mother would have given her life for my father to be a believer, but she would rather have died than have him commit the least action she would regard as sacrilege. Convinced that my father would never change his opinions, she wanted to protect him from persecution, and she would not leave him alone with the *curé* for a single instant; we took turns to guard him.[52]

The competition for the soul of this famous atheist began to grip the public's interest, and early in May Diderot took refuge, with Nanette, in Sèvres. (His enemies said later that he had been smuggled away by his *coryphées*.) Meanwhile Grimm had informed Catherine the Great of his friend's illness, and had suggested that the invalid should perhaps be found new lodgings. She replied that this must most certainly be arranged, at her expense, and a new home instantly found "for her library and its proprietor". "You should have done it without asking me; and take care that *nothing*, not the least scrap, goes astray."[53] Grimm duly looked about and found some very handsome rooms in the rue de Richelieu. They were not ideally suitable, being up a flight or two of stairs and a long way from the Vandeuls'; but they had the great advantage of removing Diderot from the parish of Saint-Sulpice and its zealous *curé*.

"He enjoyed them [the lodgings] for twelve days," continues Angélique's *Memoir*.

He was delighted with them; having lived all his life in a hovel, he found himself in a palace. But his body grew feebler every day, though his head remained unchanged. He was certain he would die very soon, but he ceased to talk about it, not wanting to add to the sadness of the people around him. In fact he did all he could to distract them; every day he would have some new scheme for the furniture or for hanging prints. On the day before his death they brought him a more comfortable bed, and the workmen argued about where it should stand. "My friends," he told them, "you are taking a lot of trouble about a piece of furniture that won't be needed for more than four days." In the evening friends would come to see him, and the conversation would turn on philosophy and the different routes that led to it. "The first step towards philosophy," he said, "is incredulity." That is the last thing I would ever hear him say. It was late, so I left him, hoping to see him the next day.[54]

All next morning, 31 July 1784, Diderot chatted cheerfully with friends and with his doctor, and then he sat down to dinner, saying he felt hungrier than he had done for weeks. He ate some soup and boiled mutton, and then seized an apricot, exclaiming blithely to Nanette, when she tried to stop him, "Good God, what harm do you think it can do me?" Having eaten it, he stretched over the table for some cherries in syrup and gave a cough. Nanette asked him a question and, receiving no answer, she looked up and saw that he was dead. It was a cheerful and becoming death, very unlike the tortured scene that religious zealots liked to imagine for an atheist.

As for the matter of Christian burial, there proved to be no real problem, for Tersac's earlier visits had fully saved appearances, aided by the large sums that Vandeul spread about the parish.

The funeral took place at the church of Saint-Roch, and Vandeul arranged things in great style. It was the custom to hire priests (at 1 *livre* apiece) as attendants at funerals, and Diderot had no less than fifty to see him into his grave. He was buried in the Chapelle de la Vierge, and his bones have long since disappeared.

24

Jacques the Fatalist

There is a better place than a deathbed to bring the story of Diderot's earthly life to an end, and this is with the last of his novels, *Jacques the Fatalist*. It has a special significance for the biographer of Diderot, for it is the one novel of his in which he presents a pattern hero; and this hero, though in a most un-statue-like way, clearly represents the person Diderot wanted to be and, in many respects, considered that he was.

> How did they come to meet? By chance, like everyone else. What were their names? What does that matter to you? Where did they come from? From the nearest place. Where were they going? Does one ever know where one is going? What were they saying? The master was saying nothing; and Jacques was saying that his captain would say that everything that happens to us on earth, whether good or evil, had been written above.[1]

So begins this novel, the history of a servant and his master, thus brusquely imposing on us one of Diderot's laws of fiction: that a fictional narrator is not obliged to be the reader's humble servant, but may be a personage with his own moods and his own rights. This novel about authority and "mastery" is, even more than *The Nun* and the stories, a fiction about the telling of fictions, and its climax is a great quarrel in which Jacques, the insubordinate servant and teller of stories, establishes his predominance and mastery for all time. One can, and should, interpret this contest in half-a-dozen relevant ways: but from one point of view it is certainly about story-telling.

In terms of sheer events there is little enough to the story of Jacques and his Master, though what there is, is magically

suggestive. Soon after we meet them, they take refuge in a
robber-infested inn. Jacques locks the robbers in and the two
escape, discussing providence as they ride. They hear a mob at
their heels and find they are *not* pursued. The Master learns what
it is to hurt one's knee. They enter, or perhaps do not enter, a
certain château. Jacques goes back to rescue his watch, retrieves it
by force from a huckster, is mobbed as a thief, is pardoned for a
seduction he has not committed and rejoins his master, who has
gone to sleep meanwhile and been robbed of his horse. They buy
another horse, which turns out to be the executioner's horse and
carries the unwilling Jacques to the gibbet . . . They reach an inn,
where after a drunken night, they have their great quarrel . . .
They set off with the Marquis des Arcis and his young secretary . .
They re-encounter their lost horse . . . We lose track of them in a
flurry of fictional excitements – homicide, prison and other lurid
themes – and are reunited with them in a happy ending, Jacques
being now married but still inseparable from his Master.

That is almost the sum of it. But, this being a fiction about
fiction-telling, their brief picaresque story is imbricated, by a
system of relays, overlays and Chinese-box effects, with a
multitude of other stories: the history, for ever interrupted, of
Jacques's *amours*; the entrancing story of Jacques's ex-master, the
Spinozan Captain, accustomed to fighting a duel every month
with his dearest friend, and dying of sheer grief when this
privilege is denied him; the landlady's great tale of Mme de la
Pommeraye, and the Marquis des Arcis's tale of Father Hudson –
stories, the one tragic, the other comic, of "mystification and
revenge"; and a score of others, including those which the
narrator says he could have devised for Jacques and his Master
but chose not to.

The episode of the quarrel in the inn-room between the valet
Jacques and his Master, and the formal treaty by which they
resolve it, is, as I have said, the "climax" of *Jacques the Fatalist*
(and must count as one of the great symbolic events of the
eighteenth century). The master has decided that, though he is
dependent upon Jacques in every way – as guide, protector,
entertainer and bosom friend – the time has come to remind him
who is master, so he orders him downstairs. Jacques's response is

that he is very comfortable where he is. "I tell you you will go downstairs," thunders his master. "I am sure that you are wrong," coolly replies the philosophical Jacques – as if all his master has done is to make an objective prediction – and he gives his master a string of good reasons why.

> It being well-known that your orders are wasted breath if not ratified by Jacques; and you having so successfully linked your name to mine that the one is found nowhere without the other and everyone speaks of "Jacques and his Master"; after this, suddenly to take it into your head to separate them! No, monsieur, that cannot be. It is written above that so long as Jacques lives, and as long as his master lives, and even after both of them are dead, people shall go on speaking of "Jacques and his Master".[2]

It is a moment of supreme crisis, as both of them know, and they fall to shouting and nearly come to blows, whereupon the hostess of the inn offers to arbitrate between them. She will do so, she says, on one condition: they pledge themselves on their honour to abide by her judgement. The two agree with great good will, and in solemn legal terms she announces her ruling: it is that equality between Jacques and his Master, established by long-standing custom, shall be formally abrogated and then immediately re-instituted. Jacques is to go downstairs, as ordered; and when he has done so he is to come up again and return into possession of all his old prerogatives. Further, the issue is never to be disputed between them again. It is the perfect solution, as the Master is the first to admit; and the moment Jacques has obediently left the room, he rushes out to embrace him, exclaiming "It is written above that I shall never part from this 'original'. As long as I live, he will be my master and I shall be his servant."

This is not quite the end of the affair, however, for Jacques insists that, to prevent any further unpleasantness, they should draw up a formal contract. It will stipulate that it is written above that the Master shall be dependent on Jacques; that Jacques shall abuse his position whenever occasion offers; that, since both parties cannot but recognise Jacques's ascendancy, Jacques shall be insolent and his Master, for the sake of quiet, must pretend not to notice; that, in brief, the Master shall have the title of authority and Jacques shall have the substance. But – objects the Master ruefully – if this is already "written" in heaven, is there any point in spelling it out? A great deal of point, replies Jacques. "All our quarrels, up to now, have come about because we have not said *clearly* that you should call yourself my master, and I should in fact be yours." "And where the devil did you learn all that?" asks the Master, in wonderment. "In the great Book . . ." replies Jacques.

The significances – political, social and literary – of that contract between master and valet positively bristle. Let us notice first that in this novel – though, like *Rameau's Nephew*, it features an antithetical pair – Diderot has not split himself up into two. We are led to expect that Jacques and his Master ("Jacques and his master" was a proverbial phrase) will be a complementary pair in the Cervantes tradition, supplying each other's deficiencies. We look for some variant on the Quixote–Sancho Panza formula as it was once analysed by Stendhal in *De l'Amour*: "The master tall and pale, the squire plump and ruddy; the former all heroism and courtesy, the latter all egoism and servility; the former always full of romantic and piquant fantasies, the latter a model of the spirit of accommodation, a collection of highly prudent proverbs, etc."[3] The narrator insists on their pairhood, as we saw Jacques doing, and tells us "They are only good together"; separated, they are worth no more than Don Quixote without Sancho or Richardet without Ferragus.[4]

However, with a cunning subversion of conventional expectations, we are shown something quite different. Equality becomes an issue in the novel, but only to be dismissed as illusory. It is not only written "above" but needs to be written in so many words on earth, that Jacques the servant is incomparably the better man, needing none of his Master's qualities to complete him. It is indeed one of his many superior qualities that he can recognise this truth. But more: Jacques is a man and his Master only the imitation of one. The Master, who only knows how to consult his watch and take snuff, and perform perhaps a couple of other such reflexes, is an automaton, much like the engineer Vaucanson's[5] famous mechanical duck or flute-player. "He has eyes, like you and me," says the narrator, "but most of the time one cannot tell if he is seeing anything. He is not asleep, he is not awake either; he simply lets himself exist, it is his habitual function."[6] What the myth of the book celebrates is not some "eternal" harmony of opposites or Renaissance doctrine of integration but a decisive transfer of authority, dictated by necessity and the nature of things.

We are invited to interpret this myth in a variety of ways – politically or socially (the relations of the aristocracy to the Third Estate), biologically (the "command-system" in the human organism), or philosophically. The reader soon intuits that, from one point of view, the partnership of Jacques and the Master represents an irreverent reversal of Descartes' account of Soul and Body, the servant Jacques standing in the masterful and directing relation of soul or mind to that inert machine, his "Master". According to Descartes, bodies, and also imperfect intelligences, are dependent on God and incapable of existing without him for a single moment – which, again, precisely describes the Master's relationship to Jacques.

But we need, above all, to ponder the "Fatalist" of Diderot's title. As *D'Alembert's Dream* is Diderot's fanciful treatment of materialism, so *Jacques the Fatalist* is his fictional rendering of determinism. He has decided, however, for all-important reasons, to handle the subject of determinism under the disguise of fatalism, which we may call the fairy-tale or *Arabian Nights* version of determinism. It is essential to fatalism that what lies in store for a human not only shall be "decreed" beforehand but shall come to that human with the force of a surprise. It is the stuff of plots and *peripeteia* and *dénouements*. There is a peculiar affinity between fatalism and writing, especially imaginative writing. The word "fate" derives from *fatum*, i.e. something "decreed" in speech or writing, and, as Diderot's Jacques continually reminds us, it envisages the vicissitudes of the world as being "written" – inscribed on a "great roll" or scroll in heaven – as it were a novel of which one has not yet reached the last pages. The *abbé* Galiani, with his usual cleverness, once pointed out that fatalism is, in a certain sense, actually the opposite of determinism.

It [fatalism] has this agreeable quality (which has not been seen, or at least has not so far been remarked on, by any philosopher, so far as I know) that it is the father of curiosity. Fatality is the most curious thing in the world; without it, there would be nothing unforeseen, nothing interesting; everything would be calculated, and the fall of a statesman would be no more interesting than the equinox and the solstice: it would have been printed ahead of time in the almanacs.[7]

By his chosen means, Diderot is in a position to make a profound critique of the *language* of determinism. For determinism, as it is commonly expressed, talks as if human beings were *compelled* to do certain things, that they were the slaves of some active force of destiny – "the idea of necessity", as Hume puts it, "seeming to imply something of force and violence, and constraint, of which we are not sensible."[8] But this is, of course, an absurd idea; for what could be the mechanism by which this force acted, and what counter-force could it be thought to be acting against? Nevertheless, "determinism" looks uncomfortably empty when shorn of such rhetoric; in fact it is very hard, perhaps impossible in the nature of language, to avoid using it.

Now, one could not ask for a better analogue to this determinist rhetoric, this appeal to an "overmastering" necessity, than the relationship of servant to master, the topic so variously explored by Diderot in *Jacques the Fatalist*. Jacques has had many masters, and by one of them he has been taught that (cosmically speaking) he is not free, for all human good and evil is "written" above. He has, that is to say, been taught fatalism as a kind of parrot doctrine, like that of Voltaire's Pangloss, fit for all emergencies. But from the same master he has also learnt the more strenuous doctrine of determinism, and we find him fully equipped to expound Spinoza. He can explain the error that, according to Spinoza, a moving stone or bullet might fall into, if it could think and feel, i.e. that it was continuing in motion by its own wish and was master of its own fate.[9] "He [Jacques] believed that man made his way as *necessarily* to glory or ignominy as a ball with consciousness of itself on a mountain slope."[10]

Along the way he gives his Master some excellent practical lessons in Spinozism. We may cite his double lesson to his

Master, near the end of the novel, when he asks him to admit that both of them are simply "living and thinking machines": machines that for most of the time function without consciousness, but no less machine-like when consciousness returns. For, as Jacques's Spinozan Captain would have said, willing is only an item like any other in the chain of causes, and to be *conscious* of willing something is only to add one more wheel or cog to the machine. The Master demurs, saying he can feel himself to possess freewill: he could prove it by taking some quite arbitrary decision, for instance to throw himself off his horse. Whereupon Jacques proceeds to show that this "causeless" volition, this "liberty of indifference", is no liberty at all, for the whole idea of throwing himself off his horse will have been caused by the need to contradict Jacques.

A few pages later, with a little assistance from Jacques, the Master's stirrup-straps give way and he falls off his horse. In his fury, he pursues Jacques round and round the horse, whip in hand, until at last Jacques asks him if he doesn't now agree. "Agree about what?" asks the Master. "Why, that for most of the time we act quite involuntarily. Lay your hand on your heart: of all you have said or done during the last half hour, was any of it consciously willed? Have you not been my marionette, and would you not have gone on being my 'Punch' for a month if I had so decided?"[11] (Jacques's "Spinozan" lesson, we are meant to note, is, among other things, a lesson about novel-writing, a form of puppet-management both suffering from and exploiting illusions of freedom.)

On the other hand, according to Spinoza, the thought of necessity gives us mastery over our emotions; and, try as he will, Jacques never learns the trick of this. He is fully aware that "we walk in the night, under what is written above, equally senseless in our wishes, our joy and our affliction." When he weeps, he often finds he is a fool to have done so, and likewise when he laughs. "All the same," he tells his Master, "I cannot stop myself weeping and laughing: that's what enrages me. I have tried a hundred times . . ."[12] In fact, as we find, the real history of Jacques's *amours*, which is not at all the salacious chronicle his Master yearns to hear but a tale of irrational acts of delicacy and generosity, enforces an important truth about determinism and Spinozism: that they are intellectually incontrovertible and quite impossible for a human being to live by consistently.

There is, in the novel, a constant conflict and oscillation between fatalism and determinism. The Master at one point wonders whether something happens because it is written up above (fatalism) or it is written above because it is going to happen (determinism). Jacques solves the problem by averring that the fact that something is or will be written up above is also written up above. It is the sort of conversational triumph that he enjoys. The Master, who is no determinist but is ready to believe in fate, enjoys it greatly when Jacques's horse carries him straight to the gibbet; it is as if destiny has given a preview of its "great scroll".

Smuggled in beside such games with "fate", however, as I say, is the sober theme of determinism. The truth conveyed is that mortals are not masters of their own actions not so much because of unforeseeable contingencies (the subject-matter of fatalism) as because what they *want* is not a matter for them to decide. One cannot *want* to want something, or at all events it would be no use if one did. This is pure determinism. It is what Hobbes held – "The will," he wrote, "is not voluntary"[13] – and Spinoza likewise. "Human freedom," writes Spinoza, "consists solely in the fact that men are conscious of their own desire, but are ignorant of the causes whereby that desire has been determined."[14] This, as I said earlier (pp. 137–8) was the heart of Diderot's own determinist position.

However, what another master (his present one) has taught Jacques, is that, socially speaking, he *is* free – for his Master is no master. This makes him feel he must clear up the whole business of "mastery". As is well-known, the manservant was a significant and contentious feature in French life at this period. With his imputed wiliness and venality and conceited aping of gentlemanly manners, he was the stuff of a hundred comedies; but, especially since the valet Damiens's attempt to assassinate Louis XV, he was also vaguely felt to be a political threat. The vetoing of Beaumarchais's *The Marriage of Figaro*[15] was to illustrate this very vividly. "The history of domestic servants is a great affair in this century," writes Michelet. "Among the various classes, the most dangerous beyond question was this one. No effort had been spared to repress and intimidate them. In vain. Their rise could not be stopped. It was said jokingly of lackeys, 'It is a *corps* of nobility all ready to replace the existing one.' "[16] Diderot's Jacques, it is true, is a valet – that is to say a confidential servant – rather than a lackey; but the term "valet" had generic force as a name for anyone who served. One finds Jean-Jacques Rousseau, who had once been a lackey, writing, apropos of Mme d'Epinay, that he "refused to be the valet of a despicable woman".

Diderot's fullest comment on the "valet", as a social problem, comes in the wonderful little scene in which Jacques and his Master re-encounter their lost horse. They catch sight of a ploughman having a furious quarrel with one of his horses, who has simply lain down in the furrow and refuses to stir. "Do you realise what you are seeing?" Jacques asks his Master.

> It is my guess that that foolish, vain and good-for-nothing animal is a city-dweller who, proud of his first employment as a saddle-horse, despises the plough; and in a word, to tell you all, it is your horse, the symbol of the Jacques you see here and all the other cowardly rascals like him, who have quit the country to come and wear livery in the capital, and who would rather beg their bread in the streets, or starve, than return to agriculture, the most useful and honourable of callings.[17]

It is a speech shot through with a dozen ironies. This is the horse (this is the servant) that the Master dreams of. The animal and he, recognising each other, have a rapturous re-union, while Jacques, looking on, mutters curses on this equine satire on himself, with his ignoble eagerness to enter a gentleman's service.

As with the "fool-problem" in *Rameau's Nephew* (who is the fool's "fool"?), the "valet-problem" expands under Diderot's hand. As he perceives, the valet has a twin in another lowly and vainglorious figure, the writer. Writers write for much the same reason as servants chatter: it gives them a sense of importance, it raises them from abjection. It is this, and not any morbid taste for cruelty, that causes humble people to flock to public executions: it will give them something to talk about when they get home. So asserts the narrator; but he confesses he gets these theories from Jacques. Jacques, indeed, is an extreme case. As a boy, he lived with his grandparents, an austere and silent couple in the secondhand goods trade, and he chattered so much that they made him wear a gag. He was gagged for twelve years (Diderot, the reader reflects, was gagged by King and *Parlement* for much the same length of time) and this explains his present loquacity. It is part of his bond with his Master that he loves talking and his Master loves listening.

All the same, Jacques being the man that he is, there is a limit to his self-mockery. If, like all writers, he is a compulsive talker, he is, as cannot be said of all writers, a talker with principles – especially the principle of never repeating oneself. He learned this attitude from his grandfather, whose faith even in the Bible was shaken by its vain repetitions. When his Master pesters him for ever more story-telling, Jacques will sometimes protest anxiously, "Monsieur is preparing a grim fate for me. What will become of me when I have nothing more to say?" "You will begin all over again," says his Master unfeelingly. "Jacques *begin again!*" replies Jacques in horror. "It is not written so above; and if I caught myself doing it, I would cry, 'Ah, if your grandfather could hear you!' and ask for my gag back."[18]

From the writer-as-valet Diderot makes a natural and easy transition to the narrator-as-valet, and here analogies between the reader–narrator and the Jacques–Master relationship pro-liferate beyond measure. From his very first words, the narrator has proclaimed himself as no man's slave: he is indeed more aggressive about his rights, perhaps because less self-confident, than the servant Jacques is about his. "Reader, you treat me like an automaton," he protests, "it is really not polite."[19] This richly suggestive complaint reminds us that, in the story of Jacques and his Master, it is not the servant but the Master who is an automaton – or as near to one as any human being can come. Moreover, his automatism closely resembles that of a certain kind of novel-reader. The motive with most power over him, and this is true of many novel-readers, is prurience – a mechanical or automaton-like reflex if ever there was one. Thus it is not any story, but the story of Jacques's *amours*, that he is so eager to hear; and in similar fashion, having been betrayed by his bosom-friend the Chevalier de Saint-Ouin, the "terrible condition" he attaches to the Chevalier's pardon is to receive a (salacious) account of his friend's night of love. Now, if listeners make such automaton-like demands on story-tellers, it is for story-tellers, as a matter of self-respect, to frustrate them – as Jacques so unrelentingly does with his unfortunate master, and as the narrator in the novel does with the reader. This business of prurience is indeed no more than an analogy. By an act of foresight Diderot could be said to have imagined all those subservient roles that, in the following century, readers would impose upon novelists, and novelists would be eager to fill: those of slave, friend, nurse, pandar and invisible and butler-like servant.

Just how richly Diderot explores this theme of automatism in fiction – the reader who is an automaton or who wants the novelist to be an automaton – can be seen when his narrator, for a second time, bridles at the Reader's literal-minded question, where are Jacques and his Master going? "Where are you going yourself?" he retorts, truculently. Most of the time, one is simply "following" (within which term is included the sense of grasping the meaning of following as we "follow" a story or an argument).

> Jacques followed his master as you do yours; his master followed
> his, as Jacques followed his master. – But who was Jacques's
> Master's master? – Well: there is no shortage of masters in this
> world. Jacques's Master had a hundred if he had one, just like
> you. But none of Jacques's Master's masters can have been any
> good, for he changed them from day to day. – He was a man. – A
> man with passions, like you, Reader; a question-asking man, like
> you, Reader. – So why did he like to ask questions? – A pretty
> question! He asked questions to learn something and be able to
> repeat it to others, like you, Reader . . .[20]

This telling pointing of the finger at the Reader must – one can feel sure – have been the inspiration for Baudelaire's famous "*Hypocrite lecteur, – mon semblable, – mon frère.*"

The "economy" of the novel comprises four leading

participants, Jacques, his Master, the Narrator and the Reader, and Diderot, taking his cue from Sterne, plays various brilliant games with them. The Narrator not only complains of ill-treatment by the Reader, he is also at times extremely rude to him. At one point he overdoes it and, having been especially insulting over his stupid parrot-cry "*In vino veritas*," he makes a becoming apology.[21] At another moment the Narrator gets into a bad tangle; he interrupts the story of Jacques and his Master in order to continue the story of Gousse ("the man with one shirt"), is then interrupted by the Reader, who wants to hear the story of "the man scraping the double-bass", and eventually, in his confusion, resumes the story of Jacques and his Master in the wrong style and as though he had actually been a participant – for which he gets sharply pulled up by the Reader.[22]

These amusements and diversions serve a deep purpose, one intrinsic to Diderot's conception of fiction as a form with its roots in fraud and deception. He presents this theme in teasing fashion. One of the Narrator's favourite ploys is to warn the Reader against automatic scepticism and against assuming that, just because there is no limit to the fictions that a story-teller can devise, everything being related is a fiction. This the Narrator then supports by an argument exactly designed to arouse scepticism. "You are going to take the history of Jacques's Captain for a story," says the Narrator, "and you will be wrong. I protest to you that I heard the tale myself, just as he told it to his Master, at the Invalides, on the day of Saint-Louis, I forget in what year, at the table of a certain Monsieur de Saint-Etienne, who was majordomo there."[23] The argument is, of course, a naive specimen of exactly the "no one would invent a detail like that" device (we think of it as the Defoe technique) that Diderot analysed at the end of *The Two Friends from Bourbonne*.

The Narrator likes to dumbfound the Reader with the freedom of the fiction-writer to make anything whatever happen. What is to stop the Narrator marrying Jacques's Master off and making him a cuckold, or despatching Jacques to the West Indies and causing him, by amazing coincidence, to be rejoined by his Master there and bringing them home in the same vessel? "How easy it is to write stories!" Some novelists have felt this godlike or monstrous freedom to be a serious problem (Thomas Hardy was one), but Diderot chooses to give the problem only joke answers: the "fatalist" answer, that he will not cause such events to happen because it is not "written" that he shall do so; or the *This Is Not a Story* answer, i.e. that what he is recounting is not fiction but truth. He also actively burlesques the problem, by creating marvellous coincidences, which, fictionally speaking, go all wrong – like Jacques' touching encounter with his beloved Captain's coffin, which turns out not to contain the Captain at all but smugglers' booty . . . or maybe a kidnapped woman . . . "Make it what you will," says Jacques' Master, who is getting bored and wants to *hear* a story, not participate in one.

When we consider the two great set-pieces of narration in *Jacques the Fatalist*, the Hostess's story of Madame de la Pommeraye and the Marquis des Arcis's story of Father Hudson, we realise Diderot's deeper intention in all this. It is important to grasp the close connection between these tales and the issues and paradoxes that the Narrator, albeit in mocking manner, has been raising about fictional veracity and the struggle for mastery between tellers of fiction and listeners. For these two narratives are stories *about* fictions and mystifications. Mme de la Pommeraye, for the purposes of her revenge on her faithless aristocratic lover, stage-manages a most elaborate charade, hoodwinking the proud des Arcis into proposing marriage to a prostitute. It is a plausible fiction such as a Richardson might have envied, and a fiction, moreover, which calls for despotic mastery on the part of its creator. Mme de la Pommeraye demands "illimitable submission" from the human instruments of her revenge, the impoverished Mme d'Aisnon and her daughter. She tells them so in so many words; they are to be her automata.[24]

Diderot is dealing here with the same knot of issues as in his short stories, and especially in *On the Inconsistency of Public Opinion*. Mme de la Carlière is a "saint", Mme de la Pommeraye is a vengeful fury, but in their overweening views, their insistence on controlling circumstances and on imposing their own rigid patterns on others, the two women are closely akin – and, in the light of what we may call the "Jacques" doctrine, they must both be accounted mad.

For the spirit in which Mme de la Pommeraye conducts her vengeful charade and determines so masterfully to manipulate appearances is the same hubristic one that led her, in the first place, to extract "the most solemn vows" of eternal fidelity from her lover. Against such exorbitant demands, Diderot's novel appeals to the known conditions of life, in a world which is in ceaseless decay and flux and in which all living creatures are hurtling into the void.

> The first vow exchanged between two creatures of flesh was made at the foot of a rock crumbling into dust; they called as witness a sky which is never for two instants the same; everything within them and outside of them was passing away, and they believed their hearts safe from vicissitudes. O children, still children![25]

This sulphurous story of wilfulness and obsession is, moreover, given a calmly and beautifully ironic conclusion: for the Marquis accepts his fate and decides to be happy with his deceitful bride. Jacques's doctrine is vindicated. "We think we are leading destiny, but it is he, every time, who is leading us."

This is one aspect of the story. Another works in an opposite direction. Just as we are induced at first to sympathise with the high-minded Mme de la Carlière, scepticism supervening only later; so, after shuddering at the pitiless Mme de la Pommeraye, we begin to find or be offered excuses for her. The Narrator takes on her defence (Jacques and his Master being otherwise occupied) and provides a very cogent one. There is at least genius and force in her action ("You may fear Mme de la Pommeraye, but you will not despise her") and also a sort of purity ("Her vengeance is atrocious, but it is not stained with the slightest trace of self-interest.") Moreover we need have no reverence for the judgement the world passes on her, for in such matters the "world" is utterly venal, inconsistent and self-interested. "You fall into fury at the name of Mme de la Pommeraye and you exclaim 'Ah, that horrible woman! That hypocrite! That criminal!'" That is how reputations are formed, and it is a shabby business. We want none of this exclaiming, this rage, this partiality, says the Narrator; instead, "Let us think about the matter reasonably."

We have here almost the whole of Diderot's "matter" as a novelist. His fiction always, in some sense, had reputation-making as its theme. *The Nun*, it will be recalled, is all about reputation-making – the agonising effort, the duplicities even, required of Diderot's Nun if she is to interest the world beyond the convent wall in her fate – and the Father Hudson episode in *Jacques the Fatalist* is an ironic version of the same theme. To protect his reputation, the rascally and lecherous Abbot Hudson shows a genius for mystification quite the equal of Mme de la Pommeraye's, and his story serves as a comic alternative to the Pommeraye one. It proves that it *is* possible to control appearances – on condition that appearances are absolutely all you care about and you do not give a damn what people really think. The story has a delicious throwaway conclusion, which is as much the ultimate comment on it as the unexpected happy-ending is on the Pommeraye one. The unfortunate (or perhaps fortunate) Richard, set on by the General of his order to expose Hudson and instead, by Hudson's superior talent, disgraced and driven out of the religious life himself, has a chance encounter with his old adversary and asks Hudson to admit, at least, that he is a dreadful rascal. The abbot demurs and spars, with his usual effrontery: then he gets bored and contemptuously floors the young man with the words: "My dear Richard, *vous vous f . . . de moi* [You take me for the most disgraceful shit], and you are perfectly right!"

It is to be noticed that what Diderot is exploring in fiction is the opposite of his "statue-building" concept of ethics. According to the latter, one must do what one does regardless of the opinion of others – by the same "fourth wall" law according to which actors and paintings ought not to address themselves directly to a spectator; though, if one's actions are virtuous, a "statue" of oneself will be erected in the minds of others that one will henceforth be loath to break. (For the *ultimate* sanction of our behaviour is, and has to be, other people's opinion.) By contrast, the Pommerayes, Hudsons and Carlières are attempting to manipulate reputation and prescribe to the world what social and moral judgements it shall pass on them – a tempting endeavour, especially for those with a genius for mystification, but in the end vain and productive of tragedy or absurdity. It is a mistake from which the "Jacques" doctrine, of letting destiny lead us, can save us.

I have spent much time on the self-subverting and anti-novel aspects of *Jacques the Fatalist*, and these are very important; but of course the novel is meant to be read in many other ways too. As Pierre Saint-Amand has pointed out, we should no doubt see in the Master and Jacques a mocking allusion to Newtonian versus non-Newtonian science, the watch-obsessed Master representing classical Newtonian time and a general fixation on measuring, as opposed to the "unoriented" time of the newer sciences.

More generally, that opening paragraph ("How did they come to meet? By chance, like everyone else," etc.) affirms determinism and materialism with all the explicitness one could ask. It evokes not only a world without purposiveness or design, but also one in which time and sequence are illusory and, by corollary, human identity is under question (hence, what need to know Jacques' or his Master's name?). For if the universe is eternal and will endure to all eternity, and not only individuals but species are transient and fleeting, it seems best to think of the world not as a sequence but as a stasis or eternal present. This is the aspect of Diderot's novel that impressed Schopenhauer, who, in his *The World as Will and Idea*, quoted what he called "that very remarkable and, in its context, astonishing passage" about the château in which Jacques and his Master sojourn: "An immense château, on the façade of which one read, 'I belong to nobody, and I belong to everybody; you were here before you entered, and you will still be here after you have left.' " Diderot's château is, for Schopenhauer, an inspired rendering of the illusoriness of time.

> To the eye of a being who lived an incomparably longer life and took in at a glance the human race in its whole duration, the constant alternation of birth and death would present itself merely as a continuous vibration. Accordingly, it would not occur to it at all to see in it a constantly new coming out of nothing and passing into nothing . . .[26]

Schopenhauer has understood Diderot very well; and not the less for the fact that, a moment later, the passage turns into political allegory – the château and its squatters (who, in defiance of the inscription, claim rights of possession over it) becoming a satire on the *ancien régime*.

I have said that in *Jacques the Fatalist* Diderot depicted himself as he would like to be and in many ways would lay claim to being. One can hardly miss the point, for Jacques is, among other things, visibly an apologia for many of his own faults, or imputed faults: his talkativeness (Jacques blames it on the gag), his officiousness, his passion for paradox, his relentless scepticism, his ribaldry and his outrageous outspokenness.

The clue or pointer in all this, biographically speaking, is "fatalism". For it was important in Diderot's mind that, buffeted as he might be by Fortune, he had been favoured in his birth. He was one of those mortals who are endowed by Nature or destiny with a whole array of virtues, talents and good qualities His addiction to self-praise finds its justification here, it being a continual and beautiful surprise to him what precious qualities, what capacities for ardent feeling or original thought, he discovered in himself. This was no occasion for vanity, for he might just as easily have had the misfortune to be born an imbecile or a criminal.

The number of shining virtues attributed to Jacques is, when one comes to count them, very large; and they are all linked to "fatalism" or respect for the necessary. "Destiny, for Jacques, was everything that touched or came near him: his horse, his master, a monk, a dog, a woman, a mule, a crow."[27] The trait is shown to be, among other things, a source of sensitivity and considerateness in his relationship to the world. As I remarked earlier, the story of his *amours* is hardly the luscious or scabrous chronicle that his Master might have hoped for, but more the history of certain unpremeditated delicacies and generosities. One recalls the scene in Desglands' château in which, in desperation, the housekeeper's daughter Denise offers herself to Jacques, who – exactly for that reason – cannot bring himself to accept.

The same respect for necessity fosters a feeling for the

"concrete", a faculty or flair from which, as we know, Diderot believed most real discoveries to spring. Jacques is doctrinaire on this subject, holding (as Diderot did) that words have a way of becoming too abstract and losing purchase on real objects; and he arranges one or two painful lessons for his Master in the experimental understanding of words.

Fatalism teaches the right kind of prudence ("He [Jacques] was prudent, with the greatest contempt for prudence") and the right kind of restraint, the kind that Diderot blamed himself for not possessing. "Jacques, you are a barbarian, you have a heart of bronze," his Master tells him. "No Monsieur, no," replies Jacques. "I have sensibility, but I reserve it for a better occasion. Those who squander such wealth find they have none left when they need it in large quantity."[28]

It is only near the end of the novel that we are given much idea of Jacques's physical appearance; and appropriately we find him, or at least his hat, to be of heroic proportions, making him (as the Narrator himself implies) a figure out of Rabelais.

> After this nonsense and other conversations of the same
> importance [Jacques and his Master have been discussing free
> will] they fell silent; and Jacques turned up the brim of his
> enormous hat, an umbrella in bad weather, a parasol in good, and
> a head-protection at all seasons, the shady sanctuary under which
> one of the best brains the world has yet seen consulted destiny on
> great occasions . . . When the wings of the hat were turned up, his
> face appeared somewhere about the middle of his body; when they
> were turned down, he could hardly see ten paces in front of him,
> and this had given him the habit of raising his nose to the wind.
> On such occasions one could say of his hat:
>
> > *Os illi sublime dedit, coelumque tueri*
> > *Jussit, et erectos ad sidera tollere vultus.*
> > [It gave to man an uplifted face and bade him stand erect and
> > turn his eyes to heaven]
> > (Ovid, *Metamorph.*, Book I, line 85)[29]

Jacques, we learn, always travels with a drinking-gourd tied to his saddle, and when, for a moment, foresight fails him, he will draw inspiration from the gourd. It is a kind of "portable oracle", silent as soon as it is empty. "At Delphi," says the Narrator, "the Pythoness, sitting bare-bottomed on the tripod with her skirts trussed up, received her inspiration from below. Jacques, on his horse, with his head turned to the heavens and his gourd uncorked, its throat tilted towards his mouth, received his from above."[30] There follows a disquisition on Jacques' disagreements with Rabelais, whom he reveres, on the subject of divination.

According to Bakhtin, the "carnival spirit", the spirit of Rabelais, takes all its inspiration from below: it is a "degradation", a descent, which "digs a bodily grave for a new birth".[29] It is an appealing fact that Diderot, after all a partisan of "enlightenment", makes Jacques adopt the opposite and heavenwards-looking posture.

25

Epilogue:
The Afterlife of Diderot

It remains to tell the story of what one might call the "afterlife" of Diderot. For it is hard to think of another great writer who has taken quite so long to come into focus, if indeed he has fully done so even now. One all-important cause of this is, of course, that it was not till many years after his death that some even of his major works were published. (His minor ones are still coming out, two centuries later.) Thus his *oeuvre* not only has looked different at successive periods, it has actually been different.

Another lesser cause lies, perhaps, with the term "The Enlightenment", which has not been much help in understanding Diderot. Naturally, I am not suggesting that it is not intensely significant how writers of Diderot's period, and Diderot himself, used the word "enlightenment" (*lumières*, *Aufklärung*) – or, for that matter, the terms *philosophe, honnêteté* and so on. My complaint is against the definite article in the phrase "The Enlightenment".[1] It is a twentieth-century coinage, and, one imagines, sprang originally from a mistranslation; for the natural sense of *Die Aufklärung* is simply "enlightenment". (After all, one would not translate *Das Kapital* as "The Capital".) What is more, "*The* Enlightenment" is a phrase it is impossible to translate into French, indeed very hard even to *think* in that language. The standard French term has remained the unpretentious one "*lumières*" ("lights").

That reifying "The", turning "enlightenment" into a discrete thing or completed event, has been a reinforcement to what you might call the *unifying* – or, to use Scholastic language, "realist" – tendency in the History of Ideas. With all the respect that one feels towards Ernst Cassirer, I cannot help thinking it a basic fallacy in his famous *Die Philosophie der Aufklärung* (1932)[2] to suppose that by meditating upon the word "enlightenment" (let alone "*The* Enlightenment") one will arrive at deeper and deeper truths about Voltaire, d'Alembert and Diderot, or Hume, Adam Smith and Kant. One sees the results of this in the manoeuvres to which he is driven to prove, by an appeal to *depth* and to *time*, that these eighteenth-century rationalists were united: to show, for instance, that they were all – at the *deepest* level and considering the *future* they unconsciously were serving – on the side of "belief". (By what sorcery could d'Alembert ever be shown to have been on the side of "belief"?)[3]

A truer way of looking at things, surely, would be to say that the beliefs and attitudes these writers agreed to share were at once exceedingly important and rather obvious – almost, as you might say, commonplaces. We have abundant need to think about Diderot's and Voltaire's and d'Alembert's attitudes towards "enlightenment" (and they were very different) but it is not going to be the key to what is subtlest and profoundest in their writings. "Diderot: always followed by d'Alembert"; Flaubert put his finger on the problem in his *Dictionary of Received Ideas*,[4] and it is just such "received ideas" that the Cassirer method seems doomed to perpetuate. It becomes, in a way, an actual obstacle to understanding, shall we say, *Rameau's Nephew* or *D'Alembert's Dream*.

For so celebrated a man as Diderot, the public reaction to his death in 1784 was rather muted. It was not news on the scale of the deaths of Rousseau and Voltaire; and indeed, during the five years still to come before the Revolution, his name was never very prominent. It was, of course, partly a matter of the very success of the *philosophique* campaigns. The "party of humanity" had become a power in the land, controlling the Académies and a large part of the press and influencing government at every level. It was even possible for such as Simon Linguet,[5] in his proto-revolutionary *Annales politiques, civiles et littéraires*, to represent them as an exclusive and repressive clique, menacing to the interests of the Third Estate. There were those who said, moreover, that d'Holbach's *System of Nature*, which was to have spelled the triumph of "philosophy", had destroyed the charm of the new doctrine by revealing its secrets all too well.[6] These last years of the *ancien régime* belonged, in the public imagination, not to Diderot and his friends so much as to Rousseau. Half France, it was said, made a yearly pilgrimage to Rousseau's grave on the Isle of Poplars and the romantic forest "hermitage" his patron the Marquis de Girardin had constructed round it.

In Diderot's own circle, his death was naturally felt as a huge event, and Angélique and Naigeon, almost simultaneously, set to work to compose memoirs of him, though for a variety of reasons, among them the Revolution, these were not published for many years, indeed not till after their own deaths. Diderot's works were still the staple of Henri Meister's *Correspondance littéraire* and would continue to be so right up to the Revolution and even briefly after it; and Meister published a tribute, *To the Shade of Diderot*, as a pamphlet in 1787. This moving and in certain ways discerning document begins with a reproach to Meister himself and his friends for their neglect.

> O Diderot! How many days have passed since your genius was extinguished, since the darkness of the tomb covered your lifeless ashes! And of all the friends to whom you sacrificed your sleepless nights, on whom you lavished the resources of your talent and the riches of your imagination, none has yet made it his business to raise a monument to you, worthy of the gratitude owed to you by friendship, your own century, and the future!

Meister speaks of Diderot as unquestionably an extraordinary prodigy, "the most naturally encyclopaedic head that perhaps ever existed."

> When I remember Diderot, the immense variety of his ideas, the astonishing multifariousness of his knowledge, the rapid soaring, ardour and impetuous tumult of his imagination, the charm and disorder of his conversation, I dare compare his soul to Nature, such as he pictured her himself: rich, fertile, abounding in seeds of every species, whether tame, wild, simple, majestic, kindly or sublime, but with no governing principle – without master and without God.[7]

Nevertheless (this was the refrain of Meister's tribute) Diderot had so squandered his energies on behalf of others that, as a writer, he had left no work that quite put him in the front rank. It meant that his was the sort of reputation that future generations would have to take on trust.

For Angélique, her father's death was a devastating blow, and she found what comfort she could in dealing with his papers. According to his wishes, when despatching his library to Catherine the Great, she also sent a copy of the manuscripts in her possession, some thirty-two volumes of them. She kept the originals, however, many of them in her father's own hand, and set to work to fulfil his plans for a collected edition, being helped, now or later, by her husband Vandeul. Naigeon, whom Diderot had appointed as his literary executor and who also possessed manuscripts, had a long-term plan for an edition on his own account, and an edginess gradually developed between him and the Vandeuls.

The work was Angélique's great consolation, but after a year or two she realised it had become a morbid obsession, so for a while she had to force herself to stop. With her father gone, she was tending to grow more religiously orthodox, and Vandeul, by now a very prosperous ironmaster, was a stickler for appearances; hence in their editing they censored and bowdlerised freely – though, to their credit, they did not obliterate the offending passages. By the time of the Revolution they were still floundering in the huge mass of material.

D'Holbach died in January 1789; thus the most important members of Diderot's circle still surviving at the time of the Revolution were Naigeon, Grimm and the *abbé* Raynal. Of these Raynal's was the most famous name. He was living in Marseilles, still partially in exile, for he was not allowed to set foot in Paris; but in August 1790 the National Assembly rescinded all remaining sanctions against him, allowing him to return to Paris. He took it as a solemn call on him to mediate between King and People, and in May 1791, upon his arrival in Paris, he and two friends[8] composed a highly critical "Address" to the Assembly, condemning the political clubs as places where "coarse and ignorant men" pronounced upon subjects they knew nothing about and attacked the sacred principle of property. On 31 May Robespierre read this Address to the Assembly, with much scorn, proposing, in view of Raynal's great reputation, that they should excuse it as the ramblings of a dotard. The Jacobin club of Marseilles forthwith moved the bust of Raynal out of their clubroom into the local lunatic asylum.

Naigeon, as might have been expected, welcomed the Revolution wholeheartedly, and late in 1790 he too drew up an "Address" to the National Assembly, attacking the moderate views of the *abbé* Morellet in some recent articles and declaring the Assembly to be entitled to limit the powers of the Crown in any way it saw compatible with the *Declaration of the Rights of Man*. But, he lamented, what a fatal error had been made by the framers of that *Declaration*, in including a reference to "the Divinity", and how much remained to be done to curb those "ferocious beasts" the clergy, men motivated almost solely by greed. It was the Assembly's duty, he said, to ensure that those "who believed nothing, and in consequence had nothing to chant", should not be obliged to pay the upkeep of a Church.[9]

This was Naigeon's last political intervention, and from now on he devoted his energies to the atheistic "Philosophy Ancient and Modern" (his rewriting of Diderot's *Encyclopédie* articles) in the *Encyclopédie méthodique*.[10] He published the third and last volume at the height of the Terror, a bold move, for by now atheism had been denounced by Robespierre as a threat to the Republic. No more principled an atheist than Naigeon has perhaps ever existed. He was as shocked by the "unprincipled atheism" of the Hébertists as by the deism of Robespierre and went about railing as loudly against the one as against the other. He survived unscathed, however, and in 1797–98 he produced the first "complete" (of course extremely incomplete) posthumous edition of Diderot's works.

As for Grimm, in his eyes the Revolution was, from the very beginning, an unmitigated disaster. On the day after the storming of the Bastille he was prophesying national bankruptcy and the taking-over of the reform movement by the "dregs" of the people. His thoughts instinctively ran to the Queen, and, as

Catherine's unofficial agent, he made extracts from Catherine's private letters to himself for the eyes of Marie-Antoinette, as proof to her of the Empress's great sympathy with the royal couple. His own position was dangerous, as the representative of a hostile foreign power, and before long he took refuge in Germany. Late in 1781, however, he ventured on one more visit to the "abyss", to rescue Catherine's letters, before retreating to Brussels. At the time of Mme d'Epinay's death he had adopted her grand-daughter, the "Emilie" of her *Conversations with Emilie*, and when war broke out they made a headlong flight through the Low Countries, before the advancing French armies, and found asylum in Gotha, which Grimm from now on made his permanent home.

Grimm had left his grandly-furnished lodgings in the rue de la Chaussée d'Antin in the charge of a servant, thinking it prudent to make no effort to remove his belongings, and hoping that he might be granted diplomatic immunity. Before long, however, he was officially declared an *émigré*, and all his possessions, including a mass of Diderot manuscripts, were sequestrated, together with his investments in government funds. When, four years later, his name was finally taken off the list of *émigrés*, the possessions had been sold and he was reimbursed in quite worthless *assignats*, together with three lace cuffs and a few lengths of muslin. He told a friend sardonically that France, it would seem, valued these pieces of fabric at 20,000 to 30,000 *livres* each.[11] Catherine and her successor Paul continued to find him some employment during these last years in Gotha, till blindness forced him to retire, but he was a disconsolate and ruined man. Goethe met him in 1801, six years before his death, in the summer-house of the Prince Augustus at Gotha, and noted: "A man of the world, rich in experience, and an agreeable fellow-guest, but not always able to conceal his profound bitterness at all he has lost."[12]

There is a famous account, said to have been found among La Harpe's papers, of a dinner-party held at the beginning of 1788 in the house of an Academician. The guests included many famous people, including Condorcet, Chamfort, Lamoignon de Malesherbes and the Duchesse de Grammont, and the tone that evening was very libertine and "*philosophique*". One guest recited from Voltaire's scandalous *La Pucelle*, and another quoted Diderot's lines about strangling the last king with the guts of the last priest. They agreed that the "revolution" they had all been working for, when superstition and fanaticism would give way to philosophy, could not now be long in coming, and they took bets as to who would witness the "reign of reason". Only one of the guests, the elderly *illuminé* Cazotte, remained silent, till, in grave tones, he told them he had a certain gift of foresight and could assure them they would all of them see their "grand and sublime revolution". They might also, he said, like to hear some of its results: such as that Condorcet would commit suicide in prison, Chamfort would cut his veins with a razor, and Malesherbes would go to the scaffold in a cart, as would the Duchess and "even greater ladies . . ." "What, princesses of the blood?" they asked . . . "Even greater," replied Cazotte: at which his host frowned and said that he was taking a joke too far.[13]

We do not have to believe this story, and in fact it would be hard to, but it reminds us of a theory of the Revolution as the more or less direct work of the *philosophes* – a notion that took a century or more to die. It was never a very convincing theory, if only because it is hard to detect that Diderot and his friends had much influence on the active leaders of the Revolution. (Whereas, perhaps significantly, two of the most relentless enemies of Diderot and his circle, Palissot and the younger Fréron, became extreme Revolutionaries.) It is true that Robespierre referred to the *encyclopédistes* as part of the "preface" to the Revolution; but he also said of them, cuttingly, "That sect, in matters of politics, always remained below the rights of the people, and in matters of ethics it went far beyond the destruction of religious prejudices. Its *coryphées* sometimes declaimed against despotism, and they were pensioned by despots."[14]

At all events, if there was relative silence about Diderot in the years immediately after his death, the same can be said of the early years of the Revolution, and his name is not often mentioned in the speeches and writings of the Revolutionary leaders. In contrast, during the Revolutionary period, Rousseau-worship mounted to extraordinary heights. At the Festival of Triumph on

14 July 1790 the bust of Jean-Jacques, carved from a stone from the Bastille and crowned with laurels, was borne through the streets of Paris, attended by six hundred white-gowned girls and troops of guardsmen, their firearms wreathed with flowers. In October, with even more lavish pomp, his ashes were brought from Ermenonville to be laid in the Panthéon. (Thérèse, not being allowed to join the procession, watched from the windows of an inn.)

Matters changed dramatically for Diderot, however, near the end of *An* IV, during the "Thermidorian" reaction. In July 1796 the *abbé* Bourlet de Vauxcelles, a journalist and miscellaneous writer once friendly with Diderot, published two important texts of his, the *Supplement to Bougainville's "Voyage"* and the sceptical *Conversation of a Philosopher with the Maréchale de ****, in a collection of pieces entitled *Opuscules philosophiques et littéraires*, and accompanied them with a violent attack on him, as being the inventor of *sansculotterie* and the man who had taught the terrorists Hébert and Chaumette their contempt for God ("the great Workman") and for magistrates and priests. Two months later a new journal, the *Décade philosophique*, the organ of a group known as "Ideologists" claiming descent from Diderot, published his poem "The Eleutheromaniacs", with its lines about strangling the last king with the guts of the last priest. Also, in the same month, the publisher Buisson issued the first editions of *Jacques the Fatalist* and *The Nun*. He was printing from manuscripts stolen from Grimm's sequestrated papers, though it so happened that, at much the same time, Frederick the Great's brother, Prince Henry of Prussia, in a much-publicised gesture, had presented the newly founded Institut de France with his own private copy of *Jacques the Fatalist*. Diderot's name was, suddenly, enormously in the news, and by October 1796 there had begun, according to an observer, "a universal onslaught" on his memory.

The two novels received a flood of reviews, some of them very lengthy, though for the most part angrily polemical, using the two books as fodder for the debate about the Revolution.[15] "It was reserved by Providence to the Anacharsis Clootses, the Gobets, the Héberts, the Chaumettes and the Fauchets," fulminated *La*

Quotidienne, "to complete the revolution which the moral author of *Indiscreet Jewels* and that of *La Pucelle* had begun so long before." There was complaint that a prince should have lent support to so "obscene" and nihilistic a work as *Jacques the Fatalist*. *The Nun* was attacked as "a masterpiece of implausibility and depraved morality" and defended, equally polemically, as "a work kept in reserve by philosophy" to repress any backsliding into "impious superstition". The journal *L'Eclair*, itself sympathetic to Diderot, remarked on what a flattering reception his two novels would have had if they had appeared ten years earlier. "But today what a chorus of imprecations against their author! He is impious! a monster! a corrupter of morals! A certain *abbé* [i.e. Bourlet de Vauxcelles], who once preferred chatting with Diderot to reading his breviary, is suddenly carried away by apostolic zeal and rends the memory of the philosopher, whom, when alive, he called his friend."

Amidst all this there were one or two discerning reviews, especially a long one on *The Nun* in the *Décade philosophique*, which spoke of Diderot's portrait of the lesbian Prioress as worthy of Racine: "It is not libertinism, it is the most ardent, the most irresistible love; it is Sappho; it is Phèdre; '*C'est Vénus toute entière à sa proie attachée.*' " It is noticeable that this, and one or two other reviews, defended Diderot's right to depict lesbian passion and praised his objective handling of it, an attitude not met again in French criticism till the days of the Third Republic. For all the fog of polemic, Diderot's two novels had established themselves, and before the end of the century there were to be several more editions of both of them, as well as translations into English and other languages.

Meanwhile the campaign to blame the Revolution on the *encyclopédistes and philosophes*, with Diderot as their ringleader, continued in full force. The great excitement of the early months of 1797 was the trial of Babeuf and his followers, for their terrorist plot against the Directory, and in his impassioned speeches in his own defence Babeuf repeatedly named Diderot as the inspirer of his communistic theories. He was referring to the *Code of Nature* – a work not in fact by Diderot at all – but his words were a gift to Diderot's enemies.

Just at this time La Harpe, who had been imprisoned during the Terror and had undergone a religious conversion, was beginning a series of lectures on literature at the fashionable Lycée in the rue de Valois; and he used it for an exhaustive and furiously hostile critique of Diderot's whole published *oeuvre*, pointing to Babeuf as the logical outcome of his theories.

La Harpe's motto, which became the epigraph of the published text, was *A fructibus eorum cognoscetis eos*, "By their fruits ye shall know them." For had not Diderot written in his *Philosophical Thoughts* of 1746 that "Only passions, and great passions, can raise mankind to great things"? What more direct encouragement could a *sansculotte* ask for?

> All the fine maxims that you have just heard me reading, and a
> thousand others in which immorality, here still half in the
> shadows, finally faces the light of day, became the code of vice and
> crime, which only needed the support of some authority. As I
> speak, it is public knowledge, and you all know it, Gentlemen, that
> it was from the very writings I have been analysing that a
> monster, whose name I can barely bring myself to utter, a name,
> however, which says everything – *Babeuf* – drew his own
> principles.[16]

As for the *Code of Nature* itself, La Harpe told his audience, it was true that it did not directly advocate massacre and pillage; but considering that the "Reason" of the *philosophes* so plainly urged the overturning of all human and divine authority, who should blame the People for obeying it in literal fashion? After all, it was not as if Diderot had not summed up and "crowned" his own doctrines, for all time, in two lines of verse: "And with the guts of the last priest, Let us strangle the last king."

La Harpe's three hundred-odd pages on Diderot make dreary reading, for he was a banal as well as a rancorous critic and has only one answer to any of Diderot's paradoxes, that it did not make "good sense"; but his lecture-course, repeated for several years running and reprinted many times in the coming century, did much to colour opinion about Diderot. It was, moreover, followed in 1798 by a more briefly famous *History of Jacobinism* by the Jesuit Barruel, which explained the Revolution as the fruit of a "triple conspiracy" of *philosophes*, freemasons and *illuminés*, and gave a lurid account of Diderot's role in the "secret committee" to which Voltaire's phrase *écrasez l'infâme* had been the password.

In Angélique's eyes this glare of publicity was good reason for withholding her father's unpublished works, perhaps for many years. To Naigeon, who had been at work on a similar enterprise, it seemed, on the contrary, a reason for hurrying the works into print; and late in 1797, to Angélique's great chagrin, he brought out an *Oeuvres de Denis Diderot* in fifteen volumes, with extensive and belligerent commentaries of his own. He explained in his Preface that he had been impelled to it by hearing that a spurious *Works* of 1772 were to be re-issued, and by the fact that, just at the moment when Diderot's ashes had become "sacred to all men of good will", writers like La Harpe were spreading "the blackest poisons on his life". The edition would moreover, he said, be a chance to serve the wishes of his old mentor, who had made him promise to publish certain passages, expressing his true opinions, that "cowardice" had caused him to suppress.

Naigeon's edition was extremely incomplete: it lacked for instance both *Rameau's Nephew*, though it appears that Naigeon at one time possessed a copy, and *D'Alembert's Dream*; and had *Jacques the Fatalist* not already been published, Naigeon would most likely not have included it either, for he thought it worthless. Nevertheless the edition was, according to his own lights, carried out very honourably, and it is an important one in the history of Diderot's text. It was, however, received with silence and indifference. The "Thermidorian" moment, and time for furious pinning of blame for the Revolution, had passed, and with it, or so it seemed, all real interest in Diderot's writings.

At last, towards the end of the Napoleonic period, there began a great and nostalgic vogue for the eighteenth century, and with this Diderot returned to view. In 1812 his old acquaintance Jean-Baptiste Suard,[17] one of the great survivors of the Revolution, published a selection from Grimm and Meister's *Correspondance littéraire*, drawing on a copy seized during Napoleon's occupation of Berlin; and this was so great a success that two further selections, one of them made by Meister himself, followed close on its heels.[18] To feed the same appetite for all things "Louis Quinze", the publisher and bibliographer J.-C. Brunet bought up the manuscript of Mme d'Epinay's semi-fictional *Memoirs of Madame de Montbrillant* from Grimm's friend de Villière and, by dint of ruthless doctoring – replacing the names "Garnier", "Volx", "René" and "Mme de Montbrillant" by the real-life names of Diderot, Grimm, Rousseau and Mme d'Epinay, and removing some of the more obviously fictional episodes altogether – he was able to present it to the public in 1818 as authentic memoirs. It was a great success, imposing on readers its partly imaginary version of events and characters for the rest of the century.

It was at this same moment (1818–19) that the publisher Belin brought out an eight-volume edition of Diderot's works, containing several previously unpublished texts – among them the *Journey Through Holland* and the *Salons* for 1761 and 1769. In his Introduction, the editor, a German historian named Depping, made large claims for Diderot, asserting that foreigners were better able to appreciate him than the French, and gave a brief résumé of *Rameau's Nephew*, but apologised for his failure to find a copy of it.

The hunt was on for Diderot texts. Naigeon, at his death in 1810, had left his Diderot manuscripts to his sister. She offered them to Angélique, who however refused to buy them, and upon this she sold them, together with her brother's "Memoirs of Diderot", to the publisher Brière. It was a very large accession, for Naigeon had by no means published everything, and on the strength of it Brière put in hand an ambitious twenty-volume edition. Depping's account of *Rameau's Nephew* had provoked some excitement about this "lost" novel – which was not in fact lost, for Angélique had a copy in her possession – and in a Prospectus published in 1819 Brière was able to promise that it would appear in his new edition.

A bizarre little imbroglio ensued. Two crooks, the Vicomte de Saur and his friend de Saint-Geniès, took it into their heads to pre-empt Brière and, making a very free and garbled translation back into French of Goethe's German version of *Rameau's Nephew*, published it in 1821 as Diderot's original. What is more, when

Brière's edition of the novel appeared, they denounced it as an obvious forgery, far too incorrect and slangy in style to be by this great author. They maintained their position with great effrontery, and it took a published declaration by Goethe to rout de Saur and Saint-Geniès. "How lightly they treat these matters in France," commented Goethe, who was as impressed, and shocked, as ever by this extraordinary work of Diderot's, "more audacious and *contenue*, more full of brilliance and impudence, more immorally moral" than anything he could have expected to meet.

Reviewers, though bewildered by *Rameau's Nephew*, at once recognised it as, for good or evil, the quintessential Diderot work. "It is Diderot face-to-face with himself, it is Diderot entire," wrote the reviewer in *Le Miroir* (5 February 1822). This infinitely complex work did not fit very well with Naigeon's picture of a single-minded, if not simple-minded, torch-bearer of "enlightenment"; and the reviewers, like Goethe, found it best to regard it historically and as giving some extraordinary, unprecedented insight into *ancien régime* manners. It should be added that Brière and his associate Walferdin cruelly bowdlerised their own text and introduced all sorts of errors, so that readers had to wait another fifty years for anything like a reliable text.[19]

Diderot's texts got themselves published in strange ways. It was true again of the next great accession, a four-volume collection entitled *Mémoires, correspondance et oeuvres inédits*, published by the firm of Paulin in 1831. On the title-page this was said to be based on manuscripts "left, at death, by the author to Grimm". In fact they had been filched from the Hermitage library in St Petersburg by a certain Jeudy-Dugour, a Russianised Frenchman who had become Rector of St Petersburg University. It was a highly important collection, including *D'Alembert's Dream* and a hundred and twenty-three of Diderot's letters to Sophie Volland, as well as Angélique's *Memoir* of her father. From the same illicit haul, the first edition of *The Paradox of the Actor* was published a month or two earlier by an associate of Paulin's, and the play *Is He Good? Is He Wicked?* was published in the *Revue rétrospective* in 1834.

Diderot was emerging from the shadows of rumour and legend,

taking shape as a thoroughly complex and appealing man and as an innovatory author whom a modern writer, not likely to go to school to Voltaire or Marivaux, might learn from. It was Angélique's touching *Memoir*, and above all the letters to Sophie Volland, that were the revelation of Diderot the man. The letters were received with acclamation and some astonishment; for it had often been said that Diderot's true greatness lay in his conversation, and so was unrecapturable, but now, after all, it seemed that one could enjoy it, or at least an excellent equivalent for it, in these letters. Nor was the Diderot who emerged from them the one of legend. Certainly one could find Meister's "most naturally encyclopaedic head that perhaps ever existed"; but he was not Barruel's and La Harpe's sanguinary *sansculotte* or inciter of *sansculottes*, nor was he just Naigeon's visionary and single-minded reformer. He was also witty, dazzlingly original, affectionate, observant and solidly planted on the earth.

The tone of critics accordingly went through a change. They began to insist, sometimes as it were against their will, on a heroic largeness about Diderot. In a succession of three articles during 1830, in the influential conservative *Journal des débats*, the critic and novelist Jules Janin progressed from very moderate praise for Diderot's *Paradox of the Actor* to an admission (it was almost an apology) that he was overwhelmed by this singular and so unclassical author.[20] For Janin it was a decisive conversion, and he later wrote a continuation of *Rameau's Nephew* taking Rameau through the Revolution.

It was somewhat the same with Sainte-Beuve, who reviewed the letters to Sophie Volland in 1830 and again in 1831.[21] The letters were a revelation to him, but, initially, the revelation of a man rather than a writer, a figure who had "spent almost all his life in a false position, in a permanent state of distraction," a genius of heroic proportions, "strong, benevolent, audacious . . . the most German of all our heads", but who had left no monument, or rather had left a monument in fragments. In other words it needed a Sainte-Beuve, with that famous biographical method of his, to reconstruct Diderot. Twenty years later, impressed anew by the *Salons*, Saint-Beuve was ready to praise Diderot much more unreservedly and called him "the directing theoretician *par excellence* of the entire eighteenth century".[22]

With Carlyle, the first English critic to deal with Diderot on any scale, it was another and more extreme case of *unwilling* conversion to Diderot. His essay, written for the *Foreign and Quarterly Review* (1833)[23] as a review of the Paulin edition, is full of noisy jibes at "our ill-starred Mechanical Philosophe-Sentimentalist, with his loud preachings and rather poor performings", and it is loudly scornful of this man, whose indecency "a pig of sensibility would go distracted if you accused him of it," and yet for all this it keeps sounding an epic note. Of Diderot's thirty years' labour on the *Encyclopédie* Carlyle writes that "only the Siege of Troy may offer some faint parallel," and of *Rameau's Nephew* that "It looks like a Sibylline utterance from a heart all in fusion: no ephemeral thing ... was ever more perennially treated." His conclusion is, in its own terms, wholeheartedly admiring:

> Nevertheless it were false to regard Diderot as a Mechanist and nothing more; as one working and grinding blindly in the mill of mechanical Logic, joyful with his lot there, and unconscious of any other. Call him one rather who contributed to deliver us therefrom: both by his manful whole spirit as a Mechanist, which drove all things to their ultimatum and crisis; and even by a dim-struggling faculty, which virtually aimed beyond this.

Meanwhile, and perhaps more importantly, this figure was being discovered by creative writers, from across the great divide of the Revolution, and looked to as an inspiration and potential model. One gets a sense of the changing face of Diderot from the scattered references that Stendhal made to him over the space of thirty years. Stendhal, whom Zola was to call "the first of Diderot's progeny", had been born in 1783, the year before Diderot's death, and thus he was aware of Diderot and his fellow-*philosophes* as a living memory. His father's clerical friends would give a peculiar grimace when pronouncing, and mangling, the names of Diderot and d'Alembert. "That grimace gave me a deep and intimate enjoyment," wrote Stendhal.[24] He never forgot it, any more than he did the gloomy look and the sermon he

received from a bookseller whom he asked for *Jacques the Fatalist*.[25]
He became a devotee of *Jacques the Fatalist* – it was the one work of
Diderot's, he noted in *Souvenirs d'égotisme*, that he really admired –
and he evidently thought of himself as in some sense continuing
the Diderot tradition. Diderot served for him as the great
example of *esprit* (wit, play of mind). *Esprit* in Diderot, he wrote,
did not become tedious, as it did in most of his contemporaries,
for he had the secret of combining it with grace, loud laughter and
bonhomie.[26]

There is, we may think, something of Diderot in the "coldness" and detachment dear to Stendhal as a novelist. In his
Journal for 1814 Stendhal writes that he has decided to reject
Rousseau's notion of the act of writing as a spontaneous
outpouring. "What I have written in a state of enthusiasm strikes
me later as frigid. I think that Diderot's dissertation on actors
could very well be right." Twenty-five years later, reading the
letters to Sophie Volland, he is by now seeing Diderot as a
monitor and example from an altogether distant culture. "Tone
of 1759. How far removed from prudery and *ennui*, the malady of
1839."

For Balzac, who was forming himself as a writer during the
1820s, the Brière and Paulin editions of Diderot came as
important events. It is noticeable, especially, that whenever
Balzac writes about art there are strong echoes of Diderot. Jean
Seznec has shown that his story *Sarrasine* is, in all sorts of
intricate ways, quarried out of Diderot's *Salon* of 1767.[27] Balzac
thought it a great pity that Diderot the novelist had not
cultivated "that beautiful side to his talent" more; for "he had
only style when telling stories," and in *This Is Not a Story* he had
written "one of the great fragments of the human heart". One of
the things that impressed Balzac in the story was the objectivity
and necessitarianism of Diderot's outlook. It is clear, writes
Balzac, that, for all his pity for the unfortunate Tanié and Mlle
de la Chaux, Diderot in the end takes the side of the ruthless
Mme Reymer and Gardeil. "Love is love, it is ungrateful and
cruel, it goes away as it came, without one's knowing why. It is
the most highly-prized of feelings precisely because it is
involuntary. The beautiful and pitiless Reymer is only

exploiting rights that Society has given her, just as Gardeil is justified under Natural Law."

What impresses him too is the uncluttered quality of Diderot's "impetuous and vivid" tale. "Like a great artist," he does not trouble the reader with the antecedents and background of Gardeil and Mlle de la Chaux. This is no mere happy chance, says Balzac, it is the very heart of his stylistic intention. "Every subject has its own special form. Diderot, in *This Is Not a Story*, sweats truth in every phrase."[28]

Partly through this enthusiasm on Balzac's part, Diderot became a father-figure for the "Realist" movement in France. The movement originated with the painter Courbet, who in 1848 declared his intention only to treat modern and "vulgar" subject-matter, and was transposed to the field of literature by the novelist "Champfleury", a great enthusiast for Diderot. Champfleury shared Balzac's special admiration for *This Is Not a Story*, and in his *Realism* (1857), a manifesto for the movement, he wrote that "Diderot first of all has given in a few lines a theory of style so clear, so new and so arresting that it could not be reprinted too often."[29] During the years 1752–54 Champfleury agitated with passion, though to no avail, to induce the *Comédie Française* to stage Diderot's *Is He Good? Is He Wicked?*, and looking back on these days thirty years later he recalled how "The philosopher was then entering the modern current in full sail," claimed by the Positivists, regarded as a master by novelists and hailed as the father of modern art criticism. "The only thing lacking to that great figure was theatrical glory."[30]

In 1856, during the first stirring days of "Realism", three of its champions, the novelist Duranty, an alienist named Thulié, and Jules Assézat, a staff-member of the *Journal des débats*, launched a journal entitled *Realism*. It was a furious affair, a "siege-engine" in the cause of Realism and the new prose fiction. (On principle, when printing verse, it laid it out without line-divisions, as if it were prose.) It lasted only for six numbers, but Assézat, twenty years later, undertook the great edition of Diderot's *Oeuvres complètes*, the one which has remained standard more or less to the present day. Thus it was under the auspices of "Realism" that Diderot reached his twentieth-century readers.

The truth is that, for the mid-nineteenth century, Diderot served two distinct and potentially contrary roles in people's imaginations, figuring for some as a corrective to the present time, and for others as an anticipator of it. For Gautier, Baudelaire and Gérard de Nerval, the second generation of Romantics, he was the perfect and necessary antidote to the ills, the sentimental rhetoric, prudery and George-Sandism of their own day. This was, likewise, precisely his attraction for Karl Marx, who once declared Diderot his favourite prose-writer[31] and loved him as much as he detested the "coquettish sentiment" and "theatrical sublimity" of Chateaubriand. In 1869 Marx sent Engels a copy of Diderot's "Unique masterpiece" *Rameau's Nephew*, together with Hegel's remarks on it in *The Phenomenology of Spirit* and a diatribe against Jules Janin's sentimental sequel.

> Janin deplores the want of a moral "point" in Diderot's *Rameau*, and remedies this defect through his discovery that the nephew's perversity stems from his chagrin at not being born a *gentilhomme*. The Kotzebuean rubbish he has smeared on this cornerstone is being melodramatically performed in London at this very moment. The passage from Diderot to Jules Janin illustrates, I suppose, what the physiologists call "regressive metamorphosis". There you have your French mind *before* the French Revolution and *under* Louis-Philippe.[32]

For the Goncourt brothers Diderot was a modern master, a living example, the originator of the novel as a sophisticated and intellectual art-form. The Goncourts, though committed "Realists", practising "documentation" and the unflinching rendering of social pathology, were aesthetes and experimenters in prose style. They possessed a much wider sense than Champfleury did of the possibilities open to fiction – like Baudelaire they were, for instance, enthusiasts for the fantastic novel *à la* Hoffmann – thus they could respond to Diderot in a less doctrinaire and more comprehensive way.

Above all, they revered *Rameau's Nephew*. "Re-read RAMEAU'S NEPHEW. What a work that is, what an inspired plunge into the human consciousness!"[33] they wrote in their *Journal*; and they would draw on it in their own *Charles Demailly*, a novel about the

"sufferings of a writer", and again in *Manette Salomon*. They noted
how Daudet had deserted his favourite Montaigne for Diderot
and how Sichel had written that Heine formed his unique
German on the Diderot model. Diderot, they wrote, resembled
Fragonard, the most marvellous of improvisers among painters.
He was the greatest *honnête homme* they had read, able to open up
houses and landscapes and make you breathe the wind. "His
honnêteté enters you, moves you to tears, like sweet summer
rain."[34] Till Diderot, they asserted, there were fictional dialogues
but no true novel (*roman*); it was he who gave fiction movement,
gesture (the Goncourts were fascinated by gesture) and dramatic
life. "The great value, the great originality of Diderot – and no
one has noticed it – is to have introduced into grave and orderly
written prose the vivacity, the *brio*, the agility and slightly mad
disorder, the *tintamarre* and feverish life, of conversation: the
conversation of men of letters, and more particularly of artists,
with whom he is the first French writer to live in real intimacy."[35]
For the Goncourts, who thought their own work was brutally
slighted by philistines, it was a shameful reflection on posterity
that Diderot, "the Homer of modern thought", should have been
put in the shade by that *cerveau de la Garde nationale*, that
"commercial travellers' rhymer", Voltaire. Take away *Candide*
from Voltaire, and what was left?[36]

Among some scientists and sociologists and radical thinkers –
Proudhonians, Positivists and the like – it became, likewise, the
fashion to claim Diderot as a "forerunner" and a nineteenth-
century writer before his day. With his speculative, conjectural,
"dreaming" approach to science, Diderot was, of course, a happy
hunting-ground for "forerunnings" and anticipations of every
kind; but as it turned out, even his scientific writings had an
influence on the nineteenth-century novelist.

Auguste Comte included Diderot as a saint in the Positivist
calendar and declared him "the greatest man of the eighteenth
century"; and Pierre Larousse, in the *Grand Dictionnaire Larousse* of
1867, said that his genius "combines all the titles which must
render him particularly dear to the nineteenth century." "Of all
the men of his time," wrote Larousse, "it is he whose works have

remained . . . by their form as much as by their content, the most interesting and the most alive." Louis Asseline, in his *Diderot and the Nineteenth Century* (1866), spoke of him even more extravagantly, claiming him as the "precursor" of practically every modern trend: his evolutionism anticipated Darwin and Lyell, his *Rameau's Nephew* foreshadowed Socialism, and his visionary materialism "contained all the tenets of the theory recently developed in Germany . . . against the metaphysics of Hegel." "Thus, you see," wrote Asseline, "all the results of the science of our own era, either proved or infinitely probable, are there in embryo in Diderot."[37]

Louis Asseline was the close friend and adviser of Diderot's editor Jules Assézat, and it helps to explain Assézat's dedication to Diderot that he was not only a "Realist" but also a committed materialist and determinist. He edited La Mettrie's *Man the Machine*, and he planned to conclude his great edition of Diderot with a full-length study of Diderot's place in eighteenth-century materialist philosophy, though he died before he could achieve it – worn out, so it was said, by his colossal labours.

Assézat's double interest in Diderot as "realist" and as determinist was shared by Zola, and as a result Diderot looms large in Zola's whole theory of the novel and of the "Naturalist" movement. Zola traced the ancestry of "Naturalism" to the eighteenth-century *philosophes*, and above all to Diderot, who, he wrote, "remains the great figure of the century, glimpsing all truths and moving ahead of his own era." It was Diderot, "the forefather of our positivists of today", who was "the first to apply the methods of observation and experiment to literature."[38] He was thus the father and creator of the "Naturalist" novel, the great claim of which, distinguishing it from "Realism", was that, in the full scientific sense, it was *experimental*. The great physiologist Claude Bernard, wrote Zola, had proclaimed, in his *Introduction to the Study of Experimental Medicine*, that the same deterministic laws applied to living creatures as to inanimate matter. "But ought one to stop there [i.e. with human tissue and organs]?" asked Zola. Clearly not; it was the task of the novelist to apply the experimental methods of science to "the passional and intellectual acts of Man".[39]

The point at stake in regard to Claude Bernard (1813–78) was vivisection. The great battle of his career had been to defeat the view, still held by Cuvier and others, that "determinism" did not apply to living creatures – that there was a "vital force" in living beings which actually acted in opposition to physio-chemical laws. On this issue hung the whole future of vivisection, in which Bernard was a pioneer; and the claim or dream of Zolaesque novelists was to practise "vivisection" and the "surgical" method in their own fiction. Thus it has a nice aptness that, in his old age, Claude Bernard developed a strong interest in Diderot. His friend George Barral, as an amusement for the lonely Bernard, arranged to come to his house every Sunday morning to read aloud to him. At first he tried poetry, but this bored Bernard; then it occurred to Barral to try him with Diderot's *Elements of Physiology*, recently published in the Assézat edition. This was such a success that Bernard dictated lengthy comments on this very "deterministic" text of Diderot's and the two friends got quite some way towards publishing an edition of it. Barral describes their initial readings.

> Claude Bernard would listen attentively, in wintertime crouching over the fire, in summer by the open window, sniffing the flowers I had brought him. He interrupted me frequently, to say: "That is a mistake, and I will explain why." "Diderot has seen clearly." "Diderot is wrong, but he could not be otherwise, considering the backwardness of physiology in his time." "That is truly a vision." "This is better still; it is a prevision."[40]

Thus by the 1870s, the time of the Assézat-Tourneux edition, Diderot had come to life as a man and a writer in several different ways: as a stimulus, a model, a contemporary and a "prophet". The idea of him as a museum-piece and fighter of forgotten battles – Flaubert's "Diderot, always followed by d'Alembert" – was still prevalent but it was losing ground. It was really literary critics, like Barbey d'Aurevilly, and literary historians, like Hippolyte Taine, who found it hardest to take his measure. As the volumes of the Assézat-Tourneux edition came out, Barbey d'Aurevilly – a royalist and man of the church, a dandy with a penchant for the "patrician" and a lifelong love-hate involvement with Diderot – reviewed the successive volumes with extraordinary *panache*, rage and unwilling admiration, later reprinting his reviews in a book, *Goethe and Diderot*. At the heart of his response lay a puzzlement. Why, given all his monstrous defects, did one warm to Diderot? Diderot was a failure in almost every direction: a grovelling materialist, totally devoid of "patrician qualities", a Germanist "mortally opposed to the French genius", a fraud and a charlatan; only in his art-criticism did he show any authenticity. Yet for all that, compared with the "icicle" Goethe ("the great Serpent of this reptile age"), Diderot was a leonine figure, a giant, and a "flame".

Taine felt something of the same bafflement. As the theorist of "Naturalism" and author of the maxim "Vice and virtue are products just like vitriol and sugar," he might have been expected to be well-disposed towards Diderot; but being the upholder of certain classical literary values – restraint, *bienséance*, clarity, good sense – he found him hard to swallow. Diderot, so he wrote in his *Origins of Contemporary France* (1875–93), is indecent without elegance; he cannot paint "pretty blackguards" with the style and finesse of a Crébillon *fils*. He represents a second, unstable generation of writers, following on the healthy one of Montesquieu and Voltaire. He "forces his tone"; he is a volcano always in eruption. He does not possess his ideas, they possess him.

This "volcano" notion of Diderot was still very widespread, only Baudelaire as yet having offered an effective revision of it; and, as we see, it is still at work when, in an extraordinary turn-around, Taine rushes to the extreme of eulogy, depicting Diderot as one of those whose greatness it precisely is that they have no idea of what they are doing.

Among so many better writers, he [Diderot] is the only one who is a true artist, a creator of souls, a mind in which objects, events and personages are born and organise themselves by their own energies, in virtue of their natural affinities, involuntarily, without external intervention, so as to live for themselves and by themselves, outside of all calculation and free of all authorial

strategy . . . This is why he is a great story-teller, a master of
dialogue, in this the equal of Voltaire and by a quite opposite
talent . . . forgetting himself, carried away by his own story,
listening to inward voices, taken by surprise by retorts which come
to him unawares . . . He has said everything on nature, art, ethics
and life in two little works [*D'Alembert's Dream* and *Rameau's
Nephew*] of which twenty successive readings will not lesson the
charm or exhaust the significance . . . There lies the advantage of
those geniuses who do not have empire over themselves.[41]

There were further large events in the afterlife of Diderot: new
espousals or appropriations of him for this or that cause, new
instalments in the picaresque history of his manuscripts – in 1891
Georges Monval came on the autograph manuscript of *Rameau's
Nephew* on a second-hand bookstall – and, from the 1950s
onwards, an absolute torrent of criticism and scholarship. But I
shall quit the story here, at this moment of excited, if puzzled,
awareness that, behind that admirable and slightly wearisome
textbook figure, the editor of the *Encyclopédie*, there lurked an
author of the utmost originality and anarchic strangeness.

Or rather I shall add just one more, decidedly eloquent, detail.
After the completion of the Assézat-Tourneux edition, Assézat's
collaborator Maurice Tourneux was commissioned by the
French government to make the journey to Russia, to draw up a
report on the Diderot manuscripts there. What he did not know
was that, in a château only a few hundred kilometres from Paris
(the Château d'Orquevaux, in the Haute-Marne), a much larger
and more important mass of papers, those of Diderot's daughter
Angélique, was still in existence. The Vandeul family had grown
very grand (Diderot's grandson was made a Peer of France under
the July monarchy), and they had become proportionally
respectable and *bien-pensant* and eager to draw a veil over their
disreputable ancestor. No Diderot admirer would be allowed to
see the papers until after the death of the last of the direct line,
Albert de Vandeul, in 1911; in fact the papers were not examined
and inventoried until after the Second World War, by which time
a number of them had gone astray, and time, rain, and most likely
mice, had done their best to ruin the rest.

Fortunately the damage, even by then, was not complete. It was not nearly so complete, that is to say, as a friend of the Vandeul family, a certain Baron Ernouf, was imagining with glee as early as 1882. Many biographers of this "too-celebrated" author, wrote the Baron that year in the *Bulletin du bibliophile*, had reported that certain of his unpublished manuscripts had been destroyed by members of his family who did not share his religious ideas; and it was quite true that Diderot's mis-named "religious" ideas were not in favour among his descendants. In this respect these descendants had absolutely degenerated, or rather (writes the Baron) been *regenerated*. But the rest of the assertion was not correct.

There still exists a collection of manuscripts which the late M. de Vandeul, Diderot's only grandson, and Mme de Vandeul his wife, who died in 1876 at a very advanced age, always refused to publish or to communicate to strangers . . . Forgotten for many years, they have been rediscovered among Mme de Vandeul's possessions. Unfortunately, or *fortunately, if you prefer* [writes the Baron with relish] these manuscripts, stowed away for many years in damp conditions, are in a state of complete degradation and only with great difficulty can even a word or two now be deciphered.[42]

Appendix

Diderot's Finances

A few notes on Diderot's finances and on prices and earnings generally may be useful. The figures are all extremely approximate.

CURRENCY

Louis = 24 livres (or francs)
Pistole = 10 livres
Ecu = 6 livres
Livre (or franc)
Sou (or sol) = ¹⁄₂₀ livre
Liard = ¼ sou

} These equivalents were subject to fluctuation

PRICES

One could get a modest meal at a *table d'hôte* for 1 *livre*. The price of bread varied from 2 *sous* a pound to 12 *sous* or more in times of scarcity. A bowl of *café au lait* at a street stall cost 2 *sous*. A cheap wig might cost 10 *livres*. A very modest seat at the *Comédie Française* cost 1 *livre*, and at the Opéra, 2 *livres*, 8 *sous*. One could send a letter within Paris by the *petite poste* for 2 *sous*. The fashionable physician Michel-Philippe Bouvard charged 6 *livres* for a consultation and the famous Théodore Tronchin charged 1 *louis*. Chairporters charged 30 *sous* for the first hour, 24 thereafter. There seems to have been a regular fare of 24 *sous* for a short journey by cab (*fiacre*). The journey from Bordeaux to Paris by *carrosse* cost 72 *livres*; the *Messageries* charged somewhat more but undertook to feed its passengers. Rousseau's *Emile* sold for 18 *livres* before it was banned, after which the price rose steeply. The last ten volumes of the *Encyclopédie* sold at 200 *livres* apiece.

RELATIVE EARNINGS

A Paris working man would be likely to earn no more than 300 to 500 *livres* in a year; a good valet earned 120 *livres* (or 180 if he could dress hair), a maid 50/60 *livres*; a clerk, 800 to 1,200 *livres*; a provincial lawyer, 2,000 to 3,000 *livres*. The stipend of a Sorbonne professor was about 1,900 *livres*, and that of a magistrate might be about the same, but he would receive many sweeteners and perquisites on top of this. A President of *Parlement* would earn 6,000 *livres* plus fees. Bishops and the incumbents of great abbeys might receive 40,000 to 100,000 *livres*. The *portion congrue* of a *curé* was 300/500 *livres*. A fashionable Paris physician might earn 8,000 to 10,000 *livres*. Diderot sold *Les Bijoux indiscrets* for 1,200 *livres* (the same amount as that for which Voltaire sold his play *L'Enfant prodigue*), and he got 3,000 *livres* for his *Pensées philosophiques* and also for his translation of Temple Stanyan's *Grecian History*. Rousseau sold his *Emile* for 6,000 *livres*. La Harpe earned 6,000 *livres* as editor of the *Mercure*, and Suard 20,000 as editor of the *Journal de Paris*. The painter Boucher earned 50,000 *livres* a year, and Voltaire's outgoings in his later years were reputedly as high as 200,000 *livres*. It has been estimated that to live "comfortably" in Paris one needed 3,000 to 4,000 *livres* a year, and to live in grand style, at least 15,000 *livres*.

DIDEROT'S PERSONAL FINANCES

Diderot began to receive payment for work on the *Encyclopédie*, not yet being a chief editor, in 1746, being paid 60 *livres* in February, 45 in March, 90 in April, 120 in June. In October 1747 he and d'Alembert signed a new contract, by which Diderot was to get 7,200 in all (1,200 to be paid on publication of Vol. I and the remaining 6,000 at the rate of 144 *livres* a month). In 1759 he entered into a new contract, as a result of which, for his work on the remaining seven volumes, he could expect 25,000 *livres*. (Voltaire, hearing this from d'Alembert, wrote indignantly: "Is it true that, for this immense work and twelve years' labour, Diderot will receive 25,000 francs, whilst those who supply bread to our armies earn 20,000 a day?") In June of the same year, Diderot's father died, and under his will his estate was divided between his three children equally, bringing Diderot an additional annual income of 1,500 *livres*. He calculated to Grimm (3/4 August 1759) that by the end of his work on the *Encyclopédie* his annual total should be 3,000 to 4,000 *livres* – sufficient for him if he were not reckless. In 1765 Catherine the Great bought his library for 16,000 *livres* and appointed him its Librarian at an annual stipend of 100 *pistoles* (1,000 *livres*). In 1766 he noted that he was receiving 4,600 a year, and in the following year he invested 70,000 *livres* with a tax-farmer. At his daughter's marriage in 1772 he gave her a dowry of 100,000 *livres*.

It is difficult to form any picture of the total that Diderot earned by his pen, apart from his work on the *Encyclopédie*. He would certainly have been paid by Raynal for his work on the *Histoire des deux Indes*. Whether he ever received payment from Grimm for contributions to the *Correspondance littéraire* is not known: the fact that there is no mention of it suggests that he did not.

Chronology of Diderot's Writings

The following list of Diderot's writings, indicating the rough date of composition, where known, the date in which a work appeared in Grimm's manuscript journal *La Correspondance littéraire*, if it did so, and the date of first publication, is somewhat selective and sketchy, but may prove helpful. For the details regarding the *Correspondance littéraire* I have mainly based myself on the "Provisional Inventory of Diderot's Contributions to the *Correspondance littéraire*" by J. Th. de Booy, published in *Dix-huitième siècle* (1969).

Title (and date of writing where known)	Included in *Correspondance littéraire*	First Appearance in print
ESSAI SUR LE MÉRITE ET LA VERTU *Essay on Merit and Virtue* [1744–45]		"Amsterdam", 1745
PENSÉES PHILOSOPHIQUES *Philosophic Thoughts* [1746]		Durand, Paris, 1746
LA PROMENADE DU SCEPTIQUE *The Promenade of the Sceptic*		In *Mémoires, correspondance et ouvrages inédits de Diderot*; Paulin, Paris, 1830–31

MÉMOIRES SUR DIFFÉRENTS SUJETS DE MATHÉMATIQUES *Memoirs on Different Subjects in Mathematics* [*c.* 1748]	Pissot & Durand	Paris 1748
LES BIJOUX INDISCRETS *Indiscreet Jewels*		Amsterdam [?], 1748
First Letter from a Jealous Citizen [1748]		Paris, 1748
LETTRE SUR LES AVEUGLES *Letter on the Blind* [1746–47]		Durand, Paris, 1749
LETTRE SUR LES SOURDS ET MUETS *Letter on the Deaf and Dumb* [1750–51]		Paris, 1751
SUITE DE L'APOLOGIE DE M. L'ABBÉ DE PRADES *Continuation of the Apologia of the Abbé de Prades* [1752]		Berlin, 1752
ARRÊT RENDU À L'AMPHITHÉÂTRE DE L'OPÉRA *Judgement Rendered at the Opera Amphitheatre* [1753]		Paris, 1753
AU PETIT PROPHÈTE DE BOEHMISCHBRODA *To the Little Prophet of Boehmischbroda* [1753]		Paris, 1753
The Three Chapters; or, the Vision of the Night from Shrove Tuesday to Ash Wednesday [1753]		Paris, 1753
DE L'INTERPRETATION DE LA NATURE *On the Interpretation of Nature* [*c.* 1753]		

L'HISTOIRE ET LE SECRET DE LA PEINTURE EN CIRE *The History and Secret of Painting in Wax* [1755]		Paris, 1755
LE FILS NATUREL *The Natural Son* [1756]		
CONVERSATIONS SUR LE FILS NATUREL *Conversations on "The Natural Son"* [1756]		With *The Natural Son*; Amsterdam, 1757
LETTRE À LANDOIS *Letter to Landois* [1756]	July 1756	
LE PÈRE DE FAMILLE *A Father and His Family* [c. 1758]		With *A Father and His Family*; Amsterdam, 1758
DE LA POÉSIE DRAMATIQUE *On Dramatic Poetry* [c. 1758]		
LA RELIGIEUSE *The Nun* [begun 1760]	October 1780–March 1782	F. Buisson, Paris, 1796
Salon of 1759	November 1759	In the published edition of Grimm's *Correspondance littéraire*; Paris, 1813
ELOGE DE RICHARDSON *Eulogy of Richardson* [1761]		In *Journal étranger*; Paris, January 1762
Salon of 1761	September–November 1761	In *Oeuvres complètes*; Belin, Paris, 1818–19, Supplement
ADDITION AUX PENSÉES PHILOSOPHIQUES *Addition to "Philosophic Thoughts"* [1762]	January 1763	In *Recueil philosophique ou mélange de pièces sur la religion et la morale* 2 vols; "London" [Amsterdam], 1770
LE NEVEU DE RAMEAU *Rameau's Nephew*		In German translation by Goethe; 1805. In translation back into French by

		Saur and St Geniès; Delaunay, Paris, 1821. In 1823 in *Oeuvres*, Brière, Paris, 1821–23.
Salon of 1763	October–December 1763	In *Revue de Paris*, 1857
LETTRE HISTORIQUE ET POLITIQUE ADRESSÉE À UN MAGISTRAT SUR LE COMMERCE DE LA LIBRAIRIE *Letter Addressed to a Magistrate on the Bookselling Trade* [1763]	1766	
ESSAIS SUR LA PEINTURE *Salon* of 1765 *Essays on Painting*	August–December 1766	F. Buisson, Paris, 1795
ELOGE DE TÉRENCE *On Terence* [1765]		In *Gazette littéraire de l'Europe*, July 1765
Salon of 1767	1767 [1768?] as an "Annexe"	In *Oeuvres*, ed. Naigeon, Paris, 1798
MYSTIFICATION *Mystification* [1768]		In *Lettres françaises*, February 1954
ENTRETIEN ENTRE DIDEROT ET D'ALEMBERT *Conversation between d'Alembert and Diderot* [1769]	June 1782	In *Mémoires, correspondance et ouvrages inédits de Diderot*; Paulin, Paris, 1830
LE RÊVE DE D'ALEMBERT *D'Alembert's Dream* [1769]	August–November 1782	In *Mémoires, correspondance et ouvrages inédits de Diderot*; Paulin, Paris, 1830
SUITE DE L'ENTRETIEN *Continuation of the conversation* [1769]	September–October 1782	In *Mémoires, correspondance et ouvrages inédits de Diderot*; Paulin, Paris, 1830

Philosophical Principles of Matter and Movement		In *Encyclopédie méthodique*, ed. Naigeon; Paris, 1792
Salon of 1769	December 1769	In *Revue de Paris*, 1857 (part)
PAGES CONTRE UN TYRAN *Pages against a Tyrant* [1769]		Ed. F. Venturi Paris, 1937
REGRETS SUR MA VIEILLE ROBE DE CHAMBRE *Regrets for my Old Dressing-Gown*	15 February 1769	In *Journal de lecture*, ed. F.-M. Leuchsenring, vol. XII; Paris. 1779
PARADOXE SUR LE COMÉDIEN *Paradox of the Actor* [1770–73]	Preliminary sketch, "Observations on a brochure entitled 'Garrick: or, English Actors' ", October–November 1770	Sautelet, Paris, 1830
VOYAGE TO BOURBONNE *Journey to Bourbonne* [1770]		Ed. M. Walferdin (Paris) 1831
ENTRETIEN D'UN PÈRE AVEC SES ENFANTS *Conversation of a Father with His Children* [1770]	1–15 March 1771	In *Contes moraux et nouvelles idylles de M.M.D. . . . et Gessner*; Zurich, 1773 (previously in German translation, 1772)
LES DEUX AMIS DE BOURBONNE *The Two Friends from Bourbonne* [1770]	December 1770	In *Contes moraux* etc., 1773
Salon of 1771		In *Revue de Paris*, 1857
Apologia for the Abbé Galiani [1770]		In *Pensée*; Paris, May–June 1954
On Women [1772]	1 July 1772	In published

		edition of *Correspondance littéraire*, 1812
CECI N'EST PAS UN CONTE *This Is Not a Story* [c. 1770–73]	April 1773 (in part)	In *Oeuvres*, ed. Naigeon; Paris, 1798
On the Inconsistency of Public Opinion Regarding our Private Actions [c. 1770–73]	May 1773 (as "Second story")	In *Oeuvres*, ed. Naigeon; Paris, 1798
SUPPLÉMENT AU VOYAGE DE BOUGAINVILLE *Supplement to Bougainville's Voyage* [1772]	September–October 1773 and March–April 1774	In Bourlet de Vauxcelles, *Opuscules philosophiques et littéraires* (Paris) 1786
LES ÉLEUTHÉROMANES *The Eleutheromaniacs* [1772]	1 March 1772	In *La Décade philosophique, littéraire et politique*; Paris, 1796
Letter to the Comtesse de Forbach on the Education of Children		In *Encyclopédie méthodique* (1792), as *Principes pratiques sur l'éducation des enfans*
Commentary on Hemsterhuis [1773]		In F. Hemsterhuis, *Lettre sur l'homme*, ed. G. May, 1964
Refutation of Helvétius [1773]	January 1783–March 1786	In *Oeuvres complètes*, ed. Assézat & Tourneux; Garnier, Paris, 1875–77
MÉMOIRES POUR CATHERINE II *Memoirs for Catherine II* [1773]		In M. Tourneux, *Diderot et Catherine II*; Paris, 1899
Political Principles of Sovereigns [1774]		In the *Correspondance secrète* of Metra, 1776 (incomplete version)

ENTRETIEN D'UN PHILOSOPHE AVEC LA MARÉCHALE DE *** *Conversation of a Philosopher with the Maréchale de* *** [1774]	April–May 1775	In *Pensées philosophiques en français et en italien*, ed. J. Crudeli, London–Amsterdam, 1777
Journey Through Holland [1773–74]	September 1780–April 1782	
Observations on the "Nakaz" [1774]		In *Revue d'histoire économique et sociale*; Paris, 1920
Salon of 1775		In *Revue de Paris*, 1857
EST-IL BON? EST-IL MÉCHANT? *Is He Good? Is He Wicked?*		In *La Revue rétrospective*; Paris, 1834
PLAN D'UNE UNIVERSITÉ POUR LE GOUVERNEMENT DE RUSSIE *Plan of a University for the Russian Government* [1775]	November 1778–June 1780	In *Oeuvres complètes*, ed. Assézat & Tourneux; Garnier, Paris, 1875–77
JACQUES LE FATALISTE ET SON MAÎTRE *Jacques the Fatalist*		In German translation by Mylius, 1792; F. Buisson, Paris, 1796
ESSAI SUR SÉNÈQUE *Essay on the Life of Seneca* [1777]		As vol. 7 of *Oeuvres de Sénèque traduites . . . par . . . M. Lagrange*; de Bure, Paris, 1778
Salon of 1781	October–December 1781	In *Revue de Paris*, 1857
Letter of Apologia for the Abbé Raynal [1781]		In H. Dieckmann, *Inventaire du fonds Vandeul*; Paris, 1951

ESSAI SUR LES RÈGNES DE CLAUDE ET DE NÉRON *Essay on the Reigns of Claudius and Nero* [*c.* 1778]		"London" 1782
Addition to "Letter on the Blind"	May 1782	
ÉLÉMENTS DE PHYSIOLOGIE *Elements of Physiology*		In *Oeuvres complètes*, ed. Assézat & Tourneux; Garnier, Paris, 1875–77
Detached Thoughts on Painting [1775–76]	February–June 1777	In *Oeuvres*, ed. Naigeon; Paris, 1798
Letters to Sophie Volland		The first substantial selection was published in *Mémoires, correspondance et ouvrages inédits de Diderot*; Paulin, 4 vols., 1830–31. Many letters were, however, not published till the edition by André Babelon, Paris, 3 vols., 1930
Correspondance littéraire		The first published edition, in 17 volumes covering the years 1753–1790, appeared in Paris in 1813.

Notes

SOURCES

It was not possible to tie all source-references to the great new Hermann edition of Diderot's works by Herbert Dieckmann, Jacques Proust, Jean Varloot and others, since it is still in course of publication. Thus, for various reasons, I have thought it best to be eclectic in my choice of source-texts.

ABBREVIATIONS

The source used for all letters from Diderot is Denis Diderot, *Correspondance* ed. Georges Roth & Jean Varloot, 16 vols. (Editions de Minuit, 1955–70), my translation. D = Diderot. SV = Sophie Volland. Thus "D to SV, 23 Nov. 1760; III, 463" means "Letter from Diderot to Sophie Volland, 23 November 1760; volume III of *Correspondance*, page 463."

A/T	=	*Oeuvres complètes de Diderot*, ed. Jules Assézat & Maurice Tourneux, 20 vols. (Garnier, 1875–77)
ENC	=	*Encyclopédie, ou dictionnaire raisonné des sciences, des arts et des métiers*, par une société de gens de lettres, mis en ordre et publié par M. Diderot . . . et quant à la partie mathématique par M. d'Alembert, 17 vols. (1751–65).
OE	=	Diderot, *Oeuvres esthétiques*, ed. Paul Vernière (Garnier, 1968)
OR	=	Diderot, *Oeuvres romanesques*, ed. Henri Bénac (Garnier, 1962)
OPhil	=	Diderot, *Oeuvres philosophiques*, ed. Paul Vernière (Garnier, n.d.)
OPol	=	Diderot, *Oeuvres politiques*, ed. Paul Vernière (Garnier, 1963)
Salons I	=	Diderot, *Essais sur la peinture*, ed. Gita May, and *Salons de 1759, 1761, 1763*, ed. Jacques Chouillet (Hermann, 1984)
Salons II	=	Diderot, *Salon de 1765*, ed. Else Marie Bukdahl & Annette Lorenceau (Hermann, 1984)
CL	=	*Correspondance littéraire, philosophique et critique par Grimm, Diderot, Raynal, Meister etc.*, ed. Maurice Tourneux, 16 vols. (Garnier, 1877–82)

Confessions = Jean–Jacques Rousseau, *Les Confessions*, ed. Jacques
                 Voisine (Garnier, 1980)
Wilson   = Arthur M. Wilson, *Diderot* (OUP, 1972)

INTRODUCTION

1 The *Salon* exhibitions, held in the *Salon carré* in the Louvre, were a
  biennial event, held under the auspices of the Royal Academy of
  Painting and Sculpture.
2 It is now in the Louvre.
3 Salons II, 253–55.
4 See Roland Barthes, "Diderot, Brecht, Eisenstein" in his *Image–Music
  –Text*, ed. S. Heath (1977), pp. 69–78.
5 D to SV, 10 Nov. 1765; V, 167–8.
6 See *post*, p.
7 M. Butor, "Diderot le fataliste et ses maîtres", *Répertoire 3* (1968).

I. DIDEROT IN YOUTH

1 See Michel Foucault, *Discipline and Punish*, trans. A. Sheridan (1979), p.
  146.
2 This and many subsequent anecdotes in this and the next chapter are
  taken from his daughter Angélique's *Mémoires de Diderot*, first
  published in 1830 in the Paulin edition of *Mémoires, correspondance et
  ouvrages de Diderot*.
3 A. de Barruel, *Memoirs Illustrating the History of Jacobinism*, trans. R.
  Clifford (2nd ed., 1798), p. xiii.
4 See Wilson, 25–27.
5 F. Venturi, *La Jeunesse de Diderot* (1939), p. 34.
6 D to Mme Riccoboni, 27 Nov. 1758, II, 97.
7 J. G. Wille, *Mémoires et journal* ed. G. Duplessis, (2 vols., 1857), I, p. 91.
8 Baculard d'Arnaud (1718–1805). Sometime during this period he did a
  spell in the Bastille, for "being a disciple of Voltaire" and publishing a
  pornographic ballet.
9 See Rousseau's *Confessions*, 334.
10 See *Salon de 1767*, A/T, XI, 127.
11 D to Nanette, 1742; I, 29.
12 T. Stanyan, *Grecian History* (1707).
13 D to Nanette,, 17 Dec. 1742; I, 35–6.
14 Didier Diderot to Mme Champion, 1 Feb. 1732.
15 D to Nanette, I, 43–4.

2. THE DUNGEON AT VINCENNES

1 He makes the comment in his *Philosophie ancienne et moderne* in the *Encyclopédie méthodique*, vol. II, p. 154.

2 Marc-Antoine Eidous, once an engineer in the Spanish army, would contribute some brief articles to the *Encyclopédie* and produced a long series of translations, including one of Walpole's *Castle of Otranto*. Melchior Grimm said that he translated into a special language of his own, not French but "Eidousese".

3 See Wilson, 44.

4 M. Foucault, *Madness and Civilisation*, trans. R. Howard (1971), p. 210.

5 J. Guéhenno, *Jean-Jacques Rousseau*, trans. J. & D. Weightman (2 vols., 1966), vol. I, pp. 130–1.

6 *Confessions*, 410.

7 The *salon* of the malicious-tongued Marquise de Tencin was one of the most famous of its period, frequented by among others Montesquieu, Fontenelle and Marivaux.

8 D'Alembert, *Oeuvres* (1805), vol. X, p. 229.

9 D'Alembert, "Essai sur les gens de lettres" in *Mélanges* (1772), vol. I, p. 322.

10 Among the immediate French precursors of the *Encyclopédie* were the *Dictionnaire universel de commerce* of Jacques Savary-Desbruslons (1723–) and the revised edition by Fontenelle of Thomas Corneille's *Dictionnaire des arts et des sciences* (1732).

11 Compare Nietzsche's remark in *Beyond Good and Evil* (Aphorism 101): "Courtly language . . . is the language of the courtier who has no special subject, and who even in conversation on scholarly matters prohibits technical expressions because they smack of specialization . . . Now that all courts have become caricatures . . . one is surprised to find even Voltaire very particular on this point. The fact is that we are all emancipated from court taste, while Voltaire was its consummation!"

12 René-Antoine Ferchault de Réaumur (1683–1757), a leading physicist and naturalist, remembered as the inventor of the Réaumur thermometer. There was, as will be seen, long-standing friction between him and Diderot.

13 A/T, XIII, 140–1.

14 J. Proust, *Diderot et l'Encyclopédie* (1962), p. 505.

15 She writes to Diderot's sister Denise, 11 Dec. 1758: "Quant au volume de l'ansiclopedy, il n'est pas encore commence, rapport a monsieur d'Aramber a qui il plait de ne reprendre qu'a la nouvelle annee."

16 See D to SV, 28 July 1765: V, 69–70.

17 She was born in 1720. Her husband Philippe Florent de Puisieux, is

mentioned in Vol. I of the *Encyclopédie* (p. xiv) as having helped Diderot in his "description of arts".

18 *Conseils à une amie. Par Madame de Puysieux.* Nouvelle ed., 1749, *passim.*

19 A. Vartanian, in *Diderot: Digression and Dispersion*, ed. J. Undank & H. Josephs (1984), p. 252.

20 OR, 58–9.

21 See *post*, pp. 397–8.

22 *Gentleman's Magazine*, vol. XIX, p. 405.

23 *Mercure de France*, Sept. 1748, p.135.

24 A. Cobban, *A History of Modern France*, vol. I (1957), p. 86.

25 See Wilson, 61.

26 Quoted by P. Bonnefon in "Diderot prisonnier à Vincennes", *Revue d'Histoire littéraire de la France*, vol. VI (1899), p. 203.

27 Voltaire to Diderot, 9 June 1749.

28 Nicolas-René Berryer, Lieutenant-general of Police.

29 The letters are printed in *Corresp.*, I, 83–90.

30 D'Alembert to Samuel Formey, 19 Sept. 1749.

31 Didier Diderot to Diderot, 3 Sept. 1749.

32 *Confessions*, 415.

33 *Confessions*, 416.

34 See D to SV, 2 Sept. 1760; III, 52.

35 See J. Seznec, "Le Socrate imaginaire", in *Essais sur Diderot et l'antiquité* (1957).

3. *Letter on the Blind* AND *Letter on the Deaf and Dumb*

1 Locke, *Essay Concerning Human Understanding* (1690), Book II, Ch. 9.

2 OPhil, 81–2.

3 See J. B. Merian, *Sur le problème de Molyneux* (1984).

4 See the discussion of the ambiguities of the word "Supplement" in Derrida's *Of Grammatology*, trans. G. C. Spivak (1974), pp. 141–164; also the examination of "Continuations" and "Supplements" in G. Genette, *Palimpsestes* (1982). On pp. 225–9 Genette discusses Diderot's *Supplément au voyage de Bougainville.*

5 See J. Spence, *An Account of the Life, Character and Poems of Mr. Blacklock* (1754), p. 60 *et ante.*

6 H. Keller, *The Miracle of a Life* (1909), p. 91.

7 OPhil, 84.

8 Ibid, 119.

9 She died in 1755. Her translation of various essays by Hume appeared under the title *Essais sur le commerce, le luxe, l'argent* (Amsterdam, 1752–3).

10 Quoted by P. H. Meyer in *Diderot Studies*, VII (1965), p. 6.

11 See C. Batteux, *Lettres sur la phrase française comparée avec la phrase latine* (1747–8).

12 Condillac mentions the idea of applying to a deaf-mute to help in tracing the origins of language in his *Essai sur l'origine des connaissances humaines* (1746).

13 Louis-Bertrand Castel (1688–1757) was in his early days a teacher at the Jesuit college of Louis-le-Grand. He first announced his "ocular harpsichord" in the *Mercure de France* in 1725. He wrote that "My aim is to make a blind man judge of colours, and the deaf to judge of sounds". While maintaining that practical application was not the heart of the matter, in 1730 he made a trial of an instrument employing coloured strips of paper and many years later he made another and more elaborate attempt employing pieces of coloured glass lit by a battery of candles. A version of his instrument was demonstrated in London a month or two after his death.

14 See *Lettre sur les sourds et muets*, A/T, I, 359.

15 See the "Life and Character of Professor Saunderson" in Saunderson's *Elements of Algebra* (1740), p. x: "It is said of Democritus that he put out his eyes, to enable him to think the more intensely".

16 *Additions pour servir d'éclaircissements à quelques endroits de la Lettre sur les aveugles* (1751); *Corresp.*, I, 120–1.

17 E. de Fontenay, *Diderot: Reason and Resonance* (1982), p.

18 *Additions*; see *Corresp.*, I, 120–1.

19 Charles Batteux (1713–80) was author of *Les Beaux arts réduits à un même principe* (1746), *Cours de belles lettres* (1753) etc. He was elected to the Académie in 1761.

20 Diderot, *Lettre sur les sourds et muets*, A/T, I, 374.

21 Ibid, p. 367.

22 G. E. Lessing, *Sämtliche Schriften*, (Leipzig, 1853), vol. III, p. 236.

4. BIRTH OF THE *Encyclopédie*

1 The best account of d'Holbach is Pierre Naville's *D'Holbach et la philosophie scientifique au 18me siècle* (1967).

2 See J. Y. T. Greig, *David Hume* (1931), p. 298.

3 The *Mémoires de Trévoux*, later known as the *Journal de Trévoux*, was founded in 1701 by the Jesuits at Trévoux, a small town near Bourg which was one of the most important centres for printing outside Paris. Its then director, Father Berthier, however, ran it from his cell in the college of Louis-le-Grand in Paris.

4 A/T, XIII, 369.

5 Ibid., 368–9.

6 *Enc.* II, 98.

7 J. W. von Goethe, *Autobiography*, trans. J. Oxenford (1974), vol. II, p. 106.

8 Ibid., vol. I, p. 97. According to Rousseau's *Confessions* (p. 420) when Grimm first arrived in France he "had not yet become a purist".

9 *Confessions*, 418.

10 Marie Fel was a ballerina and singer at the Opéra.

11 See *post*, p. 415

12 *Confessions*, 481.

13 See *post*, pp. 187–8.

14 Rousseau to de Saint-Germain, 26 Feb. 1770.

15 J. Michelet, *Louis XV, 1724–1757*, in his *Histoire de la France au 18me siècle* (1863–67), p. 258.

16 Horace, *Ars poetica*, ll. 242–3.

17 They are the astronomical observations made in Babylon over 1,900 years and reproduced in Ptolemy's *Almagest*; the calculations made in China of a solar eclipse 2,150 years before our era; and the Arundel Marbles, recording the ancient history of Greece.

18 Butor, op. cit., 104.

19 Claude Yvon (1714–91). He contributed a number of articles on religious and ethical topics to the *Encyclopedie*. It was his aim to reconcile Catholicism with enlightened rationalism. He was sharing a room with the *abbé* de Prades at the time of the "de Prades affair" and, like de Prades, took refuge in Holland, not returning to France till 1762.

20 Jean-Marie de Prades (1720–82). A police dossier described him as "a lad of intelligence, very lively and a bit mad."

21 S. Schama, *Citizens* (1989), p. 105.

22 On 8 Sept. 1713 the Pope issued the bull *Unigenitus* condemning 101 propositions in the Jansenist Pasquier Quesnel's *Moral Reflections on the New Testament*, a book first published in 1671 and re-edited in 1699.

23 Chrétien-Guillaume de Lamoignon de Malesherbes (1721–94), affectionately known as "Uncle William", was Director of Publications 1750–63. He was for many years president of the Cour des Aides and served for a time under Turgot. He drew up a damning report on the royal prisons for Louis XVI and insisted to the King that *lettres de cachet* were "a reproach which all Europe makes to France".

24 The *Nouvelles ecclésiastiques*, a series of periodical pamphlets, was published from 1728 to 1803, at first clandestinely.

25 Charles-Daniel de Caylus (1669–1754).

26 A/T, I, 482.

27 A/T, I, 483–4.

5. THE ART OF CONJECTURE

1 The story of their squabbles and of how, on his return journey, Voltaire was actually put under arrest on Frederick's orders is told in all biographies of him.

2 Georgel, *Mémoires* (1817), vol. II, p. 246.

3 See d'Escherny, *Mélanges de littérature et d'histoire*, vol. III, p. 131.

4 Diderot, *Réfutation d'Helvétius*; A/T, II, 369–70.

5 See his letter of 28 Nov. 1760 to Voltaire, about the latter's new play *Tancrede*.

6 See *Salon* of 1767; A/T, XI, 347–8.

7 Grétry relates how he asked Diderot's opinion of his efforts to set a line (*"Ah! Laissez-moi, laissez-moi la pleurer."* for his operas *Zémire et Azor*, and how Diderot, dissatisfied, declaimed the line for him, finding him exactly the rhythm he had been searching for. He told Grétry that "the model for a musician must be the cry of the man in passion." Diderot, Grétry said, had the secret of "poking the coals of genius". "It was not always wise to listen to him [Diderot] or the *abbé* Arnoud when they gave free rein to their imagination; but the first *élan* of these two burning men was of divine inspiration." (*Mémoires* (1796), vol. I, pp. 225–6 and vol. III, pp. 377–8.)

8 See his letter to Falconet of 2 May 1773 first published in H. Dieckmann & J. Seznec, "The Horse of Marcus Aurelius", *Journal of the Warburg & Courtauld Institutes*, vol. 15, pp. 217–8. "I had a student come to me. I gave instructions; he obeyed them ... His fingers modelled the clay according to my wishes. The image was in my head; I compared the work with the image, and I said 'That's it,' or 'That's not right.'"

9 See *post*, p. 116.

10 See *Lettre sur les sourds et muets*, A/T, I, 368.

11 A/T, XI, 115.

12 André Morellet (1729–1819), a prolific author and compiler, often employed as a writer in government service. He was a major contributor to the *Dictionnaire* of the *Académie* and helped secure the revival of the Academie after the Revolution.

13 A. Morellet, *Mémoires* (1821), vol. I, pp. 128–9.

14 D to Falconet, 6 Sept. 1768; VIII, 110. The "old fanatic" was Louis, Duc d'Orléans (1703–52), son of the Regent.

15 He made the remark to the artist Cochin, adding that nobody had more reason than he to be envious of Sedaine, for "that man cuts the

ground from under my feet". (Diderot to Grimm, 3 Dec. 1765; *Corresp.*, 206).

16 D to Mme Necker, Autumn 1770; X, 149.

17 Count Alessandro Verri, who accompanied Beccaria to Paris in 1766, writing to his brother, 19 Oct. 1766.

18 Jean-François Marmontel, *Mémoires*, ed. M. Tourneux (1891), vol. II, pp. 243–4.

19 Jules Barbey d'Aurevilly, *Contre Diderot*, ed. H. Juin (1986), p. 70.

20 *Mémoires sur la vie de M. de La Harpe* (1806), vol. I, pp. v–vi. Diderot thought La Harpe a pedestrian writer. He wrote to Mme d'Epinay in Sept. 1771, *à propos* of La Harpe's *Eulogy of Fénélon*, that in reading it "one is never carried away, because the orator is never carried away. As for the art of self-possession, ah! that he *does* possess."

21 Baudelaire, *Etudes sur Poe*; Pléiade ed., vol. II, p. 247.

22 See *La Nouvelle Héloise*, ed. R. Pomeau (1960), pp. 259–262.

23 The dancer and singer, see *ante*, p. 80

24 See *Confessions*, 451.

25 D'Alembert, *Eléments de musique . . . suivant les principes de M. Rameau* (1752).

26 *Confessions*, 451.

27 Rousseau to Coindet, 1766; quoted in Guehenno, *op. cit.*, vol. II, p. 172.

28 Buffon, *Histoire naturelle* (1749–67), vol. I, "Premier discours".

29 *De l'Interprétation de la nature*; OPhil, 181.

30 Ibid, 197.

31 Lucretius, *De Rerum natura*, Book 4, line 337.

32 See St Augustine, *Confessions*, Book VIII.

33 Butor, op. cit., 104.

34 See T. L. Hankins, *Jean d'Alembert* (1970), ch. 7 *passim*.

35 See Diderot's obituary article on Rouelle in *Correspondance littéraire*, A/T, VI, 405–410.

36 Goethe: "Read Diderot's *Jacques le fataliste* from 6 to 11.30, at one gulp, and enjoyed myself like the Baal of Babylon at such an enormous feast. God be praised that I can swallow such a portion at one sitting with the greatest appetite, as if it were a glass of water, and yet with indescribable pleasure. 3 April 1780."

37 Quoted in A. Cazes, *Grimm et les Encyclopédistes* (1933), p. 134.

38 Holbach's account of this incident was first published in the *Journal de Paris*, Supplement to No. 336, 2 Dec. 1789, 1567–8.

39 Rousseau, *Du Contrat social et autres oeuvres politiques*, ed. J. Ehrard (1975), p. 60.

40 *Du Contrat social* (Geneva version), chapter 2.

6. A CIRCLE WITH MAN AT ITS CENTRE

1 D to SV, 25 Sept. 1760; III, 86.
2 A/T, I, xli.
3 D to Didier Diderot, 6 Jan. 1755; I, 177.
4 Angélique de Vandeul to Henri Meister, 15 Feb. 1812; quoted in J. M. du Biest, *La Fille de Diderot* (Tours, 1949), p. 5.
5 Claude-Philippe de Tubières, Comte de Caylus (1692–1765), a well-known archaeologist, collector and traveller, author of *Tableaux d'Homère et de Virgile* (1757), etc.
6 Jean-Jacques Bachelier (1724–1806). He was "received" as flower-painter by the Academy of Painting in 1752 and in 1763 as a history-painter.
7 A/T, X, 47–83 *passim*.
8 Louis de Jaucourt (1704–79). He wrote a biography of Leibnitz (1734) which earned him membership of the Academy of Berlin.
9 *Enc.*, V, 641A.
10 Ibid., 642.
11 Ibid., 642A.
12 See Mona Ozouf, "Le Pantheon" and J. Hargrove, "Les Statues de Paris" in *Les Lieux de mémoire*, ed. *P. Nora (1987)*; also M. Billington, *The Icon and the Axe (1966), p. 300*.
13 *Enc.*, V, 646.
14 Charles Palissot de Montenoy (1713–1814. He wrote a tragedy, *Zares*, at the age of 20 and was taken up by Voltaire, but, having been elected to the Academy of Nancy, he became associated with the group who wanted to make the court of Duke Stanislaus of Lorraine a bastion of anti-*philosophisme*. He wrote a *Dunciade* (1764) in imitation of Pope.
15 See *post*, pp. 203–206

7. THE "LETTER TO LANDOIS"

1 CL, 1 July 1756.
2 See the 4th Meditation of Descartes: "Will and the freedom of choice are the only things that I experience within myself as so great that I cannot conceive the idea of any other more ample and extensive: so that it is principally these which prove to me that I bear the image and resemblance of God."
3 Schopenhauer, *The World as Will and Idea*, trans. R. B. Haldane & J. Kemp (1907), vol. I, p. 376.

8. DIDEROT AND THE THEATRE

1 A/T, VII, 19.
2 Saint-Germain-en-Laye is a suburb of Paris. The Duc d'Ayen had a

private theatre there, and it seems likely that Diderot's play was actually given one or two performances in it, thus adding a further twist to his "mystification". See J. Proust, "Le Paradoxe du *Fils naturel*", *Diderot Studies*, 4 (1963), pp. 209–220.

3 *Année littéraire*, vol. IV, 1757, p.146.

4 *The Memoirs of Chateaubriand*, ed. R. Baldick (1961), pp. 38–39.

9. "ONLY THE WICKED MAN LIVES ALONE"

1 Louise Florence de La Live d'Epinay, née d'Esclavelles (1726–83). See Perey & Maugras, *La Jeunesse de Madame d'Epinay* (1882) and *Les Dernières années de Madame d'Epinay* (1883).

2 See *ante*, p. 33.

3 D to R, 10 March 1757; I, 232–3.

4 R to Mme d'Epinay, 13 March 1757.

5 D to R, 14 March 1757; I, 234–6.

6 R to D, 16 March 1757.

7 R to Mme d'Epinay, 16 March 1757.

8 R to Mme d'Epinay, 17 March 1757.

9 D to R, 22 or 23 March 1757; I, 239–40.

10 R to D, 23 or 24 March 1757.

11 Jean-François, Marquis de Saint-Lambert, to R, 11 Oct. 1757.

12 D to R, *circa* 20 Oct. 1757; I, 248–9.

13 *Confessions*, 564.

14 Mme d'Epinay to R, 12 November 1757.

15 R to Sophie d'Houdetot, 9 Nov. 1757.

16 D to R, *circa* 15 Nov. 1757; I, 256–8.

17 *Confessions*, 573–4.

18 A great deal has been written about the "Hermitage affair" and conflicting views have been taken about the rights and wrongs of it. See for instance Rousseau's own *Confessions*, ch. 9; Guéhenno, op. cit., vol. 1, ch. 7; J. Fabre, "Frères ennemis: Diderot and Jean-Jacques", *Diderot Studies*, III; H. Guillemin, "Les Affaires de l'Ermitage 1756–1757", *Annales de la Société Jean-Jacques Rousseau*, vol. 29 (Geneva), 1941–2. Mme d'Epinay, in her *Histoire de Mme de Montbrillant*, includes a dramatic letter from "Garnier" (i.e. Diderot) to Grimm, dated 5 December 1757 and beginning "That man is a madman"; but it may well be fictional, so it seems wisest to place no dependance on it.

10. CACOUACS

1 Voltaire, *Siècle de Louis XIV*, 2nd ed., 1752.

2 Voltaire to d'Alembert, Sept. 1752.

3 Voltaire to d'Alembert, 9 Oct. 1755.

4 Voltaire to d'Alembert, 13 Dec. 1756.

5 Voltaire to d'Alembert, 2 Aug. 1756.

6 C. Palissot, *Petites lettres sur les grands philosophes* (1757).

7 A. Morellet, *Mémoires* (1821), vol. I, p. 44.

8 D to Voltaire, 19 Feb., 1758; II, 37–40.

9 Voltaire to N. C. Thieriot, 19 Nov. 1760.

10 D to SV, 25 Nov. 1760; III, 265.

11 *Réfutation d'Helvétius*; OPhil, 607.

12 D to SV, 12 Aug. 1762; IV, 100.

13 D to J.-A. Naigeon, April/May 1772; XII, 51–3.

14 D to Voltaire, 14 June 1758; II, 61.

15 Rousseau to D, 2 March 1758.

16 Rousseau, *Lettre à d'Alembert sur les spectacles* (1758), p.

17 ["Seven Rascalities"] Appendix 206, pp. 281–3.

18 Christophe de Beaumont (1703–81).

19 Abraham-Joseph de Chaumeix (*c.* 1730–90). According to Voltaire, a hostile witness, Chaumeix had been successively a vinegar-merchant, a schoolmaster, a Jansenist and a "convulsionist". He eventually retired to Russia, supporting himself by teaching, and ended his days there.

20 De la Vivotte to Malesherbes, 18 or 19 Oct. 1758.

21 D to Malesherbes, 20 Oct. 1758; II, 68.

22 D to Mme Riccoboni, 27 Nov. 1758; II, 92–3.

23 See *ante*, p. 53, and note.

24 D to Jacob Vernes, 9 Jan. 1759; II, 119 *et seq.*

25 D to Grimm, 1 May 1759; II, 119–121.

II. DIDEROT AND STATUES

1 Sophie's parents, Jean Robert Volland and Elisabeth Françoise Brunel de la Carlière, had four children: Jean-Nicolas, *d.* 1750; Marie-Jeanne Elisabeth (*b.* 1715), married in 1737 to Pierre Vallet de Salignac, "receiver of finance" to the Duc d'Orléans; Marie-Charlotte, married in 1749 to Jean-Gabriel Le Gendre, royal engineer for the Champagne district; Louise-Henriette ("Sophie").

2 D to SV, 25 Nov. 1760; III, 265.

3 D to SV, 15 Aug. 1762; IV, 107.

4 D to Grimm, 5 June 1759; 149.

5 Etienne-Noel Damilaville (1723–68). He acted as Voltaire's representative among the encyclopaedic and Holbachic clan and wrote the article on the VINGTIÈME tax in the *Encyclopédie*.

6 Henri-Charles, Baron de Gleichen (1735–1807). At this time he was

envoy of the Margrave of Bayreuth in Paris; subsequently he became Danish ambassador in Spain and then in Paris. He was a friend of de Choiseul and of Mme du Deffand.

7 The château of Marly, midway between Versailles and Saint-Germain, was built by Mansart for Louis XIV.

8 His patroness and (perhaps) lover, the Margravine of Bayreuth, had recently died.

9 D to SV, 10 May 1759; II, 135–8.

10 *De la poésie dramatique*; OE, 285.

11 D to Falconet, 5 Aug. 1766; VI, 261.

12 D to SV, 27 Jan. 1766; VI, 30.

13 *Salons* I, 251.

14 D to SV, 25 July 1762; IV, 66–7.

15 D to Grimm, 18 July 1759; II, 172.

16 D to Grimm, 3 July 1759; II, 167.

17 D to Nanette, 29 July 1759; II, 185–7.

18 D to SV, 16 Aug. 1759; II, 217 et seq.

19 D to SV, 1 Oct. 1759; II, 263.

20 D to SV, *circa* 15 Oct. 1759; II, 279 et seq.

21 D to SV, 8 Oct. 1759; II, 268.

22 Didier François d'Arclais de Montamy (1703–65), *maître d'hôtel* to the Duc d'Orléans. He was knowledgeable about chemistry and bequeathed to Diderot a manuscript on enamel-painting, which Diderot published.

23 D to SV, *circa* 12 Oct. 1759; 269–70.

24 D to SV, *circa* 14 Oct. 1759; 272–5.

25 D to SV, 30 Oct. 1759; 294–308.

26 Charles Collé, *Mémoires* (1868), vol. II, p. 236.

27 See p. 113.

28 The dramatist Poinsinet the Younger staged a parody of *The Philosophers*, entitled *The Little Philosophers*, at the *Italiens*, and in July there came a marionette play, *The Wooden Philosophers*.

29 D to S, 26 Oct. 1760; 190.

30 Voltaire to Palissot, 4 June 1760.

31 D to SV, 9/10 Nov. 1760; 247.

32 Marc-Antoine-Nicolas de Croismare (1695–1772).

33 She was named Marguerite Delamarre, and some facts about her are given by Georges May in his *Diderot et "La Religieuse"* (1954). Confusingly, in the forged letters to Croismare she writes as "Suzanne Simonin", the name used by Diderot in the novel *The Nun*.

34 CL, 15 March 1770.

35 *Eloge de Richardson*; OE, 29–48, passim.

36 CL, 15 May 1760.

37 D to Damilaville, 1 Aug. 1760; III, 40.

38 D to SV, 30 Sept. 1760; III, 97 et seq.

39 D to SV, 27 Sept. 1760; III, 95.

40 D to SV, 15 Sept. 1760; III, 66–71.

41 Ferdinand Galiani (1728–87). Through his uncle the Cardinal-bishop Celestino Galiani he gained the *entrée* to literary circles in Naples and published treatises on *Currency* (1750) and the *Grain-Trade* (1754) before joining the diplomatic service.

42 Nietzsche, *Beyond Good and Evil*(1886), Aphorism 26.

43 D to SV, 20 Sept. 1760; III, 76.

44 D to SV, 20 Oct. 1760; III, 164–70.

45 D to SV, 30 Sept. 1760; III, 98.

46 D to SV, 17 Sept. 1760; III, 72–5.

47 D to SV, 8 Oct. 1760; III, 124.

48 D to SV, 17 Sept. 1760; III, 74–5.

49 D to SV, 3 Nov. 1760; III, 219.

50 OE, 205.

51 D to unknown, XVI, 53.

52 D to Mme d'Epinay, early Nov. 1760; III, 221.

12. *The Nun*

1 OR, 247.

2 Barbey d'Aurevilly, *Contre Diderot* (1986), pp. 67–8.

3 See *Paradoxe sur le comédien*, OE, 330.

4 See Grimm's "Preface – Annex de *La Religieuse*", A/T, V, 179.

5 D to Henri Meister; 27 Sept. 1780; XV, 190–1.

6 Salons I, 55. Pierre-Honoré Robbé (1712–92) wrote a poem on the Pox.

7 OR, 307.

8 OR, 310.

9 OR, 339–40.

10 OR, 392.

11 OR, 347–8.

13. THE "MENAGERIE"

1 Chamfort, *Caractères et anecdotes*, ed. J. Dagen (1968), no. 860.

2 See L. Perey & G. Maugras, *Les Dernières années de Mme d'Epinay* (1883), p.128.

3 The full and authentic text of the *Histoire de Madame de Montbrillant* did not become available until 1951, when George Roth published his

elaborate and heavily-annotated edition, subt-titling it "Les Pseudo-mémoires de Madame d'Epinay".

4 D to Voltaire, 23 Feb. 1761; III, 292.

5 See *ante*, p. 34.

6 S. Schama, *Citizens* (1989), p. 73.

7 Quoted in Guéhenno, op. cit., I, 130–1.

8 Adélaide-Louise-Pauline Hus (1734–1805). She was a member of the Comédie Française and a rival to Clairon.

9 Louis-Léon-Félicité, Comte de Lauragai (1733–1824). He employed chemists to do research on porcelain-making for him and communicated the discovery of the so-called "true" formula for porcelain to the Académie des Sciences in 1764. It was he who, by a payment of 12,000 *livres* to the company, rid the Comédie Française stage of spectators.

10 Madeleine-Sophie Arnould (1740–1802). She made her début at the Opéra in 1757. The Goncourts wrote a life of her (1857).

11 D to SV, 7 Oct. 1761; III, 332–3.

12 St Anthony (of the Temptations) was greatly attached to his pig, whom he appointed his *grand vicaire*, and the affection was reciprocated.

13 D to SV, 7 Oct. 1761; III, 322–325.

14 *Le Neveu de Rameau*, OR, 406.

15 D to SV, 25 Nov. 1760; III, 270.

14. *Rameau's Nephew*

1 Quoted by Jean Fabre in his valuable edition of *Le Neveu de Rameau* (1977), pp. 250–2.

2 Louis-Sébastien Mercier; see Fabre, op. cit., 252.

3 OR, 397.

4 OR, 397.

5 OR, 401.

6 Etienne-Michel Bouret (1710–77), the son of a lackey, made a wealthy marriage and in 1738 was appointed *trésorier general* in the royal household, becoming a farmer-general five years later. The peak of his career was the day (30 April 1759) when he received the King at his *château* and presented him with a book entitled *Le Livre du vrai bonheur*. He died a bankrupt.

7 OR, 431.

8 OR, 487.

9 Nietzsche, *Beyond Good and Evil*, Aphorism 26.

10 OR, 448.

11 La Rochefoucauld, Maxim 563.

12 OR, 411.

13 OR, 435.

14 Hegel, *The Phenomenology of Spirit*, trans. A. V. Miller, ed. J. N. Findlay (1977), para. 522 (pp. 317–8).
15 Ibid, para. 205 (pp. 125–6).

15. THE PRIVATE AND THE PUBLIC

 1 D to SV, 12 Sept. 1761; III, 299–300.
 2 D to SV, 22 Sept. 1761; III, 313.
 3 D to SV, 7 Oct. 1761; III, 333–4.
 4 D to SV, 12 Oct. 1761; III, 334–6.
 5 D to SV, 14 July 1762; IV, 38–48.
 6 Ibid.
 7 D to SV, 25 July 1762; IV, 50–55.
 8 D to SV, 14 Oct., 31 Oct. 1762, 21 Nov. 1762.
 9 Jean Mayer, "Diderot et la quadrature du cercle", *Rev. Gen. des Sciences*, No. 52 (1955).
10 *Salon de 1767*, A/T, XI, 129.
11 E. Gibbon, *Autobiography*, ed. J. B. Bury (1907), p. 127.
12 H. Walpole to the Countess of Suffolk, 20 Sept. 1765.
13 L. Sterne to Garrick, 31 Jan. and 19 March 1762.
14 G. W. Stone & G. M. Kahrl, *David Garrick* (1979), p. 298.
15 Garrick to George Colman, 8 November 1763.
16 Quoted in A. H. Cash, *Laurence Sterne* (1975), vol. II, p. 137.
17 Hume to Hugh Blair, Dec. 1763.
18 Walpole to George Selwyn, 2 Dec. 1765.
19 D to Hume, 17 March 1769; IX, 39–40.
20 D to SV, 26 Sept. 1762; IV, 172.
21 Sterne to Garrick, 19 April 1762.
22 D to Mme Riccoboni, 27 Nov. 1758; II, 94.
23 D to M.-M. Jodin, 21 Aug. 1765; V, 102–3.
24 Salon II, 288.
25 It was included in CL, Oct.–Nov. 1770.
26 Leopold Mozart to Lorenz Hagenauer, 1 April 1764.
27 CL, 1 Dec., 1763.
28 Voltaire to D, 25 Sept. 1762.
29 D to Voltaire, 29 Sept. 1762; IV, 175–8.
30 Voltaire, *Oeuvres complètes*, ed. Moland, 29 (1879), pp. 325–7.
31 D to SV, 26 Sept. 1762; IV, 172.
32 D to A.-F. Le Breton, 12 Nov. 1764; IV, 300–6.

16. DIDEROT AS ART-CRITIC

1 *Salon de 1767*, A/T, XI, 296.
2 See Alan J. Freer, "Diderot et Stendhal", *Annales pub. par la Faculté des Lettres de Toulouse* (Littérature, 10), 11, fasc. 1 (1962), pp. 63–79.
3 Salons II, 21.
4 *Eléments de physiologie*, A/T, IX, 367.
5 "I preserve Pygmalion's character and expression, but I place him on the left: he has noticed the first signs of life in his statue. He had been squatting, but he raises himself slowly, until he is in reach of the heart. He gently lays the back of his hand on it, to see if it is beating; meanwhile his eyes, fastened on those of the statue, wait for them to open ... It seems to me that my idea is more novel, more rare and energetic than Falconet's." Salons I, 250–51.
6 Freer, op. cit.
7 Salons I, 212.
8 Salons I, 220.
9 Salons II, 117.
10 *Salon de 1767*, A/T, XI, 98.
11 Salons II, 177.
12 Salons I, 238–239.
13 *Essais sur la peinture*, A/T, X, 498.
14 Salons II, 179–183.
15 M. Fried, *Absorption and Theatricality: Painting and the Beholder in the Age of Diderot* (1980), p. 134.
16 *Salon de 1767*, A/T, XI, 238.
17 D to SV, 18 July 1762; IV, 57.
18 Salons II, 59.
19 *Salon de 1767*. A/T, XI, 372.
20 *Salon de 1767*, A/T, XI, 3 *et seq.*
21 Ibid., 113.
22 Ibid., 114.
23 Ibid., 229–230.
24 Ibid., 231.
25 *Salon de 1767*, A/T, XI, 190.

17. CATHERINE THE GREAT'S LIBRARIAN

1 D to SV, 1 Aug. 1765; V, 73.
2 Jean Meslier (1664–1733) was *curé* of Etrepigny and Brut, in Champagne. In his *Testament*, not published in full till 1864, he writes: "Nature is full of prodigies, but it is Nature herself who produces them ... and she produces them, not by design and consciously, but

mechanically and blindly, by the natural laws of motion of the insensible parts of matter which modify themselves, unite and combine in infinite sorts and manners." See P. Naville, *D'Holbach* (1967), pp. 140–7.

3 D to SV, 22 Nov. 1768; VIII, 234.

4 A.C. Kors, *D'Holbach's Côterie* (1976), p. 10.

5 Nicolas-Sylvain Bergier (1713–90) was appointed canon of Notre-Dame in 1769. The genial and corpulent Bergier, mentioned in *Rameau's Nephew*, was friendly with the d'Holbach circle and a frequenter of their dinners despite being a leading Catholic apologist. There, was, however, a certain amount of recrimination when he wrote a refutation of d'Holbach's *Système de la nature*.

6 D to unknown correspondent, summer of 1769(?); IX, 112–6.

7 Amélie Suard, *Essais de mémoire sur M. Suard* (1870).

8 D to SV, 18 Aug. 1765; V, 94.

9 S. Necker, *Nouveaux mélanges* (1801), vol. II, p. 206. There is a good account of her *salon* in R. Picard, *Les Salons littéraires* (1943), pp. 339–46.

10 Rousseau to Vernes, 24 June 1761.

11 Rousseau to Voltaire, 17 June 1760.

12 D'Alembert to Voltaire, 9 April 1761.

13 Voltaire, *Sentiments des citoyens* (1764).

14 D to SV, 25 July 1762; IV, 72.

15 Rousseau to d'Escherny, 6 April 1765.

16 D to SV, 20 Dec. 1765; V, 226.

17 See R. Friedenthal, *Goethe* (1965), pp. 103–7 for a good picture of the Darmstadt court circle.

18 In 1763 a courtier at Gotha named Wilhelm de Rothberg printed (in French) an almanack for the year 1764, and in the following year Klüpfel introduced into it some genealogical information about German ruling houses, thus founding the *Almanach de Gotha* as we know it. See G. de Diesbach, *Secrets of the Gotha*, trans. M. Crosland (1967).

19 Grimm to Caroline of Hesse-Darmstadt, *circa* 1770.

20 Ivan Ivanovitch Betzki (1704–95). He was the illegitimate son of Prince Troubetski and was rumoured to be Catherine the Great's father. He had many friends in Paris, having first come there in 1728 as a diplomatic attaché. His title of "General" was merely honorific.

21 Betzki to Grimm, 16 March 1765.

22 Voltaire to D, 24 April 1765.

23 Prince Dmitri Alexeivitch Gallitzin (1738–1813). He was Catherine's ambassador in France 1765–9 and, like General Betzki, was an habitué of Mme Geoffrin's *salon*. Gallitzin and Diderot, as we shall see, became close friends.

24 Etienne-Maurice Falconet (1716–91). He was a carpenter's son and a self-taught intellectual, who entered the sculptor Le Moyne's studio at the age of seventeen. He was a brusque- tempered and quarrelsome man, very frugal in his way of life.

25 D to Falconet, 29 Dec. 1766; VI, 369.

26 D to Betzki, 29 Nov. 1766; VI, 355–6.

27 Henri Meister's father writes to Bodmer, 12 Sept. 1771: "Diderot has written a charming tale, *Jacques the Fatalist*. The author read from it to our friend [i.e. Henri Meister] for two hours the other day". *Lettres inédites de Mme de Staël à Meister* (1903), p. 24.

28 A much-praised group exhibited at the *Salon* of 1763.

29 D to Falconet, 4 Dec. 1765; V, 207–10.

30 D to M.-M. Jodin, January 1767.

31 In 1790, the year of her death, she would address a pamphlet to the National Assembly, advocating a legislature of women. Its epigraph reads, "We are citizens too!"

18. "IS HE GOOD? IS HE WICKED?"

1 The play *Est-il bon ? Est-il méchant?* seems to have first been sketched, as "The Play and the Prologue", in 1770 or 1771.

2 D to SV, 20 Oct. 1765; V, 144.

3 E. & J. de Goncourt, *La Femme au dix-huitième siècle* (18   ), p.

4 Experiments in inoculation against smallpox began in France in the mid-1750s, amid intense controversy. The *Encyclopédie* devoted a lengthy article to the subject by the famous Théodore Tronchin, Voltaire's physician and a leading pioneer in the field.

5 After the scandalous bankruptcy of her husband Pierre Valet de Sallignac in 1762, Sophie's elder sister adopted the surname "de Blacy".

6 The section of Toland's book on "The Origin of Movement in Matter" theorises that the molecules of matter are, in their very nature, self-moving, a view adopted by Diderot in his *Philosophical Principles of Matter and Movement*.

19. *D'Alembert's Dream*

1 A sly allusion to Diderot's great debate with Falconet.

2 *Entretien entre d'Alembert et Diderot*, OPhil, 265–6.

3 See *ante*, p. 67.

4 *Le Rêve de d'Alembert*, OPhil, 287–8.

5 *Gazette de France*, 4 September 1769.

20. ANGÉLIQUE

1 C. Burney, *Music, Men and Manners in France and Italy* (1770); ed. H. E. Poole (1974), p. 225.
2 E. Stollreither, *Ein deutsche Maler und Hofmann. Lebenserinnerungen des Johann Christian von Mannlich* (Berlin, 1910),
3 J.-B.-A. Suard to the Margrave of Bayreuth, 30 March 1773: "It is certain that this story has been judged too severely. It has been found detestable more or less generally; but admitting all its faults, one finds strokes of genius on every page." Quoted in *Corresp.*, XII, 202.
4 *Voyage à Bourbonne*, A/T, XVII, 354.
5 D to Grimm, 15 Oct., 21 Oct., 1770; X, 141-7.
6 D to Jean de Vaines, 19 Nov. or Dec. 1770; X, 141-7.
7 In *Jean-Jacques Rousseau: a New Criticism* (2 vols., 1906). See P. N. Furbank, "Diderot and the *Histoire de Madame de Montbrillant*", *British Journal of 18th Century Studies*, vol. XIII, no. 2, Autumn 1990.
8 See CL, January 1770.
9 "Les Eleuthéromanes", A/T, IX, 9-19.
10 Walpole, Paris Journal for 19 Sept. 1765.
11 OE, 313.
12 OE, 310.
13 Mme d'Epinay to Galiani, 15 Aug. 1772.
14 D to Grimm, 8 Sept. 1772; XII, 121-2.
15 D to Grimm, 19 Sept. 1772; XII, 127-8.
16 D to Denise Diderot, 25 Sept. 1772; XII, 139-43.
17 Didier-Pierre Diderot to Angélique, 27 Aug. 1772; XII, 112-3.
18 D to Didier-Pierre Diderot, 13 Nov. 1772; XII, 158-76.

21. THE STORIES

1 Goethe, *Autobiography*, trans. J. Oxenford (1974), vol. II, p. 106.
2 For the purposes of this chapter I am excluding the (possibly unfinished) extravaganza entitled *Mystification*.
3 They were included there in succession during 1773 and 1774.
4 CL, April 1773.
5 *Ceci n'est pas un conte*, A/T, V, 311.
6 Salons I, 55.
7 D to SV, 14 Oct. 1762; IV, 191.
8 Butor, op. cit., 108.
9 A/T, V, 331-2.
10 P. Commerson, "Post-scriptum sur l'île de la Nouvelle-Cythère", *Mercure de France*, Nov. 1769

11 L.-A. de Bougainville, *Voyage autour du monde*, ed. J. Proust (1982), p. 230.

12 C. Lévi-Strauss, *Tristes tropiques* (1955), p. 351.

13 OPhil, 515.

22. DIDEROT IN RUSSIA

1 D to Falconet, 15 May 1767; VII, 60.

2 D to Falconet, 26 May 1769; IX, 58.

3 D to Falconet & M.-A. Collot, 30 May 1773; XII, 227–31.

4 Galiani to Mme d'Epinay, 15 May 1773.

5 The Marquis de Caraccioli, a diplomat and mutual friend, as reported by Galiani to Mme d'Epinay; see Perey & Maugras, *Les Dernières années de Mme d'Epinay*, p. 488.

6 Anecdote related by D's young friend Jean de Vaines, the visitor in question.

7 Vandeul to Mme Caroillon La Salette, 5 July 1773; XIII, 21–2.

8 D to Nanette, *circa* 15 Oct. 1773; XIII, 71–3.

9 D to Falconet, 6 Dec. 1773; XIII, 115–121.

10 *Mémoires pour Catherine II*, ed. P. Vernière (1966); no. LIII, pp. 247–9.

11 Catherine II to Mme Geoffrin; quoted in E. Scherer, *Melchior Grimm* (1887), p. 53.

12 D to Suard, quoted in M. Tourneux, *Diderot et Catherine II* (1899), p. 582.

13 *Mémoires*, no. II, p. 43.

14 *Mémoires*, no. XLIV, p. 225.

15 *Mémoires*, no. XLVII, pp. 233–4.

16 La Fontaine, "Le chien qui porte à son cou le dîné de son maître."

17 At the first Partition of Poland, by Austria, Prussia and Russia in 1772, Russia had annexed Polish territories in Livonia, and Poland itself had henceforward been in the hold of Russian garrisons.

18 *Mémoires*, no. VII, p. 56.

19 *Mémoires*, no. VII, p. 55.

20 *Mémoires*, no. XXXVII, p. 226.

21 *Observations sur le Nakaz*; OPol, 385–6.

22 *Mémoires*, no. I, p. 18.

23 *Mémoires*, no. XLVII, pp. 234–5.

24 *Mémoires*, no. II, pp. 37–44.

25 Jacques Proust thinks he may have been trying to collect data for a new Russian edition of the *Encyclopédie*. See his "Diderot, l'Académie de Petersburg et le projet d'une *Encyclopédie* russe", *Diderot Studies*, XII, 1969, pp. 103–131.

26 See D. Thiebault, *Mes Souvenirs de vingt ans de séjour à Berlin* (1804), vol. 3, pp. 140–146.

27 Quoted in Perey & Maugras, *Les Dernières années de Mme d'Epinay*, pp. 481–2.

28 Grimm to Count Nesselrode, 7 Feb. 1774.

29 Quoted by Mme Necker in her *Nouveaux mélanges*, vol. I, p. 229.

30 A/T, IX, 28–31.

31 D to C.P.E. Bach, 30 March 1774; XIII, 211–2.

32 So wrote the Swedish orientalist J. J. Bjornstahl to Christof Gjoerwell; quoted in *Corresp.*, XIV, 87.

33 OPhil, 526.

34 OPhil, 540.

35 D to Dr. Clerc, 15 June 1774; XIV, 42.

36 OPol, 343–458.

37 D to Mme Necker; XIV, 72–3.

38 *Observations sur le Nakaz*; OPol, 385.

39 Ibid., 343–5.

40 Quoted in Tourneux, op. cit., p. 519.

23. DIDEROT IN OLD AGE

1 *Journal du duc de Croy*, ed. Grouchy & Cottin (1907), vol. III, p. 153.

2 D to Catherine II, 17 Dec. 1774; XIV, 121–2.

3 A/T, IX.

4 A/T, IX, 344.

5 De la Charmotte [Vandeul's brother] to Mme Caroillon, 30 Sept. 1778.

6 D to Sartine, 12 July 1775; XIV, 152.

7 Stanislaus-Augustus of Poland to Mme Geoffrin, 17 Oct. 1774.

8 Quoted by E. Scherer, op. cit., 242 et seq.

9 Galiani to Grimm, 18 July 1772.

10 D to Grimm, end of Aug. 1776; XIV, 213–21.

11 D to Grimm, 13 or 14 Oct. 1776; XIV, 236–41.

12 Quoted in F. W. Hirst, *Life and Letters of Thomas Jefferson* (1920), p. 491.

13 Grimm to Leopold Mozart, 27 July 1778.

14 Mozart to Leopold Mozart, 11 Sept. 1778.

15 Mozart to Leopold Mozart, 26 Oct. 1778.

16 *Principes de la philosophie morale; ou Essai de M.S. *** sur le mérite et la vertu* (1745), A/T, I, 118.

17 *Essai sur la vie de Senèque le philosophe, Oeuvres complètes*, ed. R. Lewinter, vol. XII (1971); p. 567 and *fn*.

18 Ibid., 709.

19 See the Introduction to the *Essai sur la vie de Senèque*, ibid., pp. 502–7.
20 *Essai*, 699–70.
21 *Année littéraire*, vol. I for 1779, pp. 36–70 and 104–36.
22 D to Naigeon, 28 July 1780; XV, 177–9.
23 Joseph Joubert (1754–1824), later a friend of Chateaubriand, Fontanes and Mme Récamier, produced no sustained piece of writing, and his reputation rests on his *Pensées*, from which Chateaubriand made a posthumous selection in 1838.
24 See a note in Joubert's Journal for 14 Feb. 1804 referring to the year 1783, quoted in A. Beaunier, *La Jeunesse de Joseph Joubert* (1918), p. 81.
25 A/T I, xxi.
26 De Rivot to D, 11 Sept. 1780.
27 D to J. Cumming, 7 Oct. 1781; XV, 271.
28 D to M.-J. Sedaine, 11 Oct. 1781; XV, 279–80.
29 Horace Walpole to Lady Ossory, 15 June 1777.
30 Quoted by Morellet in his *Mémoires*, vol. I, p. 215.
31 The visitors were Prince Gonzague Catiglione and Bailly. See A. Feugère, *Un Précurseur de la révolution: l'abbé Raynal* (1922), p. 187.
32 D to Grimm, *circa* 1772.
33 There is much dispute as to which exactly Diderot's contributions to the work are. See M. Duchet, *Diderot et "L'Histoire des deux Indes"* (1978) and Yves Benot, *Diderot: de l'athéisme à l'anticolonialisme* (1981).
34 D to Grimm, 25 March 1781; XV, 213.
35 *Histoire des deux Indes* (1781), I, 205–6.
36 Gibbon to Lord Sheffield, 30 Nov. 1785.
37 D to Grimm, 25 March 1781; XV, 213.
38 Ibid, 213–4.
39 S.-N.-H. Linguet (1736–94) founded the *Annales politiques, civiles et littéraires du 18me siècle* in 1777 in London. It was banned in France but nevertheless circulated widely there. Linguet, a disbarred lawyer, was a virulent opponent of the *philosophes*, the Académie and the idea of constitutional monarchy, holding that "freemen in modern societies are more perfectly enslaved than subjugated men were in slave societies." He was at this time in the Bastille, and he was executed during the Terror.
40 D to Grimm, 25 March 1781; XV, 215.
41 Ibid, 223–7.
42 He means Maurepas, see p. 396.
43 Ibid, 227.
44 La Harpe supplied the Grand Duke Paul with a regular manuscript *Correspondance littéraire*, on somewhat the same lines as Grimm's; it lasted from 1774 to 1789.

45 D to Le Noir, late May 1782; XV, 302–3.
46 D to SV, 21 Sept. 1768; VIII, 178.
47 D to Angélique, 28 July 1781; XV, 252–7.
48 D to Angélique, 28 July 1781; XV, 253–4.
49 A/T, I, liv.
50 Ibid., lv
51 Vandeul to Denise Diderot, 24 April 1784.
52 A/T, I, lvi-lvii.
53 Catherine II to Grimm, 16 April 1784.
54 A/T, I, lvii.

24. *Jacques the Fatalist*

 1 OR, 493.
 2 OR, 661.
 3 Stendhal, *De l'Amour*, ed. H. Martineau (1922), vol. II, 179.
 4 Characters in the mock-heroic poem *Richardet* by Niccolo Forteguerri (1674–1731), an imitator of Ariosto.
 5 Hugh Kenner has a very suggestive passage about Vaucanson in Chapter 1 of *The Counterfeiters* (1968).
 6 OR, 515.
 7 Galiani to Mme d'Epinay, 17 Oct. 1772.
 8 D. Hume, *Treatise of Human Nature* (1739), Book II.
 9 See Spinoza, Epistle LVIII (Oct. 1674) to G. H. Schuller.
10 OR, 670.
11 OR 774–5.
12 OR, 573.
13 Hobbes, *Human Nature; English Works*, ed. W. Molesworth, vol. IV (1840), p. 69.
14 Spinoza, op. cit.
15 The story of Beaumarchais' two-year campaign to have his *Marriage of Figaro* staged, against the express wishes of the King, is a stirring piece of literary history.
16 J. Michelet, *Histoire de la France au 18me siècle* (1863–67), p. 356.
17 OR, 760.
18 OR, 608.
19 OR, 556.
20 OR, 538.
21 OR, 741.
22 OR, 575.
23 OR, 553.

24 OR, 619.
25 OR, 604. This passage reappears in slightly different guises in Diderot's *Salon de 1767* (A/T 229–230) and *Supplément au voyage de Bougainville* (OPhil, 480). Curiously it is reproduced almost verbatim in Alfred de Musset's "Souvenir":

> *Oui, les premiers baisers, oui, les premiers serments*
> *Que deux êtres mortels échangerent sur terre,*
> *Ce fut au pied d'un arbre effeuillé par les vents,*
> *Sur un roc en poussière . . .* etc.

26 Schopenhauer, op. cit., vol. III, p. 273.
27 OR, 520.
28 OR, 698.
29 OR, 759.
30 OR, 716.
31 See M. Bakhtin, *Rabelais and His World*, trans. H. Iswolsky (1984), p. 21.

25. EPILOGUE: THE AFTERLIFE OF DIDEROT

1 I discuss the verbal point in an article in the *Times Higher Educational Supplement*, 2 December 1988, p.15.
2 Translated as *The Philosophy of the Enlightenment* (1951).
3 See Cassirer's Chapter 4, on "Religion".
4 Flaubert, *Dictionary of Received Ideas*, trans. J. Barzun (1954), p. 31.
5 See ante, p. 420, and note.
6 See *Correspondance littéraire*, January 1779. The writer is no doubt Henri Meister.
7 H. Meister, *Aux Mânes de Diderot* (1787). It is reprinted in A/T, I, xiii–xix.
8 Malouet and Clermont-Tonnerre.
9 See A. C. Kors, *D'Holbach's Coterie* (1976), pp. 275–6.
10 The three volumes of "Philosophie ancienne et moderne", edited by Naigeon, in the *Encyclopédie méthodique* came out between 1791 and 1797. The whole vast *Encyclopédie méthodique*, 201 volumes in all, was not completed until 1832.
11 The anecdote appealed to Goethe's imagination, and he mentions it more than once in *Conversations with Eckermann*.
12 Quoted by Scherer, op. cit., p. 368.
13 See *Mémoires sur la vie de M. de La Harpe* (18), pp. lxii–xviii.
14 Robespierre, *Rapport sur les rapports des idées religieuses et morales avec les principes républicains*, 7 mai 1794; quoted by P. Naville, op. cit., p. 444.
15 An extensive collection of reviews and articles on Diderot for the period 1796–8 is reprinted in *Studies on Voltaire*, 33 (1965).

16 La Harpe, *Lycée, ou cours de littérature ancienne et moderne* (1801 ed., vol. 16, p. 19).

17 See *ante*, p. 262

18 A five-volume edition (1813).

19 Even Jules Assézat, in his great edition of the *Works* in 1875–77, had to make do with the Briere text, with some emendations, though – too late for his purposes – he eventually stumbled on a greatly superior text, dating from the end of the last century. This was published by his friend Gustave Isambert in 1883. The momentous discovery of the autograph manuscript was still to come (see *post*, p. 472).

20 See M. L. Charles, *The Growth of Diderot's Fame in France from 1784 to 1875*, Ph.D. dissertation, Bryn Mawr College, 1942.

21 See Sainte-Beuve, *Premiers lundis*, I, pp. 374 et seq.

22 Sainte-Beuve, *Portraits littéraires*, I.

23 Carlyle, *Critical and Miscellaneous Essays*, vol. IV (1842).

24 *La Vie de Henry Brulard*, Pléiade ed., vol. III, p. 333.

25 *Mémoires d'un touriste*, in *Oeuvres*, ed. H. Martineau (1927–37), vol. I, p. 174. *Jacques* was more than once banned during the *Restauration* period.

26 *Mélanges intimes*, in *Oeuvres*, ed. H. Martineau (1927–37), vol. I, p. 339, 23 Sept. 1814.

27 J. Seznac, "Diderot et *Sarrasine*", *Diderot Studies* IV, (1963), pp. 237–245.

28 Balzac, in the *Revue Parisienne*, 25 Sept. 1840.

29 Champfleury, *Le Réalisme* (1857), pp. 10–11.

30 Champfleury, "La Comédie posthume de Diderot au Théatre Français", *L'Art*, vol. XXXVI (1884), pp. 21–26.

31 In answer to a questionnaire by his daughter, in 1865. See S. S. Prawer, *Karl Marx and World Literature* (1976), p. 390.

32 Quoted in Prawer, op. cit. pp. 374–5.

33 *Journals*, ed. R. Ricatte (4 vols., 1956), vol. I, p. 458: 13 April 1858.

34 Ibid, vol. II, p. 282.

35 Ibid, vol. II, p. 96.

36 Ibid, vol. III, p. 537.

37 L. Asseline, *Diderot et le 19me siècle* (1866), pp. 15–17.

38 Zola, "Le Naturalisme", *Le Figaro*, 17 Jan. 1881.

39 Zola, *Le Roman expérimental* (5th ed., 1881), p. 15.

40 G. Barral, "Diderot et la médecine", *Chronique médicale*, vol. VII (1900), pp. 126–8.

41 H. Taine, *Les Origines de la France contemporaine* (7th ed.; 1879), vol. I, pp. 349–351.

42 Quoted by Herbert Dieckmann in his *Inventaire du fonds Vandeul et inédits de Diderot* (1951), pp. xxxv–xxxvi.

Index

PETER ACKROYD

Dickens

'Ackroyd's magnificent biography sets the seal on Dickens' acknowledged supremacy in the English novel. [It] is to be praised without reservation . . . I can do no more than praise, recommend, insist that you buy and read this book . . . beautifully produced and illustrated, it supersedes all other Dickens biographies'
– Anthony Burgess, *Independent*

'I couldn't bear to stop reading it: it's absolutely marvellous . . . This is an absolutely essential book for anyone who is interested in the Victorian age, for anyone who is interested in the art of biography' – P. D. James

'A breathtaking feat of scholarship' – *The Times*

'Truly magnificent . . . a book that ranks alongside Richard Ellman's *Oscar Wilde*. This is the complete, the nonesuch, the definitive Dickens. If we get a better account of his life and work this century, I shall be rather more than merely surprised' – Sheridan Morley

'Daring and utterly successful . . . A great book'
– *Literary Review*

MARGARET CROSLAND

The Passionate Philosopher
A Marquis de Sade Reader

For all his notoriety, the Marquis de Sade must head the list of writers who are more talked about than read. In this new, representative selection Margaret Crosland encourages us to take a fresh look at his work.

Sade spent more than half his life in prison, but for which he would have had scant cause to take his revenge on society through evocations of sexual cruelty. Excluded from normal life, he developed an extremist vision of the world through stories, dialogues and historical novels. Included here are extracts from his major fiction: some of the devastating fantasies in *Les Cent Vingt Journées de Sodome* as well as episodes from *Justine* and from the compulsively vicious *Juliette*.

Yet, in addition to his so-called 'obscene' writing, Sade wrote with equal fervour about idealized people and democratic societies. He was indeed a passionate philosopher, a man typical in his own way of his times but eager to pass on to later centuries his incandescent ideas about human behaviour.

Following her Introduction, Margaret Crosland provides astute commentaries on her selections, and finally a Chronology and Bibliography.

Selected and translated from the French by Margaret Crosland

Edited by MAX BROD

The Diaries of Franz Kafka

Franz Kafka is the great enigma of early twentieth-century literature. Advocates of Impressionism, Existentialism and even Christianity vie with each other in claiming him as an exemplar of their doctrines. He is seen as the successor of Dostoyevsky, the disciple of Kierkegaard and the forerunner of Sartre. Yet beside the profound searching of his great 'trilogy of loneliness' – the words are those of Max Brod, his lifelong friend and editor of the diaries – such controversy seems insignificant.

Kafka's diaries cover the period from 1910 to 1923, the year before his death at the age of forty. They reveal to us the extraordinary inner world in which he lived. Here he describes, perhaps to relieve the pain that they caused him, his fear, isolation and frustration, his feelings of guilt and his sense of being an outcast. In between come quick glimpses of the real world, of the father he worshipped and of the woman he could not bring himself to marry. And throughout this personal journal Kafka the writer is experimenting, searching for his true mode of expression.

'Perhaps the most interesting writer of his generation . . . a strange and disconcerting genius' – Edwin Muir

CATHERINE PETERS

The King of Inventors

'Wilkie Collins – the eccentric author of *The Woman in White* and *The Moonstone* – has puzzled researchers down the decades ... Up until now, the mystery surrounding him has been a hefty barrier for anyone trying to write convincingly about him. Catherine Peters has painted the first readable portrait of Collins as a human being'
– Françoise Rivière, *European*

'A wonderful case study in Victorian morals ... Catherine Peters is a careful biographer. She has uncovered much that is new ... Although writing about a sensationalist writer, her own even and measured approach commands a growing confidence. She offers a fascinating story, plainly told'
– William St Clair, *Financial Times*

'Peters provides as intelligent and comprehensive account of his work as we are ever likely to have ... What makes her book delightful is the warmth of her handling ... Her sympathy allows us to see a humorous and childlike aspect to him'
– Claire Tomalin, *Independent on Sunday*

'Peters' perceptive critical appreciations of Wilkie's dark melodramas ... undoubtedly provide an illuminating insight into the double standards of Victorian life'
– Hugh Massingberd, *Daily Telegraph*

Further Biographies Available from Minerva

While every effort is made to keep prices low, it is sometimes necessary to increase prices at short notice. Mandarin Paperbacks reserves the right to show new retail prices on covers which may differ from those previously advertised in the text or elsewhere.

The prices shown below were correct at the time of going to press.

☐	7493 0647 5	**Dickens**	Peter Ackroyd	£7.99
☐	7493 9177 4	**My Left Foot**	Christy Brown	£4.99
☐	7493 9091 3	**Pietro Citati**	Kafka	£6.99
☐	7493 9019 0	**In Search of J. D. Salinger**	Ian Hamilton	£5.99
☐	7493 9152 9	**Writers in Hollywood**	Ian Hamilton	£5.99
☐	7493 9086 7	**Sylvia Townsend Warner**	Claire Harman	£6.99
☐	7493 9070 0	**Lost in Translation**	Eva Hoffmann	£5.99
☐	7493 9005 0	**The Orton Diaries**	John Lahr	£6.99
☐	7493 9803 5	**Colette: A Life**	Herbert Lottman	£7.99
☐	7493 9014 X	**Nora**	Brenda Maddox	£6.99
☐	7493 9156 1	**What Fresh Hell is This?**	Marion Meade	£7.99
☐	7493 9082 4	**Timebends**	Arthur Miller	£7.99
☐	7493 9901 5	**Sartre**	Annie Cohen-Salal	£9.99
☐	7493 9047 6	**Friends of Promise**	Michael Sheldon	£6.99
☐	7493 9924 4	**Ake**	Wole Soyinka	£5.99
☐	7493 9170 7	**Isara**	Wole Soyinka	£5.99
☐	7493 9133 2	**Lawrence of Arabia**	Jeremy Wilson	£9.99

All these books are available at your bookshop or newsagent, or can be ordered direct from the publisher. Just tick the titles you want and fill in the form below.

Mandarin Paperbacks, Cash Sales Department, PO Box 11, Falmouth, Cornwall TR10 9EN.

Please send cheque or postal order, no currency, for purchase price quoted and allow the following for postage and packing:

UK including BFPO
£1.00 for the first book, 50p for the second and 30p for each additional book ordered to a maximum charge of £3.00.

Overseas including Eire
£2 for the first book, £1.00 for the second and 50p for each additional book thereafter.

NAME (Block letters) ....

ADDRESS ....

....

☐ I enclose my remittance for ....

☐ I wish to pay by Access/Visa Card Number

Expiry Date